NEXT-GENERATION COMPUTERS

SPECTRUM Series Advisory Board

OTHER IEEE PRESS BOOKS

SPECTRUM
S E R I E S

NEXT-GENERATION COMPUTERS

Editor:
Edward A. Torrero

IEEE
PRESS

The Institute of Electrical and Electronics Engineers, Inc., New York

IEEE Order Number: PC01883

Library of Congress Cataloging-in-Publication Data
Main entry under title:

Next-generation computers.

(Spectrum series)
Includes indexes.
1. Electronic digital computers—Addresses, essays,
lectures.   I. Torrero, Edward A.   II. Series.
QA76.5.N472   1985   004   85-14315
ISBN 0-87942-194-0

Contents

Part II: Probing the issues **93**

Part III: A tutorial review **191**

Foreword

This first in a planned series of books to be published by the IEEE PRESS was inspired by a conversation with Stephen Kahne, the IEEE's Vice President of Technical Activities. Dr. Kahne, who was at the time of that discussion director of the Division of Electrical, Computer, and Systems Engineering at the National Science Foundation, on leave from Case Western Reserve University, noted that many of *IEEE Spectrum*'s special issues could serve as ideal tutorial introductions to books on the same subject. The volume at hand represents the first realization of Dr. Kahne's idea. The chosen topic—one of interest to generalist and specialist alike—is "next-generation" computers.

During the research stages for many of *Spectrum*'s special reports a large amount of material is generated that is never published in full, but is instead distilled for summary use in the magazine. Such was the case with the special report on which this volume is based, and the editor has included in it selected valuable portions of that original research material.

Sometimes material is released or developed too late in the production cycle of a special *Spectrum* issue so that it cannot be included in the issue itself. That, too, happened in the case of the aforementioned special issue, and the editor has included pertinent portions of it in this volume.

We plan, in this new Spectrum Series, regularly to include additional appropriate articles, previously published in *Spectrum,* that relate to the topic of each volume. The advantage to the reader should be a uniform level of presentation that is useful and comprehensible not only to the specialist, but also to the scientist or engineer who is not currently practicing in the field represented by a particular book's topic.

The editors of *IEEE Spectrum* are indebted to several individuals for their important contributions in producing this volume—in particular, Professor Kahne; Professor Mac E. Van Valkenburg, Editor-in-Chief of the IEEE PRESS; W. Reed Crone, Managing Editor of the IEEE PRESS; and Emily Gross, IEEE PRESS Associate Editor.

We look forward to working with them on future books in the Spectrum Series.

Donald Christiansen
Editor and Publisher, *IEEE Spectrum*

Part I

TOMORROW'S COMPUTERS

SPECTRUM SERIES

TOMORROW'S COMPUTERS

Edward A. Torrero   Issue Editor

In April 1981 the Japanese government announced a long-range program to develop computing capabilities so advanced they would be of unrivaled usefulness in helping Japanese society prepare for the future. By the end of the decade or so, Japan proposed to extend the frontiers of computer science and engineering to the point where intelligent, superpowerful computers might be capable of serving as expert consultants to the government itself. The proposed applications would run the gamut from increasing productivity and conserving energy to providing medical, educational, and other social support.

Japanese researchers termed the project "fifth-generation computers." Whereas earlier generations could be characterized by a single, pervasive hardware building block—vacuum tube, transistor, integrated circuit, and large-scale or very large-scale integrated circuit for, respectively, the first through the fourth generations of computers—the fifth generation would be marked by advances in software and, in particular, by extensive use of artificial intelligence.

Since then, international opinion among engineers and scientists has tended to be split between two points of view. In what might be termed the nationalistic view, one group holds that Japan has embarked upon the computer-technology equivalent of the United States' 10-year Apollo program that sought to land a man on the moon and bring him back safely by the end of the 1960s. Even partial success in achieving the fifth-generation project goals, according to this opinion, would virtually ensure Japanese dominance in what has been one of the last Western bastions of high-technology supremacy.

An alternative view is that advances in computer technology are normal. Programs similar to the one in Japan were either under way or slated to be so at several research centers in the world in 1981. In fact, the Japanese program is widely regarded as largely based on the results of U.S. research, including artificial intelligence, of the last 20 years. These programs, according to this view, simply represent the next step in an ongoing, widely anticipated convergence of computer and communications technologies. Such a blending is viewed as providing evidence of a fundamental transformation of the world from an industrial economy to an information-intensive economy.

Further, because of the uncertainty of quick success by fifth-generation programs, some engineers say the resources could be better spent in developing existing large-scale computers now used in scientific applications. Commonly called supercomputers—and sometimes fourth-generation computers, because of their reliance on advanced hardware to achieve increased speed and throughput—these machines must be continually improved to meet market demands. The technology developed to enhance their performance, this argument goes, would also benefit fifth-generation computing.

These and other concerns have served to elevate discussions to the level of ''burning issues.'' Regardless of the specific forms and capabilities that may emerge from what we collectively term a new generation in computing (to encompass the Japanese project as well as comparable efforts in other nations), its elusive realization is nonetheless becoming a central concern for a growing number of individuals, both within and outside the engineering and scientific community.

The unusually malleable set of technologies entailed in next-generation computing suggests that the ubiquitous computer—perhaps best symbolized today by the pervasive personal computer—seems destined to rise to a new level of influence and importance. Despite the very formidable technical hurdles that must be overcome before fruition in any form becomes possible, the potential impacts of such a new generation on virtually every sector of professional and personal endeavors is stirring the world's decision makers as few previous technologies have.

The section in this issue of *Spectrum* entitled ''The quest'' presents a glimpse of the technology of tomorrow and describes how most of the advanced nations of the world are organizing to develop the next generation of computers. In the United States and Japan, for example, so important is next-generation computing deemed that some of the newer organizations to have emerged are radically different in structure and mission from comparable organizations of the past and would have been thought highly unusual in their respective countries just a few years ago.

The section on ''The challenges'' shows just how difficult a task researchers face. In many cases, it is a matter of synthesizing and making economical what has been only within reach in laboratories. This section concludes with an assessment of the likely technological fallout.

The final section presents a sociotechnological assessment of what the future holds and how institutions and individuals alike can prepare for this future. ◆

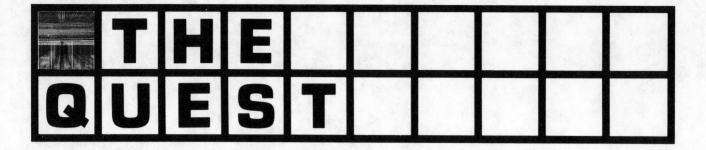

A NEW GENERATION IN COMPUTING

Microelectronics and artificial intelligence may produce advanced computers that are both fast and smart

The two perennial questions that have confronted the computing field since its inception are how machines can be made faster and how they can be made smarter. It is generally appreciated that a computer can carry out thousands or millions of basic instructions each second, but few, if any, understand how it would be possible for a machine to exhibit behavior that would be considered intelligent if done by a human. Mere rote repetition of steps, as might be involved in adding numbers, inverting matrices, or even solving certain equations, rely more on mechanics than on intellect.

Cost-effective increases in machine speed, largely due to advances in the microelectronics field, have been widely visible, particularly with the advent of high-speed microcomputer systems. A major international industry in semiconductors has emerged, and supremacy in this field is often used as a barometer for leadership in high technology. Less noticeable perhaps, but not insignificant, has been the steady progress in the field of artificial intelligence (AI) over the last 15 to 20 years. This progress has given rise to a discipline, based mainly in the universities, that has been experimentally developing and demonstrating techniques for machine intelligence. We are now at a stage where the confluence of these two disciplines—microelectronics and artificial intelligence—may indeed produce new generations of computers that are both fast and smart.

The nation that dominates this information-processing field will possess the keys to world leadership in the twenty-first century. In its brief history, information processing has affected virtually every facet of modern society. Yet we see almost unlimited opportunity for application of the technology. Better management and use of information is at the core of opportunity in the space environment. Better planning can lead to greater productivity, as well as to competitive advantage. Improved health care, education, and training may also result from judicious use of advanced information processing. Better planning coupled with effective execution of plans can be decisive in maintaining national security. And finally, a more dynamic society can result from the opportunity provided by an interactive information-based infrastructure.

It began around World War II

Digital computers reflect almost a half century's evolution of the basic sequential machine architecture that emerged around the time of World War II. In this architecture, a central processing unit (CPU) retrieves instructions one by one from a local memory, acts upon those instructions, and temporarily holds its results or deposits them back into memory. This process continues until the last instruction is executed or the machine is otherwise halted. Significant improvements in CPU architecture have been realized along the way. The basic speed with which instructions are processed has increased steadily due to numerous technological advances since that time. However, the sequential machine architecture has remained intact.

In the early days, when each bit of memory was very precious, only very small programs could be stored and executed. The development of solid-state memory and improved architectures has made feasible the storage and execution of much larger programs. By the end of this decade, conventional systems should be able to execute on the order of 100 million sequential instructions per second and to access gigabytes of memory. At that point hardware improvements alone will be insufficient to guarantee indefinite increases in computing speed for this kind of architecture.

The mere existence of a piece of hardware that can execute instructions rapidly does not, by itself, guarantee that a particular problem can be solved quickly, nor does it simplify the programming process. AI-based software systems may one day assume responsibility for some of the bookkeeping, configuration control, and internal structuring—tasks normally carried out by programmers—but the software field still appears to be far from the goal of automatic generation of programs or from creating executable specifications from initial requirements. Software and programming will be central factors in determining progress in the field.

Faster machines per se also will not produce intelligent machines. Insect behavior demonstrates levels of intelligence far higher than any computer has attained—and with relatively slow neural processing. One can only conclude that man's understanding of the nature of intelligent behavior is still quite primitive and that there is ample room for progress through research. Systems that must now be implemented with very high-speed circuits to achieve rapid response may be implementable in the future with much slower-speed circuits and completely different architectures. Conversely the existence of very high-speed circuits and greatly improved architectures may open the way for more rapid execution of intelligent behavior than has previously been encountered. It is to be hoped that this new capability can be put to work in increasingly productive ways.

What kinds of capabilities will these new machines have? How

Robert E. Kahn
Defense Advanced Research Projects Agency

will we build them? How will they be used? Based on experiments carried out in leading research laboratories and universities, it is reasonably certain that machines will be developed that can understand languages, either spoken or written, at some level of comprehension. It also appears that vision systems that can detect particular objects in an image, recognize specific locations from pictures not previously seen, or characterize the three-dimensional layout of a particular area are within reach. Likewise, display systems will be built that can automatically determine how to present textual and graphic information on a screen most effectively, based on limited user guidance. Another level of sophistication may take place inside the computer system itself as it takes over more of the task of managing its data, internal structures, and resources.

Can these machines be said to reason? Probably not—at least in the sense that most of us might apply the term. Yet it seems equally clear that they will begin to play a role in sensory processing and information management that gets closer to the central core of intelligent activity.

We know now that machines can be built that can accept English or other languages as input and process them in near real time. This should greatly ease the problem of entering complex expressions into the computer. Machines that can see and understand their environment will have significant benefit in robotic applications that are far too numerous to mention. Advanced techniques for planning and reasoning are most likely to be developed and improved over time through actual application to real problems. If initial attempts at data fusion and reasoning by analogy are only tentative, steady progress should still occur, and improvements in machine learning may also stimulate significant improvements. We expect to see marked advances in this area during the next decade.

Three basic disciplines involved

The three principal disciplines that will make a new generation of machines a reality are: (1) microelectronics, which will produce the fast, ultrasmall devices made up of large-scale chips and wafers; (2) artificial intelligence, which will guide the development and exploration of concepts and techniques for intelligent systems; and (3) computer systems and architecture that will guide development of the hardware, software, and related tools to realize working systems. Why has the merging of talent in these three fields not occurred before now, and what makes us believe the next decade or two will bring about a new generation of intelligent computers?

First, many workers in the area of computer architecture relied on discrete devices until the mid-1970s, when it became clear that access to integrated-circuit design and fabrication facilities would be needed to implement more sophisticated designs economically. During the last few years this process has begun in earnest and is intensifying. Designers in industry, and more recently in the universities, are using powerful design methods and are able to access semiconductor fabrication lines by direct negotiation with the manufacturers or indirectly via the "silicon foundry" approach. In this approach, designers submit their designs, possibly via an intermediate agent called a broker, on an arms-length basis, much like an author–publisher–printer interaction. In the VLSI domain the author is often the publisher as well.

The result is that now hundreds of architectural ideas are being explored by researchers and tested by actual fabrication all across

Five generations of computer and communications technologies

Generation	First	Second	Third	Fourth	Fifth
Years	1946–56	1957–63	1964–81	1982–89	1990–
Example computers	Eniac Edvac Univac IBM 650	NCR 501 IBM 7094 CDC-6600	IBM 360, 370 PDP-11 Spectra-70 Honeywell 200 Cray 1 Illiac-IV Cyber-205	Cray XMP IBM 308 Amdahl 580	Extensive development of distributed computing Merging of telecommunications and computer technologies Extensive modularity
Telecommunications technology	Telephone Teletype	Digital transmission Pulse-code modulation	Satellite communications Microwaves Networking Optical fibers Packet switching	Integrated systems digital network (ISDN)	
Computer hardware	Vacuum tubes Magnetic drum Cathode-ray tube	Transistors Magnetic-core memories	ICs Semiconductor memories Magnetic disks Minicomputers Microprocessors	Distributed computing systems VLSI Bubble memories Optical disks Microcomputers	Advanced packaging and interconnection techniques Ultralarge-scale integration Parallel architectures 3-D integrated-circuit design Gallium arsenide technology Josephson junction technology Optical components
Computer software	Stored programs Machine code Autocode	High-level languages Cobol Algol Fortran	Very high-level languages Pascal operating systems Structured programming Timesharing LISP Computer graphics	Ada Widespread packaged programs Expert systems Object-oriented languages	Concurrent languages Functional programming Symbolic processing (natural languages, vision, speech recognition, planning)
Computer performance	2-kilobyte memory 10 kiloinstructions per second	32-kilobyte memory 200 KIPS	2-megabyte memory 5 megainstructions per second	8-megabyte memory 30 MIPS	1 gigainstruction per second to 1 tetrainstruction per second

the United States and in other countries. Though the design process is still lengthy, the fabrication time is typically only a month or two once the design is completed. Thus innovative ideas in machine architecture can be generated and explored more rapidly by researchers, and this should accelerate progress in the area.

Second, the artificial intelligence field has only recently developed a sufficient track record of accomplishment to attract industrial interest. The commercial sector, the military, and major sectors of the health and education fields are now exploring techniques developed by AI researchers. The most notable example of accomplishment is in developing expert systems to give high-level advice or to carry out a complex function normally associated with human expertise. Examples of such systems are most prevalent in the medical area, but significant investments have also been made in such areas as equipment configuration and signal interpretation. Important earlier work in this area led to expert systems in molecular spectroscopy and symbolic mathematics. These systems incorporate numerous facts and heuristics (rules of thumb) about their domain of expertise and arrive at their conclusions through a kind of systematic application of these facts and heuristics to narrow the possibilities to explore. In this way it is often possible to arrive at a specific expert conclusion "heuristically," even with a small set of rules of thumb.

The nation that dominates this information-processing field will possess the keys to world leadership in the twenty-first century

---

Progress in AI has also been noteworthy in fields such as natural-language understanding and vision. These systems are being used, for example, to access data bases via structured English queries and, in the case of vision, to provide input to simple stationary robots. As these capabilities are refined, the applications for them will expand.

Present systems are limited

In each of these examples the systems are limited in performance in some critical way. The expert systems are restricted to simple problems because they either cannot apply enough heuristics per unit of time, cannot explore the problems efficiently enough, or are limited in acquiring the heuristics themselves. In the natural-language area, very structured sentences can be processed, but free-form text or utterances cannot yet be supported, in part because of lack of processing power and in part because basic knowledge about cognitive models is needed. Significant progress has been made in scene and image understanding, but powerful real-time systems do not yet exist.

What will intelligent systems look like? Unlike the monolithic supercomputers of today, these systems will be small, compact units that carry out a specialized function. The new generation of machines will consist of collections of these systems integrated into a whole. If a system needs vision, it can be added. Speech input can also be incorporated, but the speech system (and probably every component) will have to be given enough knowledge to do its job.

For example, it will need to know the particular language, the words to be used, and their meanings. This can all be fed in from a store-bought package (tape, diskette, read-only memory, and so on), or it can be tailored to a specific application by the user. Depending on the application, various expert systems can be ad-

ded or possibly one large expert system can have multiple areas of expertise. Thus the new generation of computers will resemble component video in appearance more than conventional supercomputers.

A major concern in planning for these new systems has been to identify effective metrics for their performance. In this way one can set measurable goals and can compare different systems on the basis of tangible criteria. Unfortunately this is proving extremely difficult. Even if we decline the challenge to develop quantifiable measures of intelligence, we are still left with the perplexing problem of quantifying expertise, or vision. To say simply that a person has 20/20 vision implies an indescribable set of capabilities for which the 20/20 attribute applies. Similarly one cannot measure an expert system by heuristics alone. One system with 1000 rules of thumb may be outperformed by another that has 500 "better" rules. Ultimately comparison testing may determine which of two expert systems is better, but the results may not be uniform, with one system outperforming the other only part of the time.

Because the AI field has chosen to focus on innovation as one of its main goals, in order to be able to solve cognitive problems that no one knows how to solve, there often is no quantifiable history of successive accomplishments that can be quantified. Unlike the development of memory chips (which went from 1 K to 250 K by multiples of 4) or processors (with speed and address space that could be measured), there is no equivalent metric for most systems produced by AI researchers. Nevertheless, progress can be measured by demonstrating how successive generations of systems perform against a defined set of benchmarks. If all the previous benchmarks are achieved by a new system, with improvements in some and degradations in none, it can reasonably be said that the new system is an improvement. Thus we can expect to see a class of benchmarks developed for intelligent systems that will be the machine equivalent of IQ tests. Obviously the utility of such tests depends upon the exact nature of the benchmarks.

Without benchmarks to test the performance of intelligent systems, we must resort to general, but imprecise, characterizations of performance or describe underlying attributes of the system, such as its overall structure or the properties of its hardware. Thus one often asks questions like, "How many million instructions per second (MIPS) are required for speech understanding?" Or how much memory is needed? These are not straightforward questions that can be answered categorically. We cannot really answer these questions about ourselves, and perhaps the questions themselves are not well formed in the context of the human brain.

In many ways LISP is the machine language of AI research. Recently significant attempts have been made to define higher-level architectures tailored to specific applications. Work on languages and systems for knowledge representation, various developments in object-oriented programming and logic programming systems reflect early attempts at creating such architectures. They may reduce significantly the effort required to develop intelligent systems, by helping to keep the user's attention focused more on the problem itself than on the implementation details of the underlying machine. In this sense, the goal of these efforts may be likened to those of high-level languages in freeing the programmer from the intricacies of assembly language. Efforts in this area are still embryonic but are developing rapidly.

Stepping up to multiprocessors

On top of this ferment comes the most fundamental development of all: the opportunity to exploit parallelism in a major way

Glossary of advanced computing terms

Artificial intelligence (AI) A discipline devoted to developing and applying computational approaches to intelligent behavior. Also referred to as machine intelligence or heuristic programming.

Atom An individual. A proposition in logic that cannot be broken down into other propositions.

Blackboard approach A problem-solving approach whereby the various system elements communicate with each other via a common working data storage called the blackboard.

Blocks world A small artificial world, consisting of blocks and pyramids, used to develop ideas in computer vision, robotics, and natural-language interfaces.

Cognition An intellectual process by which knowledge is gained about perceptions or ideas.

Compile The act of translating a computer program written in a high-level language (such as LISP) into the machine language that controls the computer's basic operations.

Computational logic A science designed to make use of computers in logic calculus.

Computer architecture The way various computational elements are interconnected to achieve a computational function.

Conceptual dependency An approach to natural-language understanding in which sentences are translated into basic concepts that are expressed as a small set of semantic primitives.

Control structure Reasoning strategy. The strategy for manipulating the domain knowledge to solve a problem.

Data base An organized collection of data about a subject.

Data-base management system A computer system for the storage and retrieval of information about some domain.

Data structure The form in which data are stored in a computer.

Declarative knowledge representation Representation of facts and assertions.

Editor A software tool to aid in modifying a software program.

Embed To write a computer language on top of (embedded in) another computer language (such as LISP).

Expert system A computer program that uses knowledge and reasoning techniques to solve problems normally requiring the abilities of human experts.

Fifth-generation computer A non–Von Neumann, intelligent, parallel-processing form of computer now being pursued by Japan.

First-order predicate logic A popular form of logic used by the AI community for representing knowledge and performing logical inference. First-order predicate logic permits assertions to be made about variables in a proposition.

General problem solver (GPS) The first problem solver (1957) to separate its problem-solving methods from knowledge of the specific task being considered. The GPS problem-solving approach employed was "means–ends analysis."

Heuristics Rules of thumb or empirical knowledge used to help guide a problem solution.

Heuristic search techniques Graph-searching methods that use heuristic knowledge about the domain to help focus the search. They operate by generating and testing intermediate states along potential solution paths.

Higher-order language (HOL) A computer language (such as Fortran or LISP) requiring fewer statements than machine language and usually substantially easier to use and read.

Inference engine Another name given to the control structure of an AI problem solver in which the control is separate from the knowledge.

Instantiation Replacing a variable by an instance (an individual) that satisfies the system (or satisfies the statement in which the variable appears).

Knowledge base AI data bases that are not merely files of uniform content, but are collections of facts, inferences, and procedures corresponding to the types of information needed for problem solution.

Knowledge engineering The AI approach focusing on the use of knowledge (for instance, as in expert systems) to solve problems.

LISP (list-processing language) The basic AI programming language.

Logical operation The execution of a single computer instruction.

Logical representation Knowledge representation by a collection of logical formulas (usually in first-order predicate logic) that provide a partial description of the world.

Means–ends analysis A problem-solving approach (used by GPS) in which problem-solving operators are chosen in an iterative fashion to reduce the difference between the current problem-solving state and the goal state.

Natural-language processing Processing of natural language (English, for example) by a computer to facilitate communication with the computer, or for other purposes such as language translation.

Object-oriented programming A programming approach focused on objects that communicate by message passing. An object is considered to be a package of information and descriptions of procedures that can manipulate that information.

Parallel processing Simultaneous processing, as opposed to the sequential processing in a conventional (Von Neumann) type of computer architecture.

Pattern recognition The process of classifying data into predetermined categories.

Procedural knowledge representation A representation of knowledge about the world by a set of procedures—small programs that know how to do specific things (how to proceed in well-specified situations).

Production rule A modular knowledge structure representing a single chunk of knowledge, usually in an If–Then or Antecedent–Consequent form. Popular in expert systems.

Programming environment The total programming setup that includes the interface, the languages, the editors, and other programming tools.

Prolog (programming in logic) A logic-oriented AI language developed in France and popular in Europe and Japan.

Propositional logic An elementary logic that uses argument forms to deduce the truth or falsehood of a new proposition from known propositions.

Rule interpreter The control structure for a production-rule system.

Search space The implicit graph representing all the possible states of the system that may have to be searched to find a solution. In many cases the search space is infinite. The term search space is also used for non–state-space representations.

Semantic network A knowledge representation for describing the properties and relations of objects, events, concepts, situations, or actions, by a directed graph consisting of nodes and labeled edges (arcs connecting nodes).

Semantic primitives Basic conceptual units in which concepts, ideas, or events can be represented.

Solution path A successful path through a search space.

State graph A graph in which the nodes represent the system and the connecting arcs represent the operators that can be used to transform the state from which the arcs emanate into the state at which they arrive.

Syllogism A deductive argument in logic whose conclusion is supported by two premises.

Symbolic Relating to the substitution of abstract representations (symbols) for concrete objects.

Syntax Order or arrangement (for example, the grammar of a language).

Von Neumann architecture The current standard computer architecture that uses sequential processing.

The preceding definitions are based on those in *An Overview of Artificial Intelligence and Robotics, Vol. 1—Artificial Intelligence, Part A—The Core Ingredients*, by William B. Gevarter, NASA Technical Memorandum 85836, June 1983.

through the use of VLSI and multiprocessor architectures. It is difficult to estimate how much the existence of sequential machines has affected the way we think about problems. It clearly affects the way we implement them. A given algorithm implemented on a multiprocessor system will surely bear little resemblance to its counterpart on a sequential machine. And multiprocessor-based LISP systems need bear no relation to a single-processor version. Conversely, we still know very little about multiprocessor architectures, concurrent programming, or parallelism. Our understanding of task decomposition strategies is still limited, and current languages, both natural and computer-based, are inadequate to represent concurrency. Since multiprocessors offer the major opportunity for realizing the hardware–software base for intelligent systems in the immediate future, it is time to address some of the key issues in this area.

First, how does one program such a multiprocessor system? What languages does one use and what performance goals should such a system have? The first question is actually two, since there is usually some underlying software system that is then used to build an end application. A main goal, aside from providing a usable, highly functional system, should be to achieve monotonically increasing speed of performance with increasing numbers of processors.

Michael Dertouzos, professor and director of the MIT Laboratories for Computer Science, has called this objective "computation by the yard." Yet multiprocessor experiments to date have shown that speed increases equal to the increase in processors (the best possible result) are achieved only over a limited range; thereafter performance will actually decrease if additional processors are used, because of a "too many cooks" syndrome.

Intelligent systems will begin to make their way into the world, but few will consider them to be really intelligent

---

The processors either use too much bandwith in the switch or they start "tripping over each others' toes." Hence a central concern in multiprocessor systems is how to use a large number of processors effectively in a given application.

Some problems do not lend themselves to much parallelism and cannot make good use of a multiprocessor system. An outstanding generic research question is how to determine the amount of performance speedup (or parallelism) possible in an application. An attendant problem is how to achieve that speedup effectively. Some problems, such as those of planning and reasoning, appear to involve a sequential component of logical development, coupled with bursts of concurrent activity to explore options and alternatives. If the concurrent operation can be performed in zero time, the maximal speedup is then determined by the residual sequential component running on the fastest sequential machine.

The piecemeal approach to speed

Alternatively, some problems that are inherently paced by real-time considerations, such as understanding speech as it is spoken, may be speeded up considerably by off-line (non–real-time) processing. For example, an hour's worth of speech may be broken into 100 segments of 36 seconds apiece, and each may be processed simultaneously for a potential hundredfold improvement over real-time processing. Neighboring segments may be given to "neighboring processors" (if the architecture has a topology suitable for neighbors) to facilitate communication between processors. The capability to break down a problem into pieces that primarily support this form of local communication is believed to be a main ingredient in developing applications that scale monotonically with the number of processors.

The author is not aware of other general paradigms that appear to guarantee asymptotic "computation by the yard," although many examples can be constructed that scale linearly for a while and then run out of communication bandwidth. If bandwidth is also allowed to scale linearly with the number of processors, other paradigms can be shown to work, such as autonomous, occasionally communicating nodes, but this requirement is usually an impractical or unachievable condition.

One would not choose to program a million-processor system one processor at a time, nor to design a million-gate chip one gate at a time. Such a process would surely be error-prone and tedious. If the software in each node is identical or substantially similar to that in all other nodes, automated means can be envisioned to tailor the system and to load it into each processor. Automated means, perhaps aided with graphics, can also be used to debug small-scale systems. Large-scale systems cannot be displayed very easily and are inherently harder to conceptualize. Effective ways to develop such systems must be sought, diagnostic procedures must be built into these systems, or they must be "applied" externally to a working system to aid in debugging.

We currently do not know how to design large-scale software systems that do not possess a great degree of regularity. As a result, we cannot predict where such "diverse systems" will be of use. Yet it is not unreasonable to expect that as our tools and techniques for software development improve and we are able to better define and specify the interfaces between system components, automated or semiautomated assembly of diverse systems will become possible.

It is possible that requirements for new system structures will be specified by humans, but the structure will be created by machine. If so, it ought to be possible to create oversight systems that co-reside with them and monitor their well-being and can take action to fix or at least report certain obvious cases of errant behavior. In fact, a symbiotic implementation in which each system oversees the other would be quite interesting to evaluate in itself.

A glimpse at the world of tomorrow

What then does the future hold? A new generation of computing technology will emerge over the next decade, based on high-performance multiprocessor systems. We will learn to use them for a wide variety of as yet unanticipated applications. Elegant ways to express parallelism and concurrency will emerge that will remind LISP experts of the power of recursion. Intelligent systems will begin to make their way into the world, but few people will consider them to be really intelligent after all. The fundamental problems of deep reasoning and understanding will become better defined but will elude all attempts to solve them. Expert systems of many kinds will become available, and limited forms of computer expertise will begin to be sold in the marketplace.

Communication networks will play an increasingly important role in connecting people and machines. Interesting examples of intelligent computing can be expected to take place involving both people and intelligent systems distributed across the nation, if not the world. Increased exploitation of knowledge in machine-processable form will occur, and strategic knowledge banks will be established for the retention of critical information. Software technology will continue to mature, with emphasis on large-scale systems and multiprocessor programming. Information management will play a key role in these systems, with emphasis on distributed data bases and interoperability. The burden of programming will be greatly eased with the aid of computer-based software-development assistants.

Completely new applications will emerge from this wealth of new technology, and computers will begin to play more important roles in planning and management throughout society. Deep strategic or tactical insights by machine may still be decades away, but the competitive use of such planning and management systems will foster even more widespread use of them, along with demands for their continual improvement.

Systems with sensory capabilities and elementary reasoning abilities will find widespread initial use in industry and the military. Expert systems will also aid in more and more sophisticated industrial and military applications. Myriads of powerful microcomputer systems will còntinue to find their way into every nook and cranny. The intellectual and technological processes that have led to this capability will surely remain the mainstay of our postindustrial society. ◆

NEEDS AND USES
Technology applied in research settings suggests that virtually everyone will use the new-generation computing systems

It is reasonable to assume that research into fifth-generation computers using technology currently available will begin to produce commercial results by the early 1990s. This assumption raises the question: What new applications will become possible and who will be the users of this new computing?

As envisioned by the Japanese, almost everybody will be users; new applications will touch almost every aspect of human life. Actually 10 broad categories of applications can be identified: industrial automation, office automation, science and engineering, computer hardware and software, aerospace, military, retailing and service industries, education, health care, and the arts, culture, and leisure [see box, p. 10]. All applications are based on technology that has already been demonstrated in a research setting; they do not require the solution of important research issues such as machines that can understand complete speech or programs that learn. A scenario, presented on pages 46 and 47, provides a user's perspective of some of the applications of new-generation computing during the course of a typical day in the future.

All the applications shown in the table rely on advances in three areas: integrated information-management systems, new computer architectures, and improved human–machine interfaces. Integrated information systems include conventional data-base systems; expert, or so-called knowledge-based, systems; and multimedia information systems combining text, graphics, images, voice, and conventional data. New computer-architectures include more powerful processors, parallel processors, and large-scale data-storage facilities to support the new information systems. And the improved human–machine interfaces include more intelligent, flexible, and easier-to-use methods of communicating with computing systems. Such interfaces will be made possible by advances in specialized hardware, user–interface design techniques, natural-language processing, speech input and output, expert systems, graphics and image processing, local- and wide-area communication networks, and cellular radio.

The major supporting components in the 10 new application areas include data-base management systems, expert systems, parallel computer architectures, software for parallel systems, speech recognition for speech input, natural-language processing, image processing and computer vision, robotics, personal work stations, high-density digital storage devices, and wide-bandwidth digital communication. Three key technologies that apply to almost every new application foreseen are expert systems, parallel processing, and improved human–computer interfaces. [These are described in greater detail in the section of this issue called "THE CHALLENGES," beginning on p. 45.]

A glimpse at the future

What might we expect within the 10 broad categories of applications for new-generation computing? An array of surprises may be in store for consumers. Not since the dawn of radio and television have there been such opportunities for electronic innovators. Here is a glimpse of some things we might expect. It is important to note that all of these potential applications have already been demonstrated as research prototypes.

Industrial automation

The last 10 years have seen an explosion in the number of industrial robots in use and in the number of companies using computer-aided design (CAD) and computer-aided manufacturing (CAM) techniques. During the same period there have been several research efforts to integrate robots with CAD and CAM systems to produce completely automated factories. Significant advances have been made in sensors for robots, such as computer vision systems, and in high-level programming languages for controlling robots. The new generation of computers will integrate these components to achieve the goal of highly automated manufacturing plants. The only economical use of today's industrial robots is to have them work in environments where a given product is manufactured continuously for several months before the assembly line is changed and retooled. One such area is the auto industry. With the new generation of computing, CAD, CAM, and high-level robot-programming languages will allow small-volume production runs to be automated as well. Autonomous vehicles and robots may also be able to replace humans operating in hazardous environments and handling dangerous materials—for example, some jobs in the nuclear-reactor industry.

Office automation

The use of computers for word processing and electronic filing is becoming ubiquitous in the U.S. office. Similarly the use of electronic mail, appointment calendars, electronic spread sheets, and data-base management systems is also growing rapidly. The new-generation systems will permit the integration, storage, and retrieval of all types of information flowing through the office. The technology to automate completely the management of office information already has been developed; its components now must be integrated into complete systems. These com-

Robert J. Douglass
Los Alamos National Laboratory

Representative applications of new-generation technology

INDUSTRIAL AUTOMATION

Users: manufacturers of goods; designers of manufactured products, product and plant engineers.

Applications: automated factories—computer-aided design (CAD), computer-aided manufacturing (CAM), and robotics; inventory management; product-cost estimating; control and routing of production runs; expert systems for design.

Components: high-speed parallel data-base storage and retrieval; software to integrate all types of information related to design and manufacturing; high-level programming languages for robots; libraries of modular designs and robot-control routines; theorem proving and planning techniques for design verification and robot control; combined expert systems and simulation for CAD; parallel processors for CAD and CAM work stations supporting high-resolution graphics.

OFFICE AUTOMATION

Users: secretaries, managers, administrators.

Applications: integration, storage, and retrieval of all types of office information; improved access to information-management systems: voice commands, voice output, natural language used for queries, data entry, and commands; integration of the telephone system with office computing systems; expert systems to assist office procedures and management decisions; teleconferences.

Components: powerful personal work stations with voice recognition and output, image digitization, and high-resolution graphics display; local-area networks linked to the telephone network and wideband networks to central mainframe computing systems; powerful data-base management software; parallel data-base machines.

SCIENCE AND ENGINEERING

Users: research scientists, design and field engineers.

Applications: expert systems for fault diagnosis; expert systems capturing and applying scientific expertise; intelligent human–machine interfaces to existing computing systems used for simulating physical processes; improved analytic tools such as symbolic algebra programs; computer-aided design; integrated data bases of scientific and engineering information, including technical papers, experimental data, and design specifications; information browsing systems and expert systems for retrieving information from scientific data bases under voice and natural-language control; expert systems for geological analysis and mineral prospecting.

Components: improved and more powerful data-base management systems including large storage systems, parallel data-base and expert-system processors; distributed data-base systems; networks for access to remote data bases; software and hardware for input and output of graphics, image, voice, and textual-data knowledge-engineering techniques to acquire and represent expertise.

COMPUTER HARDWARE AND SOFTWARE

Users: programmers, systems analysts, computer engineers, users of computer systems.

Applications: semiautomatic design and development of programs; expert systems to debug and maintain programs and electronic computer-aided design; specialized architecture for implementing firmware; expert systems for fault diagnosis of computer hardware.

Components: very high-level programming languages and hardware specification languages; integrated software-development environments; rudimentary silicon compilers; parallel processors for circuit analysis and VLSI design; high-performance work stations for software development; data-flow languages and data-flow machines; parallel programming languages and operating systems; compilers for parallel systems.

AEROSPACE

Users: pilots, air traffic controllers, scientists and engineers studying and exploiting space and remotely sensed earth resources.

Applications: air-traffic control monitors, autonomous deep-space exploration, earth-resources monitoring, semiautomatic correction and analysis of weather data, autonomous manufacturing in space.

Components: networks of ground-based and satellite-based sensors with programs for automatic data reduction and storage in large-scale distributed data bases; robots capable of autonomous planning; expert systems for fault diagnosis and repair of autonomous spacecraft; learning programs to form and verify hypotheses; self-replicating machines for space manufacturing.

MILITARY

Users: strategic planners, field and fleet commanders, intelligence analysts, weapons designers, maintenance and logistics staff.

Applications: all aspects of planning and decision support; communication, command, and control; supply and support logistics; remote sensing and surveillance; cryptography; intelligent and autonomous weapons systems; expert consultants for maintenance and fault diagnosis in the field or at sea; autonomous vehicles for hazardous environments.

Components: management information systems with remote access and distributed data bases; large-scale parallel processors and storage systems; expert systems and knowledge-acquisition systems.

RETAILING AND SERVICE INDUSTRIES

Users: consumers, retailers, advertisers, marketing department, purchasing department, sales personnel, service companies, lawyers, travel agents, advertising agencies, publishers.

Applications: computer-based catalogs for browsing and shopping; remote ordering and shopping from consumers' homes or office terminals; support for teleconferences between sales personnel and customers; accounting, billing, and invoicing systems; inventory management; automated Yellow Pages; data-base and expert systems for searching property and court records; trip and travel planning; tax and financial planning and analysis; stock-market and commodity-market information; diagnostic and troubleshooting information on cars and major appliances.

Components: hardware and software to support multimedia information systems combining image, graphical, and textual data; work stations for access to multimedia information systems; natural-language and voice commands for browsing and searching through on-line catalogues by telephone or terminal; expert-help systems; wideband networks and protocols to permit communication between user terminals and remote information systems.

EDUCATION

Users: students at all levels including professionals and adults.

Applications: intelligent computer-aided instruction (CAI) systems that permit students to direct and control the presentation of course material; computer-based training for adults and professionals; computer-based assistants that explain how to use computing systems.

Components: software and specialized processors to support voice commands, voice output, and natural-language interaction with intelligent CAI systems; specialized hardware for graphics and images; libraries and remote access to courses via digital networks; improved human–computer interfaces; cognitive modeling of the learner.

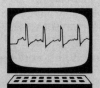

HEALTH CARE
Users: physicians, hospitals, patients, the handicapped, the disabled.
Applications: expert systems for diagnosis and prescription; data-base systems for medical records; monitoring and management of hospital patients; national data bases of information on available organs, health supplies and services, and disease statistics; automatic analysis of laboratory tests; on-line access to medical journals, textbooks, and laboratory and research results; intelligent search and retrieval entries in a medical data base; reading machines for the blind; computer-controlled wheelchairs; robot arms to aid the disabled in feeding and in manipulating objects; sensory prostheses.
Components: specialized parallel processors and software for expert systems and data-base systems; natural-language processing and voice input and output; phone and remote-terminal access to data bases and expert systems; specialized hardware to acquire, analyze, and display information from laboratory tests.

ARTS, CULTURE, AND LEISURE
Users: public at large.
Applications: multimedia computer "books" that allow browsing through images, text, and sound data; digital recording and storage of and access to music, painting, and graphic arts via digital music and image systems; a computer-based artist's palette to assist musical and graphical composition; intelligent home robots and toys.
Components: large-scale storage systems; wideband digital communication to access cultural information and entertainment; high-resolution digital sound input/output; graphical and image input/output devices, such as electronic paintbrushes and solid-state cameras.

ponents include specialized data-base processors, solid-state cameras for entering images into a data base, and improved work stations for accessing and displaying images, graphics, and text.

The new generation in computing will not only supply the hardware and software technology to support information management; it will also employ better techniques for using such systems. The user will be able to interact with the computer system through voice commands, voice output, and natural-language processing. Expert systems will furnish advice on how to use computing systems and will assist in retrieving relevant information.

Office communication will be enhanced by new-generation systems that will integrate the telephone system with office computer systems by use of digitized speech. Both local-area networks and wideband, long-distance digital communications systems will support electronic-mail and phone-message systems with teleconferences distributed over time and space.

Science and engineering

Like office managers, scientists will use new-generation computers to store, search for, and retrieve all types of information, ranging from scientific documents retrieved from librarylike data bases to experimental data acquired in real time by computer-based scientific instruments. Large-scale parallel processors will be used to analyze data collected by vast networks of small computers. For example, earthquake prediction may be possible through large-scale analysis of seismic activity collected in real time from remote stations.

Just as today the ARPAnet and CSnet computer networks allow selected scientists to work closely together as a small group even though they are physically remote from each other, ubiquitous access to such networks for new-generation users will permit scientists to collaborate with researchers at other institutions and to hold conferences without leaving their own offices.

Expert systems are already beginning to support scientific research. One such system, Dendral, has been credited with assisting in producing the results presented in more than 50 scientific publications. Symbolic processing programs, such as symbolic mathematics packages, are already aiding both scientists and engineers in problem analysis. The Prospector program developed at SRI International in Palo Alto, Calif., helps geologists locate and analyze mineral deposits.

With new hardware and better user interfaces, the new-generation computers will take advantage of expert systems to capture and apply scientific expertise. Expert systems will augment CAD systems by providing engineers with suggestions on design constraints. Improved user interfaces, when combined with traditional applications of scientific and engineering computing, will be a major advantage for the simulation of physical systems. For example, researchers at Rutgers University in New Brunswick, N.J., and at Amoco Corp. in Tulsa, Okla., have shown how an expert system and a computer menu can be used to drive a complex numerical simulation of petroleum-bearing strata more efficiently than traditional user interfaces.

Computer hardware and software

One of the primary thrusts of both U.S. and Japanese new-generation efforts is to reduce the cost of producing software. Writing, testing, and debugging software is a labor-intensive process. New-generation computing systems will include automated aids for software development, testing, and maintenance, including improved programming environments, very high-level programming languages, and programmers' assistants that keep track of certain details of a program and its formal specification. There is much interest in automatic programming—the process of automatically generating a program, given a formal specification of its inputs and outputs. Complete, general-purpose automatic programming will probably require much more basic research; however, a limited form of automatic programming might be possible for specific applications where designers can generate a program by combining a library of standard program modules.

Studies indicate that a programmer can produce approximately the same number of debugged lines of code a day, regardless of what programming language is used. Therefore, work on application-oriented, very high-level programming languages should boost the productivity of programmers using new-generation computing systems. Research on data-flow programming languages, like VAL, FGL, and Prolog, and also on data-flow machines, may make it possible to program parallel computers having a large number of parallel processors without the need for a programmer to keep track of the interaction between processors.

A few of today's manufacturers offer a powerful integrated package of programming tools, such as debuggers, editors, and file-maintenance utilities. The new generation of computing systems will offer such programming environments as standard features.

High-level electronic circuit and logic specification languages will be used in new-generation computers to improve the productivity of computer hardware engineers. Several projects in the United States are attempting to combine large-scale parallel processors for circuit analysis with CAD systems and expert systems to support VLSI design. Research with expert systems, being pursued in the United States and Japan, will assist in the design of elaborate electronics by advising on the routing and layout of circuits. The very complexity of devices, which VLSI permits, requires automated techniques for managing that complexity. One of the most important applications of new-generation technology will undoubtedly be the simulation and computer-assisted design of even newer generations of computers.

Aerospace

The new generation of computers will be applied to aerospace in such areas as air traffic control, information management for pilots, and the control of autonomous aircraft. Air traffic control could be further automated by employing a nationwide distributed data base describing the location and direction of aircraft and local weather conditions around the country. This data base would be continously updated and could be accessed by any aircraft equipped with the appropriate new-generation terminal.

Even though today's most advanced military and commercial aircraft are already largely controlled by embedded computer systems, the pilot must still cope with a tremendous flow of information coming from a complex range of instruments and displays. In the future, new-generation techniques such as voice recognition, speech output, and expert systems will help the pilot select and interpret the most important information. Computer vision systems are helping make truly self-guided autonomous aircraft possible—for example, cruise missiles that navigate by continuously comparing digitized terrain maps with images of the terrain over which they are flying.

A recent study by the National Aeronautics and Space Administration described how the new generation of computers could support intelligent earth-sensing information systems, continuously monitoring the earth's weather and resources and responding to natural-language queries for information.

The NASA study also discussed the use of new-generation techniques to control autonomous exploration missions into deep space and to support extraterrestrial manufacturing to be begun by landing a "starting kit" of machines on the surface of a planet or moon in the solar system. The kit would be programmed to replicate the plant several times to the optimal size before beginning large-scale production. Such applications will require complex robots with very sophisticated planning and problem-solving capabilities. It is doubtful that these kinds of robots will be developed within the next 10 years.

Military

Applications of new-generation computing technology here will fall into two categories. The first comprises information-management systems and expert systems to support military systems in terms of planning, decision making, and fault diagnosis. The second category encompasses the guidance and targeting of autonomous weapons.

Symbolic computing, supported by new-generation hardware, will have an important role in communications, command, and control. Possibly the greatest area of application of new-generation computing will be in information-management systems to help cope with increasingly complex problems in the logistics of supply and support, as well as with strategic and tactical planning.

Parallel architectures for analyzing radar and sonar images and for automatic planning and deduction will be incorporated in the guidance of weapons systems and in weapons defense systems. Weapons will be designed with the aid of parallel supercomputers and better computer–user interfaces. The same communication facilities that support long-range teleconferences in the office and scientific research will support worldwide digital military communication between people and data-base management systems. A number of applications of autonomous robots and weapons systems are being studied to replace humans in hostile environments. A self-guiding undersea vehicle and a robot ammunition carrier are two applications the U.S. Department of Defense has considered.

Retail and service industries

Consumers will be able to shop and buy goods, using an on-line multimedia computer catalog that contains not only textual, voice, and image and graphical descriptions of products, but that also automatically handles billing, shipping, and reordering. Tied into an electronic funds-transfer system, a retailer's computer-based catalog could automatically receive and make payments on sales and purchases, respectively.

A similar computer "book," backed by an expert system and a natural-language interface, could act as a computerized Yellow Pages that would assist a consumer in locating a company that sells a product. Improvements in speaker-independent speech recognition would allow shopping by telephone with the use of voice commands and speech output. Because present natural-language programs cannot cope with an unconstrained domain of discourse, a series of natural-language programs would have to be developed to discuss particular categories of products.

Perhaps the greatest abundance of applications of new-generation computing will come in the area of information service industries. A few representative applications are trip and travel planning, tax planning and financial analysis, stock-market and commodity-market information, access to news and weather reports on request, and diagnostic and troubleshooting information on home appliances.

The components of hardware and software needed to realize these applications have existed for some time, but the components must be integrated and more attention must be paid to developing easy, natural user interfaces both for accessing information and for entering information into knowledge bases.

Education

Computer-aided instruction (CAI) systems are currently in use at all levels of education and adult training. By offering more computing power, better user interfaces, and multimedia personal work stations, new-generation computers will make CAI available to a much larger group of users.

Networks of educational computers will offer access to a wide range of courses and will also provide such services as teleconferences with instructors. More advanced developments in new-generation computing will support intelligent computer-aided instruction, enabling a student to use natural language and voice commands to control the flow of information—both its sequence and its degree of detail. Today's research in cognitive psychology, directed at modeling human thought and problem-solving behavior, may improve CAI systems by allowing them to adjust to different learning styles and to a student's prior knowledge.

In a related area, knowledge-based computerized assistants will function as on-line "help systems" to explain how to use and diagnose problems with another system—for example, a computer application program, an automobile, an electronic device, or a manual of operation procedures. Rudimentary computer assistants exist today in research laboratories at Los Alamos, N.M.; the Massachusetts Institute of Technology in Cambridge; the University of California at Berkeley; and elsewhere.

Health care

Applications here will continue to be a prime area for expert systems. Such systems have some of their first and most successful applications in the diagnosis of diseases and medical conditions. Many problems in medicine involve the sort of classical diagnostic analysis that expert systems do well, and health care applications include many areas of specialized expertise where it is difficult and expensive to gain access to human experts.

The high cost of conventional, labor-intensive health care helps to justify the cost of building the knowledge bases for expert systems, which may reduce the overall diagnostic costs. There are, however, a number of research and social issues to be resolved, such as the medical liability of expert programs and the narrowness of knowledge that expert systems sometimes exhibit.

New-generation technology will also support aids for the handicapped and disabled. Reading machines for the blind exist today, and research on sensors and computer-controlled wheelchairs is proceeding in several laboratories. New-generation applications may also include the use of robot arms to assist disabled persons in feeding themselves and in manipulating objects.

The arts, culture, and leisure

The large proportion of the income that the entertainment industry has been able to capture in 10 years through computer-based video games is indicative of the potential for new-generation computing in this area. As true three-dimensional graphics, voice commands, and speech output become routine, computer-based entertainment will continue to spread.

Large data bases of cultural material, including digitized music libraries and "art museums," combined with multimedia personal work stations, will extend entertainment to people who want to do more than shoot down simulated alien spaceships or grapple with animated apes. Computer "books" will not only let people visit distant cities in the privacy of their own home or at the local library, but will also make it possible for art galleries, zoos, and other cultural and entertainment events to be digitized and viewed under the user's control.

Conventional video taping provides a fixed recording of an event that unfolds sequentially. Randomly accessed video disks permit users to control the presentation of information about a place or event that is not easily recorded as a sequential event. On-line libraries of conventional textual material in machine-readable format, if part of a network, could give every library in the country access to rare books and periodicals now found only in the best libraries.   ◆

This work was performed under the auspices of the United States Department of Energy.

THE TEAMS AND THE PLAYERS
Japan, the United States, and Western Europe provide striking contrasts in national interests and techniques

STRATEGIES

Within the past two years, Japan, the United States, and Europe have inaugurated major research and development programs in information technology, all feeling the urgency that, in the words of Robert E. Kahn, "the nation that dominates this information-processing field will possess the keys to world leadership in the twenty-first century" [p. 4].

In a sense, these parts of the world are following a strategy of mutual catching up. Japan has the longest-running, formal national program: its Fifth-Generation Computer Systems Project was officially inaugurated in 1981. But its aim is to catch up with the United States, which has funded research in some of the key technologies (such as artificial intelligence) for 20 years, whereas the Japanese research is virtually starting from scratch. In spite of its two decades of work, however, it was not until the Japanese announced their formal fifth-generation research project that the United States inaugurated its own concerted national research efforts toward new-generation computing.

Japan initially described its project at the International Conference on Fifth-Generation Computer Systems held in Tokyo in October 1981. The American and European scientists attending that conference concluded that Japan was announcing its intent to be satisfied no longer with taking Western technology and improving on it, but was determined to seize the lead in innovative research and development and develop unprecedented systems of its own.

That single conference spurred a dramatic response in both the United States and Europe to found similar information-technology research programs. These programs are described in the various articles in this section.

Concerns and goals

The various countries differ in their concerns and ultimate purpose of their research, and the avowed aims of each program are distinct.

The Japanese are quite clear that they are developing fifth-generation technology to meet the social needs they anticipate in the next decade. The Japanese also anticipate that exporting fifth-generation technology will improve their world economic position.

The United States is primarily concerned with maintaining its own world leadership in information technology. The United States is also concerned with the applications of fifth-generation computing technology to national security, to build up its strategic strength with respect to the USSR and the communist-bloc nations.

The Europeans are concerned about their basic economic survival in world markets. According to Horst Nasko [see page 43] the primary aim of the Europeans is to regain a strong technological base within its industries in order to reverse that negative balance of trade both in currency and patents.

These differing concerns directly influence the goals of the specific research and development programs in the various countries. Japan's goal is to build a full-fledged fifth-generation computer system and make it available for commercial use by the 1990s. The U.S. goal is to build up a greater common pool of knowledge about individual systems, both for the military and also for the use of private companies in further developing products in the usual competitive free market. Europe's goal is to rebuild a strong general industrial base through precompetitive research on various long-range projects of the kind that may not be adequately funded within individual countries.

Trudy E. Bell   Senior Associate Editor

A comprehensive overview of the research being pursued in the United States and Europe can be found in the charts beginning on page 27. No such chart could be prepared showing the research in Japan. According to a spokesperson at ICOT (Japan's Institute for New Generation Computer Technology), the Japanese "do not clearly define or distribute jobs for the fifth-generation project. All of the companies do research on each theme—on all of the research topics."

Organizational structure

The scale of the funding for all the national programs is large and roughly comparable, representing a major commitment of between half a billion and several billion dollars over the first five years. It is important to note that the programs in Japan, Europe, and England have additional financial leverage in that the companies whose research is being supported are required to match the funds they receive dollar for dollar.

All the research projects in the various countries are being pursued cooperatively between the government, private companies, and university research centers. It seems to be automatically accepted by all parties that the scale of the research challenge no longer admits of one company or laboratory being able to do the major work and that cross-fertilization is essential.

Moreover, each country, in structuring such cooperativeness, has looked to the successful examples both within itself and in the other countries, borrowing organizational concepts and applying them in innovative ways.

The Institute for New Generation Computing, with its central research center, is unique in Japan; the customary approach is to have each of the participating research institutions and companies conduct research on its own. Moreover, ICOT is contracting with outside companies and laboratories for some of the research and development—a technique familiar to U.S. defense contractors but unusual for the Japanese.

The United States, in keeping with its pluralistic decentralized pattern of pursuing scientific research and development, has three new concurrent joint research programs of national stature, each with a different structure and thrust: the Microelectronics and Computer Technology Corp. (MCC), the Microelectronics Center of North Carolina (MCNC), and the Semiconductor Research Cooperative (SRC). In addition, the Defense Advanced Research Projects Agency (Darpa) is a 25-year-old Federal agency that sponsors research and development in its own laboratories, in private companies, and in universities.

The European Strategic Programme on Research and Information Technology (Esprit) shares both similarities and differences with organizations such as ICOT and the MCC. Like both those organizations, Esprit represents a partnership between various companies, academic research laboratories, and government agencies. Unlike those organizations, Esprit also represents an international partnership.

To date, the only national European program is the recently funded Alvey Programme in Great Britain, a collaborative program between the government, universities, and private companies to support research at the various university and industrial laboratories. The Alvey Programme is consciously modeled in part on Japan's Ministry of International Trade and Industry (MITI) and on the U.S. agency Darpa.

Individual companies and universities elsewhere are pursuing information-technology research and development, but so far no other nation has yet implemented a full-fledged program. Although the French government has been considering a national research program on information technology for several years, such a program is still being discussed under the charge of Jean Claude Hirel, the director of information in the Ministry of Research and Industry in Paris. According to Pierre Aigrain, consultant to Thomson CSF and former minister for technology, it is likely that future national research programs in France will involve universities, government laboratories, and Cie. des Machines Bull (formerly CII—Honeywell Bull), which is also one of the 12 principal corporate partners in Esprit.

More questions than answers

The success of these various programs in achieving both research goals and national aims is still undetermined. The fact that the research programs in each country are as innovative in their organization as in the technology with which they are concerned suggests that the programs are also social experiments—raising more interesting questions. For example, what are the relative strengths and weaknesses of the U.S. and European tradition of doing most research in universities, versus the Japanese style of doing most of it in industry? How will the cooperative research programs in all the countries alter their traditional research structures—and serve as models for future projects as well? Only time will answer these questions.   ◆

JAPAN

Japan's reputation for productivity and efficiency notwithstanding, the country is now suffering a severe productivity bottleneck in its service industries. Production costs and consumer prices in the labor-intensive service industries continue to rise sharply, even though the same costs and prices have risen only modestly in automobile manufacturing or have even decreased in electronics. An example of the effect of this imbalance in productivity between the service industries and the manufacturing industries is the price of a dinner in a good Tokyo restaurant, which can easily cost as much as four electronic calculators.

The main reason for this imbalance is that manufacturing industries are amenable to automation by conventional computers, whereas the service industries are not. However, fifth-generation computers, with their intelligent humanlike interfaces, have the potential of partially redressing that imbalance and thus benefiting many workers in labor-intensive fields.

The fifth generation: a quantum jump in friendliness

Computers are no longer used only for science and technology, business computations, and the automated control of industrial processes; they now have penetrated our daily lives and are becoming society's central nervous system. As the developed world moves from an industrial economy to an information economy, the social structure is undergoing its greatest change since the Industrial Revolution to adapt to the new technology.

Computer technology itself is evolving. Machines are being developed that will interact naturally with human beings. Around the world the basic tools needed to fulfill this grand expectation are gradually developing. We anticipate that here in Japan our new Fifth-Generation Computer Systems Project will

Tohru Moto-oka   University of Tokyo

stimulate rapid progress toward computer systems suited to the new era.

Fifth-generation computers are expected to be used predominantly in the society of the 1990s. In addition to being capable of processing numeric data, they will handle such non-numeric data as symbols, words, pictures, and human speech. They will manipulate not only raw data, but also knowledge—that is, information judged or organized according to intrinsic characteristics, much as humans organize knowledge in their brains. Applied artificial intelligence will play a key role.

Fifth-generation computers are more than a direct extension of the computer technology that packs more integrated circuits into a smaller space. They are to be distinguished from the large and fast number-crunching supercomputers being developed for intricate scientific and engineering calculations and simulations.

Fifth-generation computer systems are expected to fulfill four major roles: (1) enhancement of productivity in low-productivity areas, such as nonstandardized operations in smaller industries; (2) conservation of national resources and energy through optimal energy conversion; (3) establishment of medical, educational, and other kinds of support systems for solving complex social problems, such as the transition to a society made up largely of the elderly; and (4) fostering of international cooperation through the machine translation of languages.

The fields in which computers will be applied in the 1990s will be extremely diversified, ranging from individual components in appliances to giant information networks with worldwide connections. Everyone will be using computers in daily life without giving it a second thought. For that to happen, however, an environment will have to be created in which a human and a computer can communicate easily through a wide variety of information media such as speech, text, and graphics—in short, the common methods by which people communicate with each other.

The changes from one generation to the next in computer technology have so far been made to accommodate changes in various devices—that is, from vacuum tubes (the first generation) to transistors, then to integrated circuits, and recently to large-scale integrated circuits. Although computers have become faster and more complex, in our view there have been no major changes in the fundamental design philosophy and objectives of computers.

With fifth-generation computers, however, the expected generation advances will be more generic changes, involving not only a change in device technology (to very large-scale integrated circuits) but also simultaneous changes in design philosophy and in envisioned application. This technological change is so great that one could even call fifth-generation systems new-era computers.

The design philosophy behind conventional Von Neumann computers in use today called for a minimum of hardware to configure systems of maximum simplicity, capable of efficient processing with software. In Von Neumann's day hardware was expensive, bulky, and short-lived, and it consumed a lot of power. Because of this, stored-program systems that were controlled sequentially were the best choice; high speeds and large capacities were pursued for economic reasons, resulting in the emergence of today's giant computers.

New directions in computer technology have led to a rethinking of this design philosophy. First, the speeds of computers now used are approaching the limit imposed by the speed of light. Second, the emergence of VLSI technology has substantially reduced hardware costs, and it soon will be cost-effective to use as much hardware as is required. To take full advantage of the mass production of VLSI chips while computing faster than the limit imposed by the speed of light, parallel processing must be used instead of sequential processing. Finally, current computers are extremely weak in basic functions for processing speech, text, graphics, and other nonnumeric data; they are also weak on artificially intelligent processing, such as inference, association, and learning.

The computer, as its name implies, was designed originally as a machine to perform numerical computations. Over the decades computer applications have expanded into such fields as control systems, the processing of multiple information media, and database and artificial-intelligence systems—but without major changes in the underlying philosophy of design. We believe that for computers to thrive in the 1990s, they must evolve from machines dedicated to numerical computations to machines that can assess the meaning of information and can understand the problems to be solved. ◆

ICOT: Japan mobilizes for the new generation

Meeting the anticipated needs of its own society in the 1990s is a cornerstone of Japan's economic planning and of its Fifth-Generation Computer Systems Project. The technology to meet these needs is being developed by Japan's Institute for New Generation Computer Technology (ICOT). ICOT's objective is to research and develop computer technology that can perform more humanlike intellectual functions: inference, association, and learning, as well as nonnumeric processing of speech, text, graphics, and patterns.

To achieve this objective, the Fifth-Generation Computer Systems Project is finding ways to supplant traditional sequential processing with parallel processing. The great speed and capacity of parallel processing are essential for developing the artificial intelligence, the vast knowledge base, and the "natural" human–machine interface envisioned for the new computers.

The net result of the Fifth-Generation Computer Systems Project will be the basic technology and prototype systems to build computers that will cooperate more fully with human beings and will extend human knowledge, perception, and intuition. The Japanese anticipate that these computers will be accepted and depended on in virtually all segments of contemporary society: manufacturing, services, science, administration, education, culture, government, medicine, finance, and other aspects of daily life.

Planning began in the 1970s

The roots of the Fifth-Generation Computer Systems Project go back more than four years, when Japan's Ministry of International Trade and Industry (MITI) began trying to envision the information society of the 1990s and the computers that would be needed then. The ministry's intent was to identify anything the government should do to help develop the computers and to propose a research and development setup to pursue these goals. For this purpose, a study group was set up in 1979 to examine the possibility of a concerted Japanese research effort.

The initial studies were conducted for two years by the Japan Information Processing Development Center. Then in fiscal 1981, based on these initial studies, the Ministry of International Trade and Industry set up its own research and study committee. Three task forces were organized. One, headed by Hajime Karat-

Spectrum Staff

su, a technology consultant from Matsushita Communication Industrial Co. in Yokohama, was responsible for addressing problems related to the social environment; its task was to identify the requirements for computers from the broad perspective of users and others. A second task force, led by Hideo Aiso of Keio University in Yokohama, was composed of technical experts charged with identifying the necessary computer architecture and hardware. The third task force, also made up of technical experts, was led by Kazuhiro Fuchi of MITI's Electrotechnical Laboratory in Ibaraki to consider basic theory and software problems. Altogether the task forces drew on the expertise of nearly 150 users and scholars.

Results of the research and the studies were compiled into a committee report in 1981 by Tohru Moto-oka of the University of Tokyo, chairman of the study group. The report described a major research project in great detail, defining its objectives, themes, plans, and a program for research and development. On the basis of this report, the Fifth-Generation Computer Systems Project was started as a national project in fiscal 1982. ICOT, the Institute for New Generation Computer Technology, was set up in April 1982 as the principal organization for executing the project.

New computers to fill many gaps

The report of Mr. Karatsu's task force, which addressed problems in the social environment, made a number of projections about the social impact of fifth-generation systems when they become commercially available.

Fifth-generation computers, with their intelligent humanlike interfaces, have the potential of benefiting many workers in labor-intensive fields, his report pointed out. For example, in education, fifth-generation technology is expected to make personalized teaching economical. Virtually everyone will have access to a wide variety of courses and will be able to study them as rapidly as or as slowly as preferred.

In medicine, remote checkups by telephone will be accepted as routine. Data banks will furnish doctors with background information on illnesses and give them medical histories of patients, even if they are treating a patient thousands of miles away.

Tedious administrative jobs can be simplified by intelligent computers that communicate with operators in a natural language. Governmental bureaucracies can thus be made smaller.

The prime aim is to make a machine that fits the needs of people instead of making people work by the rules of the machine

---

In agriculture, fifth-generation technology will bring more effective surveying of natural resources and cultivation of them. Weather will be forecast more accurately. Resources will be recycled more readily. The channels from farm to market will be more responsive in accommodating supplies and demands.

Even in Japanese manufacturing industries, fifth-generation computers will fill a critical need by controlling and reducing energy consumption. For energy-poor Japan, optimizing the operation of all types of energy-consuming systems could spell the difference between the country's success or failure as an international manufacturing power. Fifth-generation technology, with its great data-processing capability, also can aid in geological searches for conventional energy resources. With its ability to draw inferences, fifth-generation technology can aid in researching and developing unconventional energy resources.

Meeting human beings halfway

In all these uses, the prime aim is to make a machine that, according to Mr. Karatsu, should fit the needs of people instead of making the people work according to the rules of the machine. Ideally, a person who is not a computer professional will be able to handle the computer without training. "This," says Mr. Karatsu, "is the popularization of the computer in the actual sense."

A user could employ a fifth-generation personal computer that may be located in the home or office. The personal computer will have a conversational function that will allow the user to speak to it, presenting a question or a problem in the same way one person would ask another, "How much have the populations of the 10 largest cities in Japan grown each year since World War II?" If the user's question is ambiguous, the personal computer might respond with its own questions to coach the user in further defining the query. Then the computer will go to work on the problem, writing its own program and giving an answer within seconds in spoken, graphic, or printed form.

If the problem is too complex or if the machine's store of knowledge is insufficient, the personal computer will draw on the resources of larger computers and knowledge bases via networks. The answer will still be furnished in seconds, and the user will be unaware that the personal computer has gone for help.

To the user, the personal computer will act as an expert system or "intelligent assistant"—in effect, an agent that performs difficult tasks at a highly professional, expert level. It will also be equipped with some common sense: the capability to analyze problems and make inferences, judgments, and conjectures.

A combined private and government effort

The research and development for Japan's Fifth-Generation Computer Systems Project has been completely funded by the Japanese government in the intitial three-year stage. The key money to inaugurate ICOT was donated by a consortium of eight manufacturers: Fujitsu Ltd. in Tokyo; Hitachi Ltd. in Tokyo; Matsushita Electric Industrial Co. in Osaka; Mitsubishi Electric Co. in Tokyo; NEC Corp. in Tokyo; Oki Electric Industry Co. in Tokyo; Sharp Co. in Nara; and Toshiba Corp. in Tokyo. This consortium also provides the funds to run ICOT. The member companies are obliged to give ICOT their complete understanding, cooperation, and support.

These companies support ICOT equally and will share equally in the fruits of ICOT's labor. But beyond funding, they, plus the government laboratories of Nippon Telephone and Telegraph Public Corp. in Tokyo, and the Electrotechnical Laboratory of the Ministry of International Trade and Industry in Tsukuba Science City, have furnished people—42 top-flight researchers who have distinguished themselves in developing technology or in creating a good atmosphere conducive to innovation. They are the ones who will carry out ICOT's program.

All are men and all are young. Excepting the research leaders, most are under 30, and the oldest is 35—at the specific request of ICOT's director Kazuhiro Fuchi. According to Dr. Fuchi, there is good reason for this. People in middle age may have wisdom, experience, and the ability to organize and motivate. But they are not inclined to innovate—and innovation is precisely what ICOT seeks. In Dr. Fuchi's words, "Young people have fewer fixed ideas." They can follow new intellectual paths more readily, achieve new insights, and make radical departures.

At the core of ICOT is its research center, where the 42 young researchers work. Advising the activities of the research center

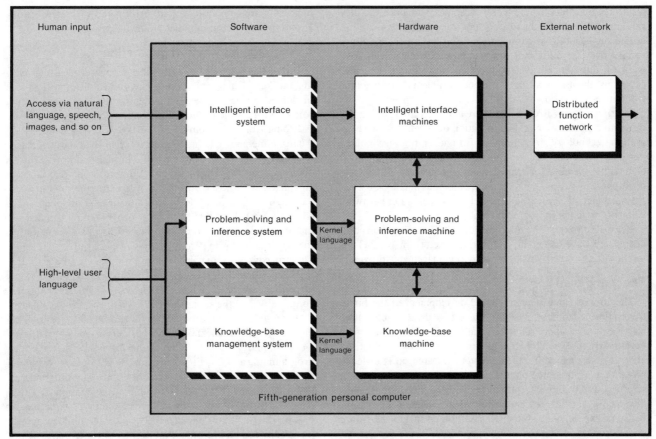

Human input	Software	Hardware	External network

The fifth-generation personal computer will consist of intelligent interface machines (corresponding to input/output channels and devices on a present-day computer), a problem-solving and inference machine (corresponding to a central processing unit), *and a knowledge-base management machine (corresponding to a memory and filing system with virtual memory). Key features of the personal computer will be ability to program itself, to perform inferences, and to communicate with other computers.*

are working groups, part of a project-promotion committee, comprising representatives of governmental laboratories, universities, and industry. The working groups advise the research work undertaken at ICOT. Supporting the activities of the research center is a General Affairs Office, which handles accounting, administration, and international relations.

With a staff of 52, ICOT is not a large organization—nor is its budget big. Starting out with a modest $2 million budget in 1982, ICOT will spend about $16 million this year and will more than double that in 1984. ICOT will spend some portion of the money for contracting with outside companies and laboratories for developing prototypes of some subsystems.

ICOT is unusual in Japan in that it is a separate, independent, neutral organization that has been established to carry out a research project; the customary Japanese approach is to have each of the participating research institutions and companies conduct work on its own. (By contrast, Japan's eight-year National Superspeed Computer Project, an independent concurrent research effort aimed at building machines 1000 times faster than the Cray 1 "supercomputer" built by Cray Research of Minneapolis, Minn., is organized along traditional Japanese lines).

Two prime hardware projects

The ICOT research center plans to approach the overall goal of a full-fledged fifth-generation system by pursuing two intermediate hardware projects of top priority: a parallel inference machine and a knowledge-based machine.

The parallel inference machine is a computer system that follows a line of reasoning to arrive at, or infer, a conclusion—

that is, it recommends a policy or action on the basis of the facts and rules presented to it. Ultimately it will be capable of 100 million to 1 billion logical inferences per second (LIPS). By way of comparison, one inference operation on a present computer is considered to require between 100 and 1000 steps; hence, one LIPS is equivalent to 100 to 1000 instructions per second.

The knowledge-based machine is a computer system that efficiently manages large amounts of knowledge—that is, data and rules—and it automatically organizes, controls, retrieves, and updates its contents. Its capacity will be between 10 billion and 100 billion bytes. It will include inference functions as well as relational algebraic functions.

The knowledge-based machine will be merged with the inference machine at the final stage of the project to form a complete fifth-generation computer. In combination, the two machines will be able to search for data relevant to the line of reasoning the inference machine is following and come up with solutions to complex problems in several seconds. The knowledge-based machine will also be able to function as a conventional data-base machine.

Intelligent software projects

ICOT's major software efforts will be oriented toward two software systems: a problem-solving and inference system for processing problems and a knowledge-based management system for accumulating and managing knowledge. These two systems will be the nucleus of the intelligent software.

ICOT's additional software efforts are directed at an intelligent interface and intelligent programming. The interface will let the machines handle speech, graphics, and images so they can interact with humans flexibly and smoothly.

The intelligent programming software will allow the machines to take over the burden of programming. Ultimately this software will automatically convert problems into efficient computer programs; the user will simply present a problem to the machine without regard to how it will be solved.

Intertwined with ICOT's hardware and software research is a program concentrating on the utilization of very large-scale integration technology. VLSI makes fifth-generation technology possible by not only reducing the cost of hardware, but also by eliminating the need for vast, virtually unmanageable quantities of software by casting it into firmware and thus making it part of the machine. VLSI and the fifth-generation computer hardware will work together in a symbiotic relationship.

Regardless of their size and function, all fifth-generation computers will have essentially the same structure: a parallel inference machine with knowledge-based management software.

The grand plan

The 10-year span of research and development of the Fifth-Generation Computer Systems Project is divided into three stages, each of approximately equal length. The initial stage began early in 1982. Its emphasis is on reviewing, evaluating, and, as necessary, restructuring current research on knowledge processing. Candidate subjects for further research are being screened, and the basic technology is being developed for the immediate stage. Hardware and software subsystems are being built for some experimental systems. These systems include hardware and software simulators, prototypes for language processing, and experimental natural-language processing systems.

The intermediate stage of the 10-year plan will establish subsystems for hardware and software. It will develop algorithms and basic architecture.

The final stage will integrate software subsystems, hardware subsystems (which have been made into VLSI circuitry), and applications software to create the first prototypes of fifth-generation computers.

Data-flow concept being developed

Conceptual designs for pilot models for both the parallel inference machine and the knowledge-based machine were completed in 1982 and functional designs were drawn up last March. These machines encompass some of the most advanced development of the fifth-generation project. They employ forms of parallel processing known as data flow, reduction, and other architectures [see "Computer architecture," p. 66]. The processing scheme is extraordinarily complex, involving intricate coordination and precise timing. Nevertheless, work on prototype hardware is under way. The inference machine's designers have taken special care to ensure that the architecture can accommodate a variety of inference methods—deductive inference, inductive inference (including guessing based on incomplete knowledge), and cooperative problem solving (solving problems based on several bodies of knowledge).

For the knowledge-based machine, the functional design includes these components:
• A mechanism for managing the execution of knowledge-based operations.
• A parallel mechanism for accumulating, updating, and retrieving knowledge, and similar functions.
• A relational data-base mechanism that stores relationships between various data so they can be retrieved as a related group.

These three components of the knowledge-based machine individually are submodules that perform the various functions. Prototypes of the submodules are being constructed.

A language for the fifth generation

Prolog has been selected as the first stepping stone for developing the kernel language, which plays the role of a high-level machine language as well as the description language for basic software for the fifth-generation computer project.

Prolog (for programming in logic) was invented in 1971 by Alain Colmerauer, a French computer scientist at the artificial intelligence unit of the University of Marseilles, and was further developed at the University of Edinburgh in Scotland. A language based on symbolic logic, it lets the computer draw inferences from a series of declarative true or false statements (called predicates). It differs from most programming languages in that it does not specify procedures to get to a result, but defines the result as following from a series of declarative statements. The procedures needed are implicit within the language itself.

This preference of the Japanese researchers for Prolog stands in contrast to the preference of the U.S. artificial-intelligence community for the language LISP (list-processing language). "There are several arguments in the Prolog-versus-LISP debate," Dr. Fuchi acknowledges in ICOT's new journal, *New Generation Computing*. "One is the difference between logic programming and functional programming. Logic programming languages have two characteristics that functional programming languages such as LISP do not. The first is a function of pattern matching through unification [a basic computational mechanism of logic programming languages]. The second is nondeterminism [the ability to search through more than one alternative to find the answer or answers to a problem]. In this sense, Prolog can be considered an extension of LISP."

Prolog as a kernel language offers special advantages to both knowledge processing and mechanized inferences. For example, Prolog is well suited to list processing, pattern matching, and a variety of other data-handling chores. The linguistic nature of logic programming languages such as Prolog also allow knowledge to be processed in parallel as well as sequentially; thus it computes by exceptionally fast methods. Moreover, Prolog incorporates many of the same functions as LISP.

The kernel language based on Prolog must be further developed to be completely suited for fifth-generation computers. A preliminary version called Kernel Language Version 0 already has been developed at ICOT for the initial phase. Kernel Language Version 0 operates sequentially and is used to design prototype hardware and software. Kernel Language Version 1, now in development, will operate on parallel machines.

Prolog in its original form does not deal with abstract data; this capability is being added for the fifth generation. Similarly the original Prolog is a simple and powerful language based on first-order logic (logic that requires every statement to be proved to arrive at a result); however, various higher-order extensions are needed to shortcut some of the repetitive time-consuming proofs, and these extensions are being introduced.

Interpreters, compilers, file systems, debugging tools, and other essential programs have to be developed. Therefore, efficient system description functions are being added to Prolog.

Software moving beyond concept stage

Both the conceptual and the functional design of the major software modules—comprising intelligent interface, intelligent programming, problem solving, inference, and knowledge-based management—were finished in 1982, including documentation.

Current work on the intelligent interface is directed along two

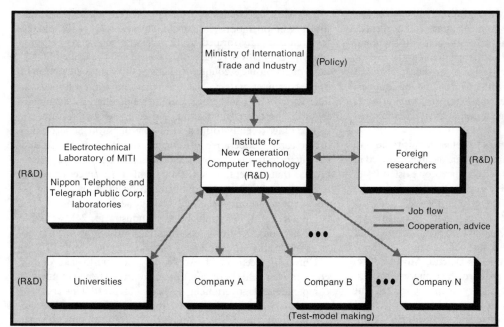

Japan's Institute for New Generation Computer Technology (ICOT) is responsible to the Ministry of International Trade and Industry, which sets the policy for ICOT's development of a fifth-generation computer system. ICOT conducts its own internal research and development and cooperates with two government laboratories, various Japanese universities, and independent foreign researchers. ICOT contracts with Japanese industries to make and test prototype hardware and software. The specific universities and companies involved vary with the individual project; participation is not limited to the consortium of eight major companies sponsoring ICOT.

lines: a high-level syntactic and semantic analysis program and a dictionary pilot system. The syntactic and semantic analysis program is aimed at devising ways for a computer to parse sentences at high speed, as well as at devising simplified algorithms for natural-language understanding.

In general, language is defined by two types of rules: syntax (the grammar of sentence structure) and semantics (the meaning of words). Since the two kinds of rules are closely related, it seems pointless to treat them separately. Thus, in ICOT's approach to natural-language processing, attention is paid to the semantics of a natural language, and application systems will therefore be built with emphasis on semantic analysis. Semantic interpretation will be performed in as formal and logical a way as possible, with due regard for the rules of syntax.

For the dictionary pilot system, ICOT is collecting various dictionaries, sentence examples, and categorized thesaurus rules. These will be recorded on a magnetic-tape data file as basic data for natural language research and as dictionaries for machine translation from one language to another.

For intelligent programming software, the immediate goal is devising basic software modules. The modules will be written in Kernel Language Version 0 and will be used on the sequential inference machine for hardware and software experimentation. These modules, scheduled to be completed by the middle of next year, will be used to help develop further programming software. The modules include:
• A conversational system to use existing programs.
• An editor system to create and modify programs.
• A debugging system.
• An analytic system to analyze and report on the contents of programs and the relationships among programs.
• A librarian system to manage the programs as a whole.

Software management verification planned

A longer-term objective for intelligent programming is a software-management and -verification program. Initially the goal is to develop a program that will manage programs in a data base according to information on their logical structures. Eventually the structure and semantics of programs and the procedures by which programs are developed will be described in

logical form. This will be used by the intelligent programming system for the automatic designing of other programs as needed.

ICOT's research on problem-solving software is focused on programming methods that will be the first step toward designing a cooperative problem-solving system. In such a system, a single problem will be solved by two or more problem-solving systems.

Work is proceeding also on the two major components of the knowledge-based management system: a large-scale relational data-base management program (to define and retrieve relationships between data) and a knowledge-representation system (for representing knowledge meaningfully and usefully). For the relational data-base management program, the initial goal is development of software to link the relational data-base machine to the sequential inference machine for conducting experiments. The ultimate goal is to develop a query system that can be used in searching a data base, including a natural-language interface. The intelligent interface module will be applied to the natural-language interface to help a user define more precisely the questions that will yield the desired information.

Work on the knowledge-representation system has shown that further development will be most productive if it is oriented toward specific applications, even at this early stage. Accordingly a knowledge-utilization submodule has been added to the knowledge-based management module, and it is being developed concurrently. The goal is to have a full-scale knowledge-utilization program ready during the intermediate stage. ◆

THE UNITED STATES

Japan's fifth-generation computer effort may have caught the imagination of the popular press, but work leading to this next generation of computing in the United States has its roots in research conducted for 20 years. Artificial intelligence is one example. The quantity of research is considerable, but it has been scattered among some 40 universities and 30 major corporations.

Mark A. Fischetti   Associate Editor

That piecemeal approach is changing, however, and engineering and computer science resources, both corporate and academic, are coming together, in part as a response to the national Japanese effort and in part due to the ever-increasing cost of microelectronics research. There is also a growing realization that cooperative research between otherwise competing commercial companies need not threaten market share, but rather is necessary for strength in a highly competitive international marketplace.

This section of *Spectrum* attempts to delineate this trend and the research being done at companies and universities involved in cooperative efforts. Four types of such cooperation exist today in the United States, with the specific goal of contributing to the next generation of computing. The efforts involve a national Government umbrella organization, an industry cooperative, two university research consortia, and individual universities that have developed expertise in a branch of computing.

Profiled is the Defense Department's Defense Advanced Research Projects Agency (Darpa), chartered by Congress to sponsor research leading to improved military weaponry [p. 21]. The agency has scheduled $1 billion in new studies over the next decade on artificial intelligence, software engineering, and computer architecture.

The Microelectronics and Computer Technology Corp. has just begun operations in Austin, Texas, as a profit-making research company formed by 13 otherwise competing corporations [p. 23]. This organization is considered the United States' most direct business counter to Japan's drive for a greater share of the computer market. The research corporation will focus on microelectronics packaging, computer-aided design and manufacturing, software engineering, and computer architecture.

Two other recently formed research groups, the Semiconductor Research Cooperative in Research Triangle Park, N.C., and the Microelectronics Center of North Carolina are really research brokers that funnel money from a number of sources primarily to universities. The semiconductor cooperative is helping to defray the enormous cost of basic research by one segment of the computer world, the semiconductor industry [p. 24], while the microelectronics center is coordinating research at five universities in North Carolina, largely with state money [p. 26].

University "centers of excellence," the fourth category of cooperative research, obtain their own grants from commercial companies and government agencies. Stanford University in Palo Alto, Calif., is a prime example [p. 25]. With numerous contracts covering VLSI, advanced architectures, and artificial intelligence, it is one of a growing number of university–industry

The challenge to U.S. supercomputers

The U.S. Office of Science and Technology Policy, under the direction of George A. Keyworth II, has come to grips with the need for large-scale general-purpose computers for scientific and engineering applications—supercomputers—and with the ongoing effort in Japan, quite apart from its fifth-generation computer program, to advance Japanese proficiency in supercomputer technology. On this issue, the science advisor to the President offers the following perspective. —Ed.

After years of domination of the supercomputer market by a few U.S. companies, we may be on the threshold of real international competition. I view this as a serious but potentially beneficial development—one that is likely to accelerate progress in computer technology.

The reasons for this approaching change stem primarily from the inevitable maturing technological capabilities of other nations. The leading aspirant to join the supercomputer club is Japan, which has made the development of an advanced supercomputer a national priority, backed by government funds. This is in addition to its program to develop computers based on artificial-intelligence concepts.

Down the road is the possibility that what is today a demand for only dozens of these expensive machines will multiply into a much broader commercial market. It is reasonable to assume that as we extend the applications of supercomputers, we will create more demand for and perhaps improve the efficiency of their production. Half a dozen industries are already experimenting with supercomputers—for modeling combustion and chemical processes, for computer-aided design, for analysis of seismic data, for optimizing distribution systems, or for generating advanced computer graphics.

We cannot ignore the reality that many of the U.S. applications of supercomputers occur in research related to national security—aircraft and weapons design, simulations, cryptology, and so on. In addition, special-purpose, high-speed machines are needed for applications such as signal processing, and the military has a growing interest in artificial-intelligence applications.

Even allowing for growing commercial demand for general-purpose supercomputers, customers will be limited, and the supercomputer market may not be able to support more than a few manufacturers. We have to be concerned about the possibility of having to rely on a foreign supplier for a critical tool for national security.

In no way am I suggesting that U.S. companies will not remain at the leading edge of supercomputer development; but I also recognize that we cannot take something as important as that for granted. We need to assure ourselves that we will not compromise our ability to meet national security needs.

How do we do that? Obviously the Federal government has a key role in supercomputer evolution, simply because it has until now been the primary customer and is likely to remain so for the foreseeable future. Because the arrangement between the Government and supercomputer manufacturers has been extraordinarily successful, earlier this year we announced our intention to follow that approach in focusing additional attention on supercomputer development. We are assessing upcoming Federal requirements for the purchase of supercomputers and expect to tell manufacturers of our needs. This assurance of a market is the incentive preferred by the manufacturers of these machines and should encourage them to go ahead with needed investments in R&D for meeting our performance goals.

We are also making sure that Federally supported research in areas like artificial intelligence, computer architecture, software, and, of course, microcircuitry is well coordinated and that important research topics are addressed.

Finally, we are looking at ways to make supercomputers more widely available to U.S. researchers, either through actual installation at major university and Government research centers or through access via a network. This is important not only to advance particular research goals, but also to make sure that next-generation researchers and computer scientists are familiar with the capabilities of these machines.

Supercomputers are important as tools in their own right, but they also drive research in a number of key areas of physics, chemistry, and mathematics. The Federal government's role in maintaining U.S. supremacy in this field will continue and will be reflected in the increasing prominence it receives in key agency budgets in the years ahead.

—*George A. Keyworth II*
Science Advisor to the President

U.S. cooperative research leading to next generation of computing

Organization/ type	Constituents			Proposed budget			Staff		Technical people at contractors*
	Univ.	Corp.	Other	Amount, $	From	To	Administration and support	Technical	
Darpa/gov't	0	0	self	1 billion 1983–90	U.S. Government	5 universities 2 corporations 2 national labs plus smaller contractors	5–10		Not recorded
MCC/corp.	0	13	0	50 million 1984	13 members	Self	15	300–400	10
SRC/ consortium	0	23	0	31 million 1982–84	23 members	30 universities	8	4	150
MCNC/ consortium	5	0	RTI**	50 million 1981–85	$43 million from state of N.C. $7 million from industry	5 universities RTI	35	30	100

*Does not include graduate students
**Research Triangle Institute

–Government cooperatives, and other schools as well could have been picked to epitomize the trend.

Following these exposes is a five-page table listing work at companies and universities involved in cooperative research. As explained on page 27, much insight can be gained into the extent of research going on in the United States. The table points to three trends. First, industry-sponsored research no longer occurs only at so-called superschools—the traditional Stanfords and MITs. Second, the temperment of industry–university cooperation is changing. It used to be that a university was inherently at odds with its industry sponsors, because of a conflict of interest between the university's commitment to teach students and a company's competitive need for fast turnaround on research. Today more and more schools are integrating industry research with teaching, to give students a more practical learning experience; companies, for their part, are taking an interest in more basic, less rushed, long-term research.

The third trend, in which universities are taking the lead in establishing industrial parks to foster joint university-corporate research, is illustrated by the Rensselaer Polytechnic Institute. Handily, Stanford University's computer research program grew up with Silicon Valley; the university was virtually next door to major corporations and other excellent computer science schools. The Massachusetts Institute of Technology, on the other hand, is adjacent to Boston's electronics industry. Cooperative research was almost ensured at both these locales. But Rensselaer is in Troy, N.Y., 120 miles from both the nearest technology-oriented school or city.

What the school has done is to create its own industrial park, centered on Rensselaer's growing electronics research program. By blending financial help from the state and commitments from a local real-estate developer and local industries, Rensselaer's president, George Low, has obtained research contracts while offering companies a new research facility and industrial park.

Individual state governments are showing similar initiative. North Carolina is a major example. It is investing more than $43 million a year in the new Microelectronics Center of North Carolina, which is allocating the money among five North Carolina universities. The state has also dedicated the Research Triangle Institute, a heavily equipped research laboratory, to the effort. Initiatives like this are catching on in other states, such as New York and Georgia, which are proposing similar research arrangements. ◆

SCS: toward supersmart computers for the military

Earlier this year, the Defense Advanced Research Projects Agency (Darpa) announced a new program called Strategic Computing and Survivability, which will foster a new generation of superintelligent computers for military use. These machines will have humanlike capabilities, allowing them to see, reason, plan, and even supervise the actions of military systems in the field. High-performance VLSI-based hardware and multiprocessor software will be developed with the goal of demonstrating them in selected military applications in the field by the end of the 1980s. Close to $1 billion may be spent over the rest of the decade toward this end.

The project is motivated by the need to support a range of military applications now well beyond the state of the art. The nation is engaged in a world competition on two fronts: with the Soviet Union politically and militarily and with its trading partners economically. Although it has a clear technological lead over the Soviet Union, the Russians have significantly outspent the United States in military hardware over the last decade. This has resulted in a gross imbalance in military potential that can only be countered by effective use of technology.

Japan's announcement of a plan to develop fifth-generation computers is also a significant initiative. The United States simply cannot afford to lose its current leadership in very large-scale integration, computers, and communications. Darpa's strategic computing program is thus a simultaneous response to military needs and the maintenance of a strong industrial base.

Darpa is well positioned to take on a major role in the development of next-generation computing technology. For many years the agency was the only significant funding source for work in artificial intelligence, which is at the heart of fifth-generation computer research. Darpa was responsible for the development of the world's first supercomputer—the Illiac IV, which was operational at the Ames Research Laboratory of the National Aeronautics and Space Administration until the early 1980s, when it

Robert S. Cooper and **Robert E. Kahn**
Defense Advanced Research Projects Agency

was replaced by one of the newer Class VI machines, the Cray-1. Darpa also funded development of timesharing and packet switching. The VHSIC (Very High Speed Integrated Circuits) program, supported by the military services, was established a few years ago to accelerate the advance of silicon integrated-circuit technology and to insert it into key defense systems. Parallel with that effort, Darpa initiated a program to stimulate innovation in VLSI, to train researchers and technologists, and to provide rapid turnaround in the fabrication of ICs for use in system development and training.

Although no special collaboration is planned with the Semi-conductor Research Cooperative in Research Triangle Park, N.C., and the Microelectronics and Computer Technology Corp. in Austin, Texas, Darpa does intend to track closely the results of their efforts, as well as other industrial R&D activities, to avoid duplication of effort and to ensure that technology from every possible source is available for application to defense problems.

The Darpa strategic computing program will span major areas of technology, including high-performance device technology and VLSI systems, multiprocessor computer architecture, and artificial-intelligence applications.

The device technology program will concentrate on gallium arsenide. It is being emphasized because it combines high speed with low power and a high degree of radiation hardness. One of Darpa's first goals for 1984 is to establish a pilot GaAs fabrication line. High-performance secondary memory technology is to be developed to support military needs for high-density bulk memory in the field. New packaging concepts, circuit techniques, and interconnections (including electrooptic) will accommodate very high-speed computing. Additional development may include high-performance bus structures and high-speed access to very high-density secondary storage.

In VLSI systems, Darpa will procure 1.25-micrometer complementary-MOS foundry services and establish the design rules and foundry interfaces for gallium arsenide. Wafer-scale integration will be pursued with the aim of fabricating very high-performance silicon and GaAs computers on a single wafer. Darpa will develop a new generation of network-based design tools that can be used to design not just single chips, but also printed-circuit boards and larger systems that will be hooked into the Arpanet

---

The Darpa program will foster a generation of computers that will have humanlike capabilities, allowing them to see, reason, plan, and even supervise military systems

---

and other commercial networks. These design tools will be made available to universities and industry for work on the project and for more general purposes.

In combination with new device technology, the computer architecture effort will have the goal of creating computers capable of performance three or four orders of magnitude greater than that of current machines. Examples are symbolic processors, data-base machines, and signal processors for real-time vision and signal interpretation. These computers will require highly parallel architectures. The initial aim will be to develop several small-scale prototype architectures, and both languages and software environments for them, and then to evaluate them in various proposed applications. The initial prototypes will be sufficiently powerful to be useful as research tools in their own right. They will be at least an order of magnitude faster than current symbolic processors but will not necessarily use high-

performance devices; they will derive their power instead from parallelism.

The construction of these machines will typically be done in joint projects between universities and industry. Darpa work is carried out at a host of universities, research facilities of the armed services, national laboratories, and corporations. Most of the experimentation with these machines will be conducted at universities, but additional units will be made available through industry and could form the basis for a new generation of machines with broad commercial applications. The development of suitable languages, operating systems, and other software for parallel processing will be an important aspect of this work. To aid in the design of advanced computer architectures and multiprocessor software, an emulation facility and a multiprocessor workbench will be constructed during the next two years. Both will be built from commercially available processors.

In artificial-intelligence applications, software will be developed in six generic areas that hold the key to military applications: speech, vision, natural languages, very large knowledge bases, graphics, and navigation. Research has been supported by Darpa in these areas for two decades, but a shortage of adequate computing power has limited the results The goal is to develop real-time processing systems that can cope with the enormous computational requirements needed for exploiting these technology areas. Efforts will concentrate primarily on developing generic multiprocessor applications software.

Work in the speech area will focus on the development of a system that can handle real-time continuous speech with a very large vocabulary—5000 to 10 000 words. Special attention will be paid to speech recognition in a fighter aircraft environment, as well as over unconditioned telephone lines. Darpa will develop real-time vision systems suitable for photointerpretation, terminal homing, and autonomous navigation and piloting systems. The natural language and very large knowledge-base efforts will deal with the problems of human–machine communication, using English and other languages. This will allow rapid retrieval of multitudinous information from large semantic networks and their use in logical reasoning about a specific problem domain.

Darpa intends to apply the computers developed in this program to a number of broad military applications. Among the most important of these are autonomous systems, such as advanced vehicles or satellite-control stations. Systems like these will require almost humanlike capabilities to sense, reason, plan, and navigate to fulfill these missions. Above all, they must be able to react effectively in the face of unexpected circumstances. They will be capable of drawing on human experience and expertise stored in massive knowledge bases and will interpret current sensor and situational information, much as a human being does, in determining future actions to be taken.

A second important group of applications are collaborative systems, in which machines aid people in controlling other machines. An example might be a pilot's assistant that can respond to spoken commands by a pilot and carry them out without error, drawing upon specific aircraft, sensor, and tactical knowledge stored in memory and upon prodigious computer power. Such capability could free a pilot to concentrate on tactics while the computer automatically activated surveillance sensors, interpreted radar, optical, and electronic intelligence, and prepared appropriate weapons systems to counter hostile aircraft of missiles. Such collaboration could elevate the role of the human pilot to that of an aircraft commander, concentrating on the strategy for carrying out the overall mission rather than that of a button-and-switch technician.

Such systems may also help in military assessments on a battle-field, simulating and predicting the consequences of various courses of military action and interpreting signals acquired on the battlefield. This information could be compiled and presented as sophisticated graphics that would allow a commander and his staff to concentrate on the larger strategic issues, rather than having to manage the enormous data flow that will characterize future battles.

Superintelligent computers can also act as expert advisors, aiding decision makers in such areas as nuclear planning, logistics, aircraft-carrier flight operations, or equipment maintenance. Finally, computers of the sort this program aims to develop will aid in the conduct of war games or, more conventionally, be used in conjunction with existing Class VI machines for aerodynamic and hydrodynamic designs for planes and ships.

Taken as a whole, the Darpa effort represents a frontal attack on a set of the most challenging technical opportunities facing the United States today. Taking full advantage of them is a challenge upon which the nation's security now depends. ◆

MCC: an industry response to the Japanese challenge

The Microelectronics and Computer Technology Corp. (MCC) is the most recent U.S. response to Japan's drive to be the first to produce the next generation of computers. The corporation's leader, Admiral Bob R. Inman, makes no bones about that. "MCC is a direct response to the Japanese success," he said. But he also added, "I have worked very hard to articulate the basic principle I'm going to use in governing MCC—we are not an anti-Japanese operation. We are a pro-competition U.S. initiative, primed to keep a technological lead."

MCC, which began operations in Austin, Texas, two months ago, is an advanced research and development corporation in which both funds and personnel are provided by 13 shareholder companies that otherwise compete in the computer and semiconductor markets. It aims to be the premier U.S. research organization that will give rise to the next generation of computers.

"We're not anything short-term," noted Adm. Inman, who resigned last year as deputy director of the U.S. Central Intelligence Agency. He brings to MCC an admittedly nontechnical background, but he does possess a strong hand and also a keen vision of what the corporation needs to do. "The whole thrust—and it's the intent for future products to be developed—is that we focus on long-term research and development," he said. This is the same view as that held by Japan's Ministry of International Trade and Industry (MITI), which is spearheading that country's effort.

Funding is private—for now

"The MITI model is similar to MCC," Adm. Inman said, "except for one critical difference: funding for it comes from the Japanese government. The MCC assembles talent from competitors as MITI does, but the shareholders are committed to it solely on the basis of their own private funding." That does not close the door on Government funding, the admiral added, "but in the next few years, at least, we're not out looking for it."

The MCC's member companies are Advanced Micro Devices

Inc., Allied Corp., Control Data Corp., Digital Equipment Corp., Harris Corp., Honeywell Inc., Martin-Marietta Corp., Mostek Corp., Motorola Inc., NCR, National Semiconductor, RCA Corp., and Sperry Computer Systems. MCC plans a working budget of $50 million in the first year. Each company's investment depends on the number of research programs it is involved in.

"We are a for-profit company," said Adm. Inman, adding, "We're not likely to make a profit for a long time, however. The

---

MCC assembles talent from competitors as MITI does, but the shareholders are committed to it solely on the basis of their own private funding

---

profit comes only from the royalties earned in licensing. All intellectual property, all patents, are the property of MCC."

Research is being concentrated in four areas: microelectronics packaging, software technology, computer-aided design and manufacturing, and advanced computer architectures. The programs will last six, seven, eight, and ten years, respectively. Companies that fund research in one or more of the four programs get licenses and a three-year lead in commercial production of the results once the program is completed. "And in this business," Adm. Inman noted, "a three-year lead is a very long lead." After that any company, member or not, can be licensed. The shortest of MCC's four research programs, packaging for microelectronics, however, is scheduled to last six years. "So it's way down the road before we see the prospect of profit," the admiral explained. "We're certainly not looking for quarterly dividends."

"The credit for the whole concept of MCC," Adm. Inman went on, "has to go to William Norris [the founder and now chairman of the board and chief executive officer of the Control Data Corp.], who believed that individual companies could not bring sufficient focus to bear to achieve breakthroughs, that we were not at a place in time where we'd gotten the quick return on capital in the information-handling industry, and that the R&D for the next series of gains were going to be substantially more capital-intensive."

He persuaded 15 companies (several of whom decided not to become members of the MCC) to outline a research corporation that they could work with and to define areas of research. "They came to concentrate on areas in which they believed accomplishments were necessary to make quantum jumps in the performance of the next generation of computers," Adm. Inman pointed out. "The four projects we're going to embark upon are the ones they ultimately concluded none of them could do by themselves."

Each shareholder company can invest money and personnel in any or all of the programs and must commit itself to a minimum of three years of funding for a minimum of one defined project. At present there are six shareholders in microelectronics packaging, six in software, nine in CAD/CAM, and six in advanced computer architectures. Work in all four areas is under the supervision of chief scientist John Pinkston, formerly the deputy director of research at the National Security Agency.

Adm. Inman elaborated on the details of the four programs. "The IC-packaging program looks at how we can accelerate use of gate-array technology in constructing chips and apply that technology to tape-automated–bonding production in a much shorter time. There are some who think that's not sufficiently ambitious, that we should know how to do that and should be at-

Mark A. Fischetti Associate Editor

tacking the next thing after tape-automated bonding. We'll be looking at that."

"The software-technology program," he continued, "began as a software productivity program. We will be looking for near-term productivity enhancements, but we'll also be looking at whether we can find totally new ways to engineer software that will let us make some quantum jumps in the cost of producing software."

The goal in the CAD/CAM program, the admiral said, is fabrication of the "one-month chip"—a system capable of laying out a chip with 10 million transistors in less than a month. It is intended to reduce design costs significantly and to improve engineering productivity.

Though Adm. Inman remarked that no program would be favored above any other, "It is fair to say," he observed, "that the advanced computer-architectures program is substantially the largest, the most expensive, and the longest running." Adm. Inman views the 10-year advanced computer-architectures program, nicknamed the alpha-omega project, as MCC's "fifth-generation computer" program, with the other three contributing to it, as well as standing alone. He would not disclose a detailed schedule of goals for the alpha-omega project, but said it was divided into four major areas: artificial intelligence and knowledge-base systems; human interfaces, including speech and image-recognition systems; data-base management; and parallel processing.

"The first three years," the admiral said, "will be spent squeezing out what we really know in all of these areas—where we need additional basic research and where to press on with advanced research. The hope is that VLSI technology will have advanced to a stage three years from now in which we can apply it across all four areas. Defining what it will do for us, and what we decide on doing, will be a major effort that's probably going to take two or three years. So we'll probably be at about the six-year point before we start dealing with the types of designs we want for computer architectures."

Some engineers are concerned that research by the U.S. cooperatives will be duplicative. Both the MCC and the Semiconductor Research Cooperative, for example, have programs in CAD/CAM and microelectronics packaging. But Adm. Inman emphasized that the MCC really picks up where SRC, for instance, leaves off, turning basic research into advanced development. "I believe we're going to turn out to be very complementary," Adm. Inman said, noting that "a number of the firms" in the semiconductor cooperative were also in MCC. All of MCC's work is being done in house and, although a small percentage of MCC technical personnel will come from outside the 13 member companies, the majority are being sent to Austin by the shareholders, a unique practice.

MCC was formed in the face of two obstacles, according to the admiral. The first, he said, was "business culture: you don't share R&D with your competitors." The second was the fear of antitrust laws. "Some firms were concerned that if they even sat down to discuss R&D," Adm. Inman noted, "somebody would say, 'Yeah, but how do you know they're not out there in the closet fixing prices?'." Such fears, in fact, kept several firms from joining, notably IBM Corp. and the American Telephone and Telegraph Co.

However, last December the U.S. Department of Justice announced it did not object to the creation of the MCC. The department will, however, be looking at each of the four programs as they develop to decide if the combination of firms cooperating in them "is something that would worry them," Adm. Inman said.

Whether publication of research results will be allowed is a concern of the researchers who are joining MCC, since all work there is proprietary. "We haven't established any publishing rules yet," Adm. Inman said, noting that whatever any employee produces becomes the property of MCC. "But I would not be at all surprised to see us ultimately with policies that are very similar to those that Bell Labs has worked on for so many years."

"We will, over the next six to nine months, be developing very detailed milestones for all four of the projects," he concluded. "And we'll have to contemplate whether we want to announce those or keep them proprietary. I'm not prepared to cross that bridge yet. I really don't know."

What he does know is the importance of making the MCC work. "The major impact, if we are successful," he said, "would be the rethinking of this country's whole approach to research and development."   ◆

SRC: the semiconductor industry draws on university resources

Faced with increasing competition from abroad and the realization that research is the foundation for its future, the U.S. semiconductor industry two years ago established the Semiconductor Research Cooperative (SRC) to increase much-needed research efforts. The cooperative is drawing on an important but underused resource: the nation's universities.

By pooling funds and contracting with research universities for priority projects, industry is accomplishing two important objectives: increasing semiconductor research and upgrading laboratories in the nation's universities, thereby attracting more students to this field of study. In 1982 close to $5 million was committed to this effort by companies participating in the cooperative. This year the commitment exceeds $11 million and the 1984 budget should exceed $13 million.

It is clear from these goals that the focus is on basic research rather than development. The research results accrue to all participants; they in turn must turn them into products for the marketplace. Joint research does not inhibit competition in the marketplace. Much work needs to be done by each company in its own way before a product is ready for market. Universities are free to publish research results, and are obligated to patent, or have SRC patent, any inventions. The natural delay in publishing results gives member companies the lead time they require for development.

Cooperating companies gain these benefits:
• Sharing of the research cost, which is increasing because of the ever-evolving complexity of the task, rising salaries for researchers, and rising equipment costs.
• Pooling of talents, which fosters the solution of problems that at times are beyond the capability of an individual company.
• Reduction of the financial risk—through sharing of the cost.
• Sharing of sophisticated and expensive equipment.

The cooperative is to concentrate on five major research areas: microstructure sciences, system components, design tools, new approaches to manufacturing, and new approaches to engineering. Research takes place on three levels. Individual contracts are awarded for a well-defined research task in a university. Centers of excellence are single universities or small inventors that have

Erich Bloch   IBM Corp.

demonstrated particular strength in a focused area of semiconductor research. Their work is primarily a large team effort, interdisciplinary in nature. In the future, "lead centers" should provide for close interaction between related efforts executed among various centers of excellence and individual contractors and should prevent overlapping research.

Research by many universities encouraged

The projects are either solicited by the SRC or proposed to the cooperative by a researcher or university. As of last May, research contracts had been granted for over $8 million. They are not going only to a few prestigious universities. An effort is being made to foster competence in many universities so more students will be attracted to the semiconductor field and so new research centers will blossom.

The cooperative is governed by a board of directors, elected by the Semiconductor Industry Association's board of directors from companies that are members of SRC. A full-time executive director, Larry Sumney, formerly director of the U.S. Department of Defense's VHSIC program, reports to the board. He is supported by a 12-person technical and administrative staff. A technical advisory board of key technicians from member companies supports the director in identifying, monitoring, and evaluating all research projects. This is a most vital function—it brings the industry's requirements into focus and ensures that the research results flow back to the participating companies in a timely way. A second advisory board comprising university faculty members has also been invaluable in providing a forum for technical matters, and administrative concerns, such as patent rights, contract wording, and other issues.

To date, 23 companies representing all facets of the semiconductor industry have joined SRC.* Close to 50 contracts have been signed with 30 private and state universities. Some contracts are for work that will be conducted over many years with major universities. Over 100 faculty members and 125 graduate students are currently working under these contracts.

The cooperative is considering extending its mission into areas other than pure research. In particular, the industry must focus on manufacturing automation and productivity improvements. Combining research with demonstration manufacturing facilities would let the industry develop products that under normal circumstances might remain undeveloped for many years. The SRC is also considering a pilot program of process definition and advanced design for a multimegabit memory chip.

Cooperatives needed to keep competitive

The Semiconductor Research Cooperative is a prototype of cooperative research that could help U.S. industries in general to improve their competitive position in world markets. The semiconductor industry has only been in existence for 30 years, but it has grown to a $15 billion worldwide industry. More important, it is now a basic industry—as basic as steel, automobiles, or oil. Semiconductor products enhance productivity in many industries. The strength of the U.S. semiconductor industry and the prime reason for its growth have been the imaginative pursuit of research and the availability of well-educated and experienced scientists and engineers.

Up to five years ago, the semiconductor industry was primarily

a U.S. industry. But in 1982 the U.S. semiconductor industry's share of the world market had eroded to 55 percent and Japan's share had increased to 35 percent, and the 1983 forecast shows further U.S. erosion. The most important product segment is that of MOS memory and logic. The increase for Japanese companies in 1982 world MOS sales was 14 percent and that of U.S.-based companies 8.6 percent. Even in the U.S. market, Japan outstripped U.S. companies in sales gains: 67 percent versus 17 percent for domestic producers. Most of this increase came from Japanese sales of 64-kilobyte memory chips.

Why this turn of events? First, foreign countries—in particular, Japan—have recognized the strategic importance of the semiconductor industry. Second, Japan specifically has targeted MOS memory products as the way to increase its market share. Third, the rapid worldwide diffusion of U.S. technology and innovation has provided a base to build on. Fourth, Japan, under the Ministry of International Trade and Industry, has fostered growth in research and development. Japanese industry also has increased its capital investment in semiconductors to the point where, in 1983, the absolute spending in Japan equals that in the United States. This fact alone should make it obvious why endeavors like the SRC are essential if the U.S. semiconductor industry hopes to remain competitive worldwide.   ◆

A university–industry–government paradigm for joint research

Virtually all research conducted in universities is supported by a sponsor. That sponsor may be the institution itself, state or Federal government, a private foundation, or industry. By a very large margin, the Federal government is the leading sponsor of university research in the United States. But a major change in this situation has occurred in the last several years and that has been the joint sponsorship of university research by groups of corporations. The Stanford University Center for Integrated Systems in Palo Alto, Calif., brings together these sponsors: it is a university–industry–Government joint venture in research.

The dual objectives of the center are to investigate concepts for very large-scale integrated (VLSI) systems and to educate new technical leaders. Nineteen corporations are sponsors of the center.* They have contributed a total of $14 250 000 for the design and construction of a 70 000-square-foot building. It will provide exceptional central facilities, including 10 000 square feet of clean rooms for the design, fabrication, testing, and application of VLSI systems. Annual contributions from sponsors will be used to support joint research and educational programs.

A faculty executive committee formulates center policies, and two codirectors, James D. Meindl and John G. Linvill, plan, initiate, and direct operations. Autonomous project teams, led by faculty members serving as principal investigators, execute the center's research program. A key feature of the center is a sponsors' advisory committee, consisting of one representative from each of the 19 corporations. More than 60 faculty, approximately

*Digital Equipment Corp., Fairchild Camera and Instrument Corp., General Electric Co., General Telephone and Electronics Corp., Gould/AMI, Hewlett-Packard Co., Honeywell Inc., Intel Corp., IBM Corp., ITT Corp., Monsanto Industrial Chemicals Co., Motorola Inc., Northrop Corp., Phillips/Signetics, Tektronix Inc., Texas Instruments Inc., TRW Inc., United Technologies Inc., and Xerox Corp.

*Advanced Micro Devices Inc., Burroughs Corp., Control Data Corp., Digital Equipment Corp., Dupont Co., Eaton Corp., E-Systems Inc., General Electric Co., General Instrument Corp., Goodyear Aerospace, Harris Corp., Hewlett-Packard Co., Honeywell Inc., IBM Corp., Intel Corp., Monolithic Memories Inc., Monsanto Co., Motorola Inc., National Semiconductor Corp., Rockwell International, Silicon Systems Inc., Westinghouse Electric Co., Xerox Corp.

James D. Meindl   Stanford University

150 members of the research staff and 300 Ph.D. candidates are now engaged in integrated systems research at Stanford. Each corporate sponsor of the center is invited to assign a member of its technical staff to participate in the effort.

Total annual expenditures in electronics and computer science research are about $30 million, of which integrated systems account for more than one third. Most of this effort is now supported by agencies of the Federal Government, most prominently the Department of Defense, Health and Human Services, the National Science Foundation, the National Aeronautics and Space Administration, and the Department of Energy.

Stanford research projects that should advance hardware and software generic to the next generation of computing include:
• *Knowledge-based VLSI design*—The application of artificial-intelligence techniques to the development of expert software systems for VLSI design, testing, and debugging.
• *VLSI information systems*—Special-purpose signal-processing algorithms and architectures; a unified high-level language for VLSI simulation and testing; a silicon compiler with an electrically based, general-purpose layout language; and statistical models for wafer-scale integration.
• *VLSI computer systems*—General-purpose architectures and design aids for VLSI; high-performance graphic work stations using the custom "geometry engine" microprocessor; and a custom 32-bit streamlined instruction set microprocessor without interlocked pipeline stages.
• *Medical and rehabilitative electronic sensors, circuits, and systems*—An auditory prosthesis for the profoundly deaf; an optical-to-tactile reading aid for the blind; a silicon gas chromatograph; and totally implantable telemetry for biomedical research.
• *A computer-aided, fast-turnaround laboratory*—Process automation using a custom high-level programming language (Fable); submicrometer electron-beam and optical lithography; and fast turnaround n-channel– and complementary-MOS wafer fabrication and testing.
• *Integrated-circuit process models*—Two-dimensional device and process models (like Stanford's Suprem program).
• *Compound semiconductor and silicon-on-insulator research*—Molecular-beam epitaxy; laser, electron-beam and ion-beam processing.
• *Fundamental studies of semiconductor surfaces and interfaces*—The use of ultraviolet and X-ray photo emission, Auger electron emission, and synchrotron radiation in materials research, including X-ray lithography.

At its highest humanitarian level, joint research makes more efficient use of human intelligence to improve the quality of life for all people. At the national level, joint research promises to stimulate innovation and to improve productivity and quality. At the corporate level, it offers a competitive advantage through early access by sponsors to both the results of research and the high-quality graduate students producing those results.

For the university, research support from industry promises better equipment, more graduate students, and faculty members of high caliber. This will increase the flow of graduates and research findings to industry. Joint research sponsorship by industry also tends to increase academic freedom, because it broadens the base of support of university research.

Solutions are being sought for the following issues as the Stanford University Center for Integrated Systems carries on its work: whether to restrict the publication of results; who owns patents and copyrights; whether industry emphasis on the development of new products that entail proprietary secrecy, highly structured management, and relatively large cost will conflict with research per se; the possibility that arts and humanities will be deemphasized with a resulting threat to quality of life; and whether potential control of research content and professorships will threaten academic freedom and creativity. ◆

MCNC: organizing research on the state level

Combining the resources of five universities, a research institute, and a $30 million industrial research facility in Research Triangle Park, N.C., the Microelectronics Center of North Carolina is providing an urgently needed support structure for the vertical integration of all stages in the process of building experimental general or special-purpose machines needed in the next generation of computing. Unlike other university-based centers, the MCNC expands upon the concept of a "center of excellence" by having dedicated equipment and a professional staff to work with the staffs of its participating institutions and in industry.

The MCNC was created as a nonprofit corporation in July 1980. Its $50 million budget for 1981-85 is fueled primarily with state monies—the state of North Carolina has already contributed $43 million. Current industrial affiliates include the General Electric Co. in Schenectady, N.Y., Airco Industrial Gases in Murray Hill, N.J., and the GCA/IC Systems in Bedford, Mass.

In addition, the MCNC staff has a core of researchers who assist in translating basic research results from all over the world into useful technology for industry and government. The staff is largely made up of people from industry, led by its president, Don S. Beilman, formerly vice president and general manager of GE's advanced microelectronics operation in Research Triangle Park, and its vice president of semiconductor research and technology, Arnold Reisman, who was formerly manager of exploratory semiconductor research at IBM Corp.

The center's participating institutions are Duke University, the University of North Carolina at Chapel Hill, the University of North Carolina at Charlotte, North Carolina State University, North Carolina A&T University, and the Research Triangle Insti-

(Continued on p. 41)

Richard B. Fair
Microelectronics Center of North Carolina

U.S. research fostering the next generation of computing

To determine to what extent research in the United States may eventually contribute to next-generation computing, *Spectrum* polled universities and companies involved in research germane to the subject as of Sept. 15, 1983. Although national research funding groups such as the National Science Foundation and the Office of Naval Research, among others, are major sources of funding (these organizations form the "Other" category), the sources called out here are so listed because they are the cooperative research groups discussed in this special report. These include the Defense Advanced Research Projects Agency (Darpa), the Microelectronics and Computer Technology Corp. (MCC), the Semiconductor Reseach Corp. (SRC), the Microelectronics Center of North Carolina (MCNC), and the Microelectronics and information Sciences Center (MEIS).

Listed is research at universities and companies that participate in these organizations. Through their involvement with these groups, they are consciously pursuing work necessary to next-generation computing. Also included are other universities and companies that are doing notable work, but were not participants in the cooperatives listed as of Sept. 15, 1983, such as the University of Utah and the Fairchild Camera and Instrument Corp. The list is not meant to be all-inclusive.

The categories of research are chosen to form a technological continuum ranging from hardware, which may advance supercomputer development as well, to software areas that form the core of next-generation computing development. Some categories could well fall under more than one superheading. Also, some categories not appearing were suggested by individual universities that have major research programs in those areas, such as fault-tolerant computing and distributed computing, at the University of California, Los Angeles, for example.

A similar profile of research being done in Europe begins on page 33.
— *Mark A. Fischetti*

Next-generation computing: research in the United States

Source of funding
A: Darpa
B: MCC
C: SRC
D: MCNC
E: MEIS
F: Internal
G: Industry
H: Other

	Arizona State U.	Brown U.	California Inst. of Tech.	Carnegie-Mellon U.	Columbia U.	Cornell U.	Duke U.	Georgia Inst. of Tech.
PRODUCTION								
Automated assembly		G H		G		F G H		
Design tools	C		A	C G		C F G		F
Computer-aided design	C G		A	C G H		C F G H		F G
Computer-aided manufacturing				G		F G H		F G
Computer-aided engineering		G H		G				
VLSI								
Physics & science	H	F			G H	C F G H		H
Materials	H	F				A C F G H	C	H
Circuits	C		A		G H	C F G H		G
Devices & components	C G H			C		A C F G H		H
Interconnections						C F H		C
Packaging						C F G		C F
Design & layout	F G		A	C G H	C	C F G H	D G H	F G
Simulation	G		A C	C G H	H	F G H		
Testing			A		H	F G	G	F G
Lithography						C F G H		
IC processing & fabrication	G H			G		A C F G H		
Wafer-scale integration						C H		
COMPUTER ARCHITECTURE								
Parallel processing	H	F G H	A G	A	H	F G H	G H	F H
Data-flow techniques						F G		F
Data-base architecture		F H				F G H		
Multiprocessors	H	F G H	A G	A G	H	F G H	G H	F H
SOFTWARE ENGINEERING								
Algorithms		F G H	A G H	A		F G	H	H
Signal processing		F G H	A G	A		A F G H	H	H
Symbolic processing		H		A G				
Image processing	F G	F G H	A G	A G		F G H	H	H
User interface		F G		A G				
Automated software engineering		F H					G H	F H
ARTIFICIAL INTELLIGENCE								
Expert systems		F H		A G H			H	F G H
Knowledge-based systems				A G H			H	F G H
Speech recognition		F G H		A		G		H
Pattern recognition		F G H		A G H		H	G H	F G H
Natural-language processing			G	A G			H	F H
RELATED								
Computer science							G H	F G H

Next-generation computing: research in the United States

Source of funding
A: Darpa
B: MCC
C: SRC
D: MCNC
E: MEIS
F: Internal
G: Industry
H: Other

	Harvey Mudd College	Illinois Inst. of Tech.	Johns Hopkins U.	Lehigh U.	Massachusetts Inst. of Tech.	Michigan State Univ.	Mississippi State U.	New York Univ.	North Carolina A&T	North Carolina State U.	Pennsylvania State U.	Princeton Univ.	Purdue U.	Rennselaer Polytechnic Inst.	Rochester Inst. of Tech.	Stanford U.	Syracuse U.	Texas A&M
PRODUCTION																		
Automated assembly				F G H									G H			A G H		
Design tools				F G H	A H							G	G	F G		A G H		F
Computer-aided design		G		F G H	A G H					F G		G	G	F G H		A G H		C F
Computer-aided manufacturing		G		F G H	A F G H								G H	F G H		A G H		G
Computer-aided engineering				F G H	A G H							G	G	C F G		A G H		
VLSI																		
Physics & science				F G H	A C F G H		A		H			A H	G H	C F H		A C G H		H
Materials				A F G H	A C F G H		C G H		D G H	H	C G	H	G H	C F G H		A C G H		
Circuits				A F G H	A C G H		A			D	C G		G	F		A G H		F
Devices & components				F G H	A C G H		A				C G H		C F G H	F G H		A G H		G
Interconnections					A C G H	A C G		D				A	G H	C F		A C G H		
Packaging				G	C G H								G H					
Design & layout	G			G	A G H	H	A	H	D	C	G	A	F G	C F G		A G H		C F
Simulation				F G H	A H		A C			G H	G	A	G	F G H		A G H		F
Testing				G	H		A C				G	A		C F G H		A G H		F G
Lithography					A C G H		A G						H	C F G	F	A G H		G
IC processing & fabrication			G	G H	A C F G H		A C G H	D	C D G	C G			G	C F G H	F	A G H		G
Wafer-scale integration					A		C G H							F G		A G H		F
COMPUTER ARCHITECTURE																		
Parallel processing		F	H	G H	A G H	H		A	G H			A G H	G H	G		A G H	H	F G
Data-flow techniques	G				A G H						G H		F G	F G		A G H	H	
Data-base architecture		F		F G H	G H						G	A G H	G H	F G		A G H	H	
Multiprocessors			H		A G H	H	A	G H	H	G				F G H	F	A G H	H	F
SOFTWARE ENGINEERING																		
Algorithms	F H	A H	H		A G H			G H	F			H	G H	F H		A G H		F
Signal processing		A G H	H	F H	H	H				G H		A H	H	F G H		A G H		G
Symbolic processing		A H			A G H								H	F H		A G H	H	H
Image processing		A F H		F G H	A G H	F				G H			H	F G H		A G H		G
User interface		A H			A G H							G	G H	F		A G H		
Automated software engineering			G H		A H								G H	F H		A G H	H	
ARTIFICIAL INTELLIGENCE																		
Expert systems	F	A H		F G	A G H								G H	F H		A G H	H	C
Knowledge-based systems		A H			A G H								G H	F H		A G H	H	
Speech recognition		F		F G	G H		H		G				H	F G H		A G H		
Pattern recognition		A H	H	F G						G H			G H	F G H		A G H		
Natural-language processing				F G H	A			H						F H		A G H		
RELATED																		
Computer science					A F G H			H				A H	H	F G H		A G H		F G H

Next-generation computing: research in the United States

Source of funding

- Darpa : A
- MCC : B
- SRC : C
- MCNC : D
- MEIS : E
- Internal : F
- Industry : G
- Other : H

U. OF ARIZONA	U. OF CALIFORNIA, BERKELEY	U. OF CALIFORNIA, LOS ANGELES	U. OF COLORADO	U. OF FLORIDA	U. OF ILLINOIS	U. OF IOWA	U. OF MARYLAND	U. OF MASSACHUSETTS	U. OF MICHIGAN	U. OF MINNESOTA	U. OF MISSOURI—ROLLA	U. OF NEW HAMPSHIRE	U. OF N. CAROLINA, CHAPEL HILL	U. OF N. CAROLINA, CHARLOTTE	U. OF NOTRE DAME	U. OF PENNSYLVANIA	U. OF ROCHESTER	
																		PRODUCTION
																		Automated assembly
	A C G H	H		H	C F G H		G H			F G			D		H			Design tools
G	A C G H	H	G	G	C F G H	F G				F G					H			Computer-aided design
	A C G H	H	G						G H	F H							G H	Computer-aided manufacturing
	A C G H	H			F G H					G					H		G H	Computer-aided engineering
																		VLSI
	A G H			H	A C H					E G H	F G					F		Physics & science
	A G H		G		C H					C E G H	F G		D F	C	H			Materials
C H	A C G H	G H	G H	G H	G H					E H	F H		A		H	F		Circuits
	A C G H		C	H						E G H	F H				H			Devices & components
G	A C G H	H		G						E				D F G				Interconnections
				F					G	E				D F G				Packaging
G	A C G H	H		G H	G H				G H		F		C D	D F	H	C H		Design & layout
G	A C G H	H			G C H					E	F		A		H	F		Simulation
G	A C G H	H			C G H	C H			H	E G H	G		A D	D			F G	Testing
	A C G H									C E	F							Lithography
H	A C G H			C		G				C E G	G		D	C				IC processing & fabrication
													C F					Wafer-scale integration
																		COMPUTER ARCHITECTURE
	A G H	A H	G	F	C G H		G	F		E H	F G	F	A H	G	G	G H	A H	Parallel processing
G H	A G H	H		G H		C			F	E G			F			F		Data-flow techniques
	A G H	H	F H	F H					F									Data-base architecture
H	A G H	A H		F	G H	H		F		E H	F G	G	A H		G	G H	F	Multiprocessors
																		SOFTWARE ENGINEERING
G	A C G H	A H	H	F	C G H		G H			E H					G	G H		Algorithms
	A C G H	H	F H	G H		H				F G	F G		G	G		G H		Signal processing
	A C G H			G H					G H						H			Symbolic processing
H	A G H	G		G H				A G H	G H	E H	F G	F G	H	G		G H	G	Image processing
F	A C G H	A H	F	F H		H			G H		F H		H			G H		User interface
		H		G H						E					H			Automated software engineering
																		ARTIFICIAL INTELLIGENCE
	A G H	H		F	G H			H	H	E H						G H		Expert systems
	A G H	H		H	G H			A G H		E H		G				G H		Knowledge-based systems
G	A C G H		H	F								F						Speech recognition
G	A G H		F H	G H				A G H		E H	F G	F	G			G H	H	Pattern recognition
	A G H	H		F	F H				G H				G	F		G H	A H	Natural-language processing
																		RELATED
	A G H			F	G H				G H	E H						H	H	Computer science

Next-generation computing: research in the United States

Source of funding
A: Darpa
B: MCC
C: SRC
D: MCNC
E: MEIS
F: Internal
G: Industry
H: Other

	U. OF SOUTH CAROLINA	U. OF SOUTHERN CALIFORNIA	U. OF TEXAS, AUSTIN	U. OF UTAH	U. OF VERMONT	U. OF WASHINGTON	U. OF WISCONSIN	WASHINGTON U... ST. LOUIS	WORCESTER POLYTECHNIC INST.	YALE U.
PRODUCTION										
Automated assembly		F					F G			
Design tools		F G H	F	A G H			F G	H		
Computer-aided design	F H	F H	F G	G H			F G	H		
Computer-aided manufacturing		F	G	G H			G			
Computer-aided engineering		H	G					H		
VLSI										
Physics & science		A F H	A F H	G			F G H	H	F H	C G H
Materials		A F G H	A F H	G H	C		C F G H	H	F H	C G H
Circuits		A F G H		A G		A G	F G	H	H	G
Devices & components		A F G H	A F H	A G			F G H			G H
Interconnections		A F G H					F G H	H		
Packaging		A H					F G			
Design & layout		A F G H		A G H		A G	F G	H		G H
Simulation		A G H	F G	A G H		A G	F G		F	G H
Testing		A F H	F G	A G H		A G	F G H	H		
Lithography		A G H					F G			G
IC processing & fabrication		A C G H	A H	G			C F G H			C G H
Wafer-scale integration		A H	H				F G			
COMPUTER ARCHITECTURE										
Parallel processing		A F G H	A H	H		H	H	H		G H
Data-flow techniques		F G H		A H				H		H
Data-base architecture		A H		A H						
Multiprocessors		A F G H	G	H		H	H	H		H
SOFTWARE ENGINEERING										
Algorithms		A F G H	H	A		H		H		G H
Signal processing	C H	A G H	H	H				H		G H
Symbolic processing		A F	H	H						H
Image processing		A H	H	H		H	F G H	H	H	H
User interface		A F G H	H	H		H	F G	H		
Automated software engineering		A G H						H		
ARTIFICIAL INTELLIGENCE										
Expert systems	C F	A F G H				H		H		
Knowledge-based systems	F	A F H	H					H		
Speech recognition	C	F								G H
Pattern recognition	H	A	H	H			H	H	H	
Natural-language processing		A F					H			
RELATED										
Computer science		A F G H				H				

Next-generation computing: research in the United States

Source of funding
A: Darpa
B: MCC
C: SRC
D: MCNC
E: MEIS
F: Internal
G: Industry
H: Other

	ADVANCED MICRO DEVICES INC.	ALLIED CORP.	CONTROL DATA CORP.	DIGITAL EQUIPMENT CORP.	EATON CORP.	FAIRCHILD CAMERA & INSTRUMENT CORP.	GENERAL ELECTRIC CORP.	GENERAL INSTRUMENT CORP.	HARRIS CORP.	HEWLETT-PACKARD LABORATORIES	HONEYWELL INC.	IBM CORP.	INTEL CORP.	MARTIN-MARIETTA AEROSPACE CORP.	MONOLITHIC MEMORIES INC.	MONSANTO CO.	MOSTEK CORP.	MOTOROLA INC.
PRODUCTION																		
Automated assembly	F	F	F			F		F		F	F	F	F		F		F	F
Design tools	B F	B F	B F	F		F	F	F	B F	F	F	F			B F	F	B F	F
Computer-aided design	B F	B F	B F	F	F	F	F	F	B F	F	F	F	F	B	F		B F	F
Computer-aided manufacturing	B F	B F	B F	F		F		F	B F	F	F	F	F	B	F	F	B F	F
Computer-aided engineering	B	B F	B F			F		F	B F	F	F	F	F	B			B F	
VLSI																		
Physics & science	F	F	E		F	F				F	E F	F	F	F	F	F	F	F
Materials	F	F	E		F	F		F		F	E F	F	F	F	F	F	F	F
Circuits	F	F	E	F	F	F	F	F	F	F	E F	F	F	F	F		F	F
Devices & components	F	F	E F	F	F	F	F	F	F	F	E F	F	F	F	F		F	F
Interconnections	F	B F	B E F	B F	F	F	F			B F	F	E F	F	F		F	B F	F
Packaging	F	B F	B E F	B F	F	F	F	F	F	B F	F	E F	F	F	F		B F	F
Design & layout	F	F	F	F	F	F	F	F	F	F	F	F	F	F	F		F	F
Simulation	F	F	F	F	F	F	F			F	F	F	F	F	F		F	F
Testing	F	F	E F	F		F	F	F	F	F	E F	F	F	F	F		F	F
Lithography	F	F	E F	F	F	F	F			F	E F	F	F	F	F		F	F
IC processing & fabrication	F	F	E F	F	F	F	F	F		F	E F	F	F	F	F		F	F
Wafer-scale integration				F		F		F		F							F	F
COMPUTER ARCHITECTURE																		
Parallel processing	F	F	B E F	B F	F	F	F		B F	F	B E F	F	F	F			F	F
Data-flow techniques	F		B E	B F	F	F	F		B	F	B E F	F	F	F	F			
Data-base architecture			B F	B F	F	F			B	F	B F	F		F				
Multiprocessors	F	F	B E F	B F	F	F	F		B F	F	B E F	F	F	F			F	F
SOFTWARE ENGINEERING																		
Algorithms	F		B E F	B F		F	F		B	F	E F	F	F	F	F		F	F
Signal processing	F	F	B F	B	F	F	F			F	F	F	F	F				F
Symbolic processing			B F	B F	F	F			B	F	F	F		F				
Image processing		F	B F	B	F	F	F		B F	F	F	F		F				
User interface	F	F	B F	B F	F	F	F		B	F	F	F	F		F			
Automated software engineering			B E F	B		F			B		E							
ARTIFICIAL INTELLIGENCE																		
Expert systems			B F	B F	F	F	F		B	F	B F	F		F				
Knowledge-based systems			B E F	B F	F	F	F		B	F	B E F	F		F				
Speech recognition	F		B F	B F		F			B	F	B F	F						F
Pattern recognition		F	B E F	B F	F	F	F		B		B E F	F		F				F
Natural-language processing			B F	B F		F			B	F	B F	F						F
RELATED																		
Computer science																		

Next-generation computing: research in the United States

Source of funding
A: Darpa
B: MCC
C: SRC
D: MCNC
E: MEIS
F: Internal
G: Industry
H: Other

	NCR CORP.	NATIONAL SEMICONDUCTOR CORP.	RCA CORP.	SILICON SYSTEMS INC.	SPERRY COMPUTER SYSTEMS	SRI INTERNATIONAL	TEXAS INSTRUMENTS	WESTINGHOUSE ELECTRIC CORP.	XEROX CORP.
PRODUCTION									
Automated assembly	F	F	F		F	F G H	F	F	F
Design tools	B F	B F	B F		B F		F	F	
Computer-aided design	B F	B F	B F		B F	F G H	F	F	F
Computer-aided manufacturing	B F	B F	B F		B F		F	F	F
Computer-aided engineering	B F	B F	B F		B F		F	F	
VLSI									
Physics & science	F		F		F		F	F	F
Materials	F	F	F		F		F	F	F
Circuits	F	F	F	F	F		F	F	
Devices & components	F	F	F	F	F		F	F	F
Interconnections	F	B F	B F		B F		F	F	F
Packaging	F	B F	B F	F	B F		F	F	
Design & layout	F		F	F	F		F	F	
Simulation	F		F	F	F		F	F	F
Testing	F		F	F	F		F	F	
Lithography	F	F	F		F		F	F	F
IC processing & fabrication	F	F	F	F	F		F	F	F
Wafer-scale integration	F		F		F		F	F	
COMPUTER ARCHITECTURE									
Parallel processing	B F		F		B	F H	F	F	F
Data-flow techniques	B F	F	F		B			F	
Data-base architecture	B F		F		B F		F	F	F
Multiprocessors	B F	F	F		B F		F	F	F
SOFTWARE ENGINEERING									
Algorithms	B F		B F	F	B F	A F H	F	F	F
Signal processing	B F		B F		B F	A F H	F	F	
Symbolic processing	B F	F	B F		B	A F H	F	F	F
Image processing	B F		B F		B	A F H	F	F	F
User interface	B F	F	B F		B F	A F H	F	F	F
Automated software engineering	B				B	A F H	F		
ARTIFICIAL INTELLIGENCE									
Expert systems	B F		B F		B F	A F H	F	F	F
Knowledge-based systems	B F		B F		B	A F H	F	F	
Speech recognition	B F	F	B F		B F	F H	F	F	
Pattern recognition	B F		B F		B	A F H	F	F	
Natural-language processing	B F		B F		B	A F H	F	F	F
RELATED									
Computer science									

Notes

Information listed in the preceding table is subject to the following constraints:

1. Several vertically integrated firms such as Honeywell Inc. and IBM Corp., among others, are working in all technology categories. Although the scope of involvement may range from "half a person" to more than a dozen, all areas have been checked to show the breadth of the firm's research.

2. E-systems Inc. of Dallas, Texas, a member of SRC, chose not to complete the table.

3. Motorola Inc. of Phoenix, Ariz., a member of MCC, chose to include only internal work, and not work being done at MCC.

4. In the "Related" category, the computer-science entry is meant to highlight universities working on new theories of computer science that may apply to the next generation of computing.

5. Among other cooperative programs not covered in this report are the University of Washington/Northwest VLSI Consortium, a cooperative funding research at the University and five Northwest technology companies, and Microelectronics Innovation and Computer Research Opportunities, supporting California industries with matching funds from the State.

6. "Other" sources of funding specified by responding universities include: Air Force Office of Science Research, Army Research Office, Defense Mapping Agency, Department of Energy, Joint Services Electronics Program, National Aeronautics and Space Administration, National Bureau of Standards, National Institute of Health, National Science Foundation, National Security Agency, Naval Avionics Center, Office of Naval Research, and the Rome Air Development Center.

The European scene: research on three levels

Europe is pursuing research toward next-generation computer technology on three levels—within the European Community, within member nations, and within individual companies.

In July, 1983 the Commission of the European Communities awarded 38 projects to universities and research centers in various combinations in nine of the community's ten member nations. France, Great Britain, and West Germany support research on relevant areas in their nations, with some companies in these countries conducting research they fund on their own.

France supports the research through such agencies as its Department of Defense's Direction des Recherches, Etudes et Techniques, an entity similar to the Defense Advanced Research Projects Agency (Darpa) in the United States. Other government support is channeled through the Centre National de la Recherche Scientifique (an arm of the Ministry of Research and Industry), through the Ministry of Telecommunications, the Commissariat à l'Energie Atomique, and universities and nationalized companies.

Support in France is in more than just money. For example, the Ministry of Research and Industry, through its Institut National de Recherche en Informatique et en Automatique, has formed the Systèmes Informatiques de la Connaissance, or Sico—a club for exchanging ideas and discussing problems related to artificial intelligence. In Great Britain, government support is channeled through the Ministry of Defence, the Department of Trade and Industry, and the Science and Engineering Research Council, an agency similar to the National Science Foundation in the United States.

In West Germany, the Federal Ministry for Research and Technology is a major source of support for research efforts. Furthermore, the Deutsche Forschungsgemeinschaft, an institution similar to the National Science Foundation in the United States, is planning to support a special research project in artificial intelligence at the universities of Karlsruhe, Kaiserslauten, and Saarbrücken.

The table identifies areas of research (not projects) supported by the Commission of the European Communities under the European Strategic Program of Research and Development on Information Technology (Esprit) marked by the letter E and by others, marked by the letter G.

Since most sources of information for this table were governmental, entries denoted by letter G represent only a sampling of research supported exclusively by companies.

—Gadi Kaplan

Next-generation computing: research in Europe

Source of funding
E: European Strategic: Program for Research and Development in Information Technology
G: Governments and companies

Research area	BELGIUM	BTMC	CATHOLIC U., LOUVAIN	SILVAR LISCO	BELGIAN INST. FOR MANAGEMENT	DENMARK	RISO	SOREN T. LUNGSO A/S	FRANCE	CERT	CEA	CERCI	CERFIA¹	CGE²	CII-HB
PRODUCTION															
Automated assembly															
Design tools											G				
Computer-aided design															E
Computer-aided manufacturing															E
Computer-aided engineering															
VLSI															
Physics & science											G				
Materials											G				
Circuits											G				G
Devices & components											G				G
Interconnections											G				G
Packaging															G
Design & layout		E	E	E							G				G
Simulation											G				G
Testing															G
Lithography											G				
IC processing & fabrication															
Wafer-scale integration											G				G
COMPUTER ARCHITECTURE															
Parallel processing		E	E	E									G		G
Data-flow techniques															
Data-base architecture														G	
Multiprocessors												G	G	G	
SOFTWARE ENGINEERING															
Algorithms		E	E	E					G						
Signal processing		E	E	E							G			G	
Symbolic processing															G
Image processing											G	G	G		
User interface					E						G	G	G		
Automated software engineering											G	E	G	E	E G
ARTIFICIAL INTELLIGENCE															
Expert systems											G		G	G	G
Knowledge-based systems							E	E	G				G	E	E
Speech recognition													G	G	
Pattern recognition											G	G	G		
Natural-language processing														G	
RELATED															
Computer science															

Next-generation computing: research in Europe

Source of funding
E: European Strategic: Program for Research and Development in Information Technology
G: Governments and companies

	FRANCE	CIMSA	CIT-ALCATEL	CNET	CRIN[1]	EFCIS[3]	ELF AQUITANE	IMAG[1]	INRIA	IRISA[1]	LAAS[4]	LCP[1]	LIMSI[1,4]	MATRA	LRI[1]	SCHLUMBERGER	THOMSON[3]	U. OF MARSEILLES	U. OF MONPELLIER	GREAT BRITAIN	BRITISH AEROSPACE DYNAMICS	BPA LTD.	CRANFIELD INSTITUTE	MINISTRY OF DEFENSE	FERRANTI PLC
PRODUCTION																									
Automated assembly								G																G	G
Design tools							G	G						G										G	G
Computer-aided design				G			G	G						G										G	G
Computer-aided manufacturing														G										G	G
Computer-aided engineering				G																					
VLSI																									
Physics & science				G					G					G										G	G
Materials				G							G			G			G							G	G
Circuits				G					G		G			G	G		G							G	G
Devices & components				G					G		G			G			G							G	G
Interconnections				G						G	G			G	G		E G	E			E		E	G	G
Packaging									G		G						G								
Design & layout				G					G	G	G			G	G		G							G	G
Simulation				G					G	G	G			G	G		G							G	G
Testing				G					G	G	G			G	G		G							G	G
Lithography				G					G		G			G			G							G	G
IC processing & fabrication				G							G			G			G							G	G
Wafer-scale integration									G		G			G			G							G	G
COMPUTER ARCHITECTURE																									
Parallel processing				G		E		G	G	G				G											G
Data-flow techniques								G	G					G											G
Data-base architecture								G	G					G											G
Multiprocessors			G	G				G	G					G											G
SOFTWARE ENGINEERING																									
Algorithms				G	G			G	G		G				G		E							G	G
Signal processing				G	G	E		G	G		G						E G							G	G
Symbolic processing				G				G	G															G	G
Image processing				G	G			G	G						G		G							G	G
User interface				G	G			G	G	G	G				G		G						E	G	G
Automated software engineering		E		G				G	G						G										
ARTIFICIAL INTELLIGENCE																									
Expert systems				G	G		G	G	G		G				G	G		G						G	
Knowledge-based systems	E			G	G			G	G	G	G				G		G							G	
Speech recognition				G	G			G	G	G			G			G	G								
Pattern recognition				G	G			G	G		G	G	G				G							G	
Natural-language processing				G	G			G	G	G		G			G			G							
RELATED																									
Computer science				G					G																

Next-generation computing: research in Europe

Source of funding
European Strategic :E Program for Research and Development in Information Technology
Governments and :G companies

Column key: 1 = General Electric Co.; 2 = GEC/Marconi; 3 = Dept. of Trade and Indust.; 4 = Inmos Ltd.; 5 = ICL; 6 = Knowledge-Based Syst. Ctr.; 7 = Logica VTS Ltd.; 8 = Marconi Co. Ltd.; 9 = Plessey Com. Syst. Ltd.; 10 = Poly of the South Bank; 11 = Racal Electronics Plc; 12 = Scicon Ltd.; 13 = Sci. and Eng. Research Coun.; 14 = Smith Industries; 15 = Stability Elect. Comp.; 16 = STL; 17 = Systems Designers Ltd; 18 = U. of Edinburgh; 19 = U. of Newcastle; 20 = U. of Southampton; 21 = U. of Sussex; 22 = Greece; 23 = U. of Crete; 24 = U. of Patras; 25 = Ireland

Topic	1	2	3	4	5	6	7	8	9	10	11	12	13	14	15	16	17	18	19	20	21	22	23	24	25
PRODUCTION																									
Automated assembly		G							G				G					G							
Design tools	E	G	G						E G				G					G							
Computer-aided design	E	G	G	G					E G				G					G							
Computer-aided manufacturing		G		G					G				G					G							
Computer-aided engineering		G		G					G				G					G							
VLSI																									
Physics & science		G	G						G				G					G							
Materials		G		G					G				G					G							
Circuits		G	G						G				G					G							
Devices & components	E	G	G	G					E G		G		G					G							
Interconnections		G		G					G		G		G	E				G	E	E					
Packaging		G		G					G		G		G					G							
Design & layout		G	G	G					G		G		G					G							
Simulation		G	G	G					G		G		G					G							
Testing		G		G					G		G		G					G							
Lithography		G		G					G		G		G					G							
IC processing & fabrication		G		G					G		G		G					G							
Wafer-scale integration		G		G					G		G		G					G							
COMPUTER ARCHITECTURE																									
Parallel processing		G		G	G				G		G							G							
Data-flow techniques		G		G	G				G		G							G							
Data-base architecture		G		G	G				G		G							G							
Multiprocessors		G	G	G	G				G		G							G							
SOFTWARE ENGINEERING																									
Algorithms	E	G		G					E									G							
Signal processing	E	G		G					E									G							
Symbolic processing		G		G														G							
Image processing		G		G														G							
User interface		G	G	G									E					G					E		
Automated software engineering		G	G		E G		G E			E			G		E	E		G						E	
ARTIFICIAL INTELLIGENCE																									
Expert systems		G	G				G		G				G					G							
Knowledge-based systems		G	G			E	G		E G E									G		E					
Speech recognition		G	G				G		G									G							
Pattern recognition		G	G				G		G									G							
Natural-language processing							G						G					G							
RELATED																									
Computer science				G					G				G					G							

Next-generation computing: research in Europe

Source of funding
E: European Strategic: Program for Research and Development in Information Technology
G: Governments and companies

	IRELAND	NAT. MICROELECT. RES. CENTER	COPS	U. OF DUBLIN	ITALY	CSELT	DATA MANAGEMENT	ITALSIEL	OLIVETTI	NETHERLANDS	CONSULDATA	NV PHILIPS	STICHTING MATH. CENTRUM	U. OF AMSTERDAM	WEST GERMANY	AEG	AEG-TELEFUNKEN[5]	ROBERT BOSCH GMBH	BATTELLE INSTITUT	EUROSIL GMBH[5]	FRAUNHOFER GESELLSCHAFT[5]	FOTON[5]	GMD[5]	INTERMETALL[5]	KARL SUESS[5]
PRODUCTION																									
Automated assembly																									
Design tools														E		E									
Computer-aided design																E									
Computer-aided manufacturing																									
Computer-aided engineering																									
VLSI																									
Physics & science																					G				
Materials																					G				
Circuits																	G		G					G	
Devices & components																	G		G					G	
Interconnections		E																			G				
Packaging																	G	G	G						
Design & layout								E								E	G	G	G			G			
Simulation								E													G	G			
Testing																					G				
Lithography																									G
IC processing & fabrication																	G		G					G	
Wafer-scale integration																									
COMPUTER ARCHITECTURE																									
Parallel processing																					G		G		
Data-flow techniques																							G		
Data-base architecture																									
Multiprocessors																							G		
SOFTWARE ENGINEERING																									
Algorithms						E						E					E								
Signal processing						E						E					E								
Symbolic processing																									
Image processing																									
User interface																							G		
Automated software engineering			E			E	E	E			E	E	E										E		
ARTIFICIAL INTELLIGENCE																									
Expert systems																	G						G		
Knowledge-based systems			E					E						E			G				G		G		
Speech recognition																	G								
Pattern recognition																	G				G				
Natural-language processing																									
RELATED																									
Computer science																									

Next-generation computing: research in Europe

Source of funding
European Strategic :E
Program for
Research
and Development in
Information
Technology
Governments and :G
companies

Research area	Krupp-Atlas Elektronik[5]	Max Planck Gesellschaft	Nixdorf Computer AG[5]	Philips Data Systems GmbH[5]	Rosenthal Technik[5]	SCS	Siemens AG[5]	Softlab Ltd.	Technical U. of Berlin[5]	Telefunken Elektronik	Triumph-Adler AG	U. of Aachen[5]	U. of Berlin	U. of Bonn[5]	U. of Braunschweig	U. of Darmstadt	U. of Dortmund[5]	U. of Erlangen/Nuer.[5]	U. of Humaburg[5]	U. of Hanover[5]	U. of Kaiserslauten[5]	U. of Karlsruhe[5]	U. of Munich	U. of the Ruhr	U. of Siegen
PRODUCTION																									
Automated assembly																									
Design tools													E												
Computer-aided design													E												
Computer-aided manufacturing																									
Computer-aided engineering																									
VLSI																									
Physics & science		G										G			G	G	G								
Materials					G																				
Circuits			G				G									G			G			G	G		
Devices & components							G									G									
Interconnections					G					E															
Packaging					G											G	G								
Design & layout							E G									G	G		G	G	G	G	E		
Simulation							E G									G									
Testing							G						G			G			G				G		
Lithography									G															G	
IC processing & fabrication							G									G									
Wafer-scale integration												G													
COMPUTER ARCHITECTURE																									
Parallel processing	G	G					G		G								G								
Data-flow techniques													G												
Data-base architecture			G	G					G						G										
Multiprocessors	G	G							G								G								
SOFTWARE ENGINEERING																									
Algorithms							E																E		
Signal processing							E																E		
Symbolic processing																									
Image processing																									
User interface						E			E			G							E G						
Automated software engineering		E					E														G	G			
ARTIFICIAL INTELLIGENCE																									
Expert systems		G																		G					
Knowledge-based systems		G					E G		G										G	G					
Speech recognition				G					G									G							
Pattern recognition							G															G			
Natural-language processing													G						G						
RELATED																									
Computer science																					G	G			

Next-generation computing: research in Europe

Source of funding
E: European Strategic: Program for Research and Development in Information Technology
G: Governments and companies

	WEST GERMANY	U. OF STUTTGART[5]	VDI—TECH. ZENTRUM[5]	VALVO GMBH[5]	WACKER CHEMIE GMBH[5]	WACKER CHEMITRONIC[5]	CARL ZEISS
PRODUCTION							
Automated assembly							
Design tools							
Computer-aided design							
Computer-aided manufacturing							
Computer-aided engineering							
VLSI							
Physics & science							
Materials						G	
Circuits		G		G	G		
Devices & components				G			
Interconnections					G		
Packaging					G		
Design & layout		G		G			
Simulation			G	G			
Testing			G				
Lithography							
IC processing & fabrication				G			
Wafer-scale integration							
COMPUTER ARCHITECTURE							
Parallel processing							
Data-flow techniques							
Data-base architecture							
Multiprocessors							
SOFTWARE ENGINEERING							
Algorithms							
Signal processing							
Symbolic processing							
Image processing							
User interface		G					
Automated software engineering							
ARTIFICIAL INTELLIGENCE							
Expert systems		G					
Knowledge-based systems		G					
Speech recognition							
Pattern recognition							G
Natural-language processing							
RELATED							
Computer science							

Abbreviations: BTMC: Bell Telephone Manufacturing Co.; Belgian Inst. for Management: Belgian Institute for Management; CERT: Centre d'Etudes et de Recherches Techniques; CEA: Commissariat à l'Energie Atomique; CERCI: Compagnie d'Etudes et de la Réalization de Cybernetique Industrielle; CER-FIA: Laboratoire de Cybernetique des Entreprises, Reconnaissance des Formes, et Intelligence Artificielle, Université Paul Sabatier, Toulouse; CGE: Compagnie Générale d' Electricité; CII-HB: Compagnie Internationale pour l'Informatique— Honeywell Bull; CIMSA: Compagnie d'Informatique Militaire, Spatialle et Aeronauticque; CNET: Centre National d' Etudes des Telecommunications; CRIN: Centre de Recherche en Informatique de Nancy, Université de Nancy; EFCIS: Etudes et Fabrication de Circuits Integrés Speciaux; IMAG: Institut de Mathematique Appliquée de Grenoble, Université de Grenoble; INRIA: Institut National de la Recherche en Informatique et en Automatique; IRISA: Institut de Recherche én Informatique et SystèmesAléatoires, Université de Rennes; LAAS: Laboratoire d'Automatique et d'Analyses des Systèmes; LCP: Laboratoire de Communications Parlées, Ecole Nationale Supérieure d'Electricité, Grenoble; LIMSI: Laboratoire d' Informatique Méchanique pour les Science de l'Ingénieur; LRI: Laboratoire de Recherche en Informatique, Université de Paris Sud; Dept. of Trade and Indust.: Department of Trade and Industry (Alvey Programme); ICL: International Computers Ltd.: Knowledge-Based Syst. Ctr.: Knowledge-Based Systems Center; Plessey Com. Syst. Ltd.: Plessey Communications Systems Ltd.; Sci. and Eng. Research Coun.: Science and Engineering Research Council; Stability Elect. Comp.: Stability Electronic Components; STL: Standard Telecommunications Laboratories; Nat. Microelect. Res. Center: National Microelectronics Research Center; COPS: Computer Organization Programming Systems; CSELT: Centro Studi e Laboratori Telecommunicazioni; Stichting Math. Centrum: Stichting Mathematisch Centrum; GMD: Gesellschaft für Mathematik und Datenverarbeitung; SCS: Scientific Control Systems GmbH; U. of Erlangen/Nuer.: University of Erlangen/Nuerenberg; VDI— Tech. Zentrum: Verein Deutscher Ingenieure—Technologie Zentrum.

Footnotes
[1]Research jointly funded by a university and the Centre National de la Rechreche Scientifique (CNRS).
[2]Esprit-related work is carried out at the company's laboratory in Marcoussis.
[3]Part of the work under the Esprit project awarded to Thomson is carried out by Etude et Fabrication de Circuits Integres, a Thomson subsidiary in Grenoble, and part by Thomson CSF, another subsidiary with laboratories in Velizy-Villycouoblay, Paris, and Morangis.
[4]Laboratory owned by CNRS.
[5]Development partially or fully supported by the Federal Ministry for Research and Technology in Boon, West Germany.

Related Esprit activities

Research activities in office automation and computer-integrated manufacturing funded by the European Strategic Program of Research and Development on Information Technology

Nation, entity and city	Activity
Belgium	
ACEC, Charleroi	Local broadband communication system for a large site
BTMC, Antwerp	Local broadband communication system for a large site
Correlative Systems, Brussels	Development of multimedia user interface for an office work station
Free University, Brussels	Development of multimedia office work station
University of Liege	Local broadband communication system for a large site
Denmark	
Dansk Datamatik Center, Lyngby	Functional analysis of office requirements; office filing and retrieval of unstructured information
France	
Compagnie Generale d'Electicité (CGE), Laboratoire de Marcoussis	Document storage and interchange standards for office automation
CGE, Puteaux	Standardization of intergrated local-area network services and service-access protocol
CII-HB, Paris	Multimedia user interface for an office work station; design rules for computer-integrated manufacturing; standardization of integrated local-area network services and service-access protocol
Institut National de Recherche en Automatique et Informatique, Le Chesnay	Multimedia office work station
Renault, Rueil Malmaison	Design tools for integration of industrial robots into computer-integrated manufacturing systems
SG2, Paris	Local wideband communication system for a large site
Thomson CSF, Marangis	Technology for handling a mixture of text, images, and voice, based on a standard architecture; local wide-band communication system; standardization of integrated local-area network services and service-access protocols
Thomson CSF, Marangis and Paris	Integrated sensor-based robot system
Université de Toulouse	Local wideband communication systems
United Kingdom	
Babcock Power, Rensrew, Scotland	Exploitation of real time imaging for arc welding
Barr & Stroud, Glasgow, Scotland	Computer-aided thermal imaging technique for real-time inspection of composite material
British Leyland Systems Ltd., Reditch	Design rules for computer integrated manufacturing systems
GEC (General Electric Co.), London	Standardization of integrated local area network services and service access protocol, integrated electronic subsystems for plant automation
Logica Ltd., London	Computer integrated production—design rules and standards
Plessey, Nottingham	Functional analysis of office requirements Office filing and retrieval of unstructured information
Queen Mary College, London	Technology for handling a mixture of text, image and voice information
Standard Telecommunications Laboratories Ltd., London	Functional analysis of office requirements
University of Strathclyde, Glasgow, Scotland	Computer-aided thermal-imaging technique for real-time inspection of composite material
Welding Institute, Cambridge	Exploitation of real-time imaging for arc welding
Greece	
Institute for Computer Science, Herakeion University of Crete	Multimedia office workstation Development of an experimental message-filing system for a mixture of message types—voice, keyboard entry, and graphics
Mnemonica, Athens	Development of an experimental message-filing system for a mixture of message types—voice, keyboard entry, and graphics
Ireland	
University College, Dublin	Office filing and retrieval of unstructured information
Trinity College, Dublin	Design rules for computer-integrated manufacturing systems

Related Esprit activities (continued)
Research activities in office automation and computer-integrated manufacturing funded by the European Strategic Program of Research and Development on Information Technology

Nation, entity and city	Activity
Italy	
Centro Studi e Laboratori Telecommunicazioni SpA, Turin	Document storage and interchange standards for office automation
Consiglio Nazionale delle Ricerca, Pisa	Development of an experimental message-filing system for a mixture of message types—voice, keyboard entry, and graphics
Comau, Turin	General-purpose sensory control system for parts production
Digital Equipment Automation, Turin	Integrated sensor-based robot system
Istituto di Ricerca sulle Onde Elettromagnetici, Florence	Computer-aided thermal-imaging technique for real-time inspection of composite material
Italsiel SpA, Rome	Work station for software development
Olivetti, Naples	General-purpose sensory control system for parts production
Polytechnic Institute, Milan	Local wideband communication systems
Selenia, Genova	Design rules for computer-integrated manufacturing
Sincon, Rome	General-purpose sensory control system for parts production
STET, Turin	Standardization of integrated local-area network services and service-access protocols
Syntax, Milan	Development of an experimental message-filing system for a mixture of message types
The Netherlands	
Philips, Eindhoven	Standardization of integrated local-area network services and service-access protocols; design rules for computer-integrated manufacturing
Stichting Mathematisch Centrum, Amsterdam	Design rules for computer-integrated manufacturing systems
University of Amsterdam	Design rules for computer-aided manufacturing systems
University of Nijmigen	Multimedia office work station
West Germany	
AEG, Frankfurt on Main	Design rules for computer-integrated manufacturing
AEG Telefunken, Seligen Stadt	Integrated electronic subsystems for plant automation
Fraunhofer Gesellschaft, Munich	General-purpose sensory control system for parts production
Olivetti, Ivria	Local wideband communication system; design rules for computer-integrated manufacturing
Fraunhofer Gesellschaft, Stuttgart	Integrated sensor-based robot system
Gesellschaft für mathematik und datenverbeitung, St. Augustin	Functional analysis of office requirements; work station for software development
Institut für Angewandte Organisations Forschung GmbH, Karesruhe	Design rules and standards; computer-integrated manufacturing
Nixdorf, Paderborn	Standardization of integrated local-area network services and service-access protocols; local wideband communication systems; broadband document communication
Oerlikon, Risenberg	Exploitation of real-time imaging for arc welding
Peripherie Computer System, Munich	Integrated sensor-based robot system
Rheinland–Westfalen Technische Hochschule, Aachen	Exploitation of real-time imaging for arc welding
Siemens, Munich	Technology for handling a mixture of text, image, and voice information
	General-purpose sensory control system for parts production; design rules for computer-integrated manufacturing
	Standardization of integrated local-area network and service-access protocols
Stollman & Co., Hamburg	Local broadband communication systems for a large site
University of Karlsruhe	Design rules for the integration of industrial robots into computer-integrated manufacturing systems

Abbreviations: ACEC: Ateliers de constructions Electriques de Charleroi; BTMC: Bell Telephone Manufacturing Co.; CII-HB: Compagnie Internationale pour l'Informatique—Honeywell Bull; SG2: Societe Generale de Service et de Gestion S.A.; STET: Societá Fínanziaria Telefonica.

(Continued from p. 26)

tute. These institutions contribute research results and joint appointments to the MCNC, but no money. Royalties from joint inventions are divided and administered according to each participating institution's policy.

Current projects are pushing design and integrated-circuit fabrication capabilities to the limit. Key development goals that the center supports are:

• A vertically integrated very large-scale integration (VLSI) design system called Vivid, a complete computer-design tool. The major components of this system, being developed at the Microelectronics Center, include a technology-independent, symbolic design methodology, a menu-driven graphics editor, a fast timing simulator, automatic routing and compacting, and a chip assembler.

• A fast prototyping capability using direct-write, thick-film hybrid techniques for building experimental architectures being developed by the Microelectronics Systems Laboratory at the University of North Carolina at Chapel Hill. The facility is expected to produce packages with up to 20 layers of interconnections and with line widths and interline spacings of roughly 1 mil. High-level packaging design will use the Vivid design system, which will have three-dimensional design capability.

• An advanced silicon-wafer fabrication facility, under construction at the Microelectronics Center. The objectives are fabrication in 3-micrometer technology in 1984 and 1-micrometer fabrication in 1985, with sufficient equipment to support advanced research in the materials and processing required for submicrometer technologies.

At present four projects are using vertically integrated capabilities available through the MCNC:

1. *Pixel planes*—Under development at the University of North Carolina at Chapel Hill, this project is attempting to bring VLSI's promise of massive parallelism to bear on the problem of updating large numbers of pixels as a screen changes.

2. *A Boolean vector machine*—Under development at Duke, this highly parallel machine will achieve computational speed unobtainable with a conventional architecture.

3. *A functional program language machine*—Being developed at Chapel Hill, this is a tree-structured machine whose machine language is functional. It also will rely on massive parallelism.

4. *An image-processing computer*—An effort at North Carolina State University, it is aimed at designing and building a computer system that is optimized to solve real-time image-processing problems with high input–output rates that also have substantial computational requirements. The key to success here also is the use of VLSI as a medium.

Research at other national programs, such as the Semiconductor Research Cooperative and the Microelectronics and Computer Technology Corp., is complementary to work at the MCNC. For example, the Microelectronics Center facility is helping SRC fulfill its mission by serving as a center of excellence in manufacturing technology research.

The board of directors comprises the chancellors of the five participating universities, a representative of the Research Triangle Institute, a representative of the state government, six citizens of North Carolina appointed to one-year terms by the governor, and the president of the Microelectronics Center. Besides the board of directors, faculty and professionals from the participating institutions and local industry advise the center. Currently over 85 people participate in these committees.

The center also offers funding for basic support for semiconductor teaching laboratories, and for a nationally competitive fellowship program.   ◆

GREAT BRITAIN

Great Britain's response to Japan's fifth-generation computer program will be a doubling of research in information technology through a new cooperative program funded by industry, by its Science and Engineering Research Council, its Department of Industry, and its Ministry of Defence. The effort will concentrate on four areas of research: very large-scale integration (VLSI), software engineering, intelligent knowledge-based systems, and man–machine interfaces. Although the objective of developing fifth-generation computers is not explicitly stated, this will undoubtedly be one of the by-products. The British program is expected to cost some $500 million over the course of its five-year life.

Participation is open to all British companies that do their research in England. The inclusion of foreign-owned companies will be considered if it can be shown that this would be in Great Britain's interest. The program, however, is not envisioned as an isolated effort.

The European Economic Community, of which Great Britain is a member, is organizing a similar program, known as Esprit, for European Strategic Programme on Research in Information Technology [see "European Common Market," p. 43]. The United Kingdom will be a major participant in Esprit; British companies are involved in more than half of Esprit's pilot projects. The British research program and Esprit will be organized to complement each other, with interlinking communications networks and common and parallel strategies. In time the two programs may well converge.

Japanese conference: an eye-opener

The British effort—known as the Alvey Programme for Advanced Information Technology, named for the chairman of the committee that set it up, John Alvey, now director of research for British Telecom—has roots that extend back to October 1981, when Japan issued invitations to a symposium on its fifth-generation computer systems project. Britain sent a team of government officials and academics, led by the head of the information technology division in the Department of Industry. The team became convinced that the Japanese plans posed a serious challenge to the world's information-technology industries and that the only way to counter the project was to take a leaf from Japan's book: to organize a British program of cooperative, precompetitive research and development in the information technologies.

The next step was a conference called in January 1982, at which most of the major companies in the British information-technology industry were represented, as well as many academics and scientists from government research establishments. The conference heard reports from the team that had attended the Japanese Fifth-Generation Computer Systems Conference. An outline program of action was drawn up by a group assembled by the Science and Engineering Research Council. The minister for technology, Kenneth Baker, was present and pledged his support for a detailed study to investigate and report on what should be done.

This led to the establishment of a committee appointed by the Department of Industry, under the chairmanship of Mr. Alvey, who had spent much of his career as a scientist in government

Brian W. Oakley   Department of Industry

research establishments. The committee consisted of about 12 people, largely drawn from the major British companies, such as General Electric Co. (GEC) of London, Plessey Co. Ltd., and International Computers Ltd. (ICL), though it also comprised additional individuals from the Ministry of Defence and the Science and Engineering Research Council, plus an eminent academic.

The committee decided that the program should be planned to run for five years and should tackle research in the main underlying fields upon which it was felt the future development of information technology depended. Working parties consulted widely in Britain, drawing up the plans for research on very large-scale integration, software engineering, intelligent knowledge-based systems, and man–machine interfaces. The proposed approach to the program was based heavily on the committee's understanding of the Japanese approach, adapted to British circumstances.

Involving top government echelons

After intensive work, a report was presented to the minister for technology in August 1982. It recommended a cooperative program of research involving all sections of the British information-technology field.

Meanwhile, the nation had already taken action on one aspect of the Alvey Committee's recommendations. It was apparent that a considerable increase would be needed in the supply of skilled research workers if the manpower for the program were to be found. Accordingly the Department of Education and Science announced in 1983 that funds were available to establish 70 extra posts in British universities, with further increases planned over the next two years. The Science and Engineering Research Council received funds to increase the number of research fellows. It also initiated a large program of postgraduate courses in various universities.

The Alvey Report was widely circulated by the Department of Industry among companies involved in information technology while the Science and Engineering Research Council sought comments from the academic world. The response was overwhelmingly in support of a program along the proposed lines, though there was some feeling that the program might come up with esoteric developments that would not be commercially exploited. Once the view of industry was clear, the Department of Industry put the case to the cabinet, and the ministers discussed it during the early months of 1983, finally announcing in April their decision to support the program.

There was only one significant change. The Alvey Committee had recommended that the research parts of the program be funded 90 percent from the public and 10 percent from industry. This was rejected by the government, which felt there was less danger of inadequate exploitation of the research work if all the costs of the program were shared fifty-fifty between the public and industrial sectors. But the academic work will be funded by the government.

The goal: a better chance to compete

The aim of the Alvey Programme is to improve the competitiveness of the British information-technology industries in the world market. Although the program includes emphasis on the development of knowledge-based systems, like the Japanese fifth-generation program it also pays attention to other aspects, some of which appear in other Japanese cooperative programs. The most obvious difference from the Japanese approach is that Great Britain does not intend to create a center for research, on the lines of the Japanese Institute for New Generation Computer

Technology (ICOT), but rather will rely on linking the British research centers through a data network and mailbox service that will allow interactive communication.

The program will be organized by a small directorate in the Department of Trade and Industry, the British equivalent of the Japanese Ministry of International Trade and Industry, led by the author. The directorate consists largely of scientists from industry—for example, GEC, Plessey, Logica, and ICL. They are being paid by their companies. There are also scientists on loan from research establishments in the Ministry of Defence and the Science and Engineering Research Council. The directorate reports to a small steering committee of senior industrialists, academics, and representatives of the funding bodies. The chairman of the Alvey Programme's steering committee is Sir Robert Telford of GEC.

Each of the main technologies in the Alvey Programme has its own director, and there is also a director in charge of networks and communications. This team will employ resources in the government and the research council, in combination with teams of industrial consultants, to administer the program.

In planning the program, the Alvey Committee used as models three active bodies around the world:

1. The Ministry of International Trade and Industry in Japan and the organization by MITI of advanced Japanese technology programs, including the fifth-generation program administered by ICOT.

2. The Defense Advanced Research Projects Agency (Darpa) of the United States and its programs, especially the work in creating the seminal ARPAnet data network.

3. The Common Valve Development organization of the British Ministry of Defence. This body was first formed during World War II, but it has survived as the body that selects and funds projects for the development of active electronic devices, including integrated circuits. The organization is widely respected in industry and the British Government as an eminent example of efficient and nonbureaucratic ways of coordinating advanced research.

Research by groups envisioned

The research work will be largely organized in small consortia—for example, two companies in information technology, together with a government research establishment team and a university team. In certain cases the consortia may be larger when the work can be readily organized on a cooperative basis—for example, by asking each organization to undertake a part of the work of developing a software system. Small companies with appropriate expertise will be encouraged to participate. In Britain there are some relatively small software houses of very high quality, though much of the information-technology hardware industry is concentrated in a few large, vertically integrated corporations. There will be a place for end-product user companies to participate in the Alvey Programme when demonstrations of products are organized.

It is expected that information will be freely exchanged within the consortia, including background information belonging to the individual companies. The work will be the property of each consortium carrying it out, and the responsibility for exploiting it will rest with the companies, with appropriate tests to ensure that it is available to other companies in the program on fair terms. In each major area of the program there will be a club-type of information exchange, with newsletters and symposia designed to increase the information flow. A network and mailbox facility will link the appropriate research centers. If foreign-owned companies participate in the program, the work will virtually always be carried out in Great Britain, with the intention of being exploited there.

Within each part of the Alvey Programme a strategic plan will be drawn up and revised from year to year. This plan will include objectives and milestones. A few large demonstration projects will be used to pace the work and determine what needs must be filled in the program. In a sense all the work of the program is directed to fifth-generation systems, and one of the demonstration projects may be specifically directed to that end. Certainly computer architectures will form a significant part of the Alvey Programme.

One technical objective is to create a widespread understanding and use of expert systems. It will be necessary to develop automatic methods for deriving the rules for rule-based or knowledge-based systems. This work will overlap that on the man–machine interfaces, where the objective must be to create friendly interfaces that actively encourage people to use information technology rather than frustrate it, as so often happens today.

The program on VLSI is not intended only to enhance the speed of integrated circuits; although the need for very large-scale integrated circuits is not obvious with today's systems outside the defense field, the ability to build in "knowledge" in the form of rule-based logic systems will rapidly create a market for larger and faster systems. This capability in turn will create a demand for software engineering, for such large systems cannot be constructed reliably and efficiently with today's manpower-intensive methods.   ◆

EUROPEAN COMMON MARKET

Since the late 1970s the general position of European information-technology industries has worsened in the world market. Most European companies are financially weak compared with their Japanese and American competitors; their information-technology products are not yet a major source of profits. The result is a negative balance of trade for Europe in this sector. In addition, studies show a negative balance of patents—evidence that European industry is losing the race to create a strong technology base for itself. The European Strategic Programme on Research in Information Technology (Esprit) was formed by the 25-year-old Commission of the European Communities (the European Common Market countries) to reverse the decline in competitiveness.

Esprit's long-range plan calls for research in five areas: advanced microelectronics, software technology, advanced information processing, office automation, and computer-integrated flexible manufacturing. Today, two years after a round-table conference in the European Economic Community that led to the formation of Esprit, the program is in the early stages of a one-year pilot phase that will run until mid-1984. Esprit has committed approximately 11.5 million ECU (economic community units, approximately equivalent to U.S. dollars) to support 23 million ECU of research for some three dozen projects.

The main program, which will involve nearly 2000 researchers and account for about 1.5 billion ECU over the first five years, is still under consideration by the European Economic Community Council of Ministers in Brussels. The council is to make its decisions before the end of this year. At that time proposals will be solicited for work in 1984–85.

Esprit shares similarities with and differs from organizations such as the Ministry of International Trade and Industry (MITI) in Japan and the Microelectronics and Computer Technology Corp. (MCC) in the United States. Like both those organizations, Esprit represents a partnership among various companies, academic research laboratories, and government agencies. Unlike those organizations, it is also an international partnership. Half of Espirit's funding will come from the 12 main corporate partners and other participating companies; the remaining portion will be provided by the Commission of European Communities.

Those 12 main partners are General Electric Co. (London), International Computers Ltd. (London), Plessey Co. Ltd. (London), Compagnie Générale de L'Electricité (Paris), Cie. des Machines Bull (Paris), Thomson Brandt (Paris), AEG-Telefunken AG (Frankfurt/Main, West Germany), Nixdorf Computer AG (Paderborn, West Germany), Siemens AG (Munich, West Germany), NmbH Philips Gloeilampenfabrieken (Eindhoven, the Netherlands), Olivetti SPA (Ivrea, Italy), and Societa Torinese Esercizi Telefonici (Rome).

Etienne Davignon, vice president of the Commission of European Communities, provided the initial impetus for setting up Esprit after observing economic trends in information technology. The world market for such products is growing at an annual rate of 10 percent—even in the present world recession. Annual world sales are perhaps 100 billion ECU. Furthermore, 30 percent of this market is within Europe.

The leading industrial nations outside Europe—namely, the United States and Japan—have had projects or programs under way for many years to help industry promote technology in this area. Hence, industrial competition from the United States and Japan has increased, especially in the very high-technology industries that are the key to growth. But the European information-technology industries, lacking a strong technology base, are increasingly dependent on foreign technology from competing companies.

Europe at a crossroads

The seriousness of this weakness was clear to Mr. Davignon: only 40 percent of the European domestic market and 10 percent of the world market in information technology were held by European industry. He saw most major European companies as being at a crossroads.

In Mr. Davignon's view, either European companies must increasingly rely on imported basic technology, at the risk of being vulnerable to embargo, or they must drop out of the race in high technology and fall back on lower-technology products. But it was clear to him that many of the world's largest growth markets were in high-technology markets.

Mr. Davignon became convinced that Europe, like the United States and Japan, must create a long-term strategy for its information-technology industries. The aim of the strategy, he contended, must place European industries in a position of at least technological equality with their competitors. Furthermore, in his view Europe could not compete by pursuing research and development along nationalistic lines. He felt it would be much more economical and useful if all countries cooperated in a Europe-wide program.

Round-table conference leads to action

In his position as vice president in charge of the commission's divisions of research and science, industry and trade, and energy,

---

Horst Nasko   Nixdorf Computer AG

Mr. Davignon invited the chairmen of the 12 leading European companies involved in information technology to a round-table conference in mid-1981. The aim was to plan a cooperative venture, to formulate its strategic objectives, and to focus on research topics—all to put European industries again in a stronger position in the world information-technology markets. The result of the round-table discussion was a plan to form Esprit.

The round-table participants and the commission installed a steering committee, which, with additional inputs from outside sources, reviewed potential areas of technology to identify those that were both necessary to compete in world markets and suitable for a cooperative European effort. The steering committee also was charged with organizing the entire Esprit project with respect to concept, size, scope of research, management, and legal questions.

Panels of experts from the 12 leading partners in Esprit, along with other specialists, established the long-range plan for research on advanced microelectronics, software technology, advanced information processing, office automation, and computer-integrated flexible manufacturing.

Major goals outlined

Advanced microelectronics is the common operational circuit technology on which all modern electronic systems rely to perform their functions. Advances in microelectronics technology are aimed at producing smaller, more reliable, and more powerful devices that can perform more functions or operations than those in use today can. The focus of the Esprit projects will be going from the present state-of-the-art processes, relying on 3-to-5-micrometer structures, to processes based on structures smaller than 1 micrometer.

Submicrometer structures will reduce power consumption and increase packing density, resulting in increased speed for reduced cost. Attaining this submicrometer technology will require developing certain lithography processes, etching techniques, and computer-aided design facilities.

Software technology is aimed at producing software more economically by automating much of the process. At present experts are needed to create software, and they are costly and limited in number. The aim of Esprit's projects will be to improve present software engineering techniques—those, for instance, needed to generate highly modular software—so that individual modules can be reused in other programs for which the same functions are required.

Advanced information-processing systems will make possible new kinds of direct communication between humans and machines, using speech and images, for instance. Moreover, their functions will more closely resemble human thought, association, and inference rather than data storage and calculation. Such artificial-intelligence systems will be knowledge processors rather than data processors. Their development will require advanced architecture and further miniaturization in microelectronics, higher reliability, and novel ideas in information science. This is a focus of the fifth-generation technology being developed both in the United States and Japan.

Office automation is expected to become the largest single information-technology market. The objectives depend on local cultural considerations. These in turn influence the architecture and software for the desired human–machine interface for creating and distributing documents, linking work stations, integrating text, voice, and images into communication systems, and retrieving organized knowledge rather than raw information. Communication is a central element of office systems. Not only will all these requirements demand greater processing capacity, but they also will bring disparate systems into contact with one another, thus making standardization between the systems essential.

Computer-integrated flexible manufacturing systems involve systematically computerizing manufacturing processes. Such systems will integrate computer-aided design, computer-aided manufacturing, computer-aided testing, and repair and assembly by means of a common data base. Such integration will require much research in system architecture and in software development.

Esprit's research programs will also focus on machine control of manufacturing, such as automated assembly, robot operating systems, imaging, and computer-controlled machine tools. Such integration will require cost-effective, highly reliable components, such as sensors and microelectronic subsystems.

Major stress in two areas of research

Most of Esprit's funds will flow to the areas of advanced microelectronics and advanced information processing. The objective in information processing is the transition from data-processing to knowledge-processing systems. Included in this objective are more user-friendly interfaces and the exploitation of very large-scale integration for a major increase in information-processing power.

The main thrust of Esprit's research and development in information processing will be in these areas:
- Information and knowledge engineering.
- Pattern recognition and man–machine interfaces.
- Computer architecture for parallel processing.
- Design objectives and computer-aided design methods.

From Esprit's overall strategy, a five-year goal has been defined by experts from the 12 main partners and outside consultants, as well as a work plan of specific projects for the forthcoming year. Once specific projects are defined, they are to be made public and proposals are to be solicited.

A building-block approach

Proposals may be submitted by research teams from any industry or university, so long as the team is composed of nationals of two or more European Economic Community countries. Companies outside the community may also participate if they do their research in the community. This setup encourages cooperation across the boundaries of corporations and states, thereby preventing parallel effort and making optimal use of limited financial and human resources.

The proposals to be approved will be selected by the commission with the help of an advisory board. The board consists of experts nominated by Mr. Davignon, mainly from industry and especially from the 12 partners. When a proposal is approved, the research team that submitted it will receive 50-percent financing to undertake the research—funding that each team is expected to match from its own research and development budget.

Compared with the U.S. and Japanese programs, the goals of Esprit are unique. The program is intended to be a building block that will improve the use of European research and development resources. Unlike the MITI program in Japan, Esprit is limited to precompetitive research; it does not intend to go so far as to develop a product like a full-scale fifth-generation computer family. At any point in the research, however, the participating companies will be free to take the information they have gained and to develop proprietary products of their own. Thus Esprit should not be in competition with national R&D programs, but rather it will reinforce them and make them more effective. ◆

THE CHALLENGES

DESIGNING THE NEXT GENERATION

Machines that are much faster, much smarter, and far more accessible than current ones require advances on a broad technological front

In 1981 a group of computer scientists in Japan proposed to leap-frog the next generation of conventional computers and build machines based on massively parallel hardware and artificial-intelligence software. Since then a number of similar projects have been proposed in the United States, Great Britain, and the European Economic Community. All the programs have their own national flavors [see "The teams and the players," p. 13], but the technology underlying them is basically the same: advanced computer architectures, advanced software engineering, very large-scale integrated circuits, and artificial intelligence.

What is the current state of those disciplines and how must they evolve to achieve the goals set out by the various national and international projects? What further progress is envisioned beyond that required for the implementation of next-generation computing systems? To answer these questions it is useful to consider the roles that different technologies will play in next-generation systems.

With the typical next-generation system, it will be impossible to point to a single device and say, "This is a next-generation computer." Links between computers can make it irrelevant which one a person is communicating with at any given time; intelligent interfaces can make that communication easy; and knowledge-based systems can extend the range of services that computers can perform.

Breakthroughs are needed

Much of this progress can be accomplished by expected advances in the current state of the art of conventional computing. But certain problems can be tackled only by machines with thousands or millions of times more processing power than current ones and by software markedly different from today's programs.

Artificial intelligence (AI) is considered by most people to be a cornerstone of next-generation computer technology; all the efforts in different countries accord it a prominent place in their list of goals. The most important subdomains of artificial intelligence for the next generation are knowledge systems, language understanding, and speech and picture recognition. Knowledge-system applications range from expert consultants in various fields to teaching systems that "understand" a student's particular difficulties, and intelligent data bases that can help their users define the information they are seeking. Language-understanding systems can be useful as interpreters for other pro-

grams, or for translation. Speech and picture recognition can speed the input of information to a computer, but it can also be helpful for autonomous devices—robots that plan their actions in response to their environment.

Today almost all of these applications founder for want of computing power. Hours of computing time may be needed to recognize seconds of speech or a few frames of video. Language-understanding systems are limited to very small subsets of human language and expert systems operate in narrow domains [see "Expert systems: powerful but limited," [p. 192]. The introduction of machines with massively parallel architectures may bring significant improvements; if the same operation can be performed on thousands of pixels (picture elements) simultaneously, or a voice signal matched against thousands of templates at the same time, or if thousands of IF-THEN rules can be checked at once to see if any of their conditions are met, then applications currently out of reach may become feasible.

Exploiting parallelism

There are, however, problems with parallelism: matching algorithms to parallel systems is one and getting all the processors in a parallel system to work efficiently is another. Often it is a case of too much or too little parallelism to be useful. In expert systems, for example, most problems require that only a few different branches of reasoning be pursued at any one time. Where the computer must search exhaustively through a set of potential solutions, the problem expands exponentially, and many millions of processors may be needed to work out the solution.

Various parallel architectures have been discussed by computer scientists, including trees, square and cubic arrays, and "data flow" structures, in which information is passed around a network until it finds a processor willing to work on it. However, only a few prototypes of any of these machines have been built and it is not yet clear whether there is any one best architecture. Some researchers have suggested that the way to approach the problem is not to look for a general-purpose parallel architecture and figure out how to match one's algorithms on it, but rather to work out parallel implementations of particular algorithms and then design architectures to execute them efficiently.

Significant problems still remain in the design of algorithms for various AI applications. In knowledge systems, there are the problems of knowledge representation and acquisition; there are certain concepts that cannot yet be satisfactorily expressed for a machine to work on; and virtually all machine knowledge comes from AI researchers coding it into machine-readable form. The

Paul Wallich   Associate Editor

Japanese fifth-generation project speaks of expert systems with tens of thousands of rules. At current rates of knowledge encoding, such systems would take nearly 20 years to build. Thus, it is obvious that automated transfer of knowledge from people to machines is a necessary step in the growth of knowledge systems.

In language understanding there are also unsolved problems. One example is what are called speech acts—questions such as "Can you hand me a wrench?" that are actually requests for an action to be performed. Language-understanding programs must have a thorough understanding of speech acts before they can be truly useful interfaces between people and computer programs. Other problems are the understanding of ungrammatical or misspelled requests and understanding novel language—for a long time to come, humans will use expressions not yet in machine vocabularies, and programs must be able to respond gracefully.

Similarly, it is not clear how to proceed in machine vision from the low-resolution, two-dimensional systems available today to high-resolution, 3-D vision. Vision, however, is one area where even experimentation with advanced algorithms is hindered by the lack of powerful enough machines. Architectures capable of performing simple operations on thousands of pixels simultaneously could be a great aid to research in computer vision.

VLSI: solution and problem

Such architectures, consisting of many simple processors, each with a small amount of local memory, are made feasible by very large-scale integration (VLSI). Once the initial circuit and its connections are designed, many processors can be put on the same chip, and large numbers of chips can be fabricated with relative ease. However, designing such circuits is not easy, and there are relatively few facilities where prototypes can be fabricated on a schedule that allows for significant experimentation. Therefore, VLSI design tools are a required element in next-generation com-

puting efforts, both to design the many chips that will be necessary for next-generation computer systems and to support the experimental designs needed along the way.

At present a number of methods are supplanting hand layout of chips. They include standard cells, gate arrays, and various kinds of silicon compliers—programs that map directly from high-level descriptions of chip function to layout. All of these methods yield chips that are slower and less densely packed than hand layouts and each method has particular disadvantages: standard cell designs may not be able to take advantage of regularities in a design; gate arrays are well known for inefficiency in implementing memories; and the silicon compilers are limited in the kinds of chips they can compile and in the floor plans they use for laying them out.

There are stages of the design process other than layout; two important ones are verification and testing. Simulating designs to make sure that they perform their intended functions at the desired speed could be significantly aided by specially designed simulation hardware; the test coverage could also be evaluated by running test vectors on the simulated design. Thus far, the massive parallelism needed for simulation hardware has been quite expensive and only very large companies have been able to afford to build large simulators.

In addition to design and verification, million-transistor chips or larger also require fabrication. At current device densities, chips with more than a few hundred thousand transistors are uneconomical to fabricate in quantity because they are too large. Furthermore, feature sizes may not shrink much more. Currently, 2-micrometer line widths are not uncommon, and chips with half-micrometer features may be possible to fabricate within the next few years. However, the physics of individual devices is more difficult to control as scales shrink, and processing requirements become more stringent because smaller flaws increase in importance. One avenue that is being explored in wafer-scale

A day in the life of a new-generation computer user

This is a fictional account of how the next generation of computers might help a user on a typical day in 1993. All technologies mentioned have already been demonstrated as research prototypes; only the specific machines and situations are fictional projections. In the scenario, the user, John Atarashi, is an actuary working for a company that develops retirement benefit plans for client companies around the world.

John Atarashi is driving down the Bayshore Freeway south of San Francisco, heading for his office in the southern San Francisco Bay Area of California. He sees traffic choked to a halt about one-half mile ahead, just beyond the next freeway exit. With a push of a button in his car, John turns on his new-generation terminal, which connects itself to his personal work-station computer at his office, using cellular radio to connect to the telephone system via conventional voice-grade lines.

With a few spoken commands, which are passed to John's office work station, digitized, and recognized by a special parallel voice-recognition system trained to his voice, John requests information on alternate routes to his destination. To answer, the office work station connects itself via a wideband digital network to a computer center of the Traffic Analysis and Routing, Bay Area Basic Information Corp. (Tarbabic). It maintains a vast array of optical disks that contain digitized maps of the entire Bay Area, and the company has a parallel supercomputer that, given an initial location and destination, can retrieve the relevant maps and perform searches to determine alternate routes.

To provide travel-time estimates, the Tarbabic machine

estimates traffic volume on different routes using a network of traffic-flow sensors that have been placed along most of the major roads and highways in the Bay Area. Tarbabic returns descriptions to John's office work station of the alternate routes and estimated times, along with a bill for the service.

John listens to the alternatives, which have been converted into spoken output by the work station and sent to the new-generation terminal in John's car. He decides to pull off at the next exit and pursue a different route. As he drives, he asks his work station to read him his electronic mail and any telephone messages that have been stored automatically and digitally on his company's central communications computer. He notes one message needing immediate attention and dictates a response. It is digitized and compressed by a special speech processor at his work station and sent to the recipient, along with copies to people he names.

One of his messages indicated that a trip to Mexico City was in order to present a benefit plan to a company there for the first time. (Although most meetings with regular clients are teleconferences, John's company long ago discovered that no technology could replace the need for human interaction when establishing rapport with a new client.) John requests that his work station reserve for him the flights and a rental car for the required dates; he decides to book his hotel later, when he is not restricted to voice commands and spoken output and can examine the hotel visually on the computer screen.

Planning a trip is a relatively complex activity, and John's company owns a knowledge-based inference system and

integration experiments is to build many more devices on a chip than are needed, probe them to see which ones work, and then interconnect them in the desired pattern.

Packaging is another obstacle to the advancement of VLSI. As chips become more complex, they require more pins to connect them to the outside world, and because they contain more devices, they dissipate more heat. Conventional packaging techniques are not sufficient for building systems from million-transistor chips; alternatives such as ceramic chip carriers and liquid cooling may have to be used in next-generation systems. One of the shorter-term projects of the Microelectronics and Computer Cooperative in Austin, Texas, is aimed at the development of high-capacity, high–heat-dissipation substrates and packages for ICs, and it seems likely that its goals will be achieved.

A need to improve software productivity

Hundreds of thousands of personal-computer users have unhappily discovered in the last few years that the most powerful hardware is of little utility without useful software. What software will the powerful machines of the next generation run and how will it be written? A major part of several national projects for next-generation computing is aimed at improving the rate at which programmers produce debugged code. Although artificial intelligence is a large part of new-generation computing, expert systems are in fact very large pieces of software: even those people selling commercial expert systems doubt that more than a quarter of their potential applications will be built in the next 30 years. Thus, conventional programming will still form the overwhelming bulk of software writing even after new-generation computers become widely available.

Several avenues are available for improving programmer productivity: software tools for tracing, debugging, and program verification; code libraries that allow many applications to be put together primarily from well-tested building blocks, automatic code-generators, or very high-level languages that translate program specifications into executable code; and structured programming techniques, which encourage the writing of modular programs on a top-down basis.

Many of these avenues have been open for a number of years, but apparently they have not been widely used. Recent surveys indicate that only a few software companies use the software productivity tools currently available. The increased use of those tools, even without major advances in software engineering, could contribute significantly to software productivity. (Some computer scientists contend that traditional software engineering approaches a dead end as programmers build more complex systems because of its emphasis on knowing in advance what the desired system looks like. They claim that "exploratory" programming environments, which take over many bookkeeping burdens from the programmer and make program modification easy, will avoid such a dead end. Such techniques as logic programming, where programs are written in declarative form and a compiler generates the necessary procedures to get results, may also supplant traditional software engineering.)

Of course, efforts to improve the current average level of 10 lines of program code per programmer per day (curiously similar to the 10 devices per engineer per day attributed to hand layout of ICs) answer only the question of how next-generation software will be written. Another significant question is: What will that software do? And there the answer is even less certain. One important feature of next-generation software, however, will be the user interface; already, graphical presentations have begun to replace tables of numbers, and it is likely that next-generation programs will interact with users in a highly graphical fashion. Voice and handwriting for input are also goals; limited successes have already been achieved, although systems capable of extensive conversation, for example, will require breakthroughs.

Another major component of next-generation software, and

---

supporting parallel hardware that runs several types of expert systems, including one that serves as an expert trip planner. John's work station passes the dates to the expert trip planner, which in turn connects to the Bay Area Travel Information Corp. (BATI), which provides flight and rental car information.

After examining John's calendar, his personal profile of travel preferences, and the flight alternatives available, the expert trip planner asks the BATI computer to make some specific reservations, remembering to request vegetarian meals for John on the plane. Billing and ticketing are handled automatically by the trip planner, the BATI computer, and the accounting system of John's company.

Having taken care of his immediate work, John completes the drive to his office while listening to selections of music he has requested. His new-generation terminal plays the requests after retrieving them from a digitized storage disk in his car.

At the office John can attend to some problems that require more powerful interaction with new-generation computers than are permitted by voice alone. At his work station, he has a high-resolution color image and graphics display, equipped with a touch-sensitive screen. He decides to use this capability to browse through a multimedia computer "book" describing Mexico City, a service provided by a company offering a library of such books for cities around the world. In response to an earlier request, the information on Mexico City has been sent via satellite and is now on an optical disk at John's work station.

His terminal calls up a sequence of images of the Zona Rosa district of Mexico City, where his meeting will be held.

Although the scene looks like a video tape of the city, John can control what image sequences are displayed by touching left- or right-turn commands on the screen, which gives him the sensation of actually walking and driving around the Zona Rosa. John sees an attractive hotel and "walks" inside to check it out. He likes the lobby, looks at a room, and decides to stay there during his business visit. He requests the expert trip-planning program to make the reservations; it looks at John's travel schedule to figure out the days for which he will need reservations and notes that it must tell the hotel's computer that his room should be held for late arrival.

Having taken care of his travel plans and obtained a feel for Mexico City, John now turns to the business-related aspects of his trip. He is putting together a package on retirement benefits for his client, the Mexican branch of a multinational corporation. He needs some expert advice about government regulations dealing with retirement benefits in Mexico and, to get it, he requests a session with his company's knowledge-based computing system.

The same parallel hardware and logical-inference software that worked out his travel plans now help him with benefit regulations by retrieving information from a different knowledge base. After an interactive session with the expert system, John is able to complete the outline of his proposed benefits plan, file it in the machine for later review, and forward copies to other members of his team for comments.

His work done for the day, John relaxes before heading home by using his office work station to wander around the streets of Tangiers.   —*Robert J. Douglass*
Los Alamos National Laboratory

Networks: wiring a nation

Fundamental to next-generation computing are networks through which computers can share each other's resources as though they were parts of the same machine. The computing power of all the computers on a next-generation network would be available at any node in the network. Personal computers would be connected to local-area networks, and local networks would be interconnected in a nationwide supernetwork. One could think of the network as a single, distributed computer, and each computer as a special part of the architecture.

The advantages to such a scheme are: efficiency, because any one computer could be used by anyone on the network; reliability, because the network would consist of modular parts that could fail without affecting the rest of the network; and flexibility, because any single computer would not be limited by its own computational capacity but by the capacity of the network.

The motivation for working toward building such a network has been fueled by advances in very large-scale integrated circuits and in telecommunications technology. Already, local-area networks carry the 10 megabits or so of information sufficient for interconnecting computers locally. Satellites and fiber-optic land lines currently being installed can carry information in the megabits-per-second range needed for interconnecting clusters of local-area networks.

The software problems, by contrast, are a long way from being solved, according to experts. Networks must be made with distributed operating systems, meaning they must be able to share resources such as data bases and divide computational tasks into loosely synchronized tasks among several computers. Distributed data bases must be implemented so that computers on a network can obtain information from and enter information into the data bases of other computers on the network.

Computers on a next-generation network must be able to translate protocols of other computers and networks. Software-translation programs must be developed so computers with different architectures can execute parts of one program, and so software written for one computer can operate on others. Making networks that can recover from errors presents special problems, since discrepancies can occur between information stored in computers at different nodes in the network. Ways must be found to ensure the reliability of data.

Distributed operating systems needed

In mainframe computers, an operating system is a program that manages the other programs running in the computer, allocating resources such as memory, the central processing unit, and peripherals. In a computer network, by contrast, no single operating system runs the entire show.

A distributed operating system, however, exists at all nodes of the network. Each computer has its own operating system, but it is coordinated with the operating systems of other computers so computational resources can be shared. For example, a program being run by a user at one node of the network might contain an algorithm that would best be executed by another computer. To implement such sharing, ways must be found to break algorithms into parts, translate software, and represent computational tasks independent of the computer that will perform the tasks.

At present, computers can transfer files and send information to other computers, but the interface between computers is relatively unsophisticated. "It is almost at the electrical level," said Thomas Love, president of Productivity Products Inc., Sandy Hook, Conn. "We need processors that can send messages to other processors like 'Do this for me: I don't care how you do it, but come back when you have the answer.'"

Many computer systems today use more than one processor, splitting a task into parts and delegating each part to a different processor. In a next-generation network, however, such interaction would be commonplace rather than occurring only in systems designed specially for certain problems and would take place at a higher level of sophistication.

Distributed data bases—a goal

An important feature of next-generation computer networks is distributed data bases. In conventional computers, a data base is a collection of information stored in such a way that a subset of the data base relevant to a query can be retrieved quickly. In a network, a computer might execute a program that requires information stored in the data bases of several other computers. The computer would issue a query, broadcasting it through the network, asking the other computers to search their data bases for relevant information. Each of the computers responding to the query in turn would communicate with each other and collect information for the computer that issued the query.

Designing the software for such a scheme presents two main problems. First, languages are being developed that deal with data in a relational rather than algorithmic way. For a computational task such as data-base query to be broadcast to several different computers, the query must be made in an abstract way and then the details of how to search for the information must be left to the computers responding to the query.

A second area of research concerns finding a way of managing a distributed data base so that computers can obtain information from the data base and modify its contents without interfering with one another. In mainframes, this problem is solved by setting priorities for different users in accessing the data base. But next-generation computer networks will involve more interaction between computers and have no central operating system. Thus, the networks will be so complex that priority access is not a solution.

The interference problem would occur when a computer's data base is accessed and modified by more than one computer in a short period of time. For example, suppose bank account A is kept on one computer and bank account B on another, and a third computer takes $1000 out of account A and begins to put it into account B. But before it can put the $1000 into account B, a fourth computer adds up the total amount of money in both accounts. The erroneous sum would show a $1000 loss. Even if the error is detected, correcting it is problematic because the sequence of events is difficult to trace. Research is on-going to make such transactions atomic, meaning that other programs cannot have access to the data needed until the transaction is completed, without significantly adding to the amount of time each transaction takes.

Translating software a focus of efforts

Since computers on a next-generation network will vary greatly in architecture and protocol, ways of translating software between computers are being developed. Compilers, the computer programs that translate high-level language into the low-level machine language, will be relied upon to apply knowledge about data structures, control structures, optimization, and parallel hardware to translate software for computers with different architectures, according to Cordell Green, director of the Kestrel Institute, Palo Alto, Calif., which is researching knowledge-based software tools.

"Next generation compilers will take a problem and configure it to the particular architecture of a computer," he said. "Now, a compiler transforms a set, for example, into a bitmap. An intelligent compiler understands several ways of representing a set for both sequential and parallel computers."

—Fred Guterl

of next-generation systems in general, will be in the realm of communications. Even the most powerful expert system will be of little value unless people can get to it to ask it questions; and the most sophisticated personal computer will not be much good unless the person using it can inform others of the results of its computations.

Where does digital-communications systems technology stand? Certainly the vision of some researchers of a world where anyone can communicate with anyone else or with any other computer is barely on the horizon. Current computer networks show signs of being electronic islands or even continents, where communication within a single network is relatively simple, but internetwork ties are difficult to use [see "Putting it together," p. 77]. Increased sophistication of computers can potentially remedy many of the problems of inconsistent message and addressing formats, but standard formats may still be desirable.

Furthermore the computer networks of the next generation are expected to be so much larger than current nets that their size may pose qualitative rather than simply quantitative differences. Current networks serve tens of thousands of users; next-generation nets, if powerful computers do indeed become part of people's daily lives, may serve millions.

Over what medium is this tremendous volume of communication to travel? Current computer nets use dedicated lines or commercial or government packet-switching services. Installing such a net for the next generation would be comparable to installing another version of a country's telephone network. The capital value of the telephone system in the United States, for example, is estimated at about $100 billion.

Here other questions arise. Are next-generation computer networks to be as ubiquitous as the telephone network? What will be the status of people without "telephones"? While these are more strictly questions of policy than technology, it is clear that the technology chosen to implement the next generation may have a significant impact on how ubiquitous it becomes.

Merging of disciplines is likely

In some cases it may be difficult to assess the state of technical disciplines for the next generation because those disciplines do not yet exist. One prime example is knowledge engineering. Although it is currently practiced only by AI researchers building expert systems, knowledge engineering may evolve as a discipline in itself as those systems are constructed for more and more commercial applications. Other examples will appear as next-generation technology matures.

Another trend, however, may be more important: the breaking down of traditional barriers between technical disciplines. For the next generation to become a reality, VLSI designers and implementors must work with machine architects, and machine architects with software researchers, and software researchers with applications specialists. The state of that cooperation today is uncertain, but its possibilities are promising.   ◆

THE BUILDING BLOCKS
Artificial intelligence, software engineering, computer architecture, and very large-scale integration will play major roles

ARTIFICIAL INTELLIGENCE

There are two major branches of research in artificial intelligence (AI): intelligent machines and cognitive science. The first branch aims at the construction of computer programs that perform at high levels of competence in cognitive tasks, while the second is concerned with modeling human processing of information. The intelligent-machines branch is a computer science and engineering approach; it is not critical whether the methods mimic the internal structure of human behavior.

The cognitive science branch of AI, on the other hand, uses the computer as a precise language with which to express hypotheses about human information processing, much as mathematics is used in physics. Once those hypotheses have been framed, a computer can predict their consequences for particular hypothetical situations, so that they can be tested and refined.

Researchers in both intelligent machines and cognitive science are motivated by a common methodology and working hypothesis. The methodology is to use programming as a laboratory to perform experiments, from which they induce theoretical ideas about the nature of intelligence. The working hypothesis is that the result will be a theory of intelligent information processing, whether that processing is done in silicon or biological tissue.

The engineering part of artificial intelligence breaks down into subdisciplines that relate to applications. For example, the area

Edward A. Feigenbaum   Stanford University

of knowledge systems is an attempt to codify the factual and heuristic knowledge of specialized areas of human endeavor and to couple that knowledge with problem-solving methods. Other subdomains of AI also deal with knowledge-based intelligent activity. For example, language understanding, whether from text or continuous speech, is heavily dependent on world knowledge.

Vision systems have the same characteristic. The data in the pixels of the image can be organized only by using knowledge of what real-world objects look like. If, for example, a program is to interpret reconnaissance photos, then it needs to know what kinds of objects will be in the pictures. It also needs to know certain facts, such as that missile silos are generally out in unpopulated areas, not in the middle of cities, so that it can know that the cylindrical objects it sees in a city are perhaps something else—like natural gas tanks.

Two other areas of artificial intelligence—automatic programming and theorem proving—are also knowledge-based. Programs that write programs need a considerable body of knowledge about programming, just as if it were a chemistry or biology problem for the computer to solve. Programs that prove mathematical theorems are also beginning to exploit techniques that expert mathematicians know and use for complex proofs.

Another important subfield of AI is intelligent robots—robots that will be able to plan their sequences of actions and take alternate actions, depending on what unfolds. Planning and problem-solving systems for robots are a central concern of AI.

AI was born in 1956 with heuristic search as its founding principle. Intelligent problem solving was viewed as the search for solutions in a maze of possibilities. The difficulty arises from the number of avenues to be explored; the problem solver achieves intelligence by using various types of knowledge to steer and prune the search—for example, looking at the best avenues first, and removing unfruitful paths.

AI spent most of its early years working out the details of search: heuristically guided generate and test, backward chaining from the goal to be achieved to facts or already proven theorems, forward chaining from known conditions, or means–ends analysis, which is the looking backward and forward from beginning point to goal and attempting to reduce the differences. In this author's view, the most powerful of these control structures for search is the blackboard model. In this scheme multiple sources of knowledge cooperate by means of a common knowledge structure that represents the emerging pieces of the solution. Each body of knowledge looks at the "blackboard" to see what it can do to build onto the emerging solution. The system achieves power from its capability to mix arbitrarily forward and backward chaining strategies, using bodies of knowledge represented at different levels of abstraction.

In the middle 1960s, after the first expert systems, such as Dendral, were built, AI underwent a shift to a knowledge-based paradigm. The principle is that, although one can not do without inference, what method one uses is not all that important relative to the knowledge the program has. Thus, the important questions are related to knowledge—how to represent it in a machine, and how to acquire it from nature or people.

Representing knowledge in the machine

What are some methods for representing knowledge? There are the formal methods drawn from mathematical logic: first-order predicate calculus, for example. Such formalisms are not necessarily convenient or understandable, so researchers have moved to other representations. There is still considerable work going on in logic programming—for example, Prolog. Prolog, in its pure form, is a descriptive rather than a procedural language, although numerous procedural mechanisms are being introduced into Prolog so that programs can be run.

The other forms that have been invented are equivalent to first-order expressions in some deep sense, but they are more transparent, interesting, and usable. The best-known form is rules—If–Then expressions, in which the "if" side is the invoking condition for the piece of knowledge and the "then" side is the action to be taken or the conclusion to be drawn.

At a more basic level, AI researchers have always had the concept of an object represented in the machine, with various attributes that themselves have values. The attribute–value structure of objects was present in the earliest list-processing languages, and it was transported right into LISP in the property-list mechanism. Current knowledge-representation systems are merely elaborate extensions of the same idea.

The major tasks now for knowledge-representation research are to extend the concepts of object description, to extend the ways in which rules can be structured, and to extend our ideas of how to represent concepts that humans encounter, such as time, ownership, and causality. These and others have to be thought through carefully before we can represent them for a machine.

Knowledge acquisition, alias machine learning, is the current bottleneck to AI progress. Right now, we are acquiring knowledge in a handcrafted fashion. An AI person must code each piece individually. Although there are ways machines can learn, there are modes of humanlike knowledge acquisition that are not yet thoroughly understood. A good example would be reasoning by analogy, and another is the discovery of new knowledge and the construction of new ideas.

The mystery that surrounds the term "discovery" must be dispensed with. Discovery is merely heuristic search in the space of old concepts and their combinations. Even though it involves a lot of computing, it's worth it, because once something new is discovered it never has to be recomputed—it becomes a piece of knowledge that lasts. Furthermore, knowledge acquisition is itself a knowledge-based task—the more you know, the easier it is to know more. With machines, just as with people, learning takes place at the fringes of what we know. It is very difficult to learn from nothing; but it's very easy to learn a little bit more.

The level of scientific activity in knowledge-acquisition research is high. The area should be well into its engineering phase in the early 1990s, because there is so much pressure for it from the expert-systems building efforts going on.

The progress into the 1990s is going to be evolutionary, rather than revolutionary. John McCarthy (professor of computer science at Stanford University in Palo Alto, Calif., and one of the pioneers of AI) likes to say that the field needs 1.7 Einsteins, but I'm not so sure. I think intelligence in a machine is gradually going to become more comprehensive. Programs will have more knowledge—for example, a program that is trying to solve a problem in area A will have knowledge about area B and will be able to exploit an analogy between the two.

The spreading of program activity from specialized areas into more general fields of human endeavor will take a very long time, because humans know so much more than machines. It requires insight from the theorists, so that we know how to represent knowledge properly. It requires an enormous amount of work in codifying human knowledge so that such knowledge can be made available to problem-solving processes. Our machines are relatively dumb, in all areas except their specialities, because they do not have enough knowledge. If we organize a major national project to collect and encode knowledge, that would change. I sometimes envision a big grassy field in which I have factories—a knowledge factory, a heuristics factory, and another factory turning out new machines that will use that knowledge effectively with those heuristics. If you look out into the future, the applications potential for such machines is enormous.

How are we going to run these programs? Do we envision running them on Crays or similar traditional supercomputers? Well, we would like to put at the disposal of the problem-solving process as much inference power and knowledge-application power as we could bring to bear. This kind of processing has almost nothing to do with arithmetic. We want logical-inference power, we want rule lookup and high-speed semantic net traversal, in contrast to the high-speed indexing of arrays.

Goals of artificial intelligence

What is the most general view of the AI enterprise? Surely, there is the desire to formulate a theory of intelligent information processing, but there are also other themes. One is the playing out of a millenia-old attraction that Pamela McCorduck documents in her book, *Machines Who Think*, the desire of people to create intelligent artifacts. It goes all the way back to the Greeks, you find it in the Golem stories, and now, in the late twentieth century people have the ability to realize those age-old aspirations for intelligent machines. AI researchers want to produce the smartest possible artifacts.

Another long-range motivation is the contribution that AI will make to the codification of human knowledge. We will have a form of knowledge that we have not seen represented before, the heuristic knowledge, the experiential knowledge of good practice —in short, "the art of good guessing." In the long-term service of humanity, it is the knowledge that is important. It may make little difference whether this knowledge is processed by machines or not.   ◆

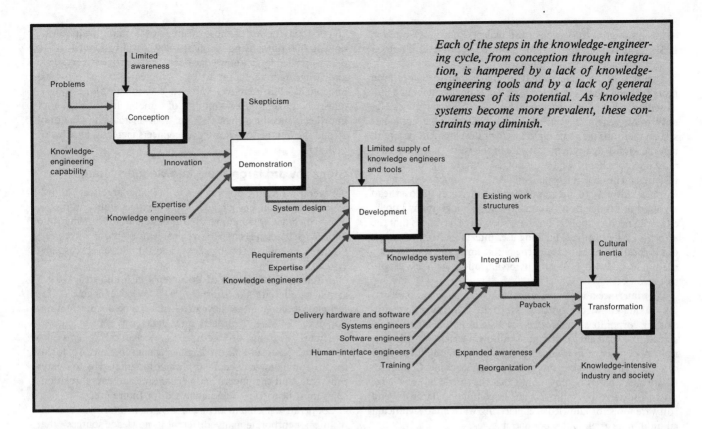

Each of the steps in the knowledge-engineering cycle, from conception through integration, is hampered by a lack of knowledge-engineering tools and by a lack of general awareness of its potential. As knowledge systems become more prevalent, these constraints may diminish.

Codifying human knowledge for machine reading

Knowledge systems are computer programs that do reasoning tasks by drawing on the encoded knowledge of human experts together with an "inference engine" to solve problems. Numerous knowledge systems containing richly varied information of both commercial and social value are intended to be a major part of the benefits of the fifth-generation computer project in Japan and also of the products of various advanced computing efforts in other nations. For such a growth of knowledge-system applications to occur, research and development programs for the next generation will have to build on the existing strengths of knowledge engineering and overcome many of its significant weaknesses.

Some parts of next-generation efforts are aimed toward improving knowledge engineering—toward advances in knowledge representation, knowledge acquisition, knowledge refinement, knowledge system architecture, and knowledge system performance. These efforts presuppose that it will be possible to reorganize the field from a craft to an industrial process. For example, knowledge representations for expert systems are currently structured on a case-by-case basis, with a different shape given to the knowledge base in each application to optimize it for domain-specific characteristics. In order to improve productivity, the Japanese fifth-generation project, among others, envisions standardized forms for knowledge representation, so that new structures do not have to be created for each application. Whether such standardization is possible without severe penalties in knowledge-system performance is unclear, although proposed

Frederick Hayes-Roth   Teknowledge Inc.

high-speed parallel architectures may make up for some performance penalties.

Building knowledge systems

Conception of a knowledge system solution to an existing problem is the first stage in system building [see figure above]. Many systems may be conceived, although fewer are carried through. Furthermore, only a relatively small number of engineers and managers are aware of knowledge systems, so the number of systems conceived and undertaken is far smaller than it might be. Feasibility demonstrations are generally the next step: building a small prototype system to demonstrate that a knowledge system would actually be useful in a given context. Currently, some prototyping can be done with existing knowledge engineering tools, such as Units, MRS, and other knowledge-representation languages, stemming from developments at Stanford University in Palo Alto, Calif., or with languages for expressing rules, such as Rosie and OPS, developed at the Rand Corp. in Santa Monica, Calif., and Carnegie–Mellon University in Pittsburgh, Pa., respectively. Most often, laboratory tools must be modified or new tools developed because novel applications are not amenable to existing knowledge-representation and problem-solving structures.

The lack of tools also hinders later stages of development. Most knowledge-engineering tools in the United States are written in a single dialect of LISP; system builders using machines that run other dialects of the language may have to build their own tools, and in any case, these tools do not generally meet commercial-quality standards for software. For this and other reasons, most knowledge-engineering tools are used mainly at the locations where they were developed, where support and advice will be available from the developers. Often, the diffusion of a tool occurs as people from one research institution or company go to another and take along their favorite tools and the expertise for using them effectively. Recently, an effort was completed to define a subset of the various LISP dialects known as Common LISP, so that more applications might be portable; it is not yet clear whether it will bear fruit.

The lack of portable, widely available tools becomes even more pressing when a knowledge system is finally integrated into its setting, where ordinary human beings will have to use it. Not only must system developers find a cost-effective computer system that runs the same dialect as their development system to run the knowledge-system software in the work place, but they must also consider new questions of user interfacing for each application. The lack of tools for interactive query systems or graphical displays to aid comprehension increases the overhead involved in producing a finished system. Though many knowledge-engineering applications have such large paybacks that the effort is easily justified, building user interfaces from scratch is not a good use of knowledge engineers' time, and it may delay the use of knowledge systems by organizations with less expansive resources.

User interface and integration considerations go beyond simply making knowledge systems easy to use and fitting them into existing corporate structures; as the systems become more widespread, they can alter perceptions of how business should function. A number of next-generation projects, among them those of Japan, Great Britain, and the European Economic Community, are based partly on the premise that the spread of knowledge systems fostered by improvements in computing hardware and software tools for knowledge engineering will lead to significant cultural, industrial, and economic changes.

Knowledge engineering: still in the research phase

Currently, building a knowledge system from conception through integration takes anywhere from seven months—for simple systems in a friendly environment with existing tools—to 15 years, for complex systems in demanding environments where fundamental R&D is required. The stages currently absorbing significant effort are demonstration, required so that projects will be funded, and integration, because knowledge systems and businesses are currently not good fits with each other. As knowledge engineering becomes more of an industry, development will become the major thrust.

As long as knowledge engineering is just emerging from the research stage, next-generation computing projects make little sense in relation to it. Only as it becomes more established and the number and scope of applications increase do the low cost and power of computing engines become important to its wide use. That optimistic view, however, presupposes that knowledge engineering will advance enough to be able to make good use of more powerful computing engines. Since plans for next-generation computing envision knowledge bases 1000 or perhaps 10 000 times the size of those existing now, computing hardware only 10 000 times as powerful as today's will be inadequate to deal with such large knowledge bases unless progress is made in knowledge representation so that problems do not grow exponentially. Furthermore, knowledge encoding alone will require an unacceptable amount of time unless the rate of knowledge encoding ("chunks" per hour) increase by a factor of 10 and the number of knowledge engineers increases by a factor of 1000.

Steps toward large-scale knowledge systems

Several promising approaches to building large-scale knowledge systems will be pursued in the next-generation projects. These include: (1) automated translation of documents into knowledge bases; (2) cooperative problem-solving architectures; (3) generic problem-solving shells; and (4) multilevel reasoning systems.

Automated translation of documents into knowledge bases can help alleviate the shortage of knowledge engineers for technical disciplines that have excellent texts or documentation. For example, several projects now under way aim to convert structural diagrams of electrical or mechanical systems into knowledge bases suitable for diagnosing malfunctions. To do this the structural design documents must be interpreted by computer programs, and the underlying mechanisms and causal relationships must be extracted and analyzed for future use.

Cooperative problem-solving architectures (blackboard architectures) incorporate many different "knowledge sources" that analyze data at different levels of interpretation and exchange results by means of a stratified global data base called the blackboard. This architecture enables system developers to work independently developing tens of individual knowledge sources that later can operate collectively in problem-solving tasks. The multilevel stratification of the blackboard serves to constrain and channel communication between functionally related knowledge sources so that communication costs remain low.

Generic problem-solving shells are "empty" knowledge systems, such as Stanford University's Emycin. These shells address a specific type of problem, such as diagnosis or computer configuration, but possess no particular knowledge about any specific disease or computer. Knowledge engineers only need to add the specifics of a particular problem to produce a consulting system. As these frameworks multiply to cover more application types, large-scale knowledge-system problems will become more tractable. For example, general schemes for symbolic modeling, data monitoring, projection, and repair will emerge to meet the needs for many specific applications of these sorts. This, in turn, will permit people to take on complex process-control tasks that must incorporate all of those generic shells as components.

Expert system goals

Area	State of the art	Intermediate goals	Next-generation goals
Knowledge bases	10^4 to 10^5 chunks* manually coded, for specific applications	Modify knowledge base to be shareable among applications	10^8 to 10^9 chunks, universally applicable
Knowledge acquisition	1 chunk per hour, without standard tools for knowledge representation	5 chunks per hour, with widespread tools for knowledge representation	10 or more chunks per hour, machine learning
Knowledge-engineering methodologies	*Ad hoc* knowledge for representations for each problem	Standard knowledge representations, standard models of physical systems and causality	Fundamental breakthroughs in knowledge encoding
User–system interfaces	Stylized language, limited graphics	Off-the-shelf, limited speech-recognition and language-processing modules	Full natural language, speech-recognition, and computer vision

*Smallest piece of knowledge—for example, in production rule system, a single IF-THEN rule

Multilevel reasoning systems may provide a basis for coping with the combinatorial explosions that plague today's attempts at building broad, knowledge-intensive systems. Generally combinatorics arise from a lack of metalevel reasoning, or meta-knowledge—higher-level knowledge required to dictate which kinds of knowledge to apply during problem solving. Without such higher-level reasoning, today's knowledge systems flounder amidst a plethora of potentially relevant but generally unproductive lines of reasoning.

A major problem in the transformation of knowledge engineering from a craft to an industry is that, for the most part, building knowledge systems involves encoding unstructured, often even unarticulated, knowledge into machine-readable forms. Because many of the formalisms allowing machines to manipulate knowledge are fairly recent, there is little generality in them, and transferring lessons learned in one application to another is difficult.

Because there are few specific generally accepted standards for representing knowledge and performing inference, knowledge engineers must work partly by trial and error. Sometimes predicate definitions must be revised, changing the precise way that a piece of knowledge is encoded so that certain kinds of inference procedures will be able to make better use of it. One example is the partitioning of rules into rule sets, so that only a few rules must be examined in a given context; another is changing the order of conditions in a rule, so that they may be checked in the most efficient order. Sometimes the constraints in a system must be stated more effectively so that the system will not wander down futile paths; perhaps the inference method itself may require tuning for a particular situation.

In some cases, the wrong problem-solving paradigm may have been chosen for a knowledge system, and it may be necessary to restructure the entire knowledge base—regrouping rules and their contexts or reorganizing the frames in which world knowledge is held. Other major reconstructions involve choosing an entirely different form for knowledge representation, such as rules instead of frames, or going back and choosing a different inference strategy: changing from backward chaining to forward chaining or even a blackboard model. The effort involved in such major restructuring is comparable to the effort required to build the knowledge base in the first place; there are no software tools available for doing such conversion.

Thus, next-generation hardware projects are no panacea for knowledge systems. Knowledge engineers will continue to convert knowledge into machine-usable forms, largely by hand, for the foreseeable future. Advances in both general-purpose and specialized machines will affect the developing industry only in an incremental and evolutionary fashion. ◆

Helping computers understand natural languages

Perhaps the most important economic factor of the current age is that, as a society, we are moving away from an economy based on the manufacture and dissemination of goods to one based on the generation and dissemination of information and knowledge. Much of this information and knowledge is expressible in English and much of the task of gathering, manipulating, acting on, and

David L. Waltz University of Illinois

disseminating it can be greatly aided by computers.

Because natural-language (NL) understanding can enable computers to interact with users in ordinary language, it can make computer power available to segments of the population that are unable or unwilling to learn a formal computer language. NL can increase knowledge productivity by providing a mechanical means for manipulating knowledge that is now expressed in natural language—for example, encyclopedias, manuals, reports, and so on.

In addition to specific applications, a substantial fraction of natural-language-understanding research has as its goal cognitive science: the identification of the principles of learning, reasoning, judgment, inference, and the architecture of the human mind. Continuing research seems likely to lead both to progressively more practical, cost-effective application systems and to a deeper understanding of the natural phenomena of NL communication.

State of the art in natural-language processing

Currently, we understand how to do a reasonably good job of literal interpretation of English sentences in static contexts and in limited, well-structured domains of application. All of the following applications are either commercial products now or could be brought to market in the next two to four years:

• *NL data-base front ends*—commercial products are available.
• *NL interfaces for operating systems, system "help" facilities, library search systems, and other software packages*—reasonably good programs exist in several university laboratories.
• *Text filters and summarizers*—script-based systems long ago demonstrated their feasibility.
• *Machine-aided translation systems*—fluent translation remains an elusive goal, though systems that do rough translations have been speeding the task of translators for years.
• *Grammar checkers and critics*—programs could perform the task of an experienced editor, detecting errors in spelling and grammar and suggesting ways to rephrase passages of text to make them more understandable and to make them conform to the patterns of high-quality language usage.
• *Systems control*—by coupling a natural-language interface with different types of devices, a range of useful applications may be produced, including systems that (1) control such complex equipment as industrial robots, power generators, or missiles; (2) furnish expert advice about medical problems, mechanical repairs, mineral exploration, the design of genetic experiments, or investment analysis; (3) create graphic displays; and (4) teach courses in a broad range of subjects, interacting with students in English. Relatively little work has been done in these areas, but there appear to be no special technical obstacles to producing systems if a concentrated effort were undertaken.

In the past, a great deal of effort was devoted to making programs small enough to fit existing computers. If a system is to accept natural language—that is, unrestricted text or what people naturally think of saying in the manner they think of saying it—it must have a large vocabulary, a wide range of linguistic constructions, and a wide range of meaning representations. A small system simply cannot be very natural.

Opportunities over the next 10 years

Because it is now possible to produce special-purpose chips with relative ease, the identification of potential parallelism in NL processing has gained importance. We can realistically consider algorithms for highly parallel word-sense selection; truly concurrent syntactic, semantic, and pragmatic evaluation of sentences; speech format extraction; and so on—with the expectation that such work can lead to novel machine architectures more appropriate for NL processing.

Numerous applications may be possible within the next 10 years. Many of these arise in conjunction with information utilities—that is, information services available via phone or cable connections. Possible public services include automatic directories of names, addresses, yellow pages, and so forth; electronic mail; on-line catalogues and ordering facilities; banking and tax services; routing directions; and access to books and periodicals. All of these services could also have on-line NL manuals and help facilities. Such services are also needed by business and the military services.

Some important applications still seem quite far away:
• *Document understanding*—reading documents and assimilating their information into a larger framework of knowledge. Programs could produce abstracts, answer specific questions, or act as librarians, directing users to especially pertinent references. We are a long way from realizing this goal for any but the simplest domains—for instance, newspaper stories.

Natural-language processing can make computer power available to segments of the population that are unable or unwilling to learn a formal language

---

• *Document generation*—translating information stored in a formal language in a computer's memory into ordinary language. For example, information encoded in a formal language describing the troubleshooting and repair of an electromechanical device could be used to generate instruction manuals in a variety of natural languages and for different audiences, such as end users, repair personnel, and engineers. Not much work has been devoted to document generation; the most serious obstacles are probably in the area of knowledge representation, rather than language processing.

Early setbacks

The first natural-language processing effort was machine translation, proposed in 1946. A great deal of work went into it during the 1950s. Researchers attempted translation by purely syntactic means: dictionary lookup of words, substitution, and reordering of sentence syntax. The effort was widely viewed as a failure: "The spirit is willing but the flesh is weak" is said to have come out as "The vodka is strong but the meat is rotten" when translated into Russian and back.

In the early 1960s, artificial-intelligence NL programs (for example, Joseph Weizenbaum's Eliza, written at the Massachusetts Institute of Technology in Cambridge) "understood" sentences by matching them directly with libraries of "meaning patterns." Thus, in Eliza, both "I am afraid of flying in planes" and "My father was afraid of heights" might match the pattern "V1 [BE] afraid of V2." Each meaning pattern was associated with appropriate replies or actions. The variables could also be used by a reply generator to produce the output strings "How long have you been afraid of flying in planes?" or "How long was your father afraid of heights?" Though programs of this sort hardly seem to understand at all, they and their descendants (including some NL data-base front ends) performed impressively.

New paradigms

Around 1970, several new paradigms emerged for NL understanding. For example, Terry Winograd's SHRDLU pro-

gram, written at MIT, used rules based on analogies between words and program fragments, sentence syntax and program-fragment ordering, and sentence and complete programs. In this paradigm, understanding a sentence was equivalent to building and running a complete, working program.

For example, from the sentence "Pick up a big block that supports a pyramid" SHRDLU constructed the following program: (1) find a block; (2) verify that it is big; (3) find a pyramid; (4) verify that the pyramid is supported by the block; and (5) pick up the block. If any step in the process failed, SHRDLU would backtrack and try again, until it either succeeded or ran out of possibilities to try. SHRDLU was able to understand—that is, construct working programs from—sentences exhibiting great linguistic variety, at the expense of only working in a narrow, specialized domain.

At about the same time, a team headed by William Woods of Bolt Beranek & Newman Inc., was completing Lunar, a question-answering system for use in conjunction with a data base of moon-rock chemical analyses. Lunar included a quite general syntactic parser that built a parse tree—a sentence diagram—which was used to construct formal queries for a standard data-base system. The data base used by Lunar was simple enough that sentences were rarely ambiguous; if in doubt, the system would query the user.

A number of data-base systems in the mid-1970s used what is called a semantic grammar—based on Eliza-like patterns—instead of a syntactic parser. For example, the Ladder system, written by Gary Hendrix of SRI International, Palo Alto, Calif., contained patterns such as "What [BE] the [SHIP-ATTRIBUTES] of [SHIP-DESCRIPTION]" that could formulate queries from sentences such as "What are the lengths and drafts of U.S. carriers?" The semantic-grammar–based Planes system, written under my direction at the University of Illinois, Urbana, filled in missing words from context by storing a history of all the items referred to in a session. It could thus handle sequences such as "Which planes had more than 30 flight hours in February 1980? . . . In March?"

The first commercial natural-language system was Robot, written by Larry Harris of the AI Corp., Cambridge, Mass., and marketed since about 1978. Robot was organized around a syntactic parser and used novel solutions to the problems of specialized vocabularies and ambiguity. Robot used all the words in a data base to form its lexicon, performed a separate search for each possible reading of a request, and then compared the number of matches for each query to guess the intended meaning. For example, faced with "Give me the salaries for New York employees" Robot would generate queries for both city and state. If there were 2000 entries in the state and 40 in the city, it would assume the city was intended; if there were none in the city and a few in the state, it would assume the intention was "New York State."

Early models of cognition

Around 1970, Roger Schank (first at Stanford University in Palo Alto, Calif., and later at Yale University in New Haven, Conn.) introduced programs for dealing with language about human actions, based on a different kind of principle: sentences were transformed into data structures, organized around a fixed number of "primitives of conceptual dependency" (or CD primitives)—abstractions of a class of related verbs. For example, the CD primitive Atrans was used to represent all verbs that involved transfer of possession, including buy, sell, give, take, or trade. A primary purpose of the primitives was to represent paraphrases similarly. Thus, "Mary gave John a bicycle" and

"John got a bicycle from Mary" were represented internally by similar Atrans structures, while "Mary gave John a shove" would be represented by a radically different structure based on the CD primitive, Propel.

Another purpose of the primitives was to organize expectations and inferences about sentences. For example, if a program had seen "John gave . . . " it would expect to encounter some object that was given as well as a recipient of the object and could use that expectation to process the rest of the sentence. Inferences were also associated with CD primitives. For example, after any Atrans (transfer of possession), the program could infer that the "recipient" controlled the "object."

Often a single sentence corresponds not only to a single action, but also to a sequence of actions. For example, consider the following story: "John took the bus from New Haven to New York. On the way, his pocket was picked. He went to Mama Leone's and ordered spaghetti. John couldn't pay the bill, so he washed dishes."

Notice that although eating is not mentioned explicitly, we readily make the inference that John ate spaghetti in the absence of any information to the contrary. Such passages were handled using "scripts" by the SAM program, written by Richard Cullingford of Yale. SAM examined the text to select scripts and then used the scripts to fill in unmentioned stereotypical actions. The restaurant script, for example, includes steps for getting seated, ordering, eating, paying the bill and tip, and so on that are assumed to occur unless the text explicitly states otherwise.

New ways of thinking about language

All this work was part of a long-term trend in natural-language research away from the view that language meaning can be constructed out of word definitions and toward the view that language understanding is a top-down process, in which words serve as cues for retrieving expectations from memory and as evidence for or against earlier expectations.

Starting in the late 1970s, the focus of NL research has shifted somewhat away from top-down processing. In part, this was because of difficulties in constructing knowledge bases. Furthermore, top-down systems had in retrospect been a way of exploiting expectation, regularity, and simplified domains to avoid the detailed analysis of language and of making it possible to construct programs that could process some body of language from beginning to end on the equipment that was available. Advances in computer hardware and software and a new view of the complexity of grammars have allowed NL researchers to realistically consider writing systems with complete coverage of English vocabulary and grammars and with facilities for handling meaning.

At the same time, our understanding of the nature of language has undergone a revolutionary change. From time immemorial, philosophers had viewed language meaning as a relationship—true or false—between sentences, on the one hand, and things and events in the world, on the other. The pioneering "speech act" work of modern philosophers, especially John Searle at the University of California at Berkeley, has dramatically enlarged our view. Linguistic utterances are now seen as one special case of goal-oriented action, in a common framework with nonlinguistic actions. An obvious example—"Can you pass the salt?"—is a speech act intended to elicit an action rather than a yes or a no response.

Parallel NL processing

The desire to find and exploit potential parallelism has triggered a recent rise in popularity of parallel language-processing

Natural-language processing milestones

Milestone	Past	1983	Future
Commercial systems for limited natural-language queries of data bases	x		
Laboratory systems that parse most grammatical sentences		x	
Programs that translate about 90 percent of text from one language to another		x	
Commercial systems that critique grammar and style			x
Commercial systems that abstract and index information from documents			x
Commercial robots that understand natural-language instructions			x

models. Observations of human actions have also helped spark interest—AI has only recently begun to take seriously the idea that some processes are best modeled as the interaction of independent agents. In similar work at the University of Rochester, N.Y., and the University of Illinois, researchers have built NL programs in which word senses compete with each other, forming coalitions with other word senses and with the discourse context to arrive at an appropriate meaning representation. For example, in Jordan Pollack's work at the University of Illinois, a system given the sentence "John shot two bucks" will select the meanings "fired a rifle at" for "shot" and "deer" for "bucks" if the system is "primed" with the concept "hunting"; but if primed with "gambling," the system will select the meanings "waste" and "dollars."

Scaling up and learning

To be useful, NL systems must be able to handle a large vocabulary and large knowledge bases. Not only must it operate efficiently when it is in possession of relatively large amounts of knowledge, but ways must also be found for building up large knowledge bases appropriate for NL understanding and for progressively expanding an NL system. Recent work by Robert Wilensky, first at Yale and later at the University of California at Berkeley, has exploited a "planner" to fill in unmentioned steps that are not necessarily stereotypical. Take the statements— "Mary wanted a radio. She went to the bank." Dr. Wilensky's system could reason that Mary probably went to the bank to get money to buy a new radio. Gerald DeJong, now at the University of Illinois, has devised related methods that allow a program to generalize such an analysis to create new scripts, thus streamlining future processing.

Learning is incremental; new concepts can be used both to process language and to participate in the learning of further concepts. This type of learning requires a system to already know a lot in order to learn anything.

Other recent NL work has been concerned with many issues such as modeling the understanding of metaphor, dealing with inconsistent input information, and judging the plausibility of sentence meanings. Plausibility judgment is necessary if a program is to understand metaphors, humor, lies, or exaggeration. It is a kind of common sense and is possible only for a program with an immense world-knowledge base. Another area of research deals with modeling characters' emotions and understanding long texts in terms of episodes and narrative units. Also important is work on context-free grammars, which use rules simpler than those of current techniques to parse sentences into a knowledge representation. Such grammars unfortunately require many thousands of rules, and so researchers are working on metarules and other procedures which would allow a program to generate the rules required to transform a particular sentence into a knowledge representation as they are needed.

Achieving next-generation goals

The Japanese fifth-generation project, for example, envisions several roles for NL processing by 1992: interactive access to knowledge bases; automatic internal indexing and reasoning; and expressing knowledge, notably knowledge input through pictures and diagrams, as well as through more traditional means. To assess what is needed to achieve the fifth-generation goals, it is critical to not merely list the desired capabilities of a system, but also to state specific performance criteria. For example: What level of misinterpretation can be tolerated? How much training (if any) would users be expected to have? How much interactive verification of understanding can be allowed? And most importantly, how general a domain must be covered?

Given moderate goals (some training, some errors, some verifying dialogues), systems can certainly be built for specific domains. Most working AI systems, though, are of limited scope. Therefore, it is no more than an act of faith to assume that current techniques will be effective with vastly larger systems.

There is a further problem in scaling up: Where is the knowledge to come from? Some of our knowledge—common sense—is "innate," while other knowledge is learned explicitly. The innate knowledge will probably have to be preprogrammed —an especially difficult problem because it is virtually never expressed in everyday life. Some learned knowledge can be acquired quickly from machine-readable encyclopedias and other texts, but much will need to be preprogrammed or learned from experience. AI learning research, while making rapid strides, is unlikely to offer adequate mechanisms for learning from experience by 1992 (remembering that we also need time for a system to *have* experiences).

Preprogramming presents staggering problems, analogous to but almost surely orders of magnitude worse than Frederick Brooks' well-documented problems developing OS 360 while at IBM Corp. It is unlikely that we could adequately specify a proper set of standard representation forms, effectively enumerate all needed knowledge, make no serious errors that would require starting over, and get an entire system working coherently—all by 1992.

Consistency is another major problem. How can a system deal with the inevitable inconsistencies it will encounter? What should it do when it finds it has added to its knowledge base a variety of inferences based on false premises? Current approaches to these problems have used brute-force techniques—for example, storing of all data dependencies so that the effects of erroneous assumptions can be tracked down and corrected.

Most critically, the number of researchers working on NL research is really rather small in the United States, Japan, and elsewhere. A recent count found only about 15 faculty NL researchers at the top 10 U.S. universities in AI, and the number of researchers at industrial labs is also small. The small number of faculty is particularly significant because it constrains the rate at which new researchers can be added to the field.

Thus, taken overall, the fifth-generation goals are almost certainly wildly overoptimistic for 1992, even allowing for breakthroughs. I do believe, however, that the fifth-generation goals will eventually be met, probably by the year 2000, and that, even before then, the technological fallout of this research will fundamentally change the ways in which we live and work. ◆

Recognizing continuous speech remains an elusive goal

To understand speech, a human considers not only the specific information conveyed to the ear, but also the context in which the information is being discussed. For this reason, people can understand spoken language even when the speech signal is corrupted by noise. However, understanding the context of speech is, in turn, based on a broad knowledge of the world. And here speech recognition by computer fails.

It is difficult to develop computer programs that are sufficiently sophisticated to understand continuous speech by a random speaker. Only when programmers simplify the problem—by isolating words, limiting the vocabulary or number of speakers, or constraining the way in which sentences may be formed—is speech recognition by computer possible.

One can already buy toys and video games for less than $100 that respond to voice commands. A number of commercial systems cost from $500 to $50 000. All have simplifying features: they restrict the vocabulary to 10 to 200 words; require training for each new speaker; demand that the words be spoken clearly, with a short pause between words; or require the use of high-performance array processors for real-time operation. Such restrictions have often led to techniques that cannot be adapted to handling continuous speech by random speakers.

Research on continuous-speech recognition (CSR) in the United States flourished in the mid-1970s because of a large effort sponsored by the U.S. Department of Defense Advanced Research Projects Agency. Since then CSR research has been relatively dormant, with exceptions—like IBM Corp.'s strong, continuous effort to develop a speech-activated typewriter.

The decoding problems of speech

Speech is based on a sequence of discrete sound segments that are linked in time. These segments, called phonemes, are assumed to have unique articulatory and acoustic characteristics. While an almost infinite number of articulatory gestures can be produced by the human vocal apparatus, the number of phonemes is limited. English as spoken in the United States, for example, contains 16 vowel and 24 consonant sounds. Each phoneme has distinguishable acoustic characteristics and, in combination with other phonemes, forms larger units such as syllables and words. Knowledge about the acoustic differences among these sound units is essential to distinguish one word from another, say "bit" from "pit."

When speech sounds are connected to form larger linguistic units, the acoustic characteristics of a given phoneme will change as a function of its immediate phonetic environment because of the interaction among various anatomical structures (such as the tongue, lips, and vocal chords) and their different degrees of sluggishness. The result is an overlap of phonemic information in the acoustic signal from one segment to the other. For example, the same underlying phoneme "t" can have drastically different acoustic characteristics in different words, say, in "tea," "tree," "city," "beaten," and "steep." This effect, known as coarticulation, can occur within a given word or across a word boundary. Thus, the word "this" will have very different acoustic properties in phrases such as "this car" and "this ship" [Fig. 1].

Raj Reddy   Carnegie–Mellon University
Victor Zue   Massachusetts Institute of Technology

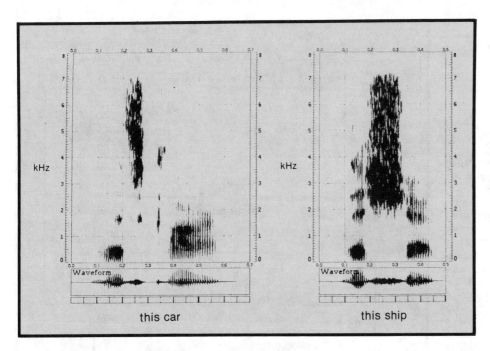

this car   *this ship*

[1] The central problem in computer recognition of continuous speech is that the way words are pronounced is modified by their context—a strictly word-by-word analysis is impossible. In addition, there are no clear breaks between continuously spoken words. In these voicegrams, which plot frequency against time (with amplitude at a given frequency being indicated by the darkness of the lines), the words "this car" are compared with the words "this ship" spoken by the same person. Note how the higher frequencies near the end of "this" are strengthened in the second example.

Over the last several decades significant advances in articulatory phonetics and acoustic phonetics have been made. Knowledge of the acoustic properties of speech sounds has increased from isolated consonant and vowel syllables to include words and sentences.

Successes in isolated word recognition

Algorithms for developing limited-vocabulary, speaker-dependent systems, called isolated-word–recognition (IWR) systems, are well understood.

Today's IWR systems share several features. They usually have an acoustically distinct vocabulary of 10 to 200 items, generally require clear pauses between words, and usually operate in a speaker-dependent mode—that is, the systems must be "trained" for a particular speaker's voice.

When each word is treated as a unit, recognition calls for matching the parameters of the input signal to the stored templates for the vocabulary items. The word with a stored template that best matches the input is selected as the intended word. The scoring algorithm uses time-alignment procedures (the most successful being dynamic programming, first introduced in Japan in 1971) designed to account for the inherent variability of the speech signal.

Within these limits, commercial IWR devices span a wide range of performance characteristics and costs. The performance of low-cost systems often varies from task to task and from speaker to speaker because of the relatively primitive methods of signal representation and recognition. For a straightforward task like digit recognition, error rates of less than 5 percent are possible. However, when the vocabulary items are acoustically similar, the error rate for even sophisticated systems increases significantly, even for small vocabularies.

Current IWR technology has severe drawbacks. Most systems require that new users receive training, and the performance varies greatly in a large body of users. Bell Laboratories and others have investigated clustering techniques to reduce the

Speech-recognition system milestones

Recognition capability	Isolated words, speaker-dependent	Continuous speech, speaker-independent	Isolated words, speaker-dependent	Isolated words, speaker-independent	Continuous speech, speaker-independent
Syntax	Limited	Limited	Unlimited	Unlimited	Unlimited
Vocabulary, words	200	1000	5000	20 000	20 000
Processing speed required, megainstructions per second	1 to 10	100	300	1000	100 000
Technology required	Acoustic pattern matching used to identify individual phonemes Dynamic programming to solve problem of variations in duration of words (Both achieved by Nippon Electric Co. commercial machines)	Beam-search strategy to narrow selection of words Better algorithms to determine word boundaries (Both achieved by Harpy)	Probabilistic approach to determine words on basis of preceding words, for use in supplementing phonetics Faster searches using selectors keyed to individual sounds (Achieved by IBM experimental system, but not in real time)	Language constraints– such as the fact that "vn" never begins English words—to narrow choices Relating acoustic signals to phonemes in form of quantitative rules	Natural-language understanding Knowledge base to use context of speech to assist in recognition Learning from errors

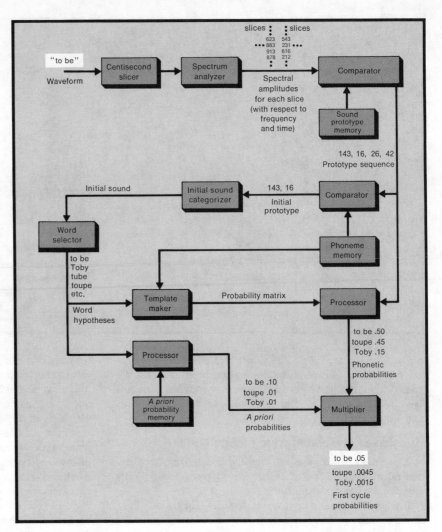

[2] One of the most advanced efforts at speech recognition is the system now under development at IBM Corp.'s Thomas J. Watson Laboratories, under the direction of Fred Jelinek and others, in Yorktown Heights, N.Y. Incoming digitized signals are broken into centisecond slices and spectrally analyzed by the system. Each slice is compared with a collection of sound prototypes and the prototype closest to each slice is entered into a sequence. The prototype sequence is then used to roughly categorize the initial sound of the word, which in turn is used to produce word hypotheses. Each word is then tested by creating a probability matrix that determines the probability that a given prototype sequence is actually that word. From this matrix and the actual prototype sequence input, a phonetic probability for each word is arrived at. Simultaneously, an a priori probability for the word existing in a given part of a sentence, following previously hypothesized words, is arrived at. The two probabilities are multiplied for each word hypothesis to give a ranking of overall probabilities. The cycle then repeats for the next word until an entire sentence is identified.

number of templates while accommodating multiple speakers, but these systems have been demonstrated only for relatively small vocabularies.

Moreover the need to train a system for each user limits the size of the vocabulary that it can accommodate. As the vocabulary increases to, say, 10 000 words, the training procedure becomes very time-consuming and renders such systems impractical. Thus, for a task like dictation, where the working vocabulary can be several thousand words, the system must be speaker-independent. Even at the isolated-word level, speaker-independent recognition from a large vocabulary is a problem of staggering complexity. The solution to this problem is unlikely to be found through extension of current IWR technology.

Feature-based recognition, an alternative to template matching, attempts to identify the acoustic features that are needed to define speaker-independent patterns for linguistic events. Speech researchers at Carnegie–Mellon University, Pittsburgh, Pa., headed by Ronald Cole, have developed a feature-based system that classifies letters of the English alphabet. The system extracts vowel features (such as formant frequencies and formant slopes) and consonant features (such as onset abruptness, voice onset time, and spectral tilt) and recognizes invariant relationships among them. At present the system has an error rate of less than 10 percent in a speaker-independent mode. The system recognizes letters in the easily confused "E set" (b, c, d, e, g, p, t, v, and z) at error rates of about 10 percent compared with error rates of 30 to 40 percent by template matching systems.

Most commercial isolated-word–recognition systems require that each word be delineated by pauses. This is necessary because in continuous speech the acoustic signal is often altered at word boundaries, making it difficult to determine where one word ends and another begins. For example, the ending and beginning s in phrases like "gas station" usually merge into a single sound. Speaking with pauses between words is unnatural and systems that require this are unlikely to find general user acceptance for many tasks. There have been attempts to generalize IWR algorithms to deal with connected words. The approach usually involves scanning across the entire utterance for all possible word matches, with a relaxation of the matching criteria at word boundaries.

A Nippon Electric Co. system, for example, achieves connected-word recognition by applying the recognition algorithm twice, once for single-word matches and once for groups of connected words. These commercial connected-word–recognition systems generally are speaker-dependent and are limited to small vocabularies and short, simple sentences.

Continuous-speech recognition: a bigger problem

Continuous-speech recognition (CSR) has long been recognized as a problem of significantly greater complexity than that of IWR. First, the acoustic properties of a given word can change significantly, depending on its position in a sentence, and such changes are particularly severe for function words (pronouns and prepositions). Second, the acoustic properties of a word can also be modified by adjacent words. Finally, syntax, semantics, and knowledge of the matter spoken of can also directly modify the speech signal.

Research in CSR was limited until the early 1970s, when the Defense Advanced Research Projects Agency (Darpa) initiated an ambitious five-year, $15 million, multisite effort to develop speech-understanding systems. The goals were to develop systems that would accept continuous speech from many speakers, with minimal speaker adaptation, and operate on a 1000-word vocabulary, artificial syntax, and a constrained task domain. The systems were to have less than a 10-percent semantic error rate and run in several times real time on a computer capable of 100 million instructions per second (MIPS). The project ended in 1976 with several system demonstrations. Two of the systems, Harpy and Hearsay-II, both developed at Carnegie–Mellon University, achieved the original goals and in some instances surpassed them.

Harpy could understand a limited-vocabulary artificial language made up of a finite number of possible sentences. With this restriction, the system could represent all possible sentences in terms of acoustical segments and a set of rules describing how the segments would change across word boundaries. To recognize a sentence, Harpy searched through the network of possible sentences, using a beam search strategy that considered only a small set of near misses around the best-match path.

Since the termination of the Darpa project in 1976, CSR research in the United States has been quite limited. The only exception is the present effort at IBM's Thomas J. Watson Laboratories in Yorktown Heights, N.Y.

The current effort at IBM adopts an information–theoretic approach to speech recognition. The speaker and the acoustic analyzer are modeled as a noisy communication channel and recognition is done by maximizing the likelihood that a sentence is the correct interpretation of an input signal [Fig. 2].

The recognition rate for IBM's 5000-word office task, in which sentences are read with pauses between words, is reported to be almost 95 percent for six speakers. While this is not a continuous-speech task, it is important because the office memos that the machine interprets are in standard English, without any restrictions on the types of sentences used.

Fred Jelinek, who directs the IBM program, is working to achieve the same performance from the system in real time, using general-purpose minicomputers. However, the IBM system, as it stands, has a number of potential drawbacks. First, it is speaker-dependent and thus requires a great deal of training data for each speaker. Second, it is quite slow, although as computing cost continues to decrease and speed continues to improve, this may become insignificant. Speaker-independence, on the other hand, is essential for large-vocabulary tasks. Researchers at IBM are working to reduce the training data, which they hope will decrease speaker dependence.

High goals with major obstacles

One of the stated objectives of the Japanese fifth-generation computer effort is to build a speech-activated typewriter with a vocabulary of 10 000 words and the capacity to handle the voice patterns of hundreds of speakers. There are difficult problems to be solved before such a system capable of taking dictation is possible. They include:

• *Large vocabularies.* As researchers go from systems that recognize a few hundred words to those that can recognize 10 000 words or more, template-based pattern-matching techniques become unsatisfactory. Acquiring the necessary learning data to create the templates becomes tedious and time-consuming and pattern-matching techniques based on dynamic programming become too slow. As more easily confused words are included, recognition errors will increase. Feature-based systems that make effective use of prosodic and phonemic features are expected to be more successful.

• *Speaker independence.* Systems that require training for each new speaker are likely to be unsatisfactory for dictation. The discovery of features that do not vary from speaker to speaker and dynamic nonintrusive adaptation for new speakers will be essential.

• *Graceful error recovery.* Perceptual confusion is not uncommon in human-speech communication. But when it does occur, people follow several accepted protocols to identify and resolve the confusion. Speech-recognition systems must follow similar protocols.

• *Cost and speed.* To be used routinely for dictation, the system must cost no more than a few thousand dollars and be able to operate at normal dictation speeds with immediate feedback. This is expected to require over 100 MIPS of computational power, which could be reduced substantially through the use of special-purpose VLSI chips.

Solutions to these problems are not likely to be found in current speech-recognition technology. But there are reasons for optimism. On the one hand, the back end of speech-recognition systems, attempting to use the context or knowledge of the subject discussed to interpret what is actually being said, can in the future borrow from a large body of artificial-intelligence techniques developed for expert systems.

On the other hand, the front end of systems, dealing with the phonetic recognition of what words have been spoken, is also improving as knowledge of human speech recognition expands. One particular achievement was demonstrated in a series of experiments carried on at the Massachusetts Institute of Technology in Cambridge and at Carnegie–Mellon in recent years, in which people were trained to identify spoken words by the examination of the spectrograms of the speech signal. The information content of the spectrograms is identical to that of the acoustic signal. While people learn to understand spoken language as infants but cannot convey to others this skill by a set of explicit rules, spectrogram reading can be taught through a set of quantitative rules. Once such rules are formulated, they can be programmed into a speech-recognition system. Given that people using a set of these rules can identify 90 percent of the phonemes from their spectrograms (independent of the speaker), there is hope that similar achievements are possible for computers.

In addition, our understanding of the constraints imposed on the sound patterns of a language has improved. An example of such a constraint in English is that the combination *rn* cannot start a word. By using this type of constraint, computer experiments at MIT have shown that the coarse classifications of sounds into only broad categories enable a machine to identify uniquely about one third of a 20 000-word vocabulary. The remaining two thirds can be narrowed down to a choice of two possible words that can be differentiated by more detailed phonetic analysis.

These developments indicate that machines that can recognize isolated words from large vocabularies—independent of speaker—may be commercially available in the next decade. Although continuous-speech recognition—independent of speaker—is much more difficult, systems capable of taking limited dictation may well be possible in the 1990s. However, given the history of speech research and the magnitude of the problems remaining to be solved, substantial resources will be necessary before we have a dictation machine. ◆

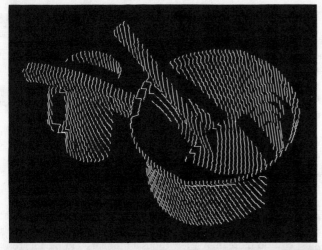

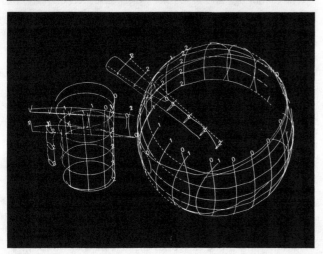

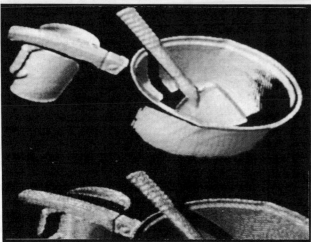

[1] One approach to determining the three-dimensional shape of an object is the use of light stripes. In this approach, applicable especially in industrial robotics, the pattern of stripes of light (top) is interpreted by the computer to determine the orientation of the surface. Here the orientations determined are color-coded (middle). Once the surface orientations are known, the computer—in the example illustrated here from work by David Smith and Takeo Kanade at Carnegie–Mellon University in Pittsburgh, Pa.—isolates each object by edges and selects certain simple geometric shapes, such as cylinders and cones, to fit to the surfaces observed (bottom). When such surfaces are correctly fitted, the computer can "recognize" the object as a cup, pan, and so on, by their descriptions in memory as combinations of simple shapes.

Computer vision: the challenge of imperfect inputs

Humans can see and understand extremely complex scenes at a glance. By contrast, the best computer vision systems now available commercially have very primitive capabilities. They can rapidly recognize and locate objects on a conveyor belt, but only under strictly constrained conditions and lighting—in essence, circumstances that reduce the objects to be identified to isolated, two-dimensional black and white silhouettes. The development of a general-purpose computer vision system that can approach the abilities of the human eye and brain is remote at present, despite recent progress in understanding the nature of vision.

Vision is difficult for a computer for a number of reasons. For one thing, the images received by a sensing device—for example, a vidicon tube—do not contain sufficient information to construct an unambiguous description of the scene observed. Most importantly, depth information is lost, and there are many parts of an image where objects overlap.

Also, many different factors are confounded in the image—a surface may appear dark, for example, because of its low reflectance, shallow angle of illumination, insufficient illumination, or unfavorable viewing angle. The interpretation of what is seen requires a large body of knowledge, not only about what various objects look like—such as cars, houses, roads, and trees—but also about how these objects can be expected to fit together.

Finally, vision involves a large amount of memory and many computations. For an image of 1000 by 1000 pixels (image elements), some of the simplest procedures require 10^8 operations. The human retina, with 10^8 cells operating at roughly 100 hertz, performs at least 10 billion operations a second, and the visual cortex of the brain has undoubtedly higher capacities.

Three steps to vision

Most computer vision systems are based on a three-step process that works upward from the raw image to some sort of scene description. Low-level processing extracts features from the image, detecting edges and then connecting edges into lines or curves or segmenting the image into regions that have more or less uniform properties [see chart on p. 62].

Intermediate-level processing derives from the image of the features of the scene—that is, the real objects that produced the image. At this point three-dimensional information, such as surface orientation and distance from the viewer, are derived from the two-dimensional image.

The highest level of processing produces a description of the scene—what is actually seen. Here the computer attempts to match models of known objects, such as cars, buildings, or trees, to the scene description and thus determine what is there.

Although this three-level process applies to many vision systems, there are some types that attempt to go from raw image to at least partial scene description in one step. In addition, most commercial vision systems omit one or more steps because they operate in a simple environment that does not require such elaborate processing.

In typical commercial systems, a gray-level image is converted into a binary black and white representation and the outlines of the objects are obtained. These outlines are then measured and

Takeo Kanade and **Raj Reddy**
Carnegie–Mellon University

compared with models stored in memory. When the observed outline and the model outline match, the object—say, a part on a conveyor belt—can be identified and its position and orientation deduced. In this instance, no 3-D interpretation is needed.

The General Motors Corp.'s Consight system, used in connection with assembly robots, is an example of a computer-vision machine. Similar vision systems are now performing such tasks as inspection, parts sorting, and the guidance function in arc welding and are assisting robots in a variety of industries.

More sophisticated systems are required to go beyond the limited factory applications to complex tasks—for example, photointerpretation or automatic navigation—where the vision system would operate in an unconstrained environment in which lighting and other variables are not tightly controlled. These systems are now only in the early stages of development. Effort has been divided mainly between the intermediate-level task of obtaining 3-D information and the higher-level task of description.

Determining 3-D shapes from images

The basic approach to determining 3-D shapes from images is to use shading, textures, shadow edges, and other image features as constraints on the shapes that may be present. Even though each constraint may allow many different shapes, a unique shape can be obtained by combining a number of constraints. Until relatively recently, most vision programs used such constraints in specialized ways. But in the past few years a powerful new approach has been formulated, and it has allowed a set of computational modules to be developed.

The new approach involves three steps. First, an image quantity, or primitive, is paired with a scene feature that it constrains. For example, the intensity or shading of an image may be matched with the surface orientation of an object in the scene. The physical and geometrical rules that govern the process of generating the image primitive from the scene primitive is then represented mathematically. For instance, the laws relating surface orientation, angle of illumination, and surface reflectance

will determine the intensity at a point on the image. By using these laws, the set of constraints on the scene primitive (in this example, surface orientation) can be derived from a set of measurements of the image (in this case, intensity).

Modules have been developed that use shading, texture, contours, shadows, stereooptical disparity, and other image qualities to produce constraints on the scene features. Though successful programs for determining 3-D shapes from arbitrary images have not yet been developed, sufficient progress has been made so that systems now can analyze images made from restricted types of scenes. For example, the shape-from-shading method developed by Berthold K.P. Horn of the Massachusetts Institute .of Technology in Cambridge, interprets images of objects that are smooth and illuminated by diffuse lighting.

One obstacle to general systems of this sort is the number of computations required to determine the constraints, especially when more than one is applied. Highly parallel, special-purpose computers are required to perform such computations in real time. Once processors are developed with capabilities of 10^{10} to 10^{13} instructions per second—comparable to those estimated for the human retina—it seems reasonable to believe that extensions of current techniques will make it possible to deduce 3-D features from arbitrary scenes in real time.

Such capabilities are already being approached in indoor applications where active lighting techniques can be used. In active lighting, the source of illumination is so structured as to give immediate clues to the 3-D shape of the objects imaged. One of the most common types of active lighting is stripe lighting, in which the source projects parallel stripes of light across the scene. The bumps and jogs in the light stripe accurately reflect the shapes of the objects independent of their other qualities, such as reflectance [Fig. 1]. This technique is already being applied in a number of products.

Thus the first problem of computer vision—perceiving the shape of a three-dimensional world from two-dimensional images—is on its way to systematic solution. More difficult is the higher-level problem of recognizing the shapes deduced as ob-

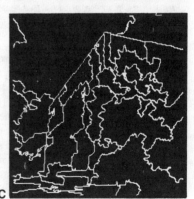

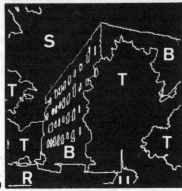

[2] Another approach to recognizing objects in a scene is to represent the world as a limited set of objects defined by certain rules, such as "buildings have straight edges." A system developed in 1980 at Kyoto University in Japan, by Yuichi Ohta and others, uses this approach. An image is first digitized (A) and then divided into small areas that have consistent coloring and shading (B). Similar adjacent patches are then grouped together into large regions (C), which are then identified using the rules (D). Here S stands for sky, B for building, R for road, and so on.

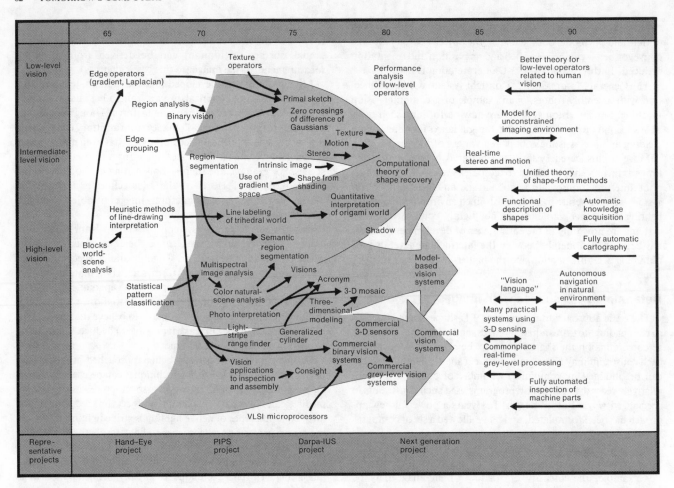

	65	70	75	80	85	90

Low-level vision

Intermediate-level vision

High-level vision

Representative projects

Hand–Eye project · PIPS project · Darpa-IUS project · Next generation project

Computer vision efforts have advanced over the past 20 years along three fronts: low-level vision, the extraction of basic features, such as edges from an image; intermediate-level vision, the deduction of the three-dimensional shape of objects from the images; and high-level vision, the recognition of objects and their relationships. Some representative research projects include the Hand–Eye robotic vision project initiated at the Massachusetts Institute of Technology in Cambridge and at Stanford University in Palo Alto, Calif.; the pattern-information processing system (PIPS) project in Japan, one of the earliest focused research programs sponsored by the Ministry of International Trade and Industry; the U.S. Defense Advanced Research Projects Agency's image-understanding system (IUS) project; and the current Darpa next-generation project.

jects and identifying them. Here progress has been more limited.

The main approach to the problem of object recognition and scene description is called model-based vision. In this approach a simplified model of the world is prepared, depending on the task at hand. For example, an urban-scene analysis program would model the world as consisting of certain types of objects— buildings, cars, trees, roads, sky, and so on. The model objects would be described in memory as having certain characteristics, and the program would attempt to match these against various parts of the image.

This task is similar to that of speech recognition, in which the program tries to match models (words) against the incoming speech signals. The difficulty in scene analysis is that a given object looks different from various angles, so the program must be capable of manipulating the model in three dimensions to match with images in many different ways.

Several approaches have been taken to match models and images. One involves performing correlations between a stored image of an object and the image itself. At the point where the object appears on the image, a correlation peak is formed. Such correlations are frequently carried out by optical means, although they can also be performed digitally.

Though correlators have been developed that recognize such objects as tanks from a variety of different viewpoints in a com-

plex background, the flexibility of this approach appears to be limited. The objects searched for must be identical with the model rather than an example of a certain type of object.

Another approach exemplified by the system, Argos, developed by Steven Rubin at Carnegie-Mellon University, Pittsburgh, Pa., used entire images of a given scene as the basic models, leaving the program with the limited task of deciding which view of the scene—say, downtown Pittsburgh—it was looking at. The approach was in part inspired by speech-understanding techniques that limited the speech input to a finite number of sentences, in one case several thousand sentences, from which the program had to decide the one that was spoken.

Argos stored each view as a network of relationships—in a form like "large brown object to left of small brown object." By searching through the network and matching the relationships against the image presented to it, Argos could identify the correct viewpoint 80 percent of the time. However, such a system has severely limited applications—such as helping a robot navigate around a small room.

A more versatile approach is to represent the world as a limited set of objects defined by a set of rules that either describe properties of objects ("buildings have straight edges") or procedures that the program should carry out under given circumstances ("if an object has straight edges, look for repeating rows of windows to confirm it is a building"). An outdoor scene system using this approach was developed at Kyoto University in Japan in 1980 by Yuichi Ohta and others. The system first portions the image into many small patches having the same color and shading. It then groups the adjacent patches into large areas, which it identifies through the rules as trees, roads, cars, buildings, sky, or a half dozen other categories [Fig. 2].

These systems, although they could label some of the objects viewed, were two-dimensional and could not give a 3-D description of the relationships among the objects. Rodney Brooks and Thomas Binford of Stanford University, Palo Alto, Calif., developed the Acronym system in 1981, which models objects three-dimensionally as generalized cylinders. Images are analyzed and divided into combinations of ribbons (cylinders) and ellipses (ends of cylinders). Then the system matches objects made up of cylinders—such as aircraft—to the images by estimating the dimensions of the cylinders and their orientations. Acronym has been applied to airport scenes, and the Hughes Aircraft Co., in Los Angeles, Calif., is using this approach to develop a photo interpretation system for port monitoring.

Urban scenes can be used to produce 3-D descriptions in the Incremental 3-D Mosaic system, under development at Carnegie–Mellon University by Marty Merman and others. This system employs block models of buildings. Several images from different angles are used, and the system builds up its model of the scene as new portions come into view. The system has successfully constructed a three-dimensional description of part of Washington, D.C.

Much research remains to be done

Clearly the general problem of recognizing objects in a scene and describing their relations in three dimensions is far from solved. Existing systems can deal only with restricted types of scenes and they operate slowly. To develop generic systems, much more knowledge of the world has to be incorporated into the program. There must be a mechanism to store large-scale spatial information about an area, from which relevant data can be extracted and into which newly acquired information can be fed.

Finally, there must be a dramatic increase in the speed of vision processors. The computing requirements can be estimated if one considers that a mobile cart developed by Hans Moravec at Stanford University navigated at a speed of 3 to 5 meters per hour while analyzing one image of its surroundings for each 1-meter lurch with a 1-million-instruction-per-second computer. To guide a similar cart at a walking speed of a meter per second will therefore require from 10^9 to 10^{10} instructions per second.

Once such high-speed processors are available, highly computationally intensive methods may be attempted that have not been tried so far, leading to more versatile systems.   ◆

SOFTWARE ENGINEERING

The power of computer hardware has improved by a factor of many thousands over the last 20 years, but programmer productivity has at best only doubled. Furthermore, as software systems have grown larger and more complex, the absolute number of bugs in them has increased, as have the potential effects of program errors. In some cases, systems have been abandoned after the expenditure of tens or even hundreds of millions of dollars.

Raymond Yeh   University of Maryland

Yet it appears that computer systems relying on increasingly complex software systems will play a growing part in people's lives in the future.

How will the software industry increase both the quality of its products and productivity? The apparent solution is automation—using the same kinds of tools that software developers have made available to others—to aid the process of creating software.

Use of software tools lags

Although a fair number of software tools—compilers, formal design methodologies, testing programs; program-design languages, and others—are available in the United States and elsewhere, they are seldom used in the software industry [see table]. Among the problems inhibiting tool use is that corporate management generally has little if any software background and therefore is not sympathetic to the need for such tools. Furthermore, there is usually no entity within a corporation to provide tools on a centralized basis; tools must generally be paid for out of the funds for a particular project and so there is little incentive for introducing them.

Some of these organizational problems hindering the introduction of software tools are less prevalent in Japan than in the United States because Japanese companies may consider the benefits versus costs of software tools over a wider base than a single project. In addition, the relative lack of mobility of Japanese software engineers leads to an increased incentive for introducing tools; programmers are more likely to reap the long-term benefits of tool use if they stay at the same company for the bulk of their careers. Yet another factor tending to favor tool use in Japan is the willingness to do postmortems on finished projects to determine what might have been done differently and what lessons might be learned from them, rather than immediately proceeding to the next project.

The progress of software-engineering techniques is also slowed because many programmers must spend a large portion of their time maintaining a huge inventory of existing, ill-structured software—estimated at over $200 billion. Software tools designed to work with well-structured programs written in high-level languages are of little use in such work, and software organizations that spend most of their time maintaining and upgrading old code have little time to apply formal methodologies to new programs. Some software organizations report spending as much as 70 percent of their time correcting errors in and making changes or enhancements to existing programs.

New alternatives are needed

All of these problems, however, may simply be masking underlying inadequacies in current program-development techniques. It is estimated that full use of all existing programming tools, starting with the requirements and specifications stages and running through unit and system testing, would reduce the cost of software development by only 40 percent. Further gains may be made because of the reduced costs of maintaining well-structured programs with good documentation, but a factor of two is about the best that can be expected in software productivity by applying existing tools.

Inadequacies in techniques come from two areas. First, it is impossible to prescribe fully the requirements of a program; the user always looks at the completed system and decides that certain operations should be carried out slightly differently or that functions must be added. Second, there are no facilities for reusing previous designs or sections of program code. To achieve the gains in software productivity that will be required for next-generation computing—gains that more closely approximate the expected gains in hardware capability and demands for applications software—an alternative to the current software life cycle must be considered.

The most difficult parts of software creation at present are at the earliest phases—in the requirements and design stages. Coding is relatively easy to automate once the software is completely specified. So the greatest opportunities for gains in productivity and quality are at the earliest stages of creation and during later maintenance.

One remedy: rapid prototyping

One major problem in building acceptable software systems is the current lack of continuing communication between users and programmers, which means that only when the programmer has produced something to look at can the user decide whether it is what was asked for. If the user's examination is delayed until the software system is supposedly ready for delivery, then much time may be wasted if the system is unsatisfactory. The user may reject software because a program does not match its original specifications. Frequently, however, a finished program may be rejected because the original specifications were not a good description of what the customer wanted.

Rapid prototyping is one approach being explored to get a good idea of how a program should be designed before too much effort has been expended in coding. A rapid prototype is an executable model of the intended system that shows in general how the final system will look to the user and how it will function. The prototype may not have all the functionality of the final system, but it will contain enough of the user's initial specifications for the system to indicate whether major changes should be made. Such a prototype can also give the programmer insight into how the final system should be implemented. It can be quickly changed until both the programmer and the user agree on its appearance, thus giving both parties a better idea of how the final system should look than if they were working from paper specifications. Having fulfilled its purpose, the prototype should generally be thrown away rather than be used as a base to develop the target system.

High-level languages that could be utilized for rapid prototyping include APL for scientific and engineering applications, Prolog for writing compilers, and C-Shell for system-building. In addition, there has been significant work in artificial intelligence

and automatic programming aimed at making executable specification languages, so the specifications of a software system—if expressed in the appropriate formal language—can be used directly as a rapid prototype. With this approach there is no need to recode the program's functionality from the specifications document into some other language.

Time to reuse program components

The generation of production-quality programs from very high-level specifications is an ideal goal. However, even though there is significant research in this area, it is not likely to bear fruit in the near future. What may be possible earlier is the automatic generation of such programs from reusable components. Reusability would not only eliminate almost the entire development process—it would also promise eventually to yield virtually bug-free programs because errors will have been corrected through previous use. With this approach, the high-level design would be completed and then the program code would be generated automatically from a library of reusable components. Maintenance of such programs would be much more efficient because changes would be made to the program specifications and then recompiled, rather than programmers having to make detailed changes in the program code, where functions and their side-effects are less apparent.

The concept of reusable software is similar to that of shareable data. Data can be shared by programs if they all use the same conventions for reading and writing it. The analogous constraints for reusable software are that it be interpretable, incorporable, and portable. Interpretable means that potential users can quickly find out what the software does, what operational environment it requires, and what other attributes the software has. Incorporable means that one should be able to use the software to build larger software systems, in much the same way that basic data objects can be used to create other data objects and abstractions from which completely different sets of conclusions may be drawn. Portable means that the software should be usable on different machines and in different operating environments.

In efforts to improve reusability, language designers have included in their language definitions declaration statements that may be used for extra information, to make programs more readable and understandable. However, the information contained in such declarations is local, intended for use within the

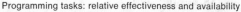

Programming tasks: relative effectiveness and availability

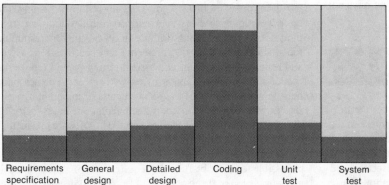

| Requirements specification | General design | Detailed design | Coding | Unit test | System test |

Most software tools currently available are aimed at converting detailed program descriptions into executable code and at testing that code once it exists. There is a lack of tools for software system design—the earliest, most crucial phase of development.

Utilization of software development techniques

Method or tool	Percent of companies using method or tool
High-level languages	100*
On-line access	89
Reviews	84
Program-design languages	60
Formal methodology	45
Test tools	27
Code auditors	18
Chief-programmer team	13
Formal verification	0
Formal requirements or specifications	0

*Every company seems to use some higher-level language, but often there is also a high use of assembly language.

program in a fixed environment. No information is included about the evolution of a piece of software, its use within its environment, or its overall functionality. All information like this is usually expressed in text documentation, which is unstructured and therefore difficult to interpret or search.

In order to make software more reusable, designers must establish specification methods, so that the desired software components can be found and integrated into a composite system. They must also develop cataloging and classification schemes, so that large software libraries can be maintained and extended. There are two ways of classifying components in the software base. One way is by application—what software systems they are used in, such as payroll, inventory control, or order processing. The second way is by task category—what functions they perform, such as user interface, printing data, or sorting records. In current applications systems, there is little or no common code; therefore, the matrix of applications and task categories has a different program in each position. In the software base, most applications programs would use the same code for a given task category. In addition to the reusable programs used in a software system, the software base would also contain the tools used for putting the software together: testers, debuggers, and analyzers.

In addition to a component data base containing all the reusable programs that are constructed and a catalogue data base to facilitate easy access to those components, the software base will also contain a property data base. This would have information on the attributes of all the various components along with "knowledge" of the development and maintenance process. The property data base would be used to verify that a finished software system does what its specifications say it does. By showing what transformations different components perform on data, it would be possible to check the ultimate correctness of program code. This verification process would be much easier using the property data base than using the original source code, because it would not be necessary to go through the proofs of what the source code does each time a component of the software base is used.

Changes in the underlying source code that did not affect program attributes would not require any change in the property data base. Program maintenance would also become easier because it would be necessary only to show that a new version of a system preserves the attributes of the old, as represented in the property data base, rather than proving its correctness starting from the source code.

Automated tools are required

Clearly, an integrated environment containing a number of automated tools will be necessary to make the concept of a software base usable. The most crucial of these is a conceptually oriented, very high-level language that will let users, working with applications specialists, design a nonprocedural system specification. Translation tools can then convert the nonprocedural specification into high-level language or into a procedural specification.

Another required tool is an intelligent software-base management system. This manager must make certain kinds of inferences so that it can check whether software components are

---

Next-generation software

The essence of a "generation" is that it marks a discontinuity in technology. The so-called fifth generation is no exception, as it proposes radical changes in the style and substance of computing. Its key characteristics are an aggressive exploitation of new VLSI technology, use of this technology to explore very different computer architectures, and software that provides significant "intelligence" or expertise in a variety of different domains.

There are at least three developments in software technology that will play major roles in the fifth generation: logic programming, object-oriented programming, and exploratory programming environments.

Logic programming, most usually associated with the programming language Prolog, regards the programming problem as one of stating the logical constraints that hold between sets of variables in a form that permits a specialized inference algorithm to solve those constraints for the values of one or more of the variables, given values for the others. In the case of Prolog, the inference mechanism is a variation on the unification algorithm from resolution theorem proving.

If a program is expressed as a series of logical dependencies between quantities, certain distinct advantages over classical programming are achieved. First, the program concentrates on stating the constraints between the variables. The task of achieving a procedural realization of a solution algorithm is left to the language interpreter. Second, because the constraints are often symmetric, programs stated in this form can be used to solve all of the variables in the set, not just one of them. Third, the lack of a procedural specification means that it is possible to use a great deal of parallelism in searching the solution space. Logic programming is an area in which there is active research and development in a number of research institutions, particularly in Europe and Japan.

Object-oriented programming, which forms the basis of systems like the Smalltalk-80 programming environment developed at Xerox Palo Alto Research Center in California, takes yet another untraditional view of the programming problem. Rather than being built as a collection of procedures or subroutines, object-oriented systems are built up as a collection of data objects, each one of which knows how to respond to a set of commands that can be given to it. Since each data object provides its own specification for each of the commands to which it responds, the behaviors of different objects can be tailored very precisely to their intended use. Object-oriented systems, in addition, usually have mechanisms that can organize objects into classes, so that they share or inherit common useful behavior specifications. Systems organized in this manner become easy to extend or to modify—simply by specializing existing objects to form new applications.

Exploratory programming is a development style that allows the incremental development of complex applications that are too difficult or uncertain to prespecify completely. Rather than requiring a complete, detailed design at the beginning of program construction, exploratory development encourages the programmer to develop possible designs by building program fragments and exploring how they work. The enabling technology is called the exploratory programming environment, an integrated set of programming tools that understand enough about programming so that they can help the programmer make, understand, and control the many changes that will be made to the rapidly developing program. In addition, these knowledge-based programming tools can automatically carry out many of the mechanical and bookkeeping activities associated with programming, in order to facilitate the programmer's exploration of many different system designs.

—Beau Sheil
Xerox Special Information Systems

being combined in ways that do not violate their input or output requirements. It must also be capable of inferring the properties of a composite program from the properties of its components.

For actually putting programs together, an intelligent editor will be needed. It will have to handle graphs, forms, texts, and structured program code. The operations that the editor performs on each of these types of information should be consistent with the logical constructs of that information: manipulation or transformation of nodes and structures for graphs, text-processing operations for standard text, and block composition or decomposition for structured program code. The intelligent editor should also maintain connections between equivalent structures expressed in different forms—a graph representing a particular piece of code should be linked to that code, and both should be linked to the appropriate specifications and documentation. Links must be preserved through changes made in any of the representations.

The editor should support the automatic generation of high-level language programs from either nonprocedural specifications or graphical specifications. To do this, the following steps must be automated: translation of the graphical or non-procedural specifications into a set of specifications for program components, retrieval of those components from the software base, generation of those components not represented in the library, and integration of all the components into an executable program.

Outlook for progress: uncertain

Where do we stand on the way to this automated software environment? Research is being done on rapid prototyping by means of executable specifications as well as by programming environments providing sophisticated aids for the programmer. Semi-intelligent editors exist for a number of languages: they can recognize statement boundaries and other program constructs and some can check syntax before compilation, thus reducing development time. The developments of models for non-procedural specifications and graphical specifications is still fairly far in the future, as is the knowledge-based technology required to transform them into actual programs or procedural program specifications.

The concept of a software base is also a long way from realization. Although program libraries exist at many software organizations, they are not standardized and they may be difficult to use even within organizations. Typical problems are lack of documentation spelling out how to use them, a lack of facilities for searching through the program library to find potentially useful components, and a lack of automated tools for integrating those components efficiently into a piece of software.

The outlook is uncertain. At some software organizations, both in the United States and in Japan, progress has been made in applying existing software tools to the problems of programmer productivity and software quality. Significant gains in productivity—sometimes by a factor of two or three—have been recorded. However, many other software organizations do not use the tools and techniques for software engineering that are available today. Such problems as organizational bottlenecks and the requirements of maintaining huge libraries of existing, ill-structured code, much of it not even in high-level languages, limit programmer productivity. Thus, software engineering faces a dual challenge: developing the techniques and programming environments that will improve productivity and quality manyfold and implementing current techniques and tools throughout the software industry, so that future developments may have an impact outside the laboratory. ◆

COMPUTER ARCHITECTURE

Despite their vast differences in hardware and performance, the first four generations of computers are all based on a single basic design: the Von Neumann processor. Such machines are sequential. They do one operation at a time, using a single processing element; a sequential centralized control unit; low-level, sequential machine language; and a linearly addressed, fixed-width memory. To speed a sequential machine, its individual parts must be run faster. Fifth-generation computers will need much higher speeds than can be achieved by this method. They will be parallel, or concurrent, machines, with architectures that allow the computer to do many operations at once.

Efforts to develop concurrent computers have been carried on for many years. Array processors exemplify commercially viable machines. These machines have been successful primarily because they integrate fairly well with the conventional, sequential instruction-stream Von Neumann programming methods. Michael Flynn of Stanford University, Palo Alto, Calif., has characterized these machines as single-instruction, multiple-data (SIMD) path architectures. SIMD machines work very well for problems where the data is primarily structured in regular dense arrays, as in image processing, matrix manipulations, and physics simulations. They are by no means as general-purpose as their single processor counterparts and are typically used as an attached processor to a Von Neumann host machine.

In addition, a number of fourth-generation machines now coming onto the market incorporate a small amount of concurrency by ganging together a small number of very large processors, connecting them by high-speed buses, packet communications networks, or some other circuit-switching structures. The Cray Corp. XMP, for example, comprises two or more Cray 1 computers.

Fifth generation to stress parallelism

These single-instruction-path machines may provide valuable experience in system design for the next generation of computers. However, in the view of many, although not all, researchers in the field, fifth-generation machines will have to employ far more parallelism, using multiple-instructions, multiple-data (MIMD) streams and using many rather than just a few processors. This would require fifth-generation designers to make a dramatic break with most of the Von Neumann architectural principles now in use. Such a break looks toward the development of new programming lanaguages, operating systems, and architectures.

While there are several dozen efforts around the world to develop such machines, the ultimate success of this research is not yet clear. Each project has concentrated on one or two of the many parts of a complete system that will eventually be needed—compilers, input/output links, and so on. In addition, for budgetary reasons, very few of the projects are using the fastest components in their machines.

Equally important, there are many unresolved fundamental issues in achieving smooth cooperation among many processors. For each problem—be it communication, control, or programming—there are many solutions. It is likely that systems capable of extremely high speed will not be developed until the ideas now being tried in parallel-processing laboratories are combined with

A.L. Davis   Fairchild Laboratory
for Artificial Intelligence Research

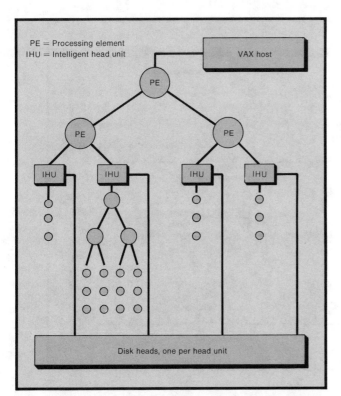

[1] Control-driven concurrent machines have a single centralized source of instructions that are passed down to many processors dealing with parallel streams of data. An example of this approach, shown here schematically, is the Non-Von-1 Machine under development at Columbia University in New York, by David Shaw and his colleagues. The Non-Von consists of a tree of 1 million processors (circles), each a tiny machine with a 1-bit ALU and 64-byte memory. These are connected to the main memory through the intelligent head units, which are disk heads with built-in processing to select the correct data from the main disk memories. The central processor sends out instructions to all the processors simultaneously.

the systems experience developing from the most advanced multiple-processor machines.

ABCs of concurrent computer architecture

With concurrent computer architectures, the main issues are control, granularity (the size of the basic processor), communication, topology, programming languages, and task allocation. A first and perhaps key decision to be made in designing a concurrent computer architecture is the type of control to be used: the operations can be controlled in either a centralized or decentralized fashion.

The centrally controlled systems face the speed problems associated with long global wires, whereas the decentralized control systems face difficulties in coordination of systems resources. Three control models have received attention to date: control-driven, data-driven, and reduction (or demand-driven).

In a control-driven system some control mechanism, such as a program counter or predicate, is used to indicate whether an activity is ready for execution. This method is the simplest extension of the Von Neumann style, and such machines typically employ centralized control [Fig. 1].

The two other control methods are usually decentralized. In data-driven systems, the arrival of the requisite operand data at a function or operator signifies that the function is ready to be evaluated. Data-driven programs can be modeled as directed

graphs, in which the data flow on the arcs of the graph and functions are associated with the graph vertices. When the input vertices contain a sufficient set of data tokens, the vertex may be executed. This causes the data to be removed from the input arcs, and new data packages called tokens are placed on the output arcs [Fig. 2].

Reduction systems, often called demand-driven systems, trigger activities by demanding results. These demands cause further demands for operands and, at some point, the demands find actual values rather than subprograms. These values are propagated back and combined operationally to yield the desired results. Demand-driven programs can also be modeled as directed graphs, in which the demands propagate over the arcs in the direction of the arc and data pass in the opposite direction. Symbolic reduction has been particularly popular among artificial-intelligence (AI) researchers for dealing with problems where the knowledge or data are incomplete. In these cases the answers can be found by symbolic simplification and substitution in a style similar to that used in performing an algebraic proof [Fig. 3].

MOS VLSI appears promising

Concurrent architectures inherently contain a number of replicated system elements. A second extremely important decision concerns the grain size of the replicated element. The grain size and choice of an implementation technology influences the element's structure, function, speed, reliability, and cost. Because of the inherently cheap replication of VLSI (very large-scale-integrated) components, the likely implementation technology for fifth-generation machines will be MOS VLSI components.

If the grain level is very small—at the arithmetic-and-logic unit (ALU) level, for example—it is likely that the VLSI physical component will contain more than one processing element per die. Such fine-grain systems are useful when the programs are structured in such a way that they can be decomposed into many concurrent pieces while minimizing the communication delay.

If the replicated element is on the order of a RISC (reduced-instruction-set computer) microprocessor, with several thousand words of storage and many registers and communication interfaces, the grain size is fairly large for VLSI implementation. With large-grain systems, it is unlikely that there will be more than a single processor on a die. With such a system, it would make more sense to place more memory on the die as the process parameters scale down than to place several smaller-capacity storage processors on a single die. These systems can support a fairly complex set of calculations locally, and therefore the communication costs can be reduced.

Importance of communication

Communication is a critical issue in concurrent machine architectures; long delays in communication may reduce the performance of the architecture to the point where the potential speed of the concurrency is negated. The design of the communication network connecting the multiple processors is thus another key choice in concurrent architecture.

The physical topology of the communicating processors has a major influence on system behavior. Many topologies are currently being investigated: tree machines; a checkerboard pattern of processors containing communication links between adjacent elements, called high-connectivity planes; rings; multidimensional cubes, such as Boolean n-cubes; and banks of processors connected by circuit-switching structures known as omega networks, banyon networks, cross-bar switches, and so on. (A Boolean n cube is a structure that has 2^n elements, and each ele-

[2] A second approach is data-driven processing. Processors carry out instructions as the data becomes available rather than when commanded by a central controller. An example of this approach is the University of Manchester machine, being developed in England by Ian Watson and John Gurd and their colleagues. The machine consists of a set of rings around which the data flow. The matching-store unit removes a data package, called a token, from the result queue and tries to match it with the other operand needed for a given operation. When the match is made, the operands are sent to the instruction store, where they pick up the appropriate instruction; the whole package is then sent to the processing unit for execution.

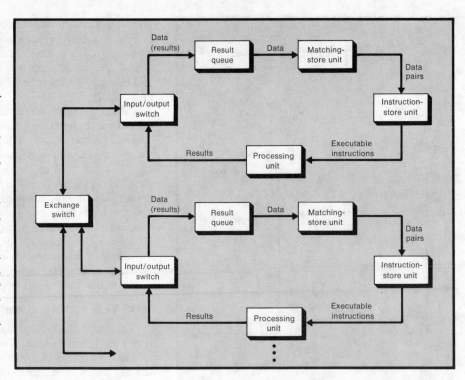

ment is connected to *n* others.)

With VLSI components, it is much easier to build a concurrent processor using automatic layout tools than it is to program one, in that conventional programming disciplines make poor use of the processing power of a concurrent architecture. If concurrent systems are to realize their performance potential, new concurrent programming methods and languages must be developed. For maximum efficiency, the control method of the programming model should match the control method of the machine. Hence, there are control-driven languages, data-driven languages, and reduction (demand-driven) languages. It is possible to evaluate other languages efficiently by translating them to an internal form that is consistent with the machine's control method.

Task allocation: a key to success

Given a particular program containing a certain amount of concurrency and a multiresource architecture capable of supporting concurrent processing, the final problem is how the concurrent program tasks should be mapped onto the physical resources of the machine—that is, which processor will do which task. This task-allocation strategy will most likely be the ultimate key to successful fifth-generation architectures.

Task allocation should not contribute significantly to the overhead of the system. If the task-allocation activity takes longer than the resulting performance increase of the concurrent evaluation, the system will be slower than a single-processor system.

In general, there are two generic types of allocation strategies: static and dynamic. Static allocations are performed once, whereas dynamic strategies continually attempt to balance the system load in a way that maximizes the utility of the system resources.

Initially the dynamic approach sounds like the best idea, and several mechanisms for this strategy have been proposed. Unfortunately, none has yet been implemented in a way that demonstrates its potential. The main issue is whether the in-

creased overhead of the dynamic load-balancing scheme can be balanced by sufficiently improved system performance. It may turn out that the simpler static methods will be sufficient. Another possibility is to combine a static-allocation strategy with a simple dynamic mechanism.

A related issue is whether to perform task allocation when the program is run or when it is compiled. Most allocation strategies are implemented when the program is run. But unless programs are extremely well suited for the particular architecture, excessive allocation times often result.

An alternative approach that has been little examined is to allocate tasks to specific processors during compilation. If a program is viewed as a directed graph, with vertices corresponding to actions and arcs corresponding to their sequence, then the physical structure of a parallel machine can be similarly viewed, with processors as vertices and the communications lines connecting them as arcs. The greater the discrepancy between these two graphs when the program is run, the greater the time will be that is expended on task allocation, and the greater communications problems will be during the run. By compiling the program in such a way that the program graph is restructured to resemble the machine graph, considerable savings can be achieved in task allocation. This approach was used, for example, in the Data-Driven Machine-II constructed by the author and his colleagues at the University of Utah.

Of course, the various choices made in designing a concurrent architecture are by no means independent. A given choice of control system or grain size, for example, will have a direct effect on the communication problem and the options available to deal with it.

A look at a few of the architectures under development makes clear some of the problems involved in concurrency and the solutions being tried. Since there are several dozen of these proposed machines [see, for example, "Computing at the speed limit," *Spectrum*, July 1982, p. 26], a complete survey is impossible in a short article. However, a sense of the ongoing work can be obtained by looking at one example of each of the three major control schemes: control-driven, data-driven, and reduction. The examples chosen here have all been supported by small-scale hardware implementations.

The Non-Von: a million processors

The Non-Von-1 Machine, being developed at Columbia University in New York by David Shaw and his colleagues, is an example of a centralized, control-flow, or SIMD, machine. The Non-Von takes as far as possible the idea that—since more processors can be placed on a given silicon chip as the area of each is reduced, while the speed of each generally decreases only linearly with the dimensions of the processor—processors should be built as small and in as great a quantity as possible. The Non-Von will eventually have a million processors, each with a tiny, 64-byte memory, eight 1-byte registers, a 1-bit ALU, and similar Lilliputian components.

Since such tiny microprocessors cannot be expected to store program instructions, they will be organized into a tree, with a central processor at the top of the tree sending out identical "broadcast" instructions to all processors. Access to the main memory will be through disk heads paired up to each small group of processing units. A certain small amount of processing ability will be incorporated in the disk heads themselves, so the heads can be instructed to select some data rather than simply read all records requested into the system.

The intimate connection of memory with each processor means that each unit can be assigned a part of the problem. In a commercial system, each individual's record would have its own processor. In a simulation, each grid point would have its own group of processors.

While all processors would get the same commands from the central processor, a designer could implement selective actions by disabling all those processors not intended to receive the message. A form of associate memory could be created in this way. Say, for example, that the memory contained employee records and the processor wanted to obtain the salaries of those in the sales department of a company. The first set of instructions would tell all processors to disable themselves if the data in cer-

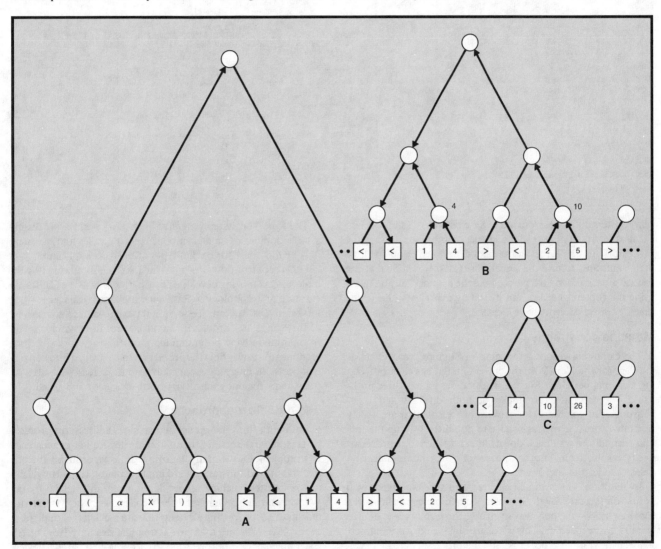

[3] The third main type of concurrent processor is the reduction, or demand-driven, machine. Processors carry out instructions when results are needed for other calculations. An example of this type is the Mago reduction (MRED) machine being developed by Gyula Mago and his colleagues at the University of North Carolina, Chapel Hill. The machine consists of T (or tree) cells and L (or leaf) cells and is designed to process FP and FFP functional programming languages. Each symbol of the instruc-tion is stored in a separate cell (A). Here, an instruction to multiply together pairs of numbers is sent up the tree and then back down in a single sweep (B). Each processor then performs the operation, sending the results to be stored in the appropriate cell (C). This way a multiplication of thousands or millions of pairs is carried out in one or two time steps. With each up and down sweep, the initial expression is further elevated or reduced until a final answer is achieved.

Computer architecture performance milestones

Performance	Less than 1 MIP	1 to 10 MIPs	10 to 100 MIPs	100 to 1000 MIPs	More than 1000 MIPs
Architecture: Control driven (instructions executed when the control program orders them)	Achieved by the earliest Von Neumann machines	Achieved by SIMD (single-instruction, multiple-data) array processors such as Floating Point Systems FPS-120B and even by nonconcurrent conventional machines such as the Cray 1	Charles Seitz's Boolean n-cube machine should meet this goal, but for more radical architectures, the issue of how concurrent programming should be done is a continuing problem. Object-oriented and functional programming models may provide a solution.	Methods are needed that programmers can use to efficiently design massively concurrent algorithms. Methods for allocation of the parallel tasks onto the processing elements of a particular architecture are also necessary. For irregular data and program structures, no clear solutions are in sight.	Incorporate very high-speed packaging and integrated-circuit technology into the implementation. Highly tuned system software is also required. Wafer-scale integration, GaAs circuits, MOSFET circuits, and thermal conduction hybrid packaging should produce the necessary performance.
Data driven(instructions executed when data is available)	Achieved by the Univ. of Utah data-flow machine and the Univ. of Manchester (England) machine	Achieved by the 12-processor single-ring Manchester system	Arvind's system, consisting of 64 LISP machines, will meet the speed goal, but for cost effective solutions, the issue of how to efficiently support large files and data structures is still not resolved in a general way. Dr. Arvind's I-structures and the Manchester tagged token with an independent structure memory offer promise.	Methods are needed for allocation of concurrent actions onto processing grains in ways that reduce communication to a tractable level. VLSI implementation, supported by the appropriate architecture, is needed to reduce the system cost. An NEC parallel processing chip uses an approach based on graph decomposition methods for the allocation problem.	Same as control-driven technology
Reduction or demand driven (instructions executed when results are needed)	Achieved by a reduction machine developed in Bonn, West Germany	Gyula Mago's MRED machine should reach this goal upon completion of the prototype.	The Mago machine architecture could be configured to meet this goal but cost is high. Advances in programming methodology and new architecture features are needed to reduce the communication overhead. Boolean n-cube topologies and high interconnection planes look good.	Arvind's stream-based demand propagation approach may alleviate some of the communication demands. Robert Keller's Rediflow concepts may provide architectural horsepower to support highly parallel evaluation structure.	Same as control-driven technology

tain registers did not correspond to the characters "sales." When the next instruction, to read the salaries, was broadcast, only the processors for employees in the sales department would still be active and thus receive the signal. The result would be that the central processor would have accessed the memory only by specifying the contents needed, not by stating explicitly where in the memory those contents were located.

Machine constraints

The Columbia group is designing VLSI chips that will act as the base for the Non–Von; the current design has eight processing elements per chip. But the machine design has three problems. The tree structure makes it both difficult and time-consuming to communicate between processors that are widely separated, because messages have to go all the way up the tree and then all the way back down. In cases where one processor needs results from another processor, such communication delays can lead to inefficiency.

In addition, the symmetrical tree structure interferes with Non–Von system growth. If a user wants more capability—say, more memory—the only way to enlarge the memory is to double the size of the machine. This is because the memory is intimately associated with the processors, and the processors are in a symmetrical binary tree.

Perhaps most significant, the choice of a very small grain size may limit the type of problems that the Non–Von can solve. For most numerical calculations, and even many symbolic AI operations, the problem cannot be broken down into millions of identical simple parts but perhaps only into hundreds or thousands. For such problems, the Non–Von processors are simply too small.

The Non–Von system will most likely work well for processing a large number of small symbolic record queries and, as such, may be quite fast for certain types of business applications.

Other control-flow designs, such as the Boolean 10-cube multiprocessor being developed by Charles Seitz at the California Institute of Technology in Pasadena, use larger grain sizes—one thousand 8086 microprocessors, in this case—and so avoid some of the Non–Von's problems. But all control-flow systems suffer from an underlying programming problem: they force the programmer to specify how the problem is to be divided into concurrent parts. In many cases this may lead to increases in software costs that wipe out gains in hardware efficiency and speed.

The data-flow approach

Both data-flow and reduction machines address this problem by creating architectures that automatically exploit concurrency in a problem. Of the many data-flow projects, probably the one that has moved furthest toward implementaton is the University of Manchester machine, under development in England by Ian Watson and John Gurd and their colleagues. The Manchester machine uses processing elements that are much larger than those of the Non–Von and that have a ring-like structure [see Fig. 2]. Each ring has 12 subprocessors, so each is itself a parallel device.

The machine uses two types of messages: data packages, called tokens, and instructions. Instructions describe what is to be done with the data, the destination to which the results are to be sent, and the number of operands to be expected at the destination. The data tokens contain the data itself, its destination, and additional information about how the data are to be processed.

Instructions are kept in the instruction store, while data passes in sequence from the result queue to the matching unit, instructions-store unit, processing unit, and an input/output switch. The cycle operates as follows. First, the matching store removes a result token from the result queue. If the token indicates that only one operand is expected at its destination, it is sent immediately to the instruction-store unit. If more than one operand is required, the memory in the matching store is searched for an entry with the same destination. The matching entry is deleted and the result pair is sent to the instruction store. Unmatched tokens are saved in the memory. Next, the destination instruction is read and transmitted to the processing unit together with the token pair for execution. The interfaces between units are asynchronous, permitting greater operational concurrency with all units operating in parallel.

An exchange switch connects the various rings into a single system. None of the storage units are shared, removing performance limitations due to finite memory bandwidth. The exchange switch has an uncomplicated structure. It consists of successive layers of token distribution, buffering, and arbitration. Tokens are routed at each distribution layer according to a particular bit in the name field. By alteration of the routing bits, faulty processor units can be isolated until they are repaired. Buffer layers decrease the effects of address interference or token "clashes" within the distribution stages.

The machine inherently requires considerable communication around each ring. In a VLSI implementation, the slow off-chip speeds will tend to reduce system performance. This may be mitigated somewhat by the capability of each ring processor to be pipelined.

Test data available

The Manchester data-flow system is one of the few advanced parallel-processing devices for which actual, rather than simulated, performance figures are available. A single ring of 12 processors can perform 1.7 million machine instructions per second (MIPS) on reasonably realistic problems. While this speed is not outstanding at first glance, one must bear in mind that the Manchester group uses relatively slow components as the basis for its prototype—each processor functions at 0.15 MIPS. State-of-the-art microprocessors are about 30 times faster. In addition a working machine will include around 30 rings, not just one. So it seems reasonable that such a machine could achieve over 1000 MIPS in actual operation.

The Manchester machine does not make any effort to bring together related computations on nearby processors or rings, so it loses efficiency in communication delays, although a number of data-flow groups have proposed ideas for automatically clustering neutral parts of a problem.

A more fundamental problem common to many data-flow machines is the difficulty in dealing with large data bases, especially data arrays, where there are many instances of a single data type. Since data are conveyed from one spot to another, tremendous communication overhead costs can be incurred in moving such large arrays.

One promising approach to this problem is the I-structure streams developed by Arvind at the Massachusetts Institute of Technology in Cambridge. Dr. Arvind's idea is basically to allow the data to remain in one place, accessible by all processors, while the commands follow the data-flow paths. The MIT group is building a prototype machine using this approach, based on 64 Symbolics Corp. 3600 LISP processors. This prototype is expected to be operating in 1985.

One further problem with the data-flow approach is that the programming implementations are often inefficient, because the division of the problem into concurrent pieces is automatically performed by the system, not the programmer. Here, hardware efficiency is traded off for ease of programming.

Finally, in handling some problems, data-flow machines can allocate tasks inefficiently, with most processors rapidly performing the easier calculations as they appear, while a few are left with the longer, harder pieces of the problem. This can lead at some point in the calculation to a processor becoming idle while waiting for the more difficult (and therefore slower) parts of the problem to catch up and make results available.

Reduction machines: the tree-and-leaf approach

Reduction machines avoid this problem by making the performance of a task depend on the result being needed for another calculation. The idea here is that processors perform work as it is needed rather than as it becomes available.

An example of a reduction, or demand-driven, architecture is the Mago reduction (MRED) machine, under development by Gyula Mago and his colleagues at the University of North Carolina in Chapel Hill. The MRED, like the Non–Von, is a tree design, but there the resemblance ends. The computer consists of two types of cells: T (or tree) cells and L (or leaf) cells. The L cells form the bases of the tree, with the T cells connecting them.

The machine is designed to evaluate expressions in FP and FFP functional programming languages [see John Backus's article, "Function-level computing," in *Spectrum*, August 1982, p. 22]. The expressions, including the data, are distributed by the T cells to the L cells, each L cell holding a single symbol. The L cells evaluate the expressions, sending results up the tree to be further processed by the T cells, and these are then sent back down again to the L cells. Cells are activated as they receive demands for results needed to evaluate an expression, and, with each sweep, a larger and larger part of the expression is evaluated.

The L cell consists of a fairly small microprocessor and associated storage, while the T cells have only very simple processing elements and serve mainly to relay instructions and data to and from the L cells.

The MRED machine, being a tree, suffers from the same communication and growth problems as the Non–Von. More generally, reduction machines suffer from an inherent communication problem, in that each step requires two-way communication—demands for results in one direction and the results themselves in the other.

A loosely coupled approach

One effort to overcome this inherent problem and at the same time deal with some of the allocation problems of data-flow machines is the loosely coupled parallel processor, known as the Rediflow, designed at the University of Utah in Salt Lake City by Robert Keller and his associates. The Rediflow is something of a hybrid between reduction and data-driven machines. Each cell has a list of priority tasks that it has been ordered to do by some other cell and each cell also has a list of available data so it can work on other, less urgent, items if data for its most urgent tasks are not yet available. The idea here is that processors are not kept waiting for demands to be passed down or for data to be passed up—they will work on what comes to hand in order of priority.

It may, in fact, turn out that none of the three main approaches is practical for high-speed computing and that hybrid designs like Dr. Keller's will eventually win out. It seems likely that no single architecture will be found universally suitable for all tasks, as has been the case with Von Neumann architecture. However, the key tests of existing ideas will not occur for two or three years, when a number of major approaches are expected to become operational. ◆

VLSI

Although software technologies are the major focus of most next-generation efforts, very large-scale integrated-circuits are the base that will allow advanced software to be run. Neither the design tools nor the fabrication techniques to build large numbers of very complex chips are available today. Progress is being made, however, in VLSI design aids; a significant step is the concept of integrating automated methods with computer-aided manual design. Fabrication technology is approaching the limits of current understanding of device behavior, but present capabilities are only a factor of between two and ten away from those required for next-generation machines.

Examples of circuits already closing in on next-generation goals are the current crop of 256-kilobit dynamic random-access memories and Hewlett-Packard's 450 000-transistor 32-bit central-processing unit. It appears that isolated examples of million-transistor chips may not be far off; however, architectural experimentation alone for next-generation computers requires that the design and fabrication of such complex ICs be not merely possible but commonly affordable. The following articles discuss these and other issues.

Reaching for the million-transistor chip

One impetus to develop next-generation computers is derived from the recognition of the vast computational power available from very large-scale integrated circuits, especially when such chips can be linked together in parallel and produced in large quantities at relatively low cost. Limitations on our ability to design and build ever more complex VLSI circuits will therefore show up as limits on the power of the resulting next-generation computers.

Integrated circuits have lowered the cost of electronics in part because of their low replication cost: once a chip has been designed and the masks have been made, the marginal cost of producing a chip falls rapidly. However, the cost of the IC design has recently been increasing faster than the complexity of the chips being designed and, except for memories, the market for chips with more transistors on them is small compared with that for simpler chips (such as those used in computer games). Thus, the amount of nonrecurring cost allocated to each chip is rising; design cost for the underlying VLSI will be a significant part of the total production cost for next-generation computers.

The architecture of next-generation computers will be affected by VLSI in two ways: the difficulty of physically putting the desired structures on silicon and the cost-effectiveness of reducing the desired architectures to patterns that can be put on silicon. These two issues are related: a structure that does not fit well onto an integrated circuit can be built—but with a long design time, poor use of silicon area, and worse than expected performance. Difficult designs or those executed with inadequate design tools will show the same results; the ease with which a design can be reduced to silicon depends both on the design and on the tools and techniques available to the designer.

Stephen Trimberger   VLSI Technology Inc.

By most estimates, next-generation computers will be built from chips containing 1 million transistors or more; that is, for example, the goal of Japan's fifth-generation project. Managing a million of anything is a difficult task, and integrated-circuit design management requires a variety of information, including functional specification, layout geometry, electrical description, and test data. The circuit designer, aided by design tools, must handle the complexity of the design by organizing the data so as to hide unnecessary detail and emphasize important features at appropriate times.

Managing complexity

There are three major methods for handling this complexity: hierarchical decomposition of the design, use of regular structures, and automated implementation. Hierarchical design is the most basic of these methods. By decomposing the design into smaller pieces along the lines of functional blocks, less information must be dealt with at any given time. Successive division of the pieces yields a design hierarchy. This top-down decomposition phase of the design proceeds until the pieces are simple enough to be completely understood and easily implemented. Each piece is then implemented independently and the pieces are assembled.

The advantage of this method is that the pieces can be implemented in relative isolation, but difficulties may arise in managing the interfaces between different segments in the hierarchy when the discrete pieces are assembled into one chip. Significant research is going on at a number of locations to develop design tools for chip assembly. Some of the tools are interactive and graphical in nature, while others are based on a text description of the desired assembly, and still others are completely automated. Generally, these tools guarantee connection of individual cells by joining predetermined connectors. Cells are either stretched to match connectors by abutting or wires are generated to route between connectors. Chip-assembly systems can also perform additional tasks, such as checking that outputs are connected to inputs, that power connections are made correctly, and that the drive capabilities of signals are sufficient for the inputs connected to them..

The designer chooses the hierarchy to simplify the conceptual model of the design, but the hierarchy can also simplify implementation by allowing reuse of existing components. For example, if the design consists of a processor, some memory, and a video generator, there may be software available to generate the memory automatically, or a video generator may already have been defined. Design-rule checking is simplified, since a piece must be checked only once, no matter how many times it is used. Other checks of correctness can also be simplified using the hierarchical design: abstract representations of circuit blocks can greatly speed simulations, and the hierarchical decomposition limits the amount of the design that must be checked at any given time.

The second major method for dealing with complexity is regularity. Every time the same cell is reproduced, design effort is saved. In very regular chips, a large amount of function can arise from a fairly small amount of design effort. Regular designs also have regular interfaces, so correctness of connections for an entire regular structure can be demonstrated by checking only one interface.

All current VLSI circuits exploit regularity. The most obvious examples are memories, but processors can also have large regular areas by using bit-slice techniques, which require the designer to specify the data path for only one bit of the processor. The other bits are identical to the first [see figure]. Regularity in processors is also achieved by using programmable logic arrays (PLAs) to implement the control structure of the processor rather than random logic. The PLAs build regular cells and interconnections and then modify individual cells slightly to produce the desired function.

An even greater level of regularity is evident in proposals for next-generation computers. Systolic arrays—very large arrays of identical processors—have been postulated on the premise that regular structures are not only desirable, but are necessary to get large numbers of processors to work on a single problem. In these structures, data flow through the array, possibly as data streams flowing in different directions, while each processor performs some computation—not necessarily the same computation—at the intersections of the streams.

A third way to deal with complexity is automation. If the function desired can be generated automatically, then the computer can take care of the complexity. Some of the more common automated layout methods currently available are gate arrays, standard-cell systems, programmable logic arrays, memory arrays, and "silicon compilers." These tools can map directly from a high-level functional specification to geometry within their areas of application.

There are a number of difficulties with current automated layout tools. Chips designed by them tend to be larger and slower than handcrafted designs. Slow circuits may be particularly unacceptable in next-generation computer designs, where high-performance parallel systems are a stated goal. Furthermore, inefficient use of silicon reduces the advantages of VLSI either by leading to chips too large to manufacture economically or by requiring more chips to perform a given function. Automated layout tools produce lower-quality designs than humans because they typically have only a single strategy for placing transistors or larger blocks and for interconnecting cells, whereas humans can call on a variety of strategies, depending on the characteristics of a particular problem.

A gate-array system, for example, must transform the desired circuit to fit on the particular array of gates with which it is designed to work. If the design calls for even a small amount of memory, it will generally be implemented inefficiently. Similarly, a traditionally standard-cell tool will be unable to take advantage of a design that can be divided into regular pipeline structures. Tools such as PLA generators and data-path compilers, which do take advantage of the structure of a design, are limited to a specific physical structure. If a particular circuit is not well suited for implementation by such a structure, then it will be implemented badly.

Automated tools can easily be integrated into a hierarchical design style where the human designer chooses the automated or manual implementation method best suited to that stage of the design. No single tool can generate the complete design, but judicious choice among a number of tools can implement most of it. Even if there is no automated tool to generate a particular part of a design, manual methods also incorporate some automation. Symbolic layout, for example, guarantees that layouts will be design-rule correct. Other symbolic tools guarantee logical connection among blocks and adjust device sizes to minimize delay in critical parts of the circuit. The size of future chips will prohibit massive gate-level checking and simulation, so good construction methodology will be necessary to ensure detailed correctness.

Currently, the major tasks of decomposing the design into the design hierarchy and of selecting the implementation strategy for each segment are left to the human designer. Silicon compilers that choose among a variety of possible floor plans for arranging functional blocks rather than using a single standard floor plan are under study, but do not yet exist in working form. University and industry researchers are also working on an expert-systems approach to VLSI design, which will incorporate the rules human designers use for selecting a strategy to implement a given function. Such a design "expert" would have access to a variety of existing specialized layout tools, as does the human designer. Since expert systems have proved successful in geological exploration and medical diagnosis, they should be able to do a credible job at integrated-circuit design.

Of course, not all the existing methods for handling circuit complexity are being used today. Hierarchy and regularity have been used extensively for years in industry and universities, but automated tools have been resisted by many designers and managers who see them as inefficient and untested. In most cases, those complaints are valid: automated tools are limited in their areas of application and do not produce designs up to handcrafted standards. On the other hand, it is becoming more and more difficult to complete large-scale designs without some automated assistance: at current rates of design productivity, a single million-transistor chip would take between 40 and 800 designer-years to lay out.

One of the major factors influencing the next-generation computers will be the ability of designers to implement particular computer architectures in silicon. (A precursor of such an effect can be seen in such projects as the University of California at Berkeley's RISC, for reduced-instruction-set computer, which features an extraordinarily regular architecture not only because of its minimal instruction set, but also because it had to be implemented by a small team of graduate students in less than one year.) Integrated-circuit designers will have to use all the techniques available to them in order to produce such complex chips, although architectures which place many identical, simple processors on a single chip may not pose significantly greater problems than current microprocessor designs. Hierarchy and regular-

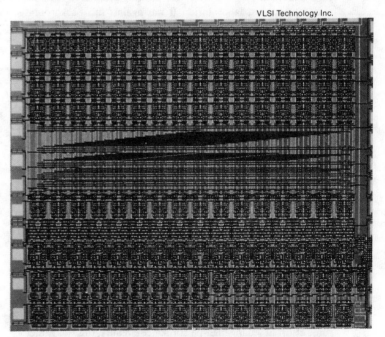

VLSI Technology Inc.

Regular structures significantly ease the layout of a 32-bit signal processor. Each of the 16 modules in the pipelined data path running vertically across the chip processes two bits of the input; the diagonal structure in the center of the circuit is a barrel-shifter, which can rotate the 32-bit word by any number of bits in a single operation.

ity will influence the structure of these designs, and automation will be used wherever possible; only the most critical parts will be done by hand. All styles of design—from fully automated through completely handcrafted—will be needed, since it is imperative that each part of a design be implemented as efficiently as possible in order to produce computers that operate at the speeds users of the next generation of computers will expect. ◆

Fabrication issues for next-generation circuits

One of the key driving forces behind the progress toward new generations of computers is the rate of advance of semiconductor circuit-fabrication technology. The well-known "Moore's Law" that the scale of integration doubled every year held good for 20 years and, although that pace shows some signs of slackening, progress during the last 10 years has been remarkable. In the early 1970s the 4096-bit (4-K) dynamic random-access memory (DRAM) was just being introduced. That circuit was characterized by minimum critical dimensions of from 8 to 10 micrometers, with one level of polysilicon and one of metal. Today's prototype circuits include the 256-kilobit DRAM with minimum critical dimensions of 1.3 micrometers, chip area of 34 square millimeters, and at least two levels of metallic interconnections [see figure, p. 75].

The last 10 years

In the early 1970s, technological progress was clearly possible in the direction of finer features and larger scales of integration. The minimum dimensions used (8 to 10 micrometers) were not at the limit of optical imaging and, moreover, new patterning technologies such as electron-beam lithography, X-ray lithography, and ion-beam etching were showing promise in research and development laboratories. It was against this background that industrywide investigations were undertaken on the advantages of finer dimensions for large-scale integrated circuitry, how to make the best use of the finer dimensions and what the constraints and limits were.

From these studies emerged a set of scaling rules based on a few initial conditions: operation at room temperature, electrical fields that do not increase as dimensions are reduced, and power dissipation per unit area that does not increase as dimensions are reduced. Among the resulting rules was that as the representative line width (for example, the channel length of an MOS transistor) was scaled down, vertical dimensions, voltage, and current per device should all scale proportionately. To prevent punch-through, doping density should scale inversely.

These rules were applied enthusiastically to MOS circuits because it was clear that by so doing the speed of MOS circuits would be comparable to that of many bipolar circuits without the complexity of bipolar circuit fabrication. A further crucial development was that by this time there was a sufficient understanding of the physics and technology of MOS structures so that both p-channel and n-channel transistors could be fabricated with high yield and consistent performance. Although there was also some effort at scaling high-performance circuitry, this was rather hampered by the fact that voltage levels were already low for high-speed logic circuits, such as emitter-coupled logic, and scal-

ing without reducing voltage levels usually led to greater power-dissipation density.

Some fundamental limits to the scaling down of dimensions were set by the minimum voltage swing needed to switch a silicon diode at room temperature—about 0.7 volts. Maintaining fixed voltage levels while scaling down dimensions led not only to increased power dissipation per unit area but also to breakdown, especially if doping levels were being increased to prevent punch-through of channel regions for MOS transistors or of base regions of bipolar transistors. A further limitation was that as device regions became very small the total number of dopant atoms in such areas became smaller, and hence statistical fluctuation in doping density would become relatively more significant. For example, a region 0.25 by 0.25 by 0.1 micrometer doped to a level of 10^{17} atoms per cubic centimeter, will contain only about 600 dopant atoms so that the standard deviation of a nominally uniform distribution of dopant atoms in such regions will be $\sqrt{600}$ (~ 24), or about 4 percent of the mean value.

Taking the above factors into consideration the consensus was that, on fundamental grounds, the limits to scaling down the dimensions of semiconductor circuitry would be at line widths of about 0.25 micrometer. Thus, it appears that we still have some way to go.

However, one trend that has been perhaps stronger than anticipated by those who enunciated the scaling rules is that, as minimum dimensions were scaled down, the chip sizes have not scaled down but have actually increased—leading to the enormous increase in the scale of integration already alluded to. This leads to two possible additional sources of limitations to progress in scaling: one is the design complexity [see "Reaching for the million-transistor chip," p. 72] and the other is the technological problem of not only achieving fine dimensions, but also of fabricating circuits with millions of components economically. How do these technological considerations apply to circuitry envisioned for supercomputers—that is, circuitry combining very high chip speed, very large-scale integration, and high-speed chip-to-chip drivers?

Patterning of fine features

The most obvious problems are those involved in making very complex and accurate patterns in the different layers of circuit material making up the circuits.

The masks can be generated with scanning electron-beam exposure of resist-coated, chromium-on-glass blanks. Such patterns have minimum dimensions of about 1 micrometer, with

Adequately interconnecting the transistors within the chip and interconnecting the chips themselves appear to be the most serious technological problems

0.1- micron repeatability of pattern placement over 100 square centimeters. Because this pattern complexity greatly exceeds even today's projected circuits, the technique can be used for exposing wafers in future circuits; this is known as "direct write."

Today, direct writing is too slow for economically mass-producing wafers but is used for producing customized and special high-performance circuitry. Thus, second-generation electron-beam systems (such as those being developed by JEOL, Varian, and Perkin-Elmer and Hughes under the auspices of the Very High-Speed Integrated Circuits program) that promise to be about an order of magnitude faster (about 10 wafer levels per hour) might well be the way to pattern the resist on crucial cir-

R.F.W. Pease Stanford Electronics Laboratories

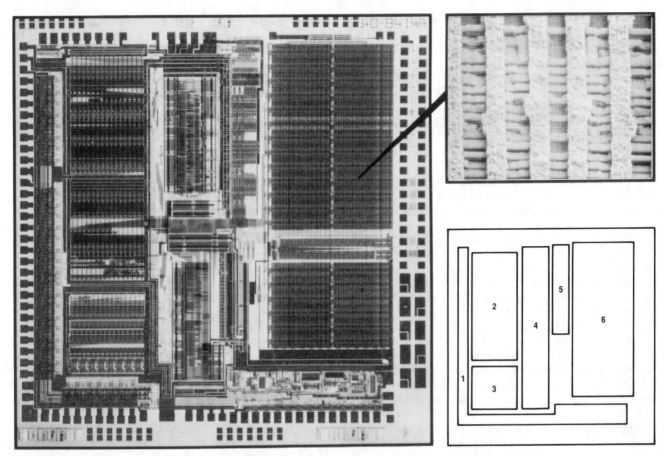

The central processor unit of the Hewlett-Packard 9000 (above) measures 6 by 6 millimeters. The packing density of transistors is not set by their dimensions, but rather by the space needed to accommodate the multitude of interconnections, as seen in the scanning electron micrograph of a small portion of the chip (above right). The wide vertical lines are second-level metal interconnections and the finer horizontal lines are the 1.5-micrometer-wide connections of first-level metal. The gaps between wires on first-level metal are 1-micrometer wide and are formed by anisotropic reactive-ion etching.

Legend:
1. Memory processor bus interface
2. Registers
3. Arithmetic logic unit
4. Programmed logic array
5. Sequencer
6. Microcode read-only memory

cuits for the next generation of computers.

Until second-generation electron-beam systems become available (about two years hence), nearly all lithography will be carried out by optical techniques. At present the best optical techniques can delineate 1-micrometer features over a 1 to 1.5 cm² field of view with an overlay accuracy of 0.2 to 0.5 micrometer. This performance might be stretched to generate 0.5-micrometer features over the same fields of view through the use not only of even better optics but also of novel resist materials and processes. During the 1980s, it is unlikely that dimensions for very large-scale integrated (VLSI) circuits will drop below 0.5 micrometer; therefore, suitable optical techniques will probably be available for the resist exposure. X-ray lithography promises line widths much below 0.5 micrometer (0.02-micron lines and spaces have been resolved), but it is unlikely that such lines will be needed within the next decade (for semiconductor computing circuits) and, moreover, it is not clear that the overlay accuracy and defect density (achievable with X-ray lithography) will be adequate.

Once the resist has been patterned, the patterns must be transferred to the underlying circuit material—usually by etching. Because the reduced lateral dimensions are now approaching that of the thickness of the material film, anisotropic etching techniques—in which lateral undercutting is minimized—are being used more and more. This pattern-transfer step has historically received less than its due share of attention, but this

shortcoming is being addressed. Anisotropic etching techniques, such as reactive ion etching, are now available for most circuit materials.

A second aspect of patterning that is beginning to receive its deserved attention concerns achieving adequate yield of very complicated patterns. The traditional approach has been to employ stringent clean-room conditions and quality control of materials and reagents; this approach has proved much more effective than predicted. More recently some form of redundancy has also been adopted so that at wafer test (for memory chips at least), one or two defects per chip can be circumvented by selectively isolating the block of flawed circuitry and connecting the spare block. Such isolation can be done by fusing links electrically, by laser-beam irradiation, or by selectively switching on (or off) interconnecting transistors with a beam of ionizing radiation. The yield problem, while still very serious, does seem amenable to the techniques at hand.

Achieving very large scales of integration

The early studies on scaling down dimensions of semiconductor circuits emphasized the advantages of scaling for individual devices—at a constant scale of integration. However, as the scale of integration has increased, two factors have emerged: (1) the largest-scale circuits have their speed performance limited by the resistance-capacitance time constants of the interconnections; and (2) only a small fraction of the total circuit area in VLSI logic circuits is taken up by the active area of the transistors (that is, the channel and isolation regions). The area is limited by the achievable density of the interconnections. Even in memories, interconnections significantly limit density.

Thus, the interconnection technology is probably the most serious technological problem in engineering high-speed VLSI circuits. Among the approaches being adopted is the development of metal silicides in place of polycrystalline silicon for at least one layer of interconnection. Such silicides have much lower electrical resistivity than silicon, yet they retain many of the good characteristics of polycrystalline silicon—such as the capability to make good electrical contact to single-crystal silicon and the capacity to form a refractory, high-performance oxide. The time constants of such interconnections are thereby lowered by reducing their resistance.

A second area of effort is increasing the number of levels of interconnection to enable the individual lines to be shorter, thus lowering both R and C. The most advanced circuits currently have from two to three levels of interconnections, and it is not clear how many can be incorporated onto a chip. In one new approach the interconnection levels are partly transferred into the package with more than 10 levels incorporated into a "multilayer ceramic" chip-carrier that is bonded to the chip. It is perhaps ironic that whereas 25 years ago the aim of circuit designers was to minimize the number of active components in a circuit, now it is the humble wires connecting them that present one of the most serious problems. Unless the interconnection problems can be dramatically alleviated, there is little point in pursuing gallium arsenide transistors for VLSI with a view to increasing speed. Moreover, scaling studies for VLSI circuits should be directed at least as much at the interconnections as at the active devices because when the active regions of the transistors occupy only a small fraction of the total area, the transistors can be left at their present dimensions without incurring an area penalty. Transconductance now becomes the dominant parameter for the performance of active devices in a VLSI circuit, raising the question of whether bipolar technology should be more actively pursued for high-speed VLSI.

Power dissipation in high-speed systems

High-speed logic circuits usually involve high quiescent power levels. For example, high-speed NMOS gates with 1-micrometer design rules have been reported that exhibit 1 milliwatt of static power; 10^5 such gates on a chip will dissipate 100 watts. When clock frequencies reach 1 gigahertz, high-speed switching may well give rise to dynamic power dissipation approaching the above figure. In addition the chip-to-chip interconnections may require powerful off-chip driver circuits that will further aggravate the power problem.

A further constraint is that to allow signal transmission between any two parts of a computing system within a single clock interval, then (for a 1-nanosecond clock interval) the system should be contained within a volume not much bigger than 1 litre. It has been estimated that the resulting power dissipation will be about 20 kilowatts in 1 liter. This figure was felt to be impractical (for room-temperature semiconductors) and other approaches—such as Josephson junction technology—involving lower power were investigated. As it turns out, optimization of liquid-coolant heat-transfer design can lead to heat exchangers that can be incorporated into the (otherwise wasted) volume of standard silicon chips and that can dissipate several hundred W/cm^2 for perfectly acceptable temperature rises (about 9 °C for 100 W dissipated in 1 cm^2 of silicon). Application of such technology will enable the 20-kW dissipation in 1 liter to be achieved, although a total liquid-coolant flow of about 1 liter per second may well be needed.

Although exotic technologies (such as those requiring 4 K) may not be needed on grounds of power dissipation, the use of liquid-nitrogen temperature (77 K) operation appears quite attractive. With liquid nitrogen as a coolant, the above heat-

---

Likely requirements for a high-speed chip containing several million transistors

If one takes memory chips as a model—because their regular structure allows extremely dense packing—integrated-circuit density has been doubling every 18 months for the last decade [see table, right]. If this rate continues, million-transistor chips could be produced in a few years. How can such complex circuits be fabricated, and how will they be integrated into working computer systems?

A chip of such complexity will occupy about 1 square centimeter, assuming that design rules call for line widths in the range of from 0.5 to 1.0 micrometer—the minimum possible with next-generation photo-optical technology.

The semiconductor single-crystal substrate and all other layers of circuit material (insulators and conductors) must be almost entirely free of functional defects over that area. In regular circuits, redundant blocks of circuitry may be activated to take the place of other blocks containing any residual defects.

The successive patterns should be overlaid with a maximum error of from 0.1 to 0.2 micrometer and line width errors must not exceed 0.2 micrometer (even less for gate electrodes of MOS transistors).

At least three levels of high-conductivity (for example, metal or metal silicide) interconnections will be needed; more are desirable.

The packaging should have provisions for:
• Liquid cooling of chips to allow power dissipation of several tens of watts/cm².
• Close spacing of all chips making up the high-speed portion of a system so that signals can be transmitted between any two points within a clock period (about 15 cm apart for a 1-nanosecond clock period).
• Many (up to 100/chip) high-speed (that is, transmission line) interconnections between the chips.
• Repair (including chip replacement) of the packaged system.   —R.F.P.

Integrated circuit milestones of the last decade (dynamic random-access memories)

Year	Circuit	Feature sizes	Interconnect
1974	4-kilobit DRAM	8-micrometer lines and spaces	1 level polysilicon 1 level metal
1977	16-kb DRAM	5-micrometer lines and spaces	1 level polysilicon 1 level metal
1980	64-kb DRAM	3-micrometer lines and spaces	1 level polysilicon 1 level metal
1983	256-kb DRAM	1.3- to 2.5-micrometer lines and spaces	3 levels polysilicon, metal silicides and metal

transfer technology becomes even more effective. More importantly, the resistances of metallic interconnections are greatly reduced, the rates of thermally activated failure-mechanisms (such as electromigration) are effectively eliminated, and, although bipolar transistors show inferior current gain, MOS transistors show superior performance.

It appears that the fundamental technology of fashioning circuit materials with increasingly fine dimensions and increasingly complex patterns can be developed rapidly enough to serve the VLSI circuitry envisioned for the rest of the decade. The limit on power dissipation, provided liquid coolant can be used, is well beyond the projected requirements for even such a power-hungry logic technology as emitter-coupled logic. Adequately interconnecting the transistors within the chip and interconnecting the chips themselves appear to be the most serious technological problems. ◆

PUTTING IT TOGETHER
An electronic panel discussion among engineers and scientists elicits a call for a national computer network that spans disciplines

A national network should connect all scientists and engineers, spanning discipline boundaries not only between computer science and related fields such as integrated-circuit design or fabrication but also between physics, chemistry, and biology: this was the recommendation of a group of U.S. scientists and engineers discussing national priorities for next-generation computer research. This discussion, initiated by *Spectrum*, took place via electronic mail on the CSnet, a National Science Foundation-sponsored network connecting computer-science researchers. "It is a scandal that it is not already in place," said Nobel-prize-winning physicist Kenneth Wilson of Cornell University in Ithaca, N.Y.

A national network, according to participants in the discussion, was among the most critical requirements for success in research aimed at producing next-generation computers. The group also examined questions of next-generation applications and computer architectures and of specific services and facilities required to make next-generation research successful, but the existence of a network to bind the research community was considered a top priority.

Such a network, according to participants in the discussion, would let computer scientists work together to build a new generation of machines without having to assemble all the people, funding, and equipment required for a project under one roof. By making the network part of the lives of researchers in other disciplines, all branches of science and engineering could share in the intellectual leverage furnished by a computer network; furthermore, by connecting people working in all disciplines to the same network, boundaries between fields could more easily be crossed, leading to further gains.

The gains in intellectual leverage from a national network would not be limited to gains from simplification of normal methods of communication, but could extend to new strategies for collaboration. Communication methods that could be enhanced by a combination of network and other technologies include sharing of computer-based tools for analysis and design, fast sharing of research results and data, and widespread access to experimental facilities that might not even be affordable if a single institution had to pay for them. There are many examples of collaborative efforts by computer scientists using the ARPAnet, a network created by the Defense Department's Advanced Research Projects Agency, and there is reason to expect that researchers in other fields would benefit too, if they were able to use a similar network.

"As for ensuring that physicists and chemists are on the network frequently, that is a question of making certain that all their routine business mail, telephone calls, paper writing, library searches, small computations, and so on are all done through the same machine that receives network mail, plus training them to use the network instead of the U.S. mail and the telephone," said Dr. Wilson, calling it "a difficult task but not insuperable."

Such communication between different fields is especially important in research and development efforts aimed at next-generation computing, the participants noted, because those efforts will focus on providing integrated service for users, and the only way to build successful systems is to involve potential users in their design from the beginning. Without such collaboration, said Randall Davis of the Massachusetts Institute of Technology, next-generation computer research is "virtually guaranteed to invent solutions for which there are no problems." Success or failure in past research projects can often be traced to the quality of communication and sharing of resources, many participants noted. One gave an example of an AI researcher who worked out a parallel-processing impementation of a particular algorithm, unaware that an equally fast single-processor implementation was possible.

The lack of interdisciplinary communications also affects projects currently under way: Norman Christ, at Columbia University in New York, reported that he and his colleagues had decided to build a special-purpose 256-processor array themselves rather than seek help from other disciplines because the cost of making their own mistakes would be less than the trouble involved in setting up the required lines of communication.

Jeffrey D. Ullman of Stanford University in Palo Alto, Calif., reported that a group of researchers from the electrical engineering and computer science departments meets weekly, so that they can all stay abreast of each other's work. "My own motivation for encouraging this process," he said, "is a perception, first of all, that computer scientists divide into subspecialities too easily. I know of too many instances where two or more groups work on the same problem unaware of each other's existence not to believe that if I had a broader outlook I would see the lack of interspecialty communication as widespread. The factionalization of what should be a unified field is probably a barrier to progress. Second, the problem of new-generation computing is among those whose solution depends on a chain of facilities working together. It is too easy for people to insist on working at one point in the chain and ignore the other links."

Dr. Ullman said that he hesitated to call the Stanford group a success at this point, "but there is no doubt that the sessions have been educational, and I predict that the minimum benefit will be the avoidance of unimplementable algorithms and languages that are easily implementable but admit no programs that do anything useful." He noted that one significant failure of the group thus far was its inability to attract much interest from the

Paul Wallich Associate Editor

artificial-intelligence community at Stanford.

According to Scott E. Fahlman computer scientist at Carnegie–Mellon University in Pittsburgh, Pa., "If a network is working right, it is possible for large design efforts to succeed, even if dozens of people are involved and they are scattered all over the country. If there is to be a national initiative, establishing a network is what should be done first." Keith Uncapher of the University of Southern California's Information Sciences Institute (USC-ISI) concurred, pointing out that the keys to past successes have been:

- A lead organization.
- An ARPAnet or equivalent network.
- The sharing of people and computing resources with little accountability.
- Almost instant surfacing of research results via informal means of communication.
- Research reports as a community effort.

Danny Cohen of USC–ISI noted that "only a few sites—such as Cornell and New York University—are able to get all of the required disciplines under one roof. It would be nice if all of us could benefit from the contribution of such groups across site boundaries, so that not each and every project at every site would have to start at square one thinking about every issue.

"Communication methods like the ARPAnet can free us from the need to organize projects according to geographic proximity. We can do better than that. We have done so in the past and we sure can do it again," said Dr. Cohen, who is associated with the MOSIS project, an MOS implementation service that provides chip fabrication to those shipping their design files over the ARPAnet to ISI. Not only does MOSIS offer silicon foundry services that none of its users could afford individually, but the ARPAnet has also made possible the sharing of VLSI design tools and cell libraries.

Network conference participants

Scott Fahlman	Carnegie–Mellon University (CMU)
Guy Steele	CMU, Tartan Laboratories Inc.
H.T. Kung	CMU
Norman Christ	Columbia University
David Shaw	Columbia University
Sidney Fernbach	Consultant
Kenneth G. Wilson	Cornell University
Forest Baskett	Digital Equipment Corp.
A.L. Davis	Fairchild R&D
Bill L. Buzbee	Computing Division, Los Alamos National Laboratories (LANL)
Robert J. Douglass	LANL
Robert H. Ewald	LANL
Randall Davis	Massachusetts Institute of Technology
Alan Gottlieb	New York University
Jack Schwartz	New York University
Larry Snyder	Purdue University
Jeffrey D. Ullman	Stanford University
Frederick Hayes-Roth	Teknowledge Inc.
Danny Cohen	University of Southern California, Information Sciences Institute (USC-ISI)
Keith Uncapher	USC-ISI
Steven Trimberger	VLSI Technology Inc.

Moderators

Chuck House	Hewlett-Packard Co.
Bert Raphael	Hewlett-Packard Co.
Alan Bell	Xerox Palo Alto Research Center
Paul Wallich	*IEEE Spectrum*

Dr. Fahlman suggested that projects for next-generation computer research would especially need a strong network because they would ideally be quite small: "Instead of huge architecture projects, we should think in terms of innovative miniprojects: a few people working on a machine that costs no more than a million dollars for maybe two years. A few of these projects will succeed and will snowball. Nothing is as sad to watch as a behemoth project that has gone sour, but that is committed to staggering on to some sort of completion years down the road."

Dr. Wilson suggested that "market forces" would be the major U.S. driver of next-generation work, rather than a single, centralized national program. He noted that, though in countries such as Japan or Sweden it might be possible to get virtually all of the top-level people in a given field together to agree on directions for research, "the activities in the U.S. in next-generation computing involve far too many people and far too much diversity to have a national program.

"It is important to assist in the market, however, and here the Government and private industry must help to make sure that people who are important to the operation of a market are able to participate in it. Many new developments—such as the minicomputer and Digital Equipment Corp.—were materially helped by just this kind of university participation in the computer market, and at the present time innovative companies like Symbolics and Denelcor need the same kind of university interaction. As long as the important players in the market can all participate in it, the United States need have no fear of Japan or anybody else."

Some areas of next-generation work, particularly those dealing with personal work stations and user interfaces, are mostly extrapolations of current efforts, according to Dr. Fahlman—"just about 10 more years of very hard work by good people." But other areas of this work, particularly machine architectures, require "innovative (and therefore risky) explorations. . . . That kind of research does not have an obvious and predictable payoff."

Cutting infrastructure costs

"It seems to me that this is where we need some sort of national initiative," he said. "We need more money for exploratory construction in the universities, more joint projects between universities and industry, better access for stimulating high-speed parallel designs so that only the most interesting ones will actually be built, and better tools for miniprojects in computer architecture (the half-million-dollar six-month project, as opposed to the five-year behemoth). The weakness of the current U.S. research and development structure is not in producing the basic good ideas and not in exploiting those ideas (however expensive) once they are shown to be right, but in doing the risky but expensive exploration in between."

The traditional problem with small projects in computer architecture, Dr. Fahlman noted, "is that it takes years and a lot of money to build the infrastructure for architectural experimentation—accumulating experienced technicians and administrators, scraping together the laboratory space and tools, building a simulation facility for work on parallel machines, and so on. Without this infrastructure the productivity of the key scientists goes way down." By sharing the infrastructure among many projects, "the support troops get a steady stream of interesting work, the cost is spread over many projects, and the incremental cost of trying out one more good idea is a small fraction of what it is now."

"The universities must be kept healthy," he said. "People are generally aware of the need for higher faculty salaries and better

Next-generation questions

In order to guide the network discussion on directions for next-generation research, the moderators posed a series of questions to participants over the course of the discussion. The participants directed their responses to the questions, but a number of the issues raised were left open. Because the questions are among the ones that scientists and engineers building the next generation should consider, they are reproduced here for comment. —P.W.

1. What does "fifth" or "new" or "supercomputer" generation computing mean? What should the goals of these programs be? What will the results of this research look like after the technology has matured? Will there be several different efforts heading toward similar goals with different names—superscientific, fifth-generation, new-generation, and so forth? How can each of them be characterized and distinguished?

2. What are the future applications for next-generation computers? What broad area do these applications fall into and what are their characteristics?

Do computer scientists have too limited breadth to envision and specify many of the new applications? What groups of people should become involved to illuminate new applications areas? How will computer scientists involve and work with these new groups?

3. How can we coordinate the creative activities of applications people, environment builders, machine architects, VLSI designers, and others so that they can learn of and build on each others work, and so that results in one discipline can build on results in others? How can we have work on a new machine at one site interact synergistically with work on a software environment at another site, for example?

What are the barriers that are keeping this kind of interaction from happening now? What needs to be done to lower them?

4. If computer networks are going to be an important part of multisite cooperation for next-generation research, who is going to sponsor them, how will they be connected, and who will have access to them? If other facilities are to spring up for such cooperation, such as hardware and software prototyping and simulation services, who will pay for them? In short, who is going to sponsor next-generation resarch, and how will the resources get where they should go? How will work sponsored by different agencies be coordinated?

---

computing facilities; this problem has yet to be dealt with. But another problem, discussed much less, is the need to pay the technicians and other staff people at something like the real-world rate. A faculty member will sometimes make financial sacrifices to stay at a university so that he (or she) can work on something really interesting. The guy who does the board layout doesn't have this added motivation."

Dr. Ullman pointed to USC-ISI's MOSIS project as an example of a central facility providing low-cost, readily accessible services over a network. He noted that although MOSIS started with chip fabrication, there have been recent experiments aimed at fabricating complete circuit boards from design files sent over the ARPAnet. Furthermore, "although it is an ARPA facility, its services have been offered to National Science Foundation–sponsored projects in a valid perception of the national interest. They are, therefore, getting fairly close to a facility available to all researchers, offering complete fabrication of experimental architectures." He suggested that funding for a MOSIS-like facility could come from a consortium of agencies, from industry, or from fees paid by users.

A similar public facility, he said, could "make working multiprocessing equipment accessible on the net of all doing software research. A big problem when dealing with unfamiliar systems is the need for resident gurus, but I almost believe I could get such expert help over the net if the people running the service were cooperative."

Dr. Ullman raised the question of whether a national project aimed at a narrowly defined goal, like the Apollo program, might not be useful to galvanize activity and procure funding for a broad range of next-generation work. "One important aspect of the moon project was that a decision about system architecture [the lunar orbiter-lander configuration] was taken fairly early, and the same would hold for a similar project in computation. One might guess that such a narrow focus would stifle work on the other computer architectures. However, I would guess that the net effect of the moon project was to facilitate the development of related but not directly applicable science and technology."

Among the possibilities Dr. Ullman mentioned for such a narrowly focused project was "a national network coupled with a usable data bank, perhaps a 'cashless society.' Maybe we could bring the educational process into the home with such a network." Another example was "to beat the Russian chess champion with a computer in 1990."

"All these efforts require the solution to technical problems that have to be regarded as open," Dr. Ullman commented. "For example, a usable data bank requires significant progress in representation, retrieval, and manipulation of massive amounts of data; maybe true understanding of natural language is needed, although I believe we can get by with much less as an interface. Processing financial transactions for a cashless society has a nasty way of requiring verifiable security, as well as control of concurrent access on a scale not heretofore contemplated."

Bill L. Buzbee of Los Alamos (N.M.) National Laboratories responded, "There is great merit in having a national goal and/or project with a specific and measurable objective. The suggestion of beating the Soviets in chess with a computer meets these criteria. Unfortunately, it would require the cooperation of the Russians and I seriously doubt that they would take the risk. Anyway, it is an excellent example of what is needed—a precise objective that will win support from 'society' and that will engender lots of good spinoff. I encourage everyone to rack their brains for such ideas."

Dr. Fahlman, on the other hand, objected strongly to the idea of a moonshot-type project: "In my opinion, it would be a terrible mistake to take the Apollo project as a model for the new generation effort in symbolic computing," he said. "Such splashy single-big-goal projects make sense when the science is pretty much in hand and agreed upon, and the problem is to marshall the necessary resources."

"As I look around, I see dozens of potentially good ideas in the general area of new-generation computing systems. A moonshot approach would cause us to select a single interlocking set of these ideas early on. These would get all the resources they need, and probably more; everything else would suffer and maybe be killed off. This is a big risk," Dr. Fahlman warned. "The political process that would govern such a selection would tend to favor a bad choice, I think.

"This sort of moon shot is what the Japanese are doing, of course. A moon shot is a good way to gain recognition and na-

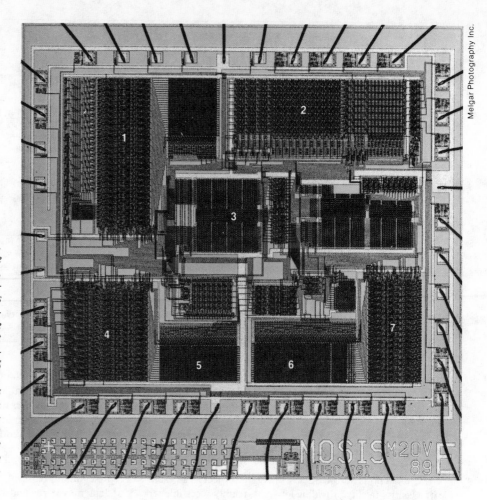

Melgar Photography Inc.

Legend:
1. Processor
2. Inteface to host computer
3. Control sequencer (program counters
   and ROM)
4. Processor
5. Memory (random-access and read-only)
6. Arithmetic-and-logic unit
7. Processor

Designed this year by Robert W. Broderson and Stephen P. Pope at the University of California, Berkeley, and fabricated by the Defense Advanced Research Projects Agency's MOSIS fabrication service, this programmable macrocell is one example of leading technology that can result from joint research in microelectronics. The 4-micrometer NMOS macrocell contains 23 000 transistors, and measures 225 by 265 thousandths of an inch. It performs linear predictive coding in low bit-rate speech communications, which can be used to compress voice signals in voice message systems, for example, or to encrypt code in secure voice communication systems.

tional prestige and a good way to build up a well-rounded technical infrastructure. Given their limited base of experience in the area of integrated hardware–software system, it makes sense to concentrate their effort for the greatest effect. In our case, however, it would make more sense to quietly pursue a large number of paths until the good ones become more apparent.''

Dr. Fahlman stressed that his comments on the dangers of a moon-shot mentality referred only to the area of symbolic computing architectures. "The building of a national network," he said, "is an area in which we have done the basic science and need only the resources and some intensive development." He doubted whether a commitment on the scale of the Apollo project would be necessary to put such a network in place.

New computer architectures an open question

All the conferees noted that the "right" computer architecture for next-generation machines was an open question. Several suggested that next-generation systems would consist of many machines linked together, each with a specialized architecture for its particular function. Robert J. Douglass of Los Alamos put forward a system description based on a day in the life of a "typical" next-generation computer system user [see "A day in the life," p. 46] in which he said, "It will be difficult to put your hand on one box, or even a set of boxes, and say that this is a new-generation computer. Instead, a new-generation computer will consist of many types of machines, I/O devices, storage systems, and communications devices interconnected in a vast network." Any given application might involve several kinds of computers from conventional Von Neumann machines to several different types of parallel systems."

A.L. Davis of Fairchild Advanced R&D in Palo Alto put the argument for such a heterogeneous system architecture more strongly. "I do not feel that supercomputers [whether numeric or symbolic] will be general-purpose in that general-purpose implies compromise and compromise implies loss of speed. If people agree with this view—many undoubtedly won't—then it would be nice to get involved in some discussion of which problem domains need supercomputers. In addition, a discussion of how these specialized supercomputers should communicate consistently also deserves comment."

A number of methods were proposed for classifying the architectures one might find in a next-generation system, from arrays of very large numbers of small processors, to small collections of high-speed processors, to parallel architectures where the interconnection patterns rather than the processors determine the information contained in a system. "If we agree that parallelism is the key to getting the kind of performance we need, what sort of parallelism do we want?" Dr. Fahlman asked. "A small number of big processors (1024 is a small number) tied together by some sort of network, with memory on one side or the other? Data flow? Something like NETL, in which the connections hold the knowledge and the processors are very simple? Systolic arrays configured for a particular task? We need a taxonomy of such systems and then a good theory of which systems are right for which tasks."

Dr. Ullman proposed a taxonomy consisting of high-flux machines, such as multidimensional cubes, with a large communication bandwidth, best suited for problems that "depend on everything meeting everything else"; tree machines, where each processor is connected to only a few other processors, suited for problems with a degree of independent parallelism; and processor arrays, which are assortments of processors specially tuned to the communication requirements of particular classes or problems, and thus are more efficient than general-purpose parallel procesors.

Dr. Fahlman proposed an orthogonal taxonomy. He suggested that machines could be classified by the kinds of connections between processors: general-purpose reconfiguration machines, equivalent to the "high-flux" category, "special-purpose machines with connectivity tailored to a specific application," and " 'connectionist' machines in which the resident knowledge is represented by the pattern of connectivity—the presence or absence of a wire between two points, perhaps with some variable weight on the wire—and not as bits inside some processor's memory."

David Shaw, of Columbia University, offered a classification based on the criteria of topology, granularity, and synchrony. Topology included "the linear array; the two-, three-, and other constant-dimensional meshes; such "nearly isomorphic" interconnection topologies as ring networks, chordal rings, and toroidal meshes; trees; and high-bandwidth machines of various kinds. Granularity referred to the number of processors involved in a given design and the relative complexity of the computing problem dealt with by any given processor. Synchrony referred to the question of whether individual processors in a particular architecture execute their instructions together (almost certainly the same instruction) or whether each is governed by completely different instructions. "It is the interaction between choices along these three dimensions that is of central interest to the architect of a new-generation machine," said Dr. Shaw.

Applications essential to design process

Guy L. Steele of CMU and Tartan Laboratories in Pittsburgh stressed the importance of knowing the application before building architectures. "Experience has shown that it is fairly difficult to take an algorithm coded with no thought for parallelism and automatically 'parallelize' it, either with a compiler or by dynamic load allocation. This leads me to conclude that successful use of architectural parallelism will necessarily be founded on proper exploitation of algorithmic parallelism. We need to identify standard paradigms of parallelism that have widespread utility and only then build hardware specifically to support these paradigms."

"Consider the stereotypical Von Neumann architecture," Dr. Steele continued, "usually conceived as having no parallelism. In fact it normally contains one very powerful parallel-processing unit: the arithmetic-logic unit (ALU). The operations of "integer" addition, multiplication, division, and so on, viewed as functions from bit patterns to bit patterns, are exceedingly complicated; their floating-point counterparts are even more complicated. Good ALU hardware performs a geat deal of bit-parallel processing to good effect. Now these operations are extremely special-purpose. They are useful only because they have an extremely powerful and well-understood model, namely the mathematics of arithmetic. Note that in this architectural context the model (arithmetic) came first; the hardware is then built specifically to support this model to the greatest extent possible. It is much better to pick a few well-understood paradigms of widespread utility, parallelize them extremely well, and package them up, than to try to be able to parallelize any general program and do only a fair job of it. The Japanese effort might or might not be an example of this approach. Certainly first-order predicate logic is a reasonably well-understood paradigm of wide utility."

Dr. Davis of MIT asked, "Imagine that someone has hooked up a million processors in an N-cube; what would you—or anyone—do with it? A few very well-defined applications have been mentioned, but that's the whole point: as Drs. Fahlman and Steele have already said far better, it will do no good to invent new architectures without a very good idea of why it's a good design to use. I find it almost vacuous to hear claims of constructing massive parallelism without any good idea of how to use that to do something."

Frederick Hayes-Roth, of Teknowledge Inc. in Palo Alto, an expert-systems firm, said, "it seems that an outside-in approach to designing new equipment would constrain us to develop machines that support the kinds of data structures, knowledge representations, intermediate structures, and control methods that prove useful in application. Work to date in AI applications does not provide enough constraint to ensure a reasonably high rate of successful architectural advances. What seems needed to me is more data and more analysis. That would put the horse before the cart. I can plainly see that advances in cart technologies—wheels, spokes, bearings, axles—need not wait for the horse. I'd just prefer to see the cart makers serving the perceived need, and to see the need itself elucidated."

There is great merit in having a U.S. goal with a specific objective, such as beating the Soviets in chess with a computer in 1990

Jack Schwartz of NYU, a researcher in that university's Ultracomputer Project, contended that "with the possible exception of designs specialized for image processing . . . there is as yet no field in which parallel algorithms are well enough understood to be a wise bet." Instead, he suggested general-purpose parallel machines as the object of a first round of exploration. "The most important organizational issue now is to get a number of really powerful parallel machines manufactured and into the hands of applications-oriented groups, so that real experience can begin to accumulate on a large scale and efficiency questions can be understood." Dr. Shaw concurred with him almost immediately on the importance of getting parallel machines into use.

Dr. Wilson put things more strongly. "From my viewpoint as a user of parallel processing for number crunching," he said, "I find myself increasingly impatient with overall discussions of network topologies and the like. Meanwhile my colleague Stewart Pawley at the University of Edinburgh (Scotland) has got himself a 4000 processor distributed-array processor from International Computers Ltd. and has proceeded to demonstrate that he can get the full 4000-fold speedup on all the problems I am personally interested in." He went on to say that he had begun a project to develop a programming environment for a large square array, working with members of the computer science and other departments at Cornell.

Dr. Douglass of Los Alamos suggested another reason one might not want to give too much weight at the present time to sophisticated architectural and other research issues. "There may be a number of unsolved issues in basic research," he said, "but if, like the Japanese, we are talking about a major national thrust to move symbolic processing research into commercial applications in 10 years, then we will be lucky to integrate, experiment with, and incorporate just the areas of AI, data-base management, and parallel processing with which we have already gained some insight." ◆

THE OUTLOOK

COMPUTERTRENDS

The high-tech, knowledge-based society will spawn a counterbalancing concern about personal and humanistic values

Technology is fueling a fundamental transformation in society, one that will see society change from the industrial economy of the last hundred years or so to an information economy, in which added value accrues not from labor but from knowledge. In the United States signs of the transformation became clear in the mid-1950s, when, for the first time, white-collar workers in technical, managerial, and clerical positions outnumbered blue-collar workers.

In another important event of the same period, the Soviet Union launched the first man-made satellite, Sputnik, thereby ushering in the era that led to modern satellite communications. An ongoing convergence of computer and communications technologies is providing the framework for the information society that is taking shape. At the same time this convergence is controlling the pace of change by collapsing what can be called the "information float"—the amount of time that information spends in transit in a communications medium. Unlike the last societal transformation, which took almost a century to complete, this one, after less than 30 years, has probably passed the halfway point.

Manufacturing industries already declining

Evidence of the transformation abounds. The current U.S. economic recovery, for example, is not a classic recovery from a recession at all. What we are actually witnessing is a "sunrise" economy overtaking a "sunset" economy; the ascending economy includes industries that generate, process, and distribute information, while the declining economy comprises the various traditional manufacturing and heavy industries.

With the decline of the automobile and steel industries, the largest U.S. manufacturing industry is now newspaper publishing, which provides a conduit of information. The largest organization in the world, as measured by the number of employees, is the Bell System in the United States. It is an organization dedicated to speeding the flow of information. Electronics already has transformed banking into an industry in which money, checks, notes, and other forms of credit exist largely in electronic form; thus, money has become information in motion and is moved around the world at the speed of light. Other such examples are bound to arise in the years ahead. By the end of the decade, the worldwide electronics industry is expected to grow to a $400 billion industry, an order-of-magnitude growth in just a decade.

Of course, manufacturing will not be displaced in the informa-

John Naisbitt (author of Mega-trends*): World industrial leadership is shifting to Japan, but it is akin to winning a championship in a declining sport.*

Jamie Phillips

tion society. Instead it will yield to even more automation, just as agriculture yielded to mechanization. Agricultural data illustrates the trend: in 1800, 90 percent of the U.S. population produced the country's food; by 1980, only 3 percent of the population produced 120 percent of the country's food, with the surplus stored or exported.

Concern has been voiced in the United States and elsewhere over the possibility of world industrial leadership shifting from the United States to Japan. This is happening, but it is akin to an athlete winning a world championship in a declining sport.

The fact of the matter is that all of the advanced nations of the world are in various stages of deindustrialization. In Asia, for example, there has been over the years a gradual, but steady, flight of less technology-dependent industries out of Japan and into such "new Japans" as Korea, Singapore, and Hong Kong, where labor and manufacturing costs are lower. The trend is clear: this world of increasingly interdependent communities, under the influence of a collapsing global information float, is becoming a global economic village.

The human touch still needed

Applied technology, even in the information society, will not be rampant. Its growth and spread will be controlled according to a formula that I describe as high-tech–high-touch: the greater the technology that is designed and built into a product, the greater the expectation from users and consumers for a counterbalancing human touch. Without this balance, the technology is likely to be rejected out of hand, regardless of any obvious benefits, in a kind of high-technology backlash.

Telephone-answering machines are a case in point, particularly when a caller has no foreknowledge that a machine, rather

John Naisbitt   Naisbitt Group

than a human, will answer the call. The resulting high-tech dissonance is probably the reason why so many unintelligible messages are left recorded on those machines. In another case, more than one bank attempting to replace its human tellers with automated versions has had to reinstate some human contacts at the insistence of customers. On a broader level, computer-privacy issues erupted at about the time that computers were finding widespread applications.

High-tech dissonance can also be expected to limit severely the use of two emerging information-age conveniences: the video conference and the "electronic cottage." The video conference allows one to attend what would usually be out-of-office meetings and conferences without leaving the office. With the electronic cottage, one can conduct business without even leaving home. In both cases the very technology that enables the convenience also precludes the counterbalancing human touch.

From a U.S. societal perspective, group therapy, which led to the personal-growth and related movements, began to gain momentum at about the time television became the national pastime. Similarly, the country, on the eve of the information age, is now experiencing a revival in humanistic and spiritual values.

New behavioral patterns emerging

In an era of instantaneously shared information, the United States is evolving from a representative democracy to a participatory one, with individuals in states, cities, and local organizations rediscovering the ability to achieve results from the bottom up. A society based on short-term considerations and rewards, and dependent on institutional help, is giving way to one with longer-term priorities and greater confidence in in-

dividual self-reliance. In business and industry, organizational decision making is shifting from a rigid hierarchical structure to an informal network of individuals.

Many of the megatrends shaping U.S. society are manifestly evident in its electronics industry. This ever-expanding industry has benefited recently from the greatest entrepreneurial boom since the last societal transformation in the previous century. In fact, entrepreneurial booms characterize societal transformations. (A corresponding trend exists in established organizations, where the individuals are known as "intrapreneurs.") The electronics industry's technology-intensive companies are considered high-risk ventures, in part because of the relatively high startup capital required, and so they must rely on investors who are unusually willing to bet on the future. Once formed, the companies tend to avoid fixed organizational barriers in favor of flexible working arrangements that encourage information exchanges and problem solving.

The rapid pace of change guarantees societal transition pains. The United States, for one, confronts a knowledge-intensive era saddled with the first generation of high-school graduates to have fewer skills than their parents. These young people will be competing for jobs that will require ever-higher entry-level skills. Moreover, throughout the world the knowledge demands that will be brought to bear over the years on large segments of the employed will alter the concept of education from a process that ends at a high-school or college graduation ceremony to lifelong education and retraining.

In stable eras, everything has settled in its place and little can be leveraged. In times of transition between eras, individuals and institutions have extraordinary leverage and influence—if they can keep a clear vision of the road ahead. ◆

NEXT-GENERATION IMPACTS
Technology watchers discuss industrial and office automation, knowledge-based systems, computer privacy, and education

More and more technology watchers say that next-generation computing is likely to affect virtually all professional and personal endeavors. To find out which institutions and individuals might be changed and to what degree, *Spectrum* invited eight engineers and social scientists from industry, government, and academia to discuss projected impacts.

The round-table, which met last June 3 at the Carnegie–Mellon University in Pittsburgh, Pa., noted these positive effects, some of which have already begun to take hold:
• More efficient manufacturing through automation will continue, with drastic reduction in the stockpiling of raw materials and even in the size of factories envisioned.
• The automating of business decisions in banking and other industries will be more pervasive and sophisticated. Whereas machines now decide in banking whether a depositor is eligible to withdraw funds, machines in the future may routinely handle more complex decisions, such as granting a loan or a letter of credit.
• Use of expert systems will be so widespread that knowledge engineering will become another engineering specialty. Expert systems will give inexpensive advice on law, medicine, and other professional fields to people who could not otherwise afford to consult a human expert.

On the negative side, the panel suggested these effects:
• A tendency toward overdependence on expert computer systems that might stifle individual initiative. The result could be slavish conformity to systems that have become all-powerful decision makers.
• Changes in jobs and work habits that might limit opportunities for low-skilled workers.

Round-table participants

Frederick Hayes-Roth, executive vice president for technology, Teknowledge Inc., Palo Alto, Calif.
M. Granger Morgan, professor and head, Department of Engineering and Public Policy and professor of electrical engineering, Carnegie–Mellon University, Pittsburgh, Pa.
Allen Newell, professor of computer science, CMU.
Raj Reddy, director of the Robotics Institute, CMU.
Marvin Sirbu, principle research associate, Center for Policy Alternatives, Massachusetts Institute of Technology, Cambridge.
Fred Weingarten, project director, Office of Technology Assessment, U.S. Congress, Washington, D.C.
Joseph Weizenbaum, professor of computer science, MIT.
Langdon Winner, visiting associate professor of politics and technology, Crown College, University of California, Santa Cruz.

Fred Guterl Associate Editor

• Threats to the privacy of individuals through the use of advanced computers to correlate seemingly irrelevant information into electronic files.

• Possible harm in education, if educators and policy makers consider computers a panacea and ignore deeper problems in the educational system.

The panelists disagreed, however, on the degree to which technology might be responsible for some of those negative effects. Some felt that invasion of privacy and problems in education, for example, were not at all related to next-generation computing. Most of the panelists agreed, however, that some sort of national planning and legislation would be required in the next few years to control computer abuses.

The formidable job of predicting

Granger Morgan, chairman of the round-table meeting and head of the department of engineering and public policy at Carnegie–Mellon University, said that predicting how the next generation of computers would interact with the rest of society was a formidable task.

In many ways, the telephone is a small-scale version of what next-generation computing will likely be, he said, noting that "there has not yet, in my view, been a good history of the telephone, despite the fact that a number of first-rate people have worked on the problem. It is an indication of how incredibly difficult a task it is: technology tends to permeate society, and one cannot clearly separate the two."

The round-table participants agreed that next-generation computing technologies could be far more malleable than previous technologies and identified several areas that would be influenced. For industry and the professions, the panelists noted that computers would continue their foray into manufacturing and offices, increasing productivity and reducing dramatically the number of low-skilled workers needed. At the same time, they said, the computers will increase the productivity of people who have been so far largely unaffected by the new technology, such as professionals and managers. Expert systems are already turning up in some narrow professional areas, and computer networks are eliminating many bureaucratic transactions.

For society, the panelists said, communication with computers over improved networks and the rise of expert systems will alter the way individuals and organizations interact with one another. The codification of information on a large scale, they suggested, can be expected to continue to raise questions about the rights of the individual to privacy versus the right of society to enforce its laws.

Clyde Hare (photos)

Weizenbaum: Great masses of people will alternate between obeying the imperatives of machines and suckling at the breast of the great bitch entertainment.

Expert systems will also change the way knowledge is passed from one generation to the next, some panelists said, and possibly lead to "homogenized knowledge" if people grow to rely too heavily on expert systems.

Rise of 'microfactories' envisioned

Next-generation computing in manufacturing industries will lead, even more than today, to the "stockpiling of manufacturing capacity rather than finished goods," said Raj Reddy, director of the Robotics Institute at Carnegie–Mellon. In other words, factories will no longer need large inventories of materials and parts but rather will store in each factory information about producing the parts.

"As advanced technologies make it possible to custom-produce a part as needed," said Dr. Reddy, "we will be able to build factories manufacturing a wide variety of parts in any region of any country. Transportation problems would be eliminated or at least substantially reduced, thereby helping to lead to the design of microfactories, ones that would cost tens of

Morgan: A choice to delay or not to adopt these technologies is equivalent to accepting a significantly lower standard of living.

millions of dollars rather than hundreds of millions, and still be able to produce virtually any part economically."

With a large number of technologies, including advanced artificial intelligence, all of which Dr. Reddy believes can be developed from today's technology, unmanned factories are to be expected, but they will not be built overnight.

"We can already do a few things without paper, people, or stockpiled inventories," the Carnegie–Mellon research director said. But other things, such as "learning to assemble a small electric motor" by observing a human assembler, will probably take a number of decades, he said.

The loss of jobs predicted as a result of automation will thus occur slowly over a long time, Dr. Reddy said. "Assuming that we do, in fact, proceed with this technical agenda, we also need to proceed on a social agenda," he observed, "one that addresses the significant dislocations widely predicted as a by-product of this new technology."

Computers to help make office decisions

In offices, next-generation computing will continue to automate so-called paper transactions, but to a greater extent than today, according to Marvin Sirbu, principle research associate at the Center for Policy Alternatives at the Massachusetts Institute of Technology in Cambridge. Computers linked by networks virtually will eliminate intermediate paper transactions, he said.

"We are proceeding through a succession of models of what office automation might be," said Dr. Sirbu. "The term 'office automation,' as coined in the 1950s, referred to using a computer for processing payrolls.

"We have gone past that now and think of it in terms of the paperless office: everything we used to do on paper, we will do electronically. We will, for example, pass forms around electronically. But even this view is beginning to be superseded by talk of functional automation, where the computer is seen as either doing a lot of work in formulating information so that a human being can make a decision or even, in fact, making a decision about the routine kinds of information-based processes."

In the insurance industry today, computers check what a claims adjuster enters on an electronic form, determine if the client meets all the proper constraints, and authorize a payment. In banking, a customer goes to an electronic teller to withdraw money, and the computer decides if enough money is in the person's account, whether he has been identified properly, and whether cash should be dispensed. It then dispenses the cash without direct supervision though bank employees sometimes check the transaction at a later date.

Citibank in New York recently automated its processing of letters of credit. "What used to be a series of steps—most of which were manual and involved several persons—was automated and turned over to a single individual who handled the entire transaction," Dr. Sirbu noted. "Now the individual deals with the customer over the telephone, updates data bases through a single terminal, and continues overseeing the operation until a letter is sent to the customer."

Hayes-Roth: Expert systems have introduced a new way of preserving knowledge.

Automation offers enormous gains in office productivity. Dr. Sirbu said, "If I write a purchase order in my company, I write it out on paper and send it to the purchasing department. They key it into the computer, which then spits out a paper purchase order." The purchase order, in turn, might be sent to another company's order-processing department and keyed into its computer to produce an invoice. "There may be four or five transfor-

The computer revolution: a perspective

Next-generation computing is an evolutionary rather than a revolutionary development, which neither detracts from its importance nor diminishes the technological accomplishments and social adjustments required to integrate the new systems into the fabric of society.

The concepts involved in next-generation computing, such as voice digitization and synthesis and pattern analysis and recognition, are logical extensions of computer fundamentals made practical by improvements and innovations in many basic and supporting technologies. As technological progress makes such extensions cost-effective, they will be implemented incrementally and most likely will not constitute a major discontinuity from developments of the past. This is consistent with the change from an analog to a digital world, exemplified by communications, mechanized activities in general, and consumer products and office automation, which has been ongoing for 30 years.

With regard to research in artificial intelligence, it covers mainly three areas: (1) the work directed toward establishing the foundation of a new science dedicated to exploring and establishing methods, approaches, and mechanisms underlying the thinking process; (2) a heuristic approach to knowledge computing; and (3) the applications of the expert-system concept to diverse but narrow fields.

Artificial intelligence can mean any one of the above or all three. Today much energy is devoted to expert systems, and a moderate amount to heuristic computing, but practically no scientific foundation has emerged. Ironically, this initially was the *raison d'être* of much of the research and enthusiasm for the field. Expert systems will be a powerful tool, providing new insight and benefits, but to market it under the label of artificial intelligence is an overstatement.

The distinction between information and knowledge, as made in discussions about next-generation computing, raises an intriguing question: Are "knowledge systems" truly a quantum leap from what computers have been doing all along? Computers and information systems, besides doing what they were designed to do, were a well-structured— sometimes too well-structured—environment for accom-

plishing a task. This latter function is often overlooked.

Expert systems do something similar: they are a record of an accumulated experience base. The programs lead the user in a logical way through many alternatives that he otherwise would have to deal with himself. Combining the know-how to solve a problem with accumulated data and experience into a computer program is a major step forward, but the claim that new knowledge is being created must be questioned. Know-how is not knowledge and training is not education no matter how important know-how and training are for an individual and society.

Continuing education and the structure of jobs in the future are important issues, but they too have not sprung up overnight. The notion of continuing education—the frequent updating of knowledge—is second nature for some professions. Medical doctors know this and engineers are learning that it applies to their profession as well. Electrical engineers have experienced the rapid transition from vacuum tubes to transistors, to integrated circuits, and now to very large-scale integration, with all the accompanying changes in design approaches and in the tools used. The task of the unskilled entry-level worker, at the same time, is becoming more demanding, broader, and less permanent. They, too, need training and retraining, as do professionals, managers, and engineers.

The application of computers to entertainment as a teaching vehicle is important, but its importance should not be overestimated. Computer literacy for everybody is a goal that needs to be stressed and should concern us greatly, and the approaches to accomplish it are many. However, it would be sad if we were to pursue a mindless dependence on entertainment, or to pursue an industrial goal where the entertainment industry will be the dominating sector, as some suggest. It is one thing to use computer games as a means to an end; it's another to see them as the end itself.

—Erich Bloch
Vice President
Technical Personnel Development
IBM Corp.

Technology and society: a complex marriage

Computers do not by themselves alter social relationships because they do not exist in a vacuum. The best empirical studies of computer-based decision systems, for instance, repeatedly conclude that the social milieu in which a technology is employed is as important as the capabilities of the technology. To arrive at useful, interesting generalizations about the impacts of computing on social life in the United States or elsewhere, or about the long-term impact of expert systems on all organizations with expert human staffs, is virtually an impossible task. What is needed is a more analytical approach to a more modest problem.

If one were to study, say, the social impacts of next-generation computing on specialists in medical decision making in urban medical centers in the United States, the problem could be approached more scientifically. A study group can produce useful inferences only if it has clear specifications for the technology and the social context in which it is adopted and adapted.

The use of cars in Southern California offers an instructive analogy. Almost all adults own their own cars, which can be driven at 80 miles per hour. However, it would be a mistake to infer that most Southern Californians commute to and from work at 80 mph, even though it is technologically possible. Just as understanding social life in Southern California is difficult from an automobile engineer's point of view, understanding the social impacts of next-generation computers is almost impossible unless analytical inquiry is made.

New technologies may have problematic social dimensions when they are woven deeply into the fabric of daily life. Thus, many of the changes in social relations that will accrue from next-generation machines and expert systems will depend upon how these technologies are integrated into the ongoing social life.

Next-generation machines are unlikely to occupy a large niche for at least 20 years, perhaps 40. Like today's expert systems, which are used by those with substantial formalized expertise, such as doctors, geologists, geneticists, and engineers, next-generation computing will offer little to the lay public—not because it does not need or desire expertise in the form of medical care, legal assistance, tax advice, and so on. Rather, the poor, the working class, and middle-income people will have little discretionary income to spend on these services, automated or not. During the next 20 years, wealthy organizations will be most able to afford the kinds of expert systems that depend upon fifth-generation machines. For most people, the benefits will trickle down.

It is critical to understand the social dimensions of the world we live in and the roles computing is coming to play, as well as the nature of our social choices. Since we can choose, it makes sense to shape major social choices in light of humanistic values. It is also critical not to overstate the contributions of otherwise interesting technologies. Improved literacy does not depend upon better computers, expert systems do not always require next-generation architectures, and computer-based systems do not always yield better decisions. The best empirical studies indicate that computer-based decision systems often play modest roles in organizational choice. Decision support systems are often persuasion-support systems and computer-based modeling is often used for legitimacy as well as insight. Computer scientists should work to ensure that claims made about the social values of computer-based technologies are accurate and reasonable.

From a social perspective, expert systems have much in common with mathematical models, and the credibility of both have often been exaggerated. If modeling computers are used by an unsophisticated cadre of technical workers, intellectual insight is gained at the expense of intuition. Expert systems allow organizations to place even less sophisticated staff in key analytical positions. Working knowledge does not come easily from an algorithm that is used uncritically under varying conditions.

The impacts of computing in a world where equipment comes first differ considerably from the impacts of the same equipment in a world where nuanced human sensitivities shape relatively unrushed technical developments. I hope the world we develop around expert systems does not loosely mirror that of Southern California, where cars and planning for physical load use came first and the quality of life for most residents was a hope or an afterthought.

—Rob Kling
Professor of Information
and Computer Science
University of California, Irvine

mations that take place between electronic and paper forms,'' which eventually should be made into one continuous electronic process, Dr. Sirbu said.

Automating transactions on the scale envisioned by Dr. Sirbu requires that system designers gain a better understanding of how companies conduct their business. They must know the procedures well enough to figure out what rules to embed for making decisions along the way, he said, and to design standard ways of exchanging information among different organizations within a company or among different companies.

The choice, Dr. Sirbu added, is between finding standard ways of exchanging information and building machines smart enough to interpret data better than they do now. For some particular applications, these problems have been solved, he observed. Some grocery chains, for instance, order goods via a computer from a warehouse. Independent agents and underwriters in the insurance business have hired IBM Corp. to build a value-added network to make each party's communications with the other more intelligible, according to Dr. Sirbu.

Expert systems will expand slowly

Expert systems constitute a major component of the technologies of next-generation computing. They are used in cases where expertise on a narrow subject or problem is needed.

Oil companies, for instance, want to employ expert systems on drilling rigs, because human experts are in short supply and delays in receiving expert guidance can cost tens of millions of dollars annually in drilling downtime.

Expert systems gained early success in chemistry and medicine because "a great deal of effort had been spent trying to write down the best-known ways to solve problems, and so there was a running start at the knowledge-engineering process," explained Frederick Hayes-Roth, executive vice president for technology, Teknowledge Inc., Palo Alto, Calif. "Also, nearly all of the knowledge in those areas is symbolic, and that's a good fit to what the technology can accommodate.

"It's already the case that one system, Internist, does as well in diagnosis as the average internal-medicine practitioner. There are places in the world where one does not have access to an average practitioner of internal medicine and I would argue that people would be better off if they had access to an artificial expert than none at all.

"Similarly, finance and accounting are professions for which concrete expertise is not generally available to the average person. One could argue that people would be better off with an artificial advisor than none at all. However, aspects of each of those professions tend to be fuzzy, intuitive, and essentially ill defined, and so do not lend themselves perfectly to expert-system applications," Dr. Hayes-Roth continued. Also beyond the capability of present technology is building a good advisor in legal matters.

Expert systems accumulate knowledge the way an apprentice worker would now. For example, "physicists pride themselves on boiling down to the essence all that is known about the fundamental laws of the universe," he said. "A good physicist recognizes when a new problem is very much like an old one and can remember in detail the way general rules had to be specialized to fit the earlier situation."

" So people have prided themselves, in general, on boiling out all that messy stuff that it actually takes to make one proficient in solving problems," he pointed out. "But except through apprenticeship, people have not bothered to attempt a direct transfer of that proficiency. With knowledge-based systems, it is possible to capture know-how and apply it as needed."

What is the growth rate for knowledge-based systems? "I think that it will not be strange to look back 20 or so years from now," Dr. Hayes-Roth said, "and see in every major organization a large number of people who are doing what we today call knowledge engineering. There may even be knowledge-engineering departments, if there are any departments at all, and as much as 30 percent of the potential applications will have been implemented."

The pluses and minuses of expert systems

By interpreting information to a greater extent than computer programs now do, expert systems promise to free people from concentration on narrow slices of knowledge and allow them to consider problems broadly. Some round-table participants, however, expressed concern that reliance on expert systems for so-called knowledge processing might lead to overdependence on computers. What might happen if artificial advisors were widely used throughout an entire profession?

Speculating on such questions, Dr. Morgan drew an analogy between computers and ecological systems. "My friends who are ecologists talk about resiliency in systems arising from diversity. They get alarmed when you start talking about producing forests where all of the trees are genetically identical," he said, pointing out that expert systems could introduce the same kind of uniformity. An ecological system exhibits remarkable resiliency when there are many different kinds of plants and animals. Likewise, knowledge can be adapted more easily to different situations when many different people rather than a program contribute to solving a problem.

Knowledge-based systems introduce new ways of preserving

Reddy: We will stockpile manufacturing capacity rather than finished goods.

Newell: Will we see societal effects from next-generation computing or from advances in the broader field of general computing?

expertise. In the past, an apprentice acquired knowledge about a profession from a master. Then he became a master and passed the knowledge on before he died. "The ecological advantage of such a system," said Dr. Hayes-Roth, "was that each new generation would grow up in a new social context. Refreshing itself as it evolved, the next generation would modify and adapt itself to its new surroundings."

A similar concern was voiced by Joseph Weizenbaum, professor of computer science at the Massachusetts Institute of Technology. "Although some people believe that the computer will introduce variety because it's such a flexible tool," he said, "most examples I can think of illustrate that it introduces uniformity and homogeneity." The widespread use of only one or a few expert systems for advice on a certain subject could lead to homogeneity, he indicated.

A current example of such a situation is the availability of data bases on timesharing networks. Expert systems rely on data bases, using them to examine huge amounts of information quickly. Dr. Weizenbaum believes that at present in many professions only a few data bases are used by many practitioners. In law, for example, the Lexis data base is widely used.

"It's hard for me to see," Dr. Weizenbaum said, "how we can avoid finding, one day, that every law office has access to Lexis. It will become the source for lawyers to look up their law. It will be the law. But what happens when a particular case gets misfiled, or just isn't in the data banks? What happens to the universe of old cases that were never machine-encoded?"

Less opportunity for low-skilled workers

With knowledge-based computers taking on higher levels of decision making in factories and offices, the opportunities for low-skilled jobs will decrease. This process of automating has many stages, Dr. Sirbu noted. At first, jobs become dull and tedious because "people are translating information from paper to electronic form or monitoring every transaction when it appears on a screen. It turns out to be dull because it's repetitive, like assembly-line work."

At later stages in the process, jobs become more supervisory and thus more interesting. In a factory, a person takes sole control of an automated machine by monitoring, repairing, and perhaps changing its program, Dr. Sirbu said.

The interesting jobs, however, will also tend to require greater worker skills. The use even today of computers for automation "implies that the level of skill and knowledge for an entry-level position is considerably higher than it previously was," Dr. Morgan said. Retraining for new jobs will have to become part of continuing education, he pointed out.

For both the long and short terms, the duration of many jobs

Winner: Are we building an electronic Panopticon, where surveillance will become a way of life?

may be short. "Different new jobs are cropping up only to disappear a few years down the road," noted Fred Weingarten, a project director at the Office of Technology Assessment in Washington, D.C. He predicted that quality checkers at semiconductor companies—people who "sit and look through microscopes, visually inspecting integrated circuits"—would soon be displaced by robots. "These people are learning skills for a category of employment that has a lifetime of only about 10 years," he said.

Such short durations mean that "the number of cycles for retraining and relearning new kinds of jobs that people are going to have to go through in a lifetime will become significant," according to Dr. Sirbu.

Even computer programmers may find themselves out of work. Dr. Hayes-Roth said he would not be surprised to find out that every programmer and every software engineer is made irrelevant by next-generation technology.

Individual privacy issue raised

Computer systems can collect vast amounts of information about a person's daily transactions; systems employing artificial intelligence will be able to do even more with that information. Today many people consider third-party use of such information as credit records and car-rental records an invasion of privacy. The cross-correlating of information stored in computers to target tax evaders or welfare cheats, for example, has raised anew the issue of the rights of society to enforce laws versus the right of the individual to privacy.

Langdon Winner, professor of politics and technology at the University of California in Santa Cruz, noted that people tend to think about the social problems of computerized data bases in very narrow terms. They worry about possible invasions of their privacy but overlook the more serious threat to public freedom. "People often say they don't need to worry about the information about them in computers because they are not doing anything that anyone would want to watch. It's precisely that attitude that I find troubling," he said.

Dr. Winner likened the scenario of everyone's transactions being collected in one large data base to the model of a prison, the Panopticon, proposed by nineteenth-century philosopher Jeremy Bentham. It was to be a circular building, several stories high, with a tower in the center. A key feature of the design was that people in its rooms could not see each other, but a guard in the center could gaze into every cell. "Such an architecture provides a powerful means of social control. A person feels he's being watched every minute of the day. The structure eliminates misbehavior and induces total compliance," he said.

"It appears that we may now be building an electronic Panopticon," Dr. Winner went on, "a system of seemingly benign electronic data gathering that creates conditions of universal surveillance. The danger here extends beyond the private sphere to affect the political freedoms upon which our privacy depends. Unless we take steps to prevent it, we could see a society filled with all-seeing data banks used to monitor an increasingly compliant, passive populace no longer willing to risk activities supposedly protected by civil liberties."

The maturation of speech-recognition technology was seen as one element in bringing about the electronic Panopticon. With advanced techniques, computers could pluck out and recognize certain key phrases from vast streams of irrelevant telephone conversations, conceivably listening in on every telephone conversation.

"People are still protected by the complexity of the data," said Dr. Weingarten. "What is now an impossible task—to listen in to all these conversations—might become feasible with this technology."

The round-table participants considered whether encryption could protect conversations from such surveillance. "Encryption technology will become inexpensive enough to use well before speech-recognition technology enables telephone conversations to be monitored by computer," Dr. Reddy noted. But having technology available does not necessarily mean that it will be used, Dr. Morgan argued: "We don't have a great track record in dealing with such situations, so though I certainly agree that such problems are largely amenable to technological fixes relatively inexpensively, I am a little less persuaded that it's a total red herring."

The danger is not so much technological as psychological, Dr. Weizenbaum observed. "If I were traveling and entered a country where they told me, 'Here they listen to all telephone conversations, but we have technical gadgets to confound them,' I would not feel very comfortable," he said. "This is what is known as the chilling effect, where people don't say certain things, in order to keep their purity. We are marching very rapidly in this direction."

The panelists disagreed on whether the potential social problems discussed at the meeting would be caused by technology. Dr. Hayes-Roth said he saw a "spurious correlation" between the two. Bureaucracies can be abusive not because of technology, he said, but because they are bad bureaucracies. Invasion of privacy can occur now, without elaborate information networks or knowledge-based systems, Dr. Reddy noted; the problem is not inherent in any technology.

"The only way to solve these problems is by social legislation, not by worrying about technological growth," he said.

Split over role in education

There was some disagreement over the role that computers would play in education. Today computer-education software forces the student to take a passive role; with artificial-intelligence techniques the students will be able to ask the computer questions, using their curiosity rather than a rigid menu as a guide. The student will be able to receive from the computer explanations for how problems are solved and for how the computer answers questions. New types of learning will present themselves as such technologies as video disks become widely available.

Home-entertainment companies are going to provide personal growth opportunities for whatever direction is called for, in the opinion of Dr. Hayes-Roth. Breakthroughs will reduce the entry costs for writing interesting and useful course programs.

Dr. Weizenbaum doubted the personal computer would prove useful in education. "I think the home computer is going to follow the example of the home movie camera. Many people bought very expensive home movie cameras, thinking that with a good camera they could make good movies. What they forgot is that in order to make good movies, one has to have an idea."

Dr. Weizenbaum fears that people will look unrealistically to computers to solve problems in the educational system. When television was introduced, he noted, educators hailed it as providing opportunity for education and enrichment; in fact, he said, it turned out to be largely an entertainment vehicle.

Present problems in education stem from social conditions, such as violence in the schools, poverty, and other ills, Dr. Weizenbaum said, and the computer may be more a problem than a cure if it distracts people from these basic problems.

Technology advances called a stampede

The technological advances that will come from the next generation of computers seems to be taking the form of a stampede, in the words of Dr. Winner. One facet of that stampede will come from the entertainment industry, according to Dr. Hayes-Roth, as labor-intensive activities become increasingly scarce. "We may end up with entertainment as the biggest industry of all," he said.

Much of the momentum for technological developments over the next 10 years is evident in two current trends, Dr. Hayes-Roth said. The first is that new people have begun to attain economic rewards on a regular basis from exploiting knowledge-based technology. "Companies that want to do it now can take on problems that are not difficult to define and that can make them $10 million to $100 million over a short period of time."

"Second, industries and governments have begun to recognize this, and they are betting with real money that this technology is going to make dramatic economic differences for them. That says to me that the next 10 years will be very competitive ones, and this technology is probably going to get capitalized and developed far more quickly than others we have seen," he said.

Dr. Weizenbaum offered his view of the effects of the computing: "The most immediate effect will be a general loss of human skills, followed closely by a decreasingly comprehensible world. Physics, for example, no longer gives us anything we can comprehend with our senses. It describes a world none of us can see or inhabit, in which we have to believe the authority of an anonymous science.

"I see an increasingly homogeneous and therefore very dull world, and a further stratification of society, most particularly of

Sirbu: Although 'office automation' now connotes the paperless office, it is coming to mean 'functional automation,' with computers making routine decisions.

Weingarten: Different new jobs are cropping up only to disappear a few years down the road.

Western society. We will have an information society populated by those whose lives are characterized by their plastic machine-readable cards. As time goes by, people's poverty of inner resources will be rendered invisible by the humanly irrelevant power of their plastic cards. Great masses of people will live out their lives alternating between obeying the imperatives of machines at their work and in their free time, suckling at the breast of the great bitch entertainment. Unless, of course, we want a better world."

The stampede also will require that some important decisions be made by governments over the next decade, several panelists said. The need for retraining workers will have to be a concern of public policy. "Our present crisis in education will in the future be compounded by the fact that we are going to be faced with fewer and fewer entry-level or low-skilled jobs," said Dr. Morgan.

Public policy intervention needed

Major policy decisions will have to be made, in Dr. Morgan's view: "If we want to maintain the economic quality of life we have enjoyed for the last decade or two in this country, we must adopt a set of the technologies we have been talking about. A choice to delay substantially or not to adopt is equivalent to accepting a significantly lower economic standard of living. We neither are likely to be able to nor should we want to adopt those technologies without simultaneously ensuring that some of the dislocations of manpower and other social impacts are properly thought about and dealt with ahead of time.

"Adopting the technology and dealing in a humane and appropriate way with the human and other social effects are not likely to occur without some sort of public-policy intervention. I do not necessarily mean single centralized Government programs. But we need something that transcends simple individual-level market choices."

A prominent public-policy issue in the next few decades will be how to train and retrain people to maintain a level of skill high enough to find jobs, Dr. Morgan continued. "What I see as a real danger is society becoming more stratified as low-level entry jobs become scarcer. In terms of maintaining ourselves as a democracy, I just don't see that we can afford to allow that kind of stratification to continue.

"Many of the situations we face are essentially matters of choice—that is, the technology has rather less imperatives for political, social, and other organizational implications than some past technologies. Some form of public policy intervention and some broad public discussion of the options and choices that ought to be made will be necessary." ◆

TO PROBE FURTHER

THE QUEST

A lively discussion of the economic and technical issues behind the international fifth-generation quest is provided by *The Fifth Generation*, by Edward Feigenbaum and Pamela McCorduck, Addison-Wesley, Reading, Mass., 1983. [A review of the book appears in the November 1983 issue of *Spectrum*, p. 16].

A textbook treatment of very large-scale integration systems and foundry methodology is found in *Introduction to VLSI Systems* by Carver Mead and Lynn Conway, Addison-Wesley, Reading, Mass., 1980.

New applications, services, and capabilities

A good source for applications of robotics and industrial automation is the Annual International Symposium on Industrial Robots. Their fourteenth symposium will be next October in Gothenburg, Sweden; contact the public relations department of the Society of Manufacturing Engineers to obtain information.

See NASA Conference Publication 2255, "Advanced Automation for Space Missions," for a fascinating and detailed description of possible space applications of next-generation computing.

Many applications of today's speech-processing technology are described in the proceedings of the '83 Voice Data Entry Systems Applications Conference, available from the American Voice Input/Output Society (Avios), P.O. Box 11, 307A, Palo Alto, Calif. 94306.

The proceedings of the Applied Natural Language Processing Conference, sponsored by the Association for Computational Linguistics and the Naval Research Laboratory in February 1983, discuss applications of natural-language processing. Several applications of next-generation computing to office automation are described in the 1982 proceedings of the Office Automation Conference, sponsored by the American Federation of Information Processing Societies, available from Afips Press, P.O. Box 9657, 1815 N. Lynn St., Suite 800, Arlington, Va. 22209.

Japan

A thorough background on the Japanese approach to science and technology can be found in the special issue of *IEEE Spectrum* called "Electrotechnology in Japan Today," September 1977.

A more recent progress report is "A Look at Japan's Development of Software Engineering Technology," by K.H. Kim, *Computer*, May 1983, pp. 26–37.

Japan's ICOT publishes two English-language journals describing current research: *ICOT Journal*, an internal magazine that can be ordered by writing to ICOT Research Center, Mita Kokusai Bldg. 21F, 4-28 Mita 1-Chrome, Minato-Ku, Tokyo 103, Japan; and *New Generation Computing*, a scientific journal available from Springer-Verlag, 175 Fifth Ave., New York, N.Y. 10010.

Proceedings of the original fifth-generation conference in Japan are available from North-Holland Publishers, 52 Vanderbilt Ave., New York, N.Y. 10017.

United States

An overview of the proliferation of joint ventures in microelectronics and computers in the United States appears in the proceedings of the 1983 University/Government/Industry Microelectronics Symposium held last May at Texas A&M University, College Station. Copies can be ordered from the Order Dept., IEEE, 445 Hoes Lane, Piscataway, N.J. 08854.

Europe

Information on Esprit, the European joint venture in microelectronics and computers, is available from the Commission of European Communities, 200 Rue de la Loi, B 1049, Brussels, Belgium. Ask for the brochure, "Esprit for Europe's Future."

The British response to Japan's announcement of a fifth-generation computer project is reviewed in "The Race for the Thinking Machine," by Peter Marsh, *New Scientist*, July 8, 1982, pp. 85–87; "Britain Rises to Japan's Computer Challenge," by David Dickson, *Science*, May 20, 1983, pp. 799–800; and "U.K. Enters Supercomputer Fray," by David Fishlock, *Defense Week*, Aug. 1, 1983, pp. 10–14.

THE CHALLENGES

Artificial intelligence

The Handbook of Artificial Intelligence by Edward Feigenbaum and Avron Barr, William Kaufman Co., Los Altos, Calif., offers a comprehensive survey of the field.

Proceedings from the American Association for Artificial Intelligence are available from AAAI, 445 Burgess, Menlo Park, Calif. 94025.

Expert systems

Spectrum has published two articles on expert systems: "Expert systems: limited but powerful," William B. Gevarter, see p. 192; and "An electronic advisor/companion," Robert Bernhard, see p. 199.

Building Expert Systems, by Frederick Hayes-Roth, Don Waterman, and Doug Lenat, Addison-Wesley, Reading, Mass., 1983, gives a detailed technical study of the field.

Speech recognition

Spectrum published a three-part report on speech recognition called "Words into action," see p. 204.

A review of commercially available devices was offered by *Spectrum* with "Speech recognition: turning theory to practice," by G. Doddington and T.B. Schalk, see p. 212.

Speech Recognition is a collection of papers presented at the 1974 International Conference on Speech Recognition, Pittsburgh, Pa., edited by D.R. Reddy, Academic Press, New York.

Automatic Speech and Speaker Recognition offers technical papers from various journals, edited by N.R. Dixon and T.B. Martin, IEEE Press, New York.

Trends in Speech Recognition, edited by W.A. Lea and published by Prentice-Hall Inc., Englewood Cliffs, N.J., offers tutorials in the field.

Production and Perception of Fluent Speech, edited by R.A. Cole and published by Lawrence Erlbaum Associates, summarizes research on how humans speak and listen.

The Proceedings of the IEEE International Conference on Acoustics, Speech, and Signal Processing from 1976 through 1983 also offers a variety of technical papers in the field of speech recognition.

Computer vision

Recent interview papers on computer vision include *Spectrum*'s "Computer that see," by Eric Lerner, see p. 219; and "Pattern recognition: a review," by David Casasent, see p. 225; also "Computational Approach to Image Understanding," by Michael Brady, in *ACM Computing Surveys*, Vol. 14, no. 1, pp. 3–71, 1983; "Survey of Model-Based Image Analysis Systems," by Thomas Binford in *Robotics Research*, Vol. 1, no. 1, pp. 18–64, 1982; "Geometric Aspects of Interpreting Images as a Three-Dimensional Scene," by Takeo Kanade in *Proceedings of the IEEE*, Vol. 71, no. 7, pp. 789–802, 1983; and "Computer Vision Techniques for Industrial Applications and Robot Control," by

Rafael Gonzalez and Reza Safabkhsh, *Computer*, Vol. 15, no. 12, pp. 17–31.

A recent textbook on the subject is *Computer Vision*, by Dana Ballard and Chris Brown, Prentice-Hall Inc., Englewood Cliffs, N.J.

The Acronym artificial-vision system is described in "Symbolic Reasoning among 3-D Models and 2-D Images," by Rodney Brooks, *Artificial Intelligence*, Vol. 17, pp. 285–349, 1981.

The 3-D Mosaic system is presented in "Incremental Analysis of a Three-Dimensional Scene Model from Images," by Marty Herman, Takeo Kanade, and Shigeru Kuroe, Carnegie–Mellon University Computer Science Department, Technical Report CMU-CS-82-139 on power analysis and machine intelligence (to appear in *IEEE Transactions PAMI*), Pittsburgh, Pa.

The outdoor scene-analysis system is fully described in Yuichi Ohta's thesis, "A Region-Oriented Image Analysis System by Computer," Kyoto University, Japan, 1980.

Software

Spectrum offers the following articles on software related to artificial intelligence: "Function-level computing," by John Backus, see p. 231; "Automating programming," by Eric Lerner, see p. 237; "Programming for nonprogrammers," by Eric Lerner, see p. 243; and "Software design: breaking the bottleneck," Alan Graham, see p. 248.

See also papers from the IEEE Compcon and Compsac conferences, both sponsored by the Computer Society.

Computer architecture

An overview of design issues in large-scale computers is given in *Spectrum*'s "Computing at the speed limit," by Robert Bernhard, see p. 256.

For a more complete description of the Mago machine see "A Network of Microprocessors to Execute Reduction Languages," parts 1 and 2, *International Journal of Computer and Information Sciences*, October and December 1979, pp. 349–85 and pp. 435–71, respectively.

The most current report on the Manchester data-flow machine, authored by John Gurd and Ian Watson, will be published in the proceedings of the Ifips 1983 conference held in Paris in September 1983. The proceedings will be available from North-Holland Publishers, 52 Vanderbilt Ave., New York, N.Y. 10017.

Details of the non–Von Neumann machine can be found in a Columbia University (New York) computer science department technical report by David Shaw entitled, "A Non–Von Super-computer," 1982.

Very large-scale integration

The progress of VLSI technology is covered in a variety of *Spectrum* articles: "More hardware means less software," by Robert Bernhard, see p. 268; "Automating chip layout," by Stephen Trimberger, see p. 286; "Fast electron-beam lithography," by John C. Eidson, see p. 294; "X-ray lithography breaks the submicrometer barrier," by Martin P. Lepselter, see p. 299; "Rethinking the 256-kb RAM," by Robert Bernhard, see p. 303; and "VLSI with a vengeance," by Larry W. Sumney, see p. 276.

See also papers from the IEEE International Solid-State Circuits Conference and the International Electron Devices meeting, available through the IEEE Electron Devices Society.

Networking

Networking is discussed in two recent *Spectrum* articles: "Telephone nets go digital," by Irwin Dorros, see p. 309; and "Local area nets: a pair of standards," by Maris Graube, see p. 315.

The September 1983 issue of *IEEE Computer* magazine was also devoted to computer networking.

Supercomputers

Recent advances and problems in supercomputer technology are covered in these *Spectrum* articles: " 'Superpower' computers," by Robert Sugarman, see p. 320; "Beyond the super-computer," by David H. Schaefer and James R. Fischer, see p. 327; and "The limits to simulation " by Robert Sugarman and Paul Wallich, see p. 333.

See also papers from the IEEE International Conference on Parallel Processing sponsored by the Computer Society, and releases of the IEEE Ad Hoc Committee on Super Scientific Computers.

THE OUTLOOK

To follow up on the round-table and megatrends discussions of the impact of computers and related technologies on society, the reader can consult the following recent books.

Megatrends, by John Naisbitt, Warner Books, New York, 1982, outlines 10 major trends the author identified in U.S. society after analyzing newspapers to determine what the public is doing and reading.

The Computer State, by David Burnham, Random House, New York, 1983, recounts the author's investigation into the use of computers in government and industry.

Other notable books are: *Technologies of Freedom*, by Ithiel de Sola Pool, Harvard University Press, Cambridge, Mass., 1983; *Computer Power and Human Reason*, by Joseph Weizenbaum, W.H. Freeman, San Francisco, Calif., 1976; *Computers and Politics*, by James Danziger, William Dutton, Rob Kling, and Kenneth Cramer, Columbia University Press, New York, 1981; *The Computerization of Society*, by Simon Nora and Alain Minc, MIT Press, Cambridge, Mass., 1980; *Autonomous Technology*, by Langdon Winner, MIT Press, Cambridge, Mass., 1977; and *The Coming of Post-Industrial Society*, by Daniel Bell, Basic Books, New York, 1982.

The proceedings of a conference on the philosophy of technology, held by the Polytechnic Institute of New York in September 1983, can be obtained by writing Carl Mitchum, Humanities Department, Polytechnic Institute of New York, 333 Jay St., Brooklyn, N.Y. 11201; telephone 212-643-8833.

The *Spectrum* special issue on data-driven automation, published in May 1983, included "An unanswered question: automation's effect on society," by Fred Guterl, pp. 89–92. ◆

Acknowledgements

Sources for spot photographs are the Department of Computer Science, University of Rochester, page 4; the Center for Integrated Electronics, Rensselaer Polytechnic Institute, page 45; and the Department of Computer Science, University of Rochester, page 82.

The table on page 5 was prepared with the assistance of Paul Cerruzzi, professor of history, Clemson University.

Sources for the table on European research efforts, beginning on page 33, are the Commission of the European Communities, Brussels; the embassies of France and Great Britain in Washington, D.C.; and the Federal Ministry for Research and Technology in Bonn, West Germany, among others. Information on French research activities was also compiled by Francoise Harrois-Monin, a member of the editorial staff of *Science & Vie*, Excelsior Publications SA, Paris.

In addition to the expert authors of the various articles in this issue, many reviewers and sources contributed to its success. Among this group are two members of the editorial board—Lynn Conway and M. Granger Morgan; and Oscar Garcia and other members of the IEEE Computer Society. Citing these individuals does not imply that they endorse any viewpoint expressed.

ABOUT THE AUTHORS

Erich Bloch (F) is vice president of technical personnel development at IBM Corp., Armonk, N.Y., and chairman of the Semiconductor Research Cooperative. He received his education in electrical engineering at the Federal Polytechnic Institute of Zurich in Switzerland and a BSEE degree from the University of Buffalo, N.Y.

Robert S. Cooper heads the Defense Advanced Research Projects Agency. He received a Ph.D. from the Massachusetts Institute of Technology, an MSEE degree from Ohio State University, and a BSEE from the University of Iowa. He has previously held posts as director of NASA's Goddard Space Flight Center and as division director at MIT's Lincoln Laboratory.

A.L. Davis coordinates the AI Architecture Group at the Fairchild Laboratory for Artificial Intelligence Research in Palo Alto, Calif. He earned the Ph.D. degree in computer science in 1972 from the University of Utah and a BSEE degree from the Massachusetts Institute of Technology.

Robert J. Douglass (M) leads a research team investigating artificial intelligence and parallel processing at the Los Alamos National Laboratory in Los Alamos, N.M. After receiving a BSEE degree from Princeton University, he earned M.S. and Ph.D. degrees in computer science from the University of Wisconsin.

Richard B. Fair (SM) holds dual appointments as professor of electrical engineering at Duke University, Raleigh-Durham, N.C., and as vice president of research program management at the Microelectronics Center of North Carolina. He received his Ph.D. from Duke in 1969.

Edward A. Feigenbaum is a coprincipal investigator at the Heuristic Programming Project at Stanford University, where he is professor of computer science. He received his degrees from the Carnegie Institute of Technology, culminating in a Ph.D. from the Graduate School of Industrial Application there in 1959.

Frederick Hayes-Roth (M) is vice president at Teknowledge Inc. in Palo Alto, Calif. He was former director of the AI research program at the Rand Corp. in Santa Monica, Calif. Dr. Hayes-Roth received his Ph.D. degree in 1974 from the University of Michigan after earning a master's degree at Michigan and doing undergraduate work at Harvard University and the Massachusetts Institute of Technology.

Robert E. Kahn (F), deputy director of the Defense Advanced Research Projects Agency, also heads Darpa's Information Processing Techniques Office. He has the Ph.D. degree in electrical engineering from Princeton Unversity and previously studied at Princeton and the City College of New York.

Takeo Kanade (M) is an associate professor of computer science at Carnegie-Mellon University where he holds an appointment within its Robotics Institute. He received the Ph.D. degree in information science from Kyoto University in Japan.

George A. Keyworth II is director of the Office of Science and Technology Policy in the Executive Office of the President and science advisor to the U.S. President. Previously, he directed the experimental physics division at Los Alamos National Laboratory in Los Alamos, N.M. He received his Ph.D. degree from Duke University in 1968.

James D. Meindl (F) is an electrical engineering professor who is codirector of the Center for Integrated Systems and director of the integrated-circuits laboratory at Stanford University. He earned his degrees in electrical engineering from the Carnegie Institute of Technology, culminating in a Ph.D. in 1958.

Tohru Moto-Oka (M) is currently a professor in the electrical engineering department at the University of Tokyo in Japan, where he received his BSEE and Ph.D. degrees. He was also visiting research assistant professor at the University of Illinois and a visiting professor at Washington University in St. Louis.

John Naisbitt is author of the best-selling *Megatrends* and chairman of the Naisbitt Group in Washington, D.C. The trends discussed in his book and summarized in the article in this issue are based on the monthly monitoring of 6000 newspapers in the United States over a dozen years.

Horst Nasko is vice president of research and development at Nixdorf Computer in Paderborn, West Germany. He has his degree from the Technical University of Graz in Austria.

Brian Oakley directs the Alvey Programme for Advanced Information Technology, a cooperative research venture in Great Britain. He was educated at Oxford University.

R. Fabian Pease (M) is a professor of electrical engineering at Stanford University. Both his graduate and undergraduate studies were completed at Cambridge University in Great Britain, where he received a Ph.D. in electrical engineering.

Raj Reddy (F) directs the Robotics Institute at Carnegie–Mellon University, where he is also a professor of computer science. Prior to joining CMU in 1969, he was on the faculty of Stanford University and was an applied science representative with the IBM World Trade Corp. He earned the Ph.D. degree in computer science from Stanford after attending the University of New South Wales in Australia and the University of Madras in India.

Stephen Trimberger (M) works at VLSI Technology Inc. in San Jose, Calif. He recently received the Ph.D. degree in computer science from the California Institute of Technology where he earned a B.S. in engineering and applied science.

David Waltz is professor of electrical engineering at the University of Illinois and a research professor at the coordinated sciences laboratory. He studied at the Massachusetts Institute of Technology, receiving his Ph.D. degree in 1972.

Raymond T. Yeh (SM) is professor of computer science at the University of Maryland in College Park. In 1966, he received the Ph.D. degree in mathematics from the University of Illinois, where he did his previous studies in mathematics and electrical engineering.

Victor W. Zue (M) currently is an assistant professor in the department of electrical engineering and computer science at the Massachusetts Institute of Technology. He received the Ph.D. in electrical engineering from MIT after studying at the University of Florida in Gainesville.

Part II

PROBING THE ISSUES

ADVANCED TECHNOLOGY

ARTIFICIAL INTELLIGENCE: A STATUS REPORT

An assessment of progress to date and an outlook for the future from renowned expert Edward A. Feigenbaum

The following is an edited transcript of an interview with artificial-intelligence expert Edward A. Feigenbaum. The interview was conducted by Associate Editor Paul Wallich on June 17, 1983 at Dr. Feigenbaum's home in Palo Alto, Calif. The full transcript was used as the basis for Dr. Feigenbaum's article on artificial intelligence in the November 1983 issue of IEEE Spectrum. (See p. 49).

—Ed.

We probably should start off by delineating the two major branches of artificial intelligence research: intelligent machines and cognitive science. The first branch aims at the construction of computer programs that perform at high levels of behavior, whether or not the methods bear a similarity to human endeavor—that is a computer science and engineering approach to the subject. It is much like the approach of aeronautical engineers who design airplanes with only slight attention to the question of how birds fly. Not that there is no similarity between birds flying and airplanes flying; there are some basic principles in common, but the designer of the new Boeing 767 did not concern himself with eagles and hawks, but rather with 747s and 727s and wind tunnels and so on.

The other branch of AI is called cognitive science. In cognitive science, the modeling of human information processing is central to the enterprise. It's not a question of engineering—that is, it's not a question of understanding how people do it so I can understand how to make machines do it—that question is the intelligent machines question. It's rather the question of how do people *really* do it?

A few comments about that: Usually the question is asked at the level of symbolic processing in people. In other words, people are talking about modeling of mind, not brain—usually. One tentacle of the field extends into the neurosciences. That tentacle was made credible by the work of the late David Marr at the Massachusetts Institute of Technology, Cambridge. That tentacle seeks to understand brain function in an effort that begins by asking the question: What computation is this piece of brain supposed to perform? If I can understand the computation, in great detail, then I can as a neurophysiologist go in and look for the mechanisms that are sufficient to accomplish that computation. That's the only tentacle AI has into neurophysiology and neuroanatomy. In the cognitive science area, the computer is used in two ways. First, it is used as a precise language with which to express one's hypotheses about human information processing in cognitive tasks, much as mathematics is used as a precise language in which to express one's physical theories in physics. Secondly, the

computer is used as a simulation mechanism to "run" the hypothesized information-processing activities. Once they are expressed, *voilà.* You have a tool sitting there. It's not just the language; beneath the language is a computer that can run off the models and generate the consequences of those models for particular hypothetical situations. Then the resulting behavior can be compared with human behavior in laboratory situations under standard, normal scientific conditions, the verisimilitude matched, the differences noted, the models changed and rerun, and so on.

People who do that are called information-processing psychologists or cognitive scientists, and the success of their enterprise is judged by how well the behavior of their models in fact explains and predicts psychological data. In short, such people behave as members of their collaborating disciplines, that is, they behave like psychologists, linguists, philosophers—those are the people who make up cognitive science.

AI applications

Now let's go back to the computer science and engineering part of artificial intelligence. That work breaks itself down into various subdisciplines that relate to applications. For example, the area of expert systems, more generally known as knowledge systems, is an attempt to codify the factual and heuristic knowledge of specialized areas of human endeavor; then to couple the knowledge with inference procedures—problem-solving methods that can be used to prove hypotheses, and for similar applications. Several other subdomains of AI also deal with knowledge-based intelligent activity.

For example, language understanding, whether from text or continuous speech, depends heavily on world knowledge. Both the natural language utterance and the speech signal are difficult to interpret and highly ambiguous except in the presence of knowledge about the surrounding context. Vision systems have the same characteristic. The information, the data that are present in the pixels of the image, can only be organized in the presence of knowledge of what real-world objects look like, and how real-world objects are seen under different illuminations, in different perspectives, by different eyes looking at the scene. That kind of world knowledge about the nature of objects needs to be in a program if the program is to interpret. If, for example, a program is to do automatic interpretation of aerial photography—photoreconnaissance—then it needs to know the kinds of objects that will show up in the pictures. For example, it needs to know what a railroad looks like. It needs to know what a road looks like. It needs to know what a reservoir looks like. It needs to know what a city looks like. It needs to know real-world information—for example, that missile silos are generally located out in unpopulated areas, not in the middle of cities, so that it can know that the cylindrical or circular objects it sees in its two-dimensional projection are perhaps something else in a city, perhaps natural gas tanks as opposed to missile silos.

Artificial intelligence has many other pieces to it; for example, robotic systems are very important. Robotics itself is a two-part discipline, of which one part has a strong interaction with artificial intelligence and the other has not. First-generation robotics, the so-called dumb robots, had little contact with the mainline of AI research; it had strong contact with mechanical engineering. The second generation of "intelligent robots" has strong contact with AI. These are robots that will be able to plan out their sequence of action and take alternate sequences of action, depending on what unfolds. We call them adaptive robots or problem-solving and planning robots. Their activity in thinking through the work they are doing is of central concern to AI researchers.

The ultimate, of course, is what are called integrated intelligent robots. Integrated intelligent robots have vision systems for input, various kinds of effectors for output, locomotion devices for moving around, and, most important, a central control, which is a planning and problem-solving process. There are very few examples of these in the history of robotics. One of the best known of the early integrated intelligent robots was Shakey at SRI [in Menlo Park, Calif.], which had a vision system, a locomotion system, and a planning and problem-solving system. It could also use its motion to push objects, so it was a primitive effector as well.

Automating programming

Another important area of artificial intelligence represents a point between AI research and research on advanced programming languages: automatic programming. AI people view programming as a task just like any other task, as if it were a chemistry or biology or engineering problem for the program to solve. Consequently, they view programs that write programs as needing a considerable body of knowledge about programming as a problem-solving process. The idea is to be able to create or design a program without having to construct all its details as we do now. Automatic programming researchers are aiming for what we call design-level or specification-level languages; the AI programs will take over from the specification and implement all the details, much as a compiler takes over from a Fortran expression and implements the details of machine code.

Yet another branch of AI deals with proving mathematical theorems as an enterprise in itself, without a special application. These programs are also turning more in the direction of expert systems; that is, they are beginning to exploit techniques that expert mathematicians know and use for complex proofs.

Now let's take an orthogonal slice through AI and look at the research issues. In 1956 AI was born with guided trial-and-error search as its founding principle—heuristic search, as it is known. Intelligent activity in problem solving was viewed as the search for solutions in a maze of possibilities. This model of problem-solving is sometimes called the maze model of a problem. Its early working out is due to the work of Alan Newell and Herbert Simon at Carnegie Mellon University in Pittsburgh and Marvin Minsky at MIT. In this view, a solution lies somewhere in the labyrinth, and the job of the problem

solver is to find it. The difficulty of the task arises from the number of avenues to be explored; the problem solver achieves intelligence by reducing the number of avenues dramatically, using various types of knowledge to steer and prune the search—looking at the best avenues first, and then removing unfruitful paths.

AI spent most of its early years working out the details of guided trial-and-error searching: breadth-first search, depth-first search, best-first-search—search theorems of all kinds that would allow a program to guide a search better. It's no accident that the beginning of the *Handbook of Artificial Intelligence* is all about search. That's what AI knows best. Search takes place in what are called problem spaces. AI has discovered and used several different methods for solving problems, using the search model. One example is heuristically guided generate and test. You generate candidates, see if they're the answer or else test to see if you're on the right path using your heuristics, and move on. Another method is backward chaining. You start with the goal to be achieved and chain backward by what is called problem reduction. You convert from problems to subproblems to further subproblems to further subproblems, until you arrive at facts or already proven theorems, that is, irreducibles. A similar model works forward, from known conditions, looking for a plausible answer, a satisfactory answer. Yet another method, called means-ends analysis, looks backward and forward from beginning point to goal, measures differences between where you are now and where you are going, and applies operators to take steps to reduce that difference.

The blackboard model

One problem-solving method in AI that I consider of great importance is the blackboard model. The blackboard model is a scheme for the cooperation of multiple sources of knowledge in a common knowledge structure that represents the emerging pieces of the solution. Each body of knowledge cooperating in the solution looks at the common knowledge structure, which represents the emerging solution, and asks: What can I add to it? What do I know that can build onto this solution? It's an incremental, opportunistic process, and a very important one—the most powerful, in my view, of all the problem-solving methods that have been invented, because it allows for arbitrary mixing of forward-chaining and backward-chaining bodies of knowledge represented at different levels of abstraction, in an arbitrary mix, opportunistically.

Once, search was the dominant paradigm of AI, and almost every research activity was aimed at understanding search better. That time has passed. We don't necessarily know everything we need to know about search, but it is no longer the primary focus of AI. AI underwent a shift to a knowledge-based paradigm in the middle 1960s, because of the needs that were uncovered in the earliest expert systems, and also the needs of the natural language understanding efforts, for which it became obvious that knowledge was the critical ingredient.

It's no accident that programs are no good at common-sense reasoning. Why? Because what we mean by common sense is an all-inclusive knowledge of almost everything that relates to the human condition and human endeavor. To have common sense means to have all of that kind of knowledge at your disposal. But we've given machines almost none of that kind of knowledge to date. At most, we've given relatively small amounts of knowledge about relatively specialized areas. Hence, machines cannot exhibit common sense, because they lack the knowledge that forms the basis of common sense. That explains why natural language understanding is hard, because it relies on common-sense knowledge of the world, which in turn implies a great deal of knowledge about the world.

Representing and acquiring knowledge

The second big problem in AI, then, is the problem of knowledge representation. The third is the problem of knowledge acquisition. (We've already talked about knowledge utilization, which is the issue of the design of the problem-solving method.) How are we going to represent the knowledge? People are using several ways. First, there are the formal methods drawn from mathematical logic. To a logician, there is no mystery about representing knowledge—you use the first-order predicate calculus or you use some higher-order calculus that may be necessary to represent the knowledge more conveniently. The first suggestion along this line came from John McCarthy, of Stanford University in California, in a paper in 1958, in which he suggested using first-order logic as a homogeneous method for representing knowledge and using theorem-provers as ways of getting from that representation to solutions to problems.

That method sat pretty much in the deep freeze until the invention of a reasonably efficient machine-oriented method for proving theorems in first-order logic, the so-called resolution method, attributable to J. Alan Robinson. There was a flurry of activity in the mid-1960s about using the resolution method in McCarthy's way, as a general problem solver. That died out as people began to become uncomfortable with the arcane and cumbersome expression of knowledge in that formalism. Formalisms may be general, and they may be powerful, but they're not necessarily convenient or understandable. So, in view of the problems of opaqueness, arcane form, and unintelligibility, the focus shifted away from these logic formalisms as a means for representing knowledge, although considerable work is still going on in that area.

The Prolog language, for example, is based on first-order logic, and it's also based on backward-chaining search. In discussing logic, one has to distinguish between logic as a universal language in which to express knowledge, and logic as a mechanism for arriving at solutions to problems. You could buy the former without buying the later. You could buy logic as a way of representing knowledge without buying the methods drawn from mathematical logic as methods for problem-solving. You may have better heuristic methods that are faster, or cheaper, or whatever. Or you could buy neither of them, or you could buy both. McCarthy, obviously, in his original paper was proposing both, and most people use neither.

AI people have invented other forms, which, of course, are equivalent to first-order expressions in some deep sense, but, ignoring that, they are more transparent, interesting, understandable, and usable. The first type is called rules. These are "if-then" expressions, where the *if* side of the expression is the invoking condition for the piece of knowledge, and the *then* side is the action to be taken or the conclusion to be drawn from that set of invoking conditions (sometimes called antecedent conditions; the *then* side is called the consequent). Rule-based representations have proven to be remarkably robust and applicable over an astonishing number of domains. The rule-based description is not primarily a descriptive representation, but primarily an action-oriented or process-oriented representation.

Although rule-based descriptions imply a verb, AI researchers have always, from the very beginning of their methodology, had the concept of an object represented in the machine, as a richly described entity. By "described" I mean having attributes, which themselves have values. The attribute-value, or property-list, structure of objects was present in the earliest list-processing languages, the IPLs out of Carnegie-Mellon University and the Rand Corporation in Santa Monica, and transported into Lisp in the property-list mechanism. The so-called frames, or units, or objects, are merely elaborate extensions of the same idea: the idea of the constellation of descriptive information, all about a single entity. The objects themselves tend to be viewed as static descriptions, except insofar as they may have rules or procedures attached to them to do something.

To use language that emerges in another area of AI, the computational-linguistics area, you might think of the objects as the nodes of a semantic net, in which the links between objects, or the ways of accessing other objects, are the relational tissue that forms the semantic net, the relational links of the semantic map. Commonly, therefore, the AI people who are not oriented toward the logic approach use a combination of rules and objects. The major tasks for the knowledge-representation people are to extend the concepts of object description, to extend the variety of structure one can put into rules (or a framework for rules), and to extend our scientific ideas of how to represent concepts that humans encounter—concepts of time, ownership, causality—all those have to be thought through carefully before we can know how to represent them for a machine.

Consequently, we have two kinds of knowledge-representation researchers: the theorists, who worry about the issues I've just discussed, and the practitioners, the engineers, who worry about the construction of usable object-oriented or rule-based systems. An example of a theorist is McCarthy at Stanford, who worries about representations of actions and time and causality, and examples of practitioners would be Mark Stefik or Dan Bobrow at Xerox Palo Alto Research Center, constructing the Loops system.

And then there's the mixture of theorists who are trying to bridge over into practical systems. These are the Prolog people. They are using a more theoretical approach, but they are trying to build practical systems to underpin that approach. It must be emphasized that Prolog itself, as a logic language in its pure form, is a descriptive language, not a procedural language. But because you have to run programs, numerous mechanisms must be introduced into Prolog to give it a procedural aspect, and some of those mechanisms have been invented already, and more are in the process of being invented.

There are ways, of course, of going from one kind of knowledge representation to another, because first-order logic is a universal representation. It's usually not convenient—although in some cases it is, and where people are trying to demonstrate the elegance and utility of mathematical logic as a formalism, you find lovely examples. In practical cases, the shift of representations is an awkward and difficult situation. Moreover, it's not done by any program—it's done by people.

Finally, one should not forget the base-level representation that's used in essentially all AI programs that have ever been done—the graph representation implicit in list structures. Remember, list processing was invented to handle the earliest AI programming problems of the Logic Theorist and other pioneering efforts. No one has abandoned that. Lists and list structures representing general graph structures have been the foundation of all AI representations. In the absence of anything else, you represent your knowledge and your data in lists, and lists of lists, and reentrant lists, and so on recursively. It's a very powerful ground-level representational tool.

Now on to knowledge acquisition. To understand the importance of knowledge acquisition, we must review a very important part of the science. In the early days of AI, the first generation of AI scientists, meaning primarily in this case Newell, Simon, and McCarthy, published papers in which they expressed strong views that the generality of a program was most important to intelligence—that is, the ability of the program to switch its attention from problem to problem without someone having to rewrite the program. McCarthy suggested theorem proving as a general problem-solving mechanism. Newell and Simon suggested a mechanism called the general problem solver (GPS), based on the very general method of means-ends analysis.

The road to Dendral

In 1965, at Stanford, Joshua Lederberg and I, plunging into the problem of modeling the behavior of scientists doing empirical induction from instrument data in chemical analysis, took the opposite view: that high levels of expertise in problem solving would be achieved by assembling a large body of highly specific knowledge about the domain of discourse—we shunned the general problem-solving methods. The motivation of the Dendral project was partly to understand how humans solved complex scientific problems, of which empirical induction was quintessential, but it was also partly to produce the smartest possible programs for doing various tasks. Performance was taken as an important goal in itself.

The insight about the importance of knowledge proved correct. When we did assemble considerable bodies of knowledge about mass spectrometry, NMR (nuclear magnetic resonance) spectroscopy, organic chemistry, stability of molecules, topology, and so one, the program performed as an excellent analyst of several families of organic chemical structures. Other "generations" of expert-systems work proved the point. The point was also proven in other knowledge-based signal-understanding systems and language-understanding systems. That led to what has been called the shift to a knowledge-based paradigm in AI.

The key result of the more than 17 years of work that has unfolded since Dendral is this: Of primary importance to the quality of problem solving by intelligent programs (and perhaps therefore by intelligent humans) is the knowledge that those programs contain. The inference procedure is of secondary importance. You can't do without inference, but whether you use the resolution method, or forward chaining, or backward chaining, or the blackboard model, or generate-and-test is not all that important relative to the knowledge that the program has.

The critical bottleneck of AI

Obviously, that makes knowledge acquisition the critical bottleneck of AI, because if programs are more intelligent the more high-quality knowledge they have, then how to get that knowledge into the system is of critical importance. Right now, we are getting that knowledge in a handcrafted fashion in which some AI scientist is codifying knowledge and putting it into objects, rules, or list structures. Knowledge engineers are working with experts in a field one-on-one, codifying rule after rule, object after object. The problem of getting knowledge automatically is not a new problem—it's been renamed recently as the knowledge-acquisition problem, but it's not new. It's been called the problem of machine learning. It's perhaps

one of the most active of all the basic research areas of AI because it's so important.

Some people in AI, including an articulate spokesman, Roger Schank from Yale, have said recently (and forcefully) that programs cannot be intelligent unless they learn. I don't subscribe to that view. I hold a *performance* view of intelligence, which says that intelligence is as intelligence does—not as intelligence comes to do better. Different people have their pet views of what constitutes intelligent activity; Schank's, at the moment, happens to be learning: namely, programs that can be highly adaptive and learn new knowledge can be "truly" intelligent, whereas other programs would be "merely" pseudo-intelligent. Other people might say that what's critical is how general programs are—that's the generality view of intelligence, which dominated AI for 10 years. Still others will say that what's critical is how well programs handle language—the "language is essential" view of intelligence: What's different between us and monkeys is that we solve problems that are more complex, and, by the way, we use language—language distinguishes human from beast.

To repeat, my criterion is performance—how hard a problem can the system solve? It is important to understand a little about this debate. Readers are constantly confused by these quirky debates in AI about what is or is not intelligence. Everyone in the field has an opinion of what's intelligent and what's not, as does everyone outside the field.

Returning to the problem of machine learning, now called the knowledge-acquisition problem for the obvious reason that we've pinned down where the real action is, AI scientists now seek methods by which knowledge can be inferred automatically from naturally occurring events that are received by the machine via data banks or sensors, or how the machine can facilitate the transfer of knowledge from humans to its own internal structures (interactive transfer of knowledge). There are other modes of knowledge acquisition on which there has not been much progress. A good example would be flexible and effective methods of reasoning by analogy, of understanding new situations as analogous to old situations. Another class of learning processes that is not yet well understood is the process of discovery of new knowledge and the construction of new ideas (though the work of Douglas Lenat at Stanford and Pat Langley and Simon at Carnegie-Mellon is promising).

In the viewpoint of those in AI, one must dispense with the mystery that surrounds the term *discovery*. Discovery is a search process, it's a knowledge-driven process, it's a process of combining ideas, finding new ideas, pruning out bad ideas. We're *just* beginning to understand how to construct new concepts out of old in programs.

Several successful experiments have been done in the automatic acquisition of knowledge from data. Dendral led to a knowledge-acquisition program called Meta-Dendral that inferred new mass spectral knowledge, later published in a scientific journal. At the University of Illinois at Urbana, there were some experiments on automatic induction of knowledge about crop diseases. But the number of experiments is very small, and scientists need to do very many more. We're in a primitive stage.

What we have come to understand can be captured in this slogan: "Knowledge acquisition is itself a knowledge-based task—the more you know, the easier it is to know more." Learning takes place at the fringes of what we know. It's very difficult to learn from nothing, but it's very easy to learn a little bit more at the fringes. This is also a common human experience.

Where do we stand now vis-a-vis the knowledge acquisition problem? The activity level is high, the research concepts are flowing. You can expect to see major breakthroughs all through the eighties; expect to see the problem well into its engineering phase in the early nineties, because the current situation is intolerable. Great pressure now exists to build expert systems. When that pressure meets the bottleneck of knowledge acquisition, that bottleneck is going to have to give. So many people are working on it, and there's such concern and such practical value, that throughout the eighties and into the early nineties there will be several major scientific and engineering breakthroughs that will lead to significant progress.

For the AI science as a whole, progress into the nineties will be evolutionary rather than revolutionary—an unfolding process without many discontinuous steps.

Gradually the activity of programs will spread from specialized areas into more general fields of endeavor. That's going to be evolutionary, too—it will take a very long time for programs to have the scope of human endeavor, because humans know so much more. But the codification of immense amounts of human knowledge in objects, semantic nets, rules, or logical expressions is a worthwhile activity for humans to undertake. It requires insights from the theorists, and it requires an enormous amount of effort to get thousands of people working on the task of codifying human knowledge so that it can be made available to computer problem-solving processes.

The 'knowledge industry'

Our machines are relatively dumb in all areas except the specialty areas—in which they are expert—because they don't have enough knowledge. The Japanese, in their fifth-generation project, speak about the "knowledge industry," and I sometimes fantasize about a big field in which I have AI factories. One of my factories has 10 000 people in it, and it's the knowledge factory. And then I have another factory that is the heuristics factory. Another factory is turning out machines, new machines that will use that knowledge effectively with those heuristics. Now here's where we get into the question of the fifth generation. If you look out into the future, the applications potential for such machines is enormous—not only for machines that have specialty functions like Mycin and Molgen and Dendral, but for machines that have more general problem-solving functions.

Now we ask the question—"we" being all scientists, including the Japanese, who have asked it in the most detail—how are we going to run these programs? Do we envision running them on DEC 2060s? Or Lisp machines? Or CRAYs? Well, you would like to put as much inference power as you could bring to bear at the disposal of the problem-solving process for those problems that require it, and as much knowledge-application power for those problems that require the application of large bodies of knowledge. That seems different from applying the power of the megaflops. What does symbolic reasoning and cognition have to do with megaflops? What do they have to do with multiplication and division and arithmetic? The answer is, almost nothing. You want to put logical inference power there, and you want to put object look-up, rule look-up, high-speed semantic net traversal, in contrast to the high-speed indexing of arrays. In the United States, we noted it first about 1975, but didn't do much about it, except to construct a Lisp machine to get Lisp out of software into firmware—a truly modest step, let me say, without trying to put down the effort. There is not an order of magnitude advantage in going from Lisp on a DEC 20/60 to Lisp on a Lisp

machine. In most cases, there's little gain.

The Japanese were the first to think through the question of progress into the nineties—what is needed for the two vital components, the knowledge base system and the inference system (hardware and software)? In addition, of course, because people have to interact with these machines, they're looking for comfortable, convenient modes of human interaction, which means some speech understanding, which requires knowledge; some picture understanding, which requires knowledge; and some natural language understanding, which requires knowledge—knowledge and inference. That's what the fifth-generation plan is all about. It's saying that we computer scientists think we can do better than just to apply conventional computer technology to the problem of knowledge-application machines and inference machines.

How do AI scientists view their enterprise most generally? What are they really after, in the long run? If artificial intelligence and cognitive science will make a contribution to the flow of great scientific thought, then what will this contribution be? Everyone in our field is motivated by a methodology and a working hypothesis. The methodology is to perform experiments using programming as the laboratory. From these experiments, we induce theoretical ideas about the nature of intelligence. The results of many experiments lead to occasional generalizations toward a theory of intelligence. The working hypothesis of the AI community is that such a theory will be theory of intelligent information processing, whether that processing is done in silicon or in biological tissue. In other words, the hope of the AI community is that there will be one theory of intelligence, not two—not a theory of machine intelligence and a theory of human intelligence, but a unified theory of *intelligent information processing*. We don't know if we can do that. We don't know if that exists. But people are striving in that direction. This striving has the effect of welding the field together and constitutes one long-range direction.

The second long-range direction for AI work is the playing out of a millenia-old theme, documented by Pamela McCorduck in her book, *Machines Who Think*, and discussed in the book *The Fifth Generation*, which I coauthored with her. It is the theme of people creating intelligent artifacts. The theme goes all the way back to the Greeks. It is found in the Golem stories, in many human myths. In the late 20th century, we are beginning to have the ability to realize those age-old aspirations of humankind for intelligent machines—machines that are truly adaptive, flexible, autonomous, intelligent. And there is a strong motivation among AI researchers to produce the smartest possible artifacts.

Of course, there is now a very strong commercial motivation to produce artifacts of high economic value, and that is rapidly becoming perhaps the dominant theme—as the world sees artificial intelligence. The increasing tempo of commercialization and industrialization is evident in the small expert systems companies, the big company laboratories. The transition of AI from university research laboratories to industry is a major event in the world of computer applications.

Another long-range motivation of AI scientists is the contribution that AI will make to the codification of human knowledge. I think that it may make little difference whether this knowledge is used by machines or not. We will have this knowledge codified—we will have a form of knowledge that we have not seen represented before, the heuristic knowledge of humankind, the knowledge of good practice, the nonrigorous knowledge, the art of good guessing, the knowledge that needs to be taught to students and apprentices. We may some-day be able to produce the equivalent of a modern-day library of Alexandria—the great coming together of all the world's knowledge—in giant machines. It will be a very great day for humankind. If you believe that knowledge is power, and the truth shall make you free, then knowing is all-important. If you believe that knowledge is more powerful than swords, then you believe that the human race ought to look down the path to greater knowledge availability, and greater knowledge of humankind's own thinking processes.

For further reading

The foundational early work in artificial intelligence is documented in the anthology *Computers and Thought*, Edward Feigenbaum and J. Feldman, eds., McGraw-Hill, 1963. The first paper advocating the use of predicate logic for knowledge representation, coupled with theorem-provers as an inference mechanism, was John McCarthy's "Programs with Common Sense" in *Mechanization of Thought Processes*, Her Majesty's Stationery Office, 1959.

A collection of papers from the second workshop on machine learning, which gives an overview of current topics in knowledge acquisition, is *Machine Learning*, edited by R. Michalski *et al.*, Tioga Press, 1983. Another useful work is *Knowledge-Based Systems in Artificial Intelligence*, by Douglas Lenat and Randall Davis, McGraw-Hill, 1982.

RESEARCH & DEVELOPMENT

ASSESSING THE TECHNICAL CHALLENGES

Present difficulties and potential solutions of next-generation computers as seen by a distinguished group of engineers and scientists

When Spectrum *began planning its next-generation computers issue [November 1983], the editors envisaged a series of roundtables in which leaders in technical and sociotechnical areas would come together to discuss likely implications of next-generation computing as well as ways that next-generation computing might be brought about. Such roundtables are notoriously difficult to arrange, especially as the level of expertise and the number of the participants increases. And, in fact, only one such roundtable—on sociotechnical impacts—was convened [see next article, p. 135].*

One member of Spectrum's *editorial board, Lynn Conway, then manager of the knowledge systems area at Xerox Palo Alto Research Center, had already been involved in computer-network–based solutions to problems of multisite cooperation between researchers, and, following her keynote address at the 1983 Spring Compcon in San Francisco, it was suggested that the roundtable dealing with technical issues be implemented via a computer network, possibly with Ms. Conway as moderator. When Ms. Conway left PARC to become computer Research Manager at Darpa, another member of the editorial board, Chuck House, corporate engineering director at Hewlett-Packard in Palo Alto, agreed to serve as a moderator, and a group was assembled, consisting of Mr. House, Bert Raphael of Hewlett-Packard, Alan Bell of Xerox PARC, and Paul Wallich of* Spectrum, *to gather a group of participants, set an agenda, and arrange a common network to which all participants could have access. [Because Hewlett-Packard and Xerox PARC are within a quarter mile of each other in Palo Alto, it was not too difficult for the group to meet.]*

Initially, there was some question about which network would be suitable for the discussion, because potential participants spanned the range from commercial to academic to industrial research, and the immediate network of choice, the ARPAnet, is generally reserved for use by people with Darpa contracts. Furthermore, Robert Kahn of Darpa expressed some concern that publication of an ARPAnet-based discussion of U.S. research aims could pose technology-transfer questions.

Dr. Raphael subsequently contacted David Farber at the University of Delaware, one of the early instigators of the CSnet network, and broached the possibility of using the CSnet as a base for the discussion. Both Dr. Farber and CSnet's sponsors at the National Science Foundation were enthusiastic about the potentials of such an experiment, and so arrangements were

made. Dr. Raphael also worked closely with the staff of the CSnet service host at the University of Wisconsin in Madison to set up and maintain a mail-distribution list for the conference and to create accounts on the service host for participants who did not have direct access to either CSnet or ARPAnet. [The CSnet is a "logical" network physically situated on the ARPAnet, Telenet, and the telephone system. Thus, CSnet sites can communicate with ARPAnet sites when all goes well.]

The resulting discussion ran from July 27 to October 3, 1983, by electronic mail, and formed the basis for the November 1983 article, "Putting it together," by Paul Wallich (see p. 77). A transcript of the messages, edited by Mr. Wallich, is presented in this section on p. 103, following a list of participants and a log of edited messages.

—Ed., March 1984

Network conference participants

Scott Fahlman	Carnegie-Mellon University (CMU)
Guy Steele	CMU, Tartan Laboratories Inc.
H.T. Kung	CMU
Norman Christ	Columbia University
David Shaw	Columbia University
Sidney Fernbach	Consultant
Kenneth G. Wilson	Cornell University
Forest Baskett	Digital Equipment Corp.
A.L. Davis	Fairchild R&D
Bill L. Buzbee	Computing Division, Los Alamos National Laboratories (LANL)
Robert J. Douglass	LANL
Robert H. Ewald	LANL
Randall Davis	Massachusetts Institute of Technology
Alan Gottlieb	New York University
Jack Schwartz	New York University
Larry Snyder	Purdue University
Jeffrey D. Ullman	Stanford University
Frederick Hayes-Roth	Teknowledge Inc.
Danny Cohen	University of Southern California, Information Sciences Institute (USC-ISI)
Keith Uncapher	USC-ISI
Steven Trimberger	VLSI Technology Inc.

Moderators

Chuck House   Hewlett-Packard Co.
Bert Raphael   Hewlett-Packard Co.
Alan Bell   Xerox Palo Alto Research Center
Paul Wallich   *IEEE Spectrum*

Log of electronic messages

Date: 27 Jul 83 15:27 PDT
From: Dorothy Sanders ⟨Sanders.HP-THOR@Rand-
        Relay⟩
Subject: **Test**

Date: 28 Jul 83 10:04 PDT
From: SHORT.HP-HULK@Rand-Relay(Moderators)
Subject: **Teleconference on new-generation computers**

Date: 30 Jul 83 00:42 EDT (Saturday)
From: Guy.Steele@CMU-CS-A
Subject: **My network address is correct**

Date: Sat, 30 Jul 1983 02:33 EDT
From: Scott E. Fahlman ⟨Fahlman@CMU-CS-C.ARPA⟩
Subject: **Teleconference on new-generation computers**

Date: Sat 30 Jul 83 13:00:24 PDT
From: Al Davis ⟨ADavis at SRI-KL⟩
Subject: **Biosketch and topics**

Date: Sat 30 Jul 83 16:17:29 PDT
From: RHAYES-ROTH@SRI-KL.ARPA(Frederick Hayes-
        Roth)
Subject: **Opening question**

Date: Sun 31 Jul 83 21:55:14 PDT
From: Jeffrey D. Ullman ⟨ULLMAN@SU-SCORE.ARPA⟩
Subject: **Favorite issues/biosketch**

Date: Mon, 1 Aug 83 08:07 PDT
From: ABell.PA@PARC-MAXC.ARPA
Subject: **Opening question**

Date: 1 Aug 83 14:11:35 MDT
From: Bill Buzbee C-DO ⟨blb@lanl⟩
Subject: **Terminology, etc.**

Date: Mon, 1 Aug 83 17:30 PDT
From: Jeffrey D. Ullman ⟨ullman@Diabolo@SU-Score⟩
Subject: **Response to question (1)**

Date: 2 Aug 1983 15:28 PDT
From: RAPHAEL@HP-HULK (Bert Raphael)
Subject: **First status report**

Date: Tue, 2 Aug 83 22:20 EDT
From: Scott E. Fahlman ⟨Fahlman@CMU-CS-C.ARPA⟩
Subject: **Reply to question (1)**

Date: Wed 3 Aug 83 13:01:46 EDT
From: David Shaw ⟨DAVID@COLUMBIA-20.ARPA⟩
Subject: **New-generation supercomputers**

Date: 3 Aug 1983 13:26:55 MDT
From: Robert Douglass C-10 ⟨rjd@lanl⟩
Subject: **Issues and biosketch**

Date: 3 Aug 83 14:59 EDT
From: Jack Schwartz ⟨SCHWARTZ.CMCL1@NYU.ARPA⟩
Subject: **The challenge is technological**

Date: Wed, 3 Aug 83 16:31:06 EDT
From: David Shaw ⟨DAVID@COLUMBIA-20.ARPA⟩
Subject: **Machines for users**

Date: Wed Aug 3 21:51:47 1983
From: trimberg (Stephen Trimberger)
Subject: **Interesting topics and short bio**

Date: 3 Aug 83 23:41 EDT (Wednesday)
From: Guy.Steele@CMU-CS-A
Subject: **Exploitation of parallelism**

Date: Thu, 4 Aug 83 00:41 EDT
From: Scott E. Fahlman ⟨Fahlman@CMU-CS-C.ARPA⟩
Subject: **Problem characterization**

Date: Thu 4 Aug 83 10:34:03 PDT
From: RHAYES-ROTH@SRI-KL.ARPA (Frederick Hayes-
        Roth)
Subject: **Exploitation of parallelism: expert systems
        approach**

Date: Thu 4 Aug 83 12:46:28 PDT
From: Jeffrey D. Ullman ⟨ULLMAN@SU-SCORE.ARPA⟩
Subject: **Data structures**

Date: Thu, 4 Aug 83 18:44 EDT
From: Scott E. Fahlman ⟨Fahlman@CMU-CS-C.ARPA⟩
Subject: **Data structures**

Date: 4 Aug 83 21:10:59 EDT (Thu)
From: kgw@Cornell (Ken Wilson)
Subject: **Issues and biosketch**

Date: 4 Aug 83 21:51:06 EDT (Thu)
From: kgw@Cornell.ARPA (Ken Wilson)
Subject: **Parallel processing**

Date: Thursday, August 4, 1983 9:53PM EDT
From: Randy Davis ⟨DAVIS%MIT-OZ@MIT-MC⟩
Subject: **Last minute . . .**

Date: Thursday, August 4, 1983 10:33PM EDT
From: Randy Davis ⟨DAVIS%MIT-OZ@MIT-MC⟩
Subject: **First question and replies**

Date: Thu 4 Aug 83 22:13:47 PDT
From: Jeffrey D. Ullman ⟨ULLMAN@SU-SCORE.ARPA⟩
Subject: **Biosketch**

Date: 5 Aug 83 01:19 EDT (Friday)
From: Guy.Steele@CMU-CS-A
Subject: **Expert systems**

Date: Fri, 5 Aug 83 09:09 PDT
From: ABell.PA@PARC-MAXC.ARPA
Subject: **Second question**

Date: 5 Aug 83 10:24:58 MDT
From: Robert Douglass C-10 〈rjd@lanl〉
Subject: **Definitions**

Date: 5 Aug 1983 10:36:32 EST
From: Larry Snyder 〈lxs@purdue.ARPA〉

Date: 5 Aug 83 23:26:56 EDT (Fri)
From: kgw@Cornell (Ken Wilson)
Subject: **Parallel operating systems**

Date: Sat, 6 Aug 1983 15:03:38 EDT
From: HT.Kung@CMU-CS-VLSI
Subject: **New gen**

Date: 6 Aug 83 18:14:51 EDT
From: gottlieb@NYU.ARPA (Alan Gottlieb)
Subject: **Biosketch**

Date: 6 Aug 83 20:55:13 EDT (Sat)
From: kgw@Cornell (Ken Wilson)
Subject: **First questions and answers**

Date: 7 Aug 83 15:55:33 EDT
From: gottlieb@NYU.ARPA (Alan Gottlieb)
Subject: **Late response to initial query**

Date: Mon 8 Aug 83 16:22:12 PDT
From: Al Davis 〈ADavis@SRI-KL〉
Subject: **First question reply**

Date: 10 Aug 83 11:52:35 MDT
From: Bill Buzbee C-DO 〈blb@lanl〉
Subject: **New-generation discussion**

Date: Wed, 10 Aug 83 16:08 EDT
From: Scott E. Fahlman 〈Fahlman@CMU-CS-C.ARPA〉
Subject: **Tasks for the new generation**

Date: 10 Aug 83 12:48 PDT
From: RAPHAEL.HP-HULK@Rand-Relay.ARPA (Bert
     Raphael)
Subject: **Mailboxes and status report**

Date: Thu 11 Aug 10:58:27 1983
From: fernbach@csnet-sh.ARPA (Sidney Fernbach)
Subject: **Answers to first two questions**

Date: Thu 11 Aug 11:17:44 1983
From: fernbach@csnet-sh.ARPA (Sidney Fernbach)
Subject: **Response to first question**

Date: Thu, 11 Aug 83 11:24 PDT
From: ABell.PA@PARC-MAXC.ARPA
Subject: **Request for info**

Date: Thurs 11 Aug 83 20:14:34 1983
From: Wallich@csnet-sh.ARPA (Paul Wallich)
Subject: **Third question**

Date: 12 Aug 83 21:15:20 EDT (Fri)
From: kgw@Cornell.ARPA (Ken Wilson)
Subject: **Third question**

Date: 14 Aug 83 09:25:31 EDT
From: gottlieb@NYU.ARPA (Alan Gottlieb)
Subject: **Third question**

Date: Sun, 14 Aug 83 22:17:42 PDT
From: ULLMAN@SU-SCORE.ARPA (Jeffrey Ullman)
Subject: **Stanford projects/barriers to communication**

Date: 16 Aug 83 15:39 PDT
From: Danny Cohen 〈COHEN@USC-ISIB〉
Subject: **Re questions (1) and (3)**

Date: Wed Aug 17 17:22:41 1983
From: wallich@csnet-sh.ARPA (Paul Wallich)
Subject: **Fourth question**

Date: Thu 18 Aug 83 13:32:16 EDT
From: Norman Christ 〈G.CHRIST@COLUMBIA-20.ARPA〉
Subject: **Biosketch and acknowledgment**

Date: Thu 18 Aug 83 13:46:39 EDT
From: Norman Christ 〈G.CHRIST@COLUMBIA-20.ARPA〉
Subject: **Parallel computation and user-driven design**

Date: Sat Aug 20 83 21:05:47 1983
From: wallich@csnet-sh.ARPA (Paul Wallich)
Subject: **Wrap-up**

Date: 21 Aug 83 00:34:10 EDT (Sun)
From: kgw@Cornell (Ken Wilson)
Subject: **Example requested**

Date: 22 Aug 1983 08:39:07 MDT
From: Bill Buzbee C-DO〈blb@lanl〉
Subject: **Bill Buzbee's biosketch**

Date: Mon, 22 Aug 83 01:47 EDT
From: Scott E. Fahlman 〈Fahlman@CMU-CS-C.ARPA〉
Subject: **Call for action**

Date: 22 Aug 83 21:59:17 EDT (Mon)
From: kgw@Cornell (Ken Wilson)
Subject: **Network**

Date: 23 Aug 83 15:57:07 EDT
From: gottlieb@NYU.ARPA (Alan Gottlieb)
Subject: **Third question**

Date: 23 Aug 83 16:11:53 EDT
From: gottlieb@NYU.ARPA (Alan Gottlieb)
Subject: **Government action**

Date: Wed, 24 Aug 83 09:43 PDT
From: Jeff Ullman 〈ullman@Diablo@SU-Score〉

Date: 24 Aug 83 09:54 PDT
From: Keith W. Uncapher 〈UNCAPHER@USC-ISIB〉
Subject: **Catch-up**

Date: Wed 24 Aug 83 15:08:19 PDT
From: Jeffrey D. Ullman ⟨ULLMAN@SU-SCORE.ARPA⟩
Subject: **Response to question (4)**

Date: 25 Aug 1983 08:58:00 MDT
From: Bill Buzbee C-DO ⟨blb lanl⟩
Subject: **Moon shot**

Date: 25 Aug 1983 12:03 PDT
From: Keith W. Uncapher ⟨UNCAPHER@USC-ISIB⟩
Subject: **Inputs**

Date: 26 Aug 1983 13:55:11 MDT
From: Robert Ewald C-DO ⟨rhe@lanl⟩

Date: Sun, 28 Aug 83 22:10 EDT
From: Scott E. Fahlman ⟨Fahlman@CMU-CS-C.ARPA⟩
Subject: **Moon shots**

From: Sanders.HP-THOR@Rand-Relay Wed Jul 27 18:40:30
       1983
Date: 27 Jul 1983 15:27 PDT
From: Dorothy Sanders ⟨Sanders.HP-THOR@Rand-Relay⟩
Return-Path: ⟨Sanders%HP-THOR.HP-Labs@Rand-Relay⟩
Subject: **Test**
Received: by HP-Venus via CHAOSNET; 27 Jul 1983
       15:30:48-PDT
To: NEW-GEN@CSNET-SH
Message-Id: ⟨428193049.7012.hplabs@HP-VENUS⟩
Via: HP-Labs; 27 Jul 83 16:32-PDT

This is a test message. The IEEE Teleconference on New-Generation Computers starts here on Thursday, July 28.

From: SHORT.HP-HULK@Rand-Relay Thu Jul 28 12:35:33
       1983
Date: 28 Jul 1983 10:04 PDT
From: SHORT.HP-HULK@Rand-Relay
Return-Path: ⟨SHORT%HP-HULK.HP-Labs@Rand-Relay⟩
Subject: **Teleconference on new generation computers**
Received: by HP-VENUS via CHAOSNET; 28 Jul 1983
       10:06:06-PDT
To: NEW-GEN@CSNET-SH
Cc: RAPHAEL.HP-HULK@Rand-Relay
Message-Id: ⟨428259967.23117.hplabs@HP-VENUS⟩
Via: HP-Labs; 28 Jul 83 10:23-PDT

The November issue of *IEEE Spectrum* will be devoted to the issues raised by the Japanese fifth-generation challenge. Paul Wallich has already discussed briefly with you some of the topics of concern, along with the proposal to conduct a month-long computer teleconference.

This message launches the teleconference. We anticipate about 40 participants, including Lynn Conway, Gordon Bell, Erich Bloch, Ivan and Bert Sutherland, and Ed Feigenbaum. Our purpose today is to outline the goals, provide some starting framework, and ask for some specific starting information. Our first question of the teleconference will follow shortly, along with procedures of conduct that we expect to follow. While the teleconference will be a short-term project, we are hopeful that a longer-term dialogue will continue after the initial needs are met.

Our aims are to produce informal commentary on what the issues are, how they are being addressed, what prospects are most promising, and what changes in direction or approach may be appropriate to recommend. This obviously is served by each of you responding to each question we pose, but more importantly, by responding to each other's inputs. It will be Paul's challenge to distill our messages into a meaningful and coherent story.

Four basic ideas

Rather than concentrating on the Japanese fifth-generation, we would prefer to focus upon American "new-generation" issues. Our preliminary thoughts revolve around four basic ideas:

(1)   What is the definition of new generation? What goals, structures, architectures, and developments are critical to its achievement?

(2)   What is the current status of new-generation research and development in America? Where are the issues being confronted, and which alternatives exist? What are the commercialization options and plans? This is germane not only in technological and capital investment arenas, but in societal impact as well.

(3)   What major new disciplines will be needed and may evolve as a result of new-generation needs—for example, knowledge engineering, advanced architecture, advanced VLSI (very-large-scale integration), network interconnection? How will the structure of disciplines as separate entities be changed by new-generation technology? (Much of computer science is impacting most engineering disciplines.)

(4)   What new infrastructures or new uses of old infrastructures will be needed to make new-generation work possible? What kinds of networks, servers, facilities, and so forth will be needed? What kind of funding will be needed for the new infrastructures—not just how much, but where will it come from, and how is it disbursed and evaluated?

A moderator will pose a question every few days, for which your answers should be addressed to NEW-GEN@CSNET-SH, which will automatically forward them to the whole group. (You will also be able to engage in private side conversations by addressing messages directly to the sender of any message. We will provide a full mailing list later.)

We'd like to pose two additional questions to help get things started. Please send your answer only to the moderators, by addressing it to NG-MOD@CSNET-SH.

(1)   What favorite issue or two do you feel is most important for our discussion agenda?

(2)   Please send us a short (one paragraph) biosketch so that we can prepare a roster of the conference by August 5.

Thanks for your involvement. Your response will serve to acknowledge that your network address is correct.

The moderators:

Alan Bell, Xerox PARC
Chuck House, Hewlett-Packard
Bert Raphael, Hewlett-Packard
Paul Wallich, IEEE

From: Guy.Steele@CMU-CS-A Fri Jul 29 23:47:01 1983
Received: from [128.2.254.192] by CMU-CS-PT with
    CMUFTP; 30 Jul 83 00:36:46 EDT
Date: 30 Jul 83 00:42 EDT (Saturday)
From: Guy.Steele@CMU-CS-A
To: ng-mod@UWISC
Subject: **My network address is correct**

Also:

(1)   I hope that issues of knowledge representation, and architectures that directly address efficient support of representations, will be touched upon. Representations first, and only then architectures. Scott Fahlman's NETL system is an example of this approach; the Japanese fifth-generation endeavor is another. A claim (that could be debated): It's silly to design hardware without a good idea of the software to be supported.

(2)   Guy L. Steele Jr. (A.B., Applied Mathematics, Harvard College, 1975; S.M., Computer Science, MIT, 1977; Ph.D., Computer Science and Artificial Intelligence, MIT, 1980) is a Member of Technical Staff at Tartan Laboratories, and Assistant Professor of Computer Science, on leave, at Carnegie-Mellon University. He has worked on the extension and maintenance of MacLISP; designed and explored with Gerald Jay Sussman the dialect of LISP called Scheme; designed Scheme-78 and helped to design Scheme-79, the first single-chip microprocessors to execute LISP directly; worked on the definition and implementation of languages to support constraint propagation; and currently is coordinating an effort to define a portable, powerful, and widely supported dialect of LISP called Common LISP.

I hope you all are aware that the IJCAI-83 and AAAI-83 conferences fall across the last half of this teleconferencing session. I'll try to get to a terminal periodically, but can't make any guarantees.

From: Fahlman@CMU-CS-C.ARPA Sat Jul 30 01:34:09 1983
Received: ID ⟨FAHLMAN@CMU-CS-C.ARPA⟩; Sat 30 Jul
    83 02:33:44-EDT
Date: Sat, 30 Jul 1983 02:33 EDT
From: Scott E. Fahlman ⟨Fahlman@CMU-CS-C.ARPA⟩
To: NG-MOD@UWISC.ARPA
Subject: **Teleconference on new-generation computers**
In-reply-to: Msg of 28 Jul 1983 13:04-EDT from SHORT.HP-
    HULK at Rand-Relay

Symbolic computation and parallelism

Issues:

(1)   If we agree with the stated Japanese view that artificial-intelligence–style symbolic computation is where the action is going to be, what would a symbol-processing supercomputer look like, as compared to a number-crunching supercomputer? If we're not after gigaflops, what are we after? How do we characterize the task? Where are the cycles going in such systems?

(2)   If we agree that parallelism is the key to getting the kind of performance we need, what sort of parallelism do we want? A small number of big processors (1024 is a small number) tied together by some sort of network, with memory on one side or the other? Data flow? Something like NETL, in which the connections hold the knowledge and the processors are very simple? Systolic arrays configured for a particular task? We need a taxonomy of such systems and then a good theory of which systems are right for which tasks.

Biographical sketch:

Scott Fahlman is a Research Computer Scientist at Carnegie-Mellon University. He received his Ph.D. from MIT in 1977. His principal research interest is the exploration of massively parallel machine architectures for AI, especially for knowledge-representation tasks and for recognition. He has also been active in the design and implementation of Common LISP and in CMU's personal-computing project (SCE).

From: ADavis@SRI-KL Sat Jul 30 17:32:58 1983
Date: Sat 30 Jul 83 13:00:24 PDT
From: Al Davis ⟨ADavis at SRI-KL⟩
Subject: **Biosketch and topics**
To: NG-Mod at CSNET-SH

Topics:

(1)   It is clear that the key to performance increases is going to be the exploitation of concurrency at all levels of system behavior. Identification of the areas in which consistent solutions are necessary would be nice. Discussion of relevant results which address these areas would be even better.

(2)   I do not feel that supercomputers will be general-purpose in that general-purpose implies compromise and compromise implies loss of speed. If people agree with this view (many undoubtedly won't) then it would be nice to get involved in some discussion of which problem domains need supercomputers. In addition, a discussion of how these specialized supercomputers should communicate in a consistent manner also deserves comment.

Biosketch:

A. L. Davis—B.S. in Electrical Engineering 1969 from MIT, Ph.D. in Computer Science 1972 from the University of Utah. Associate Professor of Computer Science at the University of Utah, Assistant Professor at the University of Waterloo. I have consulted for HP, IBM, DEC, General Research Corp., BNR, General Instruments, and Burroughs. I am presently running the AI Architecture group at the Fairchild Advanced R&D labs in Palo Alto. My main research goal is to architect concurrent systems.

Over the past 10 years I have worked in the data-flow area and built the first operational full custom data-flow processor.

Since then I have built another data-flow machine, built a data-flow graphical programming environment and high-level language, and have done a number of other things in the data-flow area. Presently I am architecting a systolic supercomputer.

Al Davis

From: RHAYES-ROTH@SRI-KL.ARPA Sat Jul 30 18:56:10 1983
Date: Sat 30 Jul 83 16:17:29 PDT
From: RHAYES-ROTH@SRI-KL.ARPA
Subject: **Opening question**
To: ng-mod@UWISC.ARPA

My favorite topics are:

(1)   Why don't we distinguish among the various factors at work in the new generation and try to focus on those few specific developments which seem to be of primary importance? This would contrast with the tendency in the United States to lump everything that's under way now as part of the U.S. response to the fifth-generation project. At least the Japanese are highly focused.

(2)   What new kinds of value-added are contributed by knowledge engineering and knowledge systems?

(3)   Is the best way to proceed with our national programs from a technology-push or demand-pull approach? It seems we have difficulty doing either well, but especially the latter.

Biosketch:

Dr. Frederick Hayes-Roth, Vice President, Teknowledge Inc., 525 University Ave., Palo Alto, Calif. 94301, 415-327-6600. Editor of the two principal references on knowledge engineering, *Pattern-directed Inference Systems* (Academic Press) and *Building Expert Systems* (Addison-Wesley). Former director of the AI research program at Rand Corp. Former principal on the Carnegie-Mellon University Hearsay-II connected speech understanding project. At Teknowledge, responsibilities include technology strategy for developing and leading the knowledge-engineering industry and management of knowledge-system development, curriculum development, and knowledge-engineering tool development. Harvard (A.B., 1969); MIT (Sloan School, 1969–1970); University of Michigan, (M.S., 1972; Ph.D., 1974). Former Visiting Associate Professor, Stanford.

From: ULLMAN@SU-SCORE.ARPA Mon Aug 1 00:00:20 1983
Date: Sun 31 Jul 83 21:55:14 PDT
From: Jeffrey D. Ullman ⟨ULLMAN@SU-SCORE.ARPA⟩
Subject: **Favorite issues/biosketch**
To: ng-mod@UWISC.ARPA

As for issues, I am quite content to let nature take its course. If I have to pick a favorite, I would like to discuss what needs to be done in the development of parallel and distributed algorithms.

Biosketch:

I guess I'm not sure what you want here. Surely you are not going to include in the roster information like prior employment, degrees, awards, publications. What exactly would you like?

From: ABell.PA@PARC-MAXC.ARPA Mon Aug 1 10:11:03 1983
Date: Mon, 1 Aug 83 08:07 PDT
From: ABell.PA@PARC-MAXC.ARPA
Subject: **Opening question**
To: NEW-GEN@CSNET-SH.ARPA
Cc: ABell.PA@PARC-MAXC.ARPA
Reply-to: NEW-GEN@CSNET-SH.ARPA

This message contains the first question to be discussed on the new-generation net conference. Please answer the question by sending a response to the whole distribution list at NEW-GEN@CSNET-SH. If you have any procedural comments or questions for the moderators, please send them to NG-MOD@CSNET-SH. A second question will be sent out in a few days.

First question:

What does "fifth" or "new" or "supercomputer" generation computing mean? What should the goals of these programs be? What will be the form of their structures, architectures, developments, and so forth? What will the results of this research look like after the technology has matured? Will there be several different efforts heading toward similar goals with different names (superscientific, fifth generation, and so forth)? How can each of them be characterized and distinguished?

From: blb@lanl Mon Aug 1 15:22:10 1983
Date: 1 Aug 1983 14:11:35 MDT
From: Bill Buzbee C-DO ⟨blb@lanl⟩
Reply-to: blb@lanl
To: NEW-GEN@CSNET-SH
Subject: **Terminology, etc.**

I'll begin with a short discussion of terminology and then offer some comments on the Japanese project.

(1)   Terminology. It seems to me that this is an "area of opportunity" for this teleconference. For example:

(a)   Fifth generation. At first blush it is easier to define fifth generation than new generation because (presumably) fifth generation is all things built out of VLSI. However, clearly the Japanese have a lot more in mind than component technology. My problem with "new" is that what is new today is old tomorrow.
(b)   Logic processing. Part of what is new in fifth generation is development and support of applications involving "nonnumeric computation." Since the phrase "symbolic manipulation" already has an established definition, we at Los Alamos have been considering the use of the phrases "numeric processing" and "logic processing" to distinguish between the

basic functionalities of computers. Have others noted a need for such, and what terms are you using?

(2) Japanese project. In this country, many people equate this project to research and development in AI. As I understand it, it is somewhat broader than that, but clearly AI is a vital component. So I'll review their objectives and offer some comments on them.

Evaluating Japanese objectives

The Japanese objectives are:

(a) Make computers easier to use, that is, usable by a large fraction of the population.
(b) Improve productivity in software development.
(c) Improve reliability and cost-effectiveness of hardware/software systems.

Comments:

Ease of use. The Japanese technical approach involves natural language processing, audio, graphics, AI, and so forth. This is an area where the U.S. personal-computer industry may be relevant because its market is proportional to ease-of-use. Some of the spread-sheet packages are conspicuous examples of this point.

Software productivity. I'm sure all of us appreciate the merits of work in this area. The Japanese technical approach involves programming enviroments and ultrahigh-level languages that have a high degree of verifiability. To what extent, if any, do the Japanese enjoy an advantage in this area because of the tremendous amount of software that the United States has in place and must carry into the future?

Reliability. The Japanese seek to further improve the reliability and performance of their components, as well as to improve fault tolerance and automatic diagnostics in their systems. This area is their forte.

Best of both worlds. The point of the previous comments is that the Japanese can make progress toward their objectives without any technological breakthroughs. This is not to discount the revolutionary aspects of the project (aspects that have already captured the imagination of the world's computing community), but to note that to some extent they can have their cake and eat it, too.

From: Ullman@Diablo@SU-Score Mon Aug 1 19:48:21 1983
Received: from Diablo by Score with Pup; Mon 1 Aug 83 17:45:59-PDT
Date: Mon, 1 Aug 83 17:30 PDT
From: Jeff Ullman ⟨ullman@Diablo@SU-Score⟩
To: new-gen@csnet-sh
Subject: **Response to question (1)**

The new generation of computers arrived this year not because of the recent Japanese preoccupation with AI, but because it suddenly became unreasonable to see computer technology progress in terms of cheaper processors. Once we have a $10 processor chip, I don't see a big future for trying to invent the 30-cent processor that can be used to control the ink flow in my 50-cent ballpoint pen. Instead, roughly from here on, progress is going to be measured by how many processors we can bring to bear on a single problem.

The primary research goals, as I see it, concern software and algorithms as much as they do architecture. Really, everything has got to fit together: the application, the algorithm, the language, the communication support, the operating system, and the hardware, or we won't get useful work out of more than a few processors.

However, I think we can classify the architectures for supercomputers into a few groups, each of which will have its place.

(1) High-flux machines, such as ultracomputers (shuffle-exchange machines), butterfly networks, hypercubes, cube-connected cycles, and so forth. These are characterized by the ability to move massive quantities of data in parallel from any set of processors to any other, quickly. I predict that these machines will have their greatest impact in the AI domain, where, despite our best attempts to narrow search, we shall find that logical inferences depend substantially on "everything meeting everything else."

(2) Tree machines. These are in a sense opposite to high-flux machines. They have a massive bottleneck at the root and cannot be used for pairing rules and data in arbitrary ways efficiently. However, they may play a role as retrieval devices for massive data bases.

(3) Arrays of proccessors, for example, systolic arrays. These are intermediate in flux between the ultracomputers and the trees. For example, they can sort n elements in a time that is proportional to the square root of n, while high-flux machines take log n and tree machines take time n. They have a crucial role to play because they are tuned well to the data-transmission requirements of a number of problems, for example, feature extraction and various numerical problems.

Date: 2 Aug 1983 15:28 PDT
From: RAPHAEL@HP-HULK
Subject: **First status report**
To: new-gen.csnet@RAND-RELAY
Cc: RAPHAEL

The two leading messages of the teleconference ("Teleconference . . ." and "Opening question") were sent to 42 network addresses. So far we have received two replies to the opening question, responses to the moderator's requests from four others, acknowledgements of participation from five more, identification of four bad addresses, and *no response from 27 people*.

We have to conclude this discussion—or at least this phase of it—three weeks from today (before several participants disappear at the American AI Conference in Washington). We anticipated almost daily interaction from most of the participants; a high level of interaction, even with brief, informal comments, is probably necessary to achieve some useful results, and should be well supported by this medium of communication.

Please send in your burning thoughts on the opening question, or your reactions to Dr. Buzbee's or Dr. Ullman's thoughts, or your complaint that it's a dumb question, *now*—so we will know you are out there and interested.

Bert Raphael

From: Fahlman@CMU-CS-C.ARPA Tue Aug 2 21:23:04 1983
Received: ID ⟨FAHLMAN@CMU-CS-C.ARPA⟩; Tue 2 Aug 83 22:20:55-EDT
Date: Tue, 2 Aug 1983 22:20 EDT
From: Scott E. Fahlman ⟨Fahlman@CMU-CS-C.ARPA⟩
To: new-gen@UWISC.ARPA
Cc: fahlman@CMU-CS-C.ARPA
Subject: **Reply to question (1)**
In-reply-to: Msg of Tue 2 Aug 83 15:50:45-PDT from Jeffery D. Ullman ⟨ULLMAN at SU-SCORE.ARPA⟩

I agree with Jeffrey Ullman's comments that the next generation is going to be largely concerned with parallelism. I also agree with his view that within the world of parallel architectures, the amount and pattern of connectivity is usually the critical question. Once we start finding microprocessors in Cracker Jacks boxes, the real bottleneck is going to be communication among the processors, and not in the amount of available processor power.

How connectivity might be used

Let me propose an orthogonal classification that complements Ullman's division into high-flux machines, low-flux tree machines, and intermediate-flux arrays. Instead of looking at the amount of connectivity, we might look at how it is used. This view gives rise to the following sorts of categories:

(1)   General-purpose machines with reconfigurable connection networks. All of Ullman's high-flux examples fall into this category: butterfly machines, *n*-cubes, and so forth.

(2)   Special-purpose machines with connectivity tailored to a specific application. A hard-wired systolic sorting network would be an example. A D-hardware retina or image-transformation processor would be another. Note that the communication bandwidth can be very high in such architectures, since you do not have to pay the price for general interconnection.

Another category might be "connectionist" machines (Jerry Feldman's term), in which the resident knowledge is represented by the pattern of connectivity—the presence or absence of a wire between two points, perhaps with some variable weight on the wire—and not as bits inside some processor's memory. Most knowledge-based machines are full of pointers; these machines just take that view a bit more literally than most. These can be viewed as custom-wired machines like those in class 2, but new connections must be added from time to time as new knowledge is added.

Of course, the real world is never so clean as our taxonomies would suggest. An Illiac-IV is sometimes used as a class 2 machine with the right connectivity to munch square arrays, and sometimes as a class 1 machine with the existing connections used to implement arbitrary patterns or virtual connectivity. A connectionist machine is a nice abstraction, but when you want to implement it you might use an *n*-cube network of processors, each representing a thousand lower-level nodes. Despite these "A masquerading as B implementing C" games, however, I have found this sort of division useful in thinking about the mapping between architectures and applications.

Scott Fahlman, CMU

From: DAVID@COLUMBIA-20.ARPA Wed Aug 2 12:03:46 1983
Date: Wed 3 Aug 83 13:01:46 EDT
From: David Shaw ⟨DAVID@COLUMBIA-20.ARPA⟩
Subject: **New-generation supercomputers**
To: new-gen@UWISC.ARPA

Colleagues:

Let me apologize in advance for what will probably be a fairly long message. Because of other commitments during the period of our teleconference, though, it will be a lot easier for me to express my thoughts in a small number of long contributions than to send quick responses on an "almost daily" basis.

I'm personally quite fond of the term "new-generation supercomputers" as a description of machines that might incorporate:

• A very large number (thousands to millions) of processing elements, and

• High-level mechanisms for the description of computational tasks.

As Bill Buzbee and Jeff Ullman pointed out, the development of such machines will depend on closely coupled advances in both the hardware and software arenas. On the basis of the mutual reinforcement that Backus and others have observed between old-generation machine architectures and old-generation programming languages, I would predict that these changes will necessarily be revolutionary, and not evolutionary, in nature. For several years now, I have also believed that such advances are likely to draw heavily on techniques and formalisms borrowed from the areas of artificial intelligence and logic programming, and on such closely related computational operations as the relational algebraic primitives.

While taxonomic classification of new-generation supercomputers is, as Scott Fahlman pointed out, often problematic, I'd like to share the scheme I've been using for three years in teaching our course on parallel architectures and VLSI systems at Columbia. This scheme assigns each "homogeneous machine" (I'll explain that term shortly) a position in each of three interacting dimensions:

(1)   Topology, which I divide into the following three categories:

(a)   Meshes. In this category, I include the linear array, the two-, three-, and other constant-dimensional meshes, and such "nearly isomorphic" interconnection topologies as ring networks, chordal rings, and toroidal meshes.

(b) Trees. In practice, these almost always seem to be binary.

(c) High-bandwidth machines. This category includes machines based on interconnection networks having a logarithmic number of stages and offering high throughput with log-time latency.

Every n-cube doesn't fit neatly into any of these slots, but is clearly related to both the first and last categories.

(2) Granularity, represented by a spectrum with the following endpoints:

(a) Coarse-granularity machines. These have a relatively small number of fast processing elements, each associated with a substantial amount of local memory.

(b) Fine-granularity machines. Such machines are characterized by a very large number of comparatively slow processing elements having very little local storage capacity.

(3) Synchrony, which is used to distinguish between the following two categories:

(a) Synchronous machines. This category corresponds to Flynn's notion of single-instruction multiple-data stream (SIMD) machines, in which each instruction is broadcast to a large number of processing elements, which execute it simultaneously on different data elements.

(b) Asynchronous machines. These are the multiple-instruction multiple-data stream (MIMD) machines, which are capable of executing independent instruction streams generated by programs stored in each of their processing elements.

Concerns of new-generation architects

In my view, it is the interaction between choices along these three dimensions that is of central interest to the architect of a new-generation machine. As an example of the interaction between topology and granularity, note that the tree-structured and linear-array topologies are "fully scalable," and can thus be used to build extremely-fine-granularity machines. The high-bandwidth machines scale very poorly, while the higher-dimensional meshes fall somewhere in between.

On the other hand, the high-bandwidth machines are able, for example, to permute data elements from all processing elements much more rapidly than the trees and linear arrays, with the higher-dimensional meshes again occupying an intermediate position. We thus observe that very-fine-granularity machines tend to employ one of the more scalable topologies, where coarse-granularity machines are free to employ more powerful, asymptotically high-bandwidth interconnection schemes.

Granularity and synchrony also interact strongly, since the finest-granularity machines, while offering tremendous raw computational power, have an insufficient amount of local memory to store their own programs locally, and must "import" them from one or more external "control processors." Such machines are thus typically synchronous. Coarser-granularity machines, on the other hand, are able to store substantial programs locally, and thus tend to take advantage of the greater algorithmic flexibility offered by asynchronous execution.

I should emphasize that this classification scheme applies to what might be called "homogeneous machines." In fact, I think there is good reason to believe that most new-generation supercomputers will ultimately be "heterogeneous" in terms of topology, granularity, and synchrony. Such machines, exemplified by MIT's Connection Machine and the emerging design for Non-Von 4, incorporate more than one kind of interconnection topology to take advantage of the benefits of different classes of homogeneous architectures.

As a final note, I think it's worth remembering Larry Synder's warning that "we don't live in Asymptopia." Although I've found the conceptual framework outlined above to be useful in practice, I wouldn't really be too surprised if some clever constant-juggler ultimately designed a superior next-generation supercomputer that represented a radical departure from the "first principles" arguments I've just advanced.

From : rjd@lanl Wed Aug 3 14:33:14 1983
Date: 3 Aug 1983 13:26:55 MDT
From: Robert Douglass C-10 ⟨rjd@lanl⟩
Reply-to: rjd@lanl
To: NG-MOD@CSNET-SH
Subject: **Issues and biosketch**
Cc: rjd@lanl

Issues of interest:

We have heard a lot about the technology (especially hardware) for the new generation, but very little about how the new generation will actually be used or who will use it.

(1) Starting from a list or discussion of applications, what are the principal software components of the new generation, and what requirements do they dictate in terms of communication, architectures, storage, and parallel and distributed computing?

(2) Given an answer to (1), what are the critical "new" components, and are they realizable in 10 years?

Sketch:

Robert J. Douglass received the B.S.E. degree in Electrical Engineering from Princeton University in 1973 and the M.S. and Ph.D. degrees from the University of Wisconsin, Computer Sciences Department, in 1974 and 1978, respectively, majoring in the area of artificial intelligence and minoring in the area of cognitive and neural modeling. His dissertation and much of his subsequent research involved computer vision systems for three-dimensional perception and parallel computer systems to support models of intelligence and perception. While a faculty member at the University of Virginia, he taught and conducted research on artificial intelligence and parallel processing. In the area of parallel processing, he has published papers on programming languages for MIMD and SIMD arrays, parallel architectures, and parallel algorithms for speech and vision. Other publications include contributions to the literature on computer vision and the application of natural-language processing and expert systems to the human-machine interface.

Currently, he is working at the Los Alamos National Laboratory, where he leads a research team investigating artificial intelligence and programming languages for parallel processing aimed at providing supercomputing power for symbolic computation and using speech, vision, natural-language, and expert-system processing techniques to improve the human-machine interface. Specific ongoing projects include developing an applicative language and dataflow implementation for the CDC AFP parallel-array computer, implementing LISP on the Cray, interfacing LISP work stations to supercomputers to achieve a high-quality programming environment coupled with high-speed execution of both numeric and nonnumeric programs, and developing a computer consultant that can explain how to use computing systems using speech input and output and English language dialogue.

From: SCHWARTZ.CMCL1@NYU.ARPA Wed Aug 3
    14:37:04 1983
Date: 3 Aug 83 14:59 EDT
From: Jack Schwartz ⟨SCHWARTZ.CMCL1@NYU.ARPA⟩
To: new-gen@UWISC.ARPA
Subject: **The challenge is technological**
Cc: Malvin Kalos ⟨KALOS.CMCL1@NYU.ARPA⟩
Message-ID: ⟨215524F7F.00C7001E;1983
    @CMCL1.NYU.ARPA⟩

I concur with the opinion, expressed by Drs. Ullman and Fahlman, that the essential new opportunity is technological, *viz.* to exploit parallelism on a very large scale, and that a first crucial question is what form of interconnection to use. I agree with Dr. Ullman's classification of interconnection architectures. Another parameter entering into design is the size of the individual processing element to be used. Suggestions have ranged from "very large, fast as possible" (leading to S1-like designs incorporating a relatively small number of 10-MIP individual processors), through "most cost-effective, high-performance one-chip microprocessors" (characteristic for the "ultracomputer" type of machine with which we are working), to "largest possible number of highly simplified processors" (characteristic for image processors, systolic arrays, and various tree machines).

It seems to me that these two parameters, namely, interconnection pattern and processor size, are the key issues which the 50-odd university architectural suggestions now extant have been exploring. Naturally enough, designs based on more substantial processors tend to use the powerful anywhere-toanywhere connections like the shuffle; many-tiny-processor machines tend to favor connections, like the tree and nearest neighbor, which lay out well on silicon.

The most important organizational issue now is to get a number of really powerful parallel machines manufactured and into the hands of application-oriented groups, so that real experience can begin to accumulate on a large scale, efficiency questions can be understood, and so forth. Software and algorithm designers will have to learn how to organize concurrent computation on a very large scale, develop operating systems, image I/O, and so forth.

Aiming for general machines

Aiming for general machines I feel strongly that, with the possible exception of designs specialized for image processing,

this first round of machines should aim at designs which are general rather than highly specialized, since there is as yet no field in which parallel algorithms are well enough understood for a large specialized engine to be a wise bet. In particular, I think it rather unlikely that Prolog will have major programming advantages, or even that the best way to move toward an efficient parallel implementation of Prolog can be understood without a great deal of penetrating research that still remains to be done. The phrase "fifth generation" is, of course, a catchword which should not be allowed to blind us to the essentially technological nature of the opportunity which fast cheap silicon now offers.

While the technology matures, I believe we will see a continuing contest to upgrade machines and to offer better price-performance, much as what we see now. It seems clear that the United States and Japan will both succeed in producing parallel supercomputers, and this within a very few years of each other. Hence, we are not so much racing for a unique golden ring as positioning ourselves for the long haul.

Jack Schwartz

From: DAVID@COLUMBIA-20.ARPA Wed Aug 3 15:32:35
    1983
Date: Wed 3 Aug 83 16:31:06 EDT
From: David Shaw ⟨DAVID@COLUMBIA-20.ARPA⟩
Subject: **Machines for users**
To: new-gen@UWISC.ARPA

I agree strongly with Jack Schwartz about the importance of getting parallel machines into the hands of application-oriented user groups.

David

From: trimberg Wed Aug 3 21:51:47 1983
To: ng-mod@csnet-sh
Subject: **Interesting topics and short bio**
Cc: trimberg

Please respond if this message was sent correctly.

Favorite issue: To what extent will the implementation medium, presumably integrated circuits, influence the design of the fifth-generation computers?

My bio:

Stephen Trimberger received his B.S. degree from the California Institute of Technology in 1977 and his M.S. degree from the University of California at Irvine while working in the data-flow architecture group.

He returned to the Computer Science Department at Caltech, where he held the position of Deputy Director of the Silicon Structures Project prior to completing his Ph.D. in 1983 in the area of integrated-circuit design tools, specifically, automated performance optimization for custom-integrated circuits.

He contributed to the definition of Caltech Intermediate Form (CIF) for integrated-circuit description and to the Caltech Silicon Structures Project Integrated-Circuit Design Software Package. His recent work includes definition of an interchange form for symbolic layout data, research into combining algorithmic and graphic-design techniques, chip-assembly software, and performance optimization of integrated circuits.

He is currently employed by VLSI Technology, Inc. of San Jose, Calif., where he is developing advanced chip-assembly tools.

From: Guy.Steele@CMU-CS-A Wed Aug 3 22:42:42 1983
Received: from [128.2.254.192] by CMU-CS-PT with
      CMUFTP; 3 Aug 83 23:34:05 EDT
Date: 3 Aug 83 23:41 EDT (Wednesday)
From: Guy.Steele@CMU-CS-A
To: new-gen@uwisc
Subject: **Exploitation of parallelism**

Experience has shown that it is fairly difficult to take an algorithm coded with no thought for parallelism and automatically "parallelize" it, either with a compiler or by dynamic load allocation. (I speculate that this is because we tend to think things out sequentially, and when we are programming we introduce unnecessary sequencing constraints unless specifically working hard to avoid such unnecessary constraints. This, however, is a matter for psychologists.)

This leads me to conclude that successful use of architectural parallelism will necessarily be founded on proper exploitation of algorithmic parallelism. We need to identify standard paradigms of parallelism that have widespread utility and only then build hardware specifically to support these paradigms.

The stereotypical Von Neumann

Let me give two examples. First, consider the stereotypical Von Neumann architecture, usually conceived as having no parallelism. In fact it normally contains one very powerful parallel-processing unit: the arithmetic-logic unit (ALU). The operations of "integer" addition, multiplication, division, and so on, viewed as functions from bit patterns to bit patterns, are exceedingly complicated; their floating-point counterparts are even more complicated. Good ALU hardware performs a great deal of bit-parallel processing to good effect. Now these operations are extremely special-purpose. They are useful only because they have an extremely powerful and well-understood model, namely the mathematics of arithmetic.

The fact that the implementation is not perfect (overflow and round-off errors are difficult to analyze) makes the operations no less useful. The model itself, in simplest form, is not necessarily inherently parallel; the simplest way to describe addition is perhaps by means of a ripple-carry chain. But the fact that there is a powerful underlying theory allows such techniques as carry-look-ahead adders to be developed and analyzed, as well as more esoteric representations such as residue arithmetic rather than two's-complement, say. Note that in this architectural context the model (arithmetic) came first; the hardware is then built specifically to support this model as well as possible.

A second example is Dr. Fahlman's NETL system. This is not at all a general-purpose parallel-processing system. It supports primarily operations on sets, notably intersection, and through them also operations on relations; thus operations such as transitive closure are fairly fast. The point is that Dr. Fahlman *first* posited a hypothesis: Set operations are sufficiently important to a wide class of applications, particularly in AI research, that it is worthwhile making them fast. This hypothesis is plausible precisely because there is a rich and well-understood theory underlying these operations. This theory in turn yields the understanding necessary to parallelize the operations. Only with this understanding is it then reasonable to go out and design hardware.

Some of what I have said may be construed as an argument for the expert-systems approach: I claim that it is much better to pick a few well-understood paradigms of widespread utility, parallelize them extremely well, and package them, than to try to be able to parallelize any general program and do only a fair job of it. The Japanese effort might or might not be an example of this. Certainly first-order predicate logic is a reasonably well-understood paradigm of wide utility. Is Prolog the correct embodiment of logic to try to parallelize?

Guy Steele

From: Fahlman@CMU-CS-C.ARPA Wed Aug 3 23:42:00 1983
Received: ID ⟨FAHLMAN@CMU-CS-C.ARPA⟩; Thu 4 Aug
      83 00:41:09-EDT
Date: Thu, 4 Aug 1983 00:41 EDT
From: Scott E. Fahlman ⟨Fahlman@CMU-CS-C.ARPA⟩
To: new-gen@UWISC.ARPA
Cc: fahlman@CMU-CS-C.ARPA
Subject: **Problem characterization**

Several of us have now made stabs at classifying parallel architectures, and I think this is a useful exercise. It seems to me that we also need to look at the structure of the most important problems that we would like the new generation of machines to solve. Where are the bottlenecks? What do the critical inner loops look like? How much parallelism is possible in these loops? Does the problem suggest some natural level of granularity or pattern of connectivity?

For example, it seems clear that image processing, both for vision and for computer-animation tasks, is one of the tasks that could use a lot more cycles than you get from even a fast uniprocessor. Most of the cycles seem to be going into the low-level analysis/generation of the pixels. These low-level operations are very simple and repetitive: For each pixel, compute some function of its inputs and those of its neighbors. At the higher levels, farther from the pixels, one finds complex logical dependencies, but at the low levels any dependencies tend to be local in nature. This task, then, seems naturally suited for a rather fine-grained SIMD machine with one processor per pixel and predominantly local (nearest neighbor) connectivity. Of course, more general architectures can be run in ways that simulate this organization, but with some waste.

I want to make a statement that will probably be controversial: In looking at AI applications, I see a lot of places with rather low inherent parallelism, and a few places with opportunities for tremendous parallelism. I don't see much in the middle. Most LISP programs and production systems sputter along on a relatively linear course, with perhaps two or three side paths to explore, until they come to a point where millionfold parallelism, of a simple sort, is possible:

- Do the operation for every pixel.
- Find the relevant fact in some huge knowledge base.
- Find the strongest connection between "lawyer" and "ambulance."
- Compare the input against all stored patterns.
- Select the next production rule to fire.
- Search the space of arm positions and velocities for the minimum-energy solution.

This suggests that for AI tasks, one wants a good serial symbol-processing machine to do the linear parts (a LISP machine or something similar, which also provides the experimenter with a livable environment) and a bunch of fine-grained, massively parallel accelerators for these key inner loops. I don't see a lot of AI tasks that map naturally into 256-way or 1024-way parallelism, except when those machines are used as a way of simulating much finer-grained architectures until we know enough to build these directly.

Anyway, that's my "1, 2, 3, infinity" model of parallelism in AI, and that's why I have been studying very-fine-grained architectures. I am not sure whether other important next-generation domains—number crunching, simulation, data-base applications—have the same character.

I want to hasten to·add that, as an exploratory tool, we will certainly need to make use of more conventional parallel architectures—1024 Cray-1's connected in a 10-D cube, or whatever. We don't want to build the massive but highly specialized machines until we've done a *lot* of simulation studies, and you can't get very far on a uniprocessor.

Scott Fahlman, CMU

From: RHAYES-ROTH@SRI-KL.ARPA Thu Aug 4 12:36:32 1983
Date: Thu 4 Aug 83 10:34:03 PDT
From: RHAYES-ROTH@SRI-KL.ARPA
Subject: **Exploitation of parallelism: expert-systems approach**
To: new-gen@UWISC.ARPA
Cc: guy.steele@CMU-CS-A.ARPA

I'd like to endorse the perspective that Guy Steele advanced. The earlier messages emphasized the technological opportunity, but Guy correctly pointed out that a great deal of constraint is required to exploit that opportunity. I'd like to amplify some of the ideas he introduced.

Importance of knowledge engineering

Various practical applications of AI methods to date have demonstrated repeatedly the importance of knowledge engineering, in two senses. First, general methods of knowledge representation and deduction have failed to provide much leverage on solving problems. Instead, people had to study carefully how practical knowledge could simplify hard tasks. Such practical knowledge provides ways to avoid blind alleys, prune large subspaces from consideration, generate promising paths first, and so forth. Often this kind of knowledge is necessary and sufficient as a basis for any solution. The second sense of knowledge engineering has concerned specific control methods for organizing heuristic problem solving. In this area, expert systems have often required invention of new data struc-

tures to hold intermediate values that make it possible to solve complex problems incrementally. Examples of this kind of fundamental work occur in Dendral, Hearsay-II, and most signal understanding tasks. In this area, knowledge engineering extends the kind of work done in analysis of algorithms. It is difficult to see how general-purpose advances in architecture will replace the need for this kind of specialization of control and data structure.

Now, it seems that an outside-in approach to designing new equipment would constrain us to develop machines that support the kinds of data structures, knowledge representations, intermediate structures, and control methods that prove useful in application. When this point was made to the Japanese (noting that they had overlooked the importance of informed demand-pull in their project), they readily accepted it and added a major thrust in expert systems. I predict that their experience in that area will strongly influence and reorient their directions over the next few years.

Experience to date seems to indicate that parallelism has many roles to play in knowledge systems. These include search, retrieval, interpretation, plan generation, and so forth. However, it also seems clear that naive notions of power are usually wildly misguided. Specifically, general-purpose designs make limited contributions to high-valued difficult applications. Rather, general architectural principles derive from practical performing systems. I would suggest that work to date in AI applications does not provide enough constraint to ensure a reasonably high rate of successful architectural advances. What seems needed to me are more data and more analysis. That would put the horse before the cart. However, I can plainly see that advances in cart·technologies (wheels, spokes, bearings, axles) need not wait for the horse. I'd just prefer to see the cart makers serving the perceived need, and to see the need itself elucidated.

Rick Hayes-Roth

From: ULLMAN@SU-SCORE.ARPA Thu Aug 4 14:53:56 1983
Date: Thu 4 Aug 83 12:46:28 PDT
From: Jeffrey D. Ullman ⟨ULLMAN@SU-SCORE.ARPA⟩
Subject: **Data structures**
To: new-gen@UWISC.ARPA

Prolog and relational algebra

I agree fully with the Steele/Fahlman view that software to utilize massive parallelism should be built around well-understood, natural, and evidently useful models. Since Prolog could hardly be excluded from consideration in this regard, we should remember that in the past 10 years there has been lots of experience translating logic into more tractable forms. I refer to the work in relational data-base systems, much of which (for example, Query-by-Example), starts from a first-order logic (relational calculus) and translates into an equivalent relational algebra expression.

The algebra is relatively easy to optimize, and while most of the optimization work has been for uniprocessors, there appears to be tremendous opportunity to build parallel implementations of the algebra.

Dave Maier suggested to me that the right way to deal with

Prolog is to develop an extended algebra (because Prolog is more powerful than relational calculus), translate Prolog to the algebra, and work on optimizing and parallelizing that.

How unique are AI data structures?

It seems that the view expressed by Hayes-Roth is diametrically opposed to the Steele/Fahlman view, and I must admit I am a bit puzzled by the implication that AI tasks require unique data structures, and that these structures must therefore drive unique hardware designs for a large number of different applications. In a sense, every large program ever written, whether it is an "AI" program or not, uses a unique data structure, if by that we take the data structure of the program to mean the full set of interconnections, explicit or logical, used in the program. Usually, we try to unify rather than emphasize the uniqueness of data structures.

We must convey data-structure ideas to the people to whom they will be useful. Volumes I and III of Knuth contain many structures that are worth conveying, because they are used time and again as components of people's data structures.

The Hayes-Roth statement that knowledge engineers are advancing the state of the art in analysis of algorithms implies to me that there are new ideas, not found in Knuth [*The Art of Computer Programming* by Donald Knuth, published by Addison-Wesley, Reading, Mass.—*Ed.*] that deserve to be taught along with them because they are going to be used repeatedly.

As Guy Steele pointed out, the natural and common structures form a good basis for the development of general-purpose tools. LISP, largely an embodiment of the tree data structure, is an example. Can anyone imagine a language based on the left-handed, triple-ended queue with three bells and two whistles?

Of course, there are some tasks that require absolutely unique facilities for their implementation. An example right now might be an Ethernet chip, since a general-purpose microprocessor is just not fast enough. However, these applications tend to fade into the background when the next speedup in general-purpose hardware is made. However, I feel it is inadvisable to perceive one's intermediate data representations as more specialized than they really are.

For example, one hears of knowledge bases as an improvement on the old-fashioned data base. I suppose that I could be criticized as out-of-date if I suggested storing a knowledge base in an ordinary relational data-base system, because such systems appear only to deal with very flat objects (relations, which are hardly more than files), while AI applications frequently need powerful structures. Yet I can build all structures out of relations by interpreting my data properly. Certain systems, like Query-by-Example, even allow the representation of "meta-knowledge" in the same system, because information about structure is automatically kept in a user-accessible relation. In fact, to turn the point around, LISP could be viewed as an attempt to keep all data in a single binary relation.

Nothing I have said negates the fact that the last factor of 2, or 10, often has to be squeezed out by taking the special-purpose route. However, general-purpose tools in compensation can receive the benefit of public thought on optimization, and tools like relational data bases have in fact benefited tremen-

dously from such thought. Thus, to ignore, or even relegate to second place, the study of general-purpose tools seems like ignoring microprocessor design and building a special-purpose chip for every application.

Jeff Ullman

From: Fahlman@CMU-CS-C.ARPA Thu Aug 4 17:45:50 1983
Received: ID ⟨FAHLMAN@CMU-CS-C.ARPA⟩; Thu 4 Aug
            83 18:44:26 EDT
Date: Thu, 4 Aug 1983 18:44 EDT
From: Scott E. Fahlman ⟨Fahlman@CMU-CS-C.ARPA⟩
To: new-gen@UWISC.ARPA
Subject: **Data structures**
In-reply-to: Msg of Thu 4 Aug 83 12:46:28-PDT from Jeffrey
            D. Ullman ⟨ULLMAN at SU-SCORE.ARPA⟩

Just a thought or two on Jeff Ullman's comments:

(1) I agree that you don't want to build a special-purpose machine for every little application that comes along. On the other hand, if a large family of important tasks (accessing AI knowledge bases or whatever) spends most of its time in a particular loop, and if the time spent in that loop is a serious limitation on what can be done, it is worth looking very hard at *that* specialization.

(2) A special-purpose architecture may only get you "that last factor of 2 or 10" if we're talking about reorganizing a single processor—getting rid of a level of interpretation or adding a couple of new data paths. But if the kind of specialization being considered is moving to a particular task-specific pattern of connectivity or trading a single general microprocessor for a thousand very simple specialized elements, the speedup can be more like 100 or 1000—maybe even more, depending on the task. This kind of a factor can make a qualitative difference in what problems we can attack and what approaches make sense (exhaustive search vs. heuristic-limited search, and so forth).

I don't want to specialize our machines too early or for too little reason, but neither do we want to limit our horizons by looking only at approaches that make sense on coarse-grained general-purpose machines.

Scott Fahlman

From: kgw@Cornell Thu Aug 4 20:12:26 1983
Date: 4 Aug 83 21:10:59 EDT (Thu)
From: kgw@Cornell (Ken Wilson)
Subject: **Issues and biosketch**
Message-Id: ⟨8308050110.AA17986@GVAX.CORNELL⟩
Received: by GVAX.CORNELL (3.320/3.14)
To: NG-MOD@CSNET-SH

I am interested in scientific number crunching and new programming environments that support number crunching. I see the main issues here as

(1) Providing an environment that supports modular programming and reusable modules, with the modules representing a logical breakdown of a programming task as seen by a

scientist rather than the much more artificial subroutines or procedures of current languages, and

(2) Putting parallel processing to work as rapidly as possible in applications where it is already known to work, and expanding this range as rapidly as possible.

Bio:

Physicist. Subfields: elementary particle physics; statistical mechanics. Ph.D., Caltech, 1961. Faculty member, Cornell University, 1963–present. Nobel Laureate, Physics, 1982. Computing interests: array processors; Monte Carlo computations in statistical mechanics and quantum field theory; optimization for horizontal microcode; and programming environments for scientific programming including a higher-level language than Fortran. Leader of the Gibbs programming environment project at Cornell (in collaboration with Cornell Computer Science Department) and member of 1982 LAX Panel on scientific computing.

From: kgw@Cornell Thu Aug 4 20:54:02 1983
Date: 4 Aug 83 21:51:06 EDT (Thu)
From: kgw@Cornell (Ken Wilson)
Subject: **Parallel processing**
Message-Id: ⟨8308050151.AA18338@GVAX.CORNELL⟩
Received: by GVAX.CORNELL (3.320/3.14)
        id AA18338; 4 Aug 83 21:51:06 EDT (Thu)
To: NEW-GEN@CSNET-SH
Cc: kgw@Cornell

From my viewpoint as a user of parallel processing for number crunching, I find myself increasingly impatient with overall discussions of network topologies and the like. Meanwhile my colleague Stewart Pawley at the University of Edinburgh (Scotland) has got himself a 4000-processor distributed-array processor (DAP) from International Computers Ltd. and has proceeded to demonstrate that he can get the full 4000-fold speedup on all the problems I am personally interested in. Since any civilized parallel processing system can handle any problem the DAP can, I have lost interest in complicated network topologies and am trying to obtain a 40-gigaflop square array as fast as possible so I can get some physics done and not wallow in the general parallel-processing mire. I also recognize that I need a civilized framework for writing down my programs including the optimization strategy for the parallelism and for the horizontal microcode likely to be required for individual nodes of a 40-gigaflop system. Hence I have started the Gibbs project with Alan Demers and David Griese of Cornell to develop a programming environment meeting my needs. Fortran is not acceptable, but I am doubtful that, for a scientist, other current languages do much better.

Ken Wilson, Cornell Physics Department

From: DAVIS%MIT-OZ@MIT-MC Thu Aug 4 23:05:12 1983
Date: Thursday, August 4, 1983 9:53PM EDT
From: Randy Davis ⟨DAVIS%MIT-OZ@MIT-MC⟩
Subject: **Last minute . . .**
To: ng-mod at CSNET-SH
Cc: davis at MIT-OZ

Sorry; read the initial message too fast and didn't notice the request for bio. Herewith the usual puffery:

Randall Davis received his undergraduate degree from Dartmouth, graduating summa cum laude, Phi Beta Kappa in 1970. While at Stanford he was an early contributor to the Mycin Project and developed the Teiresias program, a system for knowledge acquisition in expert systems. He received his Ph.D. in artificial intelligence in 1976 and spent two additional years at Stanford as a Chaim Weizmann Postdoctoral Scholar.

He joined the faculty at MIT and held an Esther and Harold Edgerton Endowed Chair from 1979 to 1981. His current research focuses on expert systems that work from descriptions of structure and function and hence are capable of reasoning from "first principles" to support a wider range of more robust problem-solving performance.

He has published widely on expert systems and serves on the editorial board of *Artificial Intelligence* and the new Japanese journal *New Generation Computing*.

He is the co-author of *Knowledge-Based Systems in AI* and presented an Invited Lecture on expert systems at the 1981 International Joint Conference on AI. He is a founding consultant of Teknowledge and a co-founder of Applied Expert Systems.

From: DAVIS%MIT-OZ@MIT-MC Thu Aug 4 23:06:43 1983
Date: Thursday, August 4, 1983 10:33PM EDT
From: Randy Davis ⟨DAVIS%MIT-OZ@MIT-MC⟩
Subject: **First question and replies**
To: new-gen at CSNET-SH

Well, I suppose it takes some disagreement to make it a discussion, so . . .

Re: Terminology. One of the worst things we could do is try to turn this into an "area of opportunity." All of the terms I have heard associated with the fifth-generation effort are either already well-defined technical terms (for example, "symbolic computation" or "fifth generation") or simply names ("new generation"). Making up new definitions or new words for existing concepts will do nothing but confuse a fairly simple issue.

"Logic processing," whatever it may be (it's just a name, apparently without a widely accepted definition) is surely not the complement of "numeric processing." Nonnumeric is a perfectly good complement, and is perhaps a tad more precise than symbolic computation (numerals are symbols, too). Regular use has in any case sanitized the latter to mean the complement of numeric, so it's perfectly serviceable. Why invent new terms?

Japanese objectives:

They're everybody's objectives. It's as straightforward a definition of much of the work in AI, architecture, programming languages, and so forth, as one could conjure up. All they did was put a national effort behind it. No small administrative and economic accomplishment, but not an intellectual one.

Nature of the parallelism problem

Dr. Ullman says, "The primary goals . . . concern software and algorithms as much as they do architecture." Agreed. There's a very serious problem in saying, as some have, that the problem is totally technical.

If you think it is, imagine that someone has hooked up a million processors in an *n*-cube. What would you (or anyone) *do* with it? A few very well-defined applications have been mentioned, but that's the whole point: As Drs. Fahlman and Steele have already said far better, it will do no good to invent new architectures without a very good idea of why it's a good design to use, and for what. I find it almost vacuous to hear claims of constructing massive parallelism without any good idea of how to use that to do something.

A few interesting exceptions to this approach that I know of (there are others) include the systolic arrays and the connection machine. For both of these the need—the problem—came first. From the first time the machines work, there will be something useful for them to do.

We do need technological breakthroughs, but to consider that the whole of the problem is to be virtually guaranteed to invent solutions for which there are no problems. First we have to understand the need for and uses for parallelism. I think the kind of comments Drs. Fahlman and Steele made are exactly the sort we need much more thought about. What, how, and where will parallelism get us? What kind of parallelism and where?

AI at this point should not be contaminated with religion and sociology. That has, I think, vanishingly little to do with expert systems. It's an issue of approach. When the problem is as ill-defined as this one is, and when it runs the risk of being technology driven, it makes good sense to try the case study/ induction approach: Get a few specific examples to work very well and then do the induction step. Doing some well-defined experiments to map out the waters is not an insight unique to expert systems.

Randy Davis

From: ULLMAN@SU-SCORE.ARPA Fri Aug 5 00:20:56
    1983
Date: Thu 4 Aug 83 22:13:47 PDT
From: Jeffrey D. Ullman ⟨ULLMAN@SU-SCORE.ARPA⟩
Subject: **Biosketch**
To: ng-mod@UWISC.ARPA

Sorry; I was having so much fun I forgot the biography. Here it is:

Biosketch—Jeff Ullman

B.S. Columbia 1963, Ph.D. Princeton, 1966. Worked Bell Labs 1966–69, Princeton, 1969–79, Stanford 1979–present. My principal intellectual contribution to the field is 11 textbooks, frequently used at the junior–to–graduate levels.

From: Guy.Steele@CMU-CS-A Fri Aug 5 00:22:10 1983
Received: from [128.2.254.192] by CMU-CS-PT with
    CMUFTP; 5 Aug 83 01:13:32 EDT

Date: 5 Aug 83 01:19 EDT (Friday)
From: Guy.Steele@CMU-CS-A
To: new-gen@uwisc
Subject: **Expert systems**

I would like to apologize for my potentially misleading use of the term "expert systems" in my previous message. This is a term that is all too easily abused because it is so popular nowadays. I used it only by way of analogy, but meant it to be applied to the lowest levels (inner loops, as Dr. Fahlman says) rather than to the highest levels (overall system behavior). I view a 74181 or a multiplier chip as an expert on a very specialized set of transformations on bit patterns. It is possible, and even easy, to use its expertise in very general ways precisely because the expertise is captured and packaged, and the rest of the system doesn't have to worry about it very much.

Also, to guard against excessive anthropomorphism, I emphasize explicitly that the expertise that has been captured in such a chip is human—that of the mathematicians and designers who think up clever models and implementations so that the users can benefit without also having to be experts on ALU designs.

Guy Steele

From: ABell.PA@PARC-MAXC.ARPA Fri Aug 5 11:14:26
    1983
Date: Fri, 5 Aug 83 09:09 PDT
From: ABell.PA@PARC-MAXC.ARPA
Subject: **Second question**
To: NEW-GEN@CSNET-SH.ARPA
Cc: ABell.PA@PARC-MAXC.ARPA

The discussion so far has been excellent, though sometimes a bit independent of the question. Many good points and issues have been raised. Several responses illustrated the importance of first understanding the application areas before creating the hardware and software systems to support them.

What are the applications where new-generation computers will be used? I would like to see us create both a taxonomy of areas and specific applications. What are the characteristics of each of these areas?

I wonder if we, as computer scientists, have too limited breadth to envision and specify many of the new applications. Is this the case? What groups of people should become involved to illustrate the application areas to us? How do we involve and work with these new groups?

From: rjd@lanl Fri Aug 5 11:36:00 1983
Date: 5 Aug 1983 10:24:58 MDT
From: Robert Douglass C-10 ⟨rjd@lanl⟩
Reply-to: rjd@lanl
To: NEW-GEN@CSNET-SH
Subject: **Definitions**

Some points on definitions and the shape of fifth/new-generation computers:

New generation computers versus super types

(1) I like the Japanese distinction between fifth- or new- (these terms I use synonymously) generation computers and supercomputers. Supercomputers seem to be the largest, highest-speed processors available (or in development). So the Cray 1, Cyber-205, and so forth are our current supercomputers; Cray 2, NEC's vector machine, Fujitsu's vector machine, the Cyber-2XX are next year's supercomputers. To a large extent, numerical simulation has driven the development of supercomputers and will probably continue to do so, leaving some traces of specialization for high-speed numeric computation. Parallelism is a key component of all the major supercomputer R&D efforts of which I am aware, and in fact vendors will be delivering the first low-scale parallel systems very shortly.

That is not to say that supercomputers will not play a role in new- or fifth-generation computing—I feel they have important fifth-generation applications in symbolic computing as well as numerical computation. Perhaps one of the most important roles they could play, as Dr. Fahlman suggests, would be to provide the processing power to model and experiment with larger-scale and specialized parallel architectures. Many of the applications bantered about for the new generation—speech understanding, natural-language processing—would not be cost-effective if they required large portions of a supercomputer's time; it would be cheaper to hire a human to perform speech recognition and translation to machine-readable format.

(2) The new generation, while dependent on VLSI and the parallelism it permits, will be a generation of advances and especially integration of software and hardware to meet new applications in the management and communication (to humans) of information and knowledge. Much of the technology exists to support a host of new applications in symbolic computing, and indeed the most formidable challenge to an American or Japanese effort to commercialize existing research advances lies in selecting between alternative technologies—different architectures, different models for representing information and knowledge—and integrating the different components.

There are of course many unsolved research issues in AI, in parallel algorithms, in parallel and distributed architectures, and for that matter in packaging; but if, like the Japanese, we are talking about a major national thrust to move symbolic processing research into commercial applications in 10 years, then we will be lucky to integrate, experiment with, and incorporate just the areas of AI, data-base management, and parallel processing with which we have already gained some insight.

(3) The "structure and look" of new-generation computing: Parallelism and parallel processors will play an important, even crucial, role in new-generation computing, but I think that what will characterize the new generation is the integration of several sorts of conventional and parallel processors, storage systems, I/O devices, and communication and networking systems into a distributed system driven by an integrated set of software components and used to provide people with specific information, advice, and information-based services through an improved human/computer interface.

It will be difficult to put your hand on one box (or even a set of boxes) and say that this is a new-generation computer. Instead, a new-generation computer will consist of many types of machines, I/O devices, storage systems, and communications devices interconnected in a vast network. Any given application might involve several types of computers from conventional Von Neumann machines to several different types of parallel systems.

A new-generation scenario

To illustrate my point, let me sketch an example:

John Silicon is driving down the Bayshore Freeway on a Monday afternoon in 1993. Out of a roiling cloud of exhaust, he sees a swelling mass of cars bringing traffic to a halt up ahead beyond the next exit. He flicks on his new-generation terminal which immediately connects him to a work-station processor in his office, using cellular radio to tie into the telephone network (conventional voice-grade lines if you like). Using voice commands, interpreted by a specialized voice-recognition processor incorporated in the office work station [NEC already markets a parallel (limited) connected-speech processor], John requests information from the "route-planner" for the Bay Area, a service provided by Tarbabi (Traffic and Routing, Bay Area Basic Information) Corp. His work station connects via a wide-bandwidth network to a large parallel processor and a vast bank of optical disks located at the Tarbabi computing center in Mendocino, a northern bedroom community of San Francisco. Using voice commands, John enters his location and asks for the quickest alternate route to his destination. The Tarbabi machine retrieves the relevant map for John's location and computes estimated transit times after deducing some alternate routes. The Tarbabi machine is tied into traffic-monitoring sensors throughout the Bay Area so it can estimate transit times based on traffic volume. The shortest route is relayed back to John's work station, converted to voice output, and sent to his new-generation terminal in his car. John heads off at the next exit while requesting his work station to receive and read him his mail and phone messages.

At a stoplight, John books a flight from San Francisco to Traverse City, Mich., using voice commands and a touch-tone key pad. To book the flight, his work station uses an expert trip-planning program running on his company's parallel expert system machine (a Stolfo tree machine or a NETL machine variant or a Prolog unification machine or whatever). The trip expert connects itself to the BATS (Bay Area Travel Service) Corp. machine to get information about available flights and make the bookings (remembering to request a vegetarian dinner for John). His work done with for the moment, John requests that his new-generation terminal retrieve (from an optical disk in the car) and play some selections of digitized music (Bach's Third Brandenburg Concerto and Golden Ring's "When the Bullet Hits the Bone").

Now that's an application of new-generation computing, and I'd like to use (and apologize for) this somewhat fictitious example to make a few points about the new generation of computing:

The new generation will serve and support people's information and problem-solving needs. To achieve this end, it must provide a very humanlike or human-friendly user interface.

All of the software and hardware components to create this scenario either are already commercially available or have been demonstrated as research prototypes in a laboratory setting. The challenge (and it is a formidable one) is to integrate these pieces—which means figuring out what types of architectures and so forth are needed and clothing them all in a software environment that permits communication and cooperation.

No one architecture or computing system can be fingered as "the new-generation computer"; rather, the new generation is the loose confederation and especially the integration of disparate and distributed hardware and software components.

From: lxs@purdue.ARPA Fri Aug 5 12:48:06 1983
Date: 5 Aug 1983 10:36:32 EST
From: Larry Snyder ⟨lxs@purdue.ARPA⟩
Reply-to: lxs@purdue.ARPA
To: ng-mod@csnet-sh

Gentlemen:

The topic of greatest concern to me has to do with the research methodology to solve these problems. There are mechanisms in place to fund projects, even massive projects, and it is not uncommon for groups to build their own "home-brewed" system. But how will fully engineered prototypes of these systems get built and put in the hands of the users? Here "fully engineered" means that the hardware and software are close enough to production quality so that we can get meaningful measurements of performance and accurately assess the operating environment.

Biosketch:

I am Professor of Computer Science at Purdue, soon to be Professor of Computer Science at the University of Washington. I direct the Blue CHiP project, ONR-funded research into highly parallel computation. We have built (equate with "works reliably") a 64 processor parallel machine, called Pringle. We have built (equate with "works reliably and is used") a complete parallel programming environment.

Larry Snyder

From: kgw@Cornell Fri Aug 5 22:29:22 1983
Date: 5 Aug 83 23:26:56 EDT (Fri)
From: kgw@Cornell (Ken Wilson)
Subject: **Parallel operating systems**
Message-Id: ⟨8308060326.AA11815@GVAX.CORNELL⟩
Received: by GVAX.CORNELL (3.320/3.14)
          id AA11815; 5 Aug 83 23:26:56 EDT (Fri)
To: NEW-GEN@CSNET-SH
Cc: kgw@Cornell

Since a taxonomy of connection networks has been presented, I would urge that a classification of operating systems models also be discussed. I am no expert here, but I believe there are at least a couple of models for such operating systems, which I call (1) the airline counter and (2) the Swiss railway system.

Details:

A modern airline counter distributes a single queue of customers to the first available clerk. This is the logical model

(with "customers" replaced by computing tasks) for the Denelcor Hep or the Ultracomputer operating system.

In Switzerland, a train leaves the station at every city every hour. In the Swiss railway model, a "data train" would leave every processor on a fixed schedule, moving over a fixed-connection system (a square or cubic mesh, for example).

In simulation, there are grid problems simple enough so no operating system is required; most of my problems are of this character. For these problems a square or cubic mesh is fine.

From: HT.Kung@CMU-CS-VLSI Sat Aug 6 14:08:37 1983
Date: Sat, 6 Aug 1983 15:03:38 EDT
From: HT.Kung@CMU-CS-VLSI
To: NEW-GEN@CSNET-SH
Subject: **New gen**
Message-ID: ⟨1983.8.6.19.1.32.HT.Kung@CMU-CS-VLSI⟩

High cost of software

The following are my responses to both the first and second questions.

First of all, I would like to point out that a new *generation* of computers means a lot more than isolated research efforts on new computer structures. For instance, $100 M would be big money for research of a new computer architecture, but is definitely not enough for the development of software and system supports needed for the widespread use of a new generation of computer. The real support must come from users. The characteristics of the next generation of computers depends on what large-user communities are looking for and will be ready for. I am afraid that researchers in computer science (including myself) will have very little impact on the next generation of computers if we don't have a good feeling on practical technology constraints and general users' needs.

However, these outside environmental factors change all the time. I may use RISC now, but may decide to switch to CISC after three years when chip density is high enough. The best we can do is to come up quickly and confidently with optimal or near-optimal architecture solutions for the current and near-future situations. Of course, long-term research on *big* ideas always has its own values, but we shall carefully not equate them to new generations of computers.

I take the definition that a *new* generation of computers has arrived only when people have a new way of looking at computers. The question is what will really change our views on computers. This can happen in many ways, including the capability of solving scientific problems that are much larger than what we can handle now and the capability of improving our programming productivity by a factor of 10 (it looks like for this we need future AI techniques).

Among other kinds of things I do, I dream of computers that can integrate *easily* various high-performance, special-purpose processors that are tailored to individual application needs. There are many important application areas where we do understand very well the requirements of special-purpose processors. Moreover, these processors can also be built cost-effectively due to powerful computer-assisted–design tools we now have and availability of highly regular and parallel algorithms suitable of hardware implementation. These tasks include "front-end processing" in areas such as vision and radar, and many simulation tasks like Ken Wilson's work in physics. At least we can try to replace those expensive, inflexible analog devices in many real-time systems with special-purpose digital processors (hopefully with similar performances). But present mechanisms of integrating these special-purpose devices into a total system are everything but easy. I don't think that breakthroughs are needed to solve this integration problem, but a solution of this problem will be a breakthrough on the way we can use special-purpose processors.

I must make it very clear, however, that tasks that can be done cost-effectively by the special-purpose approach are still very limited as far as I can tell. I made some significant effort three years ago to evaluate if it would be worthwhile to have hardware engines for operations like "join" in relational data-base systems. It turned out that disk I/O was a real bottleneck and that the software programs could really be made very efficient relative to the available disk I/O speed. Another example is that some recent CMU simulation studies have shown that there is really not too much parallelism to be explored in many of the current AI production systems for expert-system implementations.

It seems to be always very difficult to realize large speedup factors unless we do something unique that nobody has yet tried. Additional knowledge in applications and new technologies are indeed the only two things I can think of that we can rely upon.

H.T. Kung at CMU

From: gottlieb@NYU.ARPA Sat Aug 6 17:18:32 1983
Date: 6 Aug 83 18:14:51 EDT
From: gottlieb@NYU.ARPA
To: NG-MOD@CSNET-SH
Subject: **Biosketch**

Allan Gottlieb, born in New York City, received a B.S. from MIT and an M.A. and Ph.D. from Brandeis University. After teaching at the University of California at Santa Cruz, North Adams State College (Mass.), and York College of the City University of New York, he joined the Courant Institute for Mathematical Sciences of New York University in 1980. He has worked on the NYU Ultracomputer project since its inception in 1979 and is now a principal investigator. His chief academic interest is in parallel architectures for high-performance computing.

I am sorry that this is a day late. When I was telephoned about this discussion group, I mentioned that I would be away the last Friday in July and the first week in August.

While it is likely that the most significant item for discussion is how to ensure that the major computer manufacturers become involved in high-performance computing, my primary interest is in the architectural and algorithmic questions that arise.

Alan Gottlieb

From: kgw@Cornell Sat Aug 6 19:58:29 1983
Date: 6 Aug 83 20:55:13 EDT (Sat)
From: kgw@Cornell (Ken Wilson)
Subject: **First questions and answers**
Message-Id: ⟨8308070055.AA24102@GVAX.CORNELL⟩
Received: by GVAX.CORNELL (3.320/3.14)
           id AA24102; 6 Aug 83 20:55:13 EDT (Sat)
To: NEW-GEN@CSNET-SH
Cc: kgw@Cornell

I will now try to answer the four initial questions posed. (1) Definition of new-generation computers and goals, structures, architectures, and developments needed to reach them.

Answer:

I believe the primary distinction of the new generation will be that it will be much more tailored to people and their needs than the past generations. The present Black Box compilers will be replaced by work-station environments that provide much more high-level assistance to the programmer and that build programs via interactions with the user rather than accepting a complete program and then black-boxing it into machine language. The present general-purpose systems will be replaced by networks combining general-purpose switches linking special-purpose work stations and special-purpose workhorses, all (except the switches) built with thorough knowledge of the applications or range of applications served. Present universal and god-awful languages will be replaced by dialogues closer to (but not the same as) English and more interlaced with jargon of the application area than general computerese.

How to reach this goal? I think this goal is too broad to be reached, especially in the United States, by any approach more centralized than market forces. In particular I noticed on my trip to Sweden that they could assemble in one room everyone in Sweden who was concerned with a major problem (the specific example was supercomputing) and as a result any program that emerged was almost by definition a national program. I suspect the same is often true in Japan. Meanwhile, the activities in the United States in the same area involve far too many people and far too much diversity to either assemble everyone in one room or have a national program in the same sense as Sweden or Japan.

Government and industry to the rescue

Here it is important to assist the market, and here the Government and private industry must help to make sure that people who are important to the operation of a market are able to participate in it. For example, the long struggle to get supercomputing support in universities has, as one aim, to ensure that university faculty and students who can be very skilled at defining new computing applications and the associated hardware and software needs can participate in the computer market, driving innovation by their purchases. Many recent developments were materially helped by just this kind of university participation in the computer market, and at the present time innovative companies like Symbolics Inc. and Denelcor Inc. need the same kind of university interaction. As long as the important players in the market can all participate in it, the United States need have no fear of Japan or anybody else; our only problem will be to make sure that the sheer size and energy of the U.S. efforts do not crowd out everyone else (*including* Japan!).

Government expenditures should be devoted to leading-edge, long-range research, including the enabling of long-range researchers to buy equipment, rather than to more immediately practical areas which I believe are better handled through market forces.

There is one other area where help is needed. Namely, researchers in application areas, at least in science, have an abysmal knowledge of computer science and vice versa. The result is that the scientists don't realize they need help from computer science and the computer scientists don't know enough about science to provide the help unasked. An illustration of this problem is the futile interchanges that often take place when a computer scientist asks a scientist why he/she does not use PL1/Pascal/Ada/Val/C/APL and so forth instead of Fortran. These interchanges are futile because the computer scientist neither understands nor respects the features of Fortran that perpetuate its use despite Fortran's abysmal features, and the scientist hasn't the foggiest notion of the features of PL1 and the others that might make one of these languages more effective than Fortran. Computer scientists are typically unable to identify features of these languages that truly would be helpful to a scientist and explain why. A few scientists are starting to talk seriously with computer scientists about programming issues, as in the Gibbs project at Cornell; such projects deserve public support since they deal with the critical problem of the man-machine interface that has long-range forefront aspects.

Regarding the current status of research and commercialization plans, my belief is that a review is difficult, but the basic situation is that there is a healthy base of research and commercialization at the present time. Many options in hardware and software exist and are being pursued. However, I think there is a critical need to increase the relative funding of computer-based disciplines like computer science that only really started in the seventies, because they have gotten the short shrift characteristic of an expansion team of a sports league; while they get the same percentage increase in funding as older disciplines, their base for funding is too small, and so, that base should be increased.

Regarding new and old disciplines, I think it is too early to identify new disciplines—I think the terms like "knowledge engineering," implying new disciplines, are both simplistic and premature. Regarding old disciplines, the most important problem is to get interdisciplinary communication; in all my visits to Washington I have given top priority to an *open* network serving *all* disciplines in the style of the ARPAnet-CSnet-USEnet complex because of the incredible capabilities for interdisciplinary communication already demonstrated in this complex.

Infrastructures and funding

For the immediate future a strong government role is needed to establish an open replacement for ARPAnet, to help universities obtain adequate equipment, and to help computer science deal with a very high rate of increase in both teaching and research demands. However, I believe that in the longer term there will be far more private funding for universities than anybody now realizes—the essential change that will fuel this development is that the time lag of technology transfer is decreasing, and as it does so the need of industry for access to universities and their work will increase to the point where they make major expenditures to achieve this access.

The main barrier I see at the moment preventing the universities from being besieged by industry seeking access is lack of communication—industry is ignorant of the research and advanced training activities of universities; for example, a particular industry researcher or salesman or whatever rarely recognizes an occasion when university access would be helpful and, even if the need was recognized, would not know how to identify just the person who would be able and willing to help. Likewise, university personnel are even more ignorant of the revolutionary advance in technological sophistication in industry that makes industrial involvement of all kinds (I am not talking only about computers) both more important and more interesting than it ever was before. The solution: networking, again, along with training on how to get help through the network.

From: gottlieb@NYU.ARPA Sun Aug 7 15:01:27 1983
Date: 7 Aug 83 15:55:33 EDT
From: gottlieb@NYU.ARPA
To: NEW-GEN@CSNET-SH
Subject: **Late response to initial query**

Please forgive my delayed reply as I was out for the week.

Within the "high-flux" class of Dr. Ullman, one may wish to compare the machines that have multiple processors sharing a central memory (the "dance hall" architecture with all the processors on one side of the room and the memory modules on the other) with those where the processors have their own local memory and communicate via message passing. I believe that machines like the homogeneous machine (Cube) and Jack Schwartz's original Ultracomputer (shuffle-exchange) in which the memory is local and the interconnection topology is made visible to the programmer, offer higher peak performance than the current NYU Ultracomputer (dance hall), but at the cost of more difficult programming.

Indeed, we were able to obtain shuffle-exchange implementations of several important algorithms, but when we first studied the Burroughs-proposed NASF (numerical aerodynamic simulation facility—NASA's "digital wind tunnel"), we concluded that such shared-memory machines were easier to program. I know that this view is far from universal and that many believe that shared memory facilities simply lead to the creation of parallel bugs. I can only add that we have parallelized a number of medium size (up to a few thousand lines) programs and have not changed our view.

Someone has remarked that there are two problems to solve in parallel processing: communication and synchronization. For some architectures one problem is much easier than the other. For example, shared memory solves communication but makes synchronization more difficult. SIMD machines like the Illiac-IV have no synchronization problem but are poor for interprocessor communication.

An important question to ask is: How many processors does one expect to have on a single chip (or other unit with limited I/O)? If that number is large (as Non-Von postulates), then trees look favorable since 2^k processors can be placed with only four external connections. If the number is not large, then the bottleneck at the root makes trees appear unattractive.

Alan Gottlieb

From: ADavis@SRI-KL Tue Aug 9 03:24:05 1983
Date: Mon 8 Aug 83 16:22:12 PDT
From: Al Davis ⟨ADavis at SRI-KL⟩
Subject: **First question reply**
To: new-gen at CSNET-SH

I have read the comments to date, and due to their number, I will not make a point of agreeing with item X and disagreeing with item Y. The following points indicate my views on the issues raised by the initial question and the responses to date.

Fifth-generation architecture definition: I do not feel that the distinction between "new," "fifth," or supercomputer needs to be discussed, and I use the terms synonymously.

Many forms of concurrency

It is sad in a sense that the Japanese coinage of the "fifth generation" term has generated so much press, since the fourth generation will happen also. Still, the architectures of the fourth generation will mainly be based on the same architectural paradigm that supported the previous three generations. In my view, machines of this so-called fifth generation will be fundamentally based on concurrent principles. The problem is that there are many forms of concurrency:

(1) Spatial. I use this term to mean things that are independent and can therefore be distributed to different physical resource sites.

(2) Temporal—pipelining. In pipelined processing the stages of the pipe are not functionally independent but the distribution is a result of different time stages of the processing. It is certainly true that the multiple resources are also spatially distributed as well (and hence the defect in the terminology, but the idea hopefully is clear).

(3) Specific vs. "Forall" (general). In some concurrent models the concurrency is obtained by having homogeneous tasking applied to some data structure—for example, Forall × Do [some action]—while other models specifically indicate concurrent operation by doing something special:

(a) Delaying the CONS [construction of a list from components]

(b) Detecting independence and taking advantage of it.

(c) . . . [something else appropriate]

The point is that concurrency comes in many flavors and, as has been mentioned by many of the members of the net conference, the grain of the parallel operations, the type, the communication, and so forth are all important. I feel, however, that after the first round of fifth-generation attempts, the "mature" fifth-generation machines will exploit concurrency in a variety of forms at all levels of the system. Doing this will require a consistent incorporation of a number of currently disparate ideas about how concurrent systems can be constructed.

For example, at the largest-grain level, I envision future concurrent systems to look like a network-connected set of special fifth-generation engines. I do not see these engines being as "general purpose" as the mainframe machines of the past. The reason for concurrency at programming time can be made on a number of qualitative grounds, but my contention is that at run time the use of concurrency is quantitative in its goal. General purpose implies compromise and compromise implies loss of speed. At the mid-grain level we will see the types of fifth-generation multiprocessor systems (homogeneous would be my guess, but somebody is bound to try to do it the hard way, too!) that have been worked on for the last 10 or 15 years. At the lowest grain we might see very specialized pipelines for doing arithmetic, control, and memory systems that concurrently look for chunks of data that match the search criteria. My contention is that mature fifth-generation systems will consistently exploit concurrency at many levels of granularity.

I just don't think AI is intrinsically involved, and in this I concur with Dr. Ullman. Certainly some of the results from the AI community will be incorporated in a general search for machines that are qualitatively better from the human-use point of view *and* quantitatively better in terms of MIPS, KIPS, LIPS, BIPS, FLOPS, BOPS, or any other hokey metric that anybody chooses to invent. To view AI as the sole source of the ideas for the new generation of machines is absurd. There is a lot of good work out there, and it needs to be combined properly if there is to be a real win. Some data-base people feel, for example, that Prolog is a small-grain relational data-base system. Ah well—enough said.

The emphasis has got to be on the system being consistent—*not* on just the software or the hardware. The advent of the microprocessor has taught us at least two things:

(1) Significant reduction in the cost of a processor can effectively move the art of programming back to the dark ages for a while (Dijkstra essentially said this at Ifips '77 in Toronto).

(2) Multiprocessors are easier to build than to program if you are lazy and don't think about things before you design them.

Fifth generation software

New programming methods, languages, operating systems, and so forth are definitely needed. Logic programming, data flow, reduction, and similar models proliferate and only scratch the surface in my opinion, but their results are likely to form the basis for the fifth-generation software models. The topic that to my surprise has been missing so far in our discussion is the problem of how program concurrency is to be mapped onto the physical resources. I call this the resource allocation strategy. To date, there haven't been too many distinctly different approaches:

(1) Scalar data and similar topology machine—SIMD-style stuff.

(2) Logic analysis of the program structure and a "smart compiler" that generates the right set of load modules that end up in the right physical spot.

(3) Economic strategies where a first-guess allocation is made and then (usually with a great deal of overhead) things are moved later if they are in the wrong spot.

(4) Random allocation—let things just grow and hope that everything works out somehow (unfortunately, in every case that I know about in which this strategy was used, it was a failure).

The problem is that the allocation must be done so that communication delays don't effectively sequence otherwise concurrent activities.

The aims of fifth-generation research should be to incorporate enough of the sensible good ideas into a consistent, efficient system's framework, to build real systems (not just unprogrammable heaters), and to get together with the applications people to continue to develop the machine-use paradigms that will guide the work to a mature stage.

Al Davis, Fairchild AI Labs

From: blb@lanl Wed Aug 10 12:56:14 1983
Date: 10 Aug 1983 11:52:35 MDT
From: Bill Buzbee C-DO ⟨blb@lanl⟩
Reply-to: blb@lanl
To: NEW-GEN@CSNET-SH
Subject: **New-generation discussion**

For the record, this message notes some of the points made thus far that I think are particularly good. Although I occasionally reference a specific message, typically the point has been addressed by other participants as well.

(1)   A functional definition of new-generation technology. This was explicit in Ken Wilson's message of August 8 and implicit in Robert Douglass's message of August 5. VLSI, be it parallel or otherwise, is the vehicle by which functionality can be increased in a cost-effective and reliable fashion.

Also, Ken Wilson's points about market forces are important.

(2)   Put the applications in the forefront rather than in the "hindfront." Some of us who have lived through vectorization have learned the hard way that the architecture must fit the application. (See H. T. Kung, August 6.)

Suppose you had a million processors in an *n*-cube? What would you do with them? (See Randy Davis, August 4.) This is a great question, and there are some others that go with it.

Are algorithms available that can be implemented on them such that in some sense their performance can be guaranteed to exceed that on any other system?

How would applications be programmed and mapped onto the hardware? (See Al Davis, August 8.)

How would I/O be handled, both logically and physically?

What provisions for fault diagnostics/tolerance are provided?

The point is that parallel processing is a system issue (as others have noted) and must be addressed as such. This will require collaboration between people expert in applications/algorithms, software, and architecture.

Experience with parallel processing is a missing link. A recent Department of Defense/National Science Foundation study ("Highly Parallel Computing," A Report to the Information Technology Workshop, J. C. Browne, Chairman) noted:

"There is an abundance of concepts for parallel computing and abundant opportunities for developing these concepts and their applications. The current bottleneck to progress is the difficulty of executing significant experimental studies. These studies are essential to evaluation of total system concepts."

I strongly concur with suggestions by some of the participants that experimental equipment be acquired and used to supply performance data as a function of algorithm, language, architecture, and so forth. Also, I agree that this equipment and associated research be integrated into a national network.

It is my personal opinion that the overhead of interprocessor communication/synchronization will prove surprisingly significant to overall performance, and that its significance will be at least proportional to the number of processors used.

Taxonomy. More work is needed—on algorithms, architectures, and so forth. (See David Shaw, August 3; also, Alan Bell, August 5).

From: Fahlman@CMU-CS-C.ARPA Wed Aug 10 15:10:41 1983
Received: ID ⟨FAHLMAN@CMU-CS-C.ARPA⟩; Wed 10 Aug 83 16:09:10-EDT
Date: Wed, 10 Aug 1983 16:08 EDT
From: Scott E. Fahlman ⟨Fahlman@CMU-CS-C.ARPA⟩
To: new-gen@UWISC.ARPA
Cc: fahlman@CMU-CS-C.ARPA
Subject: **Tasks for the new generation**

There seem to be a couple of distinct conversations going on here, both useful, but probably worth identifying as separate. If we look at what we want the new generation of computers to do (and it would be pretty silly to build them before we have looked hard at this), we can either look at the overall picture that the new systems should present to the user or at the key low-level problems that have to be solved in order to get at some of the tasks that we cannot handle well at present. We've had several good messages on each of these topics.

When thinking about the appearance of the new generation to the user, we see the need for extremely transparent communication (text, color pictures, voice, and so forth) with other users anywhere in the world, integrated tools with good on-line training and help facilities, easily sharable program modules and data bases (either through standardization of languages or through intelligent interface managers), and so on.

All of this can be accomplished without much innovation in hardware—all it will take is something like the current LISP machines with color displays. They should be easily portable and cheap enough to be on everyone's desk, with excellent worldwide networking, and huge banks of on-line video-disk libraries. The software is the hard part, but again nothing revolutionary is required—just about 10 more years of very hard work by good people.

No revolutions required

All this is just straightforward extrapolation of what is going on now in dozens of places. It is going to happen. No major revolutions are required, and the payoff is clear enough that market forces can probably drive the whole development without any help. It would probably be helpful if there were some coordinating body to apply gentle pressure in the direction of standardizing things wherever that makes sense (or at least avoiding gratuitous incompatibility). It would also be very helpful if the necessary equipment were made available to the most active developers (universities and small innovative software organizations) as soon as possible—if these people have to wait till the hardware is cheap, they will have no opportunity to add their ideas and software to the new generation while it is still new, and the resulting systems will be much worse for this omission.

That is one thing that could be meant by "new generation," and a number of people on the list have addressed these issues. To me, this stuff is really finishing the software for the current generation of machines, but that's just quibbling over terminology—the effort is critically important, whatever we call it. I might add that at the level being discussed above, issues such as parallelism and interprocess connectivity should not come up. There is probably a lot of parallelism going on in these machines, but the less the user has to know about it, the better for us and the user.

On a different level, however, I do see the need for innovative (and therefore risky) explorations of machine architectures. While existing Von Neumann hardware (with a few special-purpose processors for graphics and communication) can handle most of what was described above, there are important tasks that require more cycles than we are going to get from such machines. One class of problems is number crunching, and a lot of work has gone into making that faster, giving rise to the Crays and HEPs and DAPs. For other tasks, these architectures seem to be inappropriate. I've listed these in earlier messages: pixel munching, animation, making intelligent use of a *lot* of assorted knowledge, recognizing things (images or spoken words or diseases or stock market trends), planning, big simulations in noncontinuous nonnumeric domains, and so on. We know that we're cycle-bound in these areas, but we won't yet agree on what to do about it, or even how to characterize where the crunch is occurring.

To me the next generation of hardware/architecture research is a matter of identifying those places where important tasks cannot be done because we lack the computing cycles, analyzing these tasks to see where the computational bottleneck is, developing a good crisp theory of what has to be done in that bottleneck and what the dependencies are, and then applying the right kind of parallelism to get the job done. Often, we will discover that the architecture developed for problem A is also useful for problem B, but that should not be a requirement.

That kind of research does not have an obvious and predictable payoff, so it is generally not done by industry. Some of the preliminary studies can be done in universities and think-tanks, but building prototype hardware has in the past been too expensive for such organizations. A single computer architecture project (with the associated software effort) has generally tied up a major chunk of university resources for a period of several years: think of Multics, Illiac-IV, the MIT LISP machine effort, among other examples.

It seems to me that this is where we need some sort of national initiative. All of the usual solutions apply: we need more money for this sort of exploratory construction in the universities, more joint projects between universities and industry (with less hassle and secrecy), better access to facilities for simulating high-speed parallel designs so that only the most interesting ones will actually be built, and better tools for miniprojects in computer architecture (the half-million-dollar six-month project, as opposed to the five-year behemoth). It looks to me like the weakness of the current U.S. research and development system is not in producing the basic good ideas and not in exploiting these ideas (however expensive) once they are shown to be right, but in doing the risky but expensive exploration in between.

Scott Fahlman, CMU

From: RAPHAEL.HP-HULK@Rand-Relay Wed Aug 10
      15:50:54 1983
Date: 10 Aug 1983 12:48PDT
From: RAPHAEL.HP-HULK@Rand-Relay
Return-Path: ⟨RAPHAEL%HP-HULK.HP-Labs@Rand-
      Relay⟩
Subject: **Mailboxes and status report**
Received: by HP-VENUS via CHAOSNET; 10 Aug 1983
      12:47:47-PDT
To: new-gen.csnet-sh@RAND-RELAY
Cc: RAPHAEL.HP-HULK@Rand-Relay
Message-Id: ⟨429392868.4728.hplabs@HP-VENUS⟩
Via: HP-Labs; 10 Aug 83 13:25-PDT

The following is the current distribution list for this teleconference, and an indication of individual participation. If there is a "?" or "0" after your name, please come on in, and help move the discussion in whatever direction you think is most important or productive.

MAILBOX	NAME	ACTIVITY
fernbach@csnet-sh	Sidney Fernbach	0
thomas@csnet-sh	Lee Thomas	?
sumney@csnet-sh	Larry Sumney	?
bsuther@csnet-sh	Bert Sutherland	?
isuther@csnet-sh	Ivan Sutherland	?
trimberg@csnet-sh	Stephen Trimberger	B
wallich@csnet-sh	Paul Wallich	M
braphael@csnet-sh	Bert Raphael (Don't use this mailbox)	
yeh@csnet-sh	Raymond Yeh	?
GJS@MIT-MC	Gerry Sussman	0
KUNG@CMU-CS-A	H. T. Kung	C
GUY.STEELE@CMU-CS-A	Guy Steele	A
FAHLMAN@CMU-CS-C	Scott Fahlman	A
david@columbia-20	David Shaw	C
KAHN@ISI	Bob Kahn	?
CONWAY@ISI	Lynn Conway	?
BASKETT@SCORE	Forest Baskett	0
ADAVIS@SRI-KL	Al Davis	A
HOUSE.HP-LABS@RAND-RELAY	Chuck House	M

RAPHAEL.HP-LABS@RAND-RELAY	Bert Raphael	M
COHEN@ISIB	Danny Cohen	?
UNCAPHER@ISI	Keith Uncapher	?
EWALD@LANL	Bob Ewald	?
BUZBEE@LANL	Bill Buzbee	C
DOUGLASS@LANL	Robert Douglass	A
DANNY@MIT-AI	Danny Hillis	?
DAVIS%OZ@MIT-MC	Randy Davis	A
GOTTLIEB@NYU	Alan Gottlieb	A
SCHWARTZ.CMCL1@NYU	Jack Schwartz	C
SNYDER@PURDUE	Larry Snyder	?
FEIGENBAUM @SUMEX-AIM	Ed Feigenbaum	0
LENAT@SCORE	Doug Lenat	?
ULLMAN@SCORE	Jeff Ullman	A
CSL.LAB.DRA@SCORE	Dennis Allison	?
RHAYES-ROTH@SRI-KL	Rick Hayes-Roth	A
waltz.uiuc@RAND-RELAY	Dave Waltz	?
ABELL@PARC-MAXC	Alan Bell	M
BOBROW@PARC-MAXC	Dan Bobrow	?
STEFIK@PARC-MAXC	Mark Stefik	?
BRIANSMITH@PARC-MAXC	Brian Smith	?
edmiston@csnet-cic	Dick Edmiston (monitoring for CSnet)	
EBLOCH.YKTVMT.IBM-SJ@RAND-RELAY	Erich Bloch	0
G.LEVINTHAL@COLUMBIA-20	Sy Levinthal	0
G.CHRIST@COLUMBIA-20	Norman Christ	0
GB28@CMU-CS-A	Gordon Bell	?
kgw@cornell	Ken Wilson	A

key:

A Active—has submitted bio and comments
B Bio submitted, but no comments
C Comments submitted, but no bio
M Moderator
0 Observing—Known to be receiving mail, but not yet participating
? No acknowledgment—unknown whether messages are getting through

---

From: fernbach Thu Aug 11 10:58:27 1983
To: new-gen
Subject: **Answers to first two questions**

(1) Favorite issues—what can be accomplished in next 10 years? Can United States muster proper spirit to beat Japan?

(2) Sid Fernbach, now a general consultant on computers, primarily supercomputers, retired from Lawrence Livermore National Laboratory where he was responsible for the computer facility for several decades.

From: fernbach Thu Aug 11 11:17:44 1983
To: new-gen
Subject: **Response to first question**

For me, it is important to distinguish between supercomputer and new or fifth generation. Supercomputers should be considered as numerical or scientific devices. New or fifth generation may or may not include them. The new generation is one that is friendly, responsive, as easy to communicate with as another human being. No doubt the architecture will derive from Non-Von concepts. The structures will vary from single processors to heterogeneous multiprocessors.

The technology will not mature for 10 to 20 years. When it does, we will have as our friends the third generation, the robots.

Yes, I believe there will be many different efforts heading to different goals. This new generation will be another intermediate one. The 21st century will bring many more into existence. We are still in childhood, not knowing what directions to take for our future goals.

From: ABell.PA@PARC-MAXC.ARPA Thu Aug 11 13:51:34 1983
Date: Thu, 11 Aug 83 11:24 PDT
From: ABell.PA@PARC-MAXC.ARPA
Subject: **Request for info**
To: New-Gen@CSNET-SH.ARPA
Cc: ABell.PA@PARC-MAXC.ARPA
Reply-To: ABell.PA@Parc-Maxc.ARPA

I would like to create a bibliography of documents related to the issues being described and to collect synopses of the projects in this area. I will distribute this information after it has been collected.

Could you please send me (ABell@PARC-MAXC) a message listing any technical reports or other documents that might be included in this bibliography. Could the project leaders of the relevant projects please send me a short synopsis (one paragraph) of your project.

Alan Bell

From: Wallich@csnet-sh Thurs Aug 11 20:14:34 1983
To: new-gen
Subject: **Third question**

So far, we've seen discussions about specific architectures move to become discussions about principles for selecting architectures, and then discussions about the need for funds and methods to experiment with architectures and applications. People also seem to agree about the need to involve applications people (including non–computer scientists) in the early stages of machine and environment development. So how do we do that?

How can we coordinate the creative activities of applications people, environment builders, machine architects, VLSI designers, and others, so that they can learn of and build on each other's work, and so that results in one discipline can build on results in the others? How can we have work on a new machine at one site interact synergistically with work on a software environment at another site, for example?

What are the barriers that are keeping this kind of interaction from happening now? What needs to be done to lower them? (For example, why are certain people sending lots of messages in this conference and others not?)

Paul Wallich
Alan Bell
Chuck House
Bert Raphael

From: kgw@Cornell Fri Aug 12 20:16:59 1983
Date: 12 Aug 83 21:15:20 EDT (Fri)
From: kgw@Cornell (Ken Wilson)
Subject: **Third question**
Message-Id: ⟨8308130115.AA09887@GVAX.CORNELL⟩
Received: by GVAX.CORNELL (3.320/3.14)
           id AA09887; 12 Aug 83 21:15:20 EDT (Fri)
To: NEW-GEN@CSNET-SH
Cc: kgw@Cornell

Bringing people together

I can only describe my own experience in dealing with bringing the relevant people together. The most important requirement is to find computer users, computing support people, computer scientists, computer designers, and so forth who have a willingness or recognized need to cooperate. Fortunately, more and more people from all these areas are recognizing a need to emerge from their niches and join forces.

This has made possible a number of projects I am involved in which combine people from different areas, as everyone recognizes is required. I have a software productivity project that combines high-energy physicists and computer scientists and will add other application areas as time goes on. Cornell is embarking on a parallel-processing project with support from both IBM and Floating-Point Systems and cooperation from scientific users, Cornell computer services, electrical engineering, and ultimately the Gibbs software productivity project. Fermilab has an experimental computer science project that brings together Fermilab researchers and outside computer scientists.

The common denominator of these efforts is to bring together members of many different disciplines, chosen because they all are needed in order to reach the project's goals and all are willing to help. I am starting a theory center at Cornell to unite all theoretical science, engineering, and agricultural disciplines at Cornell and provide a common computing support umbrella; again there is a lot of enthusiasm for this project, and both the Gibbs project and the parallel-processing project will be part of the broader theory center effort. Representatives of computer manufacturers and industrial computer users will be encouraged to participate in these efforts. The most important step needed to help this kind of effort nationwide is to make computer networking more widely known and accessi-

ble. In addition, more people need to be trained to use networking effectively.

From: gottlieb@NYU.ARPA Sun Aug 14 08:30:31 1983
Date: 14 Aug 83 09:25:31 EDT
From: gottlieb@NYU.ARPA
To: NEW-GEN@CSNET-SH
Subject: **Third question**

At NYU we have had applications people involved in the project (Ultracomputer) from the beginning. From very early on, we have had a working simulator and have run simulations of programs selected by the applications folks. Of course, due to memory constraint (and the inherent slowness of simulations), we have not been able to run the largest programs on their full data sets for the normal number of cycles, but we have done realistic examples. One tenet was that the applications people decided what portions of the program to omit and how small the data could be and still be realistic.

I must add, however, that the applications people, while not computer scientists, do use computers every day for their normal scientific work, which might be classified as computational science. How to involve so-called naive users (that is, sophisticated professionals who happen not to be familiar with computers) might well be more difficult.

In summary, for applications that are already heavily computerized, I believe that having a working simulator as a major part of the project is extremely helpful. It should also go without saying that the results of the simulations must be considered important to the entire project and that design decisions must be tested against these simulations.

Allan Gottlieb

From: ULLMAN@SU-SCORE.ARPA Mon Aug 15 02:49:44
        1983
Date: Sun 14 Aug 83 22:17:42 PDT
From: ULLMAN@SU-SCORE.ARPA
Subject: **Stanford projects/barriers to communication**
To: new-gen@UWISC.ARPA

Synopsis of projects at Stanford:

There are a number of projects at Stanford that are concerned with new-generation computing, some ongoing, some in the planning stage. As not all the principal investigators are in the survey, I'll take the liberty of summarizing them here.

(1) John Hennessy is implementing a language, SAL, that has the single-assignment property, and plans to build a memory-linked multiprocessor that supports this language, that is, it uses the special properties of single-assignment languages to avoid expensive solutions to the problem of cache consistency.

(2) Joe Oliger has been working with others on campus interested in the solution to numerical problems, in a project called Classic, to develop massively parallel solutions to numerical problems.

(3)   Tom Binford has a project to do real-time computer vision. Well along is a chip that does very fast raster processing, for low-level feature detection as well as a number of other applications.

(4)   Ed Feigenbaum is planning to develop a "blackboard machine," a special-purpose machine for solving signal detection problems via the "blackboard model," a data model where data are viewed simultaneously at several levels of abstraction, and cooperating processes make inferences about one level from data at various levels.

(5)   A group led by Mike Flynn is looking to begin work in emulation of massively parallel machines.

(6)   John McCarthy is planning the implementation of a parallel version of LISP.

(7)   I am contemplating development of some ideas in language design, where the periodic sorting of data allows communication between processes with a cost like that of closely coupled processors, even though the processors are really loosely coupled.

(8)   Christos Papadimitriou, Ernst Mayr, and I plan to do some theoretical studies of the limits of parallelism, the design of parallel algorithms, and the development of realistic models of parallel computation.

To support much of this work, we plan to buy commercial multiprocessing hardware, run as a shared facility for the above projects and others on campus interested in applications of multiprocessing or in systems aspects.

There is not too much written at the moment, but I shall try to follow up with a bibliography of Stanford publications.

Barriers to research coordination

We have also been trying to deal with the fact that supercomputer-system development is a job that requires coordination between many specialists. I would go much further than the several recent messages that support the need for applications people to sit down with computer scientists. I'm not terribly proud of the situation, but it appears that most computer science people are rather too specialized to see the big picture, even forgetting about applications that lie outside computer science proper. Therefore, a group of faculty from electrical engineering and computer science have, since March, been meeting weekly to share ideas and present their own views of their specialty. These people come from hardware, software systems, theory, network operating systems, network protocols, numerical analysis, robotics, and occasionally a few other specialties.

I don't want to speak for the motivation of the group's members, but my own motivation for encouraging this process is a perception that:

(1)   Computer scientists divide into subspecialties too easily. These subgroups develop their own notation and paradigms. I have too many examples where two or more groups work on the same problem unaware of each other's existence not to believe that if I had a broader outlook I would see the problem of interspecialty noncommunication as endemic. The faction-

alization of what should be a unified field is a significant barrier to interaction; probably it is a barrier to progress.

(2)   The problem of new-generation computing is among those where the solution depends on a chain of facilities working together, a chain such as application-area problem→algorithm→language→system support→supercomputer architecture→processor architecture. It is too easy for people to insist on working at one point in the chain, ignoring the others. The best way to avoid this problem is to have cooperating researchers, each with a good view of the overall picture.

It is too early to call the Stanford group a success; I'll claim that when people from one field start solving problems in another. But there is no doubt that the sessions have been educational, and I predict that the minimum benefit will be the avoidance of unimplementable algorithms, of languages that are easily implementable but admit no programs that do anything useful, and so on—this is the generalization to the next level of detail of the previously expressed fears concerning machines that serve only as "heaters." After a slow start, there has been a degree of enthusiasm worked up, to the extent that I can recommend the experiment to other sites wishing to try "lowering the barriers."

A significant failure has been our inability to attract much interest from our colleagues in AI. Another problem is that the group has been limited to faculty and a few others. I don't see how to expand it to the point where it serves the needs of students as well as the faculty, yet allows the sort of give-and-take that we have found valuable.

Jeff Ullman

From: COHEN@USC-ISIB Tue Aug 16 17:41:15 1983
Date: 16 Aug 1983 15:39 PDT
From: Danny Cohen ⟨COHEN@USC-ISIB⟩
Subject: **Re questions (1) and (3)**
To: New-Gen@UWISC

I apologize for joining the conference so late. I found the entries to be very interesting and educating. I would like to add to some points that did not get enough attention.

Intersite cooperation

In order to build significant machines that perform important tasks, we need the contribution of several disciplines, such as the actual problem area itself, algorithm analysis, software/programming, operating systems, architecture, and VLSI.

As a matter of style, some groups start from the problem and look for the solution, and some groups traverse this route in the opposite direction. The former risks having to face the how-do-I-solve-my-problem question. Their machines are expected to be put to good use as soon as they are assembled, or even as soon as they are partially assembled (like the Cosmic-Cube at Caltech). The latter might have to face the now-that-we-are-done-what-can-we-do-with-this-programmable-heater question. Both are interesting questions.

Doing a good job requires cooperation among several discipline. Only few sites are able to get all of them under one roof, as Cornell and NYU say. I dare suspect that not all of us can do that. It would be nice if all of us could benefit from the contribution of such groups across site boundaries, such that not each and every project at every site would have to start at square one thinking about every issue.

It would be a pity to see that a project at some site, having terrific ideas and breakthroughs in domain A (say, architecture) fails because of lack of some capabilities in domain B (say, compilers) which is perfectly handled in another site.

Communication, like the ARPAnet, can free us from the need to organize projects according to geographic proximity such that each has to invent all of its own wheels. We can do better than that. We have done so in the past, and we sure can do it again.

We should be able to share not only ideas, but also tools like programs and cell libraries, and most important, conventions that allow future use of various tools not developed or even defined yet. CIF has played an essential role for the tremendous cooperation in the VLSI community supported by ARPA in spite of it being far from perfect to the point that every researcher has his own list of CIF flaws.

I do not advocate to impose immediately premature standards (a.k.a. bureaucrats' heaven), but it is never too early to start thinking about possible coordination, interfaces (a.k.a. interchange format), and tool sharing.

The challenge of many processors

I have the feeling (sorry, no proofs) that the transition from one processor to n processors changes in nature, not just in quantity, as n changes. Some things cease to scale linearly at some point. I believe that a 64 processor system is sort of twice a 32 processor system, belonging to the same class. However, an n-thousands processor system is in another class, in which the graceful degradation issue is a cornerstone of the architecture, not just an afterthought.

Applying elementary statistics to the mean time between failures of systems with kilos of processors (megas?), each of which is powerful—probably on the order of millions of instructions per second [O(MIPS)] or O(MFLOPS)—and have enough memory to be interesting, probably O(Mbyte), yields a shockingly short time between failures.

This may suggest that logical addresses of units (that is, which task a processor performs when) are not necessarily bound permanently to their physical addresses (that is, for which other processors are directly connected). This additional level of differed binding (logical/physical addressing) has some nontrivial "switching" costs and also several significant advantages, which for large numbers of processors may outweigh the switching cost.

This separation of logical addresses from the physical addresses may also prove important for dynamic reconfiguration of the system, both for run-time bypass of failed units and for matching algorithm structures (hypercubes, trees, and other topological marvels).

Parallelizing—without paralyzing—algorithms

One cannot exaggerate the importance of "parallelizing" algorithms. It turns out that it is possible to parallelize nearly all arithmetic algorithms and to reach the ultimate n-fold speedup. IBM's Samuel Winograd has proved many interesting theorems to this effect, including even the Horner scheme, which may be the epitome of sequentialism.

This is true in general of most arithmetics, and obviously most grid-oriented problems that are typically modeled by finite differences, and—most important—obey some continuity/preservation principles.

Parallelism may be abused in many ways. It is easy to envision a "parallel matrix inversion algorithm" (suggested first by Finnegan) that is based on the search of the space of all possible matrices for the one that when multiplied by the given yields the unit matrix. Since this search can be performed in parallel, and since VLSI makes processors cheaper and smaller, we can afford many of them. (How about: Search the space of arm positions and velocities for the minimum-energy solution? How about calculus of variations instead?)

Danny Cohen, ISI

From: Wallich@csnet-sh Wed Aug 17 17:22:41 1983
To: new-gen
Subject: **Fourth question**

This conference has been taking place by means of a distribution list on the CSnet service host, which is sponsored by the NSF. Most of the participants are on the ARPAnet, which is sponsored by Darpa. Many people have reached those nets via intracompany or intrauniversity nets such as those at HP, PARC, IBM, CMU, and MIT. (There have been some adventures in trying to find people on these nets, which points to an interesting question for future cooperation.)

If computer networks are going to be an important part of multisite cooperation for next-generation research, who is going to sponsor them, how will they be connected, and who will have access to them? If other facilities are to spring up for such cooperation, such as hardware and software prototyping and simulation services, who will pay for them? In short, who is going to sponsor next-generation research and how will the resources get where they should go? How will work sponsored by different agencies be coordinated?

Paul Wallich
Alan Bell
Chuck House
Bert Raphael

From: G.CHRIST@COLUMBIA-20.ARPA Thu Aug 18 12:32:32 1983
Date: Thu 18 Aug 83 13:32:16 EDT
From: Norman Christ ⟨G.CHRIST@COLUMBIA-20.ARPA⟩
Subject: **Biosketch and acknowledgment**
To: ng-mod@UWISC.ARPA

The following is the biosketch that you requested:

I received my Ph.D. in theoretical physics from Columbia in 1966. My research has focused primarily on topics in high-energy particle physics ranging from fairly phenomenological studies of the violation of discrete symmetries to the application of differential and algebraic geometry to the classical solution of the nonlinear field equations believed to govern the interactions of quarks.

I have recently become very interested in the possibility of using numerical methods to address this problem of the physics of quarks and also of higher-energy phenomona that are very likely governed by a similar type of theory (the "Yang-Mills" or gauge theories). The numerical methods that appear promising require vast amounts of computer time—very likely hundreds of "Cray-years"; hence my interest in supercomputers. At present my colleague Anthony Terrano, two graduate students, and I are constructing a two-dimensional parallel array of single-board computers configured to address these physics problems efficiently. We expect that the final device, an array of 256 boards capable of 4 gigaflops, will make a significant impact on this physics problem.

Norman Christ

From: G.CHRIST@COLUMBIA-20.ARPA Thu Aug 18
        12:48:17 1983
Date: Thu 18 Aug 83 13:46:39 EDT
From: Norman Christ ⟨G.CHRIST@COLUMBIA-20.ARPA⟩
Subject: **Parallel computation and user-driven design**
To: NEW-GEN@UWISC.ARPA

As a physicist woefully ignorant of computer science (I'm not even sure what the previous four computer generations were!), perhaps I can best contribute to this interchange by describing the particular application that a group of us at Columbia is addressing, the parallel computer architecture that we believe will provide practical, cost-effective, near-term solution to our problem, and the approach we have taken to acquire the needed hardware. (The work that I will describe is being done with my colleague Anthony Terrano and two graduate students, all physicists.)

A physics application

We are interested in the physics of quarks and how they bind to form the more familiar protons, neutrons, pi-mesons, and so forth that are found in the atomic nucleus. This problem can be approached numerically (using a formulation due to Ken Wilson) by replacing space-time by a finite lattice of points, often a four-cube with as many as 16 points on a side. With a minimum of two real degrees of freedom per lattice site (in the form of four 3×3 unitary matrices), this is a problem with 2 million variables. Many interesting questions can be answered by averaging over an ensemble of points in this high-dimensional configuration space generated by the Metropolis method used in statistical mechanics. The interaction between these variables is nearest-neighbor and is represented as traces of products of the unitary matrices. This is currently a very important subject in high-energy physics to which the devotion of significant resources is appropriate. Estimates of the time required for a thorough treatment of the problem easily range as high as hundreds of "Cray-years." On a personal level, I am willing to devote a significant fraction of two or three years to the acquisition and exploitation of the resources necessary to answer some of the questions.

Computer architecture:

The nearest-neighbor interactions and homogeneity of the problem suggest a synchronous grid of processors (a two-dimensional torus appears best in this case). Each processor is based on an Intel 80286/287 microprocessor and is supplemented by a pair of fast TRW arithmetic chips controlled by a primitive microcode so that the repetitive matrix multiplication can be executed at a rate of 16 million 22-bit floating-point operations per second. An array of 256 of these processors will provide a 4-gigaflop speed—computational power probably adequate for at least some aspects of our problem. Since each processing element costs about $2500 and is made from off-the-shelf components, our cost-effective and near-term requirements are also met.

Acquisition of resources:

We quickly discovered the difficulties referred to in question (3) and many of the previous comments regarding useful interdisciplinary communication. In fact, we decided that the electrical engineering and computer science aspects of this project were sufficiently simple that it would be easier to learn by our mistakes than to develop the interdisciplinary communication necessary to avoid making them in the first place. Likewise, the possibility of persuading a computer manufacturer to fabricate what we needed in a short time at a reasonable cost appeared remote. Thus, we set about designing and building the system described above ourselves last winter. Because of the importance of the problem and the apparent economy of our approach, we have had no difficulty in obtaining the funding necessary to build 16 and now 64 nodes from conventional high-energy physics sources.

It is too early to pronounce our efforts a success. We have a single processor working, a second built, and are in the middle of fabricating 18 more. We remain enthusiastic and optimistic about our prospects.

Although we have decided to proceed quite independently, I am certainly interested in the problems addressed in question (3). Obviously, we would be pleased to contribute to the understanding of some of the important issues in parallel processing referred to by the other participants. Perhaps by offering time and support to computer scientists or users in other disciplines (over an appropriate network), we could get some assistance in software development for our array—especially to use it in an asynchronous mode not really required for our primary physics problem. Surely developing such fruitful communication would make some sort of collaborative, subsequent project more likely.

Norman Christ

From: wallich@csnet-sh Sat Aug 20 21:05:47 1983
To: new-gen
Subject: **Wrap-up**

Our plan was to wrap up this "teleconference" by Monday, August 22, and use the material submitted by then as the basis for the IEEE article. Therefore, this is the last formal request from the moderators:

(1)   Please review the previous questions (copy attached below), and submit any new thoughts you may have in light of the past discussion.

(2)   What is the most critical action that U.S. Government, industry, or academia should take (or should not take) with respect to these issues?

(3)   Do you think this teleconference has been worthwhile? What comments have you found most surprising, instructive, or insightful? Do you think this discussion should be reconvened, in this or some modified form, in the near future?

Paul Wallich
Alan Bell
Bert Raphael
Chuck House

From: kgw@Cornell Sat Aug 20 23:34:34 1983
Date: 21 Aug 83 00:34:10 EDT (Sun)
From: kgw@Cornell (Ken Wilson)
Subject: **Example requested**
Message-Id: ⟨8308210434.AA13962@GVAX.CORNELL⟩
Received: by GVAX.CORNELL (3.320/3.14)
          id AA13962; 21 Aug 83 00:34:10 EDT (Sun)
To: wallich@csnet-sh.ARPA
Cc: kgw@Cornell

I think the most interesting example that has already occurred at Cornell has been the Gibbs project, and more particularly the current activities of the Gibbs project. Namely, about six weeks ago I asked a graduate student of mine named Ray Renken to rewrite a program in Gibbs that he had previously written in C. There is currently no manual for Gibbs, no definition for Gibbs, not even any rules for Gibbs; but I had written a program in Gibbs myself to kick things off. I asked Ray to read my example and then do the best he could, the main aims being to write down a set of chapters which explained in complete detail what the program does, but with the chapters constructed to break down the logic of the program into logically distinct modules (we call them chapters, in analogy to the chapters of a well-written textbook) rather than the conventional modularization of C procedures.

I went over his first draft with him (P.S. Hardly any faculty, myself included, will actually *read* a student's Fortran!) and then sent him off to the computer science graduate student, Anne Nierynck, who is the lone Indian on the Gibbs project. Meanwhile, three bright undergraduates were turned over to Anne to be trained as human compliers for Gibbs: their job was now to convert Ray's program back to C, making sure that they only blindly translated whatever Ray had specified. For several weeks thereafter intensive discussion raged between Anne and Ray, both to make the Gibbs writeup precise enough to make the translation both unambiguous and correct, and to bring Ray's description to a higher, less language-specific description where he had simply transliterated the C code. Alan Demers of the computer science faculty, who is one of the chiefs (along with myself) on the project, was heavily involved as an advisor to Anne.

The conclusion of Anne and Alan from this exercise, and earlier study of my example, is that their perceptions of Gibbs has been greatly changed and enhanced by these experiences, and that Gibbs should not be given a formal definition until they have accumulated many more examples of actual scientific programs rewritten in Gibbs. We also need examples written by highly skilled programmers who already are effective in a given language, both from Fortran addicts and from users of more powerful current languages.

From: blb@lanl Mon Aug 22 15:32:59 1983
Date: 22 Aug 1983 08:39:07 MDT
From: Bill Buzbee C-DO ⟨blb@lanl⟩
Reply-to: blb@lanl
To: wallich@csnet-sh
Subject: **Bill Buzbee's biosketch**

Dr. Bill Buzbee is an assistant leader of the Computing Division at Los Alamos National Laboratory, Los Alamos, N.M. Dr. Buzbee received the B.A. and M.A. degrees in mathematics from the University of Texas at Austin and the Ph.D. degree in mathematics from the University of New Mexico, Albuquerque.

Bill's past experience was with Texaco Research, Esso Production Research, and included a sabbatical at Chalmers Institute of Technology, Gothenberg, Sweden. His specialty is numerical analysis, and he has some 20 years' experience in it. His research includes work on fast Poisson solvers, solution of inverse parabolic problems, and capacitance techniques. Current interests include vector and parallel computation.

He was an observer and contributor to the Lax Panel on Large-Scale Computing in Science and Technology. He also served on the Highly Parallel Computing Panel of the 1983 NSF/DOD Information Technology Workshop.

From: Fahlman@CMU-CS-C.ARPA Mon Aug 22 15:39:17 1983
Received: ID ⟨FAHLMAN@CMU-CS-C.ARPA⟩; Mon 22 Aug 83 16:08:32-EDT
Date: Mon, 22 Aug 1983 01:47 EDT
From: Scott E. Fahlman ⟨Fahlman@CMU-CS-C.ARPA⟩
To: new-gen@UWISC.ARPA
Cc: fahlman@CMU-CS-C.ARPA
Subject: **Call for action**

On the question of what actions government, industry, *et al.* can take to facilitate the development of the next generation of machines, here are some opinions:

The case for innovative miniprojects

(1)   It is tough to build new computer-science organizations from scratch, particularly now when there is such great demand for the limited supply of wizards. Instead of trying to build new national centers from scratch, it seems wise to reinforce the existing first-rate places and to see how many of the second-level places with an existing nucleus of good people can be upgraded to major-league status with a little more money, contracts, equipment, cooperation, or whatever. People who move take awhile to become useful again, and even with the best management it takes years for a new organization to build up the necessary critical mass of people, equipment, and software. Most such efforts fail.

(2)   Instead of huge architecture projects, we should think in terms of innovative miniprojects: a few people working on a machine that costs no more than a million dollars for maybe two years. A few of these projects will succeed and will snowball, but it is better to let this happen of its own accord than to push things in this direction. Nothing is as sad to watch as a behemoth project that has gone sour, but that is committed to staggering on to some sort of completion years down the road.

The brightest people, realizing that there's nothing left to learn, have only two ways to get free of the project: announce that it is not worth finishing (and be branded a failure for being associated with such an effort), or move to another company or university while the outside world still believes the project to be a success. Usually the solid-but-unspectacular types are left behind to finish up as best they can, just when these people are desperately needed to begin work on the next good idea. When the project dies with a whimper, years later, nobody is left to do a proper postmortem and to extract the valuable lessons—everyone wonders if the thing would have been a success if only X, Y, and Z hadn't left in the middle.

(3)   The problem with miniprojects in computer architecture is that it takes years and a lot of money to build the infrastructure for architectural experimentation—accumulating experienced technicians and administrators, scraping together the laboratory space and tools, building a simulation facility for work on parallel machines, and so on. Without this infrastructure the productivity of the key scientists goes way down— they end up spending all their time doing the things that the support troops should be doing.

One idea that some of the larger universities and industrial labs should try is to build this hardware infrastructure and share it among a lot of little projects—say, one machine being built a year, one being designed, and one being run experimentally. This way the support troops get a steady stream of interesting work, the cost is spread over many projects, and the incremental cost of trying out one more good idea is a small fraction of what it is now. Smaller organizations might group themselves together and share a regional hardware facility.

(4)   The universities must be kept healthy. People are generally aware of the need for higher faculty salaries and better computing facilities. Government and industry must help to solve these problems, somehow. Another problem, discussed much less, is the need to pay the technicians and other staff people at something like the real-world rate. A faculty member will sometimes make financial sacrifices to stay at a university so that he (or she) can work on something really interesting. The guy who does the board layout doesn't have this added motivation. Students provide useful low-cost labor for some things, but they cannot do everything that a professional support staff would do.

(5)   We need a net of at least ARPAnet quality and convenience that everyone (big companies, small companies, people in the physics and chemistry departments) can get on, along with appropriate and compatible local systems at each site. Companies should buy this service, and should not worry too much about their precious secrets leaking out—much better secrets are likely to leak in. Universities probably need a subsidy so that the cost of this service won't deter people from

using it. The ARPAnet is not the very latest technology, but if everyone who wants to get on it could do so, that would be a tremendous boost to the nation's productivity. If a network is working right, it is possible for large design efforts to succeed, even if dozens of people are involved and they are scattered all over the country. If there is to be a national initiative, this is what should be done first. As we all know, given good enough communication, we won't have to move people around.

A bit of personal experience to back up that last point:

For the past two years I have been involved in a effort to hammer out a standard for a new dialect of LISP called Common LISP. The idea was to get half a dozen distinct LISP implementation efforts, on machines ranging from the sublime to the ridiculous, to agree on a common language spec that we could all live with. We all agreed that this would be a valuable accomplishment if it could be done, especially now that AI programs are finding their way into industry. Still the task was not easy—some of the implementations in question already had working code and real users, others had special hardware requirements, and all of us had some pretty strong ideas on what did and did not belong in LISP. Naturally, some of the hardest-fought points were the ones that seem most trivial in retrospect.

The effort was coordinated by Guy Steele, though I sometimes took over this task when Guy was too busy with other things. The design was largely the work of about 10 people at five or six widely separated sites. Another 30 or so people monitored the discussion and offered suggestions or comments from time to time. We had three face-to-face meetings and used the U.S. mail to send out drafts of the 400-page manual, but perhaps 90 percent of the decisions occurred as a result of ARPAnet discussions. As of last count, there were 2300 messages sent to Guy and/or to the entire design group, a total of several million bytes. I would guess that in two years we have resolved about 800 design issues, some of them requiring the exchange and debugging of 10-page proposals. We now have agreement on the spec and the *Common LISP Reference Manual* (first edition) is in the final proofreading process prior to publication.

I mention all of this merely to illustrate the sort of cooperation that can occur given the proper network environment. A national effort to design a new generation of machines is going to need this sort of communication capability if it is to be truly national. A few observations:

(1)   The core group of people all had excellent access to old, well-established ARPAnet machines: DEC-20's, Vaxen, and LISP machines. Any problems that these machines might have had in communicating with one another were worked out years ago. A change in the ARPAnet protocol last January disrupted this smooth communication for several months, effectively freezing the discussion for that period. People on other nets tied to the ARPAnet participated, but were cut off if their net connection started bouncing messages.

(2)   All of us in the central group "lived" on our machines. All of us normally logged in several times a day—indeed, some of us spent more time on the machine than off it—and were in the habit of reading mail very frequently. This meant that we could often exchange a dozen messages and resolve an is-

sue within a day or two. Where it was important to involve the larger group, issues were normally left on the table for a week or so before discussion was closed, but people who didn't log in frequently were pretty much stuck with being observers. I'm not sure if the average physicist or chemist would use his machine in this way, but perhaps some would.

(3)   An active moderator seems to be a necessity in such an effort, not only to lead the discussion, but also to recognize when a consensus has appeared and to gavel it down before it unravels. If implementation and design are going on together, it is also necessary to have someone who can provide definitive and quick rulings as to the current version of "truth."

(4)   Fortunately, our effort was basically one of agreeing upon a manual. We could not have done this via net if we had had to exchange diagrams or even sketches. An architecture effort would require that everyone have compatible standards for graphics. Indeed, we experienced some awkwardness because not everyone used the same text-formatting and printing conventions—that was why we had to mail around hard copies of the manual.

(5)   It has been very tough cooperating with industry in this design and implementation effort, except for a few places like Symbolics and PARC that have good net connections. DEC had to put a couple of people at CMU for the duration, in part because their ARPAnet connection is inaccessible to most of the people in the company. Other companies communicate with us by phone (which wastes everyone's time) and the occasional mag tape sent by mail.

Sorry for the length of this. I wanted to get this out before leaving for AAAI tomorrow.

Scott Fahlman, CMU

From: kgw@Cornell Mon Aug 22 21:01:16 1983
Date: 22 Aug 83 21:59:17 EDT (Mon)
From: kgw@Cornell (Ken Wilson)
Subject: **Network**
Message-Id: ⟨8308230159.AA18882@GVAX. CORNELL⟩
Received: by GVAX.CORNELL (3.320/3.14)
        id AA18882; 22 Aug 83 21:59:17 EDT (Mon)
To: NEW-GEN@CSNET-SH
Cc: kgw@Cornell

A national network for all disciplines

I strongly concur with Dr. Fahlman's emphasis on a national network serving all disciplines; I plug it every chance I get in Washington and with Congress. It is a scandal that it is not already in place. The NSF must set it up, since it is too important now to put it in the hands of an agency like Darpa that does not have university support as its primary mission. I urge everyone who understands the importance of networks to push repeatedly for it from President Reagan on down. As for ensuring that physicists and chemists are on the network frequently, that is a question of making sure that all their routine business mail, telephone calls, writing papers, library searches, small computations, and so forth are all done through the same machine that receives network mail, plus training them to use the network instead of the U.S. mail and the telephone. A difficult task, but not insuperable.

From: gottlieb@NYU.ARPA Tue Aug 23 14:59:01 1983
Date: 23 Aug 83 15:57:07 EDT
From: gottlieb@NYU.ARPA
To: wallich@csnet-sh.ARPA
Subject: **Third question**

You asked me to comment further about how applications people affected the project.

(1)   We have confidence in the programmability of the machine and in our statistics, because we *know* that we are dealing with interesting problems.

(2)   A nonexpert in the applications area can easily make architectural mistakes. For example, one might think that problems formulated as finite-difference equations on a mesh would be optimally solved on a mesh-connected computer. However, the experts tell us that solution techniques such as fast Poisson solvers and multigrid methods often perform better than the natural mesh-type algorithms. These more sophisticated techniques appear to work better on the high-flux machines discussed earlier.

(3)   Let me add the following. When we were first working on concurrently accessible queues, a radiation-cascade application was being programmed. In helping to apply the queues to the application, I came to realize that I could understand radiation cascade by thinking of an operating system: The particles are tasks, secondary particle formation is task spawning, and absorption is task termination. When I commented on this to our local cascade guru, he thanked me for finally explaining the workings of an operating system.

Alan Gottlieb

From: gottlieb@NYU.ARPA Tue Aug 23 15:15:52 1983
Date: 23 Aug 83 16:11:53 EDT
From: gottlieb@NYU.ARPA
To: NEW-GEN@CSNET-SH
Subject: **Government action**

I must agree with several of the earlier responders: The experimental facilities at most universities are inadequate and need to be strengthened. In addition to supporting the call for improved networking, I can personally attest to Ken Wilson's efforts. I was at a conference at Los Alamos last week and sure enough Ken was telling anyone who would listen that better networks are needed.

Allan Gottlieb

From: ullman@Diablo@SU-Score Wed Aug 24 11:44:34 1983
Received: from Diablo by Score with Pup; Wed 24 Aug 83
        09:47:38-PDT
Date: Wed, 24 Aug 83 09:43 PDT
From: Jeff Ullman ⟨ullman@Diablo@SU-Score⟩
To: ng-mod@csnet-sh

The following references were collected from my colleagues.

From Tom Binford

Miller, A. and Lowry, M., "General Purpose VLSI Chip with Fault Tolerant Hardware for Image Processing," Proc. Image Understanding Workshop, April 1981.

Michael Lowry and Allan Miller, "Analysis of Low-Level Computer Vision Algorithms for Implementation on a VLSI Processor Array," Proc. IU Workshop Image Understanding, September 1982.

From Steve Lundstrom

Lundstrom, S. F. and Barnes, G. H., "A Controllable MIMD Architecture," Proceedings of the 1980 International Conference on Parallel Processing, IEEE Computer Society, 1980, pp. 19–27. (Printed in: *Tutorial on Parallel Processing*, by Robert H. Kuhn and David Padua, IEEE Computer Society, The Computer Society Press, pp. 165–173.)

Barnes, G. H. and Lundstrom, S. F., "Design and Validation of a Connection network for Man-Processor Multiprocessor Systems," *Computer Magazine*, vol. 14, no. 12, December 1981, pp. 31–41.

Numerical Aerodynamic Simulation Facility, Preliminary Study, Burroughs Corp., October 1977 (NASA CR-152060, CR-152061, and CR-152062).

Numerical Aerodynamic Simulation Facility, Preliminary Study Extension, Burroughs Corp., February 1978 (NASA CR-152106 and CR-152107).

Numerical Aerodynamic Simulation Facility, Feasibility Study, Burroughs Corp., March 1979 (NASA CR-152284 and CR-152285).

There are also reports on the NASF (Numerical Aerodynamic Simulation Facility) by CDC which I suspect that they will cite. If they do not, I can look them up. Note that the most important work (the system design studies for the Numerical Aerodynamic Simulator Processing System, NASPS) was not published and was generally considered to be proprietary. Burroughs has given me permission to publish the work we did, and I am in the process of preparing a number of papers on the Burroughs Flow Model Processor (the computational portion of the NASPS).

From Rod Brooks (They all deal with LISP for the S-1)

Brooks, Rodney A., Gabriel, R. P., and Steele, G. L., Jr., "Optimizing Compiler for Lexically Scoped LISP," Proceedings ACM Sigplan 1982 Symposium on Compiler Construction, Boon, June 1982, pp. 261–275.

Brooks, Rodney A., Gabriel, R. P., and Steele, G. L., Jr., "S-1 Common LISP Implementation," Proceedings 1982 ACM Symposium on LISP and Functional Programming, Pittsburgh, August 1982, pp. 108–113.

Brooks, Rodney A., Gabriel, R. P., and Steele, G. L., Jr., "LISP-in-LISP: High Performance," Proceedings International Joint Conference on Artificial Intelligence, Karlsruhe, Germany, August 1983.

From John Hennessy

Celoni, J. and Hennessy, J. L. *SAL Reference Manual*, Describes a single-assignment language for the writing of highly parallelizable code.

From Jeffrey Ullman

Ullman, J. D. *Computational Aspects of VLSI*, Computer Science Press, 1983. Covers, among other things, organizations for massive parallelism and algorithms that are appropriate for such organizations. Available September 1 (I hope).

J. D. Ullman, "A Communication-Time Tradeoff," unpublished, Stanford Department of Computer Science, 1983. Shows that for computations on an n by n grid, $ct \geq n^3$ where c is the number of values communicated between processors and t is the total time.

From: BROCK@USC-ISIB Wed Aug 24 11:58:03 1983
Date: 24 Aug 1983 09:54 PDT
Sender: BROCK@USC-ISIB
From: Keith W. Uncapher ⟨UNCAPHER@USC-ISIB⟩
Subject: **Catchup**
To: NEW-GEN@UWISC
Cc: UNCAPHER@USC-ISIB
Message-ID: ⟨[USC-ISIB]24-Aug-83 09:54:41.BROCK⟩

I've been away and hence am late in responding.

The following appear to be relevant to opportunity- and responsibility-driven facets of the architectural issue.

The dominance of the United States, in selected areas of information sciences and technology, is essential.

Aside from military superiority, a more challenging effort for all of us will be to place in the hands of the U.S. business and industrial base a principal means of establishing leadership in the international marketplace. This, coupled with the transition to an information-based society in which we must reside and flourish, is indeed a prime target of opportunity and in fact our responsibility.

Targets of opportunity

Some specific targets of opportunity are:

(1) Essential U.S. leadership in VLSI and beyond.

(2) An array of information-processing technology, which will allow dramatic change in the conduct of business and industry, in addition to creating a new business and industrial base for the 1990s.

(3) To advantage the U.S. population through the transition to an information-rich society, to populate the new business and industrial base, and to support an accompanying massive retraining and lifelong skill acquisition required for the population.

(4) To create sufficient advances in computational capability in order to cause scientists in selected areas to change their research priorities toward new areas and toward problems heretofore too difficult to solve.

One of the worst strategies we could embrace would be to create a few architectures looking for a problem(s). As one of our colleagues mentioned, getting users involved can be a very productive step.

Some specific opportunities:

• By 1990, provide run-of-the-mill users in business and industry with a smart computer-based assistant. It will require substantial computational capability per user and at an affordable cost.

• Inexpensive, very smart robots as a basic tool for modernization of the industrial United States would likely cause revolutionary change in manufacturing.

Much of the excitement and discussion these days is about supercomputers, largely from a architectural and hardware viewpoint. In the end, it's usually the software that inhibits us; hence, focus on ways to avoid software limitations should be the key to the discussions.

Regarding collaborative efforts, the following may be useful. Many of the really impressive efforts involving computer scientists/laboratories have involved multiple contractors with a mix of universities, not-for-profits and for-profits. The key to each success has been the following:

(1)   A lead organization;

(2)   An ARPAnet or equivalent;

(3)   Sharing of people and computing resources with little accountability;

(4)   Almost instant surfacing of research results via a rich communication mechanism (that is, ARPAnet) and usually via informal means of communication;

(5)   Research reports being a community effort.

What we need is a super "ARPAnet" available for largely unconstrained use by serious and committed researchers.

From: ULLMAN@SU-SCORE.ARPA Wed Aug 24 17:06:42 1983
Date: Wed 24 Aug 83 15:08:19 PDT
From: Jeffrey D. Ullman ⟨ULLMAN@SU-SCORE.ARPA⟩
Subject: **Response to question (4)**
To: new-gen@UWISC.ARPA

I guess I had hoped to see more fur flying, but I'm more surprised that a few very obvious comments were made by no one. Perhaps the comments are too trite and obvious, but that never stopped me before, so here goes.

Moon shot anyone?

I'm not saying I agree with the position, but shouldn't the conference at least examine the possibilities for and desirability of a project centered around a very clear goal (like the moon shot, and considerably more focused than the Japanese fifth generation)? The target should be something that captures the public imagination, like the moon project (sort of) did. How

about a national network coupled with a usable data bank, perhaps a "cashless society." Maybe the educational process can be brought into the home with such a network. (Sorry, that's a dumb idea, I forgot that the purpose of schools is no longer to educate; it's to help kids develop socially and have someplace to buy dope.) Maybe we ought to beat the Russian chess champion with a computer in 1990.

All these efforts, except possibly for chess, go beyond the Douglass scenario ("John Silicon is driving . . ."), in that they require the solution to technical problems that have to be regarded as open. For example, universal data access requires significant progress in representation, retrieval, and manipulation of massive amounts of data; maybe true understanding of natural language is needed, although I believe we can get by with much less as an interface. Processing financial transactions has a nasty way of requiring verifiable security, as well as control of concurrent access on a scale not heretofore contemplated.

One important aspect of the moon project was that a decision about system architecture (the lunar orbiter-lander configuration) was taken fairly early, and the same would hold for a similar project in computation. However, I guess that the net effect of the moon project was to facilitate the development of related but not directly applicable science and technology, rather than to stifle such efforts, just because of the scope of the effort.

Can MOSIS lead the way to the promised land?

Someone ought to say something nice about the MOSIS project as an example of a central facility for serving the needs of a large research community. In this case, the service involved is chip fabrication, although they are moving in the direction of providing complete boards. Although it is a Darpa facility, its services have been offered to NSF-sponsored projects in a valid perception of the national interest. They are, therefore, getting fairly close to a facility available to *all* researchers, providing *complete* fabrication of experimental architectures. Funding for such a facility could be provided by a consortium of agencies, by industry, or on a fee basis. I can see a tremendous payoff from a facility that raises the level at which designs can be stated, and therefore cuts the design time as radically as the introduction of compilers cut the software creation time (even if, as with compilers, the quality of the result was not up to hand-crafted standards).

A similar public facility would provide working multiprocessing equipment accessible on the net to *all* people doing software research. A big problem is the need for resident gurus when dealing with unfamiliar systems, but I almost believe I could get such help over the net if the people running the service were cooperative.

From: blblanl Thu Aug 25 10:02:47 1983
Date: 25 Aug 1983 08:58:00 MDT
From: Bill Buzbee C-DO ⟨blblanl⟩
Reply-to: blblanl
To: NEW-GENCSNET-SH
Subject: **Moon shot**

There is great merit in having a national goal/project with a specific and measurable objective. The suggestion of beating the Russians in chess with a computer meets these criteria. Unfortunately, it would require the cooperation of the Russians, and I seriously doubt that they would take the risk. Anyway, it is an excellent example of what is needed—a precise objective that will win support from "society" and that will engender lots of good spinoff. I encourage everyone to rack their brains for such ideas.

From: BROCKUSC-ISIB Thu Aug 25 14:07:22 1983
Date: 25 Aug 1983 12:03 PDT
Sender: BROCKUSC-ISIB
Subject: **Inputs**
From: Keith W. Uncapher ⟨UNCAPHER@USC-ISIB⟩
To: NEW-GENUWISC
Cc: UNCAPHERUSC-ISIB
Message-ID: ⟨[USC-ISIB]25-Aug-83 12:03:30.BROCK⟩

Question (1):

In the most general context, supercomputer efforts should be national objectives to place the United States in the number-one position worldwide, by a wide margin, in areas of computer science vital to the future of the United States. The focus should be the United States attaining a robust and sustained leadership on a worldwide basis in technological areas and in business and industrial areas vital to the future of the country and its people.

Hopefully, each segment of the scientific and technological thrust from the various proposed and real supercomputer efforts will be formed and judged as part of the above context.

Redundancy of effort is to be avoided, simply because there are too few key global thinkers and researchers to allow the luxury of replication.

Question (2):

Of all the scientific and technical programs being discussed or implemented, a properly conceived and implemented supercomputer-oriented set of projects will likely emerge as the premier efforts in terms of placing the United States in a required and advantaged position to enter the nineties.

Possible areas of application:

First, it is key that most elements of a supercomputer project or projects be based on applications envisioned to be essential for the nineties.

A few candidates are as follows:

(1)   A computer-based personal assistant for a major segment of the U.S. population that would amplify intellectual capability by 100 percent.

(2)   Techniques, tools, and philosophy to fundamentally change the way products are designed, fabricated, assembled, tested, and delivered to users.

(3)   Improvement of the problem-solving capability of a wide spectrum of scientists by a factor of 1–3 via computation support of enormous proportion above what is available now.

(4)   Creation of the ability to design and manufacture low-production custom systems at a price/performance ratio on a par with current high-volume–produced systems.

(5)   Placing a factor of 20–50 improvement in the delivery cycle, of the right form, to each computer scientist as a means of substantially amplifying the intellectual capital building.

Question (3):

Tough question, but there are complex strategies which, via existence-proof kind of experimentation, do seem to create dramatic change.

It is certain that a few such strategies could be developed and implemented.

Question (4):

Computer-related communication is absolutely key as many have stated. The key issue is how to provide super ARPAnet communication and resource-sharing for the bulk of the U.S. scientific community and its interaction with funding agencies, business, and industry. It is likely that an ordered list of priorities for a short list of "supercomputer" goals would place this high on the list. If it were to be so, the implementation strategy would likely evolve in good order.

Comments addressing the recent three concerns expressed by the committee:

Item (2): Escalate them as a package to the level of a national initiative on a par with putting a man on the moon.

Item (3): The teleconference has been a success in many ways, I'm sure. One way, common in such experiences, but still the most impressive to me, is the surfacing of so many great ideas in such a short time and in a form so easy to absorb and comment on.

Keith Uncapher

From: rhe@lanl Fri Aug 26 15:05:14 1983
Date: 26 Aug 1983 13:55:11 MDT
From: Robert Ewald C-DO ⟨rhe@lanl⟩
Reply-to: rhe@lanl
To: NEW-GEN@CSNET-SH

I have read with great interest the correspondence in this ARPAnet conference. Due to travel schedules and the Frontiers of Supercomputing conference that Los Alamos co-hosted with NSA last week, I have been unable to respond as the questions came in, but let me provide a few thoughts. So that you know my bias, let me provide a bit of background. We operate a very large scientific and engineering computing network with five Cray's, five CDC 7600's, three CDC Cyber-825's, and about 40 VAXes. We serve approximately 5000 users, 4000 of them locally and about 1000 around the country.

To support our using community we have historically provided state-of-the-art high-performance numeric (as opposed to symbolic) computing facilities. To get more speed from future scientific machines, we will be using parallel architectures. We have been working on parallel algorithms for some of our major programs for the past two to three years and currently believe that it will be relatively easy to use machines with small degrees of parallelism (about two–to–eight processors). We have run some experiments with good success on our Denelcor HEP-1. Higher levels of parallelism still need considerable research.

Question (1):

We are actively seeking new supercomputers to do computations that cannot now be done. Our national security and energy programs now have requirements for machines that are many times faster than today's fastest, the Cray 1 and CDC Cyber-205. It is our belief that it will be possible, with some push from users, the Government, and the industry, to produce machines that are 200 times as fast as those now available by about 1990. The Department of Energy is leading an interagency task force that is looking into how the Government can help to achieve such a machine by 1990. Although this initiative is being driven by applications and we have a huge investment in existing software, our users recognize that we may have to make substantial changes to our software to be able to take advantage of the new architectures. We, of course, would prefer to minimize the changes.

Coexistence of numeric and symbolic uses

I believe that some of the technology developed for the numeric supercomputers will also have application to symbolic computation (I have also always believed that symbolic computation will require tremendous amounts of computing power to be useful in many applications). I believe that for our types of applications we will see numeric and symbolic applications coexisting in a loosely coupled fashion in the same network, if not on the same computer. In fact, "cooperating" may be a better word than "coexisting," since it is easy to imagine expert systems controlling or interacting with numeric simulations, or numeric simulations calling on expert systems for advice when the computation becomes questionable. This cooperation will naturally cause the projects to try to converge in at least some areas.

Question (2):

Bob Douglass has listed a number of application areas in his paper for the November 1983 issue of *Spectrum*. [See p. 9.]

Question (3):

We have had numerous discussions about this area related to scientific supercomputers, and some of that may be worth repeating here. If one looks at ideas, software, and hardware, we have seen contributions to each area from different sets of people.

The academic community has many innovative ideas for new machine architecture, prototype software systems, and some real problems to be solved. American industry has real problems to be solved today; it will treat those problems, but may not be looking to the long term. The National Laboratories, due to their missions and basic research and development directions, provide many real problems and have contributed considerable software to the computing field. The computer

manufacturers have ideas for new computers, generally building on what they have already produced for compatibility reasons, and are the ones to actually produce production-quality hardware, software, communications equipment, and so forth. In the scientific market we have long asserted that we need more communication among these sets of people, and I'm sure that it is probably more important in the symbolic computation arena.

One of the things that I think might work to get some of the newer ideas for machine architecture reviewed would be to create a panel of hardware architects from the vendors and users from laboratories, universities, and business to review the various proposals for new machine architectures. This would force some communication and would review a number of proposals using the same general criteria. Finally, our experimentation with parallel architectures has proven invaluable. It has involved parallel formulation, implementation, and measurement of a few generic benchmark programs. We strongly endorse the inclusion and support of experimental equipment on national networks. In addition to providing experience, they will stimulate collaboration.

Question (4):

I will merely echo the sentiments expressed by several people—that national networks serving multidisciplinary areas are very important and should be expanded, both for new work as well as for many ongoing activities. There are user groups all over the country who have a real demand for access to other facilities and need to be able to communicate with their colleagues and are unable to do so.

Question—What is the most critical action that the Government, industry, or academia should take?

The most important thing that we should all do is to make sure that the problems we are facing in supercomputing, new-generation computing, and networking continue to receive the attention that they now are. In the scientific supercomputing business a number of actions need to be taken.

We need to continue to acquire supercomputers, and even accelerate our acquisition of them, and make them available to universities. We need to further stimulate their use in American industry. Because so few students have been exposed to supercomputing, the technical and administrative staffs of industry are generally unaware of supercomputer capability. Yet computer simulation is a cost-effective tool in developing new products and processes.

We should support new architectural approaches and make machines embodying those architectures available. We need more hands-on experience with new machine architectures, not only in the laboratories, but also in universities and industry.

We need to get academia, Government, and industry to cooperate so that each sector can feed upon the strengths of the other. I believe that the Japanese do this much better than we do.

In supercomputing, we need to help the vendors push for faster components and peripherals. We need considerable work on the problems of software, and that is a major thrust of the new-generation computing programs.

We need to make sure that U.S. industry can remain competitive in the world marketplace, which means that joint R&D activities (like the Microelectronics and Computer Technology Corp.) be allowed to exist, that R&D tax credits be investigated, and so forth.

Bob Ewald
Los Alamos

———————————

From: Fahlman@CMU-CS-C.ARPA Sun Aug 28 21:12:30 1983
Received: ID ⟨FAHLMAN@CMU-CS-C.ARPA⟩; Sun 28 Aug
            83 22:10:59-EDT
Date: Sun, 28 Aug 1983 22:10 EDT
From: Scott E. Fahlman ⟨Fahlman@CMU-CS-C.ARPA⟩
To: new-gen@UWISC.ARPA
Subject: **Moon shots**

The case against big 'Splashy' project

In my opinion, it would be a terrible mistake to take the Apollo project as a model for the new-generation effort in symbolic computing. Such splashy single-big-goal projects make sense when the science is pretty much in hand and agreed upon, and the problem is to marshal the necessary resources. The space race was probably an appropriate way to get people to feel good about contributing $100 apiece (or whatever it came to) for a piece of the rock. (I think the subsequent antispace backlash could have been avoided if the whole thing had been handled a bit more adroitly, but that's a discussion for another time.)

As I look around, I see dozens of potentially good ideas in the general area of new-generation computing systems. A moon shot approach would, as Jeff Ullman points out, cause us to select a single interlocking set of these ideas early on. These would get all the resources that they need, and probably more; everything else would suffer and maybe be killed off. This is a big risk. If we choose wrong, we have killed off a lot of good ideas to pursue a bad one. The political process that would govern such a selection would tend to favor a bad choice, I think.

This sort of "moon shot" is what the Japanese are doing, of course. In their case, it makes sense. A moon shot is a good way to gain recognition and national prestige and a good way to build up a well-rounded technical infrastructure. Given their limited base of experience in the area of integrated hardware-software systems, it makes sense to concentrate their effort for greatest effect.

In our case, however, it would make more sense to quietly pursue a large number of paths until it becomes more apparent which ideas are the good ones. The limiting factor is people with the appropriate talent, training, and experience. We've got enough good people to man a couple of dozen exploratory projects, provided that we support them properly and don't put all our resources into a couple of major projects instead. It may be that eventually a clear winner will emerge from this process and will require an Apollo-like effort to push it through to completion. More likely, if any clear winners emerge, the U.S. computer industry will take it from there. The total effort might be Apollo-like, but the scenario is very different. Seed money is the tricky part, not funding for the final accomplishment and the follow-through.

The above comments refer only to the prospect of a "moon shot" in symbolic-computing architectures. It may be that in numerical computing, we are closer to having a consensus on which paths to pursue with all available resources—I'm not close enough to that community to know. Of course, the building of a national network is an area in which we have done the basic science and need only the resources and some intensive development, but I don't think that anything on the scale of a moon shot is needed here, so maybe we don't have to sell it as a stunt.

Scott Fahlman

ASSESSING THE SOCIOTECHNICAL CHALLENGES

The promises and risks of next-generation computers as discerned by a group of technology watchers

Eight engineers and social scientists from industry, government, and academia met on June 3, 1983, at Carnegie-Mellon University, Pittsburgh, Pa., to discuss sociotechnical impacts of next-generation computing. The results of the roundtable were used by Associate Editor Fred Guterl as the basis for "Next-generation impacts," the concluding article in the November 1983 Spectrum *issue on "Tomorrow's computers" [see p. 83].*

The roundtable was chaired by M. Granger Morgan, head, Department of Engineering and Public Policy, CMU, who convened the meeting at 10 a.m. and concluded it at 4 p.m., with a lunch break in between. The meeting vice chairman was Fred Weingarten, project director, Office of Technology Assessment, U.S. Congress.

Other meeting participants consisted of Frederick Hayes-Roth, executive vice president for technology, Teknowledge Inc., Palo Alto, Calif.; Allen Newell, university professor of computer science, CMU; Raj Reddy, director of the Robotics Institute, CMU; Marvin Sirbu, principle research associate, Center for Policy Alternatives, Massachusetts Institute of Technology, Cambridge; Joseph Weizenbaum, professor of computer science, MIT; and Langdon Winner, visiting associate professor of politics and technology, University of California, Santa Cruz.

The following text contains an edited transcript of the meeting. Also included are commentaries from eminent engineers who reviewed the edited transcript and subsequently offered alternative points of view. This group included Walter R. Beam, former vice president for research and development, Sperry Corp., Great Neck, N.Y.; George H. Heilmeier, senior vice president and chief technical officer, Texas Instruments Inc., Dallas; and Willis H. Ware, corporate research staff, Rand Corp., Santa Monica, Calif. Still other commentaries are contained in Mr. Guterl's article.

—Ed.

Morgan. I am inclined to believe that, in asking us to talk about the future impacts of advanced computing, *Spectrum* has given us an unworkable problem. I think it's partly because of what I've seen of the work done on the sociotechnical history of the telephone, which in many ways is a smaller scale version of our subject matter. There has not yet been, in my view, a good social history of the telephone, despite the fact that a number of first-rate people have attempted to write one. It is an indication of how incredibly difficult a task it is: the technology tends to permeate society and one cannot cleanly separate the two. If this blurring of technology and society occurs with the telephone, I think things are probably at least an order of magnitude worse with regard to the societal impacts of advanced computing capabilities.

Newell: As I look at the broad sweep of activities in the entire field of computing, I wonder what social changes will result from fifth-generation computing, although I grant the computer field might be transformed a bit by it. In other words, are we going to see many societal effects derived directly from fifth-generation computing, as opposed to the effects to be derived from advances in the broader field of general computing?

Morgan: There is an implicit assumption in that question. It is that fifth-generation computing will make an evolutionary, not a revolutionary, contribution in the broad picture of computing.

Reddy: The potential contributions of communications in its broadest sense must also be considered. An entire spectrum of new benefits will become possible when we advance from computers talking to computers to the eventual exchange of information at high data rates among individuals around the world. Already we are beginning to not distinguish between a computer and a telephone anymore. In the future, they will be one and the same.

Hayes-Roth: If we looked at the full range of technology options that could be discussed—from communications and basic computing to knowledge-based systems—we would be talking about how to allocate all our technological resources. In effect, we would be mimicking the various national debates.

What got this whole thing rolling from my perspective was the apparent Japanese decision to put all of their computer-technology eggs on the fifth-generation end of the spectrum. Then as various countries around the world started to respond, vested interests mixed with good intentions to produce a confusing set of alternative technical programs.

Benefits for manufacturing

Morgan: I think we should begin by talking about impacts on the manufacturing sector. May we begin with a technical assessment?

Reddy: The factory of the twenty-first century will depend on a large number of technologies—for example, advanced artificial intelligence—that have yet to be developed. Although they do not exist now, they can definitely be developed. With these technologies, it will be possible to have unmanned factories for any manufacturing process one would want to select.

As advanced technologies make it possible to custom produce a part as needed, we will be able to build factories manufacturing a wide variety of parts in any region of any country. Transportation problems would be eliminated or at least substantially reduced, thereby helping to lead to the design of microfactories, ones that would cost tens of millions of dollars rather than hundreds of millions, and still be able to produce virtually any part economically.

Another way of saying the same thing is that we would be "stockpiling" manufacturing capacity rather than finished goods. As a result, companies would eliminate large inventories in warehouses because they would have the capability to produce any part as needed.

Weingarten: What kind of time frame are you talking about?

Reddy: We can already do a few things without paper, people, or stockpiled inventories, but other changeovers will likely take 30 to 50 years. For example, the attempt to automatically assemble a small electric motor using artificial-intelligence techniques based on observing a human being performing the same tasks is likely to take a long time.

According to [Nobel Laureate] Herbert Simon, any expectations for a tripling or quadrupling of present annual-growth rates in productivity of about 2.5 percent due to advances in technology alone are wholly unwarranted. At best, it might increase to a rate of 5 percent. At that rate, we have at least 20 years before we have to face up to the prospect of unmanned factories.

Assuming that we do, in fact, proceed with the technical agenda, we also need to proceed on a social agenda, one that addresses the significant dislocations widely predicted as a byproduct of this new technology.

The superautomated office

Morgan: I want to talk for a few minutes about office automation. Marvin [Sirbu], would you start us out?

Sirbu: We are proceeding through a succession of models of what office automation might be. The term "office automation" was coined in the 1950s. It referred to using a computer to do payroll and, indeed, that was office automation.

We have gone past that to now thinking of it in terms of the paperless office: everything we used to do on paper, we will do electronically. We will, for example, pass forms around electronically. But even this view is beginning to be superseded by talk of knowledge augmentation or decision support, where the computer is seen as either doing a lot of work in formulating information so that a human being can make a decision or even, in fact, making a decision about the routine kinds of information-based processes.

For example, once someone has keypunched data onto an insurance claim form, the computer can do a reasonable job of checking to see that the correct constraints have been met and to "authorize" a payment. The decision may be reviewed by a human viewing a screen, but rarely will the computer's decisions be countermanded.

The next step will be the further integration of little subdecisions into larger and larger sequences of decisions to the point where—instead of having a type of paper-processing factory with lots of people touching, handling, and making decisions about the form, one person takes responsibility for supervising an entire sequence of decisions and processes that are handled by a single machine.

In essence, we are already doing that with respect to banking transactions. I can go to an automatic-teller machine, and it decides that I have money in my account and that I may be paid the cash, with the amount debited to my account. The only thing a human learns about the transaction comes from later confirmation of it in a letter or as a result of an audit of the bank's computer records. We are going to see increasing levels of this kind of integration and a corresponding increase in the attention given to capture of information from its source.

The wonderful thing about the automatic-teller machine is that the individual who wants the cash is the same person who is first keying in the information. From then on, it's in electronic form and gets processed automatically. No one has to do the transformation job of keypunch.

Newell: That's where you get the productivity.

Sirbu: You get a lot of productivity out of that. You can handle things in electronic form for the greatest fraction of their cycle as opposed to having to do intermediate transformations.

If I write a purchase order in my company, I write it out on paper, I send it to the purchasing department, and they key it into the computer. The computer spits out a paper purchase order, which then goes to the company that keys it into their order-processing computer, which then spits out the product and invoice, and so on. There are probably four or five transformations that take place between electronic and paper forms at various stages. That should be seen as one continuous process that may eventually be electronic from the moment that I key in the order to my terminal, after deciding I want the product, to the moment when I receive a confirmation of the product arriving. All of the intermediate steps of people doing information handling can be drastically reduced.

The key things holding that up, it seems to me, are understanding the processes well enough to figure out what rules to embed for making decisions along the way and to get agreement among different organizational units within a company, or different companies, on standard ways of exchanging information to keep things in electronic form. Everybody will agree to accept a paper invoice because it can be interpreted by a human being. We have yet to agree on how to make an electronic purchase order from my computer and send it to your order entry computer automatically. We are beginning to experiment with that and the key processes here have to do with developing standard ways of referring to knowledge so that the order can be passed between machines.

Morgan: Do you think that the solution will be standardization of forms, systems that are smart enough to "read" a variety of forms, or some combination of these?

Sirbu: Some combination. In the grocery industry, where standard forms have been agreed upon, a grocery store will order goods via a computer from a food warehouse.

The insurance industry, on the other hand, decided they needed a value-added intermediary. The independent agents, and underwriters who work through the agents, have hired IBM to build a value-added network in between them that will do lots of intelligent processing so as to make what the independent agents have to say more understandable to the underwriters.

How work may change

Morgan: I'd like to hear some discussion on how the nature of work changes and how the authority and control shifts around in both the bottom end of the system that Marvin [Sirbu] described and the bottom end of the system Raj [Reddy] described. It sounds to me like there are going to be an awful lot of jobs that are going to be pretty dull.

Sirbu: A multistage process is at work here, and many of the jobs in the intermediate stage are quite dull. The intermediate stage is one where people are translating information from paper to electronic form or monitoring every transaction when it appears on a screen.

It turns out to be dull because it's repetitive, like assembly-line work. But one can, certainly in the factory and eventually in the office, move toward work involving source-data capture or toward a job that becomes more and more supervisory or interventional.

In the factory, an example of a more enriched job might be when a person takes sole control of an automated machine by monitoring, repairing, and perhaps changing its program. An example of a comparable office situation exists at Citibank, which recently reorganized its processing of letters of credit. What used to be a series of steps—most of which were manual and involved several persons—was automated and turned over to a single individual who handled the entire transaction. Now, the individual deals with the customer over the telephone, updates data bases through a single terminal, and continues overseeing the operation until a letter is sent to the customer.

Morgan: That would require skills and knowledge for an entry-level position considerably higher than now exists. It sounds to me, Raj [Reddy], that you were saying the same thing in manufacturing. So I think I am hearing that, in general, these technologies will require considerably higher levels of training and skill for entry-level jobs.

Weingarten: Different new jobs are cropping up—only to disappear a few years down the road. Consider quality checkers of integrated circuits. They sit and look through microscopes, visually inspecting the circuits for surface flaws. Surely, those jobs are going to be automatable very quickly. Yet they haven't existed very long. These people are learning skills for a category of employment that has a lifetime of only about 10 years.

Sirbu: If jobs have durations of only 10 years, on the average, the number of cycles of retraining and relearning for new kinds of jobs that people are going to have to go through in a lifetime will become significant, but a consensus is forming that this is the problem we'll be facing.

Weizenbaum: I am sure there are people who will be able to cope with a lifetime of endless learning, but the people at the entry level are simply not qualified by way of education to take the job, for example, of managing a letter of credit through an automated bank system. What we have recently learned about our educational system is that it isn't producing people who could, in fact, benefit from that kind of lifelong education, whereas Japanese citizens, on the whole, are better educated at the high-school level than ours and can perhaps take advantage of a kind of lifelong learning situation.

Sirbu: Our educational system is definitely not geared to preparing people for this kind of world. That is absolutely correct.

Preserving needed societal relationships

Morgan: Langdon [Winner], may we hear your views about political, social, and economic organization; and Fred [Wein-garten], I'm going to ask you to do the same with respect to freedom, justice, and civil liberties.

Winner: There are two related comments I'd like to make. First of all, I see a pattern emerging in many applications of microelectronics that has the effect of eliminating layers of social interaction that were previously important. For example, automated-teller machines do away with small branch banks, which were not only ways of doing business, but also places where people met, talked, and socialized.

To an increasing extent, we are removing the kinds of face-to-face contact that provide buffers between individuals and enormous sources of organized power. In contrast to this trend is the development of the factory system in the nineteenth century. For all its brutality, the factory was a profoundly sociable place; people who had previously been scattered throughout society were brought together under one roof; they could begin to know each other and recognize their common plight. Much of the impetus behind early labor movements sprang from a sense of solidarity born in the workplace.

Today we seem eager to handle our transactions in settings that do not require the presence of other human beings. Such arrangements will drastically change many social and political relationships.

Morgan: Before you go on to the second point, are you implying that in the older system there was a degree of flexibility, understandability, and adaptability that isn't as present in the newer system, or are you ascribing some other set of values to the socializing element of the problem?

Winner: Yes, flexibility and intelligiblity are sacrificed in many computer innovations. But even more important, in my view, is the creation of situations in which isolated individuals are placed in direct contact with very large sources of well-organized power. Institutions that used to serve as mediating links or buffers between people and large organizations are often ones rendered obsolete in the information age. Agencies of centralized programming now have more direct access to individuals; power can be exercised from the top down in a straight line.

Sociologists who have studied the rise of totalitarianism have often identified the destruction of intervening social layers between the individual and centralized power as one of the most dangerous political developments of this century. I find it interesting that we are now reproducing this condition in the name of technical and economic efficiency.

My second point has to do with the ways ordinary people protect their own power and interests. One thing that corporate managers find appealing in the so-called electronic cottage is that it is likely to weaken labor unions. In that totally dispersed way of doing office work, you log in on your personal computer, handle your jobs for the day, take care of your children, all in one place. There is no occasion to do what was formerly done in the office or factory—look around to see people relatively like yourself and eventually recognize your own power and authority as something you share with people in similar situations. Faced with technologies like the electronic cottage, what opportunities will people have to organize and empower themselves?

Weingarten: There is an echo of this argument in the debate about whether or not an automated criminal-justice system, in which the automation and storage of criminal-history information are designed to make the courts, police functions, and so on, more efficient, makes the whole system harsher and less forgiving because of the inefficiency of that process.

Hayes-Roth: Let me remind this group that there are examples of bureaucracies that are inept and essentially totalitarian because of that. My reaction to what I am hearing is that technology is orthogonal to the issue you are talking about and that you may create a dangerous confusion. What I see is a spurious correlation between technology and examples of social systems that either work well or don't work well and attempts to ascribe primacy of causality to technology.

Protecting individual liberty and privacy

Winner: Consider the potential threat to human freedom that arises when extensive electronic data about people's lives and activities are gathered, stored, correlated, and put to use. In the United States our tendency is to view this problem in a very narrow definition: the threat to privacy of individuals. When I talk to people about this question, citing examples in which electronic monitoring has been used as a tool for harassment and coercion, they often say that they don't need to worry about it because they're not doing anything anyone would possibly want to watch. In other words, it becomes a sign of virtue for them to say: "Thank God, I'm not involved in anything that a computer would find at all interesting." Its precisely that response that I find troubling.

A metaphor for our situation can be found in a fascinating design for a building, The Panopticon, created by nineteenth-century philosopher Jeremy Bentham. The Panopticon was to be a circular building, several stories high, with a tower in the center. It could be used as a prison, hospital, school, or factory. A key feature of the design was that people in its rooms could not see each other, but the person in the center looking out to the periphery could gaze into every cell. Bentham saw this architecture as the ultimate means of social control. There would not even need to be a guard present in the tower at all times: all one had to do was to build in such a way that surveillance became an omnipresent possibility that would eliminate misbehavior and induce total compliance.

It appears that we may now be building an electronic Panopticon, a system of seemingly benign electronic-data gathering that creates *de facto* conditions of universal surveillance. To identify problems we might face here as ones that involve nothing more than individual privacy is woefully shortsighted. The danger extends beyond the private sphere to affect the public freedoms upon which our privacy demands. Unless we take steps to prevent it, we could see a society filled with all-seeing data banks used to monitor an increasingly compliant, passive populace no longer willing to risk activities that comprise civil liberty.

Weingarten: Most of the legislation, writing, and so on, related to computers and individual privacy have been based on the view of privacy as a matter under the control of large corporations, and mainly based on what they might do with information that conceivably could be right, wrong, or incomplete. The general response has been either that it's not very serious or that there isn't anything to hide. In the past we thought, well, when I give information to, say, a loan company, it is an exchange; I am giving them information and they, in turn, are deciding whether to give me a loan.

Today, however, we are building systems that can collect a vast amount of information on an individual's daily transactions. Further, systems such as those employing knowledge-based technology can do more with that information than ever before, including the making of decisions that affect individual lives.

On a broader level, I have heard arguments to the effect that First Amendment rights are as important to society as to the individual. This is because the form of society that we have depends on the flow of information that follows from hearing, generating, and distributing new ideas. So, to the extent that computer and communication technologies may be used to control this process, I believe a potential danger exists to our society.

Morgan: You are arguing that a potential social vulnerability can be created if one builds systems in which access to information in machineable form is easy and straightforward and where there are few economic or other incentives for any given individual actor to take steps to ensure in major ways against such access. If collectively such access if not controlled, it could, under appropriate circumstances, have profound political and other implications.

Sirbu: This First Amendment issue relates to what is happening as information is increasingly treated as a commodity, as a product to be protected by copyrights. One example that Ithiel Pool, an MIT political scientist, has written about is the notion that the concept of freedom of the press may somehow be reinterpreted. We don't treat electronic-communications media the same way we treat newspapers. We accept regulations such as the FCC "equal time" provisions for broadcasters, but we find them unacceptable for newspapers. If they are eventually published electronically, will newspaper or broadcasting rules apply?

Morgan: Your point is that, because there are different technologies with different legal contexts, free flows of information may be rather different in electronic-publication media than in conventional print media. Fred [Weingarten] is making an argument that says, "because my electronic-mail system is not being encrypted, nor is anyone else's, and because I never say anything on my electronic-mail system that I want to pay very much to protect, nor does anyone else, that in a sort of global social sense, that presents some very high degree of vulnerability: for example, vulnerability to a foreign power who'd like to come in and muck up the economy by listening to a lot of transactions.

Reddy: Advanced speech-recognition technology conceivably could allow telephone conversations containing certain key phrases to be plucked from vast streams of irrelevant conversations. However, encryption technology will be inexpensive enough to use before speech-recognition technology enables conversations to be monitored by computer.

Weizenbaum: As long as the public perceives its privacy to be violated, it will not trust encryption or any other technology to restore it.

Morgan: Stop and think about situations where you can anticipate a potential problem: it takes a small act on everybody's part to prevent it. We don't have a great track record in dealing with such situations. I agree with Raj Reddy that such problems are largely amenable to technological fix through relatively inexpensive means. But this will work only if one plans for it ahead of time.

Winner: The ability to assemble and cross-correlate information from different electronic bases is already being used to punish some groups in our society. In Massachusetts last year, government officials decided to check the relationship between welfare records and bank accounts. Welfare recipients whose bank accounts had too much money according to bureaucratic rules were forced off the welfare roles. Perhaps developments of this kind are what is meant by the term "computer revolution."

Hayes-Roth: If one tried in an unbiased way to get an informed judgment from the populace at large on the things they would like to put on the social agenda for technologists to solve—even if they understood well the threats to privacy we have talked about—I believe there would be many other concerns on their agenda, such as: how am I going to keep my job? how is my company going to stay in business? and a number of things like that.

I don't think that I'm able to predict what will happen, but I would not be surprised to find out that the technology has displaced a number of highly skilled and talented individuals. For example, every programmer and every software engineer might be made irrelevant by the technology. Now, if that occurs, it will be a much bigger issue for those people, and I give that as an example because I suspect that by the time the technology that we are talking about achieves its potential, it will—like other technologies—be mixed and married with many events and cultural happenings. I don't know how to plan for new technologies because, almost by definition, they change the environment.

Distribution of power

Morgan: If you look at the early literature on social impacts of computing, you will find extensive discussions concerning a trend toward centralization of control, as well as a growing disparity between some groups in terms of access to and control over information and knowledge. In the first decades of computers, those were not inappropriate concerns; however, if you look at the directions in which computing is evolving today, with high processing power and high storage densities in stand-alone units at relatively low costs, it's not clear to me that those concerns remain as serious. Does anyone care to comment?

Sirbu: Over the next 10 years, the cost of this technology will still remain such that large fractions of the population will be excluded from it. To the extent that some of the most powerful systems are knowledge-based systems that are fairly expensive to engineer, they will remain out of the reach of all but a few people.

I have been thinking of how computers have changed political campaigning for the politicians who have used some of the best computer direct-mail systems. What happens when expert systems for advising campaigns are available to only the candidates with the largest budget? It's going to change political campaigning, as much as polling and direct mail.

Morgan: Do you have any thoughts on the gap? Is it going to grow bigger, smaller, stay the same or what?

Sirbu: In 1890, only the rich had telephones. Telephones did not advance for a fairly long time; then it penetrated universally and everyone had a telephone. Now we're going to go through a new kind of telephone expansion for a long time and only the well-to-do will have the computer videotelephone, or whatever it is, until it stabilizes again and reaches a new plateau and becomes universal at other economic levels. I think

as long as we are in a period of very rapid technological change, which I expect we will be for some time, there is going to be a differential based on money.

Weingarten: I think we are talking in a way that is sort of typical of the arrogance that technologists are prone to. We are focusing on technology, rather than on the functions that it performs. As the price of computing goes down, it seems to me that the operative question becomes whether access to information is getting cheaper, and it is not clear to me that it is.

Impacts on professionals

Morgan: I want to talk about impacts on professions, particularly on medicine, law, and finance and accounting.

Hayes-Roth: The technology of knowledge-based expert systems got its start in attempts to use computers to mimic professional expertise in narrow, well-defined areas. The first successful demonstrations were in chemistry and medicine. These areas were successful because previously a great deal of effort had been spent trying to write down the best-known ways to solve problems, and so there was a running start at the knowledge-engineering process. Also, nearly all of the knowledge in those areas is symbolic, and that's a good fit to what the technology can accommodate.

People are used to buying both knowledge and help as a commodity. Professions exist because people are willing to pay for consultant help.

Winner: From a historical point of view, that's a misleading explanation of why the professions arose. Professionalization began in the nineteenth century with an attempt to establish a monopoly of knowledge and skill in fields that had previously been open to anyone. Knowledge and practice, once part of the common culture, were redefined as commodities, available only from licensed specialists. The way you've stated it makes it sound as if consumers demanded that this change occur. That puts the cart before the horse.

Hayes-Roth: It's clear that through the recent merchandising (such as by Sears, Roebuck and Co., Chicago) of this kind of consultant help, a market exists for expanded delivery of those services. On the other hand, the knowledge and broad-based experience that is required to be a good advisor, say, in legal matters, clearly lies beyond the capability of present technology. The technology excels at recreating human specialists who deal with restricted kinds of problems.

Now that is today's limitation, but in areas such as internal medicine, it's already the case that one system, Internist, does as well in diagnosis as the average internal-medicine practitioner. There are places in the world where one does not have access to an average practitioner of internal medicine and I would argue that people would be better off if they had access to an artificial expert than none at all.

Similarly, finance and accounting are professions for which concrete expertise is not generally available to the average person. One could argue that people would be better off with an artificial advisor than none at all. However, aspects of each of those professions tend to be fuzzy, intuitive, and essentially ill-defined, and so do not lend themselves perfectly to expert-system applications.

I think the penetration of this technology will begin in those areas where the professional know-how is replicable, where there is a shortage of professionals, and where people want it badly. In industrial areas, I believe that professions will tend to shift and reorient themselves so that those areas that are heavily knowledge-intensive—and are highly symbolic or repeatable—will be reproduced in computers.

Morgan: Can you indicate rates of diffusion?

Hayes-Roth: I think that it will not be strange to look back 20 or so years from now and then see in every major organization a large number of people who are doing what we today call knowledge engineering. There may even be knowledge-engineering departments, if there are any departments at all, and as much as 30 percent of the potential applications will have been implemented.

Sirbu: Have you thought at all about how bringing in expert systems is likely to change organizations? If office automation is any guide, you bring in something that helps a person with, say, 15 percent of the things he does, so the need arises to have workloads reorganized in order to efficiently take advantage of the new system.

Hayes-Roth: Yes and no. Let me take the "no" part first. To some extent, expert-system technology will deny the necessity of a reorganization. For example, our oil-drilling advisor for Elf-Aquitaine [Paris, France] was motivated by the need for an expert on each of a company's drilling rigs. The cost of operation on a rig may be $100 thousand to $200 thousand a day and the number of drilling rigs is generally quite large. If the company could reduce drilling downtime by, say, 50 percent, the annual savings would amount to tens of millions of dollars. That alone justifies the company installing artificial advisors on its rigs.

Sirbu: What you are saying is that the job had already been concentrated so that there was someone who was putting 100 percent of his time doing the job that this expert system was going to do?

Hayes-Roth: Yes; however, the nature of human expertise today is that specialists are not generally available for all of the sites in the world where they may be needed.

Winner: The literature I've read on fifth-generation computing wants to leave the concept of "information" behind and move on to "knowledge." It's evidently "knowledge" that the Japanese will be trying to package and sell in the 1990s. I am a little unclear about how that distinction is constituted and what this supposed leap amounts to.

Hayes-Roth: The basic emphasis on the word "knowledge" reflects the fact that artificial-intelligence technology got its major impetus by implanting *expertise* in computers. When one looks at what makes an expert, even in a specialized technical area, one finds a diverse set of factors. But the power that one has tapped into is specific—namely, the capability to solve problems using facts, tricks, and wisdom gained from experience. What is being represented primarily in a knowledge-based expert system is the know-how to solve problems as an expert would. By contrast, "information" is generally taken to mean lists of facts which are generally agreed upon, or perhaps a list of data.

If I give you an information base, you are left with the problem of how to interpret it and apply it. If I give you a knowledge base, I am giving you a capability to supplement your own abilities in the ways that an expert would were he around to advise you in interpreting data, figuring out what information is relevant to your problem, and how best to solve a problem even though there may not be one probably correct way of doing it.

Winner: I find that a narrow conception of what knowledge is. It seems to me possible that the concept is being hijacked.

Reddy: That is always a problem. In fact, people are concerned about the term supercomputer, which has been a synonym for a number-crunching machine, now being used for fifth-generation machines. Basically, what we are saying is that this knowledge is information plus control.

Hayes-Roth: The crucial aspects of any kind of learning of a new skill today are experience and apprenticeship, which just reflect the way people are and the way we have evolved our knowledge-transfer systems. In physics, for example, physicists pride themselves on boiling down to the essence all that is known about the fundamental laws of the universe. In fact, if one studies the way physicists actually solve problems, one finds that a good physicist recognizes when a new problem is very much like an old one and can remember in detail the way general rules had to be specialized to fit the earlier situation. That is the kind of knowledge that I am talking about.

So people have prided themselves, in general, on boiling out all that messy stuff that it actually takes to make one proficient in solving problems. But except through apprenticeship, people have not bothered to attempt a direct transfer of that proficiency. With knowledge-based systems, it is possible to capture know-how and apply it as needed.

Morgan: The systems that we are talking about over the next decade or so are very much directed toward areas in which there is a well-defined structure, and there is a very rich set of data that one looks at and uses for inferences. This tends to reinforce the impression I had of artificial intelligence as a field that started out in the mode of looking for major insights and has increasingly moved in the direction of solving its problems by many small, incremental steps. Is that a correct impression? If so, how widely is it shared in the profession at the moment?

Hayes-Roth: I think your observation is pretty accurate. The field of artificial intelligence has branched out, but let me oversimplify by saying that today it's divided primarily between those who are looking for theoretical breakthroughs or foundational elements that are missing and those who are treating it as an empirical science that will accumulate incrementally.

The knowledge-engineering business is clearly associated with the latter of those approaches. It wasn't until people abandoned the search for the missing link and simply began focusing on application problems and on the acquisition and re-creation of knowledge, that they started making a lot of progress.

Reddy: There are a number of things we don't yet know how to do with our machines. One limitation that may take another 100 years to overcome is the ability to read a chapter in an arbitrary book and answer the questions about the chapter, and that is a goal people have been trying to achieve now for 10 years. We are nowhere near 10 percent of the solution of the problem. It is also going to become very important if we are able to deal with systems that can acquire new knowledge automatically, without help from a human being.

Another limitation are systems that can learn by observation—for example, learn to assemble small motors by observing a human operator, and to repeat and improve on it. Again, it's a fundamental problem we are faced with and it is not clear how long it will take to solve.

Still another limitation are systems that understand themselves. A solution here would get around the absurdity of having systems manuals that are heavier and bulkier than the systems themselves. In this context, we often talk of self-describing systems and self-describing factories, which could train the operators in the running of the plant.

Resiliency in diversity

Morgan: I want to ask a question that might best be posed with an ecological parallel. My friends who are ecologists talk about resiliency in systems arising from diversity. They get alarmed when you start talking about producing forests where all of the trees are genetically identical. It's probably a little early in the history of this field to raise the issue, but has anybody started to worry about the analogous problem in knowledge-based systems? If we were to plant a large number of these knowledge-based systems around the world, we would, in a different context, have built a system with virtually no resiliency.

Sirbu: I have a great example that happened recently. In Massachusetts, we now have an emissions inspection system in which a thousand or so garages in the state use a new emissions tester built by a single company. The tester had a bug in its software that was not discovered until the garages sought to record emissions tests for the month of June. On the first of that month, the machines stopped, so none of the thousand-plus systems could be used to do the emissions inspections. The malfunction was later diagnosed and corrected.

Hayes-Roth: It came as a big surprise to me to discover that one company generally did not want access to another company's expert system. One might have thought that the opposite womuld be the case.

More to the point, people who really want good advice generally seek multiple consultations. In the areas where people are paying the most for advice, say in oil exploration, it's not unusual for a single exploration site to make use of a dozen different experts from different providers.

Morgan: When I go to the hardware store now, I discover that every store in the city has the same supplier. If I can't find what I want in one place, I can't find it anywhere.

Hayes-Roth: You are not an important customer to the hardware store, basically. Still, there are places where you can go and have exactly what you want made for you.

Morgan: That's right, but at enormous cost and expense. You have been telling us about systems you are building for particular companies and how wonderful it is that I'm going to be able to go out and get better legal and medical advice. I'm worried that just as now I can only get a certain kind of hardware anywhere in town, I may only be able to get a certain kind of professional advice.

Hayes-Roth: I see this matter as a debate about "real" expertise vs. the "best" expertise currently available, and think there are examples of both kinds of knowledge now dispersed both in the industrial area and, specifically, in medicine. Actually, as a knowledge-based industry, medicine exhibits both too much standardization and a great deal of heterogeneity.

The medical business, which has been very knowledge-intensive, sets up regular activities to refresh and rewrite the knowledge in areas where new data, information, and experience accumulate very rapidly. It is done collectively on a national or world-wide basis by committees or individuals. Certain individuals write reference books that are treated as the standards, and these people are expected to rewrite those reference books on a regular basis. These standards already ensure that average patients get treated with conventional wisdom, for better or worse.

Then there are areas where there is a great diversity of opinion and practical know-how. For example, it's well known that there are real limits to the general medical community's ability to use statistical inference properly. I know people who do epidemiological studies on a regular basis, aware of which articles to ignore, and which not to ignore. Others, without this special know-how, cannot separate wheat from chaff in the literature.

Weizenbaum: General agreement appears to exist that few people who have or will have home computers are going to program their computers. They'll be making use of prepackaged software. This will lead to another kind of homogenization in our society, to what I call the Holiday Inn phenomenon. Once inside a Holiday Inn hotel anywhere in the world, one is guaranteed not to be able to tell where one is. They are made to all look the same. That doesn't help to make life very interesting.

Now consider the possibility of multiple access to the same data banks. I am thinking specifically of the legal profession's Lexis. It's hard for me to see how we can avoid finding, one day, that every law office has access to Lexis. It will become the source for lawyers to look up their law. It will be the law. But what happens when a particular case gets misfiled, or it just isn't in the data banks? What happens to the universe of old cases that were never machine encoded?

My point is illustrated by a very impressive geological map of the earth that hangs in the office of MIT physicist Philip Morrison. He likes to point out that the data for this computer-generated map postdate the year in the sixties when data needed to draw such maps became machine readable. Before that, he says, it's as if geology had not existed.

The point is this: although some people believe that the computer will introduce variety because it's such a flexible tool, most examples that I can think of illustrate that the computer introduces uniformity, homogeneity, and rigidity.

Hayes-Roth: What we are talking about are new ways of preserving expertise. In the old way, one apprentice, working for a master, learned how to be proficient at a skill. Then he became a master, passed on his knowledge to an apprentice, and died. The ecological advantage of such a system was that each new generation would grow up in a new social context. Refreshing itself as it evolved, the next generation would modify and adapt itself to its new surroundings.

Teaching versus learning

Morgan: I'd like us now to talk about teaching and learning focusing specifically on those educational tools that utilize at least some elements of artificial-intelligence capabilities. Let's talk about professional and continuing education, and also about implications for primary and secondary education.

One of the impressions that I have had with regard to primary and secondary education is that computer-based educational services are probably less likely, over the period of the next few decades, to do very much to enhance really outstanding teaching as opposed to helping to pull up the great, long lower tail to some minimum level.

Sirbu: The educational field has undergone a major transformation in its thinking about the use of computers. In the old days of computer-aided instruction, a student simply followed through a sequence of things determined by the course writer, or programmer, maybe with some branches. If the student answered a question incorrectly, what followed was determined solely by the course writer.

Gradually this approach gave way to computer systems that somehow embedded within themselves a kind of simulation of the system under study. Students could then query the system, form hypotheses, test out ideas, and, in general, control the sequence of activities and direction of explorations. I would expect knowledge-based systems to accelerate this trend, particularly in conceptual symbolic areas—as opposed to traditional geometry and physics, where we are now.

Based on previous experience with computer-aided instruction, it will be hard to predict what effect, if any, will result from the application of artificial-intelligence techniques. About the only certainty is that students will spend more time with systems that allow them to be in control than with systems in which they follow a program made out by somebody else.

Weingarten: With a kind of computer-game environment, it's fairly easy for teachers to find niches in normal course work to insert traditional computer-aided instruction to teach addition or other disciplines. If nothing else, teachers can get a little breathing space.

However, this kind of simulated resource environment that Marvin [Sirbu] referred to requires a vast restructuring of curriculum, beginning with a fundamental change in what is meant by teaching. Among the formidable hurdles to contend with is enormous bureaucratic and institutional inertia.

Hayes-Roth: I keep hearing and reading about people who are concerned that their children are not receiving relevant technological education in schools, at a time when there is a growing perception that entry-level knowledge requirements will increase as technology advances. If I had to make predictions, I'd say people will seek to exploit whatever technological opportunities are at hand, rather than wait either for social structures to catch up or for a continuing decentralization of the educational process.

Morgan: Are you arguing that the fairly widespread availability of personal computers in homes is really going to have some substantial educational impact?

Hayes-Roth: Certainly. What computer games have done is to make computers accessible to people; once interest in a game has been satiated, people begin to want to know what else they can do with computers.

I predict that what these home-entertainment companies are going to be providing is personal growth opportunities for whatever direction is called for. The resulting market pull will set the stage for a few generic breakthroughs in hardware and software, so that it will be possible, for example, to give a description of a system that someone is trying to master and have that be all that is required to produce a new course. Those breakthroughs will reduce the entry costs for writing interesting and useful courses. I believe the demand exists.

Morgan: I wish I could believe that.

Weizenbaum: I don't believe it. I think the home computer is going to follow the example of the home movie camera. Many people bought very expensive home movie cameras, thinking that with a good camera they could make good movies. What they forgot is that in order to make good movies, one has to have an idea. Good ideas are hard to come by in the domain of films, and hard to come by in the field of computation.

Morgan: Do we believe that there will be a large commercial supply of course materials?

Weizenbaum: I don't doubt it. In fact, what I see happening is that the computer in schools is beginning to serve as a technological fix for all the troubles of our educational system. That system is in profound difficulty, as we all know. Because of the mistaken belief of parents and many others that the computer for children (whether in the context of camps, schools, or anything else) is going to ensure those children jobs for the rest of their lives, computers are going to be seen as the educational system's salvation. Much time will go by before the real ills of the schools are actually attended to.

Morgan: If one goes back and looks at the very early discussions of the future of television, when it was first proposed, you would discover that those discussions are about all those wonderful cultural and educational impacts television will have.

Weizenbaum: Radio, too.

Morgan: Yes, 40 years earlier. Some of those things are indeed happening to television and radio in very incremental ways, but only after a drawn-out period.

Hayes-Roth: I think that example cuts both ways. The entire publishing and broadcasting industry produced a concentration of resources and programming as a direct result of its extreme capital intensiveness. Recent improvements in technologies and lower entry costs are only now shaking up that entire industry.

Morgan: I think the courseware is comparably expensive to develop.

Weingarten: The industry was regulated.

Hayes-Roth: I think the courseware represent just the opposite case.

Morgan: Are we saying the reason we have had lousy television programming for 20 years in this country is regulation?

Winner: Those regulations turned over most control of radio and television to the broadcasting corporations. Any cultural possibilities for the media other than ones determined by the commercial market were precluded as early as the 1930s.

Morgan: There is nothing I would like to believe more than that home computers will bring high-quality educational services into U.S. homes. I guess I have to be persuaded.

Reddy: If we take a world-wide view of this, I think that home computers may help solve one of the world's major problems—illiteracy. Computers are certainly inexpensive enough and widespread enough to help children anywhere learn how to read.

Winner: During the past two decades our society has somehow reached a sweeping decision that the profession of teaching is virtually worthless and that our young people will have to be educated more or less haphazardly, perhaps aided by various kinds of information machines—computers, video equipment, and the like.

What teachers have to offer students is not so much either knowledge or information as the ability to develop an inquiring mind. Learning how to learn is the difficult skill, one that far transcends the mastery of any particular subject matter. We have heard repeatedly today that people are going to have to be "retrained" at 5- or 10-year intervals just to stay economically fit in our society. If changes of that kind are attempted at the same time that we are tying everyone to knowledge-based systems, people are likely to become dependent on the systems and never develop truly inquiring minds that might enable them to cope with these transformations. Simply put, I don't believe that all the personal computers dumped into all the schools in this country will make a bit of difference. The problems of our educational system are chronic and stem ultimately from a lack of human care.

Hayes-Roth: The opposition that is getting set up here has to do with trying to get a feel for what the future relationship will be between education and technology.

One of the key assets of knowledge-based computers is that when they produce answers, they also are able to answer questions about how they derived those answers. Surely this ability has relevancy to education.

In this regard, these computers do three things. First, they enable people to decide for themselves whether they want to accept an answer. Secondly, people can register a lack of understanding of or agreement with the rules employed to reach answers. Finally, and perhaps most significantly, they make people more sensitive to those variables and parameters that are relevant to decisions of import, thereby enhancing individuals' abilities to focus their efforts on particular needs.

Reddy: I see a number of learning situations for which the technology can provide something not hitherto possible. Knowledge-based simulation is certainly one. Up to now we've had only aircraft-pilot training. However, active simulators can be developed for learning experiences applicable to a broad range of training, from the factory to the physics lab to the nuclear control room.

Morgan: Joe [Weizenbaum], can I ask you a question on your concern about how computers might get in the way? An alternative view might be that computers are a means to circumvent the educational establishment.

Weizenbaum: The question evokes an image of an educational system that can be bypassed, one that has system boundaries. In reality, the system is continuous with the rest of our society.

Morgan: But there is an educational bureaucracy.

Weizenbaum: I'm not saying there isn't something recognizable as an educational establishment, but that there are no hard and fast boundaries, and that, once again, we are faced with the computer in its traditional role, as a solution looking for a problem.

Let's take the case of Johnny, who can't read, and ask why he can't. An answer might have to do with his home and school environments as much as with his teacher. The point is that we see the computer as a solution to problems we won't examine. If we were to look at what the entire educational establishment is like—and that includes our society and such negative attitudes, for example, as our disrespect for teachers—then we would see that even if we could get the computer to somehow teach Johnny to read, this would be only a part of the solution. By employing merely technological means, we are not attending to the fundamental problems that underlie an educational system that is providing a human "wave of mediocrity."

Morgan: I am profoundly doubtful about a technological fix in this area. Many segments of today's educational establishment, including the training of teachers and the administration of schools, are irrelevant or, worse than that, are the problem. So when I asked about circumventing the system, somehow, I thought, one has to short-circuit a good bit of that.

Sirbu: The metaphor may not be short-circuiting, it may be unfreezing, by directing new attention to the schools. If parents begin to pay attention to the schools only to find out if there is a computer, they are at least paying attention to the schools in a way that may unfreeze the tacit cooperation by which they previously ignored the system.

Reddy: In the society of the future, the emphasis will be on computer literacy coupled with learning as a skill. Without these, access to knowledge and resources will be virtually impossible. They will be as fundamentally important as reading, writing, and arithmetic are today.

Hayes-Roth: I want to ask what will happen when it's widely recognized that the present assumptions that determine how we spend money educating people are no longer valid? Already certain segments of our society are being written off as not worth the capital investment that it would take to train them because it's too great a cost. What happens when we go beyond retraining every five years, when we get to the point where only 25 percent of the people are required to do the world's work?

Morgan: The world has a remarkable ability to find things to keep people busy. I think a much more serious likelihood is that we'll end up with a greater stratification of skilled versus unskilled labor. In a democracy, that is an untenable situation: it simply can't be allowed to develop.

Hayes-Roth: According to Nolan Bushnell (formerly at Atari and now with Pizza Time), we may end up with entertainment as the biggest industry of all, the one with the most consistent demand and the largest growth. At that point, in most industrial areas, labor-intensive activities would become passé.

Planning for the future

Morgan: Let's go round the table for any final thoughts.

Reddy: The implications of next-generation computers are that they will affect those of us who have access to these systems in a very profound way, simply by making available to us a level of problem-solving and knowledge capabilities that we just don't have now. Whatever intellectual pursuits we engage in are likely to be performed somewhat better, if not significantly better.

Sirbu: The most compelling matter for public policy is to do something about the implications for the educational level of people entering the work force and of the continuing education that will be required. The key problem is to prepare people intellectually to use this technology to change the way they work periodically, because the technology will continually change the demands for different kinds of jobs.

Hayes-Roth: I subscribe to the idea that generally, if we are talking about a period of 10 years, that the future has already happened, that the forces that will shape the next 10 years are already evident. So I'd like to point to two events that I think have occurred and that suggest the dominant forces ushered in by this technology.

The first of these is that on a regular basis new people have begun to attain economic rewards from exploiting knowledge-based technology. Companies that want to do it now can take on problems that are not difficult to define and that can make them $10 million to $100 million over a short period of time.

The second thing is that industries and governments have begun to recognize this, and they are betting with real money that this technology is going to make dramatic economic differences for them. That says to me that the next 10 years will be very competitive ones, and this technology is probably going to get capitalized and developed far more quickly than others we have seen.

Weingarten: We are going through a period of enormous technological change and it's reasonable to expect that enormous political, economical, and social consequences are waiting in the wings. Some very important choices are ahead of us; this makes it more important than ever to think through carefully the implications of this technology before they are upon us and beyond our means to influence.

Winner: Over the years, I've spent a great deal of time studying the intellectual history of the idea that "technology is out of control." In some cases notions of that kind seem to me invalid, nonsensical, even crazy. At other times, when humans seem to have relinquished moral control over their instruments, the concept of autonomous technology appears right on the mark.

As I read the literature on fifth-generation computing and listen to this conversation today, I am impressed by people's sense that we are somehow caught in a stampede and all that is left for us mortals is to rumble along with the rest of the herd. In the middle of a stampede, of course, words of caution are difficult to hear. What concerns me is that we have become so thoroughly impressed with the power of computers that we begin to ignore and even sacrifice crucial features of our culture: education, skill, family, sociability, and the integrity of human knowledge.

If we are indeed undergoing a computer "revolution," I'd like to see the revolutionaries spell out their basic ends, their program for change. Most of the writings and media presentations on this question at present are little more than hype and hoopla.

Weizenbaum: I see a number of things happening over the next several years as a result of not merely ever more powerful computers, but rather of the increasing power of high technology altogether. The most immediate effect will be a general loss of human skills, followed closely by a decreasingly comprehensible world. Physics, for example, no longer gives us anything we can comprehend with our senses. It describes a world that none of us can see or inhabit, in which we have to believe the authority of an anonymous science.

I see an increasingly homogeneous and, therefore, very dull world, and a further stratification of society, most particularly of Western society. We will have an information society populated by individuals whose lives are characterized by their plastic machine-readable cards. As time goes by, people's poverty of inner resources will be rendered invisible by the humanly irrelevant power of their plastic cards. Great masses of people will live out their lives alternating between obeying the imperatives of machines at their work and in their free time, suckling on the breasts of the great bitch—entertainment. Unless, of course, we want a better world.

Morgan: If we want to maintain the economic quality of life we have enjoyed for the last decade or two in this country, there are some economic imperatives that say that we must adopt a set of technologies that we have been talking about, that a choice to delay substantially or to not adopt is equivalent to a choice of accepting a significantly lower economic standard of living. I think a corollary to that is that we neither are likely to be able to nor should we want to adopt those technologies without simultaneously assuring that some of the human dislocations in manpower and other impacts that we are surely going to have are properly thought about and dealt with ahead of time.

Both of those things—facilitating the adoption of technology and dealing in a humane and appropriate way with the human and other social aspects of that adoption—are not likely to occur without some sort of public-policy intervention, by which I do not necessarily mean single, centralized Government programs. I do mean something that is able to transcend simple individual-level market choices.

Another set of concerns has to do with the basic knowledge and skill levels that will be necessary to function in society. What I see as a real danger is society becoming more stratified as low-level entry jobs become increasingly scarce. Our present crisis in education will in the future be compounded by the fact that we are going to be faced with fewer and fewer entry-level, or low-skilled jobs, and in terms of maintaining ourselves as a democracy, I just don't see that we can afford that kind of stratification.

We have talked about pressures that will lead to society becoming somewhat more homogeneous, somewhat more vanilla-flavored, if you will. That raises concerns about how one maintains levels of skill and competency in the broad sense of producing people who are capable and flexible. I think that computers are likely to exacerbate these difficulties, raising public-policy questions here as well.

We have talked about many of the kinds of situations that we face as being, essentially, matters of choice—that is, the technology has rather less imperatives in terms of political, social, and other organizational implications than have had some past technologies. A corollary is the fact that certain technological solutions carry with them significant social vulnerabilities. Again I think that some form of public-policy intervention and some broad public discussion of the available options and choices are going to be necessary.

Cultural roots versus classroom computers

There seems to be little doubt that learning is basically easier when the mind is young and both mind and body are uncluttered with distractions. However, whether microcomputers in the kindergarten will inspire mental discipline depends on the student's personality and his or her home environment. Even were we able to prove that development of intelligence is largely environmental, as some psychologists believe, we would still need to deal with educating students who live in a wide range of environments. Just how much personal incentive can be developed and exploited in the school, with or without computers, is unclear.

The debate about the value of the home computer for education rages on. Just as with other gadgets, some owners will soon put their computers aside. But the fact that they are available will permit the curious child (and most are) to experiment in ways heretofore impossible. Unlike, say, the home movie camera, the computer provides rapid reinforcement; even without original ideas, one has a source of inspiration in the form of precoded media.

However, the presence of a computer in the classroom may be more of an excuse than a benefit. The wave of mediocrity among today's schools seems to have deep cultural roots. In today's society, there appears to be greater comfort in being *un*exceptional, though precocious children have faced difficult peer problems ever since they were first massed in schools by hundreds of thousands. I'm inclined to believe that this cultural problem has no relationship to educational technology and precious little to do with educational philosophy.

Walter R. Beam
Former Vice President for Research and Development
Sperry Corp.

Computers as learning systems

Educators currently focus on two aspects of computers in the schools: computer literacy for most students and expanding the capabilities of the best and brightest. They seem to be missing the potential of computers to impact the problems that really concern administrators in the "trenches" in major big city school districts: test scores, discipline, and budgets.

The computer provides patient, individualized instruction, as well as drill and practice in living color. It is capable of providing personalized, self-paced, one-on-one interactions with no threat from peer pressure or embarrassment, which leads to antisocial behavior and results in disciplinary problems. It is not a computer at all but a cost-effective learning system that can impact the three major problems in a positive way.

Think, also, of the potential of a low-cost video disk combined with a personal computer, with an adaptive synergism among text, graphics, video, and processing power.

George H. Heilmeier
Senior Vice President and Chief
Technical Officer
Texas Instruments Inc.

Limits of automated tutors

The ability of a knowledge-based system to not only function as a problem-solving agent, but also to provide an explanation for how it reached the answer, certainly has relevancy to education. For example one might function as a personalized tutor or as a personalized instructor; in either case it could explain to the student the line of reasoning—the sequence of rules (the inference chain) that it used—behind the proper answer. There may be a significant limitation, however, to the ability to explain.

Knowledge-based systems being built today typically contain several hundred to a few thousand rules. Smaller ones might use an inference chain of 5 to 10 rules; larger ones, 20 to 30 rules. If such a system indicates that it has used a sequence of, say, 23 rules to reach its conclusion, one could probably comprehend what has happened. But what if educational applications require structures containing many thousands or several tens-of-thousands of rules? If one of them states that it has used a sequence of, say, 13 853 rules together with 97 specific procedures that the rules have caused to take place, how likely is it that anyone will be able to decipher what has gone on? In principle, an explanation has still been provided, but it is not a very useful nor comprehensible one. In such a circumstance, we must learn how to construct automatically, so to speak, an executive summary of a complex and extensive series of events. The same point is relevant to a knowledge-based system for any application, not just education—for example, modeling of situations or huge rule-based automata that run a complete manufacturing plant.

The point is well known to knowledge researchers, but very little research is underway on the problem of scaling today's systems upward by a factor of 10 or more.

Willis H. Ware
Corporate Research Staff
RAND Corp.

MILITARY R&D

THE DARPA PROGRAM

A proposed strategic plan for the development and application of next-generation technology for the military

Described by Robert S. Cooper and Robert E. Kahn of the Defense Advanced Research Projects Agency as a "simultaneous response to military needs and the maintenance of a strong industrial base," the agency's Strategic Computing Program is directed to developing computers that would be able "to see, reason, plan, and even supervise the actions of military systems in the field." [See p. 21.]

In October 1983, Darpa published Strategic Computing *for the U.S. Congress. The report contained a detailed look at how the agency proposed to marshall advanced computing technologies to achieve its long-range military objectives. That report is presented here.*

—Ed.

Executive summary

To meet the challenge of certain critical problems in defense, the Defense Advanced Research Projects Agency (Darpa) is initiating an important new program in strategic computing. By seizing an opportunity to leverage recent advances in artificial intelligence, computer science, and microelectronics, the agency plans to create a new generation of "machine-intelligence technology." This new technology will have unprecedented capabilities and promises to greatly increase our national security and our economic strength as it emerges during the coming decade.

The challenge. Computers are increasingly employed in defense and are relied on to help us hold the field against larger forces. But current computers, having inflexible program logic, are limited in their ability to adapt to unanticipated enemy behavior in the field. We are now challenged to produce adaptive, intelligent systems having capabilities far greater than current computers, for use in diverse applications, including autonomous systems, personalized associates, and battle management systems. The new requirements severely challenge the technology and the technical community.

The opportunity. Within the past few years, important advances have occurred in many separated areas of artificial intelligence, computer science, and microelectronics. Advances in "expert-system" technology now enable the mechanization of the practical knowledge and the reasoning methods of human experts in many fields. Advances in machine vision, speech, and machine understanding of natural language provide easy ways for humans to interact with computers. New ways to structure the architectures of computers enable computations to be processed in parallel, leading to large improvements in machine performance. Finally, new methods of microsystem design and implementation enable the rapid transfer of new architectural concepts into state-of-the-art microelectronics.

These separate advances can be jointly exploited to mechanize the thinking and reasoning processes of human experts into the form of powerful computing structures implemented in microelectronics, thus creating machine intelligence technology of unprecedented capabilities. The new requirements for adaptive intelligent military systems serve to integrate activities in the separate areas shown in Table 1 and guarantee the leveraging of the key advances.

Goals and methods. The overall goal of the Strategic Computing Program is to provide the United States with a broad line of machine-intelligence technology and to demonstrate applications of the technology to critical problems in defense. Figure 1 provides a summary overview of the program structure and goals.

The program begins by focusing on demanding military applications that require machine-intelligence technology. The applications generate requirements for functions such as vision, speech, natural language, and expert-system technology, and provide an experimental environment for synergistic interactions among developers of the new technology. The intelligent functions will be implemented in advanced architectures and fabricated in microelectronics to meet application performance requirements. Thus, the applications serve to focus and stimulate or "pull" the creation of the technology base. The applications also provide a ready environment for the demonstration of prototype systems as the technology compartments successfully evolve. To carry out this program, Darpa will fund and coordinate research in industrial, university, and

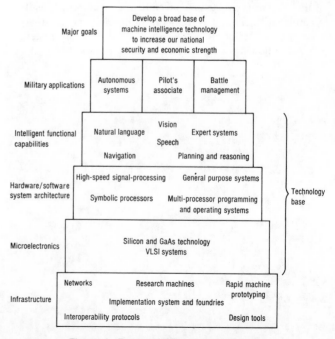

Figure 1. Program structure and goals

Major goals — Develop a broad base of machine intelligence technology to increase our national security and economic strength

Military applications — Autonomous systems · Pilot's associate · Battle management

Intelligent functional capabilities — Natural language · Vision · Expert systems · Speech · Navigation · Planning and reasoning

Hardware/software system architecture — High-speed signal-processing · General purpose systems · Symbolic processors · Multi-processor programming and operating systems

Microelectronics — Silicon and GaAs technology VLSI systems

Infrastructure — Networks · Research machines · Rapid machine prototyping · Implementation system and foundries · Interoperability protocols · Design tools

Technology base

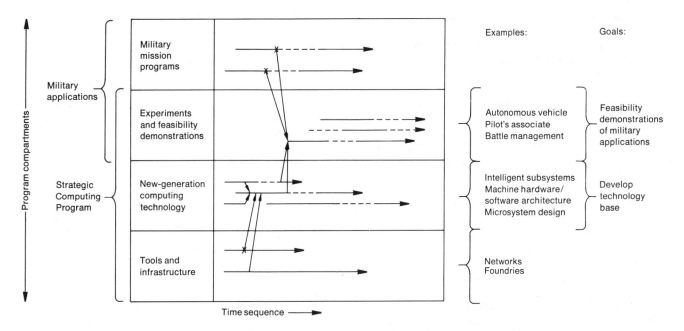

Figure 2. Visualizing and interpreting the program's compartments, elements, and timeline

government facilities, and will work with the military services and defense agencies to insure successful transfer of the resulting technology.

Figure 2 provides an overview of program activity and suggests ways of visualizing and interpreting how the various compartments of program activity will unfold over time.

Activities and plans. The initial program applications include an autonomous vehicle, a pilot's associate, and a carrier battle group battle-management system. These applications stress different compartments of machine-intelligence technology, and exert a strong pull on the overall technology. These specific examples were selected for inclusion in the Strategic Computing Program based on a weighted consideration of the following factors:

• The application must effectively employ the new technology to provide a major increase in defense capability in light of realistic scenarios of combat situations that might occur at the future time when the new systems can be procured and deployed.

• The application must provide an effective "pull" on the new-generation technology. It must demand an aggressive but feasible level of functional capability from one or more of the intelligent functions at appropriate points in the timeline.

• Development of the application must lead to new engineering know-how in artificial-intelligence software areas, such as planning and reasoning, learning, navigation, knowledge-based management, and so on.

• The application must test the efficacy of the new technology at a realistic quantitative scale of performance demands. In this way we seek to ensure against unexpected quantitative changes in system performance as a result of scaling up from models and laboratory experiments to real systems.

• The application must provide an effective experimental "test bed" for evolving and demonstrating the function(s). Stability over time, access, and visibility are thus important factors.

• The application must effectively leverage program resources. Thus an important factor is the extent to which an existing military program provides a base of capital resources and experienced personnel into which the new-generation technology can be experimentally introduced (versus this program

having to provide such noncomputing resources).

• It is important to choose a mix of applications that are jointly supportive of and involve all three services, and which are appropriately executed through each service. Only in this way can we develop the base for extension of this technology into a wide range of military systems.

• Finally, an important selection factor is the potential provided by the specific application for effecting the transfer into the services of the new machine-intelligence technology.

The planning timelines for evolving these applications have been interlocked with program timelines for evolving intelligent functions (such as machine vision, speech, and expert-system technology). The plans for creating machine-intelligence capabilities have in turn been interlocked with the program plans for system architectures that support the signal processing, symbolic processing, and general-purpose processing underlying the machine intelligence.

The planned activities will lead to a series of demonstrations of increasingly sophisticated machine-intelligence technology in the selected applications as the program progresses. Milestones have been established for the parallel development of the machine architectures required to support these demonstrations.

Attention is focused early in the program on provision of the necessary infrastructure to support and coordinate the ac-

Table 1. Areas that can be leveraged to produce high-performance machine intelligence

• Expert systems: codifying and mechanizing practical knowledge, common sense, and expert knowledge
• Advances in artificial intelligence: mechanization of speech recognition, vision, and natural language understanding
• System development environments: methods for simplifying and speeding system prototyping and experimental refinement
• New theoretical insights in computer science
• Computer architecture: methods for exploiting concurrency in parallel systems
• Microsystem design methods and tools
• Microelectronic fabrication technology

tivities of the many people and organizations that will be involved in the program. Computing facilities, network services, interoperability standards, access to rapid system prototyping and integrated-circuit implementation services must all be in place for the enterprise to succeed. This will also ensure rapid propagation of the knowledge and technology produced by the program into the community of participants and into U.S. industry.

Management and funding. Management of the Strategic Computing Program will be carried out by the Defense Advanced Research Projects Agency. Within the Department of Defense, Darpa will coordinate closely with USDRE and the military services. A Defense Science Board panel has been convened to make recommendations on DOD utilization of machine-intelligence technology. Other advisory panels and working groups will be constituted, with representatives from industry, universities, and government, to provide additional required advice in specific areas.

Table 2 shows the annual cost for the Strategic Computing Program. Program costs for the first five years of the program are estimated to be approximately $600 million. The logic of the sequencing of activities is reflected in the breakdown of spending in the first three categories. Relative spending on tools and infrastructure is higher early in the program. The large technology base activity and component of spending will likely peak in fiscal year 1987–1988. Applications activity and spending expand moderately at first, then rapidly in the late eighties, peaking near the end of the program. The entire program will peak about the end of the decade, declining thereafter as program goals are achieved.

The basic acquisition policy is that military applications will be carried out by industry, drawing upon results of research carried out in the universities. Advanced computer architectures will be developed primarily in joint projects between universities and industry. Most of the hardware and software development efforts will be competed. The most advanced artificial-intelligence ideas that seem ripe for development will be exploited with heavy university involvement. For these, expert judgment from leading participants in the field will be sought and directed selection will result. Construction and access to computing technology infrastructure will be competed.

We intend a significant effort toward technology transfer of results of this program into the military services. This effort will include: (a) use of service agents and service COTRs; (b) a process of cost-sharing with the services in the development of military applications; (c) the inclusion of technology base results from this program in service programs and test beds, and (d) training of service personnel by involvement in technology-based developments.

Equally important is technology transfer to industry, both to build up a base of engineers and system builders familiar with computer science and machine-intelligence technology now resident in leading university laboratories, and to facilitate incorporation of the new technology into corporate product lines. To this end we will make full use of regulations for Government procurement involving protection of proprietary information and trade secrets, patent rights, and licensing and royalty arrangements.

Communication is critical in the management of the program, since many of the important contributors will be widely dispersed throughout the United States. Unique methods will be employed to establish a productive research community and enable participants to interact with each other and to interlock with the program plan. Existing computer tools such as electronic networks and message systems will be used to coordinate program activities. More advanced methods will include provision to participants of remote electronic views of, and interactions with, the evolving program planning timelines.

Conclusions. We now have a plan for action as we cross the threshold into a new generation of computing. It is a plan for creating a large array of machine-intelligence technology that can be scaled and mixed in countless ways for diverse applications.

We have a plan for "pulling" the technology-generation process by creating carefully selected technology interactions with challenging military applications. These applications also provide the experimental test beds for refining the new technology and for demonstrating the feasibility of particular intelligent computing capabilities.

The timely, successful generation and application of intelligent computing technology will have profound effects. If the technology is widely dispersed in applications throughout our society, Americans will have a significantly improved capability to handle complex tasks and to codify, mechanize, and propagate their knowledge. The new technology will improve the capability of our industrial, military, and political leaders to tap the nation's pool of knowledge and effectively manage large enterprises, even in times of great stress and change.

Successful achievement of the objectives of the strategic computing initiative will lead to deployment of a new generation of military systems containing machine-intelligence technology. These systems will provide the United States with important new methods of defense against massed forces in the future—methods that can raise the threshold and diminish the likelihood of major conflict.

There are difficult challenges to overcome in order to realize the goals of a national program of such scope and complexity. However, we believe that the goals are achievable under the logic and methods of this plan, and if we seize the moment and undertake this initiative, the Strategic Computing Program will yield a substantial return on invested resources in terms of increased national security and economic strength.

I. Introduction

As a result of a series of advances in artificial intelligence, computer science, and microelectronics, we stand at the threshold of a new generation of computing technology having unprecedented capabilities. The United States stands to profit greatly both in national security and economic strength by its determination and ability to exploit this new technology.

Computing technology already plays an essential role in defense technologies such as guided missiles and munitions, avionics, and C^3I. If the new-generation technology evolves as we now expect, there will be unique new opportunities for

Table 2. Strategic computing cost summary in $M

	FY84	FY85	FY86	FY87*	FY88*
Total military applications	6	15	27	TBD	TBD
Total technology base	26	50	83	TBD	TBD
Total infrastructure	16	27	36	TBD	TBD
Total program support	2	3	4	TBD	TBD
TOTAL	50	95	150	TBD	TBD

*Out-year funding levels to be determined by program progress.

military applications of computing. For example, instead of fielding simple guided missiles or remotely piloted vehicles, we might launch completely autonomous land, sea, and air vehicles capable of complex, far-ranging reconnaissance and attack missions. The possibilities are quite startling, and suggest that new-generation computing could fundamentally change the nature of future conflicts.

In contrast with previous computers, the new generation will exhibit humanlike, "intelligent" capabilities for planning and reasoning. The computers will also have capabilities that enable direct, natural interactions with their users and their environments as, for example, through vision and speech.

Using this new technology, machines will perform complex tasks with little human intervention, or even with complete autonomy. Our citizens will have machines that are "capable associates," which could greatly augment each person's ability to perform tasks that require specialized expertise. Our leaders will employ intelligent computers as active assistants in the management of complex enterprises. As a result the attention of human beings will increasingly be available to define objectives and to render judgments on the compelling aspects of the moment.

A very broad base of existing technology and recent scientific advances must be jointly leveraged in a planned and sequenced manner to create this new intelligent computer technology. Scientists from many disciplines, scattered throughout the universities, industry, and government, must collaborate in new ways, using new tools and infrastructure, in an enterprise of great scope. Adaptive methods of planning must be applied to enhance the process of discovery. Events must be skillfully orchestrated if we are to seize this opportunity and move toward timely success.

In response to these challenges and opportunities, Darpa proposes to initiate an important new program in Strategic Computing. To carry out this program, Darpa will fund and coordinate research in industrial, university, and government facilities, and will work with the military services and defense agencies to insure successful transfer of the results.

The overall goal of the program is to create a new generation of machine-intelligence technology having unprecedented capabilities and to demonstrate applications of this technology to solving critical problems in defense. Although the achievements of the program applications' objectives will significantly improve the nation's military capabilities, the impact of non-military spin-offs on the national economy should not be underestimated. This document provides an overview of the proposed program.

II. The military challenge

Adaptive technology is important to defense. Computers are being increasingly employed to support United States military forces. The growing complexity of forces and rising level of threats have stimulated the use of ever more advanced computers. Improvements in the speed and range of weapons have increased the rate at which battles unfold, resulting in a proliferation of computers to aid in information flow and decision making at all levels of military organization. Smarter computerized weapons and forces are now depended upon to be able to hold the field against superior numbers.

A countervailing effect on this trend is the rapidly decreasing predictability of military situations, which makes computers with inflexible logic of limited value. Consider a problem encountered with a current-generation computerized system during a recent conflict. A radar designed to automatically ac- quire and track aircraft was supposed to follow all aircraft maneuvers, recognize countermeasures, and not become confused or lose track because of dropped decoys. The other side (who also had the same radar) innovated the tactic of approaching in groups of four aircraft and, as they came over the horizon, rapidly branching (*fleur dé lis*) into four different directions. The computer-controlled radar reacted by jittering around the centroid until it lost all four tracks.

The solution to this unforeseen problem is simple from a logical viewpoint, but there was no way for the forces in the field to codify and implement the solution. Instead, once the problem was recognized and diagnosed in the field, an equivalent situation was created and the solution was programmed and evaluated in the homeland, and the new software/firmware was then flown to the radar locations in the field. Even with a crash program, it took several days to eliminate the radar's inflexibility when responding to a simple change of tactics that had not been anticipated by the radar designers.

Confronted with such situations, leaders and planners will continue to use computers for routine tasks, but will often be forced to rely solely on their people to respond in unpredictable situations. Revolutionary improvements in computing technology are required to provide more capable machine assistance in such unanticipated combat situations. The military requirements for dealing with uncertainty and information saturation in life-threatening situations are far more demanding of the technology than evolving needs in the civilian sector.

Intelligent military systems demand new computer technology. The effects of increasing unpredictability are evident over a wide range of military computer applications. In certain routine military tasks—surveillance, monitoring, and recording systems—computers have actually replaced human operators. Small-scale computer systems have been applied in precision-guided munitions ("smart weapons") and some reconnaissance devices. To achieve truly autonomous systems, a variety of complex functions must be performed. However, the emergence of autonomous systems is inhibited by the inability of present computers to robustly direct actions that fulfill mission objectives in unpredictable situations. Commanders remain particularly concerned about the role autonomous systems would play during the transition from peace to hostilities when rules of engagement may be altered quickly.

An extremely stressing example of such a case is the projected defense against strategic nuclear missiles, where systems must react so rapidly that it is likely that almost complete reliance will have to be placed on automated systems. At the same time, the complexity and unpredictability of factors affecting decisions will be very great.

In many military activities, people are often saturated with information requiring complex decisions to be made in very short times. This is a severe problem for operators of complex combat systems such as aircraft, tanks, and ships. The physical environment—noise, vibration, and violent maneuvers—is extremely taxing; moreover, the information flowing to the operator increases dramatically as missions become more demanding, sensor and weapons systems become more complex, and threats to survival become more numerous and serious. The ability of computers to assist in such situations is limited because their computational capability cannot handle these highly complex unstructured environments; in addition, their interface with humans is so (cognitively) inefficient that it is doubtful the person could receive, interpret, and act on the information in time even if it were available within the machine. Improvements can result only if future computers can provide a new "quantum" level of functional capabilities.

The management of large-scale military enterprises requires large staffs to gather information, to develop and evaluate alternative courses of action, and to construct detailed plans. The trend in all areas toward faster-moving warfare severely stresses the whole staff function. Greater uncertainty in the military environment forces consideration of more options. Increasingly sophisticated methods of deception, countermeasures, and camouflage make timely acquisition of vital information more difficult. Improved weapon speed and range increase the scale of military actions. The result is a growing uncertainty in the decision making process and the evolution of large, labor-intensive military command organizations. Current computers provide only limited assistance to such decision making because they have limited ability to respond to unpredictable situations and to interact intelligently with large human staffs.

Across this spectrum of applications, from autonomous systems to systems aiding in battle management, we need computers that have far more capability for intelligent operation, improved survivability in hostile and high-radiation environments, and greatly improved man-machine interfaces. Many isolated pieces of the required technology are already being developed. The challenge is to exploit these beginnings, make new efforts to develop the full set of required technologies, and integrate components of the emerging new technology in order to create revolutionary defense capabilities. Such revolutionary capabilities can provide our nation with new, highly flexible, and significantly improved defenses against possible assaults by massed forces in the future.

III. The technical opportunity

A new generation of computing technology. Within the past few years, a series of important advances have occurred across a wide range of areas in artificial intelligence, computer science, and microelectronics. By *jointly leveraging* these many separate advances, it will be possible to create a completely new generation of machine-intelligence technology having unprecedented capabilities.

Advances in microelectronic technology have led to the manufacturability of silicon integrated-circuit chips consisting of hundreds of thousands of transistors. Because of their tiny size, the transistors in such chips function at very high switching speeds and consume very little power. New methods of microsystem design enable designers to rapidly design and implement digital systems in microelectronics.

Computer scientists have developed new insights into the exploitation of area, time, and energy tradeoffs in computing systems. This work assures the feasibility of radically new forms of computing structures. These advances in theory are now guiding computer architects in their search for ways to exploit concurrency in highly parallel systems. A number of research groups have produced workable concepts for such machines; these concepts include methods for achieving parallelism in machines that provide very high performance processing on unstructured, complex problems. Advances in system-development environments now enable very rapid prototyping of hardware and software for such new machines.

Perhaps the most stunning advances have come in the area of expert systems. The term "expert system" describes the codification of any process that people use to reason, plan, or make decisions as a set of computer rules. For example, a detailed description of the precise thought processes and heu-

ristics by which a person finds his or her way through a city using a map and visual landmarks might be codified as the basis of an "expert system" for local navigation. The methods for identifying and mechanizing practical knowledge, common sense, and expert knowledge have solidified and are now finding wide application. Expert systems, mechanized at the level of practical reasoning, now stand in great contrast to systems created using traditional computing technology. Rather than being "black boxes" whose internal workings are inaccessible to users, these systems have the ability to "explain" the reasoning used to reach decisions or take actions. The knowledge base that guides their operation can be changed quickly to cope with changes in the environment, thereby easing adaptation to situations like the "radar problem" described earlier. The methods of programming such systems promise to stimulate a movement towards articulating, codifying, and better exploiting a wide range of practical human knowledge.

Finally, there have been very important successes in other areas of artificial intelligence (AI), particularly in the mechanization of vision and visual-motor interaction, the mechanization of speech recognition, and in the understanding of natural language (see Section V).

Form and functions of machine-intelligence technology. Properly combined, all these recent advances now enable us to move toward a completely new generation of machine-intelligence technology. What kind of special capabilities would the new computers have? First, they would be able to perform intelligent functions such as:

- Understanding natural language expressions
- Information fusion and machine learning
- Planning and reasoning

They would also be able to interact with their users and environment through natural modes of sensory communication such as:

- Vision and visual-image generation
- Speech recognition and production

What form might these machines take? One important characteristic is that instead of being a single collection of microelectronics that fills all needs, the new generation of "intelligent" computer systems will be modular (conceptually; even if not physically in all cases). Each system will be created by combining modules from different specialized compartments of the new technology base, much as one might now compose a "component video system."

For example, consider a small modular computer system used to control a future autonomous vehicle. Vision modules will be included that provide basic scene-processing and object-recognition capabilities. With vision modules as input devices, a symbolic processor module would be then able to directly process fragments of pictorial, graphic, and three-dimensional scenic images. When further supported by rule-based inferencing and image understanding in a compact but powerful symbol processor and interfaced with specialized motor-control systems, these vision modules will enable the computer-controlled autonomous vehicle to "see," to move about, and to interact "intelligently" with its environment. The resulting vision, scene interpretation, and motor-control processes will be, at the very least, analogous to those found in lower animals.

This simple sketch merely hints at the possibilities. The magnitude of the opportunity before us will be seen as we explore in this document the interaction between the new-generation technology base and demanding areas of military application of machine intelligence. The "envelope" of possibilities includes not only smart autonomous systems, but also intelligent machines employed as "personal associates" to boost the capabilities of people to perform complex tasks, and as active contributors serving leaders and teams of people in the management of large enterprises.

Spinoffs from the technology base can stimulate national economy. In addition to the planned military applications discussed in this document, the value of future commercial products made available by development of the new-generation technology will be enormous. The effects will be analogous to those resulting from the replacement of the vacuum tube by the transistor, the displacement of discrete transistors by integrated circuits, and the fourth generation displacement of simple integrated-circuit technology by very large-scale integration (VLSI) now occurring in the computer and electronics industry.

The Strategic Computing Program promises the production of machine-intelligence technology that will enable yet another major cycle of new economic activity in the computer and electronics industry. If the United States aggressively competes to develop these systems, it will gain access to enormous new commercial markets that will build on top of the successes of fourth-generation technology. Spinoffs from a successful Strategic Computing Program will surge into our industrial community. They will be used by the computer industry as it creates and exploits a host of new markets for the underlying machine-intelligence hardware and software technology and by the automotive and aerospace industries as they integrate intelligent computer-aided design (CAD) into the development process and intelligent computer-aided manufacturing (CAM) and robotics into manufacturing. The consumer electronics industry will integrate new-generation computing technology and create a home market for applications of machine intelligence. In addition, a wide range of service industries will emerge that create and provide new applications for machine intelligence and new ways to leverage the production, codification, and mechanization of useful human knowledge.

IV. Goals and methods

In response to the challenging opportunity for creating and exploiting intelligent computing technology, Darpa proposes to initiate this important new program in strategic computing. The overall goal of the program is to provide the United States with a broad base of machine-intelligence technology that will greatly increase our national security and economic power. This technology promises to yield strong new defense systems for use against massed forces, and thus to raise the threshold and decrease the chances of major conflict.

To achieve this goal, a wide range of present technology and recent scientific advances must be leveraged in a coordinated manner. Engineers and scientists from many disciplines must collaborate in new ways in an enterprise of very large scope. A framework must be created for the effective, adaptive planning of the discovery and development processes in this enterprise. A skillful orchestration of events and exploitation of available infrastructure will be required to ensure a timely success.

This section sketches the methods the program will use to adaptively select and schedule program activities. The section discusses near-term planning tactics and the plans for leveraging the interaction between selected military applications and the evolving technology base. The section ends with an overview of how to visualize the program's adaptive planning process and timelines.

Figure 1 shows the logical structure of the program and its goals. The overall goals will be reached by focusing on three specific military applications to develop a new technology base. In order to conduct successful military demonstrations of these applications it will be necessary to develop new machine-intelligence functional capabilities. Although these intelligent capabilities are largely provided by software, they depend strongly on the underlying hardware architectures for high performance and efficiency. Finally, the program depends on the exploitation of faster, denser, more radiation resistant, lower-power devices provided by state-of-the-art microelectronics.

Developing and demonstrating applications to defense. Our projections for military applications of new-generation computers cover a wide spectrum of activities. They range from applications of individual machines without operators or users as, for example, in autonomous systems, to applications involving groups of machines and groups of people collectively engaged in complex tasks, as for example in battle management.

Across this spectrum of applications we find a range of requirements for machine-intelligence technology. Some autonomous systems require low-power systems, moderate performance planning and reasoning, and very powerful vision systems. At the other extreme, certain battle-management systems will require immense planning and reasoning processors, vast knowledge and data-base management systems, perhaps no vision systems, but highly complex distributed, survivable communications systems.

Specific applications are to be identified, selected, developed, and demonstrated as discussed in Section V. The applications are selected for their relevance to critical problems in defense, and for their suitability in exerting an effective "pull" on the new-generation technology base in such a way as to enable a much broader range of applications.

Creating the technology base. Although there is a very wide range of possible applications of the machine-intelligence technology, the technology base will have many elements that are commonly used in many applications. By studying many specific applications, we have developed a taxonomy of possible future intelligent systems and identified the common functions required to create those systems. For example, many future military applications will require vision, speech, hearing, and natural-language–understanding functions to facilitate easy communication between people and machines. We plan to develop these common functions as modular "intelligent subsystems," and we have evolved an initial set of technical requirements for these subsystems by detailed study of specific applications described in Section V.1 and in Appendix I.

Some of the intelligent subsystem functions, such as speech and vision, have value in a host of military and commercial systems, and generic or general-purpose software and hardware can be developed independent of the application. Other intelligent functions, such as planning and reasoning (as done for example using expert systems), and information fusion (including future extensions to include systems that learn from experience) depend strongly on and must be designed for each specific application.

The development of advanced machine architectures will accompany the development of associated software to produce integrated intelligent subsystems. The development of machine architectures will be directed toward maximizing the functional power and the speed of computation. Powerful, efficient intelligent processors, data-base machines, simulation and control systems, display systems, and general purpose systems will be needed to achieve the program performance goals and to support selected military applications. During the early years of the program, we will investigate, refine, and perfect specific computer architectures. Exploratory development, testing, and evaluation of the machines will be done in parallel with the work on software and microelectronics technology. Specific candidate architectures will then be selected for full-scale development, with their scale and configuration determined by the requirements of unfolding experimental applications.

To meet applications constraints and requirements for performance, weight, volume, power dissipation, and cost, the machine architectures will be implemented, at least initially, in advanced silicon microelectronics. The technology is widely available in industry, and accessible through implementation service infrastructure, due in part to the success of DOD VLSI/ VHSIC (very high-speed integrated circuits) programs. Later in the program, gallium arsenide microelectronics technology will be exploited for high performance in critical defense applications that require both low power and radiation hardness.

Thus, we aim to create
— *Integrated intelligent subsystems, composed of*
— *Machine hardware/software architectures, and*
— *Microelectronics, built using*
— *Tools and infrastructure.*

This last list, in fact, represents the hierarchy of development areas addressed in this plan. Specific objectives have been established for program activities in each of the technology-base areas in order to provide the functional capabilities required in the intelligent subsystems used in selected applications programs. These objectives then establish requirements for the tools and infrastructure used to support program activity.

An analysis of the technical specialties required over the long-term for this program reveals personnel shortfalls in the areas of artificial intelligence and VLSI system architecture. Efforts must be made to increase the supply of trained talent in these fields. We will encourage the offering of appropriate university courses and will encourage industry to support this process through grants, liberal retraining programs, and loan of key technical personnel for teaching. An important long-term effect of the program's technology-based development should be an increase in qualified faculty and graduate students active in all the related fields of study. This program's research is highly experimental, and significant advances require adequate computing facilities. We plan to ensure that adequate computing resources are made available to research personnel to carry out the proposed work.

Program methodology. The program begins by building on a selected set of intelligent computing capabilities that are ripe for development in the near term. The program will develop these capabilities and accumulate further intelligent capabilities under the "pull" of demanding military applications. The objective is to evolve these capabilities into a broad base of new-generation technology and to demonstrate specific applications of the new technology to solving a number of critical problems in defense.

Artificial intelligence already offers moderately developed functional capabilities in the areas of machine vision, speech recognition, and understanding of natural language. Expert systems that perform as well as capable humans at situation analysis have already been demonstrated.

Through an analysis of numerous potential military applications of machine intelligence, an initial list of *intelligent*

Table 3. Improvements in functional capabilities to be provided by the new generation of computing technology

Areas for major improvements in machine intelligence (processing and memory)	Areas for major improvements in interfacing machines to their users and environment (input and output)
Understanding of natural language	Vision
Signal interpretation	Graphics display/image generation
Information fusion/machine learning	Speech recognition and production
Planning and reasoning	Distributed communications
Knowledge and data management	•
Simulation, modeling, and control	•
Navigation	•
•	
•	
•	

functional capabilities was developed that have common utility across many applications (see Table 3). Substantial progress has already been made in the development of some of these, such as speech recognition, but others, such as information fusion, are still in an early stage of their evolution.

These initial functional capabilities can be scaled and combined in many ways to create a large "envelope" of intelligent systems in the future. The possibilities increase as we add new functions to the list.

A very large envelope of future military applications is also envisioned for new-generation computing technology. Even if we restrict our attention to a few areas, such as autonomous systems, personal associates, and computational aids for managing large enterprises, the set of possibilities is large.

It is important to note that any improvements in machine-intelligence technology capabilities expand the envelope of possible applications. But how do we focus on specific capabilities to "push" at particular times? How do we select specific applications to "pull" the technology? The key is an integrated planning framework—an active planning timeline—that derives realistic, near-term application goals from credible technology developments and simultaneously stresses that technology development by proper selection of application demonstrations to focus the research and development. That process has been used in developing this plan, based on our best understandings at this time, and is described in the following sections. As technology is developed, the situation and thus the plan will change, so this should be viewed as a dynamic process.

Visualizing program compartments and planning timeline. Figure 2 provides an overview of program activity and suggests ways of visualizing and interpreting how the various compartments of program activity will unfold over time. The figure is intended to help readers interpret more detailed plans and charts, and figures that follow later in this document.

The program goals can be visualized in the figure as guiding the establishment of specific objectives for applications, experiments, and demonstrations, and specific objectives for new-generation technology. Note that the Strategic Computing Program intersects with military mission programs in the area of applications experimentation and demonstrations. Activities in this area of overlap are based on opportunities in military mission areas *and* opportunities in the new-generation technology base, as earlier objectives are achieved in each of these areas. The figure also illustrates the role of support tools and infrastructure, and suggests how the achievement of technology base objectives depends on achievements in tool and infrastructure construction.

V. Activities and plans

We now describe the activities and plans that will be used to achieve the goals and objectives of the Strategic Computing Program. For purposes of exposition we present the key ideas by showing how sample activities proceed under the plan. These examples are selected to convey the very large scope of the enterprise and, to illustrate the methods of orchestration that will be used to stimulate activity, provide joint leveraging of technologies and direct program elements toward overall program goals.

The section is divided into four subsections. Section V.1 gives examples of planned application experiments and demonstrations. These applications drive new-generation technology requirements that are reflected in Section V.2, which describes how a mix of technology requirements will be provided under planned technology-based programs. Section V.3 next describes how programs tools and infrastructure are factored into the planning process. Section V.4 then summarizes the specific plans for initiating the overall program.

The material in this section is intended to provide an overview sufficient to enable readers to interpret detailed strategic-computing planning documents, such as the timelines in the appendices, and to have well-formed intuitions concerning the overall methods and plans of the program.

On a first reading, those who are interested in specific dimensions of the program might read the section of interest (for example, the applications) and skim the rest. Alternatively, the logic of the plan can be sampled by following the details of one chain of activities through the material (without reading all sections in detail). For example, one could follow the requirements for vision produced and passed from the autonomous vehicle (Section V.1.1; Appendix I.1) through to the section on vision subsystems (Section V.2.1.1; Appendix II.1.1), and then to the sections on system architecture, and infrastructure. In that way the interplay between the applications and technology base can be closely examined.

V.1 Experiments and demonstrations

This section describes a set of specific military applications that exploit new generation computing technology. Included is an autonomous vehicle application that will rely heavily on vision and expert system technology as enabling technologies for this application. A pilot's associate application is then described that exploits speech-recognition and expert systems. Finally, a battle-management system for a carrier battle group is described that exploits expert-systems technology and that will eventually exploit very high-performance knowledge-processing systems.

These specific examples are included in the Strategic Computing Program based on a weighted consideration of the following factors:

• The application must effectively employ the new technology to provide a major increase in defense capability in light of realistic scenarios of combat situations that might occur at the future time when the new systems can be procured and deployed.

• The application must provide an effective "pull" on the new-generation technology. It must demand an aggressive but feasible level of functional capability from one or more of the intelligent functions at appropriate points in the timeline.

• Development of the application must lead to new engineering know-how in artificial-intelligence software areas, such as planning and reasoning, learning, navigation, knowledge-based management, and so on.

• The application must test the efficacy of the new technology at a realistic quantitative scale of performance demands. In this way we seek to ensure against unexpected quantitative changes in system performance as a result of scaling up from models and laboratory experiments to real systems.

• The application must provide an effective experimental "test bed" for evolving and demonstrating the function(s). Stability over time, access, and visibility are thus important factors.

• The application must effectively leverage program resources. Thus an important factor is the extent to which an existing military program provides a base of capital resources and experienced personnel into which the new-generation technology can be experimentally introduced (versus this program having to provide such noncomputing resources).

• It is important to choose a mix of applications that are jointly supportive of and involve all three services, and which are appropriately executed through each service. Only in this way can we develop the base for extension of this technology into a wide range of military systems.

• Finally, an important selection factor is the potential provided by the specific application for effecting the transfer into the services of the new machine-intelligence technology.

The choices have been initially made on this basis, but it is recognized that further planning and the evolving technology development may lead to a change in the choice of specific application demonstrations. It might, for example, prove preferable to pursue an autonomous underwater vehicle rather than a land vehicle, and a battle-management system for land combat might prove more appropriate than that for the naval application. A panel of the Defense Science Board has been convened to make recommendations on how to best exploit machine intelligence technology within DOD, and that panel will be providing information and advice for this program. Consequently, we anticipate that some of the specifics may change over time, within the framework that is described.

An abbreviated description of each currently planned application is given in this section. Planning timelines are included in Appendix I that illustrate the detailed interactions of these applications with ongoing military programs and with the emerging new generation technology base.

V.1.1 Autonomous vehicles

Autonomous systems, as used herein, are true robotic devices: they are able to sense and interpret their environment, to plan and reason using sensed and other data, to initiate actions to be taken, and to communicate with humans or other systems. Examples of autonomous systems include certain "smart" munitions, cruise missiles, various types of vehicles possessing an autonomous navigation capability, and a wide variety of mobile and fixed robotic systems for material handling, manufacturing, and other applications. Some of these systems exist today with operationally useful levels of capability. Others, such as completely autonomous air, land, and undersea vehicles, and systems possessing more adaptive, predatory forms of terminal homing, require the kinds of significant developments anticipated in the Strategic Computing Program to fully realize their potential. These developments will both enable qualitatively different kinds of autonomous behavior in new systems and effect dramatic quantitative improvements in the operational capabilities of existing systems.

Autonomous vehicles, like other autonomous systems, are characterized by their ability to accept high-level goal statements or task descriptions. For an autonomous vehicle system one set of goal statements will define a navigation task, another will be specific to its mission, for example reconnaissance. The navigation task will usually be described both in terms of a specific destination for the vehicle and through constraints that limit the number of possible paths or routes the vehicle might use in traversing from one point to another.

Autonomous land-vehicle systems, as an example of a class of autonomous vehicles, could support such missions as deep-penetration reconnaissance, rear area resupply, ammunition handling, and weapons delivery. As an example, imagine a reconnaissance vehicle that could navigate up to 50 kilometers cross-country from one designated position to another. It would be capable of planning an initial route from digital terrain data, updating its plan based on information derived from its sensors, resolving ambiguities between sensed and prestored terrain data, and incorporating landmark prediction and identification as a navigation means. Using advanced image-understanding technology, the reconnaissance payload would perform image segmentation and other basic scene processing upon arrival in a designated area, identify target objects, and report its findings and interpretations.

To develop an autonomous land vehicle with the capabilities described requires an expert system for navigation and a vision system. The expert navigation system must plan routes using digital terrain and environmental data, devise strategies for avoiding unanticipated obstacles, estimate the vehicle's position from landmark and other data, update the on-board digital terrain data base, generate moment-to-moment steering and speed commands, and monitor vehicle performance and on-board systems. All these functions must be accomplished in real-time and near-real-time while the vehicle is moving at speeds up to 60 kilometers/hour. Scaling up from laboratory experiments indicates that such an expert system demonstration would require on the order of 6500 rules firing at a rate of 7000 rules/second. Current systems contain fewer rules, 2000 on average, and fire at a rate of 50 to 100 rules/second. ("Rules" and "firings" are terms used in expert systems. "Rules" represent the codification of an expert system process, and a "firing" indicates the examination, interpretation, and response to one rule in a particular context. In current systems, the firing of one rule can require the execution of tens of thousands of instructions, and as contexts become more complex the number of instructions for rule-firing increases.)

The vision system must take in data from imaging sensors and interpret these data in real-time to produce a symbolic description of the vehicle's environment. It must recognize roads and road boundaries; select, locate, and dimension fixed and moving obstacles in the roadway; detect, locate, and classify objects in open or forrested terrain; locate and identify man-made and natural landmarks; and produce thematic maps of the local environment, while moving at speeds up to 60 km/hr. Scaling up computing capabilities used in laboratory vision experiments suggests an aggregate computing requirement of 10 to 100 bips (billion equivalent Von-Neumann instructions per second) to accomplish the above tasks. This compares with capabilities, for example, of 30 to 40 mips (million instruc-

tions per second) in today's most powerful Von Neumann-type computers.

Of equal importance with the required computing capabilities outlined above, is the weight, space, and power required by the computing systems. For a land reconnaissance vehicle, for example, the computers should occupy no more than 6 to 15 ft^3, should weigh less than 200 to 500 pounds, and should consume less than 1 kilowatt of power including environmental support. The requirements represent at least 1 to 4 orders of magnitude reduction in weight, space, and power over today's computing systems. For certain space, air, and sea vehicles, the constraints and requirements will be even higher and will include the capability to operate in high-radiation environments.

V.1.2 Pilot's associate

Pilots in combat are regularly overwhelmed by the quantity of incoming data and communications on which they must base life or death decisions. They can be equally overwhelmed by the dozens of switches, buttons, and knobs that cover their control handles demanding precise activation. While each of the aircraft's hundreds of components serve legitimate purposes, the technologies that created them have far outpaced our skill at intelligently interfacing the pilot to them.

This mismatch seems to be characteristic of many human-controlled, complex, dynamic military systems, Further, it applies to single-operator as well as multiple-operator situations where crew communication and coordination are essential for survival. It is this type of common military problem that pulls intelligent computing technology into the realm of creating the "personal associate."

The personal associate is viewed as an ensemble of expert knowledge-based systems and natural interface mechanisms that operate in real time. In its simplest form the personal associate performs a set of routine tasks and, when prearranged, initiates actions on its own. In this way it frees the operator from routine overhead chores so he can attend to more critical tasks.

In its advanced form, the personal associate performs a set of tasks that are difficult or impossible for the operator altogether, such as the early detection and diagnosis of the subtle patterns of an impending malfunction. In this way the associate enables completely new capabilities and sophistication.

We have chosen to illustrate this concept by developing a personal associate within the context of the combat pilot. Called the pilot's associate, it is an intelligent system that assists the pilot in the air as well as on the ground, not replacing but complementing the pilot by off-loading lower-level chores and performing special functions so the pilot may focus his intellectual resources on tactical and strategic objectives.

The associate is personal to a specific pilot in that it is trained by that pilot to respond in certain ways and perform particular functions. For example, it might be instructed to automatically reconfigure the aircraft to a specific control sensitivity preferred by the pilot should the wing be damaged during combat. It also has a wealth of general knowledge about the aircraft, the environment, and friendly and hostile forces. It will have instruction on advanced tactics from more experienced pilots and up-to-date intelligence information on enemy tactics to aid the less experienced pilot on his first day of combat. These knowledge bases will be designed for easy updating to keep pace with rapidly changing tactical events. Certain classes of newly "learned" knowledge will be automatically exchanged among pilot's associates.

The approach for this application is to evolve an increasingly complex pilot's associate in increments that represent key program decision milestones. The development will be continually evaluated in full mission research simulators with representative combat pilots, eventually to be moved onboard existing research aircraft for evaluation. The three thrusts central to this development are the interface to the pilot, the knowledge bases to support the interface, and integration and interpretation processors that connect these.

The interface is based upon natural communication using advances in speech recognition (here developed for the noisy, stressful cockpit environment), speech output (particularly machine speech that can assume different speaker types and styles), and graphic or pictorial presentation of complicated information.

Knowledge bases will be developed that will be significantly larger than any previously attempted. For example, the simple monitoring of the basic flight systems (power, electrical, and hydraulic) could take several thousand rules. These will have to be processed at rates perhaps 100 times faster than the current technology allows. The knowledge bases that will be developed are:

- The aircraft/ pilot
- Tactics and strategy
- Enemy aircraft
- Communication
- Geography
- Navigation aids
- The mission
- Enemy defense
- Friendly forces

The processes that integrate and interpret the demands from the interface with the contents of the knowledge bases include functions that tie flight events to the mission plan prepared earlier, change environmental and threat situations, coordinate with other pilot's associates in the air and on the ground, continually change situational data bases for local battles as they develop, and so forth.

The demand for real-time processing eventually in small, rugged packages for onboard installation characterizes the "pull" that this application puts on the Strategic Computing Program. The knowledge gained will directly complement important service research programs such as the U.S. Air Force cockpit automation technology effort.

V.1.3 Battle management

Management of large-scale enterprises is characterized by decision making under uncertainty. The system must alert the decision maker to the existence of an incipient problem, must generate potential responses to the problem in the form of decision options, must evaluate these options in the face of uncertainty about the outcome arising from any specific option and with respect to often conflicting goals, must execute the preferred option, and monitor its execution, iterating on the above process as circumstances dictate. No examples exist today of systems which directly address each of the above steps. While many individual information processing systems, such as the World Wide Military Command and Control System (WWMCCS) and various intelligence systems, furnish data to the decision maker that support such functions as alerting and option generating, the fact remains that no systems exist that directly aid such cognitive processes as option generation, uncertainty assessment, and multiattribute value reconciliation. These are knowledge intensive and the development of aids in these and other critical areas will consequently require the kind of expert-system and natural-language developments anticipated from the Strategic Computing Program.

A battle-management system (BMS), as an example of a system to aid in the management of a large enterprise, would interact with the user at a high level through speech and natural language. It would be capable of comprehending uncertain data to produce forecasts of likely events, drawing on previous human and machine experience to generate potential courses of action, evaluating these options and explaining the supporting rationale for the evaluations to the decision maker, developing a plan for implementing the option selected by the decision maker, disseminating this plan to those concerned, and reporting progress to the decision maker during the execution phase.

For example, a Battle-Management System for a Carrier Battle Group would be integrated into the Composite Warfare Commander (CWC) battle group defense system. It would display a detailed picture of the battle area, including enemy order of battle (surface, air, subsurface), own force disposition, electronic warfare environment, strike plan, weather forecast, and other factors developed from an analysis of all available data. It would generate hypotheses describing possible enemy intent, prioritize these according to their induced likelihood, and explain the reasons for the prioritization. Drawing upon previous experience, together with knowledge of own force and enemy capabilities, it would generate potential courses of action, use an ultrarapid rule-based simulation to project and explain a likely outcome for each course of action, and evaluate and explain the relative attractiveness of each outcome considering such criteria as protection of own forces, infliction of damage on the enemy, and the rules of engagement. Once the commander selects a course of action, the BMS would prepare and disseminate the operation plan (OPLAN), and compare the effects of option execution with those developed through the simulation both as a check on progress and as a means of identifying the need to replan. At the conclusion of every phase of the engagement, the BMS would modify its expert system in the light of empirical results.

The Naval Carrier Battle Group Battle-Management System (see Chart I.3, Appendix I for details) builds upon experience and developments in the existing Darpa/Navy program to utilize expert systems and display technology on the Carrier USS Carl Vinson, and can exploit potential associated opportunities of the CINCPACFLT (commander-in-chief Pacific fleet) command center ashore.

To realize the capabilities described above will require the development of a number of expert systems and a natural-language interface. The expert systems, for the demonstration BMS will make inferences about enemy and own force air order-of-battle which explicitly include uncertainty, generate strike options, carry out simulations for evaluating these strike options, generate the OPLAN, and produce explanations. It is estimated that in the aggregate the above functions define a distributed expert system requiring some 20 000 rules and processing speeds of 10 bips. The natural language system alone will require a processing speed of about 1 bip.

Space-based signal processing requirements for surveillance and communications will require low power, very high speed, radiation hardened, integrated circuits based on gallium-arsenide technology. These circuits will operate speeds of at least 200 megahertz, with tens of milliwatts of power required for a typical 16 kilobit memory, in radiation up to 5×10^7 rads.

While the preceeding text described a Battle Management System for a Carrier Battle Group, it must be emphasized that the impact of the technology base required for this development extends substantially beyond the scope of this specific application. For example, many of the hardware and software developments would support, with different data, Army tactical battle management at the corps, division, and battalion level, logistics management, and missile defense.

V.2 The new computing technology

This section describes specific technology areas in the new-generation technology base. In Section V.2.1 we discuss three of the integrated "intelligent" functions: vision, speech, and natural-language understanding, along with expert-system technology as a means of implementation. These are areas where considerable progress has already been made, and these functions will be inserted into applications experiments early in the program.

For these areas it will be possible to codify laboratory knowledge in order to produce generic software systems that will be substantially independent of particular applications. A variety of other software areas, such as planning and reasoning, are not now as well developed. At the beginning of the program they will be pursued in the context of particular military applications in order to produce engineering know-how that can be extended to a broad range of problems. We anticipate that at a later time in the program some of these other software areas will be sufficiently well understood that they, too, can be developed to provide application independent software "packages."

A short description is given of each area, and a timeline for each area is included in Appendix II. These timelines can be cross-compared with the timelines for the functions' applications (Appendix I) and architectural implementation (Appendix II). It is important to note that a number of other intelligent functions will be competitively inserted into the program at later times, as basic research matures and as the applications environments provide opportunities for their experimental development and demonstration.

Section V.2.2 describes the technology area of hardware/software system architecture and design. This is the key area of the structural design of machines and software to implement the intelligent functions. The parameters of specific designs are set where appropriate by specific applications experiments in which the machines will be used. This section suggests the manner in which the applications and the intelligent functions' requirements will "pull" the architecture and design of new-generation machines. The reader can cross-compare the summary timeline for Section V.2.2 (Appendix II) with the timelines for Section V.1 (Appendix I) and Section V.2.1 (Appendix II).

Section V.2.3 describes the area of microelectronics. The Strategic Computing Program will place great emphasis on the effective exploitation of state-of-the-art microelectronics (see also Section V.3) in order to meet the key constraints on power, weight, volume, and performance required by the selected applications. The development of the GaAs pilot lines is specifically included within the Strategic Computing Program. The remainder of the supporting microelectronics technology is ongoing in the basic Darpa program, or under development by industry, and will contribute directly as results become available.

V.2.1 Integrated intelligent functions

V.2.1.1 *Vision*. Computer vision, also called image understanding, is the information-processing task of comprehending a scene from its projected image. It differs from related disciplines such as pattern recognition and image processing in that the process of image understanding builds a description not only of the image data itself, but also of the actual scene that is depicted. Image understanding requires knowledge about the task world, as well as sophisticated image-processing techniques.

Darpa has carried on a basic research program in computer vision for some years. The technology has matured to the point where it can now be exploited in meaningful ways. Since the autonomous vehicle application described previously stresses the technology development to a significant extent, it will serve as the initial driver of technology research. In order to meet objectives of the vehicle application, generic recognition capability will be required for both vehicle navigation and for reconnaissance. A vision subsystem will have to provide for the recognition and identification of obstacles that might deter local navigation and also for landmarks that can be used to fix vehicle position in the global navigational sense. The vision component must also be able to recognize targets and understand, at least from the standpoint of threat evaluation, what is happening to objects of interest from scene to scene. To achieve these capabilities, specific advances will have to be made in both vision software and also in the hardware that will run the necessary computer programs.

There currently exist software algorithms that perform object recognition in highly specific task domains, but techniques will have to be developed that generalize this capability. Furthermore, the recognition process will have to be robust enough to permit recognition in the face of occlusion, shadows, and differing orientations. The key to achieving this capability is significant advances in high-level modeling and use for knowledge-based recognition techniques. These concerns will receive strong emphasis in the early stages of the project. There will also be efforts to implement discrimination capabilities to differentiate objects of interest, for example, discerning obstacles as opposed to landmarks or targets. As the system evolves, it should also develop the capacity to detect moving objects within its range of vision, understand that they are moving, and comprehend the relations of their movement to other objects in the scene.

Recent progress in developing vision for navigation has been severely constrained by lack of adequate computing hardware. Not only are the machines that are now being used too large to be carried by the experimental vehicles, but current machines are far too slow to execute the vision algorithms in real time. For example, in an experimental university research program, a "corridor rover" applied a vision subsystem to navigate itself down corridors that had various obstacles in its path. The scene is reanalyzed after the cart has moved 1 meter. The current algorithms require 15 minutes of compute time for each meter moved. If the vehicle were moved at a walking pace, the computing requirements would be about 3 orders of magnitude greater. Future applications will have more complex scenes, be required to move faster, and also require the performance of various tasks en-route.

It is estimated that 1 trillion Von Neumann equivalent computer operations per second are required to perform the vehicle vision task at a level that will satisfy the autonomous vehicle project's long-range objectives. At best, current machines of reasonable cost achieve processing rates below 100 million operations per second. The required factor of 10^6 improvement in speed will have to be achieved through VLSI implementation of massively parallel architectures. In order to make use of these architectures, parallel algorithms will have to be developed. Therefore, part of the early research efforts will also concentrate on the development of suitable parallel algorithms. It is felt that low-level vision processes can be exploited in a more straightforward fashion because of the inherent parallel

Table 4. Objectives for vision subsystems

FY 86　Model and recognize simple terrain with crude objects
FY 88　Recognize and match landmarks with maps in simple terrain
FY 90　Recognize and match landmarks and obstacles in complex terrain using rich object descriptions
FY 92　Perform reconnaissance in a dynamically changing environment

nature of images and the local operations that are performed. Thus, initial emphasis will concentrate on algorithms at this level. As a better understanding of the problems is gained, the parallel-programming efforts will evolve to embrace the higher-level vision processes.

The most significant technology that will result from this effort is a generic scene-understanding capability. This technology will be exportable to a wide range of military applications, including cruise missile en-route navigation and terminal homing, as well as a wide variety of fire-and-forget weaponry (see Table 4).

V.2.1.2 *Speech recognition and production*. The program goal for speech subsystems is to enable real-time speech input to computers and the generation of meaningful acoustic output. Past efforts in speech understanding have been limited by both inadequate processing capabilities and by an inadequate understanding of the acoustic phonetics of speech. On-going basic research programs in speech are addressing a number of the basic issues. This program will capitalize on the results of this basic research.

The capabilities of a speech subsystem vary along several dimensions that include:
• Isolated word recognition to continuous speech
• Speaker dependence to speaker independence
• Quiet environments to noisy, stressful environments
• Small vocabularies in limited context to vocabularies having 10 000 or more words

This program is concentrating on developing speech recognition and generation high-performance capabilities for two generic types of applications: one in a high-noise, high-stress environment, where a limited vocabulary can be useful, such as in the fighter cockpit, and another in a moderate-noise environment where a very large vocabulary is required, such as in a battle management system. The timeline for this program is shown in Appendix II, Chart II.1.2, including specific milestones. The technology is applicable to many other tasks; the applications cited here provide a focus for the research and ensure that these specific applications will be supported with speech.

For the cockpit application, the major challenge will be to develop speech recognition algorithms which can operate in a fighter aircraft environment. This includes noise levels up to 115 decibels, acceleration to several g's, voice distortions due to the helmet and facemask, and the changing voice characteristics under the stresses of combat. The initial computational requirements are estimated to be 40 mips to demonstrate speech recognition in the cockpit, counting both the signal-processing and recognition functions. Furthermore, this hardware must be sufficiently compact so as not to exceed the restricted space and power that is available in a fighter aircraft.

The initial set of tasks focus on speaker-dependent isolated word recognition in a noisy environment. The specific use of speech recognition in the cockpit needs to be studied in detail to understand which tasks should be performed by voice, how voice will impact other systems, what vocabulary is needed,

and so on. Speaker-dependent algorithms for recognizing words in a noisy environment will be developed initially, and will later be extended to speaker-independent algorithms. A prototype architecture for performing the real-time recognition tasks will be developed and used to evaluate algorithms in a simulated cockpit environment. This initial architecture would be composed of off-the shelf hardware and would not be suitable for flight. Compact hardware will be developed, including custom hardware for performing compute-intensive functions such as template matching.

Support of spoken natural language input and output for a battle-management system will require real-time continuous speech recognition and generation of very large vocabularies of 1000 to 10 000 words with natural syntax and semantics, in a relatively benign acoustic environment. Techniques will need to be developed for the acquisition and representation of knowledge of speech variability due to alternate pronunciations, context in continuous speech, and different speakers. Efficient parallel search algorithms and hardware, combined with techniques for focusing attention on key works, will be developed for dealing with large vocabularies. Automated techniques will be developed for acquiring the acoustic, syntactic, and semantic knowledge to switch among multiple task domains. Advanced acoustic-phonetic algorithms will be needed to distinguish among similar words in large vocabularies. Integration of the speech system with the natural language system will be required to perform the overall battle-management task.

Increasing speech capabilities will be developed over time, with an initial goal of 1000-word speaker-adaptive system, and an ultimate goal of a 10 000-word speaker-independent system. We estimate that the computational requirements of the latter system will be on the order of 20 bips (see Table 5).

V.2.1.3 *Natural-language understanding*. The most common way for people to communicate is by expressing themselves in a natural-language such as English. If we can produce computer programs that can deal with a substantial subset of English meaning, we can make headway on several fronts. In the first place, we can provide natural-language interfaces so that tactical experts can be closely coupled with supporting data bases and automated expert systems. Such interfaces would accept data inputs, commands, and queries in natural language and could furnish responses either in natural language or in the form of easily understandable text and tables. We can also develop systems that understand streams of text to achieve automatic input of information transmitted in that form.

Natural-language research has matured to the point where it is finding application as a man-machine interface in various commercial equipment. However, its application to operational military environments is still limited by the lack of suf-

Table 5. Objectives for speech subsystems

FY 86　Recognition of words from a 100-word vocabulary for a given speaker under severe noise and moderate stress conditions
FY 88　Recognition of sentences from a 1000-word vocabulary with moderate grammatical constraints in a speaker adaptive mode under low noise and stress conditions
FY 89　Recognition of connected speech, independent of speakers from a 200-word vocabulary with strict grammatical constraints under severe noise and high stress conditions
FY 92　Recognition of sentences, independent of speakers, from a 10 000-word vocabulary with natural grammar under moderate noise and low stress conditions

ficient computing capacity, an inadequate understanding of semantics and discourse context, inadequate vocabularies, and the conceptually challenging and time-consuming problem of introducing sufficient knowledge and semantics into the system. Ongoing basic research programs will address some of these issues and feed into this program, but additional intensive efforts are needed to achieve the technology level necessary for meeting the requirements of the battle-management application described elsewhere in this plan.

The technology subprogram in natural language has the overall objective of achieving an automated understanding and generation capability that can be used in a variety of applications. We will undertake research that supports this objective by focusing on the technology needed to fulfill the specific natural-language requirements of the battle-management problem. This approach will not only support the implementation of a battle-management system, but progress made in this area will also be applicable to a wide class of similar problems. Meeting the requirements will entail the development of a highly intelligent natural-language interface between the user and the machine. In addition, a text-processing component will be developed that can classify text by its context, determine and store the key events, and retrieve the relevant information by contextual reference with an accuracy of no less than 95 percent. The timeline for this subprogram is shown in Appendix II.

In order to achieve the desired capability of the natural-language front end, it will be necessary to make significant advances in three specific areas. First of all, natural-language understanding programs must have a much greater comprehension of the context of the ongoing discourse between the user and the machine. This will significantly reduce the amount of dialogue that has to take place by instilling the capability within the machine to anticipate requirements of the user. Secondly, a much more sophisticated level of natural-language response on the part of the machine is required so that information can be presented in the most meaningful way to the user. Thirdly, an interactive facility for the acquisition of knowledge has to be developed. This is driven by the time-consuming requirements of incorporating new linguistic and semantic knowledge into the system. In the area of text understanding, advances must be made in the area of cognitive memory modeling and text comprehension.

In order to develop the capability we envision, several milestone systems will be built. The first of these will integrate and slightly extend existing natural-language interface techniques. There will then be a dual effort, one aimed at text processing and the other at interactive dialogue systems. Each of these efforts will result in specialized intermediate milestone systems. Finally, these streams will be joined together to achieve the full functional capability necessary to support the battle-management application (see Table 6).

The tasks described above will require substantially larger vocabularies than are currently available and significant gains in processing power in order to accomplish understanding and response in real time. It is estimated that vocabularies of 15 000 words and processing speeds of 1 billion operations/second will be needed to achieve this goal. In addition, to be useful for practical applications, this power must come in compact dimensions. These constraints will generally necessitate the utilization of massively parallel VLSI computational devices. Such an architecture will in turn demand the reformulation and development of parallel algorithms for natural-language understanding.

V.2.1.4 *Expert-system technology*. Expert-system technol-

Table 6. Objectives for natural-language subsystems

FY 86   Natural-language interfaces with some understanding of commands, data inputs, and queries (for example, interface to a database and a threat-assessment expert system)

FY 88   Domain-specific text understanding (for example, understand paragraph-length intelligence material relating to air threat)

FY 90   Interactive planning assistant which carries on task-oriented conversation with the user

FY 93   Interactive, multiuser acquisition, analysis, and explanation system that provides planning support and substantive understanding of streams of textual information

ogy has matured to become a highly exploitable application area of the science of artificial intelligence. It is characterized by the explicit use of specific domain knowledge (usually gleaned from human experts) to develop computer systems that can solve complex, real-world problems of military, scientific, engineering, medical, and management specialists.

Examples of successful applications include programs to perform electronic warfare signal analysis, medical diagnosis, geological evaluation of designated sites, oil well dipmeter analysis, maintenance of locomotives, and carrier air operations. It is a technology that is most appropriate for command and control operations, situation assessment, and high-level planning. Thus it will play a vital role in the military applications examples described elsewhere in this plan.

Expert-system technology has evolved to a point where a variety of general purpose inferencing and reasoning systems are available. These systems can be augmented with specific domain knowledge to prepare them for particular applications. Currently, the most time consuming portion of the process of constructing an expert system is the articulation of knowledge by the expert and its satisfactory formulation in a suitable knowledge representation language for mechanization by computer. Thus, the plan for expert-system technology (see Appendix II, Chart II.1.4) places heavy emphasis on knowledge acquisition and representation.

There are many opportunities for dramatic advances in the technology. These include advances in explanation and presentation capability, improved ability to handle uncertain and missing knowledge and data, more flexible control mechanisms, expansion of knowledge capacity and extent, enhanced inference capability (in terms of speed, flexibility, and power), development of inter-system cooperation, and improvement of software support tools. Intensive development attention devoted to these issues can be expected to lead to important applications of expert systems in complex military environments.

The Strategic Computing Program expert-system technology effort will exploit these opportunities by generating and extending AI techniques, by improving software support tools, and by using specialized symbolic computational hardware. Work in representation will build toward a capability for large (30 000-rule) knowledge bases. Inference techniques will be extended to handle these knowledge bases even when they contain uncertain knowledge and must operate on errorful and incomplete data. Explanation and presentation systems, ultimately using a 10 000-word speech-understanding system, will allow verbal inputs from (and discussions with) the user about the systems' assessments, recommendations and plans. The knowledge acquisition work will focus on developing facilities for automated input of domain knowledge directly from experts, text, and data. Software support efforts will lead to a progression of increasingly powerful expert-system workstations to be used in developing the needed technology.

The achievement of these complex capabilities will severly tax computational resources so that significant gains in processing power will be required to perform in real time or in simulations at faster than real time. It is estimated that hybrid expert-system architectural configurations will be required that can accommodate 30 000 rules and perform at a capacity of 12 000 rules per real-time second at rates up to five times real time. Due to compact size and cost constraints, it is anticipated that this architecture will be realized through VLSI devices incorporating massive parallelism, active semantic memories, and specialized inference mechanisms. Such configurations will require significant efforts to develop the algorithms required for parallel execution. It should be noted that the rules per second quantifications are subject to many factors, and are for comparison purposes only. Rules applied in applications late in the program will be more complex than present ones, and their contexts for firing will be vastly more complex than those common in present-day expert systems.

The results of this effort will specifically support the goals of the three sample military applications. However, the resulting technology will be substantially generic in nature so that it will significantly advance expert systems capabilities and support a wide range of applications for both the Government and industry.

V.2.2 Hardware/software system architecture

Most of today's computers are still single-processor Von Neumann machines, and the few efforts to build commercial multiprocessor systems have yielded systems containing only a few processors (generally less than 10). The underlying electronic-circuit technology is advancing at a rate that will provide a speed improvement factor of only 20 percent to 30 percent per year, at most, for such machines. For future computer systems to have substantially greater power, they must rely heavily on parallelism. While many ideas have been developed for algorithms, languages, and system software for high-performance parallel machines, practical experience with actual experimental parallel systems is still very limited, and must be greatly expanded.

Greater computing power can also be achieved through specialization of machines to particular computing functions. Such specialized machines exhibit exceptional performance, but only on the class of problems for which they were designed. Parallelism is itself a form of specialization of a machine to a class of problems. For example, array processors will out-perform a comparably priced general-purpose computer by factors of 10 to 100 on linear algebra, finite-element analysis, and similar problems. Future high-performance systems for applications such as the control of autonomous vehicles must support a diverse and demanding set of functions with high reliability. Such systems will be composed of a variety of modules configured to perform these many specialized functions efficiently, in parallel, and with redundancy appropriate to the application. For example, the control of autonomous vehicles may employ modules specialized to signal processing to handle the image processing at the lowest level, modules specialized to pattern matching to handle the scene analysis, and other modules to handle cognitive functions, control, and communications. This integration of diverse machines into complete systems depends on standardization of hardware, software, and network interfaces.

Computer architecture is concerned with the structures by which memories, processing nodes, and peripherals are interconnected; the computational capabilities of the processing nodes; and the software that is required to exploit the hardware. Ideas have been proposed for machines which are interconnected in a variety of ways, and given descriptive names such as Boolean n-cubes, trees, perfect shuffles, and meshes. Processor nodes have been proposed that are designed for floating-point operations, search operations, logic operations, and so on, and language and operating system concepts have been proposed for exploiting parallelism. It is from this collection of ideas that specific architectures have been proposed, and in some cases simulated or constructed on a very small scale.

To understand the capabilities and limitations of a proposed architecture, a prototype of the machine must be simulated or built, software must be developed, and the system evaluated on a class of problems for which the machine was designed. The role of software cannot be overemphasized. Existing languages are generally not applicable for highly parallel architectures. Special compilers are needed, as are debugging tools and tools to measure the performance of the resulting system. In evaluating a new architecture, it is more important to initially understand the applicability of the architecture to an important class of problems than to strive for high performance in a prototype implementation. Thus, to know that a 100-processor system gives a 50-fold increase over a single node of that system is more important than knowing the maximum instruction rate that can be executed or knowing the exact instruction rate achieved with prototype hardware. Once a prototype machine has been demonstrated to be promising, higher-performance versions can be built by using faster components and by scaling the entire system to have more processors.

This program will develop and evaluate new architectures in three broad areas: signal-processing, symbolic-processing, and multifunction machines. These classes of machines are described below, along with the development plans for each class. In general, several prototype systems will be developed in the early phase of the program. An evaluation phase will permit different architectural approaches to be compared. We will select from the different prototypes those that are most successful and that will be continued to develop high-performance versions.

A timeline for the development of these computer architectures is given in Appendix II, Chart II.2.2.

V.2.2.1 *Signal processing.* An important class of applications known as signal processing involves taking real-time data from a sensor and performing a series of operations on each data element. These operations might involve transformations such as an FFT, correlations, filtering, and so forth, and are dominated by performing multiplications and additions. High data rates are common, and computation rates in excess of 1 billion operations/second are needed. Military applications of such signal processing include processing data from radar, sonar, infrared sensors, images, and speech.

The exploitation of parallelism in signal processing will be based on the use of computational arrays such as systolic arrays, in which many simple, highly regular processing elements "pump" data from cell to cell in a "wavelike" motion to perform the successive operations on each element of data. An architecture based on this concept will be developed, with the goal of building a system capable of executing 1 billion or more operations/second by 1986. Other concepts that exploit signal-processing data regularity will also be investigated. By the end of the decade, the goal is to develop a system capable of 1 trillion operations/second.

The software support and programming languages for the signal-processing system will be developed in parallel with the hardware. Most of the initial programming for the prototype system will be done at the microcode level. The requirements for the operating system, programming languages, and programming environments will be developed as experience is gained using the prototype systems.

V.2.2.2 *Symbolic processing.* Symbolic processing deals with nonnumeric objects, relationships between these objects, and the ability to infer or deduce new information with the aid of programs that "reason." Examples of symbolic computation include searching and comparing complex structures (for example, partial pattern matching). Applications that make extensive use of symbolic computing include vision systems that can tell what is in a scene, natural-language systems that can "understand" the meaning of a sentence in English, speech understanding systems that can recognize spoken words, and planning systems that can provide intelligent advice to a decision maker. Most programs that perform symbolic processing are now written in the language called LISP. Special machines, called LISP machines, are now available commercially and offer computing rates in excess of 1 mip. Further development of these conventional uniprocessor LISP machines will take place under the technology infrastructure portion of the program. An ultimate performance improvement of about 50 times the current level can be achieved with these conventional techniques and the use of advanced technology.

Current applications in areas such as vision now require about three orders of magnitude more processing than is now available. As future algorithms and applications are developed, even more computing power will be necessary.

The symbolic processors of the future may well be a collection of special components which are interconnected via a general-purpose host computer or by high-speed networks. Based on software systems that have been developed for applications in vision, natural language, expert systems, and speech, several of these components have been identified. As much as four orders of magnitude speedup may be available by taking advantage of the parallelism in some of these specific areas. Some of the components include the following:

• A semantic memory subsystem—used to represent knowledge-relating concepts to other concepts in natural-language, speech-understanding, and planning domains.

• A signal-to-symbol transducer—used to make the initial step in extracting meaning from low-level signal-processing computations (for example, phonetic classification, or object identification from boundary information).

• A production-rule subsystem—a system that combines knowledge and procedures for problem solving. A system now aboard the carrier Carl Vinson uses this approach.

• A fusion subsystem—a method for permitting multiple sources of information to share their knowledge. It is used to "fuse" information in tasks such as battle management.

• An inferencing subsystem—a system that uses first-order formal logic to perform reasoning and theorem proving.

• A search subsystem—a mechanism that explores numerous hypotheses, pruning these intelligently to determine likely candidates for further symbolic processing.

The program will consist of three phases. Phase I concentrates on architecture design, simulation, algorithm analysis, and benchmark development for promising architectural ideas such as those described above. It will also include the devel-

opment and initial evaluation of the unique integrated components necessary for the implementation of these architectures. The design of concurrent LISP-like languages for programming these machines will also be addressed.

Existing high-performance scientific computers such as the Cray-1, CDC 205, Denelcor HEP, and the S-1 will be benchmarked using a portable LISP computer to determine their relative abilities to handle symbolic computation.

Phase II will engineer full-scale prototype versions of selected architectures, supporting these hardware developments with extensive diagnostic and compilation tools. The goal of this phase is implementation of a specific target problem on each of the selected architectures for benchmarking purposes.

Phase III will integrate developments of the signal-processing, symbolic, and multifunction development efforts into a composite system capable of addressing a significant problem domain. Such a system for the control of an autonomous vehicle, for example, might include a high-performance vision-processing front end based on the computational array technology, a signal-to-symbol transformer for classifying objects, a fusion subsystem for integrating information from multiple sources, an inferencing engine for reasoning and top-level control, and a multifunction processor for controlling the manipulator effectors. This phase will also pursue higher-performance versions of selected machines.

V.2.2.3 *Multifunction machines.* A multifunction machine is capable of executing a wider range of different types of computations than the more specialized machines described above, but at possibly lower performance in the specialized machine's application domain. These multifunction machines achieve high performance with parallelism. We aim to develop machines of this class having 1000 processors. The processing elements in a multifunction machine would typically be general purpose processors or computers. These elements communicate either through shared storage or networks with such interconnection strategies as rings, trees, Boolean n-cubes, perfect shuffle networks, lattices, or meshes.

On the order of six to eight prototype multifunction systems will be developed, based on custom VLSI chips, commercial microprocessor chips, or commercial processors. These systems will be benchmarked to determine how different hardware architectures and programming strategies scale in performance. Subsequently, two or three such systems will be selected in this evaluation process for continued development for advanced-technology versions and production-quality software.

Central to this program is the development of programming models and methods that will permit the convenient development of new classes of algorithms that will contain very high levels of concurrency. The way in which concurrency manifests itself in program structures can be viewed as resulting from the linguistic control method of the programming language in that the program is written. Examples of control models that will be investigated are the control-driven, data-driven, and demand-driven styles. Control-driven concurrent programming models are already evolving from existing programming languages. Examples are concurrent Pascal, parallel LISP, and so forth. In this model, program actions are sequenced by explicit control mechanisms such as CALL, JUMP, or PARBEGIN. In the data-driven model, program actions are driven into activity by the arrival of the requisite operand set. The advantage of this style is that concurrency can often be specified implicitly. The demand-driven model is based on the propagation of demands for results to invoke actions. This style has been successfully employed for parallel evaluation of LISP code. In this scheme, concurrent demands are propagated for argument evaluation of LISP functions. It is likely that new or possibly composite models such as concurrent object-oriented programming will surface, but it is also likely that advances in each area will provide highly concurrent program-based solutions for many application areas.

An important part of this project will be the implementation of new concurrent programming languages that exploit these models. The language development will need to be coupled with programming environment tools and compatible hardware and operating-system software. This development will provide the necessary computational tools to support application studies aimed at the creation of highly parallel application programs that can take advantage of the large levels of concurrency provided by multifunction machine prototypes. The long-term goal of this research is ultraspeed, cost-effective demonstrations of important application areas such as data-base access, system simulation, and physical modeling.

Given a particular instance of machine and a particular parallel program, the remaining issue is how the program should be mapped onto the physical resources in order to permit efficient exploitation of concurrency. This resource allocation problem is one of the key technical issues addressed by this program. There are two styles usually employed in the solution of this problem: static allocation and dynamic allocation.

In a static mapping strategy, the concurrency structure of the program is evaluated with respect to the topology of the physical machine. The compiler can then create specific load modules for the physical nodes of the target machine. This static method is simpler than the dynamic method but needs to be developed for each of the architectures that are being pursued. If the number of components is very large, then it is likely that component failures will occur. With the static allocation mechanism, it will be necessary to recompile the program for the current machine configuration.

In a dynamic allocation strategy, it is still important for the compiler to do some of the allocation task collection, but the output of the compiler is not in the form of specific load modules. Dynamic strategies allow the loader to define the final physical target of a compiled module based on hardware availability. Another extension to the dynamic strategy is to additionally move tasks around to balance system load. An important by-product of this program will be the development and implementation of both static and dynamic allocation strategies, but it is expected that acceptable static allocation methods will precede the more sophisticated dynamic strategies.

V.2.3 Supporting microelectronics technology

Computing technology relies heavily on microelectronics in order to achieve systems capabilities while meeting critical constraints on such factors as size, weight, power dissipation, and operating environments. Microelectronics provides computing systems with required integration complexity, switching speed, switching energy, and tolerance to hostile environments. In the case of military systems, special emphasis must be given to survival in radiation environments. Microelectronic packaging and interconnect technologies provide additional important support in meeting system constraints.

This program will place strong emphasis on the effective exploitation of such microelectronic technology. A key concept that will be used to exploit state-of-the-art microelectronics is to dramatically reduce the usual long time delays between basic research innovations in fabrication and packaging technology and their subsequent exploitation by designers. This will be done by creating a pilot line(s) for the particular technology and at the same time creating the associated designer-to-implementation system-to-foundry interfaces (design rules, process test inserts, design examples, design libraries, implementation system protocols, and so forth.). Once a new technology has been demonstrated as feasible and stable in pilot-line form, it may then be selected for inclusion in program infrastructure. [The reader should compare the microelectronics timeline (Section V.2.3) with that for infrastructure (Section V.3). (See Appendix II.)]

Silicon technology. Silicon technology will be the mainstay of this program because of its maturity and its accessibility through existing infrastructure. Early versions of the proposed subsystems prototypes will use the 3×10^{11} gate hertz/cm^2 technologies made possible by VLSI/VHSIC. More advanced technologies such as the VHSIC Phase II will also be utilized as they become available. For subsystems and/or systems that require even greater throughput this program will competitively purchase wafer-level integration technology from emerging sources. This will result in the gain of at least another order of magnitude in the computational throughput of a monolithic chip and an equally significant reduction in power consumption for a given operation by diminishing the number of required off-chip drives.

Even such gains will not fulfill the ultimate weight, volume, and speed requirements of such systems as certain autonomous vehicles that will require better than 10^{10} operations per second and 10^{11} bits of memory in less than a few cubic feet using no more than a kilowatt of power. For these requirements to be met, new fabrication technology must be developed yielding devices an order of magnitude smaller than those produced today. Ultimately, techniques now in basic research phases such as ion-beam–processing technology, laser processing, and x-ray lithography may be combined with silicon molecular beam epitaxy into a pilot-line system capable of growing multiple semiconductor and insulator layers, adding localized ion doping, etching via holes and depositing interconnect metal. If successful in moving from basic research, such efforts could eventually reduce from months to days the time required to fabricate prototype custom circuits of high complexity.

GaAs pilot lines. Survivable, space-based electronics will require the two orders of magnitude increased total dose radiation tolerance that is inherent to GaAs-based microelectronics technologies. The establishment of pilot lines, running at a throughput of at least 100 wafers/week, will place, for the first time, the production rigor on the fabrication of GaAs integrated circuits necessary to achieve acceptable yields and make GaAs circuits affordable to the military. The GaAs pilot lines will be producing low-power, radiation-hard memory and logic chips as fundamental building blocks for radiation hardened systems. Communication and surveillance systems that can survive in a strategic conflict are important components of a space-based battle management system. In addition to the primary advantage of high radiation tolerance, GaAs-based microelectronics will also produce circuits with larger operating temperature range, both lower and higher than silicon, and faster on-chip switching speed at a given power level.

Memory technology. Rapid-access, low-power memory subsystems that can be operated in the field and powered from conventional sources are needed by many applications. Today's largest disk storage systems contain on the order of a gigabyte of memory, but are too large and power-consuming for use in the field. Progress must be made in both size and power reduction. Systems needs for as large as 100-gigabyte memories with rapid access are envisioned for autonomous systems. The program will capitalize on progress in industry and in other basic research programs.

High-performance technology. The need to increase system computational speeds may be met using fabrication technology that can tailor materials properties by creating artificial compounds and super-lattices of differing materials [for example by using molecular beam epitaxy (MBE) technology]. Successful pilot lining of MBE would contribute to conventional microelectronics, microelectronics with optoelectronic I/O, and eventually to massively parallel computations using optical computing elements when available optoelectronic interconnect technology allows the number of cables and the power dissipation in large multiprocessor systems to be reduced dramatically.

As MBE systems advance into a practical production tool, heterostructure devices can be fabricated to produce high-frequency devices. Such a development will reduce transmit-receive satellite systems presently requiring 6-foot dishes to possibly hand-held devices by utilizing the 94-GHz atmospheric window. Such systems will contribute in a revolutionary manner to size, weight, and cost of battle-management communications subsystems.

Advanced computing subsystems-on-a-chip will require both high speed and high pin-count packages. The VHSIC program is developing 250-pin packages but these are only suitable up to a 40-megahertz clock rate. This program will initiate development and/or compete the selection of large pin-count packages, including those that employ microwave signal-propagation principles. Longer-term efforts directed towards achieving (optoelectronic) packages required to handle broadband operation, from d.c. to multi-gigahertz, with up to 200 signal lines in addition to power and ground leads will be factored into the program where appropriate.

V.3 Computing technology infrastructure

In order to effectively support and coordinate the activities of the large number of people and organizations in this program, we will focus our attention early in the program on the provision of adequate infrastructure for the enterprise. It is intended that this be accomplished in a manner that rapidly disseminates the technology, not only across the participants, but across U.S. industry.

There are three phases of activity in this part of the program. Beginning in the first year, major emphasis will be placed on the consolidation of state-of-the-art computing technology to enable rapid capitalization and maximum resource sharing. A second phase is designed to take advantage of early products of the program to enhance overall capabilities. A final phase is intended to bring about a transition of the activities in the infrastructure to make them self-supporting. These three phases result in a cost profile that is initially high, but is reduced over the life of the program as costs are gradually borne by recipients of the technology. High initial investment in computing equipment, services, and training also leverages the most critical resource—trained personnel.

The infrastructure is categorized by specific activities to be performed. The most immediate need is for availability of the products of computing technology so as to bootstrap the development process. We will provide common symbolic processing equipment to the selected participants in the first two years and will supplement this with more advanced equipment

as it is developed in the program. Common access to high-performance networks will be provided to facilitate communication between sites and shared use of computing resources.

Next, a set of activities address common access to services and tools that are the means of designing and building new computers. These include rapid-prototyping implementation services providing foundry access to VLSI/VHSIC and GaAs fabrication lines as well as access to higher-level system-implementation services. Computers are to be used extensively in the design and analysis of new systems and these hardware and software tools will be shared between sites by exploiting the common hardware configurations, programming languages, and network communication facilities.

Finally, the most important activities in the infrastructure accelerate the rate of progress. These activities appear as items integral to the products and services just described as well as specific activities in their own right.

The following examples are representative of the methods sought to achieve this acceleration:
- Use of state-of-the-art computing technology to develop new computing technology.
- Shared access to capital-intensive manufacturing facilities.
- Improved productivity through use of advanced design methods and system-interoperability kits.
- Rapid-turnaround implementation services.

In addition to these, specific activities encourage collaboration between researchers through the development of interoperability standards. Strong interaction with the university community is coupled with the use of the technology in the form of embedded instruction to accelerate the training and development of personnel.

The result is a powerful expansion of the traditional concept of infrastructure. The program will produce not only an advanced technology base in the form of facilities, equipment, institutions, and knowledge, but also the methods for using it and accelerating its growth.

V.3.1 Capital equipment

Hardware and software will be developed early in the program to enable widespread use of advanced symbolic computers and communication systems in both laboratory and embedded applications.

V.3.1.1 *LISP machines.* A small number (25 to 40 per year) of LISP machines will be acquired during the first years of the program for use by contractors in the conduct of research and applications development. In parallel two new classes of LISP machines will be developed by industrial manufacturers. One will be $10\times$ faster than current machines and the second will be a low-power, compact version for use in applications experiments, field trials, and demonstrations. This equipment will be supplied to contractors beginning in FY 1987.

V.3.1.2 *Research machines.* As new machine capabilities are developed and demonstrated in the program, other defense projects will be able to benefit from direct access to them. We plan to develop some of these machines and supply them with the necessary software and intelligent subsystems for use in follow-on R&D in support of the military demonstrations. Other systems will be available via a network. Industrial production of these machines will be sought where appropriate.

V.3.1.3 *Communication networks.* No element of the infrastructure is as important as the need for widening the network connection among the various participants of the program. Beyond the obvious advantages of sharing resources and facilities, the network is unparalleled as a means of promoting synergy between researchers located at different sites. We plan to work with other agencies (such as the Department of Energy, the National Aeronautics and Space Administration, and the National Science Foundation) in developing a common plan for leased wideband communication facilities to be made available by the common carriers.

V.3.2 Services

The physical construction of complex computing equipment is a difficult and time-consuming task, even when all the essential design details are understood. A set of services will be put in place that simplify this process, reduce cost, and provide rapid turnaround.

V.3.2.1 *Integrated-circuit implementation service.* Silicon VLSI/VHSIC and GaAs fabrication lines will be made available as foundries for use by selected Defense contractors. We plan to work with the vendors to develop standard design rules for this technology and provide access via network connections. This will extend the method already in use for 3-to-5-micron NMOS and CMOS of providing direct access from the designer's system over the network to the foundry service. This service will be expanded to provide access to advanced microelectronic technology as it is developed under Section V.2.3.

V.3.2.2 *Rapid machine prototyping.* A service will be established to allow the rapid implementation of full-scale systems with the goal of enabling the assembly of complete multiprocessor computer systems from initial designs in a period of a few months. This service will provide rapid turnaround services for printed circuit boards, hybrid fabrication, system packaging, power, cooling, assembly, and testing.

V.3.2.3 *System interoperability kits.* Sources will be solicited for the design and manufacture of "system kits" intended to facilitate interoperability and experimentation in new computer architectures. These standardized hardware/software environments will provide the physical means of easily integrating and assembling systems into predesigned modules using design frames for embedding unique custom designs as part of these systems.

V.3.3 Integrated system development

An advanced system-development environment will be constructed as a framework for consolidation and integration of the design and performance analysis tools that are produced by this program. This environment will set the standards for tool development and facilitate the sharing of the products of this research between sites. A major benefit of this common system development environment when coupled with rapid prototyping is that it allows hardware decisions to be deferred and an optimal balance of hardware and software achieved.

V.3.3.1 *Functional and physical design aids.* This new generation of computers will be developed using new high-level tools that are built upon state-of-the-art research in VLSI design. These tools will be extended upward to enable system level design, assembly, and test in a rapid system-prototyping environment. It is here that the use of computing technology as a tool to create new computing technology is most obvious. In the functional design of a new machine architecture, its performance can be evaluated through emulation. We expect to use dedicated hardware-emulation machines to assess a number of architectures for which construction will be difficult or costly. Likewise, advanced hardware and software approaches to physical design aids will enable more rapid and robust system design.

V.3.3.2 *Software and systems.* An integrated rapid software- and systems-prototyping capability is needed to support the development and application of multiprocessor systems. This capability will be developed by building upon advanced software and systems development environments such as ADA and LISP and extending them to support multiprocessor targets. The major problems that need to be solved to effectively apply these architectures and achieve the required performance are resource allocation for processor, memory, communication, and mass storage. In addition, the application system developers need support for using the new architectures in terms of the virtual machine interfaces that will be developed to manage resource allocation.

The software and systems activities produce the most generic software to support the application specific software. This includes programming languages, system software, and design and performance analysis tools for multiprocessor targets. As the technology matures, resource allocation will become more automatic and higher-level design environments for multiprocessor architectures will be developed.

V.3.4 Standards

To integrate hardware and software to perform basic system functions, and then to integrate those functions into systems will require interoperability research. A key ingredient will be the set of protocols that allows interaction between modules. It should be possible to access information in a knowledge base from a speech-understanding system or to make available vision or natural language to a navigation system. Outputs from any of these should be available to AI-based simulation and display systems.

We envision developing system interoperability protocols to the point where couplings of hardware, software, and peripheral devices may be selected and configured readily. This will include capabilities for speech input, vision, graphics, and a host of intelligent system tools including an expert system and a LISP machine.

V.4 Program planning

So far in this section, we have presented the key concepts of the Strategic Computing plan by showing how example activities proceed under the plan. We now step back and summarize the overall logic of the plan, list the compartments and activities to be planned, and discuss the detailed tactics to be used to *initiate* the Strategic Computing Program.

As first discussed in Section IV, and clarified by example in Section V, the top-level logic of the plan centers on the interactions of selected military applications of intelligent computing with the evolving base of technology that provides the intelligent computing. In particular,

• Applications drive requirements of intelligent functions.
• Intelligent functions drive requirements of system architectures.
• System architectures drive requirements of microelectronics and infrastructure.

In order to achieve the Program's goals, we must create on the order of a dozen different, modularly composable intelligent functional capabilities. Each one, such as vision subsystems, requires the generation of a "technical community" responsible for evolving that technology.

However, since these functions are broadly applicable to many applications, it is likely that a modest number (perhaps a half-dozen) well-selected applications will be sufficient to "drive" the whole set of intelligent functions. Each of these applications similarly requires the generation of a technical community, prime contractor, or center of excellence responsible for its evolution. A range of hardware/software architectures must also be created, systems must be implemented as microelectronics, and adequate infrastructure must be provided to support the entire enterprise.

Later, in Section VI and in Appendix IV, we provide a detailed work-breakdown structure that compartments all these program activities for planning and budgeting purposes. We now turn to the plans for initiating the program.

We are initially concerned with the development of appropriate military applications that will effectively pull the technology base. A set of three applications have been selected for initial inclusion in the program. Based on the results of a Defense Science Board task-force study (see Section VI), and a series of competitive evaluations of the most impactful applications, we plan to augment and refine the list to a final set during the first several years of the program, using selection criteria cited in Section V.1.

At the beginning of the program we will initiate work in the four areas of intelligent functions (vision, speech, natural language, expert systems) that can be exploited in the near-term, and drive these technologies using requirements set by the selected applications. At later times we will initiate activities (as basic research matures) in the other area of intelligent capabilities.

Activities will begin in system architecture on two fronts. The first will be development of systems aimed at supporting the near-term intelligent functions for selected applications (an example would be a computational array processor to support vision technology). Next, we plan competition among several large symbolic processor architectures that will be prototyped for later evaluation and selection. Such processors will be essential during later stages of the program. Additional specialized system architectures will be selected, later in the program timeline at points where they are required by applications.

Certain microelectronics technology will be developed in pilot-line form early in the program (for example GaAs), in order to position the technology for support of later program requirements.

A very key portion of the plan for program initiation is the early development and deployment of program infrastructure (see Section V.3 for details). Research machines, network communications, implementation services, and so forth, must be in place to enable program progress. A set of protocols and interoperability standards must be created to ensure later modular compatibility among Strategic Computing Program technology components. As we will see in Section VI, this means that spending on infrastructure is a moderately high fraction of program spending in the first two years (although it rapidly peaks and levels off).

Finally, appropriate program management support tools must be brought on line early in the program to ensure orderly, planned, managed progress toward program goals and objectives.

When studying the program timelines in the Appendices, note that the planning framework is not a closed-system "PERT" chart, but instead is open to accommodate available opportunities and competitively selected technologies during appropriate time windows. Thus it is the generation of the *technology envelope* that is planned, charted, and guided to achieve program goals, rather than the generation of a specific computer or specific technology module.

VI. Program management

The management of the Strategic Computing Program will be carried out by Darpa. This section describes Darpa's approach to management of the program. Because of the importance, size, complexity, and pace of this program a number of issues will be addressed.

Program coordination. The importance of the Strategic Computing Program to the national interest requires coordination with many different organizations involved in related technologies.

Within DOD, Darpa will coordinate closely with USDRE and the military services. Preliminary discussions have been held with representatives of all three services, and all have expressed strong interest in close cooperation with Darpa on this program.

An agreement for exchange of information has been reached among OSTP, DOE, NSF, NASA, DOC, and DOD representatives at a spring meeting of the Federal Coordination Committee on Science Engineering and Technology sponsored by the OSTP. This agreement called for a series of meetings specifically organized to exchange information in high-speed computing technology. The first of these meetings was held in June 1983, with the DOD chairing the meeting. Further meetings will be scheduled at regular intervals until the end of the program or until otherwise mutually agreed.

A panel of the Defense Science Board (DSB) headed by Professor Joshua Lederberg, president of Rockefeller University, has also been convened to make recommendations to the Under Secretary on how best to use the new-generation machine intelligence technology within DOD.

Program management. The Strategic Computing Program will be managed within Darpa. The Strategic Computing Program Manager will be assigned to the Information Processing Techniques Office (IPTO), the lead office. However, significant responsibilities are allocated to other offices, especially in the areas of microelectronics and applications.

It is Darpa's objective to maintain a dynamic R&D environment for this project and to manage the delicate balance between the technology-based development and the experimentation in military applications.

The number of active working relationships may be very large because other offices within Darpa, USDRE, universities, the services, and industry will all be involved. Since these relationships must be maintained to ensure integrated planning and execution, the program will use advisory panels to reach these groups. One of these will be a senior review group to provide advice as the program progresses. It will consist of representatives from the three services, OSD, other governmental organizations, and major industrial organizations and universities. In this way the program will capture the best creative ideas of Government, universities, and industry, while continually involving the ultimate user community. This group will meet quarterly with the Darpa management involved in the program.

Similarly, other panels or working groups will be constituted to provide communications and advice in specific areas and to keep other groups abreast of progress in Strategic Computing.

The Strategic Computing Program planners will continue refinement and adaptation of the program plan over time to reflect the current state of funding and development. Efforts will be undertaken to maintain program documentation, provide technical evaluation of progress, respond to congressional (and

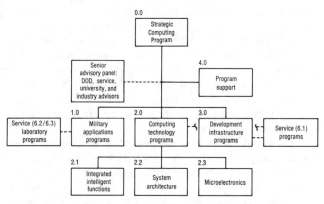

Figure 3. Darpa program management and work breakdown structure for strategic computing

other) inquiries, develop internal reporting and control systems, support program reviews, maintain technical libraries, and disseminate information in the form of technical abstracts and progress reports, as required.

Communication is a critical element of program management because many of the important contributors will be widely dispersed. Special and unique arrangements will be considered to establish an effective research community by leveraging existing computer tools and communications systems. Electronic mail and electronic bulletin boards are the simplest examples. More advanced approaches to be considered include the provision of remote electronic views of the unfolding project planning timeline to give feedback on performance to community members. This is an innovative approach that derives from successful experiences in Darpa program activities in VLSI system design. In this way we will build a planning and management infrastructure that enables new "intellectual entrepreneurs" to easily identify ways they can contribute to the program to create new elements of intelligent-computing technology and its military applications.

Program costs and work-breakdown structure. The overall scale of budget requirements is determined by the number and type of new technologies to be jointly introduced, and by past experience in the field in generating equivalent technological communities or centers of expertise. In this case we require the creation of approximately ten new "computing-technology communities" and another five to ten "applications communities." The size of these efforts must, if past experience is any guide, be at least on the order of a small research center (>100 professionals), with each community composed of two or three research laboratories, that operate over approximately an 8-to-10-year time span. This scale is consistent with past requirements for the generation of new computing technology such as timesharing, computer-networking, personal computing, and so forth. This logic provides a top-down scaling of the enterprise as requiring about 5 to 10 applications plus 10 technology communities of at least 100 persons each, and thus requires something approaching $150 million per year for a several year period around the peak of the program.

This estimate is consistent with a bottom-up budget estimate based on the detailed unfolding of actual and projected activities for the initial period of the plan where specific projections can be readily made.

A program-management and work-breakdown structure for the program is diagrammed in Figure 3. Further details of the work breakdown structure are tabulated in Appendix IV. Table 2 shows the annual cost for the Strategic Computing Program

aggregated to the program level. Program costs for the first five years of the program are estimated to be approximately $600 million.

The logic of the sequencing of activities is reflected in the breakdown of spending in the three major categories. Spending on tools and infrastructure is relatively high in the first two years, peaking early in the program. Technology base activity and spending then rises fast, and will likely peak in FY 1987–1988. Applications activity and spending expand moderately at first, then rapidly in the late eighties, peaking near the end of the program. The entire program will peak about the end of the decade, declining rapidly thereafter as program goals are achieved.

Acquisition strategy. The basic acquisition policy is that military applications will be carried out by industry drawing upon results of research carried out in the universities. The computer architectures will be developed primarily in joint projects between universities and industry. Most of the hardware and software for intelligent subsystems will be competed. There will be a selection of ideas on especially difficult topics from a set of several dozen leading contenders. The most advanced artificial-intelligence ideas that seem ripe for developing will be exploited with heavy university involvement. For these, expert judgment from leading participants in the field will be sought and directed selection will result. Construction and access to computing-technology infrastructure will be competed.

The contract personnel responsible for accomplishing the goals of this program will be largely drawn from industry and will consist primarily of engineers and systems designers. By contracting with industry we will transfer to that community computer science research results that have been developed in universities, largely with Darpa funding; we will ease the transition of the newly developed systems into corporate product lines; we will avoid a dangerous depletion of the university computer science community, with the inevitable slow-down in research and education. The magnitude of this national effort could represent a very large perturbation to the university community, but is a small percentage of the industrial engineering and system-building base.

While most of the basic technology development in this program will be unclassified, the emphasis on the industrial efforts will provide a significant control of the leakage of information outside of the U.S. industrial base.

Technology transfer. We intend a significant effort toward technology transfer of results of this program into the military services. This effort will include: (a) use of service agents and service COTRs; (b) a process of cost-sharing with the services in the development of military applications; (c) the inclusion of technology-based results from this program in service programs and test beds, and (d) training of service personnel by involvement in technology-based developments.

Equally important is technology transfer to industry, both to build up a base of engineers and system builders familiar with computer science and machine-intelligence technology now limited to university laboratories, and to facilitate incorporation of the new technology into corporate product lines. To this end we will make full use of regulations for Government procurement involving protection of proprietary information and trade secrets, patent rights, and licensing and royalty arrangements.

Evaluation. Each of the sections of this program will have a detailed evaluation plan. Specifically:

(1)   Each of the microelectronics developments will be proposed to particular performance specifications, for example, radiation hardness for GaAs, and the final deliverable will be evaluated against those specifications, driven by requirements.

(2)   Early in the program, benchmark programs will be developed for evaluation of the competitive machine architectures. For example, different signal processor designs will be benchmarked with programs drawn from radar or sonar analysis, or some other chosen signal-analysis task; different symbolic processors will be benchmarked through tasks such as evaluation of a particular production-rule set, or searching through a particular semantic set, such as one used for natural-language understanding; and, more general-purpose processor designs will be benchmarked with applications that might involve war gaming or simulation.

(3)   Performance requirements for the integrated intelligent functions, that is, vision, speech, natural language, and expert systems will be defined by the requirements of the three (or more) chosen military application areas, and evaluations will be performed toward those specifications.

(4)   Finally, the military applications developed will be evaluated using the same methods and criteria currently used by the services. This will simplify comparison. For example, the evaluation of the efficacy of the pilot's associate will be measured in combat performance—with and without—on instrumented combat flight ranges.

VII. Conclusions

We now have a plan for action as we cross the threshold into a new generation of computing. It is a plan for creating a large array of machine-intelligence technology that can be scaled and mixed in countless ways for diverse applications.

We have a plan for "pulling" the technology-generation process by creating carefully selected technology interactions with challenging military applications. These applications also provide the experimental test beds for refining the new technology and for demonstrating the feasibility of particular intelligent computing capabilities.

The timely, successful generation and application of intelligent-computing technology will have profound effects. If the technology is widely dispersed in applications throughout our society, Americans will have a significantly improved capability to handle complex tasks and to codify, mechanize, and propagate their knowledge. The new technology will improve the capability of our industrial, military, and political leaders to tap the nation's pool of knowledge and effectively manage large enterprises, even in times of great stress and change.

Successful achievement of the objectives of the strategic-computing initiative will lead to deployment of a new generation of military systems containing machine-intelligence technology. These systems will provide the United States with important new methods of defense against massed forces in the future—methods that can raise the threshold and diminish the likelihood of major conflict.

There are difficult challenges to overcome in order to realize the goals of a national program of such scope and complexity. However, we believe that the goals are achievable under the logic and methods of this plan, and, if we seize the moment and undertake this initiative, the Strategic Computing Program will yield a substantial return on invested resources in terms of increased national security and economic strength.

Appendices to
Strategic Computing

The following appendices conclude the October 1983 report by the Defense Advanced Research Projects Agency for the U.S. Congress.

A Note on collateral activities

Within the United States and abroad, there are current and planned technology programs that relate directly to the goals and activities of the Strategic Computing Program. They have been reviewed and a list and description of the activities compiled. Many relate to proprietary commercial activities and to classified military programs. Access to these data will be available to those with proper clearances and need to know. [This version of the Darpa report contains no further information on collateral activities—Ed.]

Charts on pages 168–187 prepared by Rosart Communications Design.

Appendix I Military applications plans: autonomous land vehicle

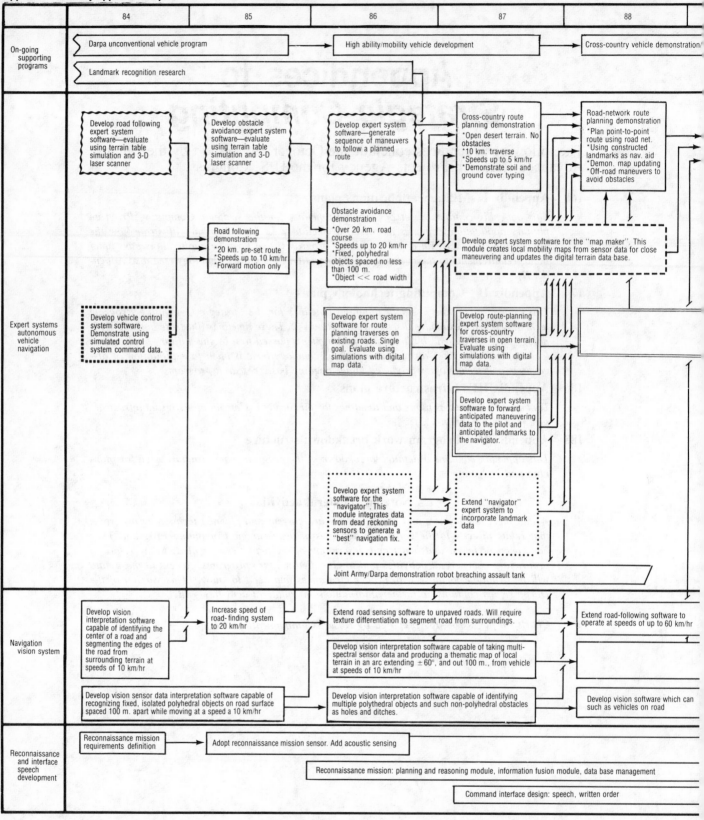

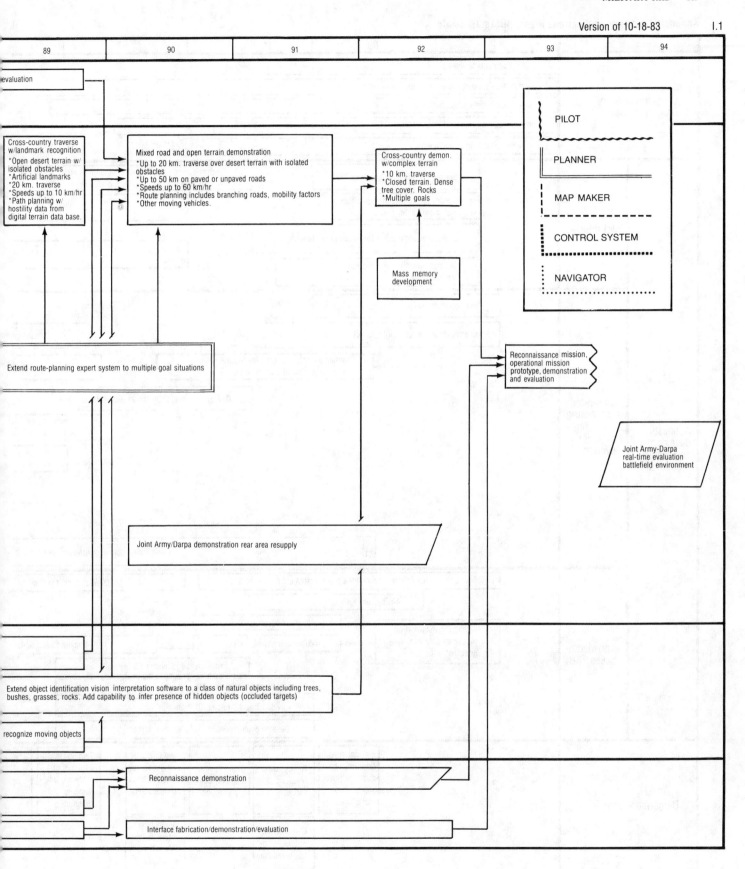

| | 89 | 90 | 91 | 92 | 93 | 94 |

evaluation

Cross-country traverse w/landmark recognition
*Open desert terrain w/ isolated obstacles
*Artificial landmarks
*20 km. traverse
*Speeds up to 10 km/hr
*Path planning w/ hostility data from digital terrain data base.

Mixed road and open terrain demonstration
*Up to 20 km. traverse over desert terrain with isolated obstacles
*Up to 50 km on paved or unpaved roads
*Speeds up to 60 km/hr
*Route planning includes branching roads, mobility factors
*Other moving vehicles.

Cross-country demon. w/complex terrain
*10 km. traverse
*Closed terrain. Dense tree cover. Rocks
*Multiple goals

Mass memory development

PILOT

PLANNER

MAP MAKER

CONTROL SYSTEM

NAVIGATOR

Extend route-planning expert system to multiple goal situations

Reconnaissance mission, operational mission prototype, demonstration and evaluation

Joint Army-Darpa real-time evaluation battlefield environment

Joint Army/Darpa demonstration rear area resupply

Extend object identification vision interpretation software to a class of natural objects including trees, bushes, grasses, rocks. Add capability to infer presence of hidden objects (occluded targets)

recognize moving objects

Reconnaissance demonstration

Interface fabrication/demonstration/evaluation

Appendix I Military applications plans: pilot's associate

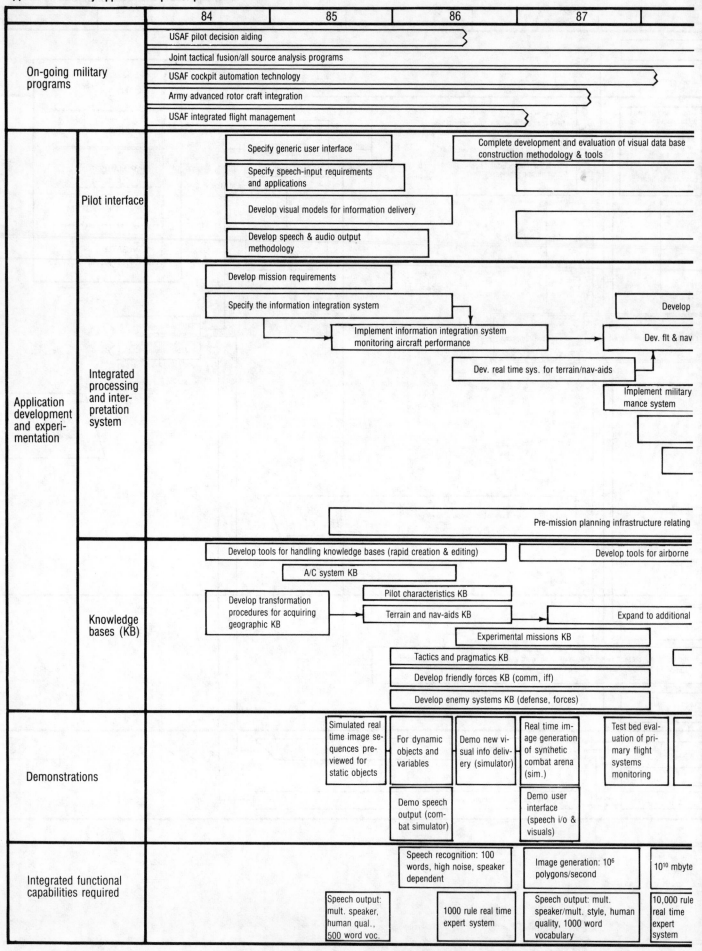

		84	85	86	87	
On-going military programs		USAF pilot decision aiding				
		Joint tactical fusion/all source analysis programs				
		USAF cockpit automation technology				
		Army advanced rotor craft integration				
		USAF integrated flight management				
Application development and experimentation	**Pilot interface**		Specify generic user interface		Complete development and evaluation of visual data base construction methodology & tools	
			Specify speech-input requirements and applications			
			Develop visual models for information delivery			
			Develop speech & audio output methodology			
	Integrated processing and interpretation system		Develop mission requirements			Develop
			Specify the information integration system			Dev. flt & nav
				Implement information integration system monitoring aircraft performance		
				Dev. real time sys. for terrain/nav-aids		
					Implement military mance system	
				Pre-mission planning infrastructure relating		
	Knowledge bases (KB)		Develop tools for handling knowledge bases (rapid creation & editing)		Develop tools for airborne	
			A/C system KB			
			Develop transformation procedures for acquiring geographic KB	Pilot characteristics KB		
				Terrain and nav-aids KB		Expand to additional
				Experimental missions KB		
				Tactics and pragmatics KB		
				Develop friendly forces KB (comm, iff)		
				Develop enemy systems KB (defense, forces)		

Demonstrations

85		86		87	
Simulated real time image sequences previewed for static objects	For dynamic objects and variables	Demo new visual info delivery (simulator)	Real time image generation of synthetic combat arena (sim.)	Test bed evaluation of primary flight systems monitoring	
	Demo speech output (combat simulator)		Demo user interface (speech i/o & visuals)		

Integrated functional capabilities required

		Speech recognition: 100 words, high noise, speaker dependent	Image generation: 10^6 polygons/second	10^{10} mbyte	
	Speech output: mult. speaker, human qual., 500 word voc.	1000 rule real time expert system	Speech output: mult. speaker/mult. style, human quality, 1000 word vocabulary	10,000 rule real time expert system	

88	89	90	91	92	93

Integrate improved speech understanding systems

Integrate improved visual display, speech, and audio output systems

coordinated mission performance

monitor. sys.

Adapt. coord. mission exec.

Dev. mission execution sys.

mission perfor-

Adaptive mission execution system

Develop mission replanning system

Develop threat detection system (enemy comm., radar, ir, ecm, visual)

Develop threat avoidance system

Post-mission evaluation

ground planning to mission modules

modification and review of KB's

geographic areas as needed

Coordinated tactics KB

Test bed evaluation of terrain/ nav-aids	Test bed evaluation of mission performance system	Test bed evaluation of coordinated mission performance	Test bed evaluation of re-planning	Prepare full scale simulator demos for integration	Flight & nav monitoring	Mission execution	Adaptive mission execution	Adaptive coordinated mission execution
				Prepare non-fighter a/c for demos	Flight & nav monitoring	Mission execution	Adaptive mission execution	Adaptive coordinated mission execution
						Prepare fighter for demo & eval	Fighter airborne eval.	

flight storage

Animated displays: 10^8 polygons/second

Speech recognition: 200 words, speaker independent, high noise

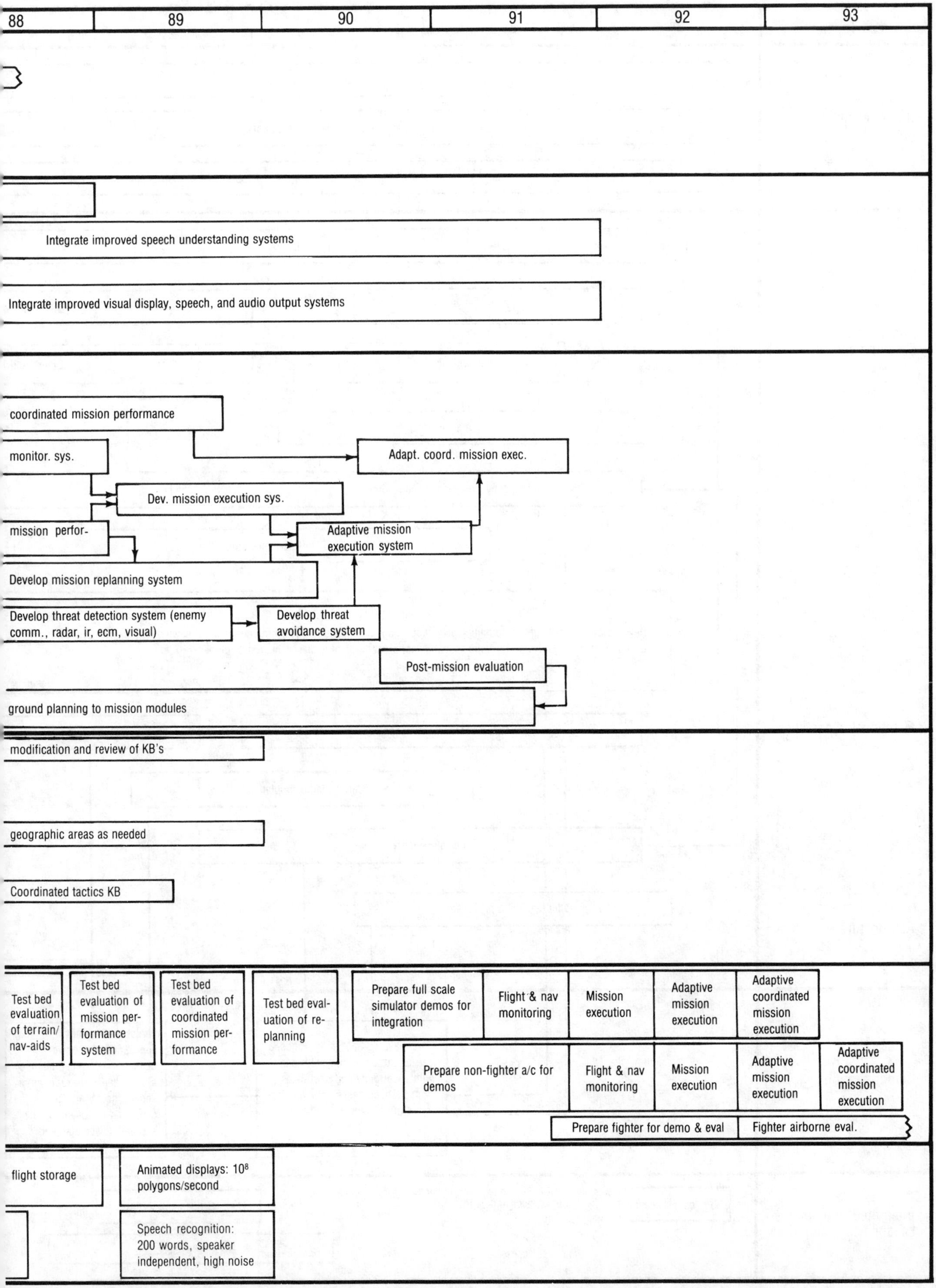

Appendix I Military applications plans: carrier battle group battle management system

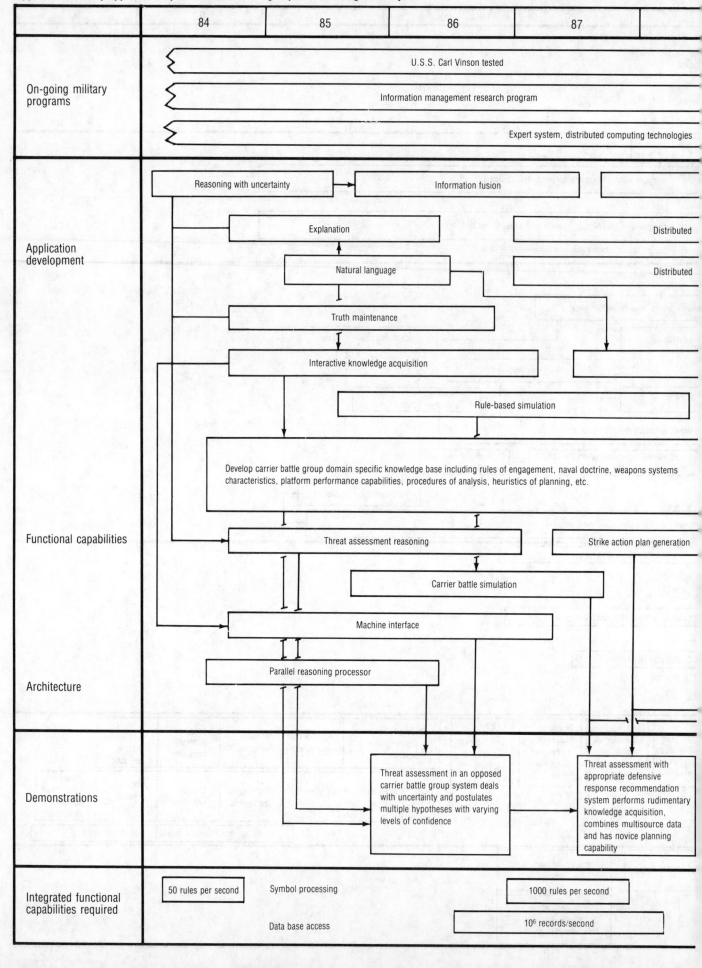

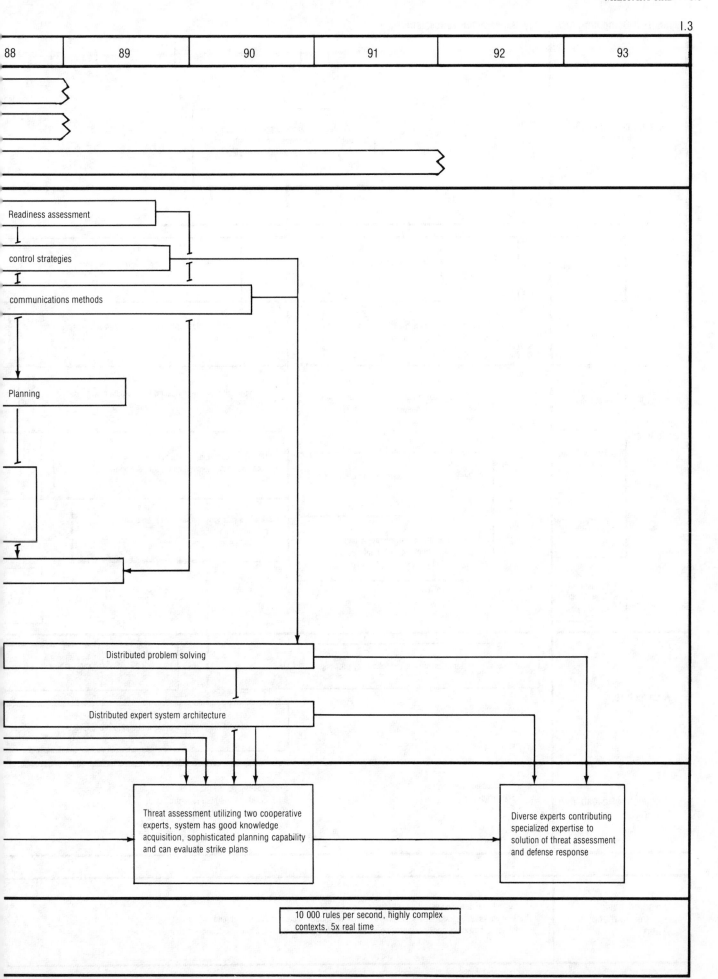

I.3

| 88 | 89 | 90 | 91 | 92 | 93 |

Readiness assessment

control strategies

communications methods

Planning

Distributed problem solving

Distributed expert system architecture

Threat assessment utilizing two cooperative experts, system has good knowledge acquisition, sophisticated planning capability and can evaluate strike plans

Diverse experts contributing specialized expertise to solution of threat assessment and defense response

10 000 rules per second, highly complex contexts, 5x real time

Appendix II Computing technology plans: vision subsystems

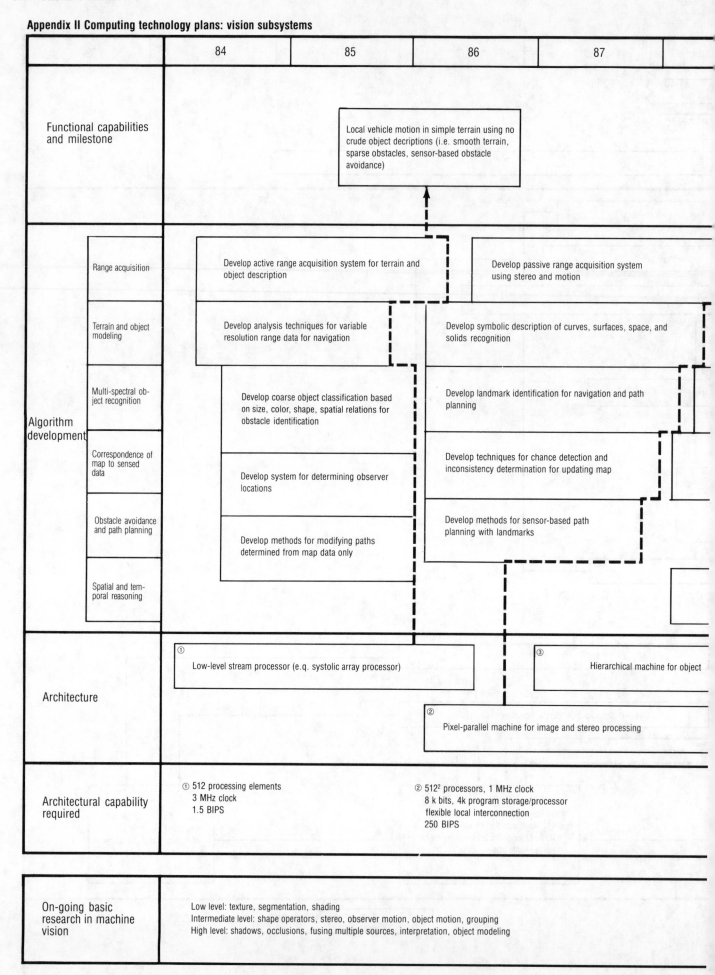

		84	85	86	87	
Functional capabilities and milestone			Local vehicle motion in simple terrain using no crude object decriptions (i.e. smooth terrain, sparse obstacles, sensor-based obstacle avoidance)			
Algorithm development	Range acquisition	Develop active range acquisition system for terrain and object description		Develop passive range acquisition system using stereo and motion		
	Terrain and object modeling	Develop analysis techniques for variable resolution range data for navigation		Develop symbolic description of curves, surfaces, space, and solids recognition		
	Multi-spectral object recognition		Develop coarse object classification based on size, color, shape, spatial relations for obstacle identification	Develop landmark identification for navigation and path planning		
	Correspondence of map to sensed data		Develop system for determining observer locations	Develop techniques for chance detection and inconsistency determination for updating map		
	Obstacle avoidance and path planning		Develop methods for modifying paths determined from map data only	Develop methods for sensor-based path planning with landmarks		
	Spatial and temporal reasoning					
Architecture		① Low-level stream processor (e.q. systolic array processor)		③ Hierarchical machine for object		
				② Pixel-parallel machine for image and stereo processing		
Architectural capability required		① 512 processing elements 3 MHz clock 1.5 BIPS	② 512² processors, 1 MHz clock 8 k bits, 4k program storage/processor flexible local interconnection 250 BIPS			
On-going basic research in machine vision		Low level: texture, segmentation, shading Intermediate level: shape operators, stereo, observer motion, object motion, grouping High level: shadows, occlusions, fusing multiple sources, interpretation, object modeling				

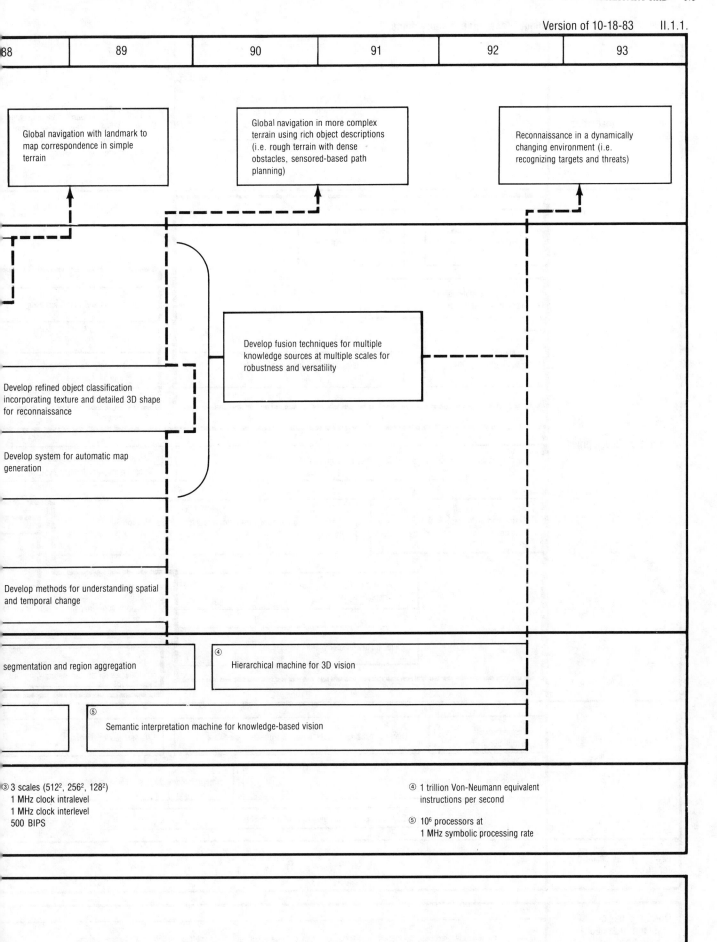

88	89	90	91	92	93

Global navigation with landmark to map correspondence in simple terrain

Global navigation in more complex terrain using rich object descriptions (i.e. rough terrain with dense obstacles, sensored-based path planning)

Reconnaissance in a dynamically changing environment (i.e. recognizing targets and threats)

Develop fusion techniques for multiple knowledge sources at multiple scales for robustness and versatility

Develop refined object classification incorporating texture and detailed 3D shape for reconnaissance

Develop system for automatic map generation

Develop methods for understanding spatial and temporal change

segmentation and region aggregation

④ Hierarchical machine for 3D vision

⑤ Semantic interpretation machine for knowledge-based vision

③ 3 scales (512^2, 256^2, 128^2)
1 MHz clock intralevel
1 MHz clock interlevel
500 BIPS

④ 1 trillion Von-Neumann equivalent instructions per second

⑤ 10^6 processors at
1 MHz symbolic processing rate

Appendix II Computing technology plans: speech subsystems

	84	85	86	87	
Functional capabilities and milestones			100 word, speaker dependent recognition, severe noise, moderate stress	1,000 word continuous speech recognition, speaker adaptive, intermediate grammar, low noise, low stress	
Algorithm development	Evaluate tactical speech environment and task	Develop speech generation capability			
	Develop noise reduction and microphone techniques			Devise noise-resistant, template	
	Develop algorithms to detect speech in noise	Develop template matching techniques for noisy speech		Develop template matching techniques for stress	
	Develop database and rules for acoustic-phonetic recognition			Develop and evaluate 1000 word continuous recognition system	
	Design knowledge representation schemes	Develop algorithms for speaker normalization and adaptation (i.e. learning)			
		Implement and evaluate alternative knowledge representation		Develop acoustic phonetic algorithms for fine phonetic distinctions	
		Develop parallel search algorithms		Develop syntax and task domain strategies for spoken natural language	
Architecture	Design cockpit recognition hardware	Develop real-time prototype from off-the-shelf hardware		Parallel search hardware*	
	Develop custom VLSI template matcher			Integrate compact speech system for cockpit	
		Develop VLSI speech input/output processor			
Architectural capability required	40 MIPS				
On-going basic research in speech recognition and generation	Multiple microphones, acoustic phonetics, speaker independence, large vocabularies, connected speech, text-to-speech conversion				

| 8 | 89 | 90 | 91 | 92 | 93 |

200 connected word recognition, speaker independent, restricted grammar, severe noise/moderate stress

10 000 word, continuous speech recognition, speaker-independent natural grammar, moderate noise, low stress

matching distance metrics

Develop search and control strategies for speaker-independent large vocabulary task

Develop and evaluate 10 000-word continuous recognition system

Develop automated technique for multi-task knowledge acquisition

Interface with natural language processing

Integrate VLSI hardware for large vocabulary continuous system

*Developed under architecture segment of program

500 MIPS   20 BIPS

Appendix II Computing technology plans: natural language subsystems

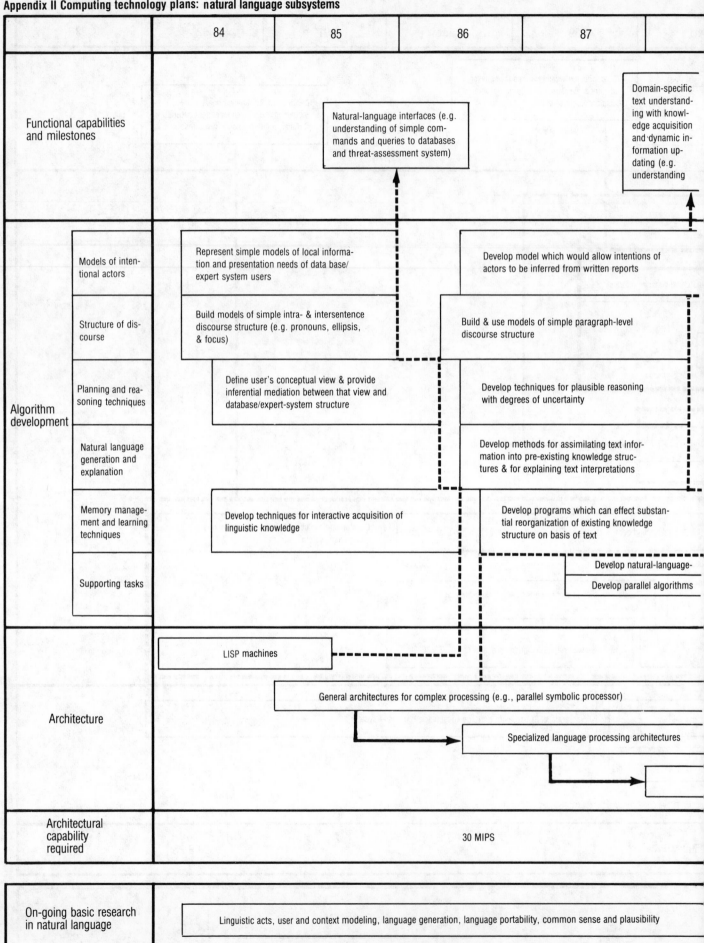

		84	85	86	87
Functional capabilities and milestones			Natural-language interfaces (e.g. understanding of simple commands and queries to databases and threat-assessment system)		Domain-specific text understanding with knowledge acquisition and dynamic information updating (e.g. understanding
Algorithm development	Models of intentional actors	Represent simple models of local information and presentation needs of data base/expert system users		Develop model which would allow intentions of actors to be inferred from written reports	
	Structure of discourse	Build models of simple intra- & intersentence discourse structure (e.g. pronouns, ellipsis, & focus)		Build & use models of simple paragraph-level discourse structure	
	Planning and reasoning techniques		Define user's conceptual view & provide inferential mediation between that view and database/expert-system structure	Develop techniques for plausible reasoning with degrees of uncertainty	
	Natural language generation and explanation			Develop methods for assimilating text information into pre-existing knowledge structures & for explaining text interpretations	
	Memory management and learning techniques		Develop techniques for interactive acquisition of linguistic knowledge	Develop programs which can effect substantial reorganization of existing knowledge structure on basis of text	
	Supporting tasks				Develop natural-language- / Develop parallel algorithms
Architecture		LISP machines	General architectures for complex processing (e.g., parallel symbolic processor)		Specialized language processing architectures
Architectural capability required				30 MIPS	
On-going basic research in natural language			Linguistic acts, user and context modeling, language generation, language portability, common sense and plausibility		

88	89	90	91	92	93

paragraph-
length descrip-
tions of intel-
ligence material
relating to air
threat with a
3000 word
vocabulary)

Interactive planning assistant
(can carry on conversation and
actively help user form a plan)

Interactive multi-user acquisition, analysis, and explanation
in a dynamic environment (e.g.
providing natural-language-
based planning support and
substantive understanding of
streams of textual information)

Build & use detailed domain-specific models of
user's goals & plans & of limitations of user's &
system's knowledge

Build & use models of cooperative & competitive planners

Model structure of complex conversation

Develop methods for handling ill-structured
discourse & errorful input

Develop techniques for reasoning under beliefs
contexts, planning communications actions, &
knowledge-based reasoning about user intent

Develop an intelligent knowledge-based plan
critic

Develop man-machine cooperative planning systems
with question-generating capabilities for obtaining
needed information from user

Develop programs for generating explanations involving new generalizations

Develop new techniques for content-based
information retrieval & the discovery of
generalizations based on meaning gleaned
from massive amounts of text

ased support for speech hypothesis testing

or planning, inference, & recognition

Compact specialized language processing hardware systems

300 MIPS

1 BIPS

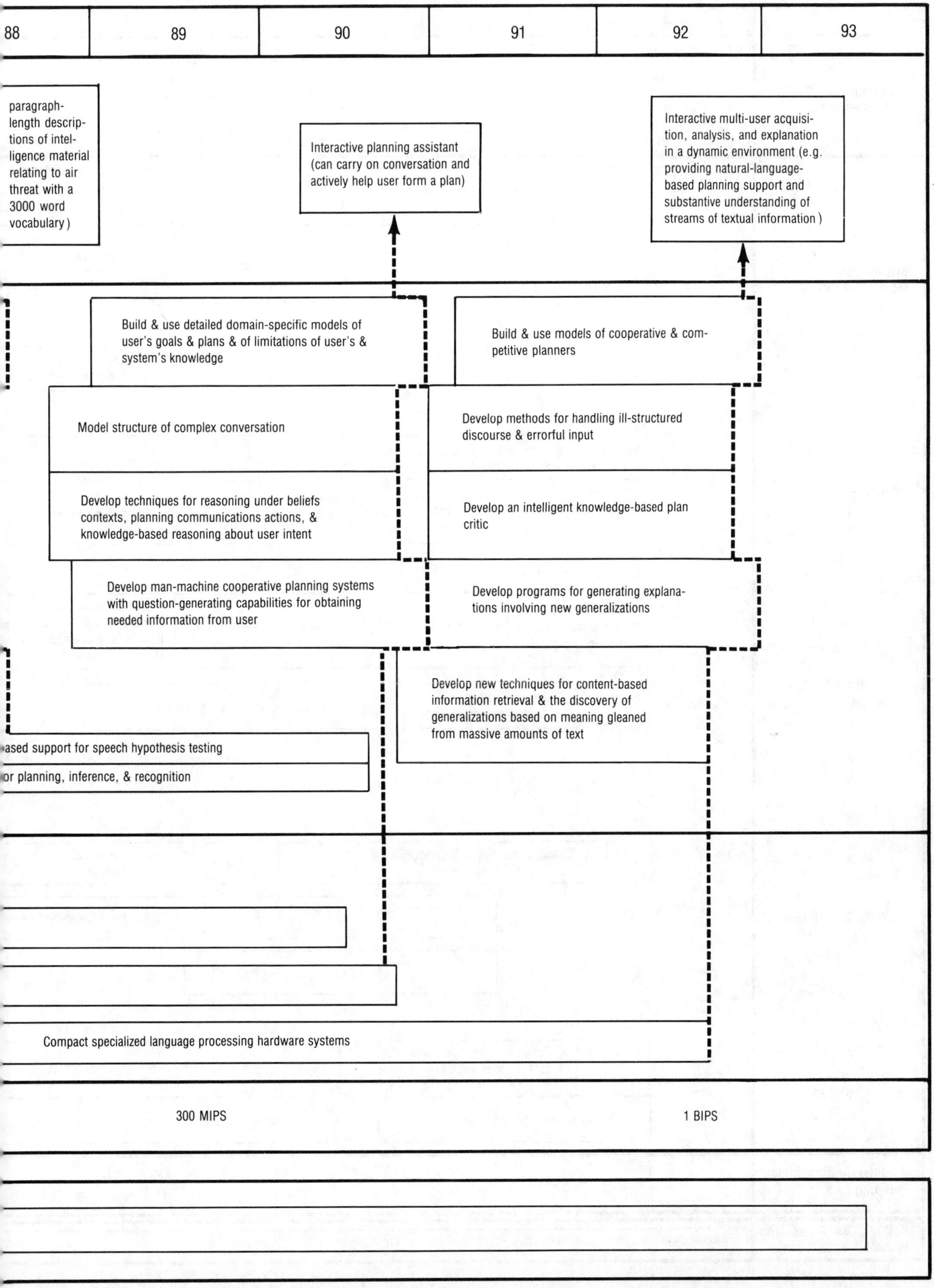

Appendix II Computing technology plans: expert systems technology

	84	85	86	87	
Functional capabilities and milestones				Situation assessment with confidence levels of conclusions, 3000 rules, 1000 RIPS,* ⅓–½x real time, modest context complexity	

*Rule inferences per second

Knowledge representation

Extend & evaluate knowledge representation strategies

Demonstrate advance

Add mechanisms to deal with causality

Add mechanisms to handl about processes

Add mechanisms to deal with multiple levels of description

Add mechanisms to handl and other expert systems

Inference

Implement strategies for problem dependent reasoning in an expert system

Demonstrate advanced inferencin

Implement techniques to deal with uncertain or missing knowledge or data

Develop symbolic simulation techniques for look-ahead

Explanation & presentation

Develop techniques for summarizing steps in reasoning process

Develop techniques for transforming signals into symbols

Develop advanced explanation techniques for discussing intermediate & final conclusions

Integrate natural language interface

Develop compact explanation and presentation aids

Integrate 1000 word speech understanding system

Knowledge acquisition

Develop techniques for knowledge base representation & refinement

Implement expert system for knowledge acquisition

Develop knowledge base browsing techniques

Develop system to identify and resolve

Develop system for maintaining knowledge bases

Support software

Design software tools and architectures for knowledge system development

Implement languages for inferencing

Implement expert system workstation

Develop knowledge description tools: objects, concepts,

Architectural capability required	10x LISP machine		Smart memory 100 MIPS	

On-going basic research in expert systems	Software engineering tools, control strategies, explanation, reasoning methods, representation and learning

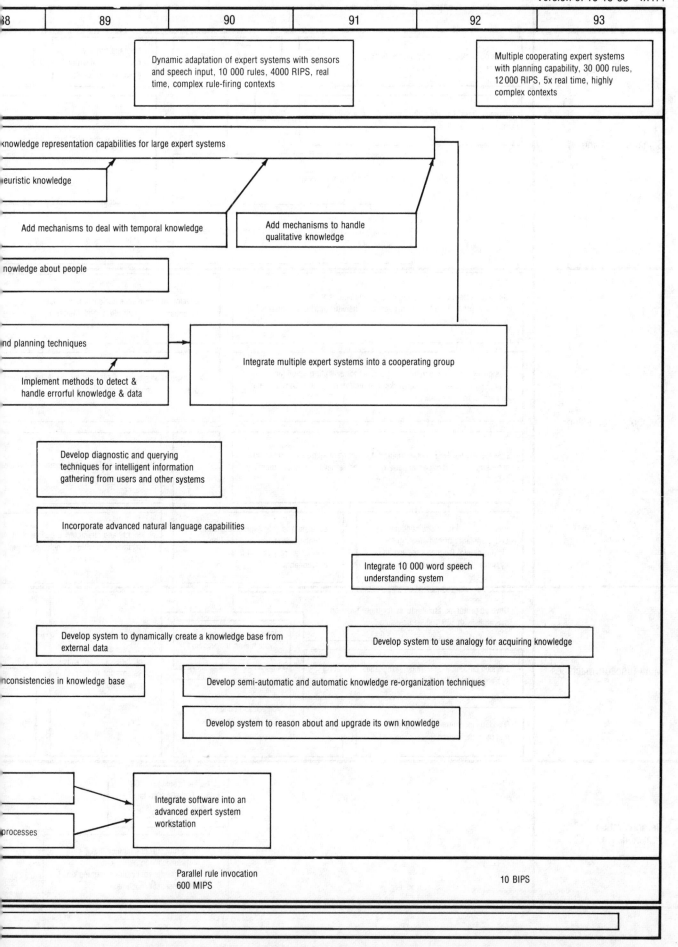

| 88 | 89 | 90 | 91 | 92 | 93 |

Dynamic adaptation of expert systems with sensors and speech input, 10 000 rules, 4000 RIPS, real time, complex rule-firing contexts

Multiple cooperating expert systems with planning capability, 30 000 rules, 12 000 RIPS, 5x real time, highly complex contexts

knowledge representation capabilities for large expert systems

euristic knowledge

Add mechanisms to deal with temporal knowledge

Add mechanisms to handle qualitative knowledge

nowledge about people

nd planning techniques

Implement methods to detect & handle errorful knowledge & data

Integrate multiple expert systems into a cooperating group

Develop diagnostic and querying techniques for intelligent information gathering from users and other systems

Incorporate advanced natural language capabilities

Integrate 10 000 word speech understanding system

Develop system to dynamically create a knowledge base from external data

Develop system to use analogy for acquiring knowledge

nconsistencies in knowledge base

Develop semi-automatic and automatic knowledge re-organization techniques

Develop system to reason about and upgrade its own knowledge

Integrate software into an advanced expert system workstation

processes

Parallel rule invocation
600 MIPS

10 BIPS

Appendix II Computing technology plans: machine hardware/software architecture

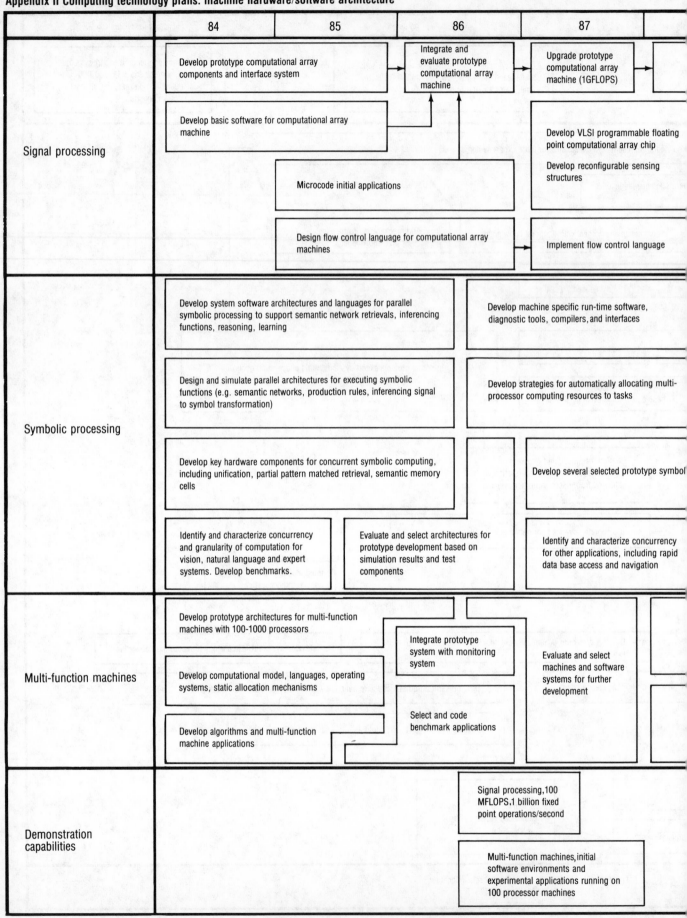

	84	85	86	87
Signal processing	Develop prototype computational array components and interface system		Integrate and evaluate prototype computational array machine	Upgrade prototype computational array machine (1GFLOPS)
	Develop basic software for computational array machine			Develop VLSI programmable floating point computational array chip Develop reconfigurable sensing structures
		Microcode initial applications		
		Design flow control language for computational array machines		Implement flow control language
Symbolic processing	Develop system software architectures and languages for parallel symbolic processing to support semantic network retrievals, inferencing functions, reasoning, learning			Develop machine specific run-time software, diagnostic tools, compilers, and interfaces
	Design and simulate parallel architectures for executing symbolic functions (e.g. semantic networks, production rules, inferencing signal to symbol transformation)			Develop strategies for automatically allocating multi-processor computing resources to tasks
	Develop key hardware components for concurrent symbolic computing, including unification, partial pattern matched retrieval, semantic memory cells			Develop several selected prototype symbol
	Identify and characterize concurrency and granularity of computation for vision, natural language and expert systems. Develop benchmarks.	Evaluate and select architectures for prototype development based on simulation results and test components		Identify and characterize concurrency for other applications, including rapid data base access and navigation
Multi-function machines	Develop prototype architectures for multi-function machines with 100-1000 processors			
	Develop computational model, languages, operating systems, static allocation mechanisms	Integrate prototype system with monitoring system		Evaluate and select machines and software systems for further development
	Develop algorithms and multi-function machine applications	Select and code benchmark applications		
Demonstration capabilities			Signal processing,100 MFLOPS,1 billion fixed point operations/second	
			Multi-function machines,initial software environments and experimental applications running on 100 processor machines	

88	89	90	91	92	93

Develop high performance computational array machine (compact, low power, reliable)

Develop system support tools for computational array machine applications

Integrate sensing technology with signal to symbol transducer

Upgrade architectures for high performance technologies, including packaging, manufacturing, and high speed processing

Build high performance computational array machines

Build high performance symbolic processors

Develop benchmark software for vision, natural language, and expert systems

Build high performance multi-function machines

processors using custom VLSI components

Design composite machine for selected military applications

Build composite machines, integrating signal processing, symbolic processing and multi-function components

Benchmark prototype machines

Develop software for composite machine

Develop enhanced architectures based on evaluation

Integrate program environment, alternate languages, and robust operating systems

Integrate dynamic allocation and recovery strategies

Signal processing, 1 GFLOPS

Signal processing, 1 trillion floating point operations/ second

Multi-function machines, advanced software environments and applications running on 1000 processor systems

Large scale applications running on 1000 processor machines

Appendix II Computing technology plans: supporting microelectronics technology

		84	85	86	87
Pilot lines		Gallium arsenide (GaAs)　　　D-MESFET			
			GaAs　　　Low power memory		
				GaAs　　　Gate array	
On-going basic research programs	Memory technology				High density memory
	High performance technology		Beam processing		
			1 GHz optical bus		
			Molecular beam epitaxy systems		

88	89	90	91	92	93

Heterostructure pilot line

Massive memory systems

Maskless fabrication system

Optical computing subsystem

8 GHz optical bus

Stripline and electro-optic packages

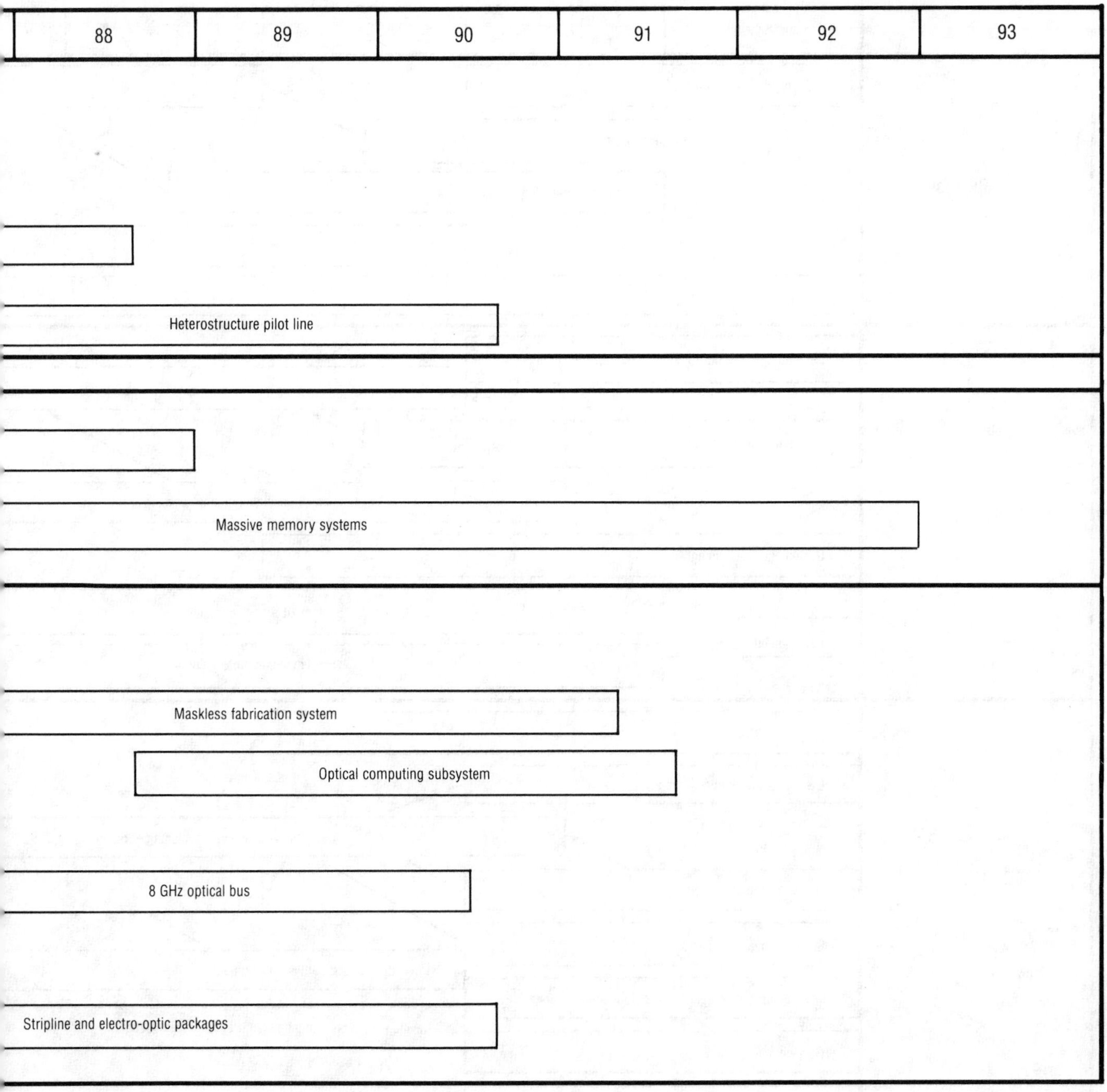

Appendix III Infrastructure plans

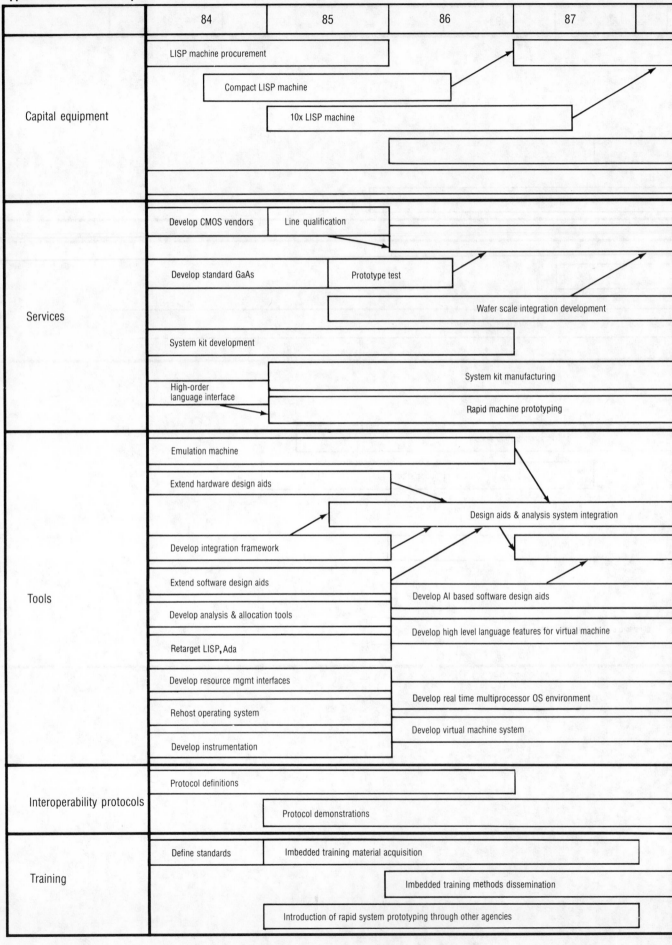

	84	85	86	87	
Capital equipment	LISP machine procurement				
		Compact LISP machine			
		10x LISP machine			
Services	Develop CMOS vendors	Line qualification			
	Develop standard GaAs	Prototype test			
			Wafer scale integration development		
	System kit development				
	High-order language interface	System kit manufacturing			
		Rapid machine prototyping			
Tools	Emulation machine				
	Extend hardware design aids				
	Develop integration framework	Design aids & analysis system integration			
	Extend software design aids				
	Develop analysis & allocation tools	Develop AI based software design aids			
	Retarget LISP, Ada	Develop high level language features for virtual machine			
	Develop resource mgmt interfaces				
	Rehost operating system	Develop real time multiprocessor OS environment			
	Develop instrumentation	Develop virtual machine system			
Interoperability protocols	Protocol definitions				
		Protocol demonstrations			
Training	Define standards	Imbedded training material acquisition			
			Imbedded training methods dissemination		
		Introduction of rapid system prototyping through other agencies			

88	89	90	91	92	93

Advanced LISP machine procurement

Research machines procurement

Network communications and support

IC implementation service

Tool dissemination & support

High level language interface to design associate

Automated resource allocation OS and DBMS

Appendix IV. Program work breakdown structure
1.0 Military applications

1.1 Autonomous vehicles
  1.1.1. Land vehicle
   1.1.1.1 Requirements analysis
   1.1.1.2 Demonstration system design
   1.1.1.3 System integration
   1.1.1.4 Functional test
   1.1.1.5 Furnished equipment
  1.1.2 Submarine vehicle
   1.1.2.1 Requirements analysis
   1.1.2.2 Demonstration system design
   1.1.2.3 System integration
   1.1.2.4 Functional test
   1.1.2.5 Furnished equipment
  1.1.3 Air vehicle
   1.1.3.1 Requirements analysis
   1.1.3.2 Demonstration system design
   1.1.3.3 System integration
   1.1.3.4 Functional test
   1.1.3.5 Furnished equipment
  1.1.4 Space vehicle
   1.1.4.1 Requirements analysis
   1.1.4.2 Demonstration system design
   1.1.4.3 System integration
   1.1.4.4 Functional test
   1.1.4.5 Furnished equipment

1.2 Operational associates
  1.2.1 Pilot's associate
   1.2.1.1 Requirements analysis
   1.2.1.2 Demonstration system design
   1.2.1.3 System integration
   1.2.1.4 Functional test
   1.2.1.5 Furnished equipment
  1.2.2 Tank crew's associate
   1.2.2.1 Requirements analysis
   1.2.2.2 Demonstration system design
   1.2.2.3 System integration
   1.2.2.4 Functional test
   1.2.2.5 Furnished equipment

1.3 Battle management
  1.3.1 Battalion battle management
   1.3.1.1 Requirements analysis
   1.3.1.2 Demonstration system design
   1.3.1.3 System integration
   1.3.1.4 Functional test
   1.3.1.5 Furnished equipment
  1.3.2 Fleet battle management
   1.3.2.1 Requirements analysis
   1.3.2.2 Demonstration system design
   1.3.2.3 System integration
   1.3.2.4 Functional test
   1.3.2.5 Furnished equipment
  1.3.3 Ballistic missile defense
   1.3.3.1 Requirements analysis
   1.3.3.2 Demonstration system design
   1.3.3.3 System integration
   1.3.3.4 Functional test
   1.3.3.5 Furnished Equipment
  1.3.4 Adaptive electronic warfare
   1.3.4.1 Requirements analysis
   1.3.4.2 Demonstration system design
   1.3.4.3 System integration
   1.3.4.4 Functional test
   1.3.4.5 Furnished equipment

2.0 Technology base

2.1 Integrated intelligent functions
2.1.1 Vision
2.1.1.1 General
2.1.1.2 Mission specific
2.1.1.2.1 Autonomous vehicle
2.1.2 Speech
2.1.2.1 General
2.1.2.2 Mission specific
2.1.2.2.1 Pilot's associate
2.1.3 Natural language
2.1.3.1 General
2.1.3.2 Mission specific
2.1.3.2.1 Battle management
2.1.4 Expert systems
2.1.4.1 General
2.1.4.2 Mission specific
2.1.4.2.1 Autonomous vehicle
2.1.4.2.2 Pilot's associate
2.1.4.2.3 Battle management
2.1.5 Application specific
2.1.5.1 Signal interpretation
2.1.5.2 Information fusion/machine learning
2.1.5.3 Planning and reasoning
2.1.5.4 Knowledge and data management
2.1.5.5 Simulation, modeling, and control
2.1.5.6 Navigation
2.1.5.7 Graphics display/image generation
2.1.5.8 Distributed communications

2.2 System architectures
2.2.1 Signal processors
2.2.1.1 General
2.2.1.1.1 Computational arrays
2.2.1.1.2 Reconfigurable sensing structures
2.2.1.2 Mission specific
2.2.2 Symbolic processors
2.2.2.1 General
2.2.2.1.1 Signal to symbol transducer
2.2.2.1.2 Semantic memory engine
2.2.2.1.3 Production rule machine
2.2.2.1.4 Fusion machine
2.2.2.1.5 Inference & control machine
2.2.2.1.6 Search machine
2.2.2.2 Mission specific
2.2.3 General purpose
2.2.3.1 General
2.2.3.1.1 Multi-microprocessor
2.2.3.1.2 Data flow machine
2.2.3.2 Mission specifics
2.2.4 Function specific
2.2.4.1 Data base machine
2.2.4.2 Simulation machine
2.2.4.3 Display machine

2.3 Microelectronics
2.3.1 GaAs D-MESFET pilot line
2.3.2 GaAs low-power memory pilot line
2.3.3 GaAs gate-array pilot line
2.3.4 Heterostructures pilot line

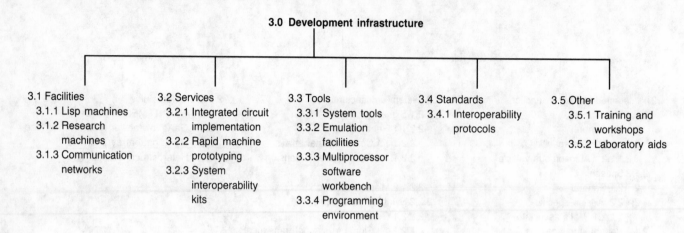

3.0 Development infrastructure

3.1 Facilities
  3.1.1 Lisp machines
  3.1.2 Research
     machines
  3.1.3 Communication
     networks

3.2 Services
  3.2.1 Integrated circuit
     implementation
  3.2.2 Rapid machine
     prototyping
  3.2.3 System
     interoperability
     kits

3.3 Tools
  3.3.1 System tools
  3.3.2 Emulation
     facilities
  3.3.3 Multiprocessor
     software
     workbench
  3.3.4 Programming
     environment

3.4 Standards
  3.4.1 Interoperability
     protocols

3.5 Other
  3.5.1 Training and
     workshops
  3.5.2 Laboratory aids

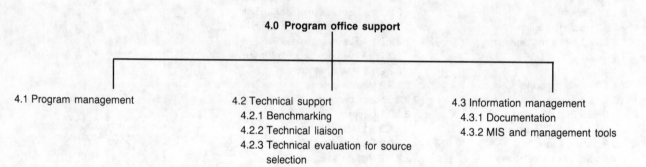

4.0 Program office support

4.1 Program management

4.2 Technical support
  4.2.1 Benchmarking
  4.2.2 Technical liaison
  4.2.3 Technical evaluation for source
     selection

4.3 Information management
  4.3.1 Documentation
  4.3.2 MIS and management tools

Part III

A TUTORIAL REVIEW

SPECTRUM S E R I E S

LIMITED BUT POWERFUL

Using a collection of facts, rules of thumb, and methods of applying those rules and making inferences, a new type of computer system is emerging

In most areas of artificial intelligence—that branch of computer science that attempts to have machines emulate intelligent behavior—programs fall far short of the competence of humans or even animals. Computer systems designed to see images, hear sounds, and recognize speech are still in fairly early stages of development. However, in one area of AI—that of reasoning from knowledge in a limited domain—computer programs can not only approach human performance, but in some cases they can exceed it.

These programs use a collection of facts, rules of thumb, and other knowledge about a given field, coupled with methods of applying those rules, to make inferences. They solve problems in such specialized fields as medical diagnosis, mineral exploration, and oil-well log interpretation. They differ substantially from conventional computer programs because their tasks have no algorithmic solutions and because often they must make conclusions based on incomplete or uncertain information.

In building such expert systems, researchers have found that amassing a large amount of knowledge, rather than sophisticated reasoning techniques, is responsible for most of the power of the system. Such high-performance expert systems, previously limited to academic research projects, are beginning to enter the software marketplace. AI programs are turning up for potential use in robots, medical diagnosis, an automatic crew-scheduling system for the U.S. Space Shuttle, and flight systems for F-16 military aircraft, among other places.

Constructing an expert system

Not all fields of knowledge are suitable at present for building expert systems. For a task to qualify for "knowledge engineering," these prerequisites must be met:
• There must be at least one human expert who is acknowledged to perform the task well.
• The primary sources of the expert's abilities must be special knowledge, judgment, and experience.
• The expert must be able to articulate that special knowledge, judgment, and experience and also explain the methods used to apply it to a particular task.
• The task must have a well-bounded domain of application.

Sometimes an expert system can be built that does not exactly match these prerequisites; for example, the abilities of several human experts, rather than one, might be brought to bear on a problem.

The structure of an expert system is modular: facts and other knowledge about a particular domain can be separated from the inference procedure—or control structure—for applying those

William B. Gevarter
National Aeronautics and Space Administration

facts, while another part of the system—the global data base—is the model of the "world" associated with a specific problem, its status, and its history.

It is desirable, though not yet common, to have a natural-language interface to facilitate the use of the system both during development and in the field. In some sophisticated systems, an explanation module is also included, allowing the user to challenge the system's conclusions and to examine the underlying reasoning process that led to them.

An expert system differs from more conventional computer programs in several important respects. In a conventional computer program, knowledge pertinent to the problem and methods for using this knowledge are intertwined, so it is difficult to change the program. In an expert system there is usually a clear separation of general knowledge about the problem (the knowledge base) from information about the current problem (the input data) and methods (the inference engine) for applying the general knowledge to the problem. With this separation the program can be changed by simple modification of the knowledge base. This is particularly true of rule-based systems, where the system can be changed by the simple addition or subtraction of rules in the knowledge base.

A need for production rules

The most popular approach to representing the domain knowledge (both facts and heuristics) needed for an expert system is by production rules (also referred to as SITUATION-ACTION rules or IF-THEN rules). A simple example of a production rule is: IF the power supply on the space shuttle fails, AND a backup power supply is available, AND the reason for the first failure no longer exists, THEN switch to the backup power supply.

Rule-based systems work by applying rules, noting the result, and applying new rules based on the changed situation. They can also work by directed logical inference, either starting with the initial evidence in a situation and working toward a solution, or starting with hypotheses about possible solutions and working backward to find existing evidence—or a deduction from existing evidence—that supports a particular hypothesis.

Not all expert systems are rule-based. Rule-based systems are particularly attractive when much of the expert knowledge in the field comes from empirical associations acquired as a result of experience. Where more causal information is available, then other representations may be more pertinent, such as networks that link state nodes (representing parts of the physical system in question) by arcs representing causal relations. Such networks allow systems to operate on a model of the situation in question. Caduceus and Prospector [see Table I] are examples of network-based expert systems.

A first step in building an expert system is to choose a problem-solving paradigm to organize and control the steps taken to solve the problem. One common approach involves the chaining of IF-THEN rules to form a line of reasoning. The rules are actuated by patterns in the global data base; depending on whether the strategy is working forward toward a solution or backward from a hypothesis, the patterns match either the IF or the THEN side of the rules.

The rule interpreter uses a control structure, sometimes encoded in terms of "metarules," to find the enabled rule and to decide which rule to apply. The basic control strategies used may be top-down (goal-driven), bottom-up (data-driven), or a combination of the two. The combination uses a relaxationlike convergence process to join the top-down and bottom-up lines of reasoning at some intermediate point, which yields the solution. Data-driven approaches sometimes have the disadvantage of generating many hypotheses not directly related to the problem under consideration, while goal-driven approaches have the disadvantage of perhaps becoming fixed on an initial set of hypotheses and having difficulty shifting focus when the data available do not support them.

One of the earliest and most often applied expert systems is Dendral. It was devised in the late 1960s by Edward A. Feigenbaum and Joshua Lederberg at Stanford University (Palo Alto, Calif.) to generate plausible structural representations of organic molecules from mass spectrogram data. The approach called for:

1. Deriving constraints from the data.
2. Generating candidate structures.
3. Predicting mass spectrographs for candidates.
4. Comparing the results with data.

This rule-based system, chaining forward from the data, illustrates the very common AI problem-solving approach of "plan, generate, and test." Dendral has been used as a consultant by organic chemists for more than 15 years and has been cited in numerous articles. It is currently recognized as an expert in mass-spectral analysis.

One of the best-known expert systems is Mycin, designed by Edward Shortliffe at Stanford University in the mid-1970s. It is an interactive system that diagnoses bacterial infections and recommends antibiotic therapy. Mycin represents expert judg-

A hypothetical expert system for space-shuttle flight operations

A simple example of an event-driven expert system using production rules can be visualized for the task of monitoring the status of a space shuttle. If, for example, a power supply—whose status is recorded in the global data base—is observed to be outside its operating limits, the following sequence takes place: "strategy" metarules—rules used to make decisions about how rules or other knowledge should be applied—select from the tens of thousands of rules in the knowledge base those having to do with power and power supplies. Similarly, "focusing" metarules select from the global data base those facts having to do with power-supply

status and the use of power by various devices aboard the shuttle.

The rules thus selected are compared with this relevant portion of the data base to determine which of them may be applicable to the current situation. "Scheduling" metarules, which deal with priorities of various actions, then select from the applicable rules the most appropriate one, such as switching in a backup power supply or turning off less important experiments. Execution of the selected rule changes the global data base that records systems status, and the cycle repeats.
—W.B.G.

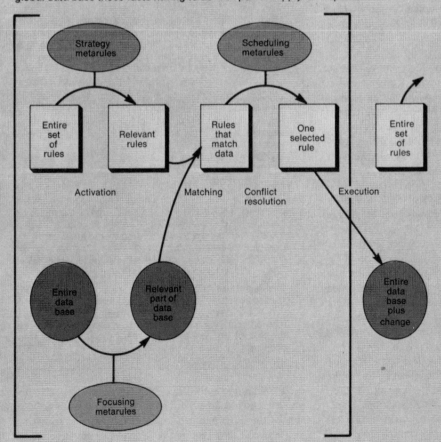

An idealized event-driven control scheme for an expert system works by using metarules—rules about what kinds of knowledge are important in a given situation—to focus its attention on a given situation, find the correct method of dealing with that situation, and then perform an action. Once the action is performed, the system repeats the process with the updated situation.

mental reasoning as condition-conclusions rules, linking patient data to infection hypotheses, and at the same time provides the expert's "certainty" estimate for each rule. It chains backwards from hypothesized diagnoses, using rules to estimate the certainty factors of conclusions based on the certainty factors of their antecedents, to see if the evidence supports a diagnosis. If there is not enough information to narrow the hypotheses, it asks the physician for additional data, exhaustively evaluating all hypotheses. When it has finished, Mycin matches treatments to all diagnoses that have high certainty values.

Another rule-based system, R1, has been very successful in configuring VAX computer systems from a customer's order of various standard and optional components [see "The stages in building an expert system," right]. The initial version of R1 was developed by John McDermott in 1979 at Carnegie-Mellon University in Pittsburgh, Pa., for the Digital Equipment Corp. in Maynard, Mass. Because the configuration problem can be solved without backtracking and without undoing previous steps, the system's approach is to break the problem up into the following subtasks and do each of them in order:

1. Correct mistakes in the order.
2. Put components into CPU cabinets.
3. Put boxes in Unibus cabinets and put components in boxes.
4. Put panels in Unibus cabinets.
5. Lay out system floor plan.
6. Do the cabling.

At each point in the configuration development, several rules for what to do next are usually applicable. Of the applicable rules, R1 selects the rule having the most IF clauses for its applicability, on the assumption that that rule is more specialized for the current situation. (R1 is written in OPS 5, a special language for executing production rules.) The system now has about 1200 rules for VAXs, together with information about some 1000 VAX components. The total system has about 2500 rules and knowledge about PDP-11 as well as VAX components.

Architecture of expert systems

One way to classify expert systems is by function—diagnosis, planning, and so on. However, examination of existing expert systems indicates that there is little commonality in the detailed system architectures that can be detected from this classification.

Rather than looking at particular functions, one can look at the complexity level and structure of the problems different expert systems are called on to deal with and try to see what kinds of control structures are best for different kinds of problems. All the approaches used to guide reasoning by expert systems are intended to reduce the amount of time spent looking for solutions among all the potential answers to a given problem; exhaustive computational searches are not appropriate because, even with a small number of different factors to consider, possibilities expand rapidly—the so-called combinatorial explosion. One method artificial-intelligence researchers use to visualize the combinatorial explosion is that of a "search space" in which solutions must be found. Each new variable that an expert system must consider adds another dimension to the search space, and each additional level of detail increases the extent of existing dimensions of the search space.

The two major categories of approaches used are: (1) finding ways to search among possible solutions in a search space most efficiently, and (2) finding ways to narrow the search to smaller, more manageable areas of the set of all possible solutions. Hardware and specially tuned algorithms can be helpful in the first approach, but the second requires advanced control structures. Because of the way combinatorial problems expand, one very

The stages in building an expert system

There are several phases to building an expert system: (1) the prototype stage, which determines if an idea is feasible; (2) development, in which the system is tested and upgraded as exceptions to its knowledge arise; (3) production, in which the system is used, although additions and corrections to the knowledge base are continually made; and (4) extension, to handle related problems. One good example of this path is R1, the expert system used by the Digital Equipment Corp. in Maynard, Mass. to configure its VAX-11 minicomputers.

R1's prototype, developed at Carnegie-Mellon University (Pittsburgh, Pa.), consisted of about 200 rules for configuring VAXs. The rules were gathered from the company's technical manuals and conversations with expert configurers. The prototype system could correctly configure slightly more than half of the sample cases given to it.

R1 was then expanded into a usable system through continued discussions with experts and more testing on sample configurations. Each time the machine made a mistake in configuration, the experts were asked what had made the existing rules inapplicable; a new rule, or sometimes a change in an old rule, was then added to the knowledge base.

When R1 correctly configured about 90 percent of its cases, it was placed in parallel with the existing DEC configuration procedure, and eventually it replaced it. Many additional rules had to be added as the program faced the plethora of real-world configuration problems. Now R1 has about 2500 rules including rules for PDP-11 computers, and its knowledge base has also been expanded to cover non-VAX computers. —*W.B.G.*

Interacting with Mycin

Mycin, an expert system for medical diagnosis, works on the assumption that a possible disease exists for the case at hand and then tries to find evidence that supports or contradicts its hypothesis. It gathers this evidence from the physician working on a case, starting with the initial choice of a possible disease. An example of dialogue follows:

Mycin: What is the infection?
Physician: Endarteritis [This is an inflammation of the inner layer of an artery and can be caused by a number of agents.]
Mycin: Is organism-1 a rod or a coccus? [This question will narrow the range of possible agents for the disease.]
Physician: Rod.

Mycin then asks additional questions about laboratory test results to help determine what organisms might be causing the disease. When it has reached its conclusions, it will recommend a particular drug therapy to combat the organism or organisms involved. So that the physician will trust Mycin's conclusions, the program is designed to answers questions about its reasoning. For example:

Physician: How did you decide that organsim-1 is E. Coli?
Mycin: I used rule 084 to conclude that organism-1 is E. Coli. This gave a cumulative certainty factor of 0.51. [The physician can question further, either by looking at the text of the rule involved, or by questioning its antecedents.] —*W.B.G.*

useful technique is to break up the problem into a number of smaller search spaces that can be tackled separately. Often the sum of the times required to search each smaller space is much less than the time required to search a single large space. Ultimately, however, because of the rate with which the set of possible solutions expands with combinatorial problems, advances in hardware are limited in the advantages they can give. Many AI researchers believe, for example, that so-called fifth-generation machines, intended to be built over the next decade and to be thousands or millions of times faster for AI than conventional computers, will not be able to deal with complex real-world problems requiring broad knowledge unless they contain advanced control structures to narrow their search spaces, as well as raw logic-processing power to sift through potential solutions.

Expert system limitations

Bruce Buchanan of Stanford University's Heuristic Programming Project and Randy Davis of the Massachusetts Institute of Technology's Artificial Intelligence Laboratory in Cambridge, among others, have pointed out limitations on current expert systems. Among them are:

• Narrow domain of expertise. Because building and maintaining a large knowledge base is difficult, only a few expert systems cover a significant range of knowledge. A notable exception is Internist [see "Internist-1: broad but shallow," p. 197], which can deal with symptoms and diagnoses of some 500 diseases. However, it achieves its broad coverage by a fairly shallow representation of associations between disease and symptoms.

• Limited knowledge-representation language for facts and relations. Certain kinds of knowledge, particularly those without immediate IF-THEN consequences, can be quite difficult to represent efficiently in current knowledge-representation languages.

• Relatively stylized languages for input and output. Users must describe problems in a strictly defined formal language.

• Stylized and limited explanations of the reasons behind a system's decisions or conclusions.

• Laborious construction. At present, a "knowledge engineer" must extract knowledge from a human expert and laboriously build it into the knowledge base. In some cases, knowledge-acquisition systems have been built for existing expert systems so that human experts could add to the knowledge base directly; one example is Teiresias, built by Dr. Davis while he was at Stanford to extend the knowledge base of Mycin.

• Need for a single expert as "knowledge czar." Expert-systems developers are currently limited in their ability to maintain consistency and resolve conflicts between overlapping items in the knowledge base. Thus, though several experts may contribute to a project, one must maintain absolute control to ensure the quality of the knowledge base.

• Fragile behavior. Most systems do not deal well with problems at the boundaries of their knowledge. Furthermore, they general-

Existing expert systems

Function	Domain	System	Institution
Diagnosis	Medicine	PIP	Massachusetts Institute of Technology (MIT)
	Medicine	Casnet	Rutgers University
	Medicine	Internist/Caduceus	University of Pittsburgh
	Medicine	Mycin	Stanford University
	Medicine	Puff	Stanford University
	Computer faults	DART	Stanford University
	Medicine	MDX	Ohio State University
	Computer faults	IDT	Digital Equipment Corp. (DEC)
	Nuclear Reactor Accidents	Reactor	EG&G Idaho
Data analysis	Geology	Dipmeter Advisor	MIT/Schlumberger-Doll Research Center (SDRC)
	Chemistry	Dendral	Stanford University
	Chemistry	GA1	Stanford University
	Geology	Prospector	SRI International Inc.
	Protein crystallography	Crysalis	Stanford University
	Determination of causal relationships in medicine	RX	Stanford University
	Determination of casual relationships in medicine	Abel	MIT
	Oil-well logs	ELAS	Amoco Corp.
Analysis	Electrical circuits	EL	MIT
	Mechanics problems	Mecho	Edinburgh University
	Naval task force threat analysis	TECH	Rand Corp. and Naval Ocean Systems Center
	Earthquake damage assessment for structures	Speril	Purdue University
	Digital circuits	Critter	Rutgers University
Design	Computer system configuration	XCON/R1	Carnegie-Mellon University and DEC
	Circuit synthesis	SYN	MIT
	Chemical synthesis	Synchem	State University of New York, Stony Brook
Planning	Chemical Synthesis	Sechs	University of California at Santa Cruz
	Robotics	NOAH	SRI
	Robotics	Abstrips	SRI
	Planetary flybys	Deviser	Jet Propulsion Laboratory
	Errant planning	OP-Planner	Rand
	Molecular genetics	Molgen	Stanford University
	Mission planning	Knobs	Mitre Corp.
	Job shop scheduling	ISIS-II	CMU
	Design of molecular genetics experiments	SPEX	Stanford University
	Medical diagnosis	Hodgkins	MIT
Learn from experience	Chemistry	Metadendral	Stanford University
	Heuristics	Eurisko	Stanford University
Concept-formation	Mathematics	AM	CMU
Monitoring	Patient respiration	VM	Stanford University

ly do not have the knowledge built into them to determine when a given problem is beyond their capacity or outside their field. As a result, even some of the best systems come up with verifiably wrong answers for problems just outside the borders of their domain. And even within a domain, systems can sometimes be misled by complex or unusual cases.

• Need for a knowledge engineer to operate the system. Often, only the builders of a system or others with comparable detailed knowledge can successfully operate an AI system, properly framing questions for a given problem and extracting appropriate—that is, plausible—solutions. Most system developers have not constructed friendly interfaces for their programs.

Nevertheless, even with these limitations, there have been some notable successes. A workable methodology has been developed for representing formal knowledge. And five systems using such methodologies for representing and using empirical associations have been routinely solving difficult real-world problems: Dendral, Macsyma, Molgen, R1, and Puff. The first three all have serious users who have only minimal contact with the original system designers. Macsyma is in fact available commercially from Symbolics Inc., of Cambridge, Mass., a company that manufactures computers optimized for running the artificial-intelligence language LISP. (Some do not consider Macsyma an expert system because it uses algorithms to transform equations; however, it does use mathematical knowledge and heuristics in deciding what transformation algorithms to apply.) Dendral, which analyzes chemical instrument data to determine the underlying molecular structure, is the oldest of these expert systems and has been the most widely used. R1, which is used internally at Digital Equipment Corp. to configure VAX computers, has been reported to be saving DEC millions of dollars a year and is now being followed up with XSEL, a program that ensures orders are correct before they are filed. Dozens of other systems have been constructed and experiments are being conducted with them [see table].

A wide-open future

Many expert systems are also under development. Their application areas include medical diagnosis and prescription, medical-knowledge automation, chemical-data interpretation, chemical and biological synthesis, mineral and oil exploration, planning and scheduling, signal interpretation, military threat assessment, tactical targeting, space defense, air-traffic control, circuit analysis, VLSI design, equipment fault diagnosis, computer-configuration selection, speech understanding, computer-aided instruction, knowledge-base access and management, and

Existing expert systems (continued)

Function	Domain	System	Institution
Use advice	Structural analysis computer program	Sacon	Stanford University
Computer-aided instruction	Electronic trouble-shooting	Sophie	Bolt, Beranek & Newman (BBN)
	Medical diagnosis	Guidon	Stanford University
	Mathematics	Excheck	Stanford University
	Steam propulsion plant operation	Steamer	BBN
	Diagnostic skills	Buggy	BBN
	Causes of rainfall	Why	BBN
	Coaching of a game	West	BBN
	Coaching of a game	Wumpus	MIT
	Coaching of a game	Scholar	BBN
Knowledge acquisition	Medical diagnosis	Teiresias	Stanford University
	Geology	KAS	SRI
Expert system construction		Rosie	Rand
		AGE	Stanford University
		Hearsay III	University of Southern California Information Sciences Institute (USC-ISI)
		Emycin	Stanford University
		OPS 5	CMU
		Rainbow	IBM
	Medical diagnosis	KMS	University of Maryland
	Medical consultation	Expert	Rutgers University
	Electronic systems diagnosis	ARBY	Yale University/ITT
	Medical consultation using time-oriented data	MECS-AI	Tokyo University
Intelligent assistant	Battlefield weapons assignments	Battle	U.S. Navy Center for applied research in artificial intelligence
	Medicine	Digitalis Therapy Advisor	MIT
	Radiology	Raydex	Rutgers University
	Computer sales	XSEL	CMU/DEC
	Medical treatment	Oncocin	Stanford University
	Nuclear power plant configuration	CSA	Georgia Tech
	Diagnostic prompting in medicine	Reconsider	University of California at San Francisco
Management	Automated factory	IMS	CMU
	Project management	Callisto	DEC
Automatic programming	Modeling of oil-well logs	Phoenix	SDRC
		CHI	Kestrel Institute
		Pecos	Stanford University
		Libra	Stanford University
		SAFE	USC-ISI
		Dedalus	SRI
		Programmer's Apprentice	MIT
Image understanding		Visions	University of Massachusetts, Amherst
		Acronym	Stanford University

Internist-1: broad but shallow

Researchers at the University of Pittsburgh, Pa., have spent 15 person-years developing Internist-1, an experimental computer-based diagnostic consultant for general internal medicine. The program, based on the expertise of internal-medicine specialist Jack Myers, can deal with about 500 diseases, and it is also able to diagnose multiple simultaneous diseases, in contrast with systems that attempt to ascribe all symptoms to a single ailment. It thus covers about three quarters of major known diseases.

For each disease, the program develops a profile by listing symptoms and their associated evoking strength, a measure of how specific each symptom is to a certain disease. It also notes the frequency of each symptom—how often the symptom will actually appear in patients who have the associated disease. The data base is then inverted, so that for given symptoms the associated diseases are indicated.

To use Internist-1, a physician enters patient data [see illustration], and, as each manifestation is entered, the program retrieves the diseases associated with it. Each disease hypothesis is scored, based on the evoking-strength and frequencies associated with the evidence from the manifestations entered. The resulting disease hypotheses are ranked by score, and Internist-1 then partitions the top hypotheses into groups of competitors. (Two diseases are considered competitors if, taken together, they explain no more of the manifestations than either alone.) Internist-1 then seeks more data from the physician to assist in selecting one hypothesis from the diseases in the various competing groups.

When a diagnosis is chosen from the group, all observed manifestations explained by that diagnosis are removed from further consideration. The program then recycles to try to explain the remaining manifestations.

Thorough trials indicate that Internist-1 is about as good at diagnosis as the average clinician; nevertheless, it has major deficiencies. These include:
• Inability to attribute findings to their proper cause.
• Inability to synthesize a general overview in a complicated multisystem problem.
• Inability to recognize subcomponents of an illness.
• Shallow explanation capability.
• Inadequate representation of causality.
• Exhaustive listing of disease profiles in terms of manifestations, rather than in terms of intermediate states.
• Inability to allow for interdependency of manifestations.
• Inability to reason anatomically or temporally.
• Inability to recognize severity.

As a result, new programming approaches have been developed for complex reasoning processes, so that Caduceus, the successor to Internist-1, can synthesize a broad overview of a patient's condition incorporating evidence from causal relationships. Caduceus reasons by means of a model of the human body and its workings; thus, it can make inferences based on interdependencies of different organs. It also incorporates time-based reasoning abilities, so that it can draw inferences from data about the progression of disease symptoms as well as from non-chronological lists. It also has refined control structures that allow it to deal with symptoms that may be due to a number of different underlying diseases.

This move from purely empirical associations toward a system based on a model of functional relationships in the problem under consideration is typical of the current evolution of expert systems. System builders have found that explicit representation of such knowledge can improve the abilities of an expert system and also allow its empirical knowledge to be used for other purposes, such as teaching. —W.B.G.

Internist-1: Enter case name
[The physician enters the case name.]

Internist-1: Initial positive manifestations

Physician: + Age gtr than 55
+ Arthritis HX
+ Depression HX
+ Sex female
+ Chest pain lateral sharp
+ Liver enlarged moderate
+ Feces guiaiac test positive
. . .

Internist-1: Initial negative findings

Physician: −Alcoholism chronic HX
−Diarrhea chronic
−Fever
−Uric acid blood increased
. . .

Internist-1: Disregarding: Depression HX, weight increase recent HX, chest pain lateral exacerbation with breathing, chest pain lateral sharp.
. . .
Considering: Age gtr than 55, sex female, urine dark HX, anorexia, feces light colored, jaundice, liver enlarged moderate.
. . .
[Focus of Internist-1's attention is on the problem area formed by the competing top scoring disease hypotheses and their associated manifestations.]

Internist-1: Please enter findings of lipid(s) blood
[Seeking additional generic information to assist in selecting among top hypothesis.]

Physician: Go
[Physician has no additional information to enter in response.]

Internist-1: Cholesterol blood decreased? [Asks the single specific item that prompted the generic question that the physician couldn't answer.]

Physician: N/A [not applicable]
...
[The interaction continues until Internist-1 reaches a diagnosis.]

Internist-1: Conclude: Hepatitis chronic active [Internist-1 now recycles to the next group of competing hypotheses and continues until all symptoms are explained.]

Internist-1, an expert system capable of dealing with more than 500 diseases, interacts with physicians by means of a specialized vocabulary. It focuses on possible disease symptoms, considering both manifestations that are present and those that are absent.

expert-system construction.

There appear to be few constraints on the ultimate use of expert systems. However, the nature of their design and construction is changing. The limitations of rule-based systems are becoming apparent: not all knowledge can be structured as empirical associations. Such associations tend to hide causal relationships, and they are also inappropriate for highlighting structure and function.

The newer expert systems are adding deep knowledge about causality and structure. These systems promise to be less fragile than current systems and may yield correct answers often enough to be considered for use in autonomous systems, not just as intelligent assistants.

Another change is the increasing trend toward non–rule-based systems. Such systems, using semantic networks, frames, and other knowledge-representation structures, are often better suited for causal modeling. By providing knowledge representations more appropriate to the specific problem, they also tend to simplify the reasoning required. Some new expert systems, using the "blackboard" approach, combine rule-based and non–rule-based portions, which cooperate to build solutions in an incremental fashion, with each segment of the program contributing its own particular expertise.

The growth of expert systems, coupled with increased computer capability and greater access to computers by the public, promises to give virtually everyone access to expertise. This will lead to profound changes in our society.

To probe further

An overview of the entire field of artificial intelligence is given by Avron Barr and Edward A. Feigenbaum in their three-volume *Handbook of Artificial Intelligence* (William Kaufman, Los Altos, Calif., 1982). Vol. 2 deals primarily with expert systems. Other sources for principles and issues in expert systems include "Expert Systems: Where are we now? And where do we go from here?" by Randy Davis of MIT, in *AI Magazine*, Vol. 3, no. 2, Spring 1982; "Expert Systems" by David Nau in *Computer*, Vol. 15, no. 2, February 1983; *Knowledge-Based Systems in Artificial Intelligence*, by Dr. Davis and Douglas Lenat of Stanford University's Heuristic Programming Project (McGraw-Hill, 1982); and "The Organization of Expert Systems: a tutorial," in *Artificial Intelligence*, Vol. 18, pp. 135–73 (1982), by Mark Stefik of Xerox Corp.'s Palo Alto (Calif.) Research Center, among other authors. Stanford University's Heuristic Programming Project issues reports on its work, which covers most areas of expert systems.

Detailed discussions of particular expert systems and their construction are also available. Examples are *Applications of Artificial Intelligence for Organic Chemistry: the Dendral Project*, by R.K. Lindsay, Bruce Buchanan, Dr. Feigenbaum, and A. Lederberg (McGraw-Hill, New York, 1980); "Internist-1, an Experimental Computer-Based Diagnostic Consultant for General Internal Medicine," by Miller, Pople, and Myers, published in *The New England Journal of Medicine* (Vol. 307, no. 8, Aug. 19, 1982, pp. 468–76); "R1, A rule-based Configurer of Computer Systems," by John McDermott, in *Artificial Intelligence*, Vol. 19, pp. 38–88, 1982. Information on other systems or on AI issues in general may be found in *AI Magazine, Artificial Intelligence*, or in the proceedings of various AI conferences. The most important are those of the American Association for Artificial Intelligence (AAAI) and the International Joint Conference on Artificial Intelligence (IJCAI). Information on ordering is available from the AAAI, 445 Burgess Drive, Menlo Park, Calif. 94025.

Mycin

If: 1) The infection which requires therapy is meningitis,

And 2) the patient has evidence of a serious skin or soft tissue infection,

And 3) Organisms were not seen on the strain of the culture,

And 4) The type of infection is bacterial,

Then: There is evidence that the organism (other than those seen on cultures or smears) which might be causing the infection is staphylococcus-coag-pos (.75) or streptococcus (.5).

A

R1

If: The most current active context is assigning a power supply,

And an SBI module of any type has been put in a cabinet,

And the position it occupies in the cabinet (its nexus) is known,

And there is space available in the cabinet for a power supply for that nexus,

And there is an available power supply,

Then: Put the power supply in the cabinet in the available space.

B

(A) Mycin assigns certainty factors between 0 and 1 to its rules by chaining back through the deductive process. Thus the certainty factors illustrated assume that all the antecedents to the rule are known with absolute certainty. If the certainty factors for a rule's antecedents are less than 1, then the certainty factor for the rule's conclusion will be reduced accordingly. (B) R1 operates by matching IF conditions to the current situation. If more than one rule applies, the program performs the action for the rule with the largest number of IF conditions.

This year's conferences are Aug. 8–12 in Karlsruhe, West Germany (IJCAI) and Aug. 21–24 in Washington, D.C. (AAAI).

About the author

William Gevarter (M) is currently completing work on a series of reports on artificial intelligence and robotics for the National Aeronautics and Space Administration and the National Bureau of Standards in Gaithersburg, Maryland. He will return to NASA full time to lead a research group in artificial-intelligence applications at Ames Research Laboratory (Moffet Field, Calif.) with emphasis on expert systems. Prior to his work at NBS, he was manager of automation research at NASA headquarters and, before that, a policy analyst for the space agency.

Dr. Gevarter has been chairman of the Washington chapters of the American Society for Cybernetics and the IEEE Systems, Man and Cybernetics Society. He received his Ph.D. in aeronautical and astronautical engineering from Stanford University in 1966, his M.S. in electrical engineering from the University of California at Los Angeles in 1955, and his B.S. in aeronautical engineering from the University of Michigan in 1951.   ◆

AN ELECTRONIC ADVISOR/COMPANION

Computers able to function as personal consultants require breakthroughs in the field of artificial intelligence

Some people are going through life with an electronic "companion." No bigger than a portable radio, it "grows up" with a person, learns his or her habits and personality traits, picks up knowledge of the person's business affairs, and learns enough law, medicine, and finance to render simple advice in these areas. Expert consultant systems like these are being used by pace-setting physicians, scientists, and lawyers in the 1990s.

Other consulting systems drilled in techniques for automobile, home or electronic repairs are being used by do-it-yourself enthusiasts, as well as maintenance and repair personnel. No programming knowledge is needed by the user, since the devices understand natural language spoken in strings of up to 25 words and have effective vocabularies of at least 100 words. Quick release connectors allow the devices to interface with TV, radio or time-shared computer terminals.

Smarter computers assume those managerial functions that occupy most of an executive's time, but do not involve overall policy or final decisions: discovering and defining problems, generating alternative strategies for marketing, manufacturing, pricing, and labor negotiations.

The software profession, meanwhile, is in process of writing itself out of business. Programmers have supplied computers with programs for self-programming, even for developing new programming tricks. Automatic programming solves the current software crisis, the ever-rising cost of writing reliable software. In time, it will abolish most programming jobs and turn software engineering over to the users.

The smarter computers have the ability to "know what they know:" to explain the reasoning behind their decisions, reason about their own knowledge, and encode new knowledge about reasoning strategies. Nevertheless, a new software crisis arises. Because computers no longer follow step-by-step instructions, it is often impossible to trace a machine's line of reasoning or source of error. Computers may not have the same reaction to identical stimuli on different days, since intervening experience may cause the machine to change its software.

The software enterprise, at any rate, is now closely tied to behavioral science, which supplies the innovative ideas for computer technology. Computer behavior gradually becomes unfathomable to the same degree as human behavior.

—Based on the more optimistic projections
of specialists in artificial intelligence

Sooner or later, visionaries say, computers will be thinking rings around people, pursuing their thoughts beyond the step-by-step programs fed to them, reasoning along lines befitting average Ph.D.s in any subject. The forerunners of those computers are reputed to be in the laboratory or in limited use, and they attempt to emulate human reasoning power. They do not just substitute rote memory or mathematical models for human insight. What is debatable, however, is whether these computers do have the knack of human thinking—or are on the verge of getting it—or whether they are just a bag of programming tricks that can give machines the appearance of independent thinking.

The technology for producing computers that may emulate our own thinking processes is basically a software enterprise called artificial intelligence (AI). AI workers have, in fact, developed software packages called "expert consultants"—systems that equal human experts in limited areas of science, medicine, and mathematics. The systems solve conceptual problems—such as creating new ways to synthesize drugs and diagnosing medical problems—through heuristics. The latter are general concepts and rules of thumb, gleaned from experts in various fields, for guiding reasoning and using experience to improve performance.

Many AI workers believe that expert consulting systems will be marketed within 5 to 10 years and will represent first approxima-

tions to the ultimate computer—the self-sufficient machine. That machine would learn natural language as people do, gain knowledge and reasoning power through experience, not just spoon-fed instructions, and be able to solve the gamut of problems that humans can solve. One group of AI researchers maintains that the principles for building such machines are already at hand; that the heuristics now in place need only be extended to further applications. Most researchers, however, acknowledge that the principles have not yet been developed and that very basic problems remain. These problems are best understood through the criticisms that have been lodged against AI research since its beginnings over 15 years ago.

AI workers have long been accused of making exaggerated claims, while failing to redeem their most basic pledge: to lead behavioral scientists in developing the first detailed models of human thinking. These would be models with enough "nuts and bolts" to build computers or software with the full range of human intelligence. AI research has had spinoffs that are now in the mainstream of computer science—such as higher-level languages, data base querying systems, and image processors—but these are hardly the results that AI workers have been forecasting for 15 years.

No computer has captured the essence of human thinking, nor can it do so in the foreseeable future, according to critics, for a simple reason: No one knows what the essence is, and no general agreement is evident even on the meaning of such terms as

Robert Bernhard   Associate Editor

"thinking," "intelligence," or "creativity." The expert consulting systems, moreover, are based on rules of thumb and programming strategems that appear to "work" under foreseen conditions, but they contain no general theory of how the human mind reasons either verbally or nonverbally.

Most AI researchers concede that they have produced no widely accepted theory of human thinking. However, they do claim to be producing the next best thing for practical purposes: a new discipline called knowledge engineering—or how to represent knowledge and how to acquire and use it in solving problems. Advances, therefore, are needed in four major areas to develop more intelligent computers:

(1) Techniques for modeling and representing knowledge.
(2) Methods for allowing computers to think in terms of natural language. Natural language underlies man's ability to think and manipulate symbols; theories of reason and memory are based on understanding how language works, how meaning is mapped into the structure of language.
(3) Techniques for common-sense reasoning, deduction, and problem solving.
(4) Strategies for heuristic search—or how to use heuristics to focus quickly on a small number of most-likely solutions among a multitude of possible solutions.

Nevertheless, along with the expert consulting software already developed, the mid-1980s will witness an explosion of microprocessor-based consulting systems in such areas as medical diagnosis, chemistry, geology, mathematics, and management strategies, according to a pioneer AI researcher, Donald Michie, professor of computer science at Edinburgh University in Scotland. However, this forecast is based on the doubtful assumption that computer manufacturers will apply major funding to the field by 1982 or 1983. Whether they do or not, the present consulting packages are different by any measure from conventional computer systems; they can reason on their own, after a fashion.

Software matches human capabilities

Computers programmed with the expert consultants INTERNIST or MYCIN, for example, can diagnose certain diseases as accurately as medical specialists. The programs DENDRAL and SECS command as much reasoning power in chemistry as do many Ph.D.s in this subject. DENDRAL infers the structure of large organic molecules from their mass spectrograms and chemical formulas—a task often given to chemists in postdoctoral training. SECS develops new methods for synthesizing complex organic chemicals, and it has created valid methods never before reported in the literature. It is now used routinely in several pharmaceutical research laboratories.

A software package called the General Problem Solver, though not as general as its name suggests, is a flexible scheme for reasoning about any subject. It has developed proofs of many theorems that are found in the famous textbook on the foundations of mathematical logic, *The Principia Mathematica*, by Bertrand Russell and A.N. Whitehead. PROSPECTOR analyzes geological data and judges whether the data signifies the presence of economic minerals. PECOS develops alternative computer programs for implementing specified algorithms.

Chess-playing computers can defeat many top players, and some chess analysts expect that a computer will beat the world champion in about 10 years. The world champion backgammon player was recently defeated by a computer program.

Commercial, rudimentary AI systems are being marketed today for such limited applications as controlling robots, recognizing handwriting (in some British banks), inspecting printed-

A successful artificial intelligence system now used in some chemistry laboratories is SECS (Simulation and Evaluation of Chemical Syntheses), which numbers among its credits the discovery of 8 of the 11 known ways to make the economically important pesticide grandisol (A). The final intermediate compounds on each of the discovered synthetic paths are labeled, respectively, a through h. The program (B) selects and guides chemical reactions—thousands of reactions may be possible at each of many steps—while chemists working with the program decide which syntheses should be explored further. The chemist uses a light pen to draw the 2-D structure of the target molecule on the CRT; the program then analyzes the structure for chemical species, cycles, functional groups, stereochemistry, and symmetry, and builds both a 3-D ball-and-stick model and a quantum mechanical model. The "chemistry module" then applies chemical transformations that generate possible precursors to the target. The evaluation module examines each precursor for chemical soundness.

A

B

circuit boards, interfacing natural language to computers, and real-time image processing for target-finders on missiles.

The MYCIN program helps physicians diagnose infections, and it is an example of an AI system that is capable of deductive reasoning. The basic reasoning power of MYCIN, therefore, could be applied to other subjects by reformulating some elements of the program and applying it to a different data base. MYCIN is designed to give advice in desperate cases, where therapy must be started at once with disease-specific drugs and time cannot be taken to identify the infectious agent positively. MYCIN talks to physicians in English, and informs itself about a particular case by requesting information about the patient. The

Knowledge may be represented in artificial intelligence systems by fact lists (A), networks of related nodes (B), or "frames" (C). The facts about simple arches, for example, may be stored as shown below, where lists and nodes may be well suited for simple descriptions, but frames appear to be better for more complicated descriptions. A frame is a data structure for representing such stereotyped information as the characteristics of objects or situations. The top level of a frame is fixed and represents things that are always true about the supposed object or situation. The lower levels, or "slots," are filled with specific instances or data. Collections of related frames are linked together to form frame-systems. When humans encounter a new situation or change their minds about a problem, they extract what amounts to a frame from memory. Frames may be changed to match the changing details of reality. The passage from one related frame to another represented a shift of attention or emphasis.

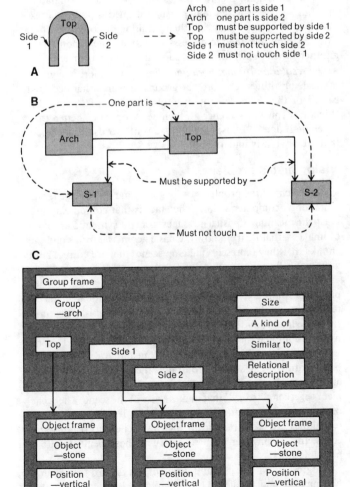

questions start as if they were unreeled from a memorized list, but the queries then vary as the patient's condition unfolds.

MYCIN contains a pool of knowledge about bacterial infections, and it works in a domain where deductions are rarely certain. A typical bit of knowledge is: *If the patient has bacteremia* (infection in the bloodstream), *then a probable point of entry is the gastrointestinal tract, and there is evidence that the bacteria are gram negative.* MYCIN uses this information and works backward toward primitive facts known from clinical observations and laboratory data. MYCIN checks every possible hypothesis—no economy of search is sought—and so conversations with the physician are guaranteed to stick with one hypothesis until it is exhausted.

Forward-running systems, such as DENDRAL, can jump from one hypothesis to another, gathering evidence for any line of reasoning in random order. DENDRAL has a pool of knowledge about both the stabilities of various molecular substructures and the methods for generating the mass spectrograms of all possible structures composed of these substructures. When given the chemical formula of a molecule, together with the mass spectrogram, the program uses its knowledge of the stabilities to reduce the number of plausible structures from thousands to tens. DENDRAL then generates a predicted spectrogram for each plausible structure and compares it with the actual spectrogram. The best match yields the most-plausible structure.

The MYCIN and DENDRAL procedures may seem simple from these superficial descriptions, but years of effort have gone into developing them from strategies that experts use. Ferreting out what the experts know and how they work has revealed a frustrating fact: the more expert the individuals, the more heuristic and less explicitly logical their reasoning—and the less able they are to describe how they work.

Critics of AI research, therefore, see the consulting systems as triumphs of performance, but with no ability to *originate* the thinking that was extricated from human experts and coded into the systems. These systems do not think independently, but consist rather of programming tricks that are added over time until the system performs as it should. Instead of emulating human thought, they are a projection of the operation of certain black boxes—the human experts, whose inner workings remain as mysterious as ever.

Knowledge representation the key

Most research in knowledge engineering aims at general principles for organizing and manipulating knowledge within structures known as tree graphs. These graphs represent information as clusters of linked nodes. A single cluster of nodes may deal either with single sentences, events or related pieces of knowledge. Superclusters of related clusters—called frames—apply to more complex objects, events or chunks of knowledge.

Heuristics seek solutions to given problems by searching through frames in tree graphs. Two basic approaches are used that generate solutions by looking only at likely solutions and avoiding unlikely ones. In one, the tree graph is expanded, and the problem is reduced to subproblems with likely solutions. The other transforms the problem into that of finding a path through a space of subproblems, which leads from the initial position to the goal. The rules developed through interviews with experts are used to generate the likely paths toward solutions, establish milestones, and evaluate the acceptability of solutions.

Tree-searching methods dovetail with methods for solving managerial problems as well as scientific problems. Investigators at the IBM T. J. Watson Research Center in Yorktown Heights, N.Y., have found that managers solve complex problems by checking lists of subproblems that may contribute solutions. The hierarchical process stops when subproblems are isolated that can be solved either by a decision or action, or that require more information or expertise for further analysis.

The ability of computers to use natural language depends on the organization of common-sense knowledge about physical objects, events, thoughts, and human personality. Because humans share so much common-sense knowledge of the world, natural language possesses a powerful form of ambiguity: People normally include just enough detail in utterances or writing to hint at what they mean, or to allow assumptions to be made about the detail's relevance to a conversation. Providing computers with a similar store of knowledge is more a problem of organization and complexity than of memory size or manipulation.

What is needed most here is a closed natural language system: a general theory of language that would apply to all languages and handle unrestricted dialog, whatever the subject and however poorly the information is organized. Many systems are now available for limited dialogs in tightly specified subjects, and they

An electronic expert consulting system could use voice dialogs to teach assembly workers how to assemble an air compressor, as in the example shown. The dialog is from a transcript of an experimental run of a system developed by Dr. Peter Hart of Stanford Research Institute International. The consultant has a hierarchical plan for transforming any initial state of the compressor to the final desired state. The worker executes the plan, while the system keeps up with the current state. The replies "OK" and "How" tell the consultant either to go to the next step, or to explain the current step in more detail.

Electronic consultant: "Try to assemble the air compressor."

Assembly worker: "How?"

Consultant: "Install pump . . . Install pump brace . . . Install pump pulley . . . Install belt housing cover . . . Ready for questions."

Worker: "Show me the pump."

Consultant: (A laser beam moves and points to the pump.) "Ready for questions."

Worker: "What is this?" (Points with wand to tank platform.)

Consultant: "Tank platform . . . Ready for questions."

Worker: "None."

Consultant: "Install pump."

Worker: "How?"

Consultant: "Get 4 1/4-inch #5/16 hexagonal bolts, and 4 #9/16 flat washers, and 4 5/16 hexagonal nuts."

Worker: "Okay."

are used as natural language "front ends" for simple applications. The systems have limited grammars and highly constrained branching factors—the average number of words that may precede or follow a given word. The applications are primarily with data bases to answer factual questions.

Language problems ahead

The major research now concerns solving problems that would make today's consulting systems more powerful. The problems include:

• *Closure*. Two schools of thought predominate. One is based on the age-old principles of learning theory; it asserts that language, like many other mental attributes, is learned through experience. No special circuitry in the brain is present from birth that can generate or understand language. The second school, developed by Noam Chomsky, professor of linguistics at the Massachusetts Institute of Technology, advances a revolutionary idea: People are born with deep structures built into their minds for coding language in understandable, if not grammatical, stretches. Language, in short, is a biological organ, though learning and experience play a role in its maturation.

• *The control of inferences*. A combinatorial explosion of inferences would occur if the computer treated as new inputs all the inferences triggered by words and sentences. Humans, of course, control inferences by focusing on the most relevant ones in the context of the message. They do so naturally by referring to their store of experience and knowledge. Inference-related problems occur in consulting the systems as the so-called "termination dilemma." The program may pursue extraneous paths that experts would ignore because of their intuition or common sense. The programs also tend to digress—skip from one hypothesis to another, when new information suggests a new possibility.

• *The resolution of anaphora and elipses*. Anaphora are grammatical substitutes for words or groups of words that occurred earlier in the sentence—for example, the use of "does" for "operates" in the sentence "Machine A operates better than Machine B does." Elipses are omissions of words in sentences that are obviously understood.

Vision also a problem

Equivalent to the problems of language and knowledge representation is computer vision. That fact is that computers must grasp the meaning of visual messages from the syntactic structure of images—that is, from how the basic geometric forms and the chunks that they represent make up scenes that are correct both grammatically and semantically.

Workers in this field are split into two camps. One group approaches vision as a problem in pattern analysis, not artificial intelligence. Hardware algorithms extract characteristic features from the image, and then statistical classification techniques are used to combine the features into meaningful images. Parsing processes are sometimes used to build meaningful images from basic features. The second group uses the AI approach: Scenes are analyzed by use of knowledge bases and semantic networks to piece together a "story" that makes sense of the scene. The scene often consists of a digital image obtained by TV camera. Various techniques are used to segment the raw scene into regions and edges; the AI program then reconstructs these elements into a plausible story.

Progress in AI research and development is hard to measure, benchmark, and predict. The research is virtually inseparable from the development phase, and both involve the most poorly understood characteristics of human behavior: thinking and vision. Predictions here are just guesses about the next break-

Is everything computable?

One wing of workers in artifical intelligence believes that humans are, to put it bluntly, as simple as computers where information processing is concerned. This view was represented by one of the most senior AI researchers, Herbert A. Simon, professor of computer science at Carnegie-Mellon University, at a recent symposium sponsored by the National Academy of Sciences.

Humans and computers are quite simple, said Professor Simon. They only seem complex because they seek to adapt to very complex environments. According to this belief, the principles are already at hand for creating true thinking machines: The limited heuristic programs that are now in place can be extended indefinitely to cover the gamut of human thought. It is just a matter of time.

Are humans really reducible to computer software? The short answer to this question takes a long time to explain. It may be sought in two widely different fields: the mathematical theory of computability, which indicates the basic limits to what computers can do, and the science of neurophysiology, which explains the structures and functions in the brain.

Computability theory says, in a nutshell, that Professor Simon could be right—or, at least, that he is not speaking of the impossible. There is, of course, the mystery of consciousness. Computers are said to lack self-awareness, and therefore cannot be said to think. By this view, the only way to be sure that a computer or a human is thinking is to be the computer or person and "feel" the thinking. The mystery of consciousness, at any rate, need not be solved before there is an answer to computability questions in terms of technological applications.

To turn momentarily to neurophysiology: Despite a popular notion among engineers, the facts here reveal almost nothing in machine terms about how humans may think or process sensory information. The brain is too complex to understand its behavior from the study of its circuits. Methods do not even exist for identifying the wiring diagram. The black-box approach of psychology, moreover, has been bogged down for generations.

Computability theory, however, indicates that computers can do anything that can be defined by an effective procedure: rules stating unambiguously what to do from one moment to the next. Certain theoretical conditions do prevent people from computing everything that they may wish to; practically speaking, however, effective procedures, or programs, can generally be found when the behavioral rules of a phenomenon are known.

Computability theorists have proved two remarkable facts: First, a special type of automaton called a Universal Turing Machine (UTM) can imitate the behavior of any other Turing machines, no matter how large or complex. (Question: Is the human brain a Turing machine?) Second, a modified type of UTM has the ability to reproduce physically either itself or another Turing machine that is less complex than itself.

A Turing machine is an abstract automaton described in 1936 by the late English mathematician Alan M. Turing. It moves a tape back and forth, reading and changing marks on a single square at any one time, as it goes from one internal state to another. The marks are zeros or ones, though any other marks may be made without altering the nature of the conclusions. The behavior of the Turing machine is completely described, when, for every mark under its reading head, the description states the following: the mark the automaton is to write, the state it is to go into, and whether it is to shuttle the tape one square backward or forward. Most modern computers, when stripped of their sophisticated parts that make practical computation possible, are UTMs.   —R.B.

---

through in cognitive psychology or computational linguistics.

Hardware problems do exist, but these are more predictable and easier to solve than the software problems. The primary needs here are higher speed, more memory, and further miniaturization, so the consultants can fit into small boxes.

Throughputs suitable for real-time processing will almost certainly be achieved within five years. Miniaturization will allow consulting systems to be built with multiprocessor assemblies of microprocessors. The memory requirements can already be met. A representative AI program—SECS—contains 25 000 to 50 000 lines of code for a PDP-10. That includes at least 5000 lines of assembly language plus 5000 to support a graphics display.

The throughputs achievable today are inadequate, however, for consulting systems that must respond within seconds to requests made in unrestricted natural language. Grammatical compilers today take about one second to parse unrestricted English text on a computer with the capabilities of a PDP-10. Similar speeds are expected within five years for the more difficult task of semantic interpretation. These speeds must be more than doubled to compensate for the time needed to process requests and thus keep total processing to a few seconds.

Speech understanding systems lag text systems in performance and applications. Speech recognition currently requires about 30 million instructions per second for every second of speech—or 10 to 30 times real time for the computers used. The recognized sentences must then be interpreted semantically.

AI workers have done little research on gaining public acceptance for consulting systems. The marketing successes in AI are confined largely to military applications. The military originally sparked AI research and has always sought advanced AI systems.

Commercial markets will pose a far stiffer challenge.

Studies indicate that most physicians, for example, are opposed to diagnostic computers, no matter how well such machines perform. Initial resistance was overcome in certain areas, however, where the computer could offer at least two benefits: allow physicians to do jobs they could not do before, such as manage the complex rules of chemotherapy for cancer patients, and let the practitioners upgrade their skills by using the consulting system as a teacher.

More money and management?

Marketing problems aside, staggering amounts of engineering research have gone into AI in the last 20 years. All this suggests a vast, powerful enterprise, intricately organized and coordinated. Actually, however, it has been a scattered, poorly funded business that somehow evolved mainly at four centers: M.I.T., Stanford University, Carnegie-Mellon University, and Stanford Research Institute International. Some observers contend that the technology could be ordered up more quickly with more money and sterner management. One trouble with this view is that it attributes to AI a much greater store of usable information, with coherence and connectedness, than actually exists.

Nevertheless, Dr. Peter Hart, director of the Artifical Intelligence Laboratory at Stanford Research Institute International, believes that AI is one of the three breakthrough technologies of modern times. The others, in his view, are genetic engineering and, of course, microelectronics. The policy-makers must soon choose: whether to devote more money and management or to let AI develop further on its own—as a matter of course.   ◆

SPEECH RECOGNITION

WORDS INTO ACTION I:
Spoken advice can be recognized and converted to standard digital commands

Automatic speech recognition is entering a crucial phase. While users of the first systems are assessing the benefits and weighing them against costs, researchers are vigorously continuing to explore even more advanced systems. Development of the newer systems is not going to be easy.

The unknowns span vast areas—from basics of human perception of language to the organization of and access to large, associative memory data bases and the selection, storage, and comparison of features of speech signals.

Speech recognition researchers are eagerly awaiting large, low-cost data-processing power through very-large-scale integration semiconductor devices. Some think that this, rather than basic knowledge, is what is needed to leap into an era of communication with computers by natural, conversational speech.

Even if these researchers are proved to be wrong, one thing is clear: The technology is moving toward making computers available to more and more people without special skills. Speech is our most natural means of communication. Unlike keyboard input, direct speech requires no special skills or training. It allows the talker to be mobile or remote from a computer input terminal. It permits the talker to use his hands and eyes for other aspects of the task.

Speech is also about twice as fast as keyboard input by a skilled typist. With speech input, a data-processing system can eliminate intermediate data preparation and entry steps.

A relatively recent development

Automatic speech recognition emerged from the laboratory only a few years ago. While the market today is quite fragmented, its potential is vast. It spans industry, homes, offices, the military, communication systems, schools, hospitals, transportation, and other areas of human endeavor.

However, an essential ingredient for success is acceptance and satisfaction by users. Widely advertised failures could seriously damage this fledgling industry.

Human factors in the man/machine interface are all important, cautions James L. Flanagan, head of the Acoustics Research Department at Bell Laboratories, Murray Hill, N.J. He notes that automatic speech recognition systems must compete with existing modes of man-machine communication, such as keyboards, graphic devices, and carefully designed control panels.

While working in the "pristine laboratory environment," researchers often ignore this, Dr. Flanagan says. Automatic speech recognition systems must be resistant to noise and other interfering sounds, he observes. The systems must be easy to "train" and to "correct" in case of error.

At least seven manufacturers are selling automatic speech recognition systems (Table I). Most can only recognize isolated words—an unnatural mode of speech—by one talker from a relatively small vocabulary, and most systems must be separately trained for each talker. Nevertheless, they are useful. Speech recognition systems are helping to save time and increase throughput in such operations as sorting and the routing of parcels or quality control. Psychological aspects are very important here. In a large package-sorting facility, for example, operators use familiar football team names as codes. They found them easier to memorize than ZIP code numbers.

In laboratories, where more advanced systems are under study, at least two goals can be identified. On the one hand, researchers in such establishments as Bell Laboratories in Murray Hill, N.J.; Nippon Telegraph and Telephone in Tokyo; and the French National Center for Telecommunication Studies (CNET) in Lannion, are striving to expand the usefulness of telephone services. Researchers at Bell, for example, are using experimental systems for automatic directory inquiry and airline reservation to study problems of human-machine communications.

At IBM's T. J. Watson Research Center in Yorktown Heights, N.Y., on the other hand, researchers are working toward a more ambitious goal: automatic transcription of spoken English into typed text.

Systems extract acoustic features

The steps to automatic recognition, at least for isolated words, are straightforward (see "One way to talk to computers," *Spectrum*, May 1977, pp. 35–39). Speech creates air pressure variations, and one must first transduce these, by microphone, into an electrical signal. Then, there is spectral analysis of this signal. The signal's acoustic features are detected and stored. Because a word does not necessarily have the same length each time a speaker says it, one must "time-align" its length. A computer does this and then compares the features of the aligned word against those of a vocabulary stored in its memory. The computer decides whether two sets of features coincide to a reasonable extent.

The computer thus "recognizes" words. It also rejects any word whose features are too remote from those stored.

Each of these steps, however, has problems. For example, in transducing pressure into voltage, how does one cancel or reduce undesirable noise, be it high-level background machine noise in a factory or coughing or sneezing by the talker himself? How to best analyze the signal is another tough question. Several techniques are available. Among them are bandpass filtering, time-domain analysis or a linear prediction coefficient technique that models the human vocal tract as an acoustic system with resonance frequencies. The shape of the tract (and the resonances) change during speech.

Then comes the question of which features are vital for correct recognition. Because of limits on computer memory and the need for fast response, one would like to limit the stored data to the minimum essential for correct recognition. Storing one second of good quality speech requires about 50 kilobits of computer

Gadi Kaplan   Associate Editor

memory. Coding techniques can reduce this figure substantially without compromising intelligibility. Also crucial are techniques for accessing the stored data, word by word, and for comparing them with the spoken word. Yet another constraint is the choice of criteria for recognition and rejection. In many cases, the time alignment of the unknown and stored utterances is intertwined with their comparison (pattern matching). A case in point is the use of dynamic programming techniques for nonlinear time warping of the unknown utterance.

In connected, natural speech, the problems are compounded even more. Unlike typed text, where one can clearly distinguish between consecutive words, natural speech waveforms do not show clearly when one word ends and the next one starts, and the time alignment problem is far more difficult with connected speech than with isolated words. Not only does one have to align individual words, but one must also repeat this for groups of words or whole sentences. Once an input word is recognized, the computer must decide which word is most likely to follow the input word.

Focus on three systems

Several systems for connected speech recognition are under study (Table II). Three are of special interest:
1. Harpy, developed by Raj Reddy and Bruce Lowerre of Carnegie-Mellon University in Pittsburgh. It was one of the first systems to demonstrate, in 1976, continuous-speech recognition directed by syntax rules and employing a large vocabulary.
2. A dynamic programming technique developed by Yasuo Kato and co-workers with the Nippon Electric Co. to overcome variations in the length of a word spoken at different times. The technique is used in the company's commercial DP-100 system.
3. A statistical model of the entire speech process, a technique being used by Frederick Jelinek and co-workers at IBM's T. J. Watson Research Center in Yorktown Heights, N.Y. The model includes the production of sentences, pronunciation by a speaker, and the processing of the speech signal by an acoustic processor. The IBM researchers have been using a vocabulary of 1000 words taken from descriptions of laser patents. The IBM group recently reported that, using this vocabulary, their experimental system recognized correctly more than 91 percent of the words in natural speech by one speaker. Processing time is lengthy, however—about 200 times longer than the speech utterance itself. Under more constrained conditions, IBM's success rate was much higher.

Two years ago, Dr. Jelinek reports, the IBM system recognized perfectly sentences generated by an artificial grammar using a vocabulary of 250 words.

Both Dr. Reddy and Dr. Kato demonstrated their systems last Dec. 4–5 at the 1979 IEEE Acoustics, Speech, and Signal Processing Society workshop at Carnegie Mellon University. They describe their systems in the accompanying articles.

Gaps in basic knowledge

Researchers in automatic speech recognition note that it took some 25 years of effort to move the technology to its present state, and there are three main schools of thought on why it has taken so long. Some say that what is lacking is fundamental scientific knowledge; others blame technological or financial hurdles; and still others feel the reason is a combination of both.

Because automatic speech recognition is difficult, researchers with the acoustics research department at Bell Laboratories, for example, are very cautious in their approach to the problem. They are studying two categories of systems for well-defined tasks which they feel are very likely to succeed.

Bell researchers are, of course, interested in the general problem of unconstrained speech recognition, but they prefer to embark on modest investigations, building carefully on what they believe to be solid foundations. Says Dr. Flanagan:

"The problem of automatic speech recognition has not been solved, primarily because the speech communication process is a very subtle one. Many of its fundamentals are not well understood. For example, while most researchers recognize that a short-time frequency spectrum of speech bears important information, the human ear and brain are not a laboratory spectrum analyzer. We do not completely understand the inner ear, and what happens beyond the auditory nerve is almost a total mystery."

Dr. Flanagan also points out that speech synthesis, a closely related field, is an area where researchers lack fundamental understanding. He explains that synthetic speech today does not sound natural, although it may be relatively intelligible. *Spectrum* has recently shown how difficult it is to write computer programs that convert text to continuously varying frequency domain parameters needed to imitate speech. (See "The computer speaks," *Spectrum*, August 1979, pp. 18–25.)

Some of the unnatural aspects of synthetic speech stem from simplifying assumptions, Dr. Flanagan maintains. He feels that models for speech synthesis can be improved by better understanding of the physics of human speech generation. He also feels that some of the shortcomings of synthetic speech reflect a lack of understanding of linguistic and higher-level—semantic and pragmatic—aspects of speech.

It's hard to model speech

A number of researchers believe that it is difficult to accurately model speech. They say that such a model require enormous memory capacity, with rapid access to it. They maintain that the data structure of human memory, as determined by psychophysical experiments, seems to be associative. These researchers feel that today's technology does not permit the construction of large, fast-access associative memories. Even if such devices were available, they claim, it is not clear what to put in them or how to load them.

Another gap in research knowledge relates to adaptive processes, according to Stephen Levinson of the Bell group. "Speech is an acquired ability," he explains. "It is not present at birth, but learned by a child over years of interacting with the world. What is present at birth is the ability to adapt to surroundings. However, researchers in automatic speech recognition do not use the adaptive strategy, largely because not enough is known about adaptive systems of such complexity. It is unrealistic, though, to think that natural language communication can be so well understood by an individual or even a team that a deterministic computer program for its simulation can be written."

Most researchers also believe that hardware and software are a major stumbling block to commercial automatic recognition systems for connected speech. Dr. Jelinek says:

"Computers are still too slow and too expensive. Ten years ago they were even too slow to carry out research in speech recognition. New research is possible, but continuous-speech recognition products, by present techniques, would be quite costly."

"Because programming, even in today's high-level computer languages, is difficult, research is slow. It takes a very long time to test out the simplest experimental idea."

Dr. Jelinek also points out, in a view supported by others, that large companies, up to now, have not been eager to spend time and money on speech recognition. As a result—since speech recognition requires complex processing—"researchers have

I. Characteristics of selected commercial automatic speech recognition systems for isolated words

Manufacturer and System	Vocabulary Words per Speaker	Response Time, seconds	Test Conditions and Recognition Accuracy[4]			Accuracy percent	Unit Cost, dollars
			Telephone Speech?	Training Times	Other Conditions		
Auricle Inc. Cupertino, Calif.[1] AUR-1	32	0.30	No	4	Trained speaker	97	1995
Centigram Corp., Sunnyvale, Calif. MIKE	32	0.03	No	3–4	Trained speaker	97	2750
Dialog Systems Belmont, Mass. 1800[2]	12	Real Time	Yes	None		98	62500
Heuristics, Sunnyvale, Calif. H2000	64	0.25	Yes	1–2		95	259
Interstate Electronics Anaheim, Calif. VDES	to 800	Real time	Yes	7	8 male and 2 female speakers spoke 42 words each	99.4	22500
VRM	40	0.15	Yes	7	8 male and 2 female speakers spoke 42 words each	99.4	1550
Nippon Electric Co. Ltd., Tokyo, Japan DP-100[3]	to 1000	0.30	No	1	6 speakers; 8400 words total; vocabulary: 120 names of Japanese cities	99.3[6]	67000
Threshold Technology Inc., Delran, N.J. 580	to 256	0.05	No	10	Trained speaker	>99	13800

[1]Subsidiary of Threshold Technology Inc.   [2]Accommodates unlimited number of speakers   [3]Recognizes connected speech   [4]Laboratory results except for Dialog Systems (telephone switching office) and Heuristics (office environment).   [5]Legend: Int.: interface with a host computer; VR: Voice response; NC mike: noise-canceling microphone   [6]Average for six speakers

II. Connected speech recognition—selected experimental results

Researchers	System Identification	Total Vocabulary, words	Average Branching Factor[1]	Perplexity[12]	Test Conditions and Results[5]			
					Number of Speakers	Training, words/speaker	Test, words/speaker	Maximum Background Noise, dB
James L. Flanagan et al, Bell Laboratories	Airline system[14]	127	—	4	3	127	500	Quiet computer room
	Connected Digits[13,14]	10	10	—	6	—	2700	Telephone line
William Wood et al, Bolt Beranek & Newman	HWIM[13]	409	67	—	3		248	office
Stephen L. Moshier, Dialog Systems	Model 1800[11]	20[2]	10	10	3 men 2 women	200	2000[3]	85
Frederick Jelinek, IBM	Artificial task	250	7.5	7.3	3	8000	700	Office
	Natural task	1000	1000	24.1	1	19000	1250	Office
Yasuo Kato et al Nippon Electric Co., Ltd.	DP-100[11]	10 (Japanese digits)	10	10	3	20	500[4]	
Sadaoko Furui et al, Nippon Telegraph & Telephone Laboratories	Connected speech	≤30		—	7	1 sample/word	200	70
	Speech understanding	112			8	7-word sentence per speaker[7]		70
Leon Ferber et al, Perception Technology Corp.	Air-traffic control data entry[15]	53	18		37 men 13 women	53	~540	Office
Timothy C. Diller, Sperry Univac	Alphanumeric sequences	36	18		6[5]	646 Utterances of 2 or more words by 7 male speakers	263 Utterances; all test speakers	Moderately absorbing room
	Data-management commands	63	7					
Raj Reddy and Bruce Lowerre, Carnegie Mellon University	HARPY	1011	33	14.5	3 men 2 women	~100	~500	65 (dBA)
Jean Paul Haton, University of Nancy	MYRTILLE I	40			1			

[1]Average number of alternative words that can follow an input word.   [2]Digits and 10 command words.   [3]Test utterances have three-digit strings and five-digit strings with 10 command words.   [4]Test samples included two- to five-digit strings for each speaker.   [5]Test speakers include three of the training speakers and three new ones.   [6]Average word recognition per speaker.   [7]For training of vowels and the one nasal "N" sound. The system uses vowel and vowel-consonant-vowel patterns, but it requires training only for the vowels.   [8]Phrase recognition.   [9]The result is for connected two-, three-, and four-digit strings, with a total vocabulary of 10 words.   [10]The system's recognition accuracy can be improved to 99.1 percent through 3.2 question and answer pairs, on the average.   [11]Commercial system.   [12]Anti-logarithm of entropy. (Entropy is a measure of the average information content coming from a source).   [13]System is independent of speaker.   [14]Telephone speech.   [15]Work supported by U.S. Air Force.

Options at Added Cost[5]	Comments
None	Developmental system.
Int.; VR; NC mike	Cost includes keyboard serial and parallel interfaces, and four-digit display
Int.; VR	Accepts eight simultaneous telephone inputs; can increase vocabulary to 128 words; "trains" itself to user.
NC mike	Must be connected to an Apple computer (made by the Apple Computer Corp.). Serves mostly the hobby computer market
Up to four simultaneous inputs; attachment to printers; Int.; large character display	Vocabulary splits between the inputs
Added memory for up to 100 words; two serial interfaces	Single-board processor; can interface many computers
Two simultaneous inputs; peripherals compatible with minicomputers	Recognizes up to five connected words. Has remote user terminal; interfaces with a host computer.
Peripherals	Recognizes word strings with short pauses between the words. The number of words is limited only by the machine's vocabulary. Can operate up to a rate of almost three words per second.

Correctly Recognized Words, percent	Response Time, multiples of utterance length	Comments
90	100	Using constrained grammar
>95	100	
52 (sentence recognition)	1050	Part of U.S. Department of Defense Advanced Research Project's Agency's project, terminated in 1976.
99.5	1	Using tapes recorded during mail bag sorting
96	15	Using grammar called New Raleigh
91.3	200	Using words from laser patent disclosures
99.6[4,6]	0.3 seconds	
99.3[9]	1	Training words/speaker can be reduced to 12 at no significant degradation
86.08[8]	5	Interactive system for train reservation[10]
96.7 (digits) 99 (other words)	3	Accepts up to 2.4 seconds of speech at a time
90.5[6]	50	
95[6]	50	
98	∿12	Abstract retrieval task
95 (sentence recognition)		Using 40 syntax rules

been taking shortcuts, dictated by what they perceived was economic necessity rather than by sound principle," Dr. Jelinek says.

George White, president of Auricle Inc. in Palo Alto, Calif., represents the middle-of-the-way approach. He says that, for recognition of unrestricted, natural language, one must resort to theories of artificial intelligence. On the other hand, technology today has resolved the problem of recognizing isolated words from small vocabularies by known speakers. Dr. White adds that the problems become "more theoretical as we increase the number of words in the vocabulary, the number of unknown speakers, the speed of the speech, and the ambient noise."

Two philosophical approaches

There are two philosophical approaches to continuous-speech recognition. Many researchers believe that a continuous-speech recognition system must include and reflect knowledge about many aspects of the language, such as its acoustics, phonetics, syntax, and prosody. Researchers, however, are puzzled about how much knowledge is essential for acceptable recognition. Other questions are how to represent such knowledge and how to use it effectively in a speech recognition system.

A particular approach is taken by Dr. Jelinek at IBM's Watson Research Center. He feels that we must "let the recognizer organize itself automatically from the processing of speech data," rather than imposing linguistic rules as the researchers understand them.

VLSI could advance speech recognition

Certain hardware and software developments must occur before there can be wide use of automatic speech recognition. Very-large-scale integrated circuits could help by dramatically reducing the cost of storage and processing. Several integrated circuit companies, including Intel and Texas Instruments, have been trying to increase the memory and arithmetic power of microprocessors. They are also looking at ways to mix analog and digital signal processing on one semiconductor chip.

Bandpass filtering on a single chip has been announced by Bell Laboratories and Nippon Electric Co. and Fourier transforms on a single chip will soon be available. One expert said that a complete isolated-word recognition system for a vocabulary of 20 words will be available on four large-scale integration semiconductor chips next year. In the next five years, he projected, single-chip isolated-word recognizers for vocabularies of 50 words will become available.

Dr. Reddy of Carnegie Mellon is more specific. He says that a semiconductor chip costing a few hundred dollars and capable of processing a billion instructions per second could lead to a continuous-speech recognition system that would sell at about $1000, but we are still far from that. This speed is about 1000 times faster than that of the fastest single processor chip today.

Cheap and fast parallel processing may help the researchers circumvent one of the toughest problems they are facing: a method of organizing associative data bases. Such bases are essential for fast access to words that are acoustically and phonetically similar to part of an input utterance. To quantify such similarity, the computer must make detailed calculations for each of the candidate words. To speed the process, both the retrieval of candidate words and the computation itself should be simultaneous.

Evaluation criteria are proposed

Manufacturers and researchers alike recognize that evaluation of system performance is critical—and there difficulties arise immediately. Should isolated-word and connected-speech systems be evaluated by similar or different criteria? What should criteria be? Do all criteria carry similar weight? For example, is size of vocabulary as important as the number and sex of speakers or the system's response time? Should the criteria apply equally well to different languages or to dialects of one language? Should the criteria be universal, or should each task have its own criteria?

IBM's Dr. Jelinek proposes the following general parameters for evaluating any system:

• Is the system intended for a designated speaker or for many speakers?
• How long does it take to train a system to a speaker or a set of speakers? How little human intervention is required?
• Does the system operate in real time, and if it doesn't, what is its response time?
• What quality of speech input is required? What frequency band? What background noise? Is it telephone speech?
• Is the system intended to be a commercial product or is it a research tool?
• What recognition task is the system designed for?
• Is the task an artificial one circumscribed by a man-developed grammar, or is it a natural task so system performance can be evaluated by recognizing spontaneous utterances?

Researchers, however, disagree on how to measure the complexity of a continuous-speech recognition task. The most commonly used criterion is the "branching factor," or the average number of alternative words that can follow an input word. Dr. Jelinek and co-workers at IBM have proposed "perplexity," which they feel is a better measure. Perplexity is the antilogarithm of entropy, which in itself is a measure of the average information content coming from a source. For example, Claude Shannon has estimated that the entropy of natural English is 5.5 bits per word. A laser patent task presently under study at IBM has an entropy of 4.6 bits per word.

Jean Paul Haton, professor at the data processing research center of the University of Nancy in France, says that measuring the "difficulty" of a vocabulary is a problem, even with isolated-word systems. Some 100-word vocabularies, he notes, turn out to be easier to recognize than the alphabetic and digit vocabularies.

How to measure success is another problem. For example, one researcher has suggested that, with isolated words, one ought to establish both the percentage of correct recognition on a large set of data, as well as that of rejected words.

Measuring success rate in a connected-speech recognition system is considered to be much tougher. For example, at what level should one measure success? Should it be with phonemes, words or sentences? Evaluating a recognition score for a sentence would require pronunciation of a very large number of sentences to be statistically meaningful. And, of course, the size and complexity of the grammar must be taken into account. Renato De Mori of the University of Turin in Italy observes that the stability of error and rejection rates over time are important, too. Then comes the question of how exhaustive can a test be? Test through samples may well be the answer for continuous-speech recognizers with large vocabularies—the systems of the future. A word of caution: Laboratory tests rarely reflect field results.

It goes without saying that the IEEE has a role in establishing test standards. The Technical Committee on Speech Recognition and Understanding of the IEEE Computer Society is trying to draft a standard for speech recognition devices.

For further reading

Speech Recognition, Invited papers presented at the 1974 IEEE Symposium, a book edited by Raj Reddy published by Academic Press, 1975, addresses systems, parameter and feature extraction, acoustics and phonetics, syntax and semantics, and system organization.

Automatic Speech and Speaker Recognition, edited by N. Rex Dixon and Thomas B. Martin, an IEEE Press book published in 1979 and distributed worldwide by John Wiley and Sons, New York, gives reviews, system descriptions, and experimental results. The book carries 38 carefully screened papers published since 1970.

The book, *Digital Processing of Speech Signals,* by L.R. Rabiner and R. W. Schafer, Prentice Hall, 1978, shows how digital signal processing can be applied to speech telecommunication.

"Special issue on Man-Machine Communication by Voice," *Proceedings of the IEEE,* April 1976, discusses theories and applications of automatic speech recognition and synthesis.

Editor Wayne A. Lea addresses the latest *Trends in Speech Recognition* in a book published by Prentice-Hall in January 1980. ◆

SPEECH RECOGNITION

WORDS INTO ACTION II: A TASK-ORIENTED SYSTEM

Harpy is an experimental, continuous-speech recognition system that exploits a low-cost minicomputer

Automatic recognition of continuous speech can be accomplished if the vocabulary is restricted and the sentences limited to those used for a specific task. This is amply demonstrated by Harpy, one of the first such successful experimental systems. It showed in 1976 that it could retrieve documents upon voice request. Using a low-cost minicomputer, Harpy recognizes correctly 98 percent of the words in connected speech by a male or a female speaker, in almost real time, from a vocabulary of more than 1000 words.

Harpy was developed by Bruce Lowerre, the author, and others at Carnegie Mellon University in Pittsburgh. Though complex in operation, it has but two basic parts. One is the speech analyzer—all the hardware and software to process the incoming speech. The other is the collection of knowledge sources—all the stored information on the expected characteristics of the incoming speech.

A knowledge source is a catalog of information on an aspect of

Raj Reddy   Carnegie Mellon University

[1] Straight-line segments depict possible paths through the logic network in a recognition process. Rectangular boxes are nodes, or points in time where phonetic comparisons are performed. Within each box is the symbol for the actual sound at that point, together with the English word from which the sound is taken. Numbers to the left of each box are negative logarithms of the cumulative probability of match (the lower the number, the better the match). The cumulative probability is the total probability from the first node up to that particular node. Numbers to the right of a box describe the degree of match for that node only (the smaller the number, the better the match).

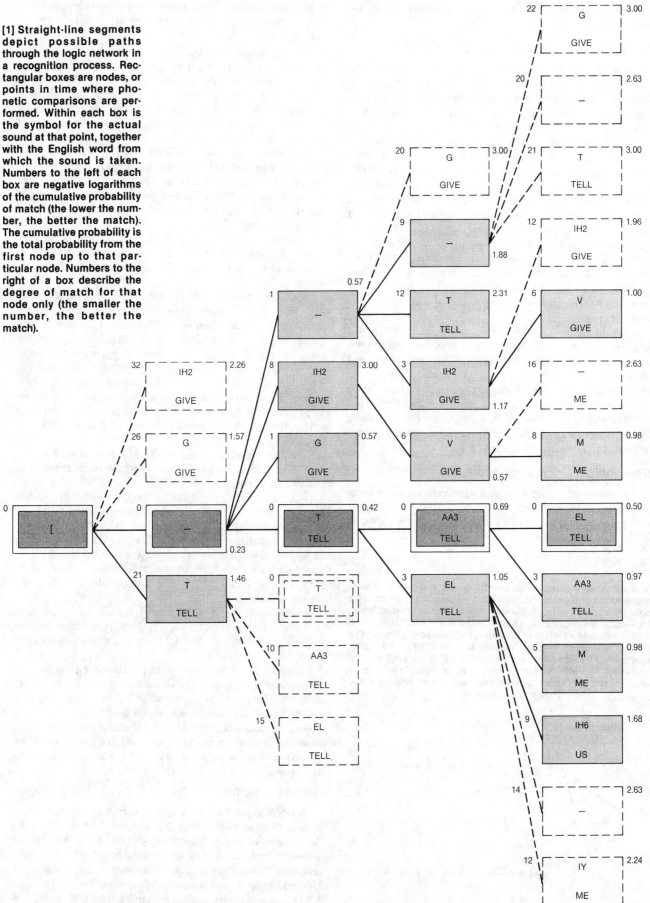

language, such as the arrangement of words in a sentence (syntax), sound variations within each word (phonological phenomena), and what happens to the sound at word boundaries (juncture rules).

Sentences based on 1011 words

Harpy's vocabulary is restricted to 1011 words, and sentence structure is limited to that used in the retrieval of abstracts of documents relating to computer technology. What Harpy's inventors have done is to take all words in the vocabulary and to trace out the allowable combinations of these words. Even for 1011 words, the number of possible sentences is astronomical—beyond the capabilities of present computers. Special encoding schemes, however, were devised by the researchers to generate a manageable representation of all possible sentence combinations.

This, in itself, would have been an enormous task, even if each of the 1011 words had just one sound, but most words have a number of different sounds and groups of sounds. Moreover, some sound characteristics depend on their location in a word or in a sentence. The information had to be organized into a unified format. Pronunciation, for example, is in a format different from that of syntax or juncture rules. Much of Harpy's success can be attributed to the unified framework that was created of the diverse knowledge.

Translating these knowledge sources—originally represented in different notations—into a single computer-accessible symbolism requires a special knowledge compiler. The method is not unlike that of translating programs specified in a high-level language into a machine code. It took over 13 hours on a DEC-1090 to compile the 1011-word vocabulary into a "15 000-state" network—that is, a graph structure containing 15 000 nodes representing possible combinations of sounds (phonemes) in the abstract rtetrieval task.

Recognition: a comparative process

Recognition of a sentence in Harpy proceeds according to the following sequence:

The incoming signal from a microphone undergoes low-pass filtering at 4.5-kHz cutoff frequency. It is then sampled at a 10-kHz rate. The sampled signal is divided into segments, based on the signal's amplitude and zero crossings. Each segment is then automatically analyzed to determine its detailed spectral characteristics.

Next, the measured characteristics of each segment are compared against all 90 phones (basic sounds) stored as a knowledge source in the system. These phones are collected using a set of known sentences by one speaker. These sentences are analyzed to generate a set of "phone templates," to characterize each sound.

After the acoustic comparison, Harpy begins the recognition process. The goal is to find an optimal sequence of sounds and words that will satisfy two criteria: The sequence must be a "legal path" through the knowledge network—that is, it must obey all the rules of syntax, vocabulary and structure, that have been built into the knowledge sources—and the sequence must consist of sounds with high acoustic match probabilities. Researchers call this a "beam search" technique, in which a group of near-miss alternatives are examined in parallel. By searching many alternatives simultaneously, this method avoids the need for backtracking. Here is a crude, somewhat simplified example of such a search:

Suppose Harpy recognized the word "give." Suppose, further, that the words most likely to follow "give" are "me," "you," "him" or "it." Harpy then performs segment-by-segment patching of the sounds of all these words. It computes the probability of occurrence of each sound. It also computes the cumulative probability that a sequence of sounds, or a path, will occur. The procedure continues for many paths simultaneously. Any candidate path whose cumulative probability falls below an acceptable threshold is eliminated. Of the paths that survive at the end of the utterance, the one with the greatest probability is the solution.

Figure 1 analyzes the recognition process for two words—"tell me." The degree of complexity that would result from many more words is evident.

Figure 2 portrays part of the permissible sequences of sounds for "tell me," according to the knowledge sources. Two word strings are possible: "give me" or "tell me." The initial word "give" is immediately rejected as of low probability (dashed line, dashed box, Fig. 1). Of the remaining opening choices, the silence sound (indicated by a hyphen) provides the best acoustic match. However, the sound "T" is also a candidate, although with poorer probability.

An important step in the sequence is the rejection of the three nodes following the first "T" node. Harpy rejects these because they are redundant with the "T" node following the first silence node.

The numbers shown to the left of each box in Fig. 1 represent the negative logarithm of the probability. Using the log of the probability simplifies the computation. Rather than multiplying probabilities, the computer adds their logarithms.

Harpy's success bodes well for the future. It carries with it the hope that computer recognition of connected speech would be cost-effective for constrained tasks such as retrieval of data and documents.

About the author

Raj Reddy, professor of computer science and director of the Robotics Institute at Carnegie Mellon University in Pittsburgh, developed the Harpy speech recognition system with Bruce Lowerre. Prof. Reddy is on the editorial boards of *Artificial Intelligence, Image Processing and Computer Graphics, Bioscience Communications,* and *Journal of Cognitive Science.* He has a Ph.D. degree in computer science from Stanford University. ◆

[2] A knowledge network has several possible states, with each represented by a circle. The notations within each circle are symbols for specific sounds. Certain symbols have obvious meaning—for example, "EL" is a sound in the word "tell." The symbol AA3 represents a variant of the sound "A," and so on. The bracket symbol indicates the start of a sound sequence, while the hyphen symbol represents silence that can occur at the beginning or anywhere else within a sound string. For example, in voicing the word "octal," the vocal tract is closed momentarily during the articulation of the "K" and "T" sounds.

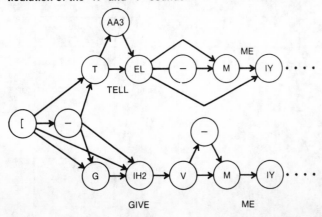

S P E E C H   R E C O G N I T I O N

WORDS INTO ACTION III:
A COMMERCIAL SYSTEM

Dynamic programming handles varying word lengths in this pioneer continuous-speech recognizer

One of the first commercial systems to recognize continuously spoken words automatically was the Nippon Electric Co.'s DP-100. With an identification capability of approximately 100 different words, the DP-100 is aimed at such applications as routing and inventory control in warehouses. Direct voice input here is cost-effective.

The DP-100 is designed to overcome two serious handicaps that cause inaccuracies in automatic speech recognition systems. The first is variation in the rate, or speed, at which particular words are spoken—even by the same person. The second is the general problem of continuous-speech recognition. Words spoken in a connected string are much more difficult to identify automatically than words spoken in isolation. To recognize continuous speech, a system must discover the boundaries between words, and these boundaries are smoothed and concealed.

Commercial systems other than the DP-100 generally get around the speed problem by having the speaker pronounce each word a number of times. The automatic speech recognition system then takes the average of all the entries for that particular word and generates a typical sound pattern. The pattern is converted to a set of signals and stored in a memory. Such an averaging procedure compensates, to some extent, for the variations in rate of speech for the different pronunciations.

Nippon Electric resolves this speed problem by a dynamic programming technique that optimally adjusts the time bases of stored sound patterns to those of an unknown utterance. This technique shows higher recognition accuracy than that demonstrated by methods that fix the length of the sound pattern.

Nippon Electric's technique to overcome the second problem —that of continuous speech—is to apply a dynamic programming matching technique twice, once for each word and then again on entire groups of words. Such a two-level system allows automatic recognition of continuous strings of up to five words.

The basic operations of the DP-100 are similar in some respects to those of other speech recognition systems. Spoken sounds enter the system via a noise-canceling microphone. They are then sampled and digitized about 12 000 times a second.

The next step is spectrum analysis by digital filters. This generates every 18 ms a set of data—a multidimensional vector—that represents the relative amplitude of each important spectral component of the sound.

During the "registration," or learning, cycle the speaker pronounces each word once, and the resulting spectral pattern, or multidimensional vector, is stored in the system's memory. In the "recognition" mode, a special matching processor compares the vector with the previously stored patterns.

In this comparison, the time axis of the stored pattern is automatically contracted or expanded in a process called time axis normalization (Fig. 1) to achieve optimum match with the fluctuating length of the input signals. Thus, the system automatical-

Yasuo Kato   Nippon Electric Co.

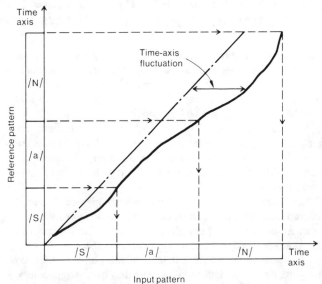

[1] **Optimal variation of the time base of stored word reference patterns is based on dynamic programming in the Nippon Electric DP-100 speech recognition system. Here, the technique is applied to the Japanese word "san" (three).**

[2] **The DP-100 two-level matching scheme applies dynamic programming twice, once for single-word matching and then for a group of connected words. The technique is applied here to the Japanese words, "san jon ni" (the number 342).**

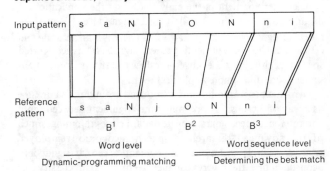

ly compensates for variations in speech by one speaker.

A special computer algorithm provides for automatic pattern matching of single words, followed by the matching of entire groups of words with stored patterns (Fig. 2). This two-level matching technique is repeated. The process is continuous and simultaneous with the time-axis normalization process. A built-in, general-purpose microcomputer controls the entire operation.

About the author

Yasuo Kato directed the development of Nippon Electric Co.'s system, DP-100, the first commercial system for automatic recognition of connected speech. He heads the communication research laboratory of Nippon Electric Co.'s central research laboratory in Kawasaki City, Japan.   ◆

SPEECH RECOGNITION

SPEECH RECOGNITION: TURNING THEORY TO PRACTICE

New ICs have brought the requisite computer power to speech technology; an evaluation of equipment shows where it stands today

Ten years ago speech scientists were predicting that automatic dictation and other sophisticated applications of electronic speech recognition would not be possible in this century, if ever. Today the outlook appears more optimistic. Such applications may be commercial by 2000—perhaps earlier.

What has made the difference? Advances in semiconductor technology, especially integrated circuits, have broadened algorithmic horizons to the point where computer scientists can cope with the staggering complexity of electronic speech recognition at reasonable cost.

Low cost is the key, made possible by high-performance microprocessors and programmable signal processors. Such circuits are beginning to be produced by Nippon Electric and Bell Laboratories, and it is not unreasonable to expect much faster second-generation versions with more memory and versatility by mid-decade. These devices, along with less expensive memory, will dramatically reduce the cost of implementing current speech recognition technology. They will also be a basis for implementing more advanced technology.

Speech recognizers commercially available today are effective only within narrow limits. They have relatively small vocabularies and frequently confuse words. Users must develop the skill to talk to the recognizer, and the machine's performance often varies widely from speaker to speaker.

A key development in the early 1970s was the application of linear predictive coding (LPC) to speech signals [see "How computers recognize speech," p. 214]. LPC analysis is an accurate and efficient method of representing speech signals. It has accelerated speech technology because it allows standardized, well-understood, and simple implementation.

Dynamic programming was introduced around the same time as a way of establishing optimum time alignment between input and reference speech data. Before dynamic programming, much of the advanced research in speech recognition employed relatively simple techniques to segment a speech signal into acoustic units, then very complex techniques to classify the segments and recover from segmentation errors. Scientists gradually came to realize that the signal could not be segmented reliably without prior knowledge of the acoustic sound class, and this realization led to the introduction of techniques that hypothesize acoustic events and then test and evaluate these hypotheses at an acoustic level. Dynamic programming, a prime example of such a technique, provides a springboard for future advances.

This hypothesize-and-test approach needs abundant computer power—a fact that has inhibited its use. Processors are needed

that can do upward of 1 million 16-by-16-bit multiply-and-accumulate operations per second. Such processors will become available commercially, of course, and will create a mutually reinforcing combination of performance and business potential for speech recognition.

With sufficient computing power, it becomes possible to address a more basic problem—that of teaching computers to hear speech almost as easily as human beings. Speech perception at an acoustic level is critical to advanced recognition capability. Commercial word recognizers do not "hear" the way human beings do, and this lack of adequate acoustic-level perception is the source of most of the shortcomings of these machines. Phoneticians already know a great deal about how speech is recognized acoustically, yet there has so far been little activity in transferring this knowledge to machines.

Likely areas of application

Assuming such problems are solved, consumer products seem likely candidates for the first applications: voice-controlled television sets and microwave ovens, wristwatches answering polite verbal requests for the time of day, electronic chess games dutifully responding to the words "pawn to king four." But in these applications, speech input contributes little or nothing to tasks that already may be manually performed quickly, reliably, and inexpensively. They may also demand relatively high-performance recognition, partly because of the user's inexperience with machine speech recognition. Furthermore, cost considerations will limit recognition capability in consumer products, at least for the next few years, to current technology.

Though there appears to be little near-term intersection of application needs and technical capability in speech recognition for consumer products, an exception may be the home computer market, in which the consumer is likely to be relatively wealthy, willing to learn, and more forgiving of recognizer problems.

Much more promising are applications that can be solved effectively only by speech input, or for which speech input possesses some strong and clearly defined advantage over other inputs. One such application is in automatic telephone transaction systems. The ability to conduct and consummate transactions over the telephone is a powerful tool in business. With the centralization such a system affords, the speech recognition subsystem can be at once large and sophisticated, yet still economical. And many applications could be supported by a relatively small vocabulary and simple syntax. Telephone transaction systems are, of course, already in use, notably for airline reservations and inquiries, but the human operator is an expensive element. Totally automated systems with push-button telephones are in early use, but these systems suffer from customer resistance to the clumsy input protocol and from a limited base of telephone instruments. Speech input offers the

George R. Doddington and **Thomas B. Schalk**
Texas Instruments Inc.

promise of a good user interface, low cost, and perhaps even speaker identification for completing sensitive transactions.

Verbex, the first company to exploit this opportunity, now has a number of installations. Verbex's success is moderated, however, by overall limitations in speech technology. Widespread use of such voice transaction systems will depend upon recognition of limited vocabularies—10 to 20 words—with an accuracy of better than 97 percent. Such recognition must occur in connected speech, and the system must be able to recognize any speaker, not just one it has been "trained" to recognize. This will probably be possible by the mid-1980s.

Office automation is another promising business application, considered by some, in fact, to be critically dependent on automatic speech processing. "You can't automate the office until you automate speech," experts frequently say. Such automation is beginning in the form of digital voice-message transmission and storage. This promises to be a true revolution in voice communication, linking people efficiently without a one-on-one contact.

However, although limited capabilities in speech recognition may find application in the office, the grand quest for automatic dictation will likely remain unfulfilled during the 1980s. The first successful efforts in this difficult task will probably be in Japan, because the Japanese language is more amenable to machine recognition than English is and because, with the many characters in its alphabet, it is relatively difficult to transcribe. But even in Japan, automatic dictation systems will probably not become a commercial reality before the 1990s.

The three questions most often asked about the capabilities of a word recognizer are: "Can it recognize connected speech?", "Is it speaker-independent?", and "How big a vocabulary can it recognize?" The answer is frequently not clear-cut.

The easiest question involves the connected-versus-discrete-speech issue. Most currently available recognizers depend on a small period of silence—typically 200 milliseconds—between words to determine the end points of the words. These are clearly discrete-speech recognizers. Some—notably those from Nippon Electric and Verbex—can recognize words without explicit knowledge of their end points. This capability tends to be expensive, because it requires much more intensive data comparison than if the word's end points were known. However, even these connected-speech recognizers do not perform as well with connected speech as they do with discrete speech because the acoustic variation of words spoken in connected speech is greater than when the words are spoken discretely. This is attributable to the "coarticulation" of neighboring sounds: the positions of the tongue, jaw, and lips in one speech sound are affected by their previous and future positions (Fig. 1).

On the speaker-independence issue, there are two factors to consider. First, machines are sensitive to speaker characteristics

[1] *A speech sound is affected by the sounds that have preceded it and will follow it, as indicated by this spectrogram of the utterance of two identical word pairs: "Eight two eight two." The energy distributions are not identical. There are large differences in the second formant frequency of the two "eight"s, and the words share the "t"s. Such coarticulation variations in the pronunciation of the same word complicate speech recognition.*

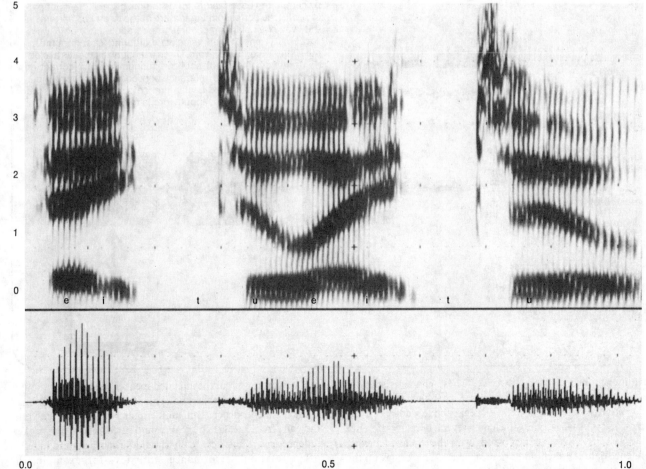

How computers recognize speech

Whether the listener is a computer or a human being, a key element in recognizing the information in spoken sound is the distribution of energy with frequency. The formant frequencies—those at which the energy peaks—are particularly important. The formant frequencies are the acoustic resonances of the mouth cavity and are controlled by the tongue, jaw, and lips. For a human listener, determination of the first two or three formant frequencies is usually enough to characterize a sound (Fig. A).

Similarly, machine recognizers invariably include some means of determining the amplitude spectrum of the incoming speech signal. This first step in speech recognition is referred to as preprocessing, or feature extraction (Fig. B). It transforms the speech signal into features or parameters that are recognizable and reduces the data flow to manageable proportions.

The most common means of feature extraction is direct measurement of spectrum amplitude, with, for example, a set of 16 bandpass filters. Another means is measurement of the zero-crossing rate of the signal in several broad frequency bands to give an estimate of the formant frequencies in these bands. Yet another means is representing the speech signal in terms of the parameters of a filter whose spectrum best fits that of the input speech signal. This technique, known as linear predictive coding (LPC), has gained popularity because it is efficient, accurate, and simple.

The recognition features extracted from speech are typically averaged over 10 to 20 milliseconds, then sampled 50 to 100 times per second. At this point the data are digitized (if they are not already in digital form), and the ensuing recognition steps are performed by a programmable digital processor.

Time alignment: a tough problem

The next recognition step is the comparison of the actual input features with those of the various reference patterns. But first the input features must be time-aligned, or synchronized, with the reference patterns so that the input "l" in Figure A, for example, is compared with the reference "l" and the input "s" with the reference "s." Time alignment is one of the toughest problems for a speech recognizer.

Usually alignment is established by the beginning and the end of a word as determined by energy criteria: the word begins at the onset of significant speech energy and it ends when the speech energy drops below some threshold for a while. The recognition pattern is constructed by selecting input features based on the beginning point and end point established for the input word. Usually the format consists of time slices—that is, a fixed number of features, typically 16, equally spaced in time between the word's end points.

The input pattern is now ready for comparison. For each reference vocabulary word, a measure of similarity is computed by comparing each feature for each time slice of the input pattern with the corresponding feature of the reference pattern. In this way N similarity measures are computed (for an N word vocabulary), and the reference word differing least from the input is the "recognized" word. Often a recognizer applies a rejection criterion to prevent spurious recognition of incorrect or nonspeech input. If the difference between reference and input is too large, or if the next-best reference is nearly as good as the best reference, then the input word is rejected.

—*G.R.D. and T.B.S.*

[A] The speech spectrogram for the word "listen" (above) plots the energy in the speech signal as a function of both frequency and time. The energy is represented by the darkness of the plot—the darker the plot, the more energy present at a given frequency and time.

[B] The essential processes in machine speech recognition (right) prepare the words of a speaker (the input) for use by a host system (the output).

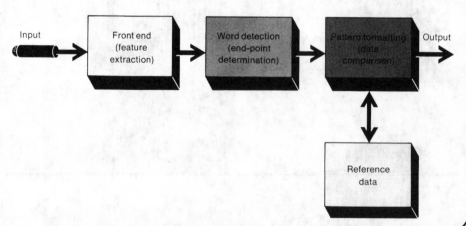

that human beings barely perceive. These characteristics invariably degrade performance when speaker-independent recognition is attempted. Where speaker independence is attempted, it is usually done by including several or many reference patterns for each vocabulary word, with the intent of having reference data represent almost all speakers. This brings up the second factor: quite frequently a speaker-dependent recognizer

that performs well for the intended speaker will perform passably well for a different speaker too. This often gives an impression of speaker independence. But, unfortunately, performance varies radically from speaker to speaker, and performance for speaker-independent recognizers really should be characterized in terms of population performance statistics—for example, the recognizer performs with E percent or less error on the best P

I. Evaluation of speech recognizers

Manufacturer	Model	Speaker-independent	Connected-speech	Nominal price, dollars*	Number of substitutions	Errors for men	Errors for women
Verbex	1800	Yes†	Yes†	65 000	10 (0.2%)	2	8
Nippon Electric	DP-100	No	Yes†	65 000	60 (1.2%)	1.4%	1.0%
Threshold Technology	T-500	No	No	12 000	73 (1.4%)	1.2%	1.7%
Interstate Electronics	VRM	No	No	2 400	147 (2.9%)	2.0%	3.7%
Heuristics	7000	No	No	3 300	300 (5.9%)	4.4%	7.3%
Centigram	MIKE 4725	No	No	3 500	366 (7.1%)	6.3%	8.0%
Scott Instruments	VET/1	No	No	500‡	646 (12.6%)	11.2%	14.0%

* Actual price depends on several factors such as date of quote and vocabulary size. The prices listed here are only a general guide.
† Not tested. Testing was performed only in the speaker-dependent discrete-word mode.
‡ The VET/1 is designed as a home-computer peripheral. The listed price includes only the software and the peripheral hardware.

Note: Recognizers evaluated in the Texas Instruments study are listed in order of increasing substitution error rate. All the manufacturers received copies of the evaluation data, and some now claim better performance as a result of changes suggested by their analysis of the data. Scott Instruments, for example, reports an error rate of 6.4 percent for its VET/2. Such improvements underline the need for formal system evaluation and the benefit of algorithm changes based on such evaluations.

II. Summary of test conditions

Manufacturer	Sound source	Test location	Test date	Vendor present
Verbex Corp. Bedford, Mass.	Tape	Bedford, Mass.	3/22/81	Yes
Nippon Electric Co. America Melville, N.Y.	Tape	Dayton, Ohio	2/11/81	No
		Atlantic City,* N.J.	7/23/81	Yes
Threshold Technology Inc. Delran, N.J.	Digital	Dallas, Texas	11/1/80	No
Interstate Electronics Corp. Anaheim, Calif.	Digital	Dallas, Texas	11/20/80	No
Heuristics Inc. Sunnyvale, Calif.	Tape	Sunnyvale, Calif.	3/2/81	Yes
Centigram Corp. Sunnyvale, Calif.	Tape	Sunnyvale, Calif.	3/18/81	Yes
Scott Instruments Inc. Denton, Texas	Digital	Dallas, Texas	11/6/80	No

*At the request of Nippon Electric, a different DP-100 was tested to confirm the original measurements. The test was conducted on July 23 in Atlantic City, N.J., and a Nippon Electric engineer witnessed the test. During this second test, the DP-100 made 58 substitutions, two rejections, and two insertions. This compares closely with the 60 substitutions exhibited during the first test (see Table I).

percent of the population. The objective of speaker-independent recognizers is to minimize E and maximize P. The bottom line, however, is that speaker-dependent recognizers perform better than speaker-independent recognizers.

On the vocabulary size issue, there are also two factors to consider. First, can the machine do the work? Since the computer processing time is usually dominated by a comparison of input and reference data and since the amount of comparison required is linearly proportional to the size of the vocabulary, can the recognizer keep up with the incoming speech data? The second factor is usually the more important: what happens to recognition performance as the size of the vocabulary is increased?

Often performance degrades to an unacceptable level before the machine reaches its processing capacity. Of course, error rate is not strictly a function of vocabulary size; more important is how acoustically similar the words in the vocabulary are. Performance tends to be better for vocabularies comprising long multisyllabic words. Most important, however, is the particular composition of the vocabulary in terms of the acoustic similarity of the various vocabulary words to one another. Even a two-

word vocabulary—one comprising "seen" and "seem," for example—might be impossibly difficult to handle.

Of all the difficulties that burden speech recognizers, probably the greatest is in determining word end points reliably. Misaligned end points are responsible for almost all word-recognition errors. This is true, of course, only for discrete-word recognizers that base reference comparisons on an initial end-point determination. This end-point detection problem is solved more comprehensively for connected-speech recognizers, so these have potentially better performance even in discrete speech applications. Speech sounds have wide-ranging amplitude and time profiles, and it is sometimes very difficult to distinguish them from noise.

Word articulation also varies considerably—for example, a speaker will sometimes release a final stop (a consonant that involves a complete closing of the breath passage) and sometimes not. On the other hand, the "noise" most harmful to the recognizer is often generated by the speaker himself: aspiration after speaking a word and quick inhalation or lip pops immediately before speaking. Such noises do not occur for all words, but if the performance goal is 1 percent error, it is reasonable to demand satisfactory end-point detection at least 99 percent of the time, regardless of speaker-created noise and variations in articulation.

The worst time to make mistakes in end-point detection is during enrollment, when the machine creates reference speech patterns for the speaker. Often a "bad enrollment" occurs—the pattern for a word does not really represent the speaker's usual pronunciation—and the speaker must be reenrolled with the offending word. Reenrollment at the time is inconvenient, but the real problem is that bad enrollment goes undetected until there have been significant negative results.

Consistency is an elusive goal

Running a close second to the end-point detection problem, and in fact contributing to it, is the inconsistency of word pronunciation. Speech produced during a single interval is much more consistent than that produced over a long period of time. The variation may not be totally attributable to the speaker, however. Changes in the environment—particularly as they affect noise and reverberation—and in microphone placement—especially important for close-talking, noise-canceling microphones—can contribute to inconsistency.

Usually a new user, perhaps intimidated by the system, tends to speak too softly. The microphone is typically no farther than an inch from the mouth, which would seem to require a very low speech level, but low speaking levels lead to inconsistency and reduced signal-to-noise ratio. Shouting is acceptable, except that consistency would be lost as the user grows hoarse, and it has obvious social drawbacks. The preferred speech level is that of authoritative, confident, across-the-desk conversation. Aside from the user's experience, a very strong individual variable in recognition performance still remains. This has been observed many times and has given rise to user categories designated "sheep" and "goats." It appears that recognition systems generally work quite well for the bulk of the population (the sheep), whereas most of the problems are created by a small segment of the population (the goats).

Statistics gathered from a voice verification system, in use at Texas Instruments for the last six years to control entry to its corporate computer center, substantiates such categorizing. A primary performance parameter of this system is the probability that a valid entrant will be rejected because of voice mismatching. These rejection statistics show that the rejection rate for more than three quarters of users is lower than average, and that the typical (median) user has a probability of rejection of less than half the average value.

Probably the greatest problem for human beings is maintaining the separation between words required by discrete speech recognizers. Speaking discretely is not an intuitive or easily acquired skill—one must learn to speak crisply and to leave the required gap, plus a safety margin, between words. And the implicit demand for high recognition throughput requires that the safety margin be no greater than necessary. (A sense of how much is necessary is honed by the experience of committing word-gap violations.) Connected-word recognizers, in contrast, have the advantage of a gradual, "graceful" degradation of performance with decreasing size of the gap between words.

Another human limitation concerns the size of the machine's vocabulary. For larger vocabularies, some users have had trouble remembering which words are in the vocabulary, particularly if portions are seldom used. This limitation may be overcome by experience or by a visual display of menus, but it is a problem that needs to be considered by potential users in judging the suitability of their applications.

Setting up an evaluation test

TI's Central Research Laboratories has been called upon frequently to consult with other groups at TI on the use of word recognition, to make recommendations regarding the purchase of word recognizers, and to project system performance. It was eventually concluded that the only responsible way to perform these tasks was to formally evaluate the performance of candidate systems.

The main criterion for the evaluation was recognition error rate. It is computed by presenting an equal number of tokens (actual utterances by particular speakers at different times) of each vocabulary word to the recognizer and tallying the correctly recognized words. The number of errors is the difference between the number of tokens and correct recognitions, and the error rate is this difference divided by the number of tokens.

There are two main types of errors: substitution errors, or the mistaking of one word for another, and rejection errors, or refusal to classify a word. The latter are less troublesome; recognition algorithms are often programmed to reject words whose identities are questionable.

The overall error rate increases when a rejection criterion is included in the recognition strategy. Typically, about two to four rejections will be produced for each substitution that is eliminated. Recognition performance may now be measured quantitatively by assigning appropriate costs to substitution and rejection and then computing an average cost of error per word.

Another kind of error, however, which occurs in the recognizer when the input speech violates its rules, complicates performance evaluation. The user causes these errors primarily by speaking rapidly with too short a pause between words or by producing words or sounds outside the prescribed vocabulary. The correct response to these spurious inputs is rejection. Measuring performance on spurious input is clearly difficult, but 50 percent false recognition of spurious utterances is not uncommon.

Finally, there is the question of how much data should be collected in an evaluation. Although it is important to establish significant results, it is also important to limit the cost and effort of evaluation. Accordingly, a "confidence interval" and "confidence level" are often used to quantify the notion of "significant" results. For example, if an error rate of E percent is measured, it might be asserted that the "true" error rate of the recognizer falls within 30 percent of this measured value (the confidence interval is from $0.7\,E$ to $1.3\,E$). Further, this assertion might have a probability of 0.9 of being true (the confidence level is 90 percent). If all of the tokens of word samples are statistically independent, it turns out that exactly 30 errors are required to provide this $\pm$ 30-percent interval with 90-percent confidence. More errors give a tighter confidence interval or higher confidence level. The implication is that the greater the performance, the more data that must be collected to prove it.

And the tokens must be statistically independent. Unfortunately words spoken by different subjects in the same test session are not statistically independent, having been spoken under identical physiological conditions. Moreover, the tokens for one speaker are not statistically independent even in different sessions. So the number of truly independent events is really the number of speakers, not the number of tokens or sessions. If an error rate of 1 percent is expected, and thus the true error rate is to be measured within 0.3 percent, 3000 statistically independent

[2] *The 16 speakers in Texas Instruments' evaluation varied in their effectiveness in using speech-recognition machines. Here they are ranked from left to right in order of decreasing skill. Men are represented by circles and women by solid dots. The relative error for each subject is averaged over all speech recognition machines, except for the Verbex machine, which had an error rate so low that it would have distorted the values.*

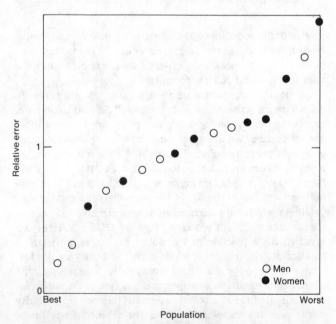

trials must be conducted, and the implication is that data should be collected from 3000 subjects. A compromise must obviously be made.

In the TI evaluation, a 20-word vocabulary was used, consisting of the 10 spoken digits "zero" through "nine" and 10 command words: start, stop, yes, no, go, help, erase, rubout, repeat, and enter. The words were selected because they seemed likely to be used frequently. They yielded a total of 5120 test tokens, which gave reasonably significant results because error rates were fairly high.

The subjects were eight women and eight men. About half of them had had some experience with word recognizers. There were nine sessions for each speaker, stretching out for nearly two months.

The first session was enrollment, in which 10 tokens of each word were collected. (The words were collected in rotation, with 10 passes through the vocabulary, rather than collecting all tokens of each word at once.) The next eight were test sessions, where two tokens of each word were collected. (The 92 tokens were collected in a different random order for each test session.) Utterances that were incorrect, or that stuttered or were corrupted in some obvious way, were not used in the evaluation because the goal was not to measure the performance of the speakers, but rather the pure performance of the recognizers alone. Only discrete speech was used, and the recognizers were tested only for speaker-dependent operation, even if they also had speaker-independent capability.

Seven recognizers in all were evaluated (see Tables I and II). Verbex and Nippon Electric systems alone claimed connected-speech-recognition capability. It is not surprising, therefore, that these two systems performed better than the others. It is also not surprising that they were substantially more expensive.

All seven systems used rejection criteria to allow substitutions for the usually less noxious rejections. During the tests, however, rejection was inhibited to allow a more direct comparison of recognition performance. The errors in Table I are thus all substitution errors.

Although the Verbex machine exhibited the best substitution performance, it made an error the other machines did not. On nine occasions it made an insertion, recognizing a word when none was spoken. This is an addition to the 10 errors counted in Table I. These insertions occurred because the Verbex machine does not explicitly use an energy-based word-detection algorithm.

Men versus women speakers

That machine recognizers perform better for men than they do for women is supported by the tests: although the performance difference was not great, all the recognizers except Nippon Electric's did better with men.

The tests also bore out the fact that some speakers are consistently better than others. The "sheep and goats" population distribution was estimated by computing the proportion of errors a recognizer made for a particular speaker and then averaging this proportion over all recognizers (Fig. 2). The Verbex machine was excluded from the estimate, because it made no errors for 11 of the 16 speakers.

Error rate did not correlate at all with the length of time be-

III. The most troublesome words

Manufacturer	Model	Correct word	Number of times missed	Most frequent substitution	Number of times substituted
Verbex	1800	eight	4	repeat	4
		go	2	no	2
Nippon Electric	DP-100	go	11	no	8
		stop	9	five	4
		start	7	rubout	3
		help	6	no	3
Threshold Technology	T-500	no	19	go	18
		nine	12	three	3
		eight	11	repeat	6
Interstate Electronics	VRM	no	23	go	18
		nine	22	five	14
		go	16	no	8
		help	13	no	6
Heuristics	7000	go	62	no	36
		no	38	go	24
		start	29	stop	24
		stop	24	start	16
Centigram	MIKE 4725	start	55	stop	22
		no	42	go	26
		go	42	no	32
		help	25	go	7
		seven	25	start	9
Scott Instruments	VET/1	stop	63	start	45
		no	57	go	30
		start	55	stop	46
		go	48	no	12
		help	40	start	9

Note: The words listed here are those most frequently missed and account for 50 percent of the substitutions made by each of the seven recognizers. The first entry should be read as: the Verbex unit misrecognized "eight" four times, and of those misrecognitions, "repeat" was substituted four times.

tween enrollment and test—not a surprising result. Different sessions, if separated by enough time (one day minimum in TI's tests), should provide statistically independent physiological conditions.

Certain word pairs were frequently confused in the tests (Table III). Very common was the confusion of "go" and "no" and of "start" and "stop." These are understandable confusions. More unusual was the confusion of "help" with a variety of other, dissimilar words.

Most recognizers used all 10 tokens of each word for enrollment. The only exception was the NEC DP-100, for which five were used. The DP-100 could not use 10 tokens because of the memory limitation of the machine (each enrollment token is stored individually rather than averaged into a single pattern). Two recognizers, the Centigram MIKE 4725 and the Verbex 1800, used the enrollment data many times. The Centigram machine made two complete passes through all 10 tokens and the Verbex machine made three through all 10 tokens. Furthermore, prior vocabulary knowledge was used by Verbex—the recognizer began the enrollment procedure with preexisting reference data for each word (independent of the enrolling speaker, of course).

The test results were obtained for a high-quality data set and therefore the performance achieved may not hold up in a work environment. The noise level was low, the acoustic environment unvarying, the speech level was tightly controlled, and most important, all errors in speech input were eliminated.

Evaluation is a difficult task at best, primarily because of the limitations of current word recognizers and because of their sensitivity to application parameters. But standards are needed, as systematic evaluation is likely to become more common as word recognition becomes more important economically.

Certain crucial issues will have to be resolved before standards can be established. What should test conditions be? How large should the vocabulary be, and what words should it include? How can growing data sets be accommodated? How can uncontrollable differences in the same equipment models be accounted for?

A statistically convincing data set appears impractically large at present primarily because of the many subjects that would be required. The alternative is relative performance measurement, such as that done by TI.

Not only the population, but also the acoustic noise background, rate of speech, microphone characteristics, and—most importantly—vocabulary specification can have a dramatic impact on recognizer performance. The complexity of parameter combinations prevents any comprehensive prediction of recognizer performance. Although attempts are being made to model the effects of these parameters upon recognition performance, probably the only reliable means of estimating performance for a particular set of application parameters in the foreseeable future will be actual measurement of the performance.

As for vocabulary, the spoken digits and the letters of the English alphabet should be adopted as evaluation for equipment. The alphabet is not now a commonly used recognition vocabulary, partly because it is a difficult vocabulary to recognize. But in fact this difficulty especially recommends the alphabet because it provides the same statistical confidence as an easier vocabulary having a smaller evaluation data set.

This brings up yet another ominous problem: as the performance of word recognizers continues to improve, the size of the required evaluation data set will continue to grow. Enrollment may also become a nasty evaluation issue. With the development of improved recognition algorithms, it is quite possible that speaker-dependent enrollment strategies may become so idiosyncratic that they will not accept a standard prerecorded enrollment data set.

Software or hardware may also have idiosyncrasies that adversely affect recognition performance—ones that would be difficult to evaluate without explicit foreknowledge. For example, several of the recognizers that TI tested, such as the Threshold Technology T-500, were sensitive to input speech amplitude. Recognition performance deteriorated substantially, with as little as a ± 6-decibel change in input speech level. The Texas Instruments evaluation data set was controlled to within ± 3 dB from word to word, however, and so amplitude sensitivity was not a factor.

Other recognizers, such as the Interstate Electronics VRM, accept no speech input while they format the just-detected word. The initial portion of the next word will therefore be truncated if it is spoken with too short a pause between it and the previous one. Although the TI evaluation did not test this shortcoming, truncation will surely compromise recognition performance.

And then there is the variation that occurs over time or within an ensemble of "identical" recognizers. Most front-end feature extraction is currently performed by analog circuitry, and it is here that such variations may be expected to degrade performance. If occasional reenrollment is highly undesirable, or if a number of different recognition units must use the same speech reference data, the effect of such analog circuitry variation must be considered.

As recognizer performance improves, evaluation becomes more difficult, although perhaps less consequential, since machine limitations will be less serious. So yet another incentive for improving speech recognition technology is to hasten the day when evaluation is no longer such an important task.

For further reading

George R. Doddington gives detailed forecasts of speech-recognition applications, technology, and performance in "Whither speech recognition?" in *Trends in Speech Recognition,* Prentice-Hall, 1980.

Important techniques that promise to help speech-recognition technology reach its full potential are described in two papers: "Speech analysis and synthesis by linear prediction of the speech wave," by Bishnu Atal and Suzanne Hanauer, *Journal of the Acoustical Society of America,* Vol. 50, no. 2, 1971, and "A Dynamic Programming Approach to Continuous Speech Recognition," by H. Sakoe and S. Chiba in *Proceedings of the International Congress on Acoustics,* 1971.

A three-part article in the June 1980 issue of *Spectrum,* "Words into action," reviews current voice-recognition technology and describes two important systems, one a research model and one a commercial unit [see p. 204].

About the authors

George R. Doddington (M) directs research on advanced speech processing at Texas Instruments, including speech recognition, coding, and synthesis. He previously worked for the Federal Communications Commission and Bell Laboratories. He received a B.S. in electrical engineering in 1964 from the University of Florida and an M.S. and Ph.D. in 1967 and 1970 from the University of Wisconsin.

Thomas B. Schalk is a member of the technical staff in the Central Research Laboratories at Texas Instruments, where he conducts research on speech recognition. He received a B.S. in electrical engineering from George Washington University in 1973 and a Ph.D. in biomedical engineering in 1979 from Johns Hopkins University.   ◆

COMPUTER VISION

COMPUTERS THAT SEE
Solutions to this difficult challenge may reside in hardware rather than software, or a combination of both

Computer vision—the automated analysis of visual data—has long been one of the most intractable problems in automation and robotics. While simple types of vision devices, capable of recognizing isolated two-dimensional forms, are now being commercialized, more general vision tasks have remained out of reach. Most researchers in the field believe that the current predominant approach, which regards computer vision as primarily a software problem broadly similar to speech understanding, will eventually achieve useful vision capabilities. However, a growing minority feel that real automated vision will require not just better software, but also hardware that is radically different from present digital computers, hardware more capable of mimicking human vision.

Key applications at stake

Important industrial and other applications are at stake. The computer vision devices, just beginning to be applied industrially, can identify isolated, two-dimensional objects on a conveyor belt and define their location and orientation, so they may be manipulated by a vision-controlled robot and assembled with other components. Still to be developed is computer vision that can make sense out of arbitrary three-dimensional scenes and recognize objects within that scene.

The General Motors Consight system and a system by the Machine Intelligence Corp., based on research done at SRI International, are the two leading representatives of present commercial computer vision. Consight is being introduced in a few GM assembly operations, while the Machine Intelligence Corp. device has been on the market since last February. Brown Boveri and Automatix Inc. also market vision systems based upon the work done at SRI. Both the GM and the SRI systems operate on nearly identical principles.

The image of the object is obtained via a video scanner as a rectangular grid of about 10 000 gray-scale elements, or pixels. Object outlines are then derived by conversion of the gray-scale image to a binary image; a threshold is used to separate the light background from the darker object in front of it.

Only transitions recorded

In the Consight system, only the transitions from black to white and back again—the threshold crossings—are recorded; this is to reduce processing time. Once outlines are obtained, a set of measurements is applied to the outline—such as area, number of holes, area of holes, maximum extent in x and y directions, location of center of largest hole, maximum and minimum x and y coordinates, and so on. The measurements, which are invariant to rotation and translation, are compared with other measurements made on models of the objects to be identified, and the closest match statistically is the object recognized. The remaining

measurements are then used to relate the position and orientation of the observed object to that of the standard model.

With this relatively straightforward technique, these devices can identify up to 15 different parts with cycle times of about 1 second, and they can provide accurate enough position and orientation information for successful manipulation of the parts by robots.

But, while such systems can be applied to a number of industrial assembly operations and can be assisted by cleverly designed constraints, they are a far cry from what is needed in most vision situations (see "The blue-collar robot," *Spectrum,* September p. 52).

Ideal industrial robots should recognize three-dimensional parts that are not isolated, that may be seen against a complex background, such as in a jumbled bin of parts, and that may be seen from a variety of three-dimensional viewpoints under changing lighting conditions. Similarly, vision systems intended for military use must be able to analyze real scenes and pick out likely targets from any angle. The most generalized vision systems should be able to handle non-rigid objects, human faces, unknown objects, and other sophisticated problems. It is in this realm of generalized vision that computer vision researchers find their real challenges.

'Linguistic' approach used

The dominant approach to this exceedingly complex problem is perhaps best described as "linguistic," in that the overall method is similar to that used by those attempting to devise machines that understand speech. Dr. David Marr of the Artificial Intelligence Research Center at the Massachusetts Institute of Technology defines vision as the "process that produces from images of the external world a description that is useful to the viewer and not cluttered by irrelevant information"—in other words, the extraction of symbolic information from images, as speech understanding extracts such symbols from sound.

Just as speech is seen by most computer theorists as constructed "bottom-up" by sounds forming words, which in turn construct meaningful sentences, so the predominant approach to computer vision assumes that vision is essentially a local process, with objects being built from the correlation of points, lines or small regions, and scenes similarly constructed from objects.

From this standpoint, the basic steps in computer vision analysis of complex scenes consist of segmentation, or the breaking apart of a scene into its constituent objects; recognition, or the identification of each object; and interpretation, or the analysis of the relations among the objects in the scene. Again, the method is conceptually similar to first breaking a stream of speech into words, identifying the words, and then obtaining from strings of words the meaning of sentences.

In practice, very serious difficulties have been encountered with even the first step of the process segmentation, as Harry Barrow of SRI International has pointed out. The initial attempts to

Eric J. Lerner Contributing Editor

divide a scene crudely into regions of relatively constant intensity suffer from problems such as these: Changes in intensity may or may not indicate the borders of an object that has been defined either by physical boundaries or changes in color or shading on the surface; the changes may equally likely be caused simply by sudden changes in illumination, such as shadows. Another serious drawback to such simple methods is that they tend initially to treat the scene as two-dimensional, while in the general case it is merely a two-dimensional projection of three-dimensional objects.

Acquiring three-dimensional data

The acquisition of three-dimensional depth information—a task accomplished very effectively by human vision—is, in fact, one of the most active areas in computer vision today. One approach is to obtain depth information directly by use of laser range finders. Richard Duda and David Nitzan of SRI have designed an experimental system that does this. Once the data is encoded, the system finds planar surfaces by first separating out the points at a known range of distances, then eliminating smaller surfaces by thinning, and then finding all major horizontal and vertical surfaces. The system is designed to work in a man-created environment where planar surfaces, mostly horizontal and vertical, predominate. Obstacles arise in more complex environments, where curvilinear surfaces are more common.

Another direct method of determining depth is stereoscopically, but again serious problems are encountered when attempting to determine which parts of the two stereo images should be matched.

Dr. Marr and Dr. T. Poggio (at the Max Planck Institut fur Biolgische Kybernetik in Tubingen, West Germany) have collaborated on some work attempting to explain and duplicate the capacities of human stereo vision. Their theory is based on the observation that human vision seems to detect certain spatial frequency patterns, which are then matched between the two eyes to obtain measures of stereoscopic divergence. They have proposed a computational system using a series of four or more spatial frequency filters or masks. The system attempts to match zero-crossings of the second derivatives of the images passed through each of the four filters to obtain progressively finer measures of divergence, storing tentative matches in a memory "sketch" of the scene or object observed.

'First step' in vision analysis

An alternative approach of much greater potential is being developed by another SRI group headed by Dr. Barrow and J. Martin Tannanbaum. Dr. Barrow's work is based on the idea that the first step in machine vision analysis, prior even to segmentation, must be to derive the three-dimensional and other intrinsic characteristics of the scene from two-dimensional intensity input, much as the human eye can derive three-dimensional data from flat photographs or even line drawings.

To find the intrinsic characteristics which include inherent reflectivity (albedo), Dr. Barrow and Mr. Tannanbaum rely principally on the physical constraints provided by the actual process of formation of images. They argue that the intensity characteristics at or near the edges of intensity areas can be used to determine unambiguously the intrinsic properties of the underlying surfaces. While there may be ambiguities for each local area, the combination of all areas into a coherent whole will eliminate such confusion, they say.

Most of their work has been done in an artificially simplified world in which all surfaces are relatively smooth, have constant albedo (no surface markings), and are illuminated by a combination of a point source at infinity and a diffuse background (sun and sky lighting). In this simplified world, which resembles a Salvador Dali painting, each type of intensity edge can be characterized by the way in which the intensity varies on each side of the edge.

Three kinds of intensity identified

Intensity variations on each side of the edge are identified as being in one of three categories: constant, tangent, or varying. Tangent refers to the condition in which the extremum of a curved object forms its apparent edge, where the line of sight is tangent to the object. At this type of edge, the surface orientation

[1] The "sun illustration," the perception of a circle that does not exist on the paper, can be explained by the brain's imposition of a three-dimensional structure—in this case, through the perception of an occluding disk—as the reason for the sudden termination of the lines.

[2] Random dot moire patterns such as this, formed by the superimposition of identical patterns slightly rotated relative to each other, are illustrations of visual gestalts. While some researchers feel that the bull's-eye illusion can be explained by purely local visual processes, others point out that the illusion disappears when only part of the pattern is seen (right). The implication is that a global perception process is involved.

is immediately observable, and the light variation along the edge is predictable. Conversely, if the light variation along an unknown edge fits the prediction, the edge must be a tangential one. If the light variation along an edge neither meets this criterion nor is constant, it is classified as varying.

After classification of the illumination conditions on both sides of an edge, the edges formed by shadows and those formed by one object occluding another can be tentatively distinguished from one another. Much of the remaining ambiguity can be removed by application of similar classification rules to the junction between edges.

Once the situation at the edges is determined, these intrinsic characteristics of the surface (orientation and reflectance) are "propagated" by a relaxation algorithm into the interior of the regions. In the case of tangential edges, where the orientation is known, the assumption of continuity can be used to derive the reflectance of the entire surface, while the use of a simple equation gives approximately the orientation of each segment of the surface.

The theory can be generalized to less restricted worlds if new types of edges are introduced. The assumption of constant reflectance can be dropped by introduction of a "reflectance edge," which is distinguished by the property that the ratio of image intensities across the edge is always constant. Similarly, the assumption of smoothness can be dropped by introduction of an "intersection edge," which represents a discontinuity in surface orientation and also has inherent distinguishing properties.

Dr. Barrow feels that further generalization of the method is possible, because as the variety of objects increases, so do the physical constraints that can be used to produce distinguishing characteristics. Such a method, once generalized, can provide a natural basis for segmentation, Dr. Barrow says. Each segment is defined as a single smooth surface of constant reflectivity, which at a higher level of analysis can be combined with other such segments into recognizable objects.

This process of obtaining intrinsic three-dimensional data from images is, the SRI group hypothesizes, the basis for the early stages of analysis in human vision. They explain certain classes of optical illusions as the result of the brain's imposition of three-dimensional interpretations on two-dimensional patterns (Fig. 1).

Need for specialized processors

These methods and the conceptually related ones developed by Dr. Marr at M.I.T. and others are all designed to be carried out on digital computing equipment. However, they are ill-suited to present serial architecture of general-purpose machines. Most practical applications will require some form of parallel, specialized processors, probably employing very-large-scale integration. Considerable initial design work and thinking has been done by a number of groups concerning development of such processors.

Dr. Barrow and his colleagues, for example, have suggested a design consisting of a stack of registered arrays connected to each other by parallel local operations. These processes will act to modify the intensity values in the image to make them consistent with the constraints of continuity and to insert and delete edge elements, which, in turn, limit the effects of the continuity restraints. In the course of processing the image from one layer of arrays to the next, intensity edges are detected, then interpreted according to a catalog, and then reinserted as various labled types of edges—such as shadows and object limits. In this manner, similar processes will be carried out on each small part of the image simultaneously.

The system as a whole will operate iteratively, repeating the same processes until complete consistency of continuity con-

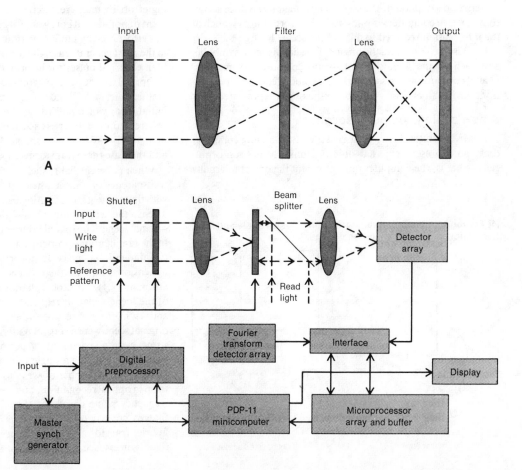

[3] Schematics show the functions of various types of optical processors. The optical frequency plane correlator is the basic type (A). Joint transform correlator with digital hybrid controls is useful when the reference pattern is changed frequently (B).

straints, edge effects, and other physical constraints implicit in the program are all satisfied.

However, even if such a method produces accurate three-dimensional segmentation, the problems of recognition remain extremely difficult. To match three-dimensional objects in a scene against three-dimensional stored models, each model must be rotated in three axes. Unless there are very few objects to be compared, such a system becomes computationally impossible, even without the additional complexities of non-rigid objects and object that don't quite match their models. Because of this, the accomplishments of digital computer vision systems have remained fairly modest: No general three-dimensional recognition systems have been demonstrated, even in the laboratory.

Basic methodology questioned

A number of researchers say the problem is the basic methodology and hardware used in the predominantly software-oriented approach. Martin Fischler of SRI contends that the linguistic model of vision that transforms images into symbols is itself inaccurate and does not reflect the actual working of human vision. "The requirement to describe a scene as a network of relationships among a small number of discrete named entities," he contends, "cannot be satisfied in a practical manner because of the complexity of most real-world scenes."

Mr. Fischler notes that while human vision derives symbolic information from images—during reading, for example—it also preserves iconic information about the objects' shapes, colors, locations, and so on. When a human recognizes a peach, for example, its image is not replaced with a symbol "peach" but is perceived as a specific peach with definite coloration, shape, and orientation.

Thus, perceived visual scenes, Mr. Fischler says, contain much more information than could be contained in a purely symbolic, or verbal, description of the scene. The attempt to reduce scenes to symbols in computer vision systems therefore destroys much of the information required to analyze the scene, he argues.

Mr. Fischler attributes the origins of the linguistic, or symbolic, approach to the limitations of digital computers themselves. Digital computers necessarily process symbols (coded representations having an arbitrary relation to the object represented).

A new analog computer sought

In Mr. Fischler's view, what is needed is an analog computer that can represent external objects iconically or isomorphically—that is, the computer must represent the object internally in such a way as to preserve its spatial relations in the same way that a map preserves the relations of a territory. Further, such a computer must be able to mimic the physical processes and transformation that objects undergo (rotation, translation, deformation), while maintaining the constraints of the real situation.

Conventional digital computers can, of course, manipulate simple line drawings fairly readily, and they do so in computer graphics systems. However, when images of continuous surfaces are involved, manipulation with conventional computers becomes impracticably difficult. Therefore, while significant work can be done with existing hardware, Mr. Fischler says, new computer architecture will ultimately be essential.

Some computer vision researchers have replied that digital equipment is theoretically capable of carrying out any conceivable operation. Most agree that highly parallel digital architectures will eventually be needed for real-time applications, but they question the need for analog devices.

Other researchers have criticized the second main premise of the predominant computer vision approach: the assumption that visual processing is primarily local. Many workers in the field have pointed out that human vision seems based, at least in part, on gestalts—conceptions of whole objects or scenes against which local details are compared (Fig. 2). At the same time, human visual memory appears to be stored in a distributed rather than localized fashion, so that entire images are compared globally against whole object-memories, rather than by a point-by-point comparison. If this is the case, then computer vision methods that are purely local may be inherently incapable of duplicating the capacities of organic vision.

Research in optical processing pressed

While Mr. Fischler has not put forward any concrete suggestions for alternative computer hardware, a very active and growing effort by many researchers is being devoted to the development of non-digital hardware for computer vision. Virtually all of this effort is being put into various forms of optical processing—in the most general sense, the use of electromagnetic waves rather than electrical pulses for information processing.

Optical processing originated in 1964 from the work of mathematician A. Vander Lugt on spatially matched filters. The initial idea, which still forms the basis of the field, was to use coherent optical interference methods—in essence, a form of holography—to produce spatial Fourier transforms of objects and then use these transforms to recognize the objects.

When coherent light, such as from a laser, passes through a transparency of a scene, the light becomes amplitude modulated with that scene. If the resulting beam is then focused on a plane by a lens, the lens produces a spatial Fourier transform of the original scene. The spatial Fourier transform is directly analogous to the familiar time Fourier transform, breaking a signal up into a two-dimensional space frequency spectrum rather than a one-dimensional time-frequency spectrum. The intensity of light at any point (x,y) in the focal plane is proportional to the magnitude of the scene's spatial frequency component kx in the x direction and ky in the y direction, where k is a constant. Thus, if the original scene were a vertical pattern of evenly spaced, sinusoidal stripes with a spacing of M per millimeter, the spatial Fourier transform would be a single spot of light at point $(0,kM)$.

There are a number of ways to use the spatial Fourier transform in optical recognition, but the most widely used system is the frequency plane correlator (Fig. 3). In this, a matched spatial filter is created by the interference of a plane wave with the Fourier transform of the reference object to be recognized. The filter is, in essence, a hologram of the object, although it may not

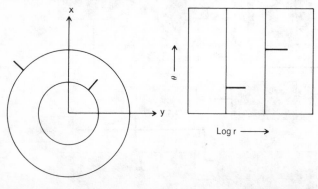

[4] The logarithmic-polar transformation changes scale and rotation distortions into translational shifts.

Original scene   Transformed scene

have the same appearance as a conventional holograph, since it is recorded as a *focused* image.

The input scene is then correlated with the matched spatial filter when laser light is focused through a transparency of the scene onto the filter. The resulting interference pattern indicates the presence of the reference object in the input scene: in the output plane, a single point of light results at location (x,y) for every appearance of the object at the corresponding point in the input scene.

The process is closely analogous mathematically to the phenomenon of resonance in the time domain. Just as an oscillatory system will resonate when the frequencies of its natural modes are inputted to the system, so the identity of the spatial frequencies of the reference and input objects produces the equivalent resonance in space—in the form of a beam of light. (Some research in human vision has indicated that the brain uses a form of spatial Fourier transform, or is at least sensitive to spatial frequency data in images. The evidence previously mentioned demonstrating the use of spatial frequency analysis in stereopsis is among the best known of this research.)

Rapid response by light modulators

In a real-time system, both the input scene and the matched spatial filter must be capable of rapid response. The devices that accomplish this task are known as spatial light modulators, and they are typically electro-optic crystals. In one system, the input scene is scanned onto the crystal with an electron gun, thereby altering the transparency of the crystal in proportion to the intensity of the beam. A laser beam is then passed through the crystal to produce the desired amplitude-modulated beam. When the object to be recognized is changed, a similar electro-optic crystal at the transform plane can be scanned with the pattern of the matched spatial filter. As a rule, the most sophisticated correlators are digital-optical hybrids that use digital equipment for control and interfacing.

In alternative systems, such as the joint transform correlator, both the reference object and the input scene are in the same plane, an advantage if the reference is changed rapidly.

The two basic advantages of such optical processing systems over digital computer vision devices are their speed and their ability to deal with scenes in a global manner. While two-dimensional Fourier transforms are performed by digital process, that approach is very time-consuming; the optical processor does the job in a highly parallel manner at the speed of light. The correlators compare entire objects or scenes against entire reference patterns, thus avoiding one of the main problems with the localist approach of purely digital systems. As a result, simple optical correlators can pick out objects from very complex background scenes, something not yet possible with digital systems.

Problems with optical processors

However, these relatively simple types of optical processors have severe drawbacks. Potential users in industrial applications find that they are too rigid, requiring objects to be correctly oriented, and are also incapable of dealing with changes in illuminations and scale. Delays in putting data into and out of the optical system often destroy any time savings from the processing itself. Even researchers who are critical of digital systems, such as Mr. Fischler, contend that optical systems also have very weak isomorphism to objects, not being able to represent them in true three-dimensional character.

Optical processing researchers are attempting to develop devices that overcome at least some of these problems. David Casasent, head of Carnegie-Mellon University's optical process-

ing laboratory, thinks that the problem of data input and retrieval is not the most serious.

"In either an optical or digital approach," he says, "you are mainly limited by the millisecond times of TV scans. In general, retrieval of data from computer memories is slower than optical processing input and output."

The most significant efforts are thus being focused on expanding the flexibility of optical systems. The simplest part of the problem is to make the systems capable of recognizing input patterns irrespective of scale and rotation, while still preserving scale and rotation data. Ordinary optical correlation breaks down with rotations of a few degrees and scale changes of a few precentage points.

Dr. Casasent and his associates are developing transformation more sophisticated than the simple Fourier to deal with scale and orientation variations. They use a logarithmic transform, $(x',y') = (\log x, \log y)$, to convert scale distortions into shifts in one axis. Combining the logarithmic transformation with a Fourier transform yields a Mellin transform and provides invariance to scale. Similarly, a polar transformation is used to convert rotation to a second positional shift (Fig. 4). By obtaining a Fourier transform of an input (which is itself invariant to position), then taking its magnitude, then applying a logarithmic and polar transform, and then correlating the output, one gets a system that is invariant to position, scale and rotation.

However, in taking the Fourier transform of the input twice, one loses information. This means that only two simultaneous distortions can be dealt with at once—such as scale and orientation or position and rotation—but not all three. The loss of information in Fourier transforms is, in fact, a general limitation of such processors. Dr. Casasent has developed combined digital-optical methods of reconstructing the phase of the input from a Fourier transform, thus making possible systems that can identify objects regardless of scale, rotation, and position, while identifying the magnitude and direction of all three distortions.

Dr. Casasent's systems use digital processing to create the nonlinear transforms required for invariant operations, and this approach tends to negate in part the parallelism of the optical processing.

Imitating the human brain

A simple method for performing such nonlinear transforms in parallel has been proposed by George Chaiking of the Goddard Institute for Space Studies and Carl Weiman of General Electric. Their work was inspired in part by findings that such mappings were used by the human visual system.

In the human brain, the nerve fibers leading from the retina are continuously deformed as they approach the brain, creating automatically the logarithmic-polar mapping. Mr. Weiman and Mr. Chaikin proposed to imitate this design by using a bundle of optic fibers that will perform continuously the desired nonlinear mapping, thereby eliminating the need for time consuming digital processing.

Systems capable of identifying two-dimensional patterns in a cluttered background, irrespective of size, orientation, and position, are apparently within reach of optical processing technology and could have a wide range of applications. Word recognizers that are insensitive to page misalignments or distance variations are one possibility being investigated, as are various sorts of industrial inspection systems.

Far more useful, but more difficult to design, would be systems that could deal with changes in three-dimensional aspect and illumination. Dr. Casasent and researchers at the U.S. Army's Redstone Arsenal in Alabama are attempting to perfect such systems by using multiple filters that have recorded on them a target object, as seen from a variety of orientations. Experiments have shown that multiplexing only five to eight images can give good recognition and discrimination over a wide range of angles.

Such industrial tasks as picking components from a bin require, in addition, the ability to recognize partly obscured objects. Some optical processing techniques have been developed for producing entire scenes from fragments—a form of "associative memory." When certain types of spatial filters are illuminated with light from only a fragment of the original scene, the entire scene is formed as an output. In multiple exposed holograms, a fragment of one scene will produce an image of that original scene and no others, providing the possibility of discriminating among a class of objects recognized.

Two big final hurdles

By combining these techniques, a system may be able to locate an arbitrarily oriented object in a complex scene by first transforming the image and then using the result to select a single aspect image on a multiplexed filter. Even with these more advanced designs, however, a number of problems remain. First, there is a limit to how much information can be usefully stored on a single two-dimensional filter and, therefore, it is very difficult to create practical systems that can identify any significant number of different objects. Systems of parallel filters rapidly degrade the input and become cumbersome.

Serial systems, which effectively store information three-dimensionally, would be far more desirable, but information is rapidly lost through the amplitude modulation of successive filters. As with digital systems, existing optical systems destroy optical information as they process it.

A second problem is the rigidity of optical systems to minor variations in the input other than simple geometric distortions—a result of the ultimate linear character of spatial frequency correlators. For such systems to recognize similar objects, a nonlinear correlation, which responds to nearby frequency patterns, is required. Ideally, such a system would function in a way analogous to nonlinear oscillators in the time domain; these respond not only to natural, but also to nearby frequencies.

One possible solution to both problems is to combine spatial frequency with time-domain frequency analysis. One might do this by encoding part of the image data as frequency or phase modulation in time rather than purely as space amplitude modulation. This would immediately add a third dimension to the data and allow the signal to interact more easily with information stored in a three-dimensional array, since the frequency or phase modulation patterns would be preserved. (In contrast, amplitude-modulated information would be distorted by the earlier elements in the array before they could interact with later ones.) Frequency modulation would also allow the use of nonlinear electrical oscillators, whose nolinear characteristics would be much more easily controlled than those of purely spatial optical elements.

Systems under study

Dr. Casasent has proposed a combined spatial time-frequency correlator system that would use some combination of coherent light and acousto-optic cells. Such cells can phase-modulate light at frequencies up to 1 GHz, well within the range of microwave circuitry. In particular, a single system using a two-dimensional array or arrays of such cells could combine electromagnetic processing in the optical and microwave spectrum with digital controls and interfaces.

While it may be difficult to produce arrays of nonlinear oscillators that are sufficiently compact with existing LSI technology, superconducting Josephson junction devices now under development may help, since junctions with dimensions of a few microns act as nonlinear oscillators with frequency response in the gigahertz range.

Such a system of nonlinear oscillators, sensitive to space-time electromagnetic patterns, would be a fulfillment of ideas first proposed by the mathematician Norbert Weiner in the early 1960s. He suggested that such arrays might mimic the self-organizing features of human perceptual processes. Recent neurophysiological research has also tended to support the idea that the brain uses such space-time electromagnetic patterns in both visual processing and higher functions. In fact, strong, apparently resonant, interactions between human or primate brains and weak environmental electromagnetic fields have been repeatedly observed. Furthermore, it has long been known that visual data is encoded as frequency modulated signals as well as spatially organized ones.

Once developed, such combined systems may have the flexibility to produce workable vision systems that overcome the limitation of both existing digital and optical systems. Dr. Casasent is seeking funding for initial studies of space-time correlators. In the meantime, overall funding for all computer vision approaches seems certain to increase as the technology approaches the stage at which major applications become practicable.

For further reading

A good overview of digital-based systems for computer vision, as well as a description of techniques used at SRI International by a group headed by Harry Barrow, is provided by "Prospects for Industrial Vision" by Jay M. Tannanbaum, Harry G. Barrow, and Robert C. Bolles in *Computer Vision and Sensor-Based Robots*, Plenum Press, 1978.

The views of Martin Fischler of SRI International are summarized in "On the Representation of Natural Scenes" in *Computer Vision Systems*, Academic Press, 1978.

David Casasent of Carnegie-Mellon University gives a survey of optical processing methods in "Coherent Optical Pattern Recognition," *Proceedings of IEEE*, Vol. 67, No. 5, pp. 813–825 (May 1979).

The use of multiple filters for three-dimensional objects is discussed by B.D. Guenther, C.R. Christiansen, and Juris Upatnieks in "Coherent Optical Processing: Another Approach," *IEEE Journal of Quantum Electronics,* Vol. QE-15, No. 12, pp. 1348–1363 (December 1979).

Dr. David Marr's theory of stereopsis is presented most fully in "A Theory of Human Stereo Vision," M.I.T. Artificial Intelligence Laboratory Report No. 451.

Carl Weiman and George Chaikin discuss the use of logarithmic transforms in "Logarithmic Spiral Grids for Image Processing," *Proceedings of IEEE Conference on Pattern Recognition and Image Processing*, pp. 25–31 (1979).

Some neurophysiological evidence on how human vision works is surveyed in "Computer Vision Looks to the Brain" by Eric J. Lerner, *High Technology*, May 1980, pp. 40–50.

About the author

Eric J. Lerner is a contributing editor to *Spectrum*. He is currently president of Advanced Technologies Enterprises Inc., an R&D firm, and has written numerous articles on a wide variety of scientific subjects. He was, until recently, a contributing editor to *High Technology*. He received a B.A. in physics from Columbia University in 1968 and did graduate work in high energy and astrophysics at University of Maryland.　◆

COMPUTER VISION

PATTERN RECOGNITION: A REVIEW

Optical techniques developed to discern military targets are being studied for industrial and commercial applications

Optical pattern-recognition systems—systems that use optical interference to process incoming signals—have long attracted attention because of their highly parallel operation and high speed. Until now, most research in the United States has concentrated on military applications, such as missile guidance and electronic warfare. However, although the emphasis remains primarily on military applications, recent advances in optical system components, system architecture, and pattern-recognition algorithms suggest development of systems with potential commercial applications in robotics, automated product inspection, and other civilian fields.

Pattern recognition is the identification of a given pattern of data, frequently visual data, within a mass of extraneous signals. Typical applications include the location and identification of a target, such as a tank, in a terrain, or the location of a part in a bin. It is a difficult task to automate, both because of the large amount of data that must be rapidly processed and because the pattern to be identified may differ in practice from the ideal reference pattern.

While there are many digital electronic pattern recognition systems, optical methods have certain definite advantages. The most notable one is that the entire pattern is processed at once through some form of optical interference with the reference pattern. This is a potentially much quicker method than the sequential processing of each picture element, or pixel, that is typical of digital methods.

Optical data processing therefore represents an attractive alternative to conventional digital electronics for pattern-recognition problems. A number of such optical systems are now in advanced stages of research and development for military applications, and there has been some limited commercial development.

How it works

The basic principles of optical pattern recognition (OPR) are best illustrated by looking at the most common type of system used (Fig. 1). An input scene is illuminated by laser light and a diffraction pattern is formed. The pattern is then focused by a lens on a plane. An optical filter, produced from a reference object or pattern, is located at the focal plane. The optical filter (called a matched spatial filter or MSF) diffracts the incoming pattern of light, thereby producing a second diffraction pattern. This resultant pattern is then refocused by a second lens onto the output plane. The filter is obtained by the interference of laser light that had passed through the reference pattern with an unmodulated laser beam.

If the reference pattern is present in the input scene (for example, if the tank is in view, or the part is in the bin) the output contains a peak of light whose location indicates the location of the reference pattern in the scene.

The device works by optically obtaining the correlation function of the reference pattern and the input scene. The first lens produces the spatial Fourier transform of the input scene. The filter is similarly the Fourier transform of the reference pattern. The interaction of the two Fourier transforms is the product of the transforms. Finally, the second lens produces the inverse Fourier transform of the product, which is the correlation function.

This type of system is called a frequency plane correlator because the correlation function is formed by multiplication in the frequency, or Fourier transform, plane.

In such an OPR system, the input laser light operates in parallel on all pixels within the input plane. Thus, parallel processing of 8×10^6 bits of data, or a $10^3 \times 10^3$-pixel image with 8 bits intensity level, is trivial in an optical processor. Moreover, the processing time required in an optical system is the time it takes light to travel from input to output. Since light travels at 3 m/ns, the processing time in an optical system is negligible. In any real system, of course, the processing time, per se, is not the total time between input and output: The transfer of data into and out of the device takes much longer than 3 ns. These real-time and parallel processing features have intrigued researchers in many disciplines for over 15 years.

Military applications dominate R&D

Considerable research has gone into developing such processors for missile guidance, reconnaissance, and similar military applications. In such cases, the input data is a real-time sensed image, and the reference pattern is a matched spatial filter that is similar to a hologram of the reference object, or image area being sought. The MSF of the reference object is stored on board the missile or satellite, and the image is the scene within the sensor's field of view. The coordinates of the output correlation peak provide the information for the missile's guidance system, or indicate where to point a secondary sensor.

Projected sensor systems are expected to provide high-resolution data at frame rates that can yield over 10^{11} bits per second of data. With such numbers, the ability of sensor systems to acquire data has vastly exceeded the ability of users of the systems to process and analyze such data intelligently. It has been estimated, for example, that the National Aeronautics and Space Administration has looked at less than 1 percent of the sensor data it has acquired so far from Landsat surveys. It is thus no wonder that projected advanced sensors require advanced image processing techniques with high throughput and parallel processing. The basic pattern-recognition problem—determining the presence of a reference object and its location in an image—is quite analogous to similar ones that arise in artificial intelligence, autonomous robots, product inspection, and computer vision.

Optical data processing systems are not without problems. To realize the real-time and parallel processing advantages of such systems, real-time and reusable two-dimensional spatial light

David Casasent   Carnegie-Mellon University

modulator transducers are needed to convert input electrical or noncoherent ambient image data into a form suitable for spatial modulation of a coherent laser beam. A leading optical transducer that shows promise is the liquid-crystal light valve addressed by a charge-coupled device (Fig. 2). This device is under development at Hughes Research Laboratories in Malibu, Calif.

In this unit, 2-D raster-recorded electrical input data from a TV or similar sensor is fed to the CCD. When a new line of data has entered, it and all prior ones are shifted down until the full image frame is present in the CCD structure. The charge is then coupled to the electrooptical liquid-crystal layer, producing a spatial electric field distribution across the liquid crystal. Polarized laser light incident from the liquid-crystal side of the unit emerges spatially modulated and proportional to the spatial electric field. This and similar transducers offer the low cost, size, and weight necessary for both military and commercial optical processors.

The three major shortcomings of optical processors have been their accuracy, rigid stability requirements, and ability to perform only limited operations. In the practical OPR problem, the input and reference object differ for many practical reasons that depend upon the application. For example, geometrical differences of scale and rotation and textural differences, if different

sensors are used, are common.

The simplest uses of optical processing do not involve the production of a correlation function, but merely the detection of the Fourier transform itself.

The Fourier transform operation is the hallmark of optical processing. It converts the normal spatial description of an image into a spatial frequency pattern. If low spatial frequencies are present in the image, peaks of light appear near the center in the Fourier transform plane. Higher frequencies produce peaks further off axis. The radial locations of peaks of light in the Fourier transform pattern thus denote the presence of different spatial frequencies in the input image and the amplitudes of these peaks of light are proportional to the amount of each spatial frequency that is present in the input data. The angular locations of different Fourier transform plane peaks convey information on the orientation of the different spatial frequencies in the input data.

Wedge-ring detector: a commercial device

A useful method of determining such Fourier transform plane information about an image involves use of a wedge-ring detector placed in the Fourier transform plane. This unit contains 32 angular and wedge-shaped detector elements on each half of a 2.5-cm diameter device. The wedge-shaped detector elements provide orientation information and the ring-shaped detector elements provide spatial frequency information on the input object. These data are available in parallel on 64 wires from the detector that can be fed to an electronic support system for further analysis.

Many commercial applications of this detector system have been pursued. These include: product inspection of paper and cloth goods, IC boards, and biomedical image screening, among others. Because the magnitude of the Fourier transform is shift

[1] **The basic type of optical pattern recognition system is the frequency plane correlator. Laser light illuminates an input pattern (such as A) at P_1. A lens L_1 then focuses the diffracted light onto a filter at P_2. (The filter is produced from a reference pattern such as B). The resulting interference pattern is then refocused by L_2 on P_3 to produce the correlation function between the input and reference patterns. If the reference pattern is present in the input, a peak of light intensity, as C (actually a computer-generated plot of light intensity in plane P_3) appears in the correlation function, at a location corresponding to the location of the reference pattern in the input.**

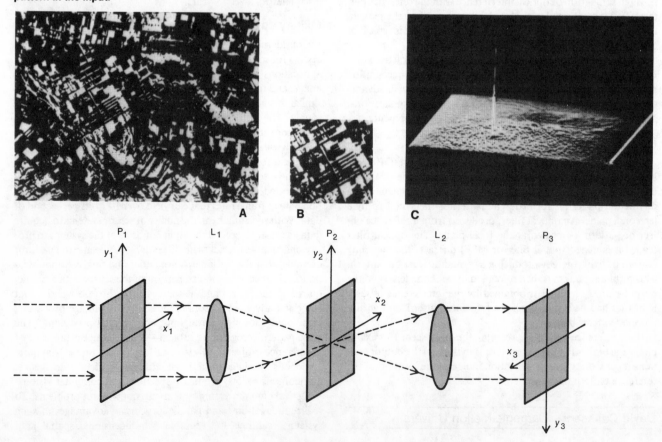

A   B   C

invariant (input image displacements in the input plane or along the optical axis will not change the magnitude of the Fourier transform), this system is quite rigid and practical for industrial use. It also provides a large data reduction from over 10^6 input pixels to 64 output pixels. A commercial version of this system is currently available from Recognition Systems in Van Nuys, Calif. This is one of the very few optical processing systems that have been commercialized.

Need for hybrid optical-digital systems

For most applications, real-time operations are necessary. In general, these involve hybrid optical-digital systems.

Such a system is under development at the Engineer Topographic Laboratory in Fort Belvoir, Va., and will be delivered later this year. In this system, regions of the input image are sequentially scanned. The Fourier transform of each region is focused on to a wedge-ring detector and an image of each region is produced by a 32-by-32-element solid-state detector. This dual-frequency and image-plane processor uses extensive digital post processing, including statistical analysis, to determine the content of the different regions of the input scene. Such a system is of direct use in robotics and computer vision, as well as in the automatic analysis of aerial photographs for which it is being fabricated.

Hybrid optical-digital processors give the optical system increased flexibility by allowing use of more sophisticated software pattern recognition algorithms. In such architectures, the optical system is used to address the digital processor and to give it data and image features in various formats. Proper combinations of optical system operations and new digital algorithms that operate on such optically produced data promise practical systems for general pattern-recognition applications. Recent detector advances have yielded smart sensors that can do considerable on-chip image preprocessing. The combination of digital preprocessing and postprocessing is shown in the general optical-digital architecture of Fig. 3 with both off-line and on-line digital preprocessing functions denoted, together with the use of synthetic discriminant functions.

Beyond matched spatial filtering

The architecture of Fig. 3 provides a general framework for several new approaches to OPR. These examples are representative of the new wave of research that uses techniques besides matched spatial filter correlation. Such work aims to increase the flexibility of an optical processor and the operations it can perform, as well as to capitalize on recent advances in microprocessors, detectors, smart sensors, and digital processing. This effort has brought optical and digital processing researchers close together, since many of the new techniques have their basis in conventional mathematical pattern-recognition literature. The use of hybrid optical techniques has made realization of such algorithms more practical.

One of the simplest preprocessing operations possible is a coordinate transformation. When the proper coordinate transformation is chosen, the correlation of coordinate transformed functions results in an optical processor that is invariant to selected geometrical image distortions. For example, a logarithmic transform converts the distance from a central point into a displacement, thus making all similarly shaped objects identical in size. The combination of a Fourier and logarithmic transform, called a Mellin transform, is thus scale invariant. Similarly, a polar transformation converts rotations around a point into displacements, yielding a rotation-invariant transformation. Several researchers have suggested that the human brain and eye

function as a Mellin transform space-invariant processor and that this is how people recognize objects independent of their scale and rotational orientation. Thus, researchers in vision, artificial intelligence, and optical data processing share some common algorithms.

In many practical pattern-recognition cases, the orientation from which the object will be viewed cannot be controlled. Such a case arises in robotics when an object is to be selected from a bin and in other automated product line systems. A related military application is the location of a tank from infrared imagery. When the reference object is mobile, such as a tank, different input images result, depending upon the aspect angle between the object and the sensor. A 3-D pattern-recognition search problem results. Infrared imagery introduces yet other problems, such as contrast reversals and the loss of different parts of the object, depending on its temperature and its prior activity.

New optical pattern-recognition techniques have been employed to solve this problem. To overcome the contrast reversal and data drop-out effects of infrared imagery, edge enhancement, histogram equalization, and bandpass filtering preprocessing have been employed. In the military tank problem, a set of images of a tank, taken from different aspects, was obtained and preprocessed, as noted. The objective was to determine one synthetic filter function that would be capable of recognizing the input tank object independent of its 3-D aspect.

Toward this end, a covariance matrix was first obtained: The entries of the matrix were equal to the values obtained from the correlations of all possible pairs of tank images. Then the matrix was diagonalized. The diagonalization resulted in a new description of each image as a weighted summation of orthogonal basis functions. The synthetic filter function was written as a similar expansion of the same basis function set. By requiring the cor-

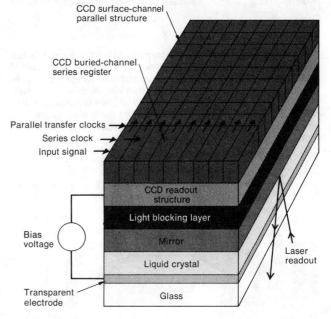

[2] For real-time applications, an input scene must be converted to a transparent pattern in order to modulate the laser light in an optical pattern recognition device. One transducer that can accomplish this conversion is the charge-coupled-device liquid-crystal light valve. In this device, under development at Hughes Research Laboratories, data from a sensor is fed to the CCD on the top layer. This produces a spatial electric field distribution on the liquid crystal layer below. When polarized laser light is reflected through the bottom layers, it emerges spatially modulated by the original input pattern.

CCD surface-channel parallel structure

CCD buried-channel series register

Parallel transfer clocks

Series clock

Input signal

CCD readout structure

Light blocking layer

Mirror

Liquid crystal

Bias voltage

Transparent electrode

Glass

Laser readout

relation of the filter function with each image function to equal a constant, the relation between the weighting coefficients of the filter and the images was found. Thus, the necessary composite synthetic discriminant function can be found.

In effect, what is done here is analogous to the breaking down of a vector into its orthogonal components. The basis functions are the orthogonal axes that define the multidimensional space which contains all the images. Each image can be viewed as a vector if the pixels are arranged in a linear order (as they are in any scanning system). By the above mathematical manipulations, the part of the hyperspace that the images are located within is defined. The synthetic filter acts as the boundary plane of this portion of the space, so that any image input that has a good correlation with the filter will lie in the designated part of the space; in other words, the input image will be recognized as resembling the reference object, even if it is viewed from an orientation different from that of any of the training set, the set of images used to create the synthetic discriminant period.

Thus, the process of producing the synthetic filter determines mathematically what are the elements common to all views of a given object.

This entire process was performed off-line on a digital computer for the training set used. The synthetic discriminant reference function was produced, and it correlated with all of the images in the training set; it thus was capable of recognizing all inputs within the training set.

In this case, and for analogous product-line inspection and robotic applications, off-line synthesis of such a synthetic discriminant function is possible because the training set exists. Once the filter has been produced, it can be permanently recorded and used in the system. Only when the object being searched for is changed do we need to generate a new filter function. This represents one of the newest and most organized approaches to OPR. It also demonstrates the use of synthetic discriminant functions or combinations of them.

This OPR technique has not yet been incorporated into a system and is still a subject of further development. The problem of discrimination of false targets is not yet fully resolved.

Another OPR technique that represents quite a radical departure from the conventional MSF correlation approach is the computation of the invariant moments of an image. These seven moments are invariant to any space-invariant geometrical distortion of an object. Thus, calculation of these moments for a given

input scene, and comparison with the values for the object being searched for, should suffice to determine if the reference object is present in the input or not. These invariant moments are quite complex combinations of the ordinary moments (such as the location of the effective center of mass) of a function or image.

In a new hybrid optical-digital system concept, one can compute all moments for an input function on-line by optical methods. These values are then fed to a dedicated digital postprocessor, which computes invariant moments. The optical system to compute the moments in parallel is a simple imaging system using a fixed mask, with the necessary transfer functions for each of the moments encoded on a different spatial frequency carrier.

Nonmilitary application: a case study

Case studies illustrate both the uses to which OPR can be put and which systems are appropriate for a given application. The simplest optical correlators are, as stated, based on matched spatial filters. However, in most military applications, simple matched spatial filtering is not adequate because of the many differences in scale, orientation, etc. that arise in the representation of the reference object at the system's input. Carnegie-Mellon University recently performed for the Central Intelligence Agency a detailed case study of a nonmilitary application for which optical MSF correlation was found to be adequate. The problem was to determine all pages within the CIA's microfilm data base for which a given key word (the name of a person, city, etc.) was pre-

[3] The most flexible type of optical processing system combines optical and digital electronics components into an optical-digital hybrid. Digital electronics preprocesses the images, and produces synthetic discriminant filters that can be used in the subsequent optical processing. After a correlation function or other optically obtained pattern is produced by the optical processor, more digital circuitry determines the presence and location of the reference object in the scene.

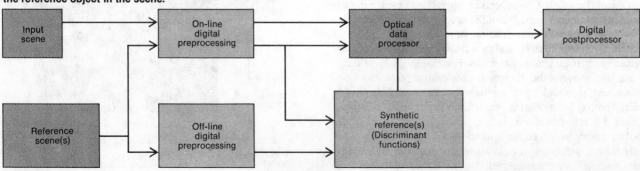

sent and to make copies of all such pages. This set of hard copies could then be used to assemble rapidly a file and report on a given person or subject. Microfilm information represents a data base with adequate control; an unsupervised 3-D aspect-angle pattern-recognition search is not necessary.

In many automated product inspection applications, the orientation and scale, as well as the location of the object, are similarly controlled to quite fine tolerances during fabrication. Thus, simpler OPR techniques should be adequate for many commercial applications.

Although the optical word-recognition problem is quite different from product inspection, a discussion of it and the resulting system design provide considerable insight into an optical MSF correlator system.

Since optical processors have limited gray-scale response, the binary (black and white) nature of microfilm data is an attractive feature. Because the data base is sufficiently controlled, the system need maintain correlation only over ± 10 percent scale differences (caused by different point sizes of text) and ± 5° rotational differences in the reference word. Microfilm data is already available as a transparency and is thus suitable for direct input to an optical processor without need for a real-time noncoherent-to-coherent optical transducer converter.

Analyzing an entire microfilm page

Previous OPR techniques for automated text reading recognized characters rather than words, but word recognition greatly decreases output false alarms and increases the system's discrimination ability. Because of its parallel and 2-D nature, an optical system such as the one in Fig. 1 can analyze an entire microfilm page in the same time it can analyze one line of text or one word. Thus, the high processing speed necessary to search such a large data base in a reasonable time is available.

Another feature of this problem is that the system output need only be a yes or no answer on whether the key word is present on a given page. It is not necessary to know the exact line where the word exists or its position on the line, since a hard copy of the entire page and the two adjacent pages will always be made. This greatly simplifies the decision logic needed in the detector at the output of the optical correlator. These and other specific features make this optical word-recognition problem attractive for an OPR solution. A study like this is necessary for each pattern-recognition problem.

From an analysis of the microfilm data base, the data were grouped into three distinct classes: printed, typewriter, and teletype. Printed data can be in any of 20 to 30 different text fonts. Typewriter data can use mono or proportional spacing. Teletype data is more noisy, and small rotational differences are present in the orientation of each letter. Thus, each class of data is characterized by a different problem.

If each word is viewed as a spatial modulation about a carrier frequency determined by the stroke width of each character, then it is necessary only to look in a region of the Fourier transform plane about this carrier spatial frequency to locate all information on the input text. When this is done, the three classes of data are found to be characterized by different carrier spatial frequencies, and thus, the class of input data could be determined from the outputs from three photodetectors placed at three different spatial frequency locations in the Fourier transform plane.

To produce a single MSF capable of recognizing the key word with the necessary scale and rotational differences, weighted MSF synthesis is employed. To understand this, recall that the MSF is formed off-line, with the reference object in the input plane by interference of its Fourier transform with a plane-wave reference beam. This is analogous to the formation of Fourier transform holograms for 3-D image displays. During synthesis of the MSF, the intensity of the reference and signal beams are set equal at a specific spatial frequency location in the frequency plane. This controlled the modulation level, or emphasis given to different input spatial frequencies during the subsequent correlation process. When lower spatial frequencies are emphasized, such a weighted MSF could easily provide the small scale and rotational tolerances required in this problem.

The optical word-recognition system employs three different output detection techniques to increase the probability of detection, reduce the probability of false alarm, and improve the system's tolerance scale and rotational differences. These correlation plane detection criteria are: (1) conventional thresholding, (2) requiring the area of the correlation peak at a given threshold level to exceed a present value, and (3) requiring the

[4] Benchtop optical processing system, built by Ampex, is being used by the Army Missile Command to study the feasibility of using optical processors in missiles and airplanes. (Special-purpose optics would be used to reduce the size of the system to that required for practical applications.) The input image and the reference pattern are displayed side-by-side on a monitor (M), whose image is focused onto a liquid-crystal device (A). This input pattern then diffracts a laser beam (L), thereby producing a Fourier transform pattern on a second liquid crystal (B). In turn, this pattern again deffracts a laser beam, and a second Fourier transform is produced on a vidicon detector (C). This detected pattern can then be analyzed to determine the presence and location of the reference object in the scene.

volume under the correlation peak above threshold level to exceed a preset value. These are referred to as threshold, area, and volume detection.

All three operations are easily realized with simple comparator, monostable, and peak detector circuits in the detection electronics. Tests show that volume detection was superior to area detection and that both provide better system performance than does conventional threshold detection.

Another application that optical processors are being applied to is in the detection and tracking of moving objects—important in both military and commercial fields. In general, these applications use optical-digital hybrids.

One example is a search and track processor developed by TRW in Redondo Beach, Calif. In the search mode, the processor locates moving objects in a star-field background pattern. In the track mode, it provides time history outputs of all moving objects. This system represents a different approach to pattern recognition, since the optical system provides time history data to a digital postprocessor, which then determines the objects in the system's field of view that are of interest. This system is also noteworthy because it is fully real-time, using no film, and because a tabletop version of it was fabricated and delivered by TRW to the Ballistic Missile Defense Advance Technology Center of the Army in Huntsville, Ala. It performed successfully and represents the type of OPR system that has been used outside the laboratory.

In the search mode, the time sequential output signal from a sensor is fed to an electrooptical light modulator in synchronism with an x-y raster deflector to produce an image of the sensor's field of view on the modulator. The modulator is an Itek Corp. Pockels Readout Optical Modulator, and when many time-sequential images are superimposed on it, moving objects (targets) produce streaks of light, whereas stationary objects (for example, stars) appear as points. To determine the position and angle of the streaks, and hence the necessary target information, the Fourier transform of different regions of the composite image is formed sequentially with a He-Ne laser. Each Fourier transform output is sensed by a wedge-ring detector. The time of occurrence of the output peak determines the location of the target, and the wedge-shaped detector element on which the output occurs indicates the angular trajectory of the target.

In the track mode, a subset of the sensor array is pointed at the target, and the sensor's output at different times is written on different lines of the optical modulator. The LED source shown is used to read out this data, which is then imaged onto a linear detector array. The time output from an element of the scanning linear detector array is the desired time history information of a given moving object in the sensor's field of view.

In another moving target detector being studied by Lockheed Missile & Space Co. in Palo Alto, Calif., successive frames of data from a sensor are optically correlated. The location of the correlation peak allows registration of the two successive images to an accuracy better than a single pixel in the image. The registered frames are then subtracted to yield a difference image, in which only objects that have moved between the frames appear. This represents a large reduction in data and hence is also useful for bandwidth compression.

Optical processor ruggedness improved

A number of other military applications are illustrative of improvements in the ruggedness and compactness of optical processors, qualities also required in commercial use. One system under development uses holographic optical elements rather than fragile lenses. The MSF in this system is formed with a convergent reference beam.

The resulting pattern is an MSF plus a Fourier transform lens, or a so-called lensless MSF. The resulting system thus requires no rigid positioning tolerances between the MSF and the second transform lens and, in fact, the only lens in the system is the simple imaging lens (which can also be made as a holographic element if desired). The low cost, size, and weight of this system and the new OPR architectures it suggests are of use in both airborne and commercial systems.

Another example of a relatively resilient system is the joint transform system recently fabricated by Ampex Corp. in Redwood City, Calif., and delivered to the Army Missile Command in Huntsville, Ala. The two images to be correlated are displayed side-by-side on a monitor. The monitor's image is focused onto an optically addressed liquid-crystal device. This recorded pattern is then read out in laser light, and its Fourier transform is formed on a second liquid-crystal light valve. The Fourier transform of this pattern, in turn, is produced. This second transform contains the desired correlation. A benchtop version of this system is shown in Fig. 4.

The system operates at one frame per second on imagery of 256×256 pixels with 8 bits of gray scale and with a system dynamic range of 38 dB. A second system, with more efficient light coupling from the vidicon to the first liquid crystal, has operated at 30 frames per second.

The reductions in cost and improvements in durability of optical systems for military use counter some of the main objections to such systems in the factory. Military-developed applications, such as identification of objects from arbitrary orientations and location of moving objects, are directly transferable to the industrial field. What is needed now is industrial and commercial funding to apply this useful technology to civilian endeavors.

For further reading

Robotics applications and the role of optical processing are also described in: "Computers that see," Eric Lerner, *Spectrum*, October 1980, pp. 28-33 [see p. 219].

A general view of coherent optical pattern recognition techniques is contained in: "Coherent Optical Pattern Recognition," David Casasent, *Proceedings of the IEEE*, May 1979, pp. 813-825.

A more in-depth treatment of optical processing is available in: "Optical Pattern Recognition," *Proceedings of the Society of Photo-Optical Instrumentation Engineers*, Vol. 201 (1979).

A recent discussion of the similarity and roles of optical and digital processing in diverse applications can be found in a two-volume special issue of *Optical Engineering*, March/April and May/June, 1980.

A more global survey of optical computing exists in the *Proceedings of the IEEE, Special Issue on Optical Computing*, January 1977 and in the various *Proceedings of the International Optical Computing Conferences* noted therein.

Two of the most notable textbooks on optical processing include: *Introduction to Fourier Optics*, J.W. Goodman, McGraw-Hill, 1968, and *Handbook of Optical Holography*, H.J. Caulfield, Academic Press, 1979.

About the author

David Casasent (F) is a professor of electrical engineering at Carnegie Mellon University, where he is head of the Hybrid Optical-Digital Signal and Image Processing Laboratory. He is the author of numerous articles and book chapters and the editor of many special journal issues on optical data processing. He is also a Fellow of the American Optical Society and of the Society of Photo-Optical Instrumentation Engineers.   ◆

SOFTWARE

FUNCTION-LEVEL COMPUTING

A new programming method linked to radically different architectures, may greatly simplify software development

Computer hardware has advanced tremendously in the last 25 years, going from vacuum tubes to very large-scale integrated circuits. In the same period neither the architecture of computers nor the programming languages used to control them have changed significantly. As a result, the expanding capabilities of VLSI are not being fully exploited and the costs of much-needed programs are soaring. Recognition of this fact has focused attention on a style of programming called functional programming, which offers the prospect of much cheaper programs and new machine architectures that exploit VLSI. The functional approach rejects the model of computing conceived by the mathematician John von Neumann and others. The von Neumann model is based on a computer consisting of a central processing unit (CPU), a store or memory, and a connection between them that transmits a single unit of data, or "word," between the CPU and the store. Because today's programming languages are modeled on such computers, programs are complex, concerned with the smallest data entities, and seldom reusable in building new programs.

The most unfortunate result has been the enormous cost of software. While computing power and hardware costs get cheaper every year, the writing of software becomes more expensive. The programs to make a given microprocessor useful may cost considerably more to develop than the microprocessor itself. Such costs and the expertise required to write programs discourage millions of people from using computers.

There are two functional programming styles, one—exemplified by the LISP language—was developed over 20 years ago. But while function definition is its central notion, LISP retains some features of von Neumann programming. The second style, called function-level programming, has been developed since the mid-1970s by a number of researchers, including this writer.

In this style, existing programs are put together with so-called program-forming operations to form new programs, which can again be used to build even larger ones. This approach allows parallel operations to be expressed easily; it suggests hardware designs built from large numbers of identical units that can achieve highly parallel operation, designs well suited to VLSI technology.

Function-level computing is still in its infancy; only relatively small resources are being devoted to its development. In part this is because it is more a revolutionary than an evolutionary approach to computing. Many theoretical and practical problems remain to be solved before it can become a reality in the

marketplace. Nevertheless interest in function-level computing is steadily growing because it is one of very few approaches that offer a real hope of relieving the twin crises of computing today: the absolute necessity to reduce the cost of programming and the need to find computer designs that make much better use of the power of VLSI and of parallelism.

The von Neumann bottleneck

The key problem caused by the original design of computers is in the connection between the CPU and the store [see Fig. 1]. Since the huge contents of the store must pass, one word at a time, through this connection to the CPU and back again, one might call this the "von Neumann bottleneck."

This bottleneck blocks parallel operation and the effective use of more VLSI circuits, but, more critically, it is the model for serious drawbacks in programming languages. Programs in present languages alter the data stored in memory one word at a time. Variables in the programs are used to designate the storage cells, and one entire assignment statement is needed to alter the

John Backus IBM Research

The software challenge

The growth of computer use in the last few years has been fueled by the wide availability of cheap hardware, but it is becoming more and more clear that software is the limiting factor in putting raw computer power to use. Software packages may now cost more than the machines they run on, and even the several hundred thousand professional programmers in the United States cannot keep up with the demand. Programming, although it is becoming easier, is still too complex and tedious for the average computer user to pick up, and so the ultimate users of computing power—businessmen, accountants, scientists, and engineers—still require a middleman to communicate with their machines.

Some of the attempts at making programming easier and more efficient are aimed at relieving professional programmers of drudgery—by shifting repetitive tasks to the machine—while other attempts are aimed at simplifying and automating program generation so that nonprogrammers can set up complex tasks. These approaches are dealt with in the second and third articles in this special report, "Automating programming" [p. 237] and "Programming for nonprogrammers" [p. 243].

A more radical approach is presented by John Backus of IBM Research in San Jose, Calif., in "Function-level computing" beginning on this page. Mr. Backus, the originator of the Fortran computer language, believes that the problem lies in the basic architecture of current machines and current languages. He proposes that new basic designs for computers and corresponding new programming styles will make far easier the tasks of building complex programs from simple modules.

One thing is clear from these articles: while software automation is on the way, it is not yet here. Some simple tasks have been automated, but automatic generation of complex programs is still some way off.　　—*Ed.*

data for each variable. Thus programs consist of repetitive sequences of instructions, with control statements governing how many times and under what conditions the sequences of assignment statements are to be repeated.

If programming is to be really simplified, it is absolutely crucial to be able to build high-level programs from existing programs; and one must be able to do this knowing only the purpose of each constituent program without a lot of other details. [To understand how existing programming languages fail in this, see "The stores problem," p. 236].

A shift in focus in programming

Both von Neumann and LISP-style programs are more concerned with "object" building than with program building. For example, "average(x,y) = half(x + y)" defines an "object-level" program that transforms any pair of objects, x and y, into the desired result-object, their average. It uses object-forming operations (half, +) to build the objects x + y and then half (x + y). It says how to build an object, not how to build the program.

Function-level programming seeks to shift the focus and the level of programming from the combining of objects to the combining of programs (programs are now simply mathematical functions or mappings). The goal of this shift from object-level to function-level description of programs is to emphasize the main issue of programming: how programs are put together, rather than how objects are put together.

Instead of describing how to form the result-object for a program by applying object-forming operations to objects, the function-level style constructs the program directly by applying program-forming operations (PFOs) to existing programs. For example, the function-level description of average is "average = half ∘ +". Here average is built from two simpler programs (half, +) with the PFO "composition," denoted by the small circle (∘), which means "do the right operation (+) first, then do the left one (half) to the result." Thus, average applied to a pair of numbers is simply the half of their sum.

In the function-level style half a dozen or more PFOs can be used to construct programs. In each case the meaning of a program built by a PFO is simply related to the meanings of the programs from which it is built. The program P ∘ Q always represents the composition of the purpose of P with that of Q, and P ∘ Q is always meaningful if it makes sense to apply P to the things that Q produces.

It is this ability to build up meaningful programs from either simple or complex ones that is the principal strength of the function-level style. It can describe programs that have no object-level counterparts; these tend to be concise, well structured and nonrepetitive.

Another program-forming operation is "construction," which is denoted by square brackets. The construction of two programs does both operations to its argument and returns a pair of results. Thus the program [half, double] applied to 4 gives < 2,8 >. If one now starts with three given programs P, Q, and R and builds the program P ∘ [Q,R], then its meaning is clear: first do [Q,R] to form a pair of objects, the first the result of applying Q, the second the result of applying R (a pair of objects is also an object). Then do P to that pair. P ∘ [Q,R] will be meaningful if it makes sense to apply P to pairs produced by Q and R.

In addition to the power that PFOs provide for building meaningful programs at all levels of complexity, they also have other important properties. For example, composition and construction satisfy the distributive law [f, g] ∘ h = [f ∘ h, g ∘ h], for all programs f, g, and h. Notice that the program on the right side can be made more efficient by transforming it into the one on the left

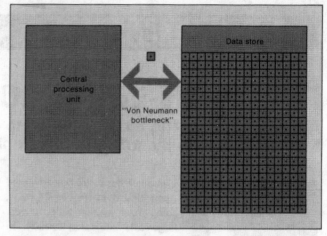

[1] The von Neumann machine operates on one word of data at a time, even when the same operation must be performed on thousands of words. Finding the location of a piece of data in memory and bringing it to the CPU therefore limits computational speed.

left, since the latter uses h only once. Thus even this simple law can be used to improve many programs. There are dozens of similar laws from which many theorems about programs can be derived; these can represent a large body of knowledge that can be used again and again to prove the correctness of programs and to guide their construction.

Some program-forming operations express parallel operations very naturally, whereas von Neumann programs are essentially sequential. When the program [P,Q] is executed, it makes no difference whether P or Q is done first or whether both are done together. This potential for parallelism in function-level programming, if incorporated into new computer architectures, would lead to a better use of VLSI.

To see why such languages may some day cut the cost of programming by a larger factor than Fortran achieved 25 years ago when it replaced machine languages, it may be helpful to contrast function-level programming languages with von Neumann languages in five major areas:

1. *Program domains*

Present programs map stores into stores, whereas their real purpose is to map objects into objects. The structure of data objects in the store is known only to the programs that use it; changing the size or structure of the data means changing the programs.

Function-level programs map objects into objects and thus a program directly represents the transformation that is its purpose. Objects can be numbers or symbols or even sequences of other objects. The structure of a data object is part of the object, rather than part of the program, so the same program can treat objects of different structure and size.

2. *Program building*

In the present approach, unless programs have a common data-storage plan, a composite program built from them is meaningless. In the function-level approach, programs can be freely built from others that have suitable purposes. The purpose of a program is simply related to those of the programs from which it is built.

3. *Program structure*

Present programs contain three kinds of structures: programs, expressions, and variables or constants. A program is built from subprograms the simplest of which are the assignment statements (variable: = expression); these in turn are built from expressions (for example, $2x + y$), and expressions are built from variables and constants.

Function-level programs are built only from programs, and the simplest programs are given at the outset.

4. *Program-forming operations*

Present programs are built with three PFOs: composition, if-then-else, and while. Function-level programs can be built using six or more PFOs: composition, condition, construction, constant, apply-to-all, insert, and others [see "Function-level programming in action," below, for descriptions].

5. *Algebraic treatment of programs and correctness proofs*

With present programs, PFOs satisfy few algebraic laws. There are few general, practical theorems about programs; most apply only to a single program or a small class of programs (for

---

Function-level programming in action

Function-level programs consist of objects, functions, functional forms, definitions, and one operator called "application." Objects are numbers, symbols, words, or sequences. A sequence $< x_1, x_2, \ldots, x_n >$ of objects consists of x's which are either numbers, symbols, words, or sequences.

"Application" is the operation of applying a function to an object. For example, to apply the addition function (+) to the object $< 1, 2 >$ we write:

$$+ : < 1, 2 > = 3$$

Primitive functions, like all functions, transform one object into another. Examples are:

1. Selector functions, which choose an element of a sequence:

$$1 : < x_1, x_2, \ldots, x_n > = x_1$$
$$2 : < x_1, x_2, \ldots, x_n > = x_2$$

2. Arithmetic functions, such as $+, -, \times, \div$, and so on.

3. Transpose:

$$\text{trans}: << 1, 2 >, < 3, 4 >> = << 1, 3 >, < 2, 4 >>$$

4. Distribution functions, such as distribute from the left:

$$\text{distl}: <x, <y_1, y_2, \ldots, y_n >> = <<x, y_1 >, <x, y_2 >, \ldots, <x, y_n >>$$

Functional forms are expressions denoting programs that are built from existing programs using program-forming operations (PFOs). Some examples of PFOs and simple functional forms built with them are:

1. Composition (of f and g):

$$(f \circ g) : x = f : (g : x)$$

In words: the composition of f and g, f∘g, applied to x gives the result of applying f to the result of applying g to x. If f = arctan and g = sin, then f∘g is the arctangent of the sine.

2. Construction (of $f_1, f_2, \ldots, f_n$):

$$[f_1, f_2, \ldots, f_n] : x = < f_1 : x, f_2 : x, \ldots, f_n : x >$$

3. Condition (of p, f and g):

$$(p \rightarrow f; g) : x = f : x \text{ if } p : x \text{ is true;}$$
$$= g : x \text{ if } p : x \text{ is false}$$

4. Constant (of an object y; constant makes a constant-valued function out of an object):

$$y : x = y \quad \text{for any x, the function y gives the result y}$$

5. Insert (of f):

$$/ f : < x_1, x_2, \ldots, x_n > = f : < x_1, / f : < x_2, \ldots, x_n >>$$

6. Apply-to-all (of f):

$$\alpha f : < x, x_2, \ldots, x_n > = < f : x_1, f : x_2, \ldots, f : x_n >$$

Definitions define new functions in terms of old ones. Thus **Def** f = g∘[h, k] means that f is to stand for the function g∘[h, k]

The difference between function-level and von Neumann programs can be illustrated.

Vector inner product. The vector inner product is obtained by multiplying pairwise the elements of two vectors and adding these products. For example, in a billing system, a vector of the prices of all items would be multiplied by the vector of orders for each item to give the total bill.

(a) Von Neumann program:

```
c : = 0;
for i : = 1 step 1 until n do
      c : = c + a ( i ) × b ( i )
```

(b) Function-level program:

Define   Inner Product = (insert +) ∘ (apply-to-all ×)
                                                    ∘ transpose

Or in abbreviated form:

Def   IP = $(/ +) \circ (\alpha \times) \circ$ trans

This program is executed from right to left and can be expressed as follows: "The definition of inner product is: transpose the pair of vectors (pair their elements), multiply each pair together, and sum the resulting vector." A preprocessor or "translator" program would not have much trouble in translating language like the above into the FP definition.

To see this program in action, take the vectors $< 1, 2, 3 >$ and $< 4, 5, 6 >$ as an example and apply IP to this pair:

1. Composition gives:

$$(/ +) : ((\alpha \times) : (\text{trans}: << 1, 2, 3 >, < 4, 5, 6 >>))$$

2. Transpose gives:

$$(/ +) : ((\alpha \times) : << 1, 4 >, < 2, 5 >, < 3, 6 >>)$$

3. Apply-to-all gives:

$$(/ +) : < \times : <1, 4 >, \times : < 2, 5 >, \times : < 3, 6 >>$$

4. Multiply gives:

$$(/ +) : <4, 10, 18>$$

5. Insert gives:

$$+ : < 4, + : <10, 18 >>$$

6. Addition gives:

$$+ : < 4, 28 >$$

7. Another addition gives:

$$32$$

The von Neumann and functional programs for inner product have several differences:

1. The functional program is hierarchically built from three generally useful, preexisting programs (+, ×, trans). All the components (the two assignment statements and the 'for' statement) of the other program must be specially written for it alone.

2. The von Neumann program is repetitive—to understand it, one must mentally execute it, or use special mathematical tools. The FP program is nonrepetitive; if its components are understood, its meaning is clear.

3. The von Neumann program computes one word at a time by repetition. The functional program operates on whole conceptual units, not words, and does not repeat any steps.

4. The first program mentions the length, n, of the vectors; hence it lacks generality. The functional program is completely general.

5. The von Neumann program names its arguments—it will only work for vectors called a and b. The functional program can be applied to any pair of vectors without naming them.

—J.B.

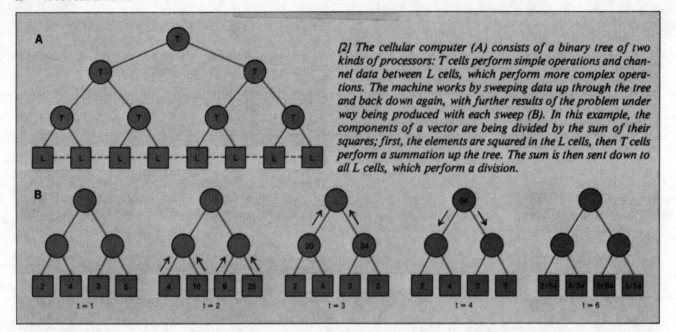

A

B

t = 1   t = 2   t = 3   t = 4   t = 6

[2] The cellular computer (A) consists of a binary tree of two kinds of processors: T cells perform simple operations and channel data between L cells, which perform more complex operations. The machine works by sweeping data up through the tree and back down again, with further results of the problem under way being produced with each sweep (B). In this example, the components of a vector are being divided by the sum of their squares; first, the elements are squared in the L cells, then T cells perform a summation up the tree. The sum is then sent down to all L cells, which perform a division.

example, "Theorem: this program is correct").

With function-level programs, PFOs satisfy dozens of algebraic laws that yield many general theorems about program equivalence and about solving equations for programs. Proofs about large classes of programs are possible, and other proofs can be greatly simplified by drawing on standard general theorems, as in mathematics.

This comparison indicates that function-level languages have overcome many of the principle problems in von Neumann languages. However, these languages are very distant from the von Neumann model of computing, and this means that either many problems of optimization must be solved before they can be run on von Neumann computers with acceptable speed or else that new, non–von Neumann computers must be designed to execute function–level programs efficiently.

A non–von Neumann computer

A number of efforts are seeking to develop such a computer. Two projects are typical of these efforts. One is being led by Professor Gyula Mago at the University of North Carolina at Chapel Hill, the other by Professor Arvind at the Massachusetts Institute of Technology's Laboratory for Computer Science in Cambridge.

Prof. Mago's design is the more radical of the two, since the parallelism inherent in functional programs is carried out to the fullest in the structure of the computer, in which storage and processing units are intimately linked. The computer consists of an arbitrarily large number of cells, each of which is one of two types: leaf, or L, cells and tree, or T, cells [see Fig. 2]. The tree cells are connected to form a binary tree, with each cell communicating with one parent cell and two child cells. The leaf cells form the base of the tree, each cell being the child of a T cell; each L cell is connected to its two neighboring L cells in addition to its parent T cell. All L cells are identical, as are all T cells, so that the overall design of the computer is simple and well adapted to VLSI technology.

In operation, functional program expressions, including their data, are fed into the L cells. The T cells then partition the expression, breaking it down into independent subexpressions. Each subexpression is composed of a function and the data to which it is being applied; each can be evaluated at the same time as all the

others. The partitioning of the T and L cells in this way divides the whole machine into a number of subtrees. Each subtree is a smaller machine applying its own program to its own data.

The L cells act both as storage units and as processors, while the T cells manage communication between the L cells. By its very structure, the cellular computer avoids the problem of addressing, since its operation ensures that when the moment comes to apply any subprogram, its data will be in the adjacent L cells to its right.

The operation of the computer consists of a series of upward and downward sweeps of information as increasingly large parts of the functional expression are computed. The process begins with the innermost parts, which can be calculated immediately, and ends when the entire expression has been evaluated.

The T cells distribute the microprogram required by each L cell to apply the operational part of the expression to data in neighboring cells. For example, a microprogram might instruct the L cell to send its contents to the T cells above that are working to evaluate the same expression. Thus, during each machine cycle, information will sweep up to the top of the subtreee working on a given subexpression, and the information collected there will be sent down for further use by the L cells. At the end of each downward sweep, another stage in the evaluation of the subexpression will be completed.

Each cell of the machine is a fairly simple microprocessor containing both a CPU and a very small store. The L cells have a small store for microprograms, local storage for the symbol stored in the cell, its level of nesting in the expression, some condition registers, and a CPU.

The T cells are still simpler, basically containing only data registers and very simple processing units to direct the data and perform simple operations on it.

The basic simplicity of the cells and the fact that there are only two kinds means that the cost of designing and building such computers, even very large ones, should be manageable. Prof. Mago envisions computers with as many as a million cells, each with a few thousand circuits, with a number of cells on each VLSI chip.

Prof. Mago has made detailed calculations of the speed of operation of such computers. Performance of several billion instructions per second may be feasible in some applications. Yet, because of the simplicity of construction, such computers might be no more expensive that current large von Neumann machines. Since these machines implement both primitive programs and program-forming operations with microprograms, their machine language is a higher-level language than current so-called high-level languages.

At present, Prof. Mago is designing the elementary chips for the cellular computer and expects to produce the first prototype chips in a couple of years.

An alternative approach

An important alternative approach to implementing functional languages is the data-flow architecture of Prof. Arvind at MIT (data-flow ideas were first elaborated by Jack Dennis at MIT and later by Paul Kosinski at IBM Research Center, Yorktown Heights, N.Y.). Unlike the Mago machine, Prof. Arvind's design is intended for use with any functional language, not just the language we have been discussing. All such languages are compiled into a graphical data-flow language.

The Arvind machine itself consists of up to several thousand identical microprocessors connected by a packet communication network that allows any unit to send "tokens" to any other unit. Each token contains a piece of data and a "tag" telling to what processor the token is to be sent and with which other tokens its data is to be combined. When any processor receives a token, it matches it with its mate, performs the appropriate operation on the data of the token pair, forms a new token with the result, and sends it to the appropriate processor for further treatment.

Each processor has several sections [see Fig. 3]. A token normally arrives at the waiting-matching section, which contains tokens waiting for their mates. When a pair of matching tokens is formed, it is sent to the instruction-fetch section, which retrieves the needed instructions from its program memory and sends them with the data from the tokens to the arithmetic-and-logic unit (ALU). The ALU combines the data using the instructions to form a result. Finally this result is sent to the output section where it is incorporated into a new token whose tag is computed from the tags of the input tokens and from the addresses given in the instructions.

As much as possible, code related to a single loop within a pro-

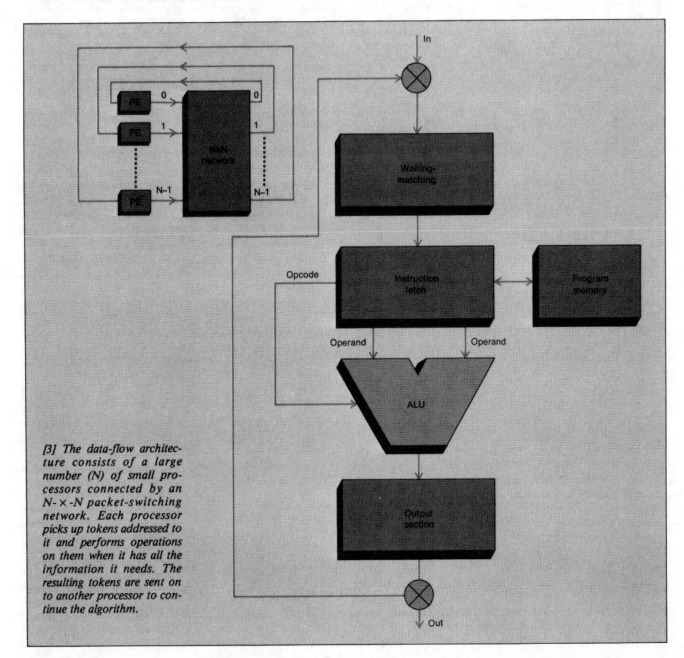

[3] The data-flow architecture consists of a large number (N) of small processors connected by an N- × -N packet-switching network. Each processor picks up tokens addressed to it and performs operations on them when it has all the information it needs. The resulting tokens are sent on to another processor to continue the algorithm.

The stores problem

Von Neumann programs depend on the details of the storage plan that positions their data in the store (a store is a set of named cells, each cell containing a word of problem data). Programs must also provide the structure for their data, which resides in the store as an unstructured set of words. Thus larger programs can be built only from smaller ones that share a common storage plan (where is the data and what is its structure?), with the result that they must all be planned and written together. This prevents building up large collections of programs that can be used over and over to make larger ones.

The word-at-a-time nature of programs is another important factor, along with the need for storage plans that interferes with their universal applicability.

The net result of these difficulties is that programming takes a great deal of time to learn and a great deal of time to do. In addition, prepackaged programs are often so inflexible as to severely limit their use, or they offer so large a catalogue of options and features that it is very difficult to learn how to use them. Thus the accomplishments of the vast army of programmers is not even cumulative.

One way to understand the basic problems of von Neumann programming languages is to observe that their programs always map stores into stores. However, the *purpose* of a program is to map objects into objects—for example, to map a matrix into its inverse, or a file of transactions into a file of responses. The purpose of a program is *never* to map stores into stores, yet this is what all von Neumann programs do. Thus the programmer must translate the purpose of his program—say, to map matrices into their inverses—into a mapping of stores in which the input matrix occupies certain cells and the results others.

This disparity between the purpose of a program, on one hand, and its actual store-to-store mapping, on the other, is the source of the difficulty in building von Neumann programs from smaller ones. Suppose there are two programs, one to invert matrices, the other to transpose them, but they have not been planned together. Now a program to calculate the inverse of the transpose of a matrix is desired. It would seem a simple matter to form the composition of the two program, which first does "transpose" and then does "inverse," to get the desired program. But unless both programs have a common storage plan (and independent programs generally do not), with the output cells of "transpose" coinciding exactly with the input cells of "inverse," the composition of the programs will not achieve the composition of their purposes: the resulting program will be meaningless.

It is possible to write special von Neumann programs called subroutines whose storage plans can be altered when they are *used*, rather than being fixed when they are written. Such subroutines can be reused more easily than ordinary programs but are less convenient for building larger programs than functional programs, which do not depend on storage plans.   —*J.B.*

gram is assigned to a physically related group of processors so that communication time between processors is minimized.

Prof. Arvind's group is now working on the detailed design of a 64-processor prototype machine, which they expect to be operating by the end of 1985.

It is too early to say which of these approaches to functional-style hardware will prove more fruitful, or whether some other approach may in the end be more suitable than either. Once prototypes are operating, it will be possible to compare the actual performance and costs of the various designs.

Problems remaining

A significant number of issues in functional programming need elaboration before commercialization can be considered. The most important relates to the handling of secondary and permanent storage. In addition, hardware must be built and tested, microprogramming systems elaborated, and problems run.

Before any of the projects developing parallel computers for functional programs have built a cost-effective model, some simple sequential computers for functional languages may evolve to fill the gap between today's computers and the parallel, non–von Neumann computers of tomorrow.

Were non–von Neumann computing to be widely adopted, its impact would likely be profound. Not only would programming time be reduced and repetitive programming of similar problems be largely eliminated, but programming of many applications could be simplified so that each one of millions of potential users could write programs for his own needs without the help of a professional programmer. Combined with the increased speed that would be possible with new computer architectures and VLSI design, a vast expansion of computer applications is entirely conceivable. Many tasks, such as visual recognition and computer graphics, involving many parallel computations could become much easier with such an approach. Finally, the design and manufacturer of hardware based on many identical parts could become much cheaper than current hardware. Overall, the possible advantages of non–von Neumann computing seem to justify a much larger commitment of resources to its rapid development than is currently being made.

To probe further

The problems of conventional programming methods are discussed in "Can Programming Be Liberated from the von Neumann Style? A Functional Style and its Algebra of Programs," by John Backus, *Communications of the ACM*, August 1978, pp. 613–41. The difference between the function-level style and the LISP style of programming is elaborated in "Functional-level programs as mathematical objects," *Proceedings of the Conference on Functional Programming Languages and Computer Architecture*, October 1981, pp. 1–10, Association of Computing Machinery.

For a more complete description of the Mago machine see "A Network of Microprocessors to Execute Reduction Languages," Parts I and II, *International Journal of Computer and Information Sciences*, October and December 1979, pp. 349–85 and pp. 435–71.

"The U-interpreter," by Arvind and Kim P. Gostelow, IEEE *Computer*, February 1982, pp. 42–49, contains a description of the Arvind machine; a further description is found in "A multiple-processor data-flow machine to support generalized procedures," by Arvind and Zinod Kathail, *Proceedings of the Eighth, International Symposium on Computer Architecture*, IEEE and ACM, pp. 291–302.

About the author

John Backus is an IBM fellow at the IBM Research Laboratory in San Jose, Calif. He headed the group that produced the Fortran language and its first compiler. He also participated in the design of the international programming language Algol and proposed the language called Backus-Naur Form, or BNF, used to describe its syntax. A member of the National Academies of Sciences and of Engineering, Mr. Backus holds B.S. and A.M. degrees in mathematics from Columbia University.   ◆

SOFTWARE

AUTOMATING PROGRAMMING
Researchers are beginning to shift the growing burden of programming to the computer itself

Though some researchers consider radical changes in the way computers work to be essential to break the programming bottleneck, such an approach inevitably will take a number of years to bear fruit. In the meantime, others are working on more evolutionary approaches: leaving the computers as they are but automating the tedious job of programming them. In essence, these computer scientists are taking the development of programming languages one step further. Twenty years ago Fortran and other high-level languages were developed to enable programmers to generate many machine-language commands from fewer high-level instructions. Today's efforts are aimed at producing languages that will allow a simple statement about the purpose or behavior of a program to generate the entire high-level language algorithm to carry out the operations, thus eliminating the need for applications progammers.

These new languages, some of which are on the verge of commercialization, are collectively termed "nonprocedural," in that they allow the user to state merely *what* operations he or she wants performed, not, as with conventional languages, *how* the computer is to perform them. These languages are called "data flow" because the compiler program uses the relationships among the data groups to determine the sequence in which procedures are to be carried out. In contrast, with conventional "control flow" languages, the sequence of procedures is spelled out in the program itself.

Compiler analyzes statements

In data-flow programming, the compiler determines the sequence of procedures by analyzing the statements entered and requiring that a given operation not be executed until its input operands are available. Take the problem of computing a payroll from a list of pay rates, hours worked, and taxation tables. With a conventional programming language, a repetitive sequence of operations must be specified in instructions such as the following:

```
n = 1
Do n,1,1140
PAY(n) = HOURS(n)*RATE(n)
n = n + 1
```

This would be followed by a similar, explicitly laid out procedure for calculating the taxes.

But with a data-flow language, all that is necessary is to state the relations among the data:

Eric J. Lerner   Contributing Editor

```
PAY = HOURS*RATE
TAXES = .15*PAY, IF PAY LESS THAN 200.00
TAXES = 30.00 + .18*PAY, IF 200.00 LESS THAN PAY,
PAY LESS THAN 250.00
```

and so on. The compiler itself determines from these statements that PAY must be calculated before TAXES and sets up the appropriate loops to do this for all employees. With many data-flow systems, the compiler has the capability to send queries to the user to clarify the statements.

Because so much of the work of programming involves deciding the sequence in which instructions are carried out, the data-flow languages, which automate these decisions, vastly reduce the difficulty of programming. In addition, they facilitate the use of modules, since the meshing of subprograms is performed by the compiler in a standard way, not by the programmer according to preference.

As an idea, data-flow programming is not new; it originated over 15 years ago. However, only in the last few years has dissatisfaction with existing languages led to intense interest in and development of data-flow methods.

Automatic programming system developed

One of the most developed examples of a data-flow language is the Model language developed by the automatic program generation project of the Moore School of Electrical Engineering at the University of Pennsylvania in Philadelphia. In this system two types of statements define and describe the data aggregates, and assertion statements describe logical or arithmetical relations among the data categories. The statements can be entered in any order, as they come to the user's mind. The Model processor analyzes the statements given to it as a whole and then queries the user when it detects ambiguity or incompleteness. It uses the relations among the assertions to produce a finished program.

The capabilities of the system are illustrated by its application in three projects. In one, funded by the National Science Foundation and administered by the departments of economics and computer science at the University of Pennsylvania, more than 20 institutions around the world are collaborating on the formulation of econometric models. Each institution is designing a mathematical model of its own country's economy, with the aim of combining the models into a single predictive model of world trade and development.

With conventional programming languages, such a project could become a major headache to all concerned. Economists would have to spend much time programming their models or working with programmers. The differences between the computer models of each country would in addition make the integration of the models into a single global system an enormous programming problem.

However, with the automatic program-generation system, development has been much easier. Economists can enter their models into the system as sets of equations, while the system itself generates a program and automatically takes from each model the terms for imports, exports, and balance of payments, integrating these into the global model. Virtually no manual programming time is involved in the whole process.

For use in the project, the Model language was expanded to accept matrix and vector expressions and operations, such as matrix multiplication. Such expressions can be entered in the same form that they are written in conventional mathematical notation. This is useful not only for economics, where matrices are used to represent the input-output connections among industries, but also in the physical sciences, where matrix notation is widely used. Without such labor-saving modifications to the language, the complexity of the global model, including up to 70 000 equations, would make the project nearly impossible. In addition, the ease with which the model can be modified through the entry of new equations makes it practical to change the country models frequently in response to changes in economic policies or conditions.

A second expansion of the language is the definition of aggregate data structures and operations—operations that select one set of data from another or merge two sets of data. These operators can be expressed by a single statement for each set of data, rather than by statements defining how each element in a set is to be processed.

At present the first steps in implementing the economic project have been completed, and the full system is expected to be operational by 1984.

Problems with business applications

The effort toward automatic program generation in business applications has been less successful. Accountants and other business users have been trained to use the system to set up accounting and inventory-control programs. But the need for careful, standardized descriptions of the data sets and their relationships require that the users learn a simplified form of programming language, which, although elementary, is very different from English. Furthermore, the description of the relations between the data uses algebraic equations, with which many users are unfamiliar.

"Basically, there is always a human-engineering problem in these cases," commented Noah Prywes, the director of the project at the Moore School. "Users need to know enough basic math and logic to formulate what they want done, even if they don't need to know programming. This is why we have had somewhat better results working with professionals such as scientists, who have mathematical training, than with business types, who don't."

A third effort by the University of Pennsylvania group, using a related language called Nopal, aims at automating entirely the programming of automatic test equipment (ATE). The generation of programs for testing electronics equipment has become increasingly expensive. ATE software generally costs 10 times more than ATE hardware, and total ATE costs are a major contributor to computer-maintenance expenditures. The Nopal automated system generates its programs from the circuit characteristics to be tested.

Nopal consists of two subsystems. The first, or "top," part takes a circuit diagram, entered in standard form, and other test criteria and uses an electrical-engineering data base to produce a test specification. The second, or "bottom," part of the system then takes the test specifications and converts them into a test program.

Thus far Nopal has generated test programs for boards with up to 100 components. However, the present system is not fully automatic; it requires a good deal of interaction with a highly skilled operator to check a test specification. The bottom part of the system can be used separately to generate programs from manually prepared test specifications.

Steps to automatic programming

The automatic programming generator creates the program via a series of separate steps [Fig. 1]. The first step is a syntax analysis. In this stage the compiler analyzes and categorizes each statement, identifying variables and conditions. Then it produces a graphical representation of the dependency of each variable on the others. This directed graph [Fig. 2] shows which variables

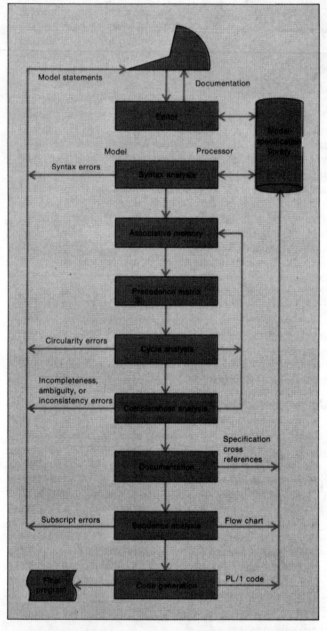

[1] The Model system takes a logical specification and turns it into a computational process. It queries the user when there are errors in syntax or logic, or when the logical specification is ambiguous. In addition to producing a final program, it also produces a specification, a flow chart, and program code to go into a library for later reference and reuse.

must be calculated first, which variables are dependent on them, and so on.

The third state is the detection of errors in the source specification. Here the compiler searches for three broad problems: (1) ambiguities when the same name is assigned to different data; (2) incompleteness caused by the lack of definition of some variables; and (3) inconsistencies in definition. If such errors are noted, the compiler either suggests a resolution to the user or requests a correction.

Once an error-free specification is prepared by the compiler, the compiler creates a flow chart of the program, based on a directed graph. The flow chart details the order in which program steps are to be carried out. In preparing the flow chart, the compiler first looks for cycles in the graph of the specifications. These cycles represent either a circular definition of a variable, in which case an error message is sent to the user, or a set of simultaneous equations, in which case either an exact solution or a numerical approximation technique is set up. Then the compiler takes each data aggregate—for example, a payroll—and breaks it down into a series of DO loops, or repetitive calculations, on each element of the aggregate—say, each employee in the payroll.

Once an initial flow chart is devised, the compiler attempts to optimize the efficiency of the program by consolidating iterations, thus reducing the number of input and output operations and the number of calls to external memory.

Finally, each block of the flow chart is translated into high-level language code (either PL/1 or Cobol).

Model versus Nopal system

In the Model system, the user presents a solution and obtains a program to implement it, but in the Nopal system the user presents only the problem and the computer supplies both the solution—the test specifications—and the program. The basic input to the system is a circuit description, node by node and component by component. For each component, tolerances are

entered. In addition, failure definitions, initial conditions, and test objectives—such as isolation of a fault in a group of components—may also be entered.

The system then generates stimuli and measurements for tests using, in turn, three different strategies. As Dr. Prywes describes it:

"First, small voltage stimuli (dc or ac, depending on the type of components involved) are connected to connecting points of the unit under test (UUT), with the objective of measuring impedances at the connection points. This is referred to as the *cold-circuit* strategy. Next, the UUT is powered with the nominally specified dc power sources, and voltage and current measurements are conducted at the available nodes. This strategy is referred to as a *dc nominal*. Finally, an ac signal is applied to input connecting points, and user-specified tests are conducted. This strategy is referred to as *ac signal*."

The circuit behavior is then simulated, with each component modeled with a failure condition. The simulation provides the outputs for each test when each component is in the failure condition. Then the results are compared with the test objectives to see if the objectives have been met—that is, if the failures can be clearly distinguished by the tests. Each strategy is examined in turn, until the objectives are met or the strategies are exhausted.

If the objectives are met, the program optimizes the text program by eliminating as many tests as possible without loss of fault isolation.

The top part of the system then produces a complete set of test specifications in Nopal code and passes them to the bottom part. The bottom part of the system first sequences the tests according to criteria such as:
- Component protection—the concept that a critical component must be tested before other components that depend on it.
- Fault isolation—meaning that more general faults are tested first.
- Failure likelihood—testing for most likely failures first.

The system produces a flow chart for the test sequence, and finally it converts the chart into program code in the Atlas test language. At present, the Nopal system is compatible only with RCA Equate AN/USM-410 automated test equipment and its Equate Atlas compiler, although only the final step is machine- or language-dependent.

Knowledge-based programming

A second major effort to develop an automated programming system is the knowledge-based programming effort at the Kestrel Institute in Palo Alto, Calif. Two systems, PSI and CHI, are under development by a group led by Cordell Green. The PSI system produces finished programs from high-level descriptions. The CHI system, a successor of PSI, can also participate in algorithm design when completely autonomous program generation is not feasible. CHI has a knowledge-based programming environment that lets programmers carry out difficult steps while relieving them of the simpler parts of program generation.

PSI consists of a set of closely interacting modules, called "experts" [Fig. 3]. The programming process, which is highly interactive, begins when the user enters his description of what the program is to do into the system. The parser/interpreter module parses the sentences entered and converts them into a more standardized set of statements about the program. This module uses extensive programmed control structures (such as loops and procedures), and various other algorithms. With this knowlege base, the module can assign a meaning to an unknown word on the basis of context.

The dialogue-moderator expert questions the user to elicit a

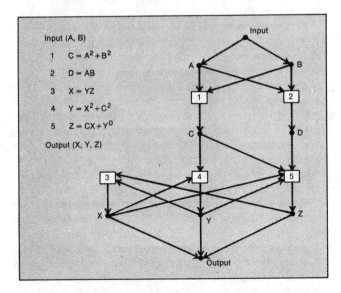

Input (A, B)

1   $C = A^2 + B^2$

2   $D = AB$

3   $X = YZ$

4   $Y = X^2 + C^2$

5   $Z = CX + Y^D$

Output (X, Y, Z)

[2] *The directed graph is a basis for producing a sequential program from interrelationships among variables. Given the series of equations above, the Model system extracts a graph showing which variables depend on which other variables, and therefore what the order of computational steps must be. If the directed graph shows circular dependencies, then the user will be required to modify the specifications.*

Automated software on the market

Although the generation of general-purpose programs from a functional description is still a subject of university and industry research, program generators in certain limited areas are available commercially. (One that has been in existence for many years is IBM Corp's RPG, which generates reports in tabular and other formats by searching through a data base for the relevant information.) Most of these systems are designed for business use: inventory control, management information, data base management and similar tasks. In these areas, some automatic program generators perform quite well.

There are two programming methods that commercial program generators use to go from user descriptions to code. The first is the "self-contained" or interpretive method, which executes the user's instructions directly by calling on a series of subroutines contained within the program generator; thus very high-level specifications can be executed, but a penalty in memory requirements and speed may be exacted. The second method is to produce a set of high-level language instructions from a library of routines; the generated program is then compiled and executed separately from the program generator itself. Depending on the application, either method may have advantages or disadvantages.

One example of a self-contained system is PRO-IV, developed by Data Technical Systems Inc., Honolulu, Hawaii, and licensed for a number of minicomputers. The system relied on a displaced set of problem-definition forms or programming menus to speed applications programming for such tasks as data-entry. The forms constrain a programmer's choices, but by doing so they also make setting up a new applications program a matter of choosing between options at various points in a basic scenario rather than building a program from scratch.

Many automatic program generators write programs for applications such as data-base manipulation, querying a data base for particular information such as:

```
Accounts: Past due   > 30 days and
          Balance    > $10 000
```

Where data-base query languages are unavailable or inadequate, automatic program generators can be used and can repeat searches at regular intervals simply by rerunning a program. Informatics Inc. of Woodland Hills, Calif., produces a generator called Mark-V for calculations using IBM machine languages. It can access data bases such as payroll or accounts receivable and perform calculations on the data. The generated programs can call subroutines written in any of IBM's languages and thus can interface efficiently with existing program libraries, as well as become part of a library of generally available programs. Another similar system is QBE [see "Programming for nonprogrammers," p. 243].

There are many other program generators on the market of various capabilities, from simple systems suitable for production scheduling to more sophisticated systems capable of writing programs for computation-intensive statistical analysis. Many of the simpler programs run on microcomputers; the Visicalc series is one example, as are Ashton-Tate Inc.'s dBase II, Micropro International Corp.'s Infostar, Fox & Geller Associates Inc.'s Quickcode, and a host of others. Most of the microcomputer-based automatic software generators are self-contained, and all those which do produce independent programs do so in high-level languages. Automatic programmers for large machines are also mostly self-contained, but those that do produce independent code are somewhat more likely to produce it in fast-executing assembly language.

Commercial program generators clearly are not suited to complex scientific and engineering applications, much less to writing business operating and accounting systems, but within their limited areas of expertise they should make computing power far more available to casual users.   —Ed.

---

further description of the program. This module collects questions from the other modules that are working on the program, determines what the topic under discussion is, and decides which questions are appropriate. It then passes the questions to the explainer expert.

The explainer expert converts questions generated by the system in an internal language into English before passing them to the user. It phrases questions in terms related to either the problem area the program deals with or to previous sentences in the dialogue between the user and the system.

One other expert deals with communication between the user and the system: the example/trace expert. This module analyzes examples given by the user to illustrate what the program is to accomplish and deduces statements about the program from the examples.

The domain expert contains knowledge about specific applications areas. Thus, for an electronics engineering program, relations and definitions frequently used in electronics are programmed into this module. The domain expert uses this knowledge base to help the parser/interpreter and the example/trace experts figure out what the user means.

The remaining three modules do the actual work of taking the specifications and converting them into a program. The model-building expert applies knowledge of what constitutes a correct program to convert the program net—a set of statements derived from the user specifications and dialogue—to a model or outline of the program. The model-building expert fills in missing parts of the model and analyzes the model for consistency. Where necessary, it asks questions of the user, passing them to the dialogue expert, or its queries the other experts or makes inferences from the available data.

Finally, the coding expert converts the program model into a final program in the desired programming language, while the efficiency expert works with the coding expert to determine which of various possible implementations will run the fastest.

The coding expert, called Pecos, was developed by David Barstow of the Kestrel Institute and uses a set of 400 programming rules to transform the program model into an actual program. The model defines the program in terms of data structure and operations on those structures, such as mappings. The programming rules are basically "translations" of such program relationships into the target language, LISP, or into forms that are a step closer to LISP.

When a number of different rules can be applied to the same part of the program model, the efficiency expert, called Libra, decides which rule should be applied and what part of the program model should be acted on next. Libra, developed by Elaine Kant of Kestrel, makes these decisions based on both the estimated ultimate efficiency of the implementation of the program and the amount of effort the PSI system must expend to develop such an implementation.

Currently the PSI system can be used by an experienced user for certain limited applications. It has produced a number of simple programs. The problem areas currently covered include symbolic computation, list processing, searching and sorting, and data storage and retrieval. However, Dr. Green believes that

[3] PSI consists of a series of interacting experts and the programmer that produces a program from a high-level description of the program's behavior. If there are no ambiguities in the original description of the program, the user does not play a role in the program-building process, but if the system requires extra information or clarification, it will ask the user for them. The domain expert may recognize that a datum needed for a particular application is missing, sending a request for it through the parser and interpreter, or the explainer may translate the machine's internal representation of the problem back into English to see if it is correct.

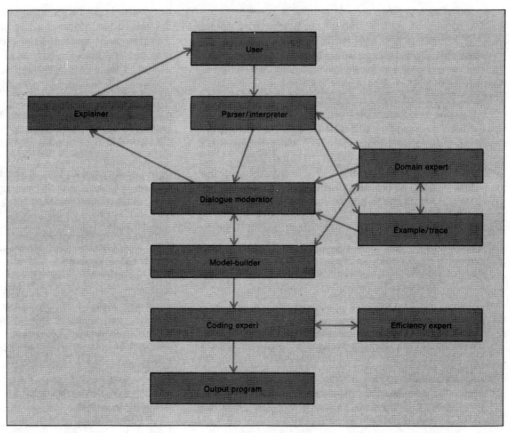

other applications could be included fairly easily by the development of new domain-expert modules.

The CHI system is designed to be helpful in general programming as well as in the programming of knowledge-based automatic programming systems, including itself [Fig. 4]. CHI is defined in a programming language called V, which both is used by the system and is the language in which the system is written. The structure of CHI is such that it can be made to operate on its own program.

While other systems based on languages, such as Smalltalk, use such self-referencing, CHI differs from them in that it is a knowledge-based system—that is, it includes rules for programming that can be used, at least partly, to automate the programming process. An experienced programmer communicates with the CHI system in V, a very high-level language much like English. The programmer can direct the system, using very high-level instructions (basically English sentences), to carry out programming processes or to implement changes in its own structure. For example: "Add a new synthesis rule that does . . . [some programming process]."

CHI differs from PSI in that it does not simply generate programs from a user description, but rather carries out high-level programming instructions from the programmers. Essentially it acts as an intelligent programmer's assistant. CHI does the detailed work of programming, so the programmer can concentrate on decisions at the highest level.

To do this, CHI uses a number of modules that are broadly similar to those used in PSI. These modules use programming rules to carry out the most straightforward aspects of programming, such as data structuring. However, one module now under development would go further and develop algorithm design modules that could be used in either PSI or CHI systems to further simplify the job of the user.

The algorithm design project has so far formulated a number of machine-implemented rules that simplify problems and produce useful algorithms for solving them. The rules are based on a description of algorithms that involves generators to produce sequences of elements, mappings that map elements into some function of the elements, constraints that filter out elements that satisfy them, and orderings that arrange elements into a predetermined order. Some constraints may seem trivial, but they are capable of greatly shortening the implementation times of complex problems, such as finding primes or the shortest path (a problem that crops up in applications from delivery-route scheduling to cruise-missile guidance).

A third approach to automated programming is being developed by Robert Balzer and collaborators at the University of Southern California's Information Science Institute in Marina Del Rey. Their system is not fully automatic, since the user must decide certain optimization issues, working interactively with the system. However, within this interactive mode, the system can transform abstract program specifications into final programs.

The core of the system is a process of transformations similar in overall concept to those used by the coding expert in the PSI system. The system takes a program specification written in a formal but very high-level language called GIST and under the guidance of the user transforms it step by step into the final implementation. The specifications define what must be done by the program, not how it is to be done.

As in PSI, the system applies rules to transform the specifications into a program, but the user, rather than an efficiency module, decides what transformation is to be applied where and when. This has the advantage of letting the programmer optimize the program more effectively than an efficiency module can, but it also has a drawback: the programmer needs to be involved throughout the programming process, even though the implementation of each decision is made automatically.

The necessity of starting with a specification in a formal language, rather than a natural one like English, is also potentially burdensome. Dr. Balzer's group has been working on a subsystem that would produce formal specifications from informal ones written in English.

The subsystem first analyzes the informal input, separating the statements into descriptions of structure and descriptions of process—objects of some type and what is to be done to them. It then produces formal-language equivalents of the statements and completes from the context any partial structural descriptions. It then analyzes the resulting set of processes by trying to see what data flows where—where new objects are "produced" and where they are "consumed" by another state of the program. The subsystem thus generates a sequence of processes that show their interrelationships. Finally, the subsystem evaluates the formal specification by logically checking through it to see if basic programming criteria hold—such as, that objects must be produced somewhere, that they must be used in some way, that they must be "produced" before being "consumed," and so on.

At present, the ISI system has succeeded in translating a number of informal specifications into formal languages, but they remain limited in the range of subject that can be correctly interpreted. On the other hand, the inverse subsystem, which paraphrases GIST specifications in English, has been quite successful and has often made obvious program deficiencies that did not show up in the formal-language specification.

For example, a program for a shipping company might deal with ships carrying different cargoes among several ports. Each port has several piers at which a ship can dock, and the proper cargo must be brought to the proper pier. If the user does not give the number of piers at each port when writing the initial specification, GIST will set that number to 1, and the program will malfunction. An English paraphrase of the specification would bring out such a conceptual error immediately. Similarly, the paraphrase could bring out inconsistencies in the kinds of cargo that can be carried by the same ship—fuel oil and grain cannot be carried at the same time, for instance, but a user without a programming background might not bother to make such a caveat in the initial specification.

The outlook is mixed

Though at present there are no commercially available compilers for automatic program generation, these do not appear to be far off, especially for engineering and scientific applications. Systems such as Model could be modified to accept direct entry of differential and integral expressions, as well as other mathematical formulations used in the natural sciences. When combined with existing capabilities, such modifications could make possible the entry of virtually any scientific operation with no instructions other than those required in conventional mathematical and Boolean logical notation.

Some computer experts, such as John Backus of IBM [see "Function-level computing," p. 231], question whether automatic program generation with existing computer hardware and object languages will really solve the problems raised by the software explosion. The multilevel compilers, which first translate specifications into high-level languages and then into machine-language instructions, may prove to be too slow and cumbersome. It may be more effective to redesign computers and languages radically—as in functional programming—rather than merely automate existing practices.

However, because automatic program generation uses existing hardware, it seems likely that such systems will be implemented much sooner than functional programming or other approaches requiring new hardware design. With the implementation will come, it seems virtually certain, greatly expanded computing power for those who have until now been stymied by the cost and complexity of handmade software.

For further reading

A good overview of the automatic-program-generation project at the University of Pennsylvania is offered by Noah Prywes in "Automatic generation of computer programs," *Advances in Computers*, Vol. 17, Academic Press Inc., 1978, pp. 57–123.

Dr. Prywes and C. Tinaztepe describe the work of the project in program generation for automated test equipment in "Use of Nopal in generating programs for testing analog systems and circuit boards," *Proceedings of the IEEE International Conference on Circuits and Systems*, October 1980, pp. 924–27. More detailed descriptions of Model, Nopal, and the economic modeling project can be obtained from the Technical Reports of the Automatic Program Generation Project, a report series available from the University of Pennsylvania, Moore School of Electrical Engineering, Philadelphia.

A description of other approaches to nonprocedural languages is contained in "What versus how: a view of nonprocedural programming in the 1980s," by P.A. Thomas, *Proceedings of the Canadian Information Processing Society Session 1980*, pp. 282–84.

An overview of recent progress in knowledge-based programming is provided by the Kestrel Institute report KES.U.81.2, "Research on knowledge-based programming and algorithm design—1981," by Cordell Green *et al.*, August 1981 (available from the Kestrel Institute, 1801 Page Mill Rd., Palo Alto, Calif. 94304). PSI and CHI are both outlined in *The Handbook of Artificial Intelligence*, Vol. 2, William Kaufman, Publishers, pp. 326–35.

Robert Balzer gives a brief introduction to the ISI system in "Transformational implementation: an example, in *"IEEE Transactions on Software Engineering*, Vol. SE-7, no. 1, January 1981.

Details of the system can be found in three papers—"Operational specification as the basis for rapid prototyping"; "Using symbolic execution to characterize behavior," and "Mappings for rapid prototyping"—given at the Association for Computing Machinery's Sigsoft workshop on rapid prototyping in April 1982. ◆

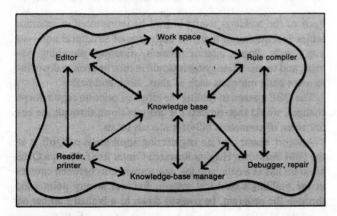

[4] CHI can be considered a closed set of tools for working on itself: each part of it interacts with the others and with the user so that the system itself can constantly be extended. CHI is, of course, also useful for programming problems other than knowledge-based program generators.

SOFTWARE

PROGRAMMING FOR NONPROGRAMMERS

New languages are helping those who are not professionally trained communicate with computers

The boom in personal computers and the rapid expansion of computing systems built on small computers has brought large numbers of people who are not professional programmers into direct contact with computers. As a result, more and more engineers, businessmen, accountants, and secretaries are discovering how frustrating it can be to get a computer to do what they want it to. Conventional programming languages seem to be too cumbersome, complicated, and time-consuming for easy use by those with little computer training.

Now, new languages and programming systems are being developed and marketed to come to the aid of the growing ranks of nonprofessional programmers. The aim of these systems is to simplify programming radically, making it accessible to those who have little or no previous programming knowledge, or have no time to use more laborious conventional programming methods.

The new systems include some that have already come into widespread use, such as IBM Corp.'s Query-by-Example, and those that are just beginning to go into circulation, like Xerox Corp.'s Smalltalk. Their aims also vary considerably; some, like QBE, attempt to help the user with no previous experience, while others, like Smalltalk, are for virtually any small computer user who needs to work faster.

What all of the systems have in common is that they are at least to some degree "nonprocedural"—that is, they allow the user to specify *what* has to be done, rather than specifying the *procedure* by which it is done. In addition, all these systems rely heavily on an interaction between the user and the computer and on extensive use of graphic displays.

Though a number of such systems are in various stages of development or implementation, the clearest way to view the field is by looking in some depth at the two best-known ones—QBE and Smalltalk. These systems also exemplify two different approaches to the general problem of simplifying programming for nonprogrammers.

Query-by-Example

The Query-by-Example language was first introduced by IBM in 1978. It was developed by Moshe Zloof and his colleagues at IBM's Thomas J. Watson Research Center in Yorktown Heights, N.Y. It is now in widespread use and is currently being expanded to include all office-type procedures. Research on the expanded

language—Office-Procedures-by-Example, or OBE—is being conducted by IBM.

The basic idea of QBE is to give instructions to the computer in the form of tables, which has examples of the sort of information desired as output. The language is therefore suitable for all business or engineering applications where data can be represented conveniently in tabular form.

An example of how QBE works is the construction of an invoice [Fig. 1]. The user defines a table containing the items to be included in the invoice, such as customer name, materials purchased, prices, and so forth, and then sets up another table with examples defining the relationships between different items in the table. QBE takes these specimen tables and does the indicated operations on whatever data the user directs.

Any program that can be entered in such a tabular form is suitable for QBE. Another example would be a program for a bill of materials, where the user would set up a series of tables showing various end-products, the amounts of raw materials needed for each end-product, and the costs of each raw material. Changes in prices or product mix could rapidly be reflected in new cost and materials estimates.

One large French construction firm is using just such a QBE bill-of-materials system for a billion-dollar construction project in the Middle East. The project involves the purchase of large quantities of materials and elaborate design specifications. The recalculation of the total bill of materials and cost estimate for the projects, which becomes necessary periodically as materials prices and specifications change, used to take over six months. Now it can be run in 3 hours on a QBE system.

In this case, the system uses a process called transitive closure, involving a number of steps. The overall plan might call, for example, for a given quantity of each of several types of buildings. Each of the buildings would in turn be represented in separate tables as requiring so many of each type of structural unit—so many walls, floors, interior dividers, windows, plumbing systems, and so on. These systems would in turn be broken down into more basic materials such as glass, steel, and nails.

The QBE system, in finding the effect of price on requirement changes, would then process the changes down through the entire chain of connected bill-of-materials totals.

Another example of an engineering application of QBE is at the IBM Yorktown Heights Research Center itself. Here, a QBE program has as a data base the interconnections between circuits in the building's electrical system. Failures at any point can, through the program, be tracked down to a limited number of circuits that may have caused the failure and therefore should be checked out.

However, the QBE system is designed primarily for business rather than engineering applications. One limitation is its inability to handle any but the simplest mathematical expressions—those

---

Eric J. Lerner Contributing Editor

that can be written as relatively short combinations of basic arithmetic operations and exponentials. But custom-designed technical programs that carry out specific mathematical manipulations can be "plugged into" a QBE or OBE system and used as black boxes, thus giving a degree of flexibility in handling the data that the mathematic program may itself lack. Such hybrids of QBE and technical programs could considerably improve productivity in dealing with both engineering and scientific problems.

Office-Procedures-by-Example

The Office-Procedures-by-Example language now being developed by IBM expands the concept of QBE to include all office activities, including word processing, report writing, graphics, and electronic mail. Nonprogrammers like secretaries can set up menus of programs according to specifications from executives without recourse to a programming staff. One program on the menu, for instance, might allow an executive to review his messages, another to see specified summary reports, and another to send messages automatically according to predetermined conditions.

One of the key advantages of the OBE system is that it makes possible the gradual automation of an operation in a step-by-step way. Initially, a user can limit the system to simple bookkeeping operations and then later, as the user gains experience, add more sophisticated decision-making functions, such as credit-rating assignment, inventory management, ordering, and so on.

The OBE system has other features useful in business programming. By simple instructions, the program can be told to group all invoices from a given customer together for processing and to total the entries from a set of forms onto a single form. Through the same tabular instructions used throughout the language, a program can be instructed to perform a series of clerical operations, such as posting journal entries from an accounting table into a permanent ledger. OBE makes it easy to formulate subprograms and sub-subprograms that are included only as tables inside larger tables. Conditions and branchings can be specified to determine at what point any subprogram can be called.

The OBE system allows users to manipulate two-dimensional objects on a screen much as they would shuffle papers. The screen consists of multiple windows—boxes containing formatted data. The windows can be overlapped, since each is assigned a different "depth" level. In this way, various tables can be seen and compared.

The forms, letters, graphs, and other objects that appear on the screen are prepared by the user by combining and modifying a small number of primitive preprogrammed objects: rectangles, skeleton tables, skeleton graphs, and so on. Seven function keys perform the graphical manipulation of the screen objects: EXPAND, ERASE, MOVE, SCROLL, LOCATE, ZOOM, and PUSH DOWN. The effect of these few function keys varies according to where the cursor is placed when the key is depressed. Thus if a cursor is on the vertical border of a rectangle when the EXPAND key is pressed, the rectangle expands vertically. If the cursor is on the horizontal border, it expands horizontally; if it is between two words in a text, the space between them will expand.

The ERASE, MOVE, and SCROLL functions are obvious from their names. LOCATE lets the user find any string of characters typed in within a window or text. ZOOM scales down objects, such as text, so that they are visible within the screen, even if they are inherently larger than the screen area. PUSH DOWN moves the plane of the windows relative to one another, bringing different windows to the "top" when the windows overlap on the screen—the electronic equivalent of paper shuffling.

Using these functions, virtually any letter or report format can be generated and the forms linked together via programs essentially identical to, although more powerful than, those in QBE. One simple program could send a message ordering more of a given commodity once inventory and/or sales level drops below a given ratio, or it could send another alert message if the ratio rises above another point, indicating excessive inventory accumulation [Fig. 2].

The program has built-in graph-making capabilities. A graphics program can simply define by example the data to go into the graphs and the axes of the graph. It then automatically adjusts both x and y scales to take advantage of the space available and plots the graph. Thus, in general, the OBE system will be capable of carrying out all of the computer-based procedures of virtually any small- or even medium-size firm without programmers.

A user can perform any number of processes simultaneously on OBE simply by moving the various windows around. A user could, for instance, interrupt a data-processing inquiry, or a letter being composed, to send a message or retrieve other data, and

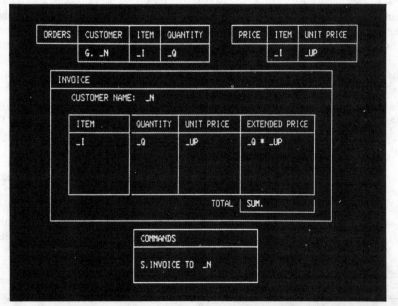

[1] The Query-by-Example language allows users to set up programs through the use of examples and tables. Here, a user needs a program to calculate total costs in an invoice from item quantities and unit costs. The program is built in the form of a table, with examples showing how elements in the input and output tables are connected.

then return to the exact point where he left off.

It should be noted that QBE and OBE require a high degree of programming sophistication in their compilers (which are written in PL-1) in order to achieve a high degree of simplicity in use. Both languages are two-dimensional, in that the compiler cannot simply read instructions line by line sequentially, but must take into account all data that is on the screen at any one time.

Smalltalk

Smalltalk is intended to make life easier for those who know some, or even a great deal of, programming and wish to be able to do broader tasks than the Query-by-Example approach can handle. Smalltalk has been developed over the past 10 years by the Learning Research Group at Xerox in Palo Alto, Calif., and will be released this year to the public.

The key idea of Smalltalk is modularity. One of the great frustrations of anyone trying to program a computer is the notion that he or she is repeating the work done by thousands of other programmers who have similar problems to solve. The catch is that simple subroutines cannot in general be fit together to build up any desired program. They are highly individualized, and a subroutine designed for one program cannot, as a rule, be easily plugged into another. The designers of Smalltalk have, in contrast, made the concept of subroutine basic to the language so that in all cases subroutines of various sorts can be interlinked to create more and more complex programs from simple building blocks.

The way this is done is by basing the structure of the language on a system of "objects" that send "messages" to one another. Each object is a package of information and a description of how the data can be manipulated (a set of procedures). The messages merely say *what* is to be done with the information contained in the objects, not how to do it. The messages are thus nonprocedural—the procedures are all contained in the "objects."

Each object in effect has its own set of subroutines. Since the messages do not define procedures, objects and their subroutines can be plugged into a simple overall structure to build up more complex programs. In addition, since the language defining the procedures within each object uses the same object-message

[2] With OBE, orders and requisitions can be sent out based on present target inventory levels. A complete version of this table would include preparation of a purchase order.

structure, there is no limit to how many layers of hierarchy can be built up.

In a conventional procedural language, like Fortran or Cobol, by contrast, the procedures are defined in each instruction, and therefore the procedures in the overall structure of the program must be tailored to be compatible with the procedures in each individual subroutine. This is what ensures that most subroutines cannot arbitrarily be transferred from program to program.

A unit of Smalltalk programming consists of one message. The message contains the object to which the message is sent, called the receiver; a name defining the type of manipulation to be carried out, called the selector; and, in some cases, another object that helps define the manipulation required, called an argument. Thus, for example, if the designed manipulation is to move a piece of text called "numbers" to a location on the screen defined as "x,y," the instructions would be written "NUMBERS MOVE X,Y," with the first word being the receiver; the second, the selector; and the third, the argument.

A program as a whole consists of sets of definitions of objects, which define the procedures each object uses as well as the sequence of messages that ties the objects together. Each of the procedures that an object uses is termed a "method." Groups of similar objects can be described by a single definition as a "class."

To understand how the Smalltalk approach works, the example used with the QBE system can be examined. The user wants a program that takes an order and the bills of materials for each component and a price list for the materials, producing an overall bill of materials and overall cost for the order as a whole. Mathematically, this problem can be treated as a series of vector and matrix multiplications [Fig. 3]. The order (a vector) can be multiplied by the bills of materials (a matrix) to yield the overall amounts of materials (another vector). This in turn can be "dot-multiplied" by the vector representing the prices of each material to yield the total cost (a scalar, or ordinary number).

To turn this procedure into a Smalltalk program, the user would begin by defining a class of objects as "matrix." The class definition would include the variables that would be needed to define each matrix: height, width, and the contents—a string of values. The definition would also include the messages the matrix objects could respond to and what they would do when they received such messages. These messages would be, say, multiply, invert, add, and retrieve components (i,j). Each method would state how these procedures would be carried out. In the case of a matrix, the user might take advantage of the fact that Smalltalk has built in the object class "vector" and matrices could be defined as ordered strings of vectors.

Once the basic object "matrix" has been defined, the rest of the program is simple, since the messages of the overall program that multiply one vector by a matrix and then the result by another vector can be written out in terms of the already defined objects.

Of course, this program is more complex to implement in this example than was the same operation with SBA. But in compensation the programmer has achieved a higher degree of flexibility. Suppose, for example, that the user having programmed his definition of matrix is now working on an entirely different problem, in which certain manipulations are defined in terms of ordinary scalars. He now finds that it would be convenient to do the same manipulation in terms of matrices. All that must be done throughout is to substitute the appropriate matrix object for the existing scalar object.

Because the matrix object has embedded in it a set of matrix operations for addition, multiplication, and so on, corresponding to the scalar arithmetic operations, the messages that are sent to it remain the same. When the matrix object receives those messages, however, it interprets them differently than a scalar object would.

This ability to use the same message to carry out several different procedures depending on the object it is sent to is one of Smalltalk's major strengths. Procedures that are conceptually similar but different in detail can be represented by the same message—for example, the message "sort" could cause an object that contained a list of numbers to sort them in ascending order, an object that contained a list of titles to sort them alphabetically, and an object that contained a list of dates to sort them in chronological order. The replacement of scalar objects by vector or matrix objects is only one example of the flexibility of Smalltalk.

This flexibility has important implications for the development of canned programming. Since many problems in business, engineering, and science can be easily expressed as matrix and vector manipulations, once Smalltalk is in circulation it would be reasonable to expect packaged programs to be sold that include definitions of the class of object "matrix." In fact, programs could be sold that are little more than "class dictionaries" defining a number of useful objects. Then, a user who had purchased this dictionary could create programs that use these objects—in effect calling subroutines—without having to know anything in particular about them except the standard messages they may receive. In other words, the user would need to know only what the objects can do, not how they do it. Unlike packaged subroutines in conventional languages, which must be specifically called and must be imbedded in programs that are compatible with their data structure, Smalltalk objects can be used as "black boxes" that can be incorporated in any program. At the same time, the distributors of such packages can allow users to modify the black boxes as desired, since the language in which the objects are described is identical to the one in which the users write their programs.

Thus, although Smalltalk initially may not prove to be particularly simple for novice programmers, as more sophisticated canned dictionaries go on the market in the coming years, it could become much easier to use. In fact, since the production of such programs will itself become simpler as more and more dictionaries are built up out of more and more building blocks, highly complex yet flexible definitions would become available, enabling nonprofessionals to create relatively sophisticated programs easily.

This emphasis on modularity makes Smalltalk similar in approach to a number of other nonprocedural-type languages, such as functional programming [see "Function-level computing," p. 231]. Both Smalltalk and functional programming aim at reducing to an absolute minimum the number of different types of concepts that programmers must deal with and at allowing easy creation of hierarchically built-up programs. Smalltalk, however, does not share FP's emphasis on parallel operation and new types of computer hardware.

Graphically, Smalltalk anticipates OBE: the screen is broken up into a number of overlapping windows that can be expanded and shuffled at will. Smalltalk is also designed for use with Xerox's new personal computer, the Star, which comes equipped with a graphic device called a mouse that controls a pointer with which a user can draw on the screen. The mouse has a set of wheels that roll as the user moves the mouse about. The motion of the wheels conveys to the computer the mouse's change in position, which is translated as a change in position of the pointer on the screen.

The position of the pointer on the screen determines what ef-

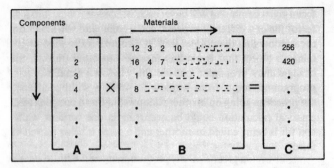

[3] The bill of materials example used to demonstrate QBE can also be represented as a series of vector and matrix multiplications for programming in Smalltalk. Here, a vector composed of the amounts of each item in an order is multiplied by the matrix showing the amount of raw material required for each item to yield another vector, the total amount of materials needed to fill the order.

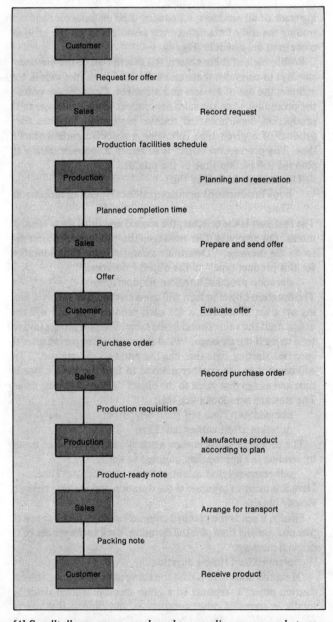

[4] Smalltalk programs are based on sending messages between objects. In this example, a chain of actions occurs when a customer sends an order to a manufacturing facility.

fect a given command will have: each window is a view into a different file or a different process, and a command will affect only the window that the pointer is in. (Of course, if the window contains an object that is sending messages to other objects, then changes may propagate outside the window.) Smalltalk lets a programmer move from window to window without affecting the processes going on in other windows, so that a complex mathematical calculation could be occurring in one window while a text file is being edited in another and a game is being played in a third.

The hierarchical structuring in Smalltalk is illustrated in another example from Tyrgve Reenskaug of the Central Institute for Industrial Research in Oslo, Norway. It involves a small manufacturing job shop with two departments, sales and production. The Smalltalk program treats each of these departments as objects, with additional objects being customers. The sales objects would have the tasks of generating products proposals, reserving the necessary resources in production for the product and sending contracts and other communications to the customer. The production object would have the functions of keeping track of all products, scheduling their manufacture and controlling the use of manufacturing resources to get the products completed on schedule [Fig. 4].

Within each of these objects is a description of the methods it employs to carry out these tasks. Each of these methods in turn includes the use of objects and messages. Consider the point in the procedure when the sales department sends a message to the production department to reserve production facilities for a product of a given type following a specified earliest starting time. The production object is to return a message stating the planned completion time of the product.

The message looks like this:

bookProductionFacilities:productTypeafter:earlieststartTime

The first part is the selector; the second and third parts are arguments. On receiving this message, the production object first sends the message, "Determine manufacturing time (duration) for this product type" to the object "duration."

duration productDuration: productType

The duration object in turn will use a method that involves looking up a list of durations for each product type and will then assign itself the value found in the table. Second, production will send to itself the message, "Find the earliest free period after the specified starting time that has the duration determined." This will cause it to use another method to find the earliest starting time and assign that value to the object "planned starting time." The message here looks like this:

plannedStartTime self findFreePeriod:

duration after: earlieststartTime

The production object then actually reserves the time needed by sending the appropriate message to itself.

self reservePeriod: durationfrom: plannedStartTime.

Here it is using as arguments the duration and starting time previously obtained.

Finally, it sends the planned completion time, which is just the planned starting time plus the duration, back to the sender of the original message.

plannedStartTime + duration

Of significance here is that the subroutine describing the production object's response to a given message is itself described totally in terms of other subroutines and objects that execute them. Just as the sales object merely tells the production object what to do—"Give me the completion time and reserve a slot in the production schedule"—so the objects within production are also just told *what* to do, not how to do things: "Determine the starting time," "Find the earliest open slot," and so on. In this way, the task is broken down into simpler and simpler units until only at the lowest-level objects are instructions totally explicit.

It should also be noted that Smalltalk can be made relatively self-documenting once a user is familiar with it. Each of the above messages can be turned into English by inserting a few words. For example, the second messeage of the method can be written in English as "*To find the* planned starting time, find *the first* free period *of the given* duration after *the given* earliest starting time." Only the italicized words need be added to the actual Smalltalk instructions.

Is help on the way?

At the moment, both Query-by-Example and Smalltalk still fall far short of the ideal solution to the headaches neophyte computer users face with their small computers. QBE and its related systems remain restricted to a certain category of problems, while Smalltalk, just emerging onto the market, is not yet sufficiently friendly to suit the average beginning programmer, nor is it intended to be. However, the current rapid growth of personal-computer capabilities and numbers combined with the proliferation and refinement of new languages that emphasize modularity and ease of use may together lead to a takeoff in computer usability. A large market for canned programs, together with a reduced cost of producing programs through easier programming languages and a greater flexibility of programs through easily manipulated user-oriented languages, could begin to break down the logjams that users face today. For many of the simpler computing problems that small computers are used for, this process could lead to a relatively rapid replacement of conventional languages, such as Fortran, Basic, and Cobol, as the favorites of the nonprofessional programmer. If that happens, the power of the computer may quickly become available to a much larger group of users than is currently possible.

In not too many years, an average engineer or executive may be able to use some hybrid language that incorporates the ease of use of QBE and the modularity of Smalltalk to piece together cheap canned modules into whatever programs he or she needs. For someone struggling today with tangled codes and endless error messages, that is indeed a vision of Utopia.

To probe further

Information on QBE is available from IBM Corp.; for example, the QBE Terminal User's Guide, #SH20-2078, is available at IBM branch offices. A technical look at QBE is contained in "QBE: a database language," by Moshe Zloof, in the IBM Systems Journal, Vol. 16, no. 4, 1977, pp. 324–43. "QBE/OBE: a language for business and office automation," by Dr. Zloof, *Computer*, May 1981, pp. 13–22, gives an overview of the principles of both QBE and OBE. Another article by Dr. Zloof, "Security and integrity within the QBE database-management language," examines the question of maintaining accurate and secure files in a system designed to be used by nonprogrammers; it is available as research report RC 6982 from the IBM Thomas J. Watson Research Center, Yorktown Heights, N.Y. 10598.

Articles are available on the earlier versions of Smalltalk, such as "The Smalltalk-76 Programming System: Design and Implementation," by Daniel H.H. Ingalls, *Proceedings of the Principles of Programming Languages Symposium*, 1978, introduces the language as it existed then. A book on the current version of Smalltalk, Smalltalk-80, will be published by Addison-Wesley in the spring of 1983, entitled *Smalltalk-80: the language and its implementation*, by Adele Goldberg and David Robson. ◆

SOFTWARE

SOFTWARE DESIGN: BREAKING THE BOTTLENECK

A visionary approach is recommended in place of the piecemeal policy now in effect

The software design crisis, the extraordinary manpower cost of programming new information systems, could be eased by 1990—or it could last until the year 2020. It all depends on whether computer developers adopt a visionary approach that actively seeks a fully integrated programming support system, or whether they continue the present ultracautious, piecemeal development.

The crisis is created by the labor-intensive nature of today's design methods: the cut-and-fit approach to program specification and writing, the barriers between software tools, the duplication of efforts on different hardware by different software suppliers, and the mountains of paperwork used in administering large software projects. The crisis will end when computer technology offers:

• Automated programming aids.

• Direct access to computers by end users, so that professional programmers will not be necessary for routine data processing.

• Project-information management that exploits the benefits of computers in the interpersonal communication, record keeping, and documentation essential to major software development projects.

The technological innovations needed to implement fully integrated programming support are either already available or can be readily developed. But taken separately, they offer only marginal improvement, for each widens only one of many bottlenecks. But when they are integrated, they will revolutionize the industry.

To a surprising extent, the computer industry resembles the aircraft industry of the late 1920s and early 1930s, when it was growing rapidly amid both technological promise and economic disappointment [see "The evidence for long waves," p. 249]. Innovations such as radial, air-cooled engines, retractable landing gear, monocoque bodies, wing flaps, and variable-pitch propellers were available earlier, but they were not integrated in one aircraft. Individually these innovations offered only minor improvements. When they were finally integrated in the DC-3, they made the modern air-transport business possible [see "Why is a computer like an airplane?" p. 254].

There are parallels. Computers are clearly a growth industry. Yet as an economic force, the value of hardware and software produced by the computer industry is small, amounting to 0.67 percent of the gross national product in 1980. In fact, the computer industry is just now beginning to tap a very large market. In 1980, 48 percent of all United States employees were engaged in information handling (as opposed to industry, services, and agriculture). In 1979, the spending for offices (whose work is information processing) came to about $800 billion, or about 35 percent of the gross national product.

The parallel to the earlier aircraft industry leads one to believe that programming is on the verge of a breakthrough. What keeps the computer industry from tapping the market more fully? The answer is problems of reliability and cost for both hardware and software.

Hardware reliability problems are certainly on the way to being solved by redundant hardware, speedy diagnosis over telephone lines, and gradual improvements in device reliability. But hardware is only about 30 percent of the cost of information processing. The rest is in various software activities. Thus, even if the hardware were free, expenses would come down only about 30 percent.

Electronic information processing is most economical if many customers can use the same program. The most widespread applications of computers are highly standardized operations, such as in payrolls and inventory control. Even here, minor variations in customer needs add a substantial programming and operating burden. It seems clear that if computers cannot be more easily programmed, applications will remain standardized and narrow. Computer use will grow substantially only when programming costs are reduced.

For U.S. software producers, the motivation for opening the programming bottleneck transcends efficiency and economics. The U.S. leads the world both in research on programming methodology and in commercial software production. But there is no guarantee at all that it will lead in applying that research to commercial production. A parallel situation occurred around

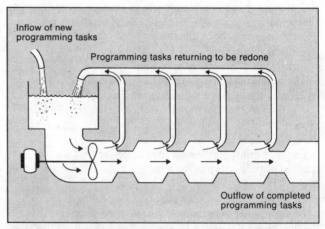

[1] *Hydraulic analogy compares programming work flow to the flow of a liquid through a pipe containing a series of bottlenecks and taps that return part of the flow to the source. The bottlenecks are like nonautomated programming activities, and the return flow is like software that must be revised because of flaws.*

Alan K. Graham
Massachusetts Institute of Technology

1950, when the U.S. steel industry had both technological and production dominance. But Japanese companies exploited the technology far more aggressively than their U.S. counterparts and thus came to dominate world markets. It is difficult to see what would prevent similar events in software, other than the U.S. computer industry's aggressively following a vision of future software technology. Without such a vision, world leadership might be a temporary condition.

Programming is a handicraft

For airplanes in the 1920s, the difference between current technology and next-wave technology was size and speed. For computers in the 1980s, the difference must be productivity in developing and maintaining software. With exceptions, programming is currently a handicraft: write specifications, write flow diagrams and code, submit a deck, analyze printed output, and repeat as needed. Programmers go through this cut-and-fit, write/run cycle by hand until the program is acceptable. Management-control systems are similarly manual, with requirements, reports, and documentation handwritten or typed and then physically circulated and filed.

In a hydraulic analogy, these hand operations are like bottlenecks in a pipe [Fig. 1]. New programming tasks are pumped into the pipe along with needed revisions of past tasks. Programming here denotes a broad spectrum of activities, ranging from talking with clients to formulating specifications, through

---

The evidence for long waves

Technology is often regarded as if it were an unchanging, inexorable process. That may be true from one year to the next. But from decade to decade, the pace of technological progress can change dramatically [see illustration]. There were very sharp peaks or surges of basic innovation around the 1760s, the 1830s, the 1880s, and the 1930s. In other words, the progress of technology is not at all smooth; it proceeds in cycles of about 50 years' duration. In several respects, the era whose technological prospects were most like those of the present occurred not in the immediate past, but about 50 years ago [see "Why is a computer like an airplane?" p. 254].

The innovation surges initiated waves of economic development, each using a distinctive ensemble of dominant technologies. In communication, the 1830s to 1870s saw limited telegraphy. The following wave introduced transcontinental telegraphy and short-distance telephones. The onset of electronic amplification in the 1930s created the present wave of television, radio, and worldwide telephony. Similarly in transportation there were wood-fired steam locomotives from the 1830s to 1870s. The succeeding wave featured coal-fired and much more sophisticated locomotives for intercity use, as well as electric trolleys for urban use. This was the "Great Age of Steam," which ended when the present wave began in the 1930s with diesel-electric locomotives and competition from trucks.

The illustration suggests that another surge of innovation may begin over the next 10 years and that the predecessors of those innovations exist right now as laboratory prototypes or highly specialized, limited-applications technologies. (This is called the invention stage.) For example, of the 11 basic innovations of the 1920s and 1930s listed, 8 had reached the invention stage by 1920. Statistics imply that in 1981 most of the next-wave basic innovations became working inventions, half started development, and a decision to market was made on fewer than a quarter, but very few were commercially available.

Innovation does not go at its own inexorable pace. Rather, technologies are developed by people responding both to their technological vision and to economic forces; during the surge in innovations, technologies move from laboratory prototypes to routine application four times more quickly than technologies invented earlier. Likewise, the accompanying article suggests how the pace of innovation in software might be increased.

Innovation is but one of several arenas where a 50-year cycle is revealed. Studies and simulation modeling at MIT suggest that long waves originate from the dynamics of physical capital formation: at the peak of a long wave, a variety of mechanisms have encouraged the overbuilding of plant, equipment, and infrastructure. Demand for these capital goods falls and the economy enters a depression. Eventually, accumulated depreciation creates a need for new building, which sets the stage for a period of expansion (and innovation), peaking, and again depression. As might

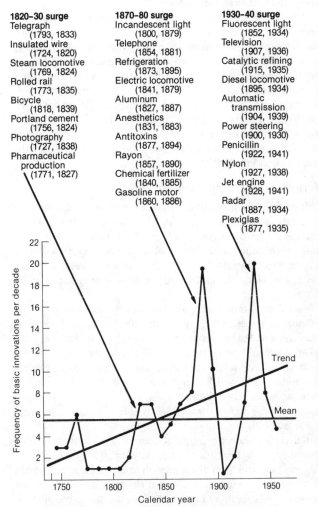

1820–30 surge
Telegraph
　(1793, 1833)
Insulated wire
　(1724, 1820)
Steam locomotive
　(1769, 1824)
Rolled rail
　(1773, 1835)
Bicycle
　(1818, 1839)
Portland cement
　(1756, 1824)
Photography
　(1727, 1838)
Pharmaceutical
　production
　(1771, 1827)

1870–80 surge
Incandescent light
　(1800, 1879)
Telephone
　(1854, 1881)
Refrigeration
　(1873, 1895)
Electric locomotive
　(1841, 1879)
Aluminum
　(1827, 1887)
Anesthetics
　(1831, 1883)
Antitoxins
　(1877, 1894)
Rayon
　(1857, 1890)
Chemical fertilizer
　(1840, 1885)
Gasoline motor
　(1860, 1886)

1930–40 surge
Fluorescent light
　(1852, 1934)
Television
　(1907, 1936)
Catalytic refining
　(1915, 1935)
Diesel locomotive
　(1895, 1934)
Automatic
　transmission
　(1904, 1939)
Power steering
　(1900, 1930)
Penicillin
　(1922, 1941)
Nylon
　(1927, 1938)
Jet engine
　(1928, 1941)
Radar
　(1887, 1934)
Plexiglas
　(1877, 1935)

A surge of basic innovation occurs at intervals of approximately 50 years. Basic innovations are defined as those that create new industries or transform existing ones. Representative innovations are listed for the three most recent surges. The numbers in parentheses indicate the year of the invention (functioning as a laboratory prototype) and the year of innovation (commercially available or in widespread use).

be imagined, the effects radiate throughout the economy; statistical evidence suggests 50-year cycles not only in innovation, but in capital intensity of production, unemployment, prices, interest rates, energy sources, and even political attitudes. —A.K.G.

coding, to maintaining the software. In other words, it takes in the entire software cycle.

Some phases of programming have been automated, such as the compiler's function of keeping track of storage locations and symbol definitions. The automated parts are represented in the figure by smooth flow through a pipe large in diameter. Other phases involve creative, but fallible, human programmers. The flow of programming tasks is not only more difficult at these points, shown as a narrower pipe, but also errors inevitably cause some of the programming tasks to flow into the reservoir of tasks needing more work.

At present, a given programming task will typically recirculate several times before leaving as a finished product. Although this analogy is obviously greatly simplified, it has the same essential structure as that emerging from several detailed studies of the research-and-development process.

What is the cost-effectiveness of eliminating bottlenecks, perhaps through innovation? Getting rid of the first few does not eliminate much of the impediment to smooth flow. If anything, more pressure and more errors would be expected in the remaining bottlenecks. Only as the last few bottlenecks are eliminated does the cumulative effect of the earlier eliminations become apparent, with dramatically increased throughput. In other words, bottleneck solutions must be integrated. These fall into three areas: automating programmer activities, avoiding programming through direct computer access by end users, and managing software project information.

Automating programmer activities

It used to be (and often still is) that programmers did by hand such tasks as allocating absolute addresses and registers and tracing the causes of program failures [Table I]. Eventually these tasks were automated by such tools as compilers (for translating higher programming languages into machine language) and debuggers (for help in determining how a program is going astray).

But these automated tools are still surrounded by other manual activities, which constitute substantial bottlenecks as they consume manpower and produce errors. For example, compilers must still be created manually; software for automatic translator production would eliminate that task. Multiple documents must still be compared by hand; multiple-window cathode-ray-tube displays that show specifications, program listings, and program output side by side would ease that task considerably.

On a larger scale, a principal bottleneck arises from the lack of portability and standardization in software. It is a trivial but extremely powerful form of automation to use existing programs in a variety of circumstances. But differences in languages (or dialects), machines, and operating systems, not to mention inadequacies in documentation, make it very difficult for one organization to use programs developed by another. Each tends to write its own software, duplicating programming efforts elsewhere.

There is also duplication in software tools. Hundreds of compilers and text editors certainly exist, most restricted to a single type of computer and operating system. It should come as no surprise that more advanced software tools are seldom available, given the difficulty of creating software that will work for a variety of installations.

Users facing three bottlenecks

For business and many other types of computer applications, three bottlenecks now stand between the user and the machine:

(1) users lack physical access to a computer; (2) they do not know how to find information; and (3) they do not know how to process information. When these bottlenecks are eliminated and users no longer need programmers, it will be because the software is flexible and friendly enough to facilitate routine tasks without reprogramming. With just a little training, even an inexperienced user will then be able to set up a computer for such day-to-day jobs as querying a data base or generating reports. Of course, programmers will still be needed for complex or unusual programming.

The first two areas of congestion can be easily eliminated. First, end users can have convenient access to information systems through either a remote terminal or an inexpensive small computer. Second, users will be able to locate what they want in a massive amount of information if the information is organized as a data base—all information is collected in a single uniform format designed for flexible access. Then professional programmers will not be needed to guide the user through different file formats, data organizations, and other complexities.

The third bottleneck, learning how to process information, implies that computers must be made easy for nonprofessional users to direct and control. Ease of use in turn implies that computers must have a generous amount of front-end interfacing as well as considerable built-in flexibility. These requirements may be furthest from being met.

Only recent word processors can be said to possess, as a class, any kind of capability to show a novice the ropes. There is considerable research under way, however, on both query-by-example (in which the user simply gives the computer an example of the required response) and natural-language data-base query systems. Major innovations in these user-oriented interfaces may need to wait for innovations in other areas of programming, for user interfaces themselves can be major programming tasks.

As a practical matter, at any one of the three bottlenecks most end users call for a professional programmer. Only when all three are eliminated can a user's needs be met without programmers.

Managing project information: a promising area

One of the most promising areas in software productivity is project management, which broadly includes not only planning, scheduling, and organizing, but also communicating with clients and users and designing software to make the project manageable. These activities can be regarded as processing various kinds of information about the software-development project.

Information about a project resides in various mediums: human memory, memorandums, program annotations, code, and manuals. Such diversity causes many difficulties. Important information is sometimes not even recorded. Formats are often inconsistent, and usually information in one medium is only minimally cross-referenced to that in other mediums. Because different people are custodians of different pieces of information, any one person's ability to access the body of information is extremely limited. If this total body of information generated by a typical project is viewed as a data base, it must be called a chaotic one [Fig. 2].

Several innovative communication tools have already been designed to bring order to chaos. Formal specification and validation procedures make some communication links more orderly and electronic word processing speeds production, distribution, and storage of typed documents. Program annotations are intended to convey information from one programmer to another in the form of clarification and explanation of program features. But as Table II indicates, each of these innovations is still surrounded by other bottlenecks—communication links that are vague in format, difficult to use, and intermittently effective.

A programming support environment (PSE) that fully integrated programming and communications tools would have these features:

• A single, compatible storage format for all documents, programs, and data files, so they can form a fully integrated data base.

• Software tools meshing easily with one another.

• Facilities for reporting and supervision that allow quick surveys of progress on schedules and specifications without special efforts by supervisors or programmers to generate those surveys.

• Facilities for communication among programmers, including both electronic mail and "voice mail" (electronic storage and forwarding of voice messages).

• Facilities for disciplined programming, proceeding directly from the specification and planning documents.

• Means of updating and annotating programs without destroying the original, so a history of why the program has been designed as it has is preserved.

• Provision for creating pointers that connect new documents or programs to existing information.

• An information-display management system with which a user can examine any cross section of the available information base. For example, the user will be able to view simultaneously a statement in machine language, the high-level language statement that generated it, and the original specification of its function.

• Documentation for publication, derived straightforwardly and semiautomatically from the integrated data base. Documentation will not be a separate and belated activity.

An end to chaos envisioned

This kind of support will benefit the more mechanical aspects of programming in two major ways. It will boost efficiency in everyday tasks, because the tools are designed to work together. And it will have programming and project management expertise, because of well-tested built-in standard procedures and a variety of routine, automatic checks. This would leave programmers and managers more time and attention for subtler problems.

Fully integrated support would considerably affect project management. The natural progression for creating a program would start explicitly from a formal specification document and other planning documents to prevent several problems. If the specifications were inadequate, that fact would show up immediately, instead of going unnoticed until a user discovered the program did not do everything required. If the architecture is inadequate, the programmers can change it before programs are written, instead of scrambling parts of the program later to make ends meet. If clear documentation becomes an enforced custom, programmers will be more prone to write straightforward, understandable, and portable programs, instead of programs that depend on idiosyncrasies of the language and machine being used.

Certainly maintenance would be much more effective with an integrated information base. Links within the project information base would allow a maintenance programmer trying to fix a particular error to find the corresponding part of the program, what module it is part of, what that module should do, and how it relates to the original specifications. Another programmer would have access to a complete history of changes made to that part of the program and the memorandums explaining each and thus could rapidly approach the expertise and familiarity of the original programmer.

Finally, an integrated programming support system would lead to more effective project supervision—now limited because meetings or reports take time away from the task itself. But if the entire project-information base were available on computer, early detection of schedule slippage or excessive bugs could become almost automatic.

Next long wave of progress

The long-wave hypothesis is that most of the technologies that will dominate the next long wave of progress exist now as experimental prototypes and limited-application technologies, waiting for the right circumstances to pull them into full development and widespread use. This is certainly true for the integrated program-support environment (PSE). The pieces are functioning and available, and there are several examples of computer systems that could integrate such tools.

As an example of a limited application of integration, there are systems available that integrate word processing, production, work management, and communications—but for the newspaper industry, not for programming. Perhaps more important, there are programming support systems deliberately designed to facilitate growth and integration of software tools, notably UNIX (a trademark of Bell Laboratories), a general-purpose operating system for minicomputers, and Interlisp, a programming system used for artificial-intelligence research. Both these systems have a history of flexibility and expandability. The result has been user-created software features substantially more advanced than those originally built into the system.

The portability and standardization problem is attacked in several ways. The p-code system for microcomputers interprets a standardized machine language that works on a variety of microcomputers, for complete program portability. Standards are being specified for existing languages, emerging languages like Pascal, and languages still being designed, like the Defense Department's Ada. Even programming environments are moving toward standardization and portability. In addition to a specification for Ada, there is also a nascent specification for an Ada programming support environment (APSE). Both UNIX and APSE architectures make implementing standardized programming support systems much easier than for traditional architectures. Both relative portability and expandability have made UNIX extremely popular; future systems with more of these features are likely to be similarly well received.

The specifications for APSE also explicitly provide for a database that not only integrates all software tools, but also is "the repository for all information relevant to a project throughout its life cycle," according to one of its developers. It may be that these features, when widely available, will ultimately eclipse the significance of the Ada language itself.

Still more ambitious technologies are being developed in the laboratory. For example, the Artificial Intelligence Laboratory at the Massachusetts Institute of Technology has both hardware and software based on a language (LISP) that treats everything—system programs, user programs, and text, for example—uniformly as data. This uniformity has allowed the evolution of a well-integrated PSE and, as might be expected, programming efficiencies estimated to be several times greater than those for standard commercial programming. Representing programs uniformly as data has also eased the ongoing development of a "programmer's apprentice" that in a sense understands programming tasks. For example, the programmer's apprentice converses with a programmer about the task, supplying variants of standard algorithms, such as those for sorting, and prompting

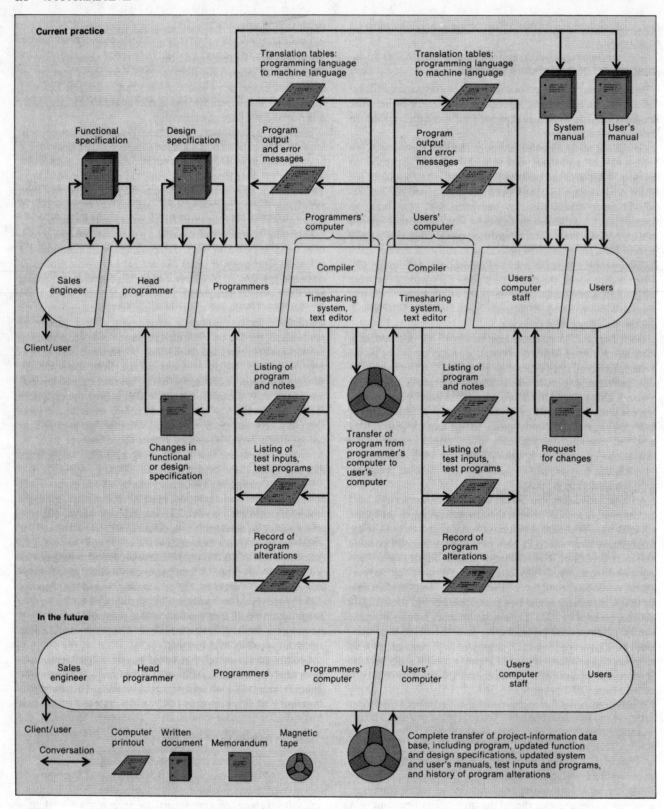

Current practice

Functional specification

Design specification

Translation tables: programming language to machine language

Program output and error messages

Translation tables: programming language to machine language

Program output and error messages

System manual

User's manual

Programmers' computer

Users' computer

Sales engineer

Head programmer

Programmers

Compiler

Timesharing system, text editor

Compiler

Timesharing system, text editor

Users' computer staff

Users

Client/user

Changes in functional or design specification

Listing of program and notes

Listing of test inputs, test programs

Record of program alterations

Transfer of program from programmer's computer to user's computer

Listing of program and notes

Listing of test inputs, test programs

Record of program alterations

Request for changes

In the future

Sales engineer

Head programmer

Programmers

Programmers' computer

Users' computer

Users' computer staff

Users

Client/user

Conversation

Computer printout

Written document

Memorandum

Magnetic tape

Complete transfer of project-information data base, including program, updated function and design specifications, updated system and user's manuals, test inputs and programs, and history of program alterations

[2] In current programming practice, virtually every movement of information requires changing the transmission medium. The result is a plethora of separated caches of information—in people's heads, computer printouts, manuals, memoranda, and magnetic tape. Only a small fraction of the information about a program is actually given to the users' computer staff, which, in effect, must create from scratch the information already produced by the original programming project. But even within a single organization, opportunities for error and confusion abound. Changes in one place will rarely be adequately cross-referenced to information elsewhere, and outdated information can be used unknowingly. Thus, program tests may not actually check to see that the program does everything that the user wants. Or a programmer can inadvertently undo someone else's repairs to a program, because nothing records the original problem or its solution. In the integrated project-information management of the future, in contrast, information flows electronically from one step of the program development process to the next. There are no gaps; even the apparent gap between software producer and user is bridged by tape.

the programmer when some detail has been neglected, such as initializing counters.

Integration of prototypes needed

So more than enough technology for a fully integrated PSE exists as various prototypes, waiting to be pulled together. The designers of Ada even visualize such an integrated system to some extent.

Cost is not really a barrier, although the PSE components are numerous and ambitious and probably will be expensive to develop. Adding to the initial software costs, the data bases for entire programming projects would be maintained on line, requiring more expenditure for hardware. But continuing to economize on hardware may be penny wise and pound foolish. In the not-too-distant future, hardware costs will be down to 20 percent from the present 30 percent, and software development and maintenance expenses will be 80 percent of the computer bill. When that happens, the break-even point for tradeoffs between programming and hardware costs might be surprising: reducing programming costs by 25 percent could be traded off evenly against *doubling* hardware costs.

How fast will integration happen then? In one scenario, economic prudence forces new system development to be highly certain of success. Each generation of systems therefore would be only incrementally different from the previously successful systems. Large-scale innovation would be virtually impossible, because precedents would be required to justify expenditures for each new incremental development. In this scenario, integrating even the technologies that exist today would require many generations of systems stretching over decades. Indeed, incrementalism may explain some of the slow pace of programming innovation in the past.

An alternative scenario would have clarity, consensus, and commitment to a vision of what the software system of the future will look like. With such a vision, system designers would incorporate more innovations in each new system than are possible with incrementalism. The number of generations of new systems required to achieve a fully integrated programming support system would be shrunk accordingly [Fig. 3]. The minimum time for that achievement would be a generation beyond the first Ada systems, perhaps by 1990. The maximum time, judging from the history of structured programming and the older languages, could be 20 years or longer. Of course, in both cases nationwide programming productivity would improve continuously because of gradual acceptance of the new systems. But the pace could differ by a factor of 2 or more.

It may seem novel that vision could change the pace of innovation so substantially. But looking at the aircraft industry again, all of the major technologies that marked the difference between the World War I airplane and the 1935 DC-3 were invented by 1925. The 10 years from 1925 to 1935 were spent making incremental changes in a whole series of airplane designs. Knowing how to integrate the technologies in 1925 would have increased by a factor of 2 the pace of innovation.

Similarly, in computers, John Mauchly and John Eckert, who built the Eniac and later the Univac, observe, "The Eniac could have been invented 10 to 15 years earlier, and the real question is, why wasn't it done sooner?...In part, the demand wasn't there. The demand, of course, is a curious thing. People may need something without knowing they need it." In other words, a technological vision that spurs development may be lacking.

Even with complete consensus and a clear view of future software technology, a fully integrated programming environment is still some years away. It seems like at least a five-year process to complete the first APSE; have users and computer companies migrate modestly integrated programming tools to it from systems like UNIX (or migrate Ada-like project-information handling to existing systems); experiment with a variety of mechanisms needed to integrate the pieces of a programming support environment; and finally, incorporate those mechanisms into a standard, widely available system. Both the hydraulic analogy and experience suggest that as automation and integration eliminate bottlenecks, new ones (that is, new opportunities for further automation and integration) will come to the fore. Even in a very optimistic projection, another five-year generation of PSEs would be needed before these features could be achieved. The earliest that a truly integrated PSE will appear, then, would be in the beginning of the 1990s.

Without a compelling vision, any one of several events could be the trigger for full integration, much as molten metal solidifies around a single small crystal. For example, use of cathode-ray-tube displays for developing programs might create a demand for links between software tools such as the editor and the compiler. Automatic syntax checks could alert the programmer immediately if an error were made. A light pen or cursor could specify stopping points in the program; the programmer would simply point to the proper place on a program listing displayed on the screen. The program would then run only to that point and stop, so that the program events could be inspected. The result would be an enormous speed-up in debugging.

Another phenomenon that could trigger full integration—either singly or in combination with CRT editing—is greater programmer acceptance of common programming environments. The trend is already evident as UNIX and p-code and other stan-

I. Programming activities that have been and those that remain to be automated

Manual operation	Automated by:	Remaining manual operations	To be automated by:
Allocating absolute addresses and registers	Compiler	Running, consulting listing, editing, rerunning	Syntax-checking editor, high-level debugging package
Decomposing algebraic expressions and so on		Manually creating compiler tools	Automatic translator production
Retrieving off-line output, key punching, submitting checks	Interactive terminals and editors	Making and comparing listings	Multiple-window cathode-ray-tube displays
Tracing cause of program failure	Debugger	Mapping between source and object codes	High-level debugging package

Why is a computer like an airplane?

The modern airplane evolved rapidly in the 1930s through the integration of several existing technologies. The circumstances during the 1920s and 1930s that set up those breakthroughs are remarkably similar to the circumstances today in computer software.

Clearly the airplane industry was off the ground technologically well before the 1930s. The Wright brothers flew in 1903, and airplanes were used in World War I. Lindbergh had already flown the Atlantic in 1927. In the 1920s, airplanes were a growth industry—between 1926 and 1930 the revenue miles flown per year went from 4 million to 32 million. Yet, as an economic force, the airplane industry was minuscule. In 1930, the value of aircraft production was 0.066 percent of the gross national product.

Although small during the 1920s, the airplane industry had just begun to tap a very large market for rapid transportation—most notably of mail and later of people. The alternatives were telegraph, train, automobile, or ship. The airplane had a big future if it could be made safe and cost-effective —progress in pilot training and navigation procedures had made air travel safer, but the size, range, and speed of the 1920s airplane made air transport relatively expensive.

By the mid-30s, aeronautical engineering was producing larger, faster, and more cost-effective planes. What might be called the first modern airplanes were the DC-3 in 1935 and the Lockheed Electra in 1936. It was said at the time that the DC-3 was the first airplane able to support itself economically as well as aerodynamically. The technological superiority rested on five innovations, but none was particularly effective when installed alone in an older airplane. The innovations were:

• Radial air-cooled engines, which offered substantial increases in power-to-weight ratio over earlier designs. The first radial air-cooled engine came out commercially in 1921. But installing larger and larger engines often had only marginal effect, because older airplane design was not streamlined: older planes had canvas-covered wings braced with struts and landing wheels and struts protruding below.
• Retractable landing gear, which greatly reduced aerodynamic drag.
• Monocoque bodies, with stressed metal skin and single internally braced wings. Streamlining had long been attractive to airplane designers: monocoque construction (with wood) and an all-metal monoplane had both been tested in Europe before World War I. But streamlining to achieve fast, capacious airplanes was not pursued aggressively, because large airplanes were notoriously difficult to land and take off. The airplane wing was shaped to give efficient (low-drag) high-speed flight, but it did not produce adequate lift at low speeds. Landings were dangerous with such wings, unless wing flaps were used.
• Wing flaps, which alter the shape of wings to give more lift at low landing and takeoff speeds. Although the technology for variable aerodynamic surfaces had been part of powered flight from the very beginning, wing flaps were not used on the smaller, slower aircraft of the time because the small improvement in aerodynamics did not justify the added weight of the mechanisms.
• Variable-pitch propellers, which can move through the air at a shallow angle when the plane is standing still and at a larger angle when the airplane is moving rapidly, so the engine can operate at maximum propulsive force regardless of airspeed. (Variable-pitch propellers have the same function as gear shifts in cars.) Variable-pitch propellers were tried during and after World War I. But, again, the weight and complexity of the mechanism did not justify its use in early planes, which flew at relatively slow speeds, so the difference between cruising and takeoff speeds was smaller.

By 1933, the Boeing 247 had incorporated all of these innovations except wing flaps and was manifestly superior to any existing transport plane. But its size and power had to be reduced below its original specifications precisely because the lack of wing flaps would have caused landing difficulties. When Douglas added wing flaps in 1935, more powerful engines and larger size became feasible for the DC-3. Thus in 1937 it was the DC-3, not the Boeing 247, that carried 95 percent of civilian air traffic.

The analogy to today's computer industry lies in the fact that the airplane industry of the 1920s, in general, still represented a minority component of the GNP, but had decades of technological innovation behind it. It was a growth industry just beginning to tap a large market; the technical barriers to tapping a wider market could be broken through by integrating several existing technologies, which were not cost-effective when implemented singly within older technology.

The computer industry fits the same mold. There are over three decades of technological innovation the industry can choose from: Whirlwind I, the first modern computer (electronic switching, stored programs, magnetic-core memory, parallel-processing arithmetic), was in full stride by 1953. Machines with some modern features were developing during the early 1940s, including the first production computer, Univac I, which emerged in 1951. High-level languages have been available since Fortran was introduced in 1954. A computer was put on a single silicon chip in 1969.

Economically, the computer industry—at least partly because of the long wave—stands out as a growth industry in the midst of general malaise. Of course, the ensemble of technologies that dominates the next long wave will contain other technologies—genetic engineering and new materials, to name two. Nonetheless, few doubt the future growth of the computer industry in all its forms: manufacturing, programming, services, and applications. The market for all forms of information processing is huge and just beginning to be tapped by the computer industry. Programming costs are a substantial barrier, even though a promising variety of software technologies exists. There will be a breakthrough only when these programming technologies are fully integrated.

—A.K.G.

dardized systems become more popular. As more programs are written to work with such systems, additional programmers will be encouraged to adopt them.

Or perhaps integration of project management and communication will trigger full integration; several of today's trends create a demand for it. The APSE is designed to work from a project-information data base, and programming for the Department of Defense will use it. Some programmers are already using electronic filing and electronic mail and can thus communicate with other programmers through their computer consoles. With such telecommuting, they work at home much of the time and communicate with co-workers via home terminals and telephone.

Another potential trigger phenomenon is the arrival on the market of artificial intelligence. If research on artificial intelligence produces a system that is clearly more effective than anything else in speeding up programming, commercial copies are bound to follow. MIT's programmer's apprentice is a step in this direction; it is on the border line between automatic aids and fully automatic programming. When fully developed, the programmer's apprentice will perform routine and repetitive programming, leaving difficult programming and concept development to the human programmer. Such a system is further in the future than CRT editing, a common programming environment, or integrated project management and communication.

These predictions do not exclude other innovations; technologies in other fields and other computer technologies will play an important role in coming decades. New applications of electronic information processing will give rise to new types of hardware in banking, communication, commerce, cars, the home, and elsewhere. But programming bottlenecks will still limit the pace of such innovations. Indeed, as hardware devices proliferate, the inadequacies of the software that engineers use to design hardware will impose an ever more serious limitation. The implication is that other advances in the computer field are increasingly dependent on advances in programming technology. The important message for the computer industry is that vision—seeing what lies ahead—can make a vast difference in how rapidly the software bottleneck opens.

To probe further

The IEEE's *Computer* magazine has several issues that highlight key topics in programming. Ada was covered in the June 1981 issue, office-information systems in May, and programming environments in April.

R.C. Waters describes an important artificial-intelligence aid to programming in "The Programmer's Apprentice: Knowledge-Based Program Editing," *IEEE Transactions on Software Engineering*, Vol. SE-8, no. 1, January 1982.

Alan K. Graham and P.M. Senge explain technological and economic cycles in "A long-wave hypothesis of innovation," *Technological Forecasting and Social Change*, no. 17 (1980), pp. 283–311.

J.B. Rae examines the development of aircraft manufacturing in *Climb to Greatness: The American Aircraft Industry 1920-1960*, MIT Press, Cambridge, Mass. (1968).

K.C. Cooper describes a model-based method for quantitative analysis of research and development in "Naval Ship Production: A Claim Settled and a Framework Built," *Interfaces*, Vol. 10, no. 6 (1980) pp. 20–36.

The illustration showing intervals of about 50 years between surges of basic innovations [p. 249] is adapted from one on page 130 of the book *Stalemate in Technology* by Gerhard Mensch (Ballinger, Cambridge, Mass., 1979). Its author is one of the major researchers in areas of innovation and long-wave theory, and the book's German edition was a best-seller.

Several recent books published by the IEEE Computer Society cover the basics, as well as advanced techniques, of software engineering. They can be ordered from the IEEE Computer Society, P.O. Box 80452, Worldway Postal Center, Los Angeles, Calif. 90080. Among them are the following (prices shown include fourth-class book-rate shipping):

II. Manual bottlenecks in communication tools used for programming

Communication tool	Remaining manual operations
Formal specification and validation procedures	Memos to programmers; programmer review of documents while programming
Word processing	Typing in documents; shuffling through and skimming documents to find relevant information
Program annotation	Typing in notations (partly redundant with specification documents); locating relevant notation among other notations and code; maintaining discipline to notate adequately; rephrasing for documentation

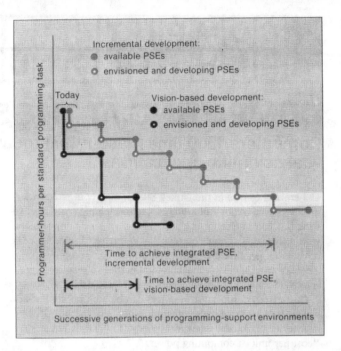

[3] *The pace of integration depends on the clarity of vision of those who develop and implement programming technology. An integrated programming support environment (PSE), represented by the wide horizontal line, will be realized slowly if just the new features already developed by users or other companies—only those features for which a clear demand exists—are incorporated in new PSEs. But development based on a vision can arrive at an integrated PSE in a far shorter time because it incorporates more features in each PSE generation. This is feasible because development based on a vision of future technology does not require coming up with fundamentally new ideas, but rather more actively developing and implementing ideas that already exist.*

A broad survey of software-engineering methods, with an emphasis on newer approaches, offered by Peter Freeman and Anthony I. Wasserman in their *Tutorial: Software Design Techniques* (Third Edition), 1980, 425 pp., 300 (EHO 161-0); members $15, nonmembers $20.

Techniques for writing exact specifications for what a prospective computer system is supposed to do, given in Kenneth J. Thurber's *Computer System Requirements* 313 (EHO 168-5) 1980, 364 pp.; members $15, nonmembers $20.

About the author

Alan K. Graham (SM) is the director of research for the System Dynamics National Model Project in the Sloan School of Management at the Massachusetts Institute of Technology, Cambridge. The project's objective, which is in the process of being reached, is to develop a computer simulation model of the U.S. economy with a methodology, system dynamics, that is based on engineering control theory. The model represents the effects of individual decisions—hiring, buying, capital investment, and so on—on the whole economy and can simulate economic change over decades and even centuries. Research on innovation and software technology has grown out of the long-term economic research. Dr. Graham previously served as assistant professor at the Sloan School and as a consultant. He has applied system dynamics to a variety of other fields, including engineering management, endocrinology, and urban development. He received a B.S. in electrical engineering and a B.S. in management in 1973, an M.S. in electrical engineering the same year, and a Ph.D. in electrical engineering in 1977, all from MIT.   ◆

COMPUTER ARCHITECTURE

COMPUTING AT THE SPEED LIMIT

Computers 1000 times faster than today's supercomputers would benefit vital scientific applications

Unheralded efforts in the United States, mainly in universities, have removed major stumbling blocks to building cost-effective superfast computers for scientific and engineering applications within five years. These computers would have sustained speeds of billions of floating-point operations per second (flops), whereas with the fastest machines today the top sustained speed is only 25 million flops, with bursts to 160 megaflops.

Cost-effective superfast machines can be built because of advances in very large-scale integration and the special software needed to program the new machines. VLSI greatly reduces the "cost per unit of computing power."

The development of such computers would come at an opportune time. Although the U.S. leads the world in large-scale computer technology, its supremacy is now threatened, not surprisingly, by the Japanese. Publicized reports indicate that the Japanese government is funding a cooperative effort by commercial computer manufacturers to develop superfast computers—about 1000 times faster than modern supercomputers. The U.S. computer industry, by contrast, has balked at attempting to boost computer power so sharply because of the uncertain market for the machines and the failure of similar projects in the past to show significant results.

Many architectures proposed

But while there is good news, there is also bad. There is no common agreement on which of the many architectures proposed for superfast computers over the years could tackle the broadest variety of problems. Nor is there any indication that such agreement will be reached in the next few years. Moreover, a problem may have a number of different solutions, each achieved by only one architecture, and there is no body of theory or experience for predicting which problems are most suitable for solution on the different architectures. Many computer scientists suspect that no such theory exists at all.

A further snag is that most computer manufacturers lack the necessary experience to assemble large numbers of concurrently working processors. "They do not know how assemblages of microprocessors will function, who will use them, and above all, who will buy them," according to Kenneth Wilson, James A. Weeks Professor of Physical Science at Cornell University and a specialist in computational physics. "They face major hardware- and software-development projects to take advantage of the opportunities microprocessors will provide." And, finally, Dr. Wilson noted, "there is a history of parallel-processing projects that have failed to take hold, starting with the Illiac IV."

Superfast computers have always been needed to predict the behavior of such systems as fusion power reactors, turbulent flow around ships or planes, the weather, or the flow of oil in underground deposits. These systems do not lend themselves to

computer analysis within reasonable time and cost limits with the machines now available if realistic three-dimensional models are used. Instead relatively simplistic two-dimensional models are used, which have serious drawbacks [see "3-D models need higher speed and more memory," p. 260].

In addition to computing practical problems, the superfast computers are needed as research tools for achieving a better understanding of three-dimensional systems through simulations. In some cases, full-scale experiments with the systems are too expensive or realistic physical conditions cannot be reproduced in inexpensive small-scale models.

To achieve superfast performance, scientists have developed new types of highly parallel architectures—thousands of processors that can work concurrently on different parts of the same problem. This was necessary because a limit to higher speed had been reached with brute-force approaches employing faster switching devices. Faster components made with gallium arsenide or Josephson junction devices can increase computer speed only 10 times if current uniprocessor architectures are used; however, with the new architectures, there is hope of increasing speed 100 to 1000 times [Fig. 1].

Two major stumbling blocks had to be overcome before the multiprocessor architectures could be developed: (1) the interconnection network was more expensive than the rest of the system; and (2) new methods were needed to exploit the concurrency in problems, either through the execution of different programs simultaneously or with a single, highly concurrent program. The recent development of so-called banyan networks [Fig. 2] has solved the interconnection problem, and new algorithms and compilers have shown how to exploit concurrency.

U.S. sponsoring university research

Most research on highly parallel machines is being done in university centers and is sponsored by the National Science Foundation, the Defense Advanced Research Projects Agency, and the National Aeronautics and Space Administration. The leading candidates for the architectures of the future are multiprocessors and data-flow systems [Fig. 3].

The multiprocessor system is the most flexible when each processor is a programmable unit that can execute its own general-purpose program. Multiprocessors may be organized as an MIMD (multi-instruction stream, multidata stream) or SIMD (single-instruction stream, multidata stream) machine.

In the MIMD architecture, the computing problem is partitioned by the programmer (and compiler) so the processor can compute it by operating concurrently on different data streams with different instructions. The slower-speed, lower-cost SIMD system can operate with either separate programs or a single program. Multiprocessors, in any case, require complex controls and software to mesh the results of different concurrent computations with a minimum of recursions (computations that depend on the updated results of other, concurrent computations,

Robert Bernhard   Senior Associate Editor

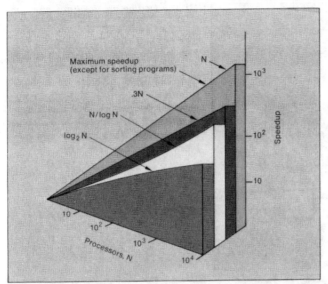

[1] The speedup that can be achieved with N processors working concurrently on a single problem is in theory N times the speed of one of the processors (although it may be higher for certain problems that include sorting operations). But the speedup in practice is less, since some processors are idle at a given time because of conflicts over memory addresses or communication paths and inefficient algorithms for exploiting the natural concurrency in the computing problem, among other reasons. Various estimates of the actual speedup range from a high of .3N, based on simulations of relatively simple Fortran programs, to a lower bound of $\log_2 N$. The truth may lie between 0.3N and N/logN.

so that some processors remain idle while awaiting results from other processors).

Data-flow machines, by contrast, have no controls to speak of. The algorithm for computing a given problem is first written in a special programming language designed for data-flow applications. The program, which now has the appearance of a directed graph, is then implemented directly by a network of hardware units corresponding to the graph. Each unit performs a single step of the algorithm whenever the data needed for the computation arrive at the unit.

In multiprocessor systems, hundreds or thousands of processors may also be interconnected so as to mirror the basic geometry of the computing problem as well as of the algorithm. In determining airflow over a wing, for instance, each processor can do the computing for one of the many regions, each having differing physical characteristics, within the airflow. The largest regions would be in the free stream—farthest from the wing—where flow is smooth and free of turbulence. The regions would be smallest close to the wing and trailing edge, where there is turbulence and the most rapid changes occur in the velocity and pressure of the airflow.

The major projects today [Fig. 4] include a multiprocessor called TRAC (Texas reconfigurable array computer) at the University of Texas in Austin; the FMP (flow model processor), being built by the Federal and Special Systems Group of the Burroughs Corp. in Paoli, Pa., and proposed for the NASA Ames Research Center in Mountain View, Calif.; the CHIP (configurable highly parallel) multiprocessor at Purdue University in West Lafayette, Ind.; and data-flow machines at the

[2] The networks needed to interconnect thousands of processors with memory modules must perform all possible connections of inputs and outputs, yet be relatively cheap and simple. The conventional crosspoint network (A) is too expensive for more than about 50 processors—the cost and complexity increase as N^2—so designers today have turned to various banyan networks (B, C, D), in which cost and complexity increase only as NlogN. A simple banyan network (B) has two lines entering each switching node (spread of two), two lines leaving each node (fanout of two), and three levels (apex to base). The network could link eight processors with eight memories or input/output devices. The omega network (D) is made with stages that are actually "perfect shuffle" interconnections (C) followed by a column of four-function interchange boxes. The term "perfect shuffle" comes from card playing when there is a perfect mix of each half of the deck.

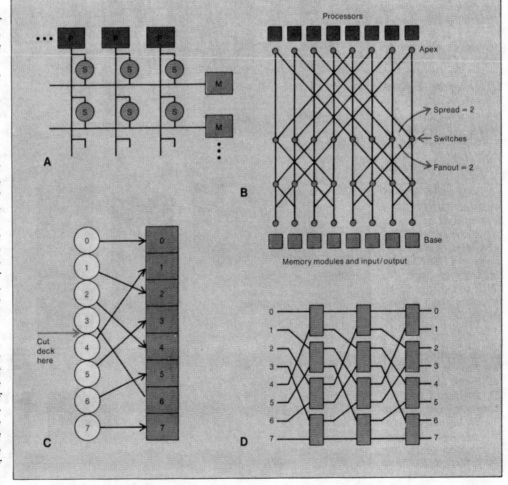

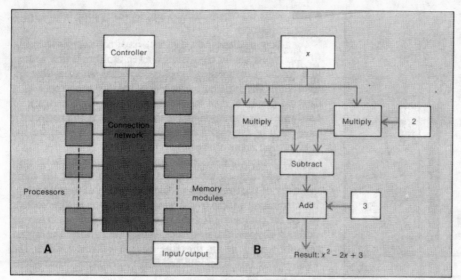

A
Controller
Connection network
Processors
Memory modules
Input/output

B
x
Multiply   Multiply ← 2
Subtract
Add ← 3
Result: $x^2 - 2x + 3$

[3] The leading architectures now for superfast computers are multiprocessors (A) and data-flow machines (B). The multiprocessors are more or less general-purpose machines that share data and work together on a single problem. Data-flow systems implement the computing algorithm directly, although they can also be built as a multiprocessorlike system or with cell-block architecture [Fig. 4E].

[4] The Burroughs flow-model processor, which has 512 processors, is interconnected in an omega network (shown in A for 16 processors). The actual system has nine stages with 256 two-input, two-output switches. The same interconnection plan is envisioned for the Ultracomputer by researchers at New York University's Courant Institute. The Ultracomputer, described by its designers as a paracomputer, actually executes data-flow language. Two multiprocessors that can be reconfigured through software for different problems are the configurable highly parallel processor (CHIP), under development at Purdue University, and the Texas reconfigurable array computer (TRAC) at the University of Texas. The CHIP can change its architecture from a mesh pattern (B), for example, to a tree (C). The TRAC is reconfigured through a banyan network (D). The data-flow machine with cell-block architecture (E), envisioned by Jack Dennis of the Massachusetts Institute of Technology, has the synchronization of concurrent operations built into the hardware.

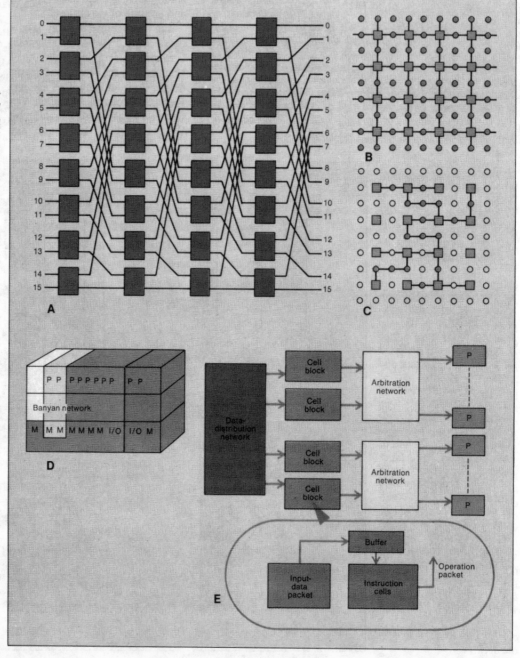

D
P P P P P P P P
Banyan network
M M M M M M I/O I/O M

E
Data-distribution network
Cell block
Cell block
Arbitration network
Cell block
Cell block
Arbitration network
P
P
P
P
Buffer
Input-data packet
Instruction cells
Operation packet

Massachusetts Institute of Technology in Cambridge.

The Ultracomputer, being developed at New York University's Courant Institute of Mathematical Sciences in New York, simulates an abstract machine called a paracomputer. Although built with identical microprocessors, and thus superficially resembling a multiprocessor, it operates on a data-flow language with data-flow principles.

These machines are still in the early stages of development, but hopes were raised that such projects would be successful when Denelcor Inc. of Denver, Colo., last year introduced the HEP (heterogeneous element processor). The HEP is the first commercial computer that is potentially expandable to thousands of processors, according to Dr. Wilson of Cornell, although it now has just 16 processors and a reported speed of 160 megaflops.

Whatever the architecture of superfast computers, scientists have been speculating for decades on exactly how much speedup can be achieved by highly parallel architectures. Common sense suggests that, in theory, a multiprocessor with N independent processors can compute a given problem at most N times faster than one of the processors. This ideal is known as linear speedup. But the speedup in practice is less than the ideal, primarily because of the following four factors, which are in addition to delays caused by input/output or inefficient algorithms or compiled programs:

1. Several processors may simultaneously request data from the same memory addresses, so that some remain idle for several memory cycles until the data become available.

2. Processors vying for the same communication paths to other processors or to memory can also slow computation until paths become open.

3. Many processors may simultaneously attempt to read or update an array index, so a significant amount of time may be spent waiting for clearance to read an index.

4. Because of these delays, processors that start out in synchrony tend to lose synchrony during a lengthy computation. Computation must therefore be slowed periodically to resynchronize the system.

For example, the Illiac-IV, built at the University of Illinois in the late 1960s and operated at Ames Research Center until it was decommissioned last year, had 60 processors that could work concurrently. It was designed to execute 200 megaflops, but it never achieved more than 25 megaflops. This illustrates a major frustration in designing superfast machines—namely, the general methods for predicting the performance of a given design are "big-O" theories. The theories can estimate the relative advantages of different designs in terms of orders of magnitude, but they tend to underestimate or ignore the slowdowns in speed caused by such practical items as wire length and I/O delays.

The most widely known speculation about the realistic speedup probably comes from Marvin Minsky, professor of computer science at MIT. In 1970 he conjectured that the use of N concurrently operating processors would result in a speedup of, at most, $\log_2 N$ [Fig. 1]. Accordingly, 1024 processors could result in 10 times faster computing speed.

However, Dr. Minsky's theory appears to have underestimated the potential speedup, according to Jack Worlton, assistant division leader of the computing division at the Los Alamos Scientific Laboratory in New Mexico. He has calculated that the maximum speedup is $N/\log 1.78N$, based on a widely accepted formula called Amdahl's law [see "Using Amdahl's law," p. 261]. With current components, this means that 10 000 processors would be needed to achieve a thousandfold speedup over today's fastest machines; 1000 processors could provide the thousandfold speedup only if they were built with advanced gallium arsenide or Josephson junction circuits.

Using different assumptions, other researchers have concluded that the maximum speedup may be $0.3N$, which is higher than the other estimates. This result is a projection from simulated runs of Fortran programs, which have indicated that 32 processors could achieve a tenfold speedup, while 135 processors could yield a fortyfold speedup. This suggests that the thousandfold speedup could be achieved with 3000 processors.

Scientists have a long way to go, however, in learning how to assemble or program optimally 1000 or so parallel processors; but their task is further complicated because there is no inexpensive way to predict which problems are best implemented on specific architectures. The programs are generally so expensive and time-consuming to run that software developers are often unable to test adequately for convergence, accuracy, or efficiency before running them. Moreover, no systematic method exists to guarantee beforehand that a given numerical method will solve the three-dimensional partial differential equations that describe fusion reactors or hydrodynamic or aerodynamic flow.

While research continues in these areas, software methods have been developed to exploit as far as possible the practical speedups. Ideally, the shortfall in linear speedup that is caused by memory conflicts would be minimized if three conditions could be met: (1) the processors all started out in synchrony; (2) special algorithms were used to organize the memory to avoid conflicts; and (3) each processor accessed its own portion of memory in the common memory.

In the FMP, for instance, address 1 is in memory module 1, address 2 in module 2, and so on. In the simplest type of memory-access pattern, each processor (1, 2, 3, ...) is associated with an index (I = 1, 2, 3, ...) that refers to computations done in each processor. During a computation, therefore, any reference to a vector, $A(I)$, in the program causes the processor with index I to access the vector element with subscript I. The addresses are separated by a constant "skip" distance, so that the memory address of $A(I) = A(O) + pI$, where $A(O)$ is the offset of the base address of the vector and p is the skip distance.

Although memory conflicts can be avoided in these ideal cases, they are inevitable in other situations, such as practical aerodynamic computations. Here most memory use involves simultaneous access to the elements of two-dimensional subsets of three-dimensional arrays, $A(I,J,K)$. Simulations of the FMP have shown that with 512 processors no conflicts occur when the memory is accessed in the "first easy direction"—where parallelism is assigned to I and J while K is kept constant across all processors. However, up to 72 processors may be blocked from accessing the memory when access occurs in the "second easy direction" and the "hard direction." The second direction refers to a pattern where I is fixed and each processor has separate values of the pair J, K; the hard direction refers to a fixed J while each processor has separate values of I, K.

In practice, in any case, the processors gradually become desynchronized and tend to access memory randomly. The random pattern, the FMP simulation has shown, leads to increased memory conflicts and more idle processors at any given time. Another measure to prevent conflicts in this case is scrambling—or "hashing"—according to Dr. Wilson. The hashing process, performed before memory requests are sent to the memory, translates regular sequences of addresses into random sequences and is designed to increase the probability that a given address will be available to a maximum number of processors. Hashing has long been used in setting up data-base records, where it allows data to be entered into records without having to reorder the addresses in the entire record.

3-D models need higher speed and more memory

Huge increases in computer speed and memory are needed for what is probably the oldest reason for making digital computers at all: to obtain numerical solutions to the partial differential equations (PDEs) of applied physics. For more than 30 years now, scientists have used, first, fast mainframes and, later, supercomputers to compute the PDEs representing two-dimensional models of turbulent flow in hydrodynamics, aerodynamics, the weather, and the behavior of plasmas in fusion power reactors or of materials in response to complex patterns of mechanical stress. But the leap to more realistic three-dimensional models has been all but impossible because the expanded calculations require computers 1000 times faster than supercomputers and primary memories 1000 times larger.

The limitations cannot be overcome by increased computer power alone. The problems involve complex questions in physics that are still poorly understood. Complexity here refers to physical systems with a prohibitively large number of degrees of freedom—and that is where more powerful computers come in.

The computing requirements are illustrated by the simulation of three-dimensional turbulent flow around a plane or ship's hull (the problem is similar for models of the weather, oceanic circulation, or fusion power reactors). Turbulence implies chaotic motion or many excited degrees of freedom in the fluid. In nonturbulent flow, by contrast, all layers of the fluid move in parallel in the direction of flow. In turbulence, random changes occur in pressure and velocity, and the details of the flow are unpredictable. As a result, a plane or ship in the turbulent fluid will encounter increased frictional forces that slow it, or forces that tend to destabilize its motion.

Two-dimensional models of turbulent flow have been successful to a degree, because of various methods for averaging the chaotic motions on the molecular scale over larger regions of the fluid. Still, physicists have always needed better tools—including 3-D models—to understand in fuller detail the behavior of the fluid on a small scale. But the simulation of better models requires coordinate systems with an estimated 10^9·mesh points, and these have to be computed at each step in time. Moreover, each step involves about 10^{10} scalar variables—or 10^9 mesh points multiplied by the sum of 1 pressure, 1 temperature, and 3 velocity variables, for both the current and previous time step. At each step, meanwhile, 10^{12} to 10^{15} arithmetic operations are needed, depending on the method for numerically solving the PDEs describing the fluid.

The computations are estimated to require a primary memory of 10^{10} words. The most powerful computers today, by contrast, can do about 10^9 operations per time step, and they have a primary memory of about 10^6 words.   —R.B.

These problems take different forms in data-flow machines. In contrast to multiprocessors, the speedup of data-flow machines is estimated by the number of computations needed for a given problem and the clock rate of the machine. For instance, one study has shown that a data-flow system can multiply two $N \times N$ matrices in a time of order N, the number of time steps required for the computation. A conventional process requires on the order of N^3 steps for the same computation. A study by Jack Dennis, professor of computer science at MIT, has indicated that a data-flow system with a 150-megahertz clock rate can do weather-prediction computations 100 times faster than an IBM 360/95.

Nevertheless, for large values of N, a prohibitively large number of memory accesses may be needed in a data-flow system. This was suggested by studies indicating that for a system in which the processors were connected by a ring bus, N^2 memory accesses and N^3 operations would be needed to switch data through the single ring connection. A ring bus, however, is a notoriously inefficient way to link many processors.

A data-flow system envisioned by Dr. Dennis creates no memory conflicts, since all hardware units are represented by an acyclic, directed graph and each unit has its own memory. That architecture may be too expensive, however. An alternative proposal by Dr. Dennis is the sharing of data structures wherever possible to reduce the number of hardware units or memory modules.

Data-flow machines with 512 processing units, each operating at the state-of-the-art speed of 2 million flops, could perform 1 billion flops, according to Dr. Dennis. A system with 512 cell blocks [Fig. 4E] could, he believes, be interconnected through 1000 message-packet routers, each fabricated as a 100-pin large-scale integrated circuit.

Another alternative to the excessive storage in data-flow systems is the so-called I structure—but this reintroduces memory conflict. The I structures are data arrays in memory addresses that are allocated before the data are generated by computations. The structures must, therefore, be optimally distributed among many processors to minimize both the traffic through the network and the conflict between processors for the same addresses.

In multiprocessors, in contrast with data-flow machines, another form of conflict between processors that arises is over communication links and switching elements that interconnect processors or link processors to memories. No such contention would occur in processors connected by a nonblocking crosspoint network. In crosspoint interconnections the right data are always available to the right processor because all pairs of processors are connected.

But crosspoints are too expensive for systems with 50 or more processors. Among the many alternatives to the crosspoint switch, most designers of advanced systems have chosen various types of banyan networks, including shuffle-exchange and omega networks. While these are more cost-efficient than crosspoint networks, there is increased conflict for communication paths.

Crosspoints are themselves a special—though the least efficient—type of banyan network. Whereas the complexity of a crosspoint grows as N^2, other banyans grow in complexity as $N \log N$. The other banyans, moreover, can be adapted to specific applications by selecting the "fanout" and "spread." Fanout is the number of lines fanning out from each node towards the next lower level; spread is the number of lines fanning into each node.

Beyond these generalizations about networks, it is difficult to pin down the advantages of one network over another in terms of such practical design criteria as bandwidth, which here means the expected number of requests that a given network can handle in a unit of time. Analytical methods and numerical simulations have been used to calculate bandwidths, but they have been limited to relatively simple cases. However, these approaches have shown that multistage networks, which include many banyans, will probably allow MIMD systems to execute 1 billion flops and yet cost as little as one twentieth the price of a crosspoint switch.

A detail often overlooked in predicting computer performance concerns conflicts between processors that attempt to read and update an array index simultaneously. The processors instead must take their proper turn, so the index will be updated in the right sequence. The conflict is generally resolved with software, but most methods cause significant delays. In the HEP, on the other hand, requests to use the index are handled by hardware that reportedly avoids appreciable delays.

When implemented as a banyan network, the replace-add is executed through a special memory and integer adder in each node of the network. Each node can add two simultaneous requests to increment the index and then process the updated index that is returned to the node from the memory. With this procedure each processor can update a unique subset of array elements that is always within the range of the update finally applied to the index.

The principle of highly parallel processing—albeit with 16 processors—will receive its first commercial test with the HEP. One HEP has been delivered to the University of Georgia Research Center in Athens, two more will be delivered soon to the U.S. Army Ballistics Research Laboratory in Aberdeen, Md., and another will be shipped to Dr. Wilson's laboratory at Cornell.

Each of the 16 processor modules in the HEP can execute a peak rate of 10 million instructions per second, so that 16 modules running concurrently on the same problem could, in theory, execute 160 million instructions per second. The system is limited now to 16 modules because of a tradeoff between cost and the system's mean time between failures. A notable characteristic of the overall design is that it gives the appearance of being an MIMD architecture; however, each module can execute many independent programs that are actually interleaved and thus executed as in a SIMD system. This has come about because the modules have much higher clock rates than memory rates, so they had to be slowed; but the slowdown was offset by a design allowing each module to run from 8 to 64 independent processes. The processes in each module are executed in round-robin fashion; upon completing an instruction for a given process, the module is stepped to the next process, and so on.

Computational physicists are waiting not only to see how well the HEP works, but also to see whether other computer manufacturers will decide to compete with it.

To probe further

A special issue of *Computer*, entitled "Highly Parallel Computing," appeared in January 1982. It contains an overview of general principles by Leonard S. Haynes *et al.* of Carnegie-Mellon University in Pittsburgh. Other articles in the same issue focus on details of the flow-model processor, the configurable highly parallel processor, the Ultracomputer, and so-called systolic architecture (largely for image-processing applications).

Data-flow systems are described in the February 1982 issue of *Computer*, with one article, by D.D. Gasjke of the University of Illinois at Urbana and others, sharply criticizing the concept. The main objections are that data-flow systems are unnecessary complications that contribute nothing conceptually to the technology. They are plagued, the authors say, by the same problems as multiprocessors and also need special programming languages that have yet to be perfected.

The programming of concurrent processors—a major issue not discussed in the above article—has a voluminous literature that is surveyed in "Exploiting Program Concurrency in Computing Systems," by Phillip C. Treleaven of the University of Newcastle upon Tyne, England, in the January 1979 issue of *Computer*.

Most of the programming languages that can be used to implement concurrent programming—including PL/1, Algol, and concurrent Pascal—are modifications of old fashioned sequential-flow computation. In PL/1, for instance, instructions such as FORK, JOIN, CALL, or WAIT allow various streams of instructions to be executed concurrently, while synchronization instructions coordinate sequential operations. The FORK instruction, for example, would allow the execution of the instruction immediately following the FORK, while a JOIN would bring separate instruction streams back together.

In the data-flow computer, by contrast, a program is a directed graph. As such, the nodes of the graph are the subroutines of the program that can be executed as synchronous instructions. The arcs of the graph are data paths that specify the flow of data between operations. A subroutine can be either a single primitive operation, such as division or multiplication, or a series of instructions interconnected by data paths. The data paths are first-in, first-out buffers that store partial results.

A number of specialized data-flow languages have been developed that have capabilities similar to those of conventional languages, but quite different semantics. Whereas the semantics of conventional languages are more or less independent of the architecture or hardware of a specific computer or problem, the semantics of data-flow languages correspond to the directed graph (representing a given program) and thus to a specific data-flow machine for a given problem.   ◆

Using Amdahl's law

Amdahl's law states that a computer with both high-speed and low-speed modes of operation may be dominated by the low-speed mode, even if the high-speed one is infinitely fast. The law was first stated in 1967 by Gene Amdahl, founder of the Amdahl Computer Corp. in Sunnyvale, Calif., and it has since passed into computer lore. The designers of superfast multiprocessors who ignore it are doomed to failure, according to Jack Worlton, computing specialist at the Los Alamos Scientific Laboratory in New Mexico. What the law implies, in Dr. Worlton's opinion, is that though a mix of low- and high-speed modes may be alright for general-purpose computers, the designers of superfast machines will do better at exploiting concurrency in the computing problems if they use a smaller number of fast processors instead of a larger number of slower processors.

With Amdahl's law, the number of results that a computer can generate per unit of time can be computed with the expression $1/(F_h T_h + F_l T_l)$, in which F_h and F_l are the fractions of results generated in the high- and low-speed modes, respectively, and T_h and T_l are the periods of time needed to generate a single result in each mode. Dr. Worlton used the law to derive his estimate of the speedup resulting from the use of multiprocessors. He used a multiprocessor version of the law, where F now referred to the fraction of computer tasks done by a given number of processors.

This version came out to be

$$\frac{N}{\sum_1^N \dfrac{f}{i}}$$

where N is the number of processors and i refers to the ith processor. Dr. Worlton then evaluated the equation for the case where the computing tasks are distributed equally among all processors—that is, when $f_i = 1/N$. The result was

$$\frac{N}{\sum_1^N \dfrac{1}{i}}$$

which, when expanded, approaches the value of

$$\frac{N}{\log N}$$

for large values of N.   —R.B.

COMPUTER ARCHITECTURE

DATA-FLOW ARCHITECTURE

A decentralized structure based on the flow of data will permit future computers to operate at even higher speeds

ADVANCED TECHNOLOGY

COMPUTERS

The development of a new generation of faster, more intelligent computers—the goal of major projects in the United States, Japan, and Europe—requires not only the perfection of faster devices but also new ways of linking chips. In the view of many computer scientists, the key to obtaining much higher speeds is the abandonment of the conventional Von Neumann architecture and the adoption of new designs, in which calculations are performed in parallel rather than in a fixed sequence.

But how can this be done? Of the various competing ideas of how a parallel computer can be built, the best known and most developed is called data flow. In data-flow computers, each of many identical processors calculates results as the data for a given computation become available. This contrasts with the procedure in a conventional computer, where a single processor does the calculations specified in a sequential program.

A half dozen major groups and some two dozen smaller ones around the world are now involved in the development of data-flow machines. The work is concentrated at laboratories in the United States, Great Britain, and Japan (where the research is integrated with that country's government-backed Fifth-Generation Computer Systems Project, which seeks to develop intelligent, high-speed computers). Those in the field believe that data-flow machines can be developed in the course of the 1980s that are many times faster than the fastest existing supercomputers.

The move toward parallelism

Data-flow machines must be placed in the context of the broader efforts to develop parallel computer architectures. This development is motivated by the need for greater speed. Typical scientific and commercial applications of computers involve the use of the same procedure on a large number of entities, be they particles in a simulation of plasma or payroll accounts. For example, an astronomical simulation of the gravitational interactions of a thousand stars requires for each time step the calculation of the force applied by each star on every other one. In nature, the effects of all on each other are felt simultaneously. But for a conventional serial computer to simulate the interaction, the program must take each star one by one and have the effect on it of each other star calculated in sequence. A computer that could in a single time step perform the same set of calculations on all the stars at once would, obviously, be much faster than a serial computer.

The advent of very large-scale–integrated (VLSI) technology has made the development of highly parallel computers a practical possibility. Single VLSI chips, costing only a few dollars to manufacture, may soon have the computing power of large present-day mainframe computers. If many of these chips could be joined in a larger structure to work in parallel, computers of great power could be built.

Eric J. Lerner   Contributing Editor

The main technical question in achieving this goal is how to divide up the computing work required among the individual processors so that none are either overworked (leading to bottlenecks and delays) or idle (leading to wasted computing power). In the real world, an individual entity, such as the star in our example, can be influenced by many other entities at once. In a digital computer, however, each processor can only deal with a few inputs simultaneously. Thus, the allocation and scheduling of tasks must be such that for each processor there are enough data, but not too much, to match the input capability at all times.

The problem is analogous in a broad way to the problem of organizing a work force to carry out some function in an enterprise, such as the designing of a circuit or the production of automobiles. The work must be arranged so that each individual has sufficient tasks, materials, and tools to be occupied productively, but not so much that a backup occurs.

Three major approaches for achieving optimal allocation and

Defining terms

Associative memory: a memory in which the data are stored and indexed by content, as in a dictionary, in contrast to the storage of a random-access memory.

Control-flow machine: a parallel-processing architecture with a single central sequence of instruction, carried out by many processors.

Data-flow machine: a parallel-processing architecture in which each processor acts on instructions when the data needed become available.

Demand-driven machine: a parallel-processing architecture in which processors carry out instructions when the results of a processing step are demanded.

Functional language: a programming language that uses exclusively expressions to be evaluated.

Graphical language: a programming language that expresses programs in a graphical form resembling flow charts.

List-processing language: a programming language that is widely used in artificial-intelligence research to manipulate categories or lists of items.

Reduction machine: a parallel-processing architecture that reduces expressions (often used synonymously with demand-driven).

Single-assignment language: a programming language that allows only one value to be assigned to a variable in a single expression.

Tag: a label attached to a piece of data in a data-flow computer that says where the data are to be used in a program.

Token: the information package that contains a piece of data and a description of its location in the program.

Von Neumann machine: the conventional type of computer architecture in which instructions are carried out sequentially.

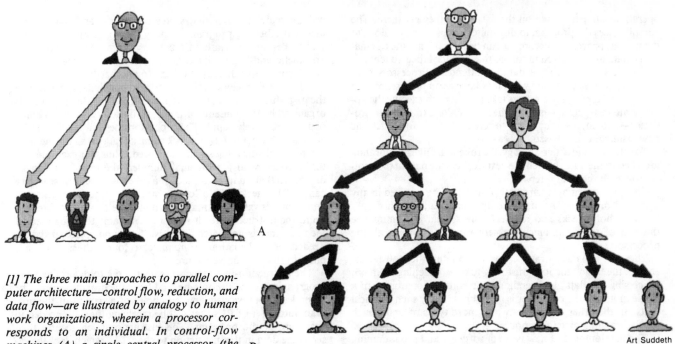

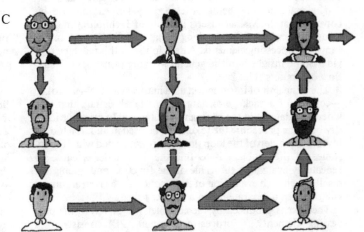

Art Suddeth

[1] The three main approaches to parallel computer architecture—control flow, reduction, and data flow—are illustrated by analogy to human work organizations, wherein a processor corresponds to an individual. In control-flow machines (A) a single central processor (the "boss" figure) sends out instructions to many processing elements, which have associative memories. In reduction (demand-driven) machines (B) processors break up an expression of the programming language into subexpressions, thereby distributing the work. Elements at the bottom do the actual calculations and send the results up. In data-flow machines (C) each processing element carries out instructions as soon as it receives the necessary data, then transmits the results to another processor. Implementations for each architecture can have a number of variations of the simplified forms shown.

scheduling of tasks have been proposed for parallel computer architectures. They are termed control-flow, reduction (or demand-driven), and data-flow machines [Fig. 1].

Control-flow machines use a centralized control of scheduling similar to that in conventional Von Neumann machines. A central processor or controller determines the schedule and allocation of tasks to large numbers of subsidiary processors.

The idea of this structure is similar to the method of operation of many small offices or factories, where one manager sets up the schedule for the completion of a task, informs each subordinate of the task and the deadline by which it is to be completed, and supervises the carrying out of the schedule. The main problem in this approach is that the whole responsibility for devising a good, efficient allocation and scheduling of work rests on the central controller, and in complex problems this control function could become unwieldly, just as the centralized control of an enterprise tends to develop problems as the number of employees grows.

A second approach, on which rather more work is being done, is called variously reduction or demand-driven architecture. Tasks coming into an initial group of processors are systematically divided into subtasks and passed to other units, so that many processors perform the needed calculations and send the results back to be combined into the final result. Such machines are termed reduction machines because they act to reduce an expression in the programming language to a final result. Alternatively, they are called demand-driven, because processors execute commands when an expression demands such a calculation for its reduction.

This type of organization has its analogy in the large corporation in which a hierarchy of managers delegate tasks to several levels of subordinates, tasks actually carried out by those at the bottom of the pyramid. The difficulty to be avoided here, as is the case with human bureaucracies, is that too much time is

wasted while orders are being passed down the tree or results are being sent up.

The third approach, perhaps farthest from conventional computer organization, is data flow, and it is on this idea that the most work has been done. Data-flow machines are highly decentralized, with each processor working cooperatively on the same level as all others, rather than subordinated to a central controller or organized into a hierarchy. The organization of the data-flow machine is contained in the program that dictates the flow of data—where results go. Each processor works asynchronously (rather than to a set schedule), calculating the results as soon as it has the data to do so and forwarding the results directly to another processor.

In terms of our analogy to human work organization, data flow would be similar to a small team of individuals all equally knowledgeable about their jobs, who, without a set schedule, work as fast as they can and, when finished with one task, automatically pick up on whatever remains unfinished. The problem here is to ensure that with a large number of processors the work automatically gets divided evenly, without a controller there to do the dividing.

How data-flow computers work

The basic idea of data-flow machines is quite simple. The data-flow program is a graph that shows where the data go and what operations are performed on the data when they get there. The compiler uses the program to distribute groups of instructions to the various processors before the run begins. During the calculations, data are packaged in tokens that include labels to identify the process for which the data are intended. Processors continuously receive data, and when they have a complete set of data for a given label, the processors take the data and execute the appropriate instruction—passing the results along to another processor—and change the tokens to reflect the task for which the new results are to be used.

To return to the office analogy, the tokens are like memoranda attached to the data that tell the next workers the part of the project to which the data refer.

There are two major hardware obstacles to be resolved in any data-flow machine. The first, already mentioned, is the necessity to avoid bottlenecks and idleness. The second is to minimize the cost of the communication network that connects all the processors.

There are two main strategies for surmounting these obstacles. In one, the basic functions of storing tokens, matching them up, processing the data, and sending the results are combined in a single unit, and the computer is made up of many such identical units. In the other, there are two or more types of units, each specializing in a given function.

The development of new types of software and programming languages suited to data-flow computers will be crucial to the success of these types of machines and is also extremely difficult.

The machine now being developed by Dr. Arvind and his coworkers at the Massachusetts Institute of Technology in Cambridge is an example of the designs that use all-identical, multifunction processing elements. A description of this machine provides some insight into the general working principles of dataflow computers [Fig. 2].

The basic unit of information used in this machine—the token—consists of a package of data and the label, or tag, that says where the data fit in the program. The tag will in principle identify both the procedure the token is to be used in and, if a loop is involved, the step of the loop the data are connected with. For instance, if the problem is to find the area under a curve by repeatedly evaluating the value of the function and adding the results, then each evaluation of the function for a given argument will be given a separate tag in a distinct token.

The tokens produced by the compiler will be fed to the processing elements. A processing element (PE) consists of a waiting–matching unit that stores the tokens and matches up identical labels, a program memory, an instruction-fetch unit that takes appropriate instructions from the memory, an arithmetic-and-logic unit (ALU) to perform the instructions, and an output unit to direct the tokens to another PE.

When a PE receives a token, it tries to match its tag against all the tags in an associative memory. That is, the memory is organized by the contents of the tags, like a dictionary, so that a search is relatively rapid. The processor does not need to check each tag in turn but only to check against that part of the memory where the identical tag should be stored. Thus, for example, if a tag is coded with a sequential number, the processor can go directly to that number to check if a token is there, just as a clerk can swiftly check a list of credit-card holders to see if the card before him is valid. If a match is found, the two tokens are sent on to the instruction-fetch section. (The same thing happens if the token needs no match—that is, if only one piece of data is needed for a calculation.) If no match is found, the new token is put into the associative memory.

The instruction-fetch section reads the tag to determine what program instruction should be read from the program store. The compiler has previously entered copies of a section of the program into a set of PEs that will be receiving the data needed in that part of the program. The instruction-fetch section then sends the data in the instruction to the ALU, which does the required calculation.

The ALU then conveys the result to an output section, which uses rules specified in the tag to create a new tag and to decide on a new PE address to which the result will be delivered. The output section then transmits the new token to the communication network that passes it along to the designated PE.

Dr. Arvind and his colleagues have noted a number of crucial aspects of this machine design. First of all, the associative memories must be sufficiently large so that a token is likely to find a mate before the memory fills up. There is an overflow memory; however, the overflow memory is a simple random-access memory, which means that its contents must be checked one at a time for matches. To avoid having the associative-memory overflow, the program on the compiler must ensure that there is not too long a delay between one piece of data becoming available and its match becoming available.

Second, there has to be a provision for loading related bits of a program into physically close PEs, or the amount of time wasted in transferring tokens back and forth across the entire machine

n x n routing network

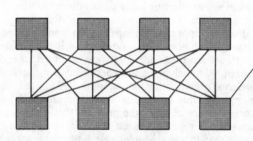

A processing element

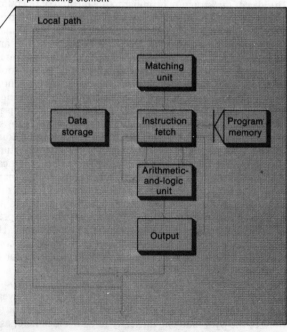

[2] In one version of a data-flow machine, developed by Dr. Arvind and his colleagues at the Massachusetts Institute of Technology in Cambridge, all processing units are identical and are connected by an n × n *network. Each processing element contains a matching section that stores incoming data tokens and compares them with each other to find sets that together make some calculation possible. When such pairs are found, the instruction-fetch section gets the appropriate instruction from the program memory and passes it to the arithmetic-and-logic unit for processing. When the results are obtained, they are passed to the output unit for packaging into another token and transmission to another processor.*

Local path

Matching unit

Data storage

Instruction fetch

Program memory

Arithmetic-and-logic unit

Output

becomes prohibitive. In Dr. Arvind's design, this is accomplished by the compiler.

Dr. Arvind's group plans to construct a 64-unit prototype of this machine. Another group at the University of Manchester in England, under Ian Watson and John Gurd, has already built a small-scale prototype of a generally similar machine and has obtained some preliminary performance results that appear to confirm the importance of the problem of token memory size and buffers in general.

The Manchester machine uses processing elements that are structured as rings. A token first goes into a token queue, then to the matching unit, then (once matched) to the node store to pick up instructions for the processing unit, then to the processor, and finally out of the PE again. Each ring has 12 processors and is therefore itself a parallel device, and many rings can be connected through a switching system.

While operational data-flow machines can be expected to use the fastest available devices and VLSI processors, for economic reasons the Manchester prototype uses relatively slow components. Only one ring is currently being tested, so the resulting speed is only a few million instructions per second (MIPS).

The current machine uses 96-bit tokens containing 32 bits of data, a 36-bit label, 18 bits for destination, and 10 bits for control. The period of the ring is set at 200 nanoseconds. A relatively slow Digital Equipment Corp. LSI-11 computer serves as the host computer and handles the input and output of the ring processors.

The Manchester group ran a number of test programs on the machine in order to simulate what would happen in a real data-flow machine with a number of rings. They found that as the number of processing units is increased, the speed of the machine at first increases linearly but then levels off at around 1 MIPS [Fig. 3]. If a program is used that bypasses the matching section,

however, because each instruction needs only one piece of data to execute, then the speedup is linear with the number of processing units and shows no upper cutoff. Drs. Watson and Gurd concluded that the problem was that at times there are gaps in the sequence of results, causing processors to become idle. The solution was a buffer of matched tokens, a so-called reservoir, to smooth out fluctuations in the supply of pairs.

Another key problem in data-flow architectures is the increasing cost of the communication network as the number of processors increases. A network that connects all processors with all others, as in the Arvind design, requires n^2 connections for n processors, an eventually prohibitive requirement as n increases. One solution to this problem is embodied in the data-flow design being developed by Makoto Amamiya and his colleagues at the Musashino Electrical Communication Laboratory of the Nippon Telegraph and Telephone Public Corp. (NTT) in Tokyo. This design uses ring processors similar to those at Manchester but connects them up in an array, so that each processor only has direct communication with its immediate neighbors. Such an array allows communication links to increase only linearly with the increasing number of processors but puts a high premium on keeping long-distance communication to a minimum. This may be possible in many scientific calculations, especially simulations. In these applications, processors can be assigned to individual grid points and thus need to receive data only from their physical neighbors.

Another way to minimize communication costs is to employ a treelike hierarchical structure. Although such structures seem more natural for reduction than data-flow machines, they can be used with data flow as well. Such a structure has been used in the Data Driven Machine #1 (DDM1), designed and built in 1976 by Al Davis, then at the University of Utah in Salt Lake City and now with Fairchild Camera and Instrument Corp. in Palo Alto, Calif. The DDM1 and its faster successor, the DDM2, organize their PEs in an eight-branch tree—a tree in which each node has eight daughter nodes, rather than two as in a binary tree. A potential problem with this scheme is that because work is allocated from parent to child cells or elements, it is possible that some cells may remain idle while work remains to be done in a distant part of the tree.

Separating the functions

The data-flow designs that concentrate all the functions in a single type of processor have an inherent problem in allocating work: some processors may get many enabled instructions—that is, matched pairs of tokens—while others may get too few to keep busy. The alternative is to separate the functions of matching up tokens and processing them into different elements. This is the approach taken by the Topstar machine under development at the University of Tokyo under the direction of Tatsuo Suzuki, Tohru Moto-oka, and their associates. Topstar contains two types of elements: control modules (CMs) and processing modules (PMs). Each PE is connected to a number of CMs, and each CM is connected to a number of PMs. When a PM needs an instruction to process, it requests a matched pair of tokens from a CM. If it cannot get one from that CM, it sends a request to another CM. Once the enabled instruction is obtained, the PM processes the result and sends it back to one of the CMs. The CMs store tokens and match them up, making them available when matched to requesting PMs. The net result of all this is that CMs with many enabled instructions can service many PMs at once, while those with few or none serve few PMs.

Similar principles are used in another data-flow design at MIT being developed by Jack B. Dennis and others. (Dr. Dennis was among the first to work on data-flow designs.)

New languages required

Because all of the data-flow machines described here have structures quite different from those of existing computers, it is not surprising that existing programming languages do not provide efficient ways of communicating with data-flow computers. Conventional languages are by their nature sequential—that is, they are sequences of instructions. For a calculation that involves parallelism, programming in conventional languages means that the programmer must convert a parallel process into a sequential one and then have the compiler convert it back into a parallel one.

To eliminate such conversions, three new types of languages are being developed that can be used on data-flow machines—graphical, single assignment, and functional. Many of the machines described use a graphical language as the machine-level language, and programs can be written directly in such languages. Graphical-language programs greatly resemble flow charts: operations are nodes in the graph and arrows connect the nodes, showing where the data go [Fig. 4]. An example of such a language is the Graphical Programming Language (GPL) developed at the University of Utah. In GPL, various types of expressions can be written into each node, making possible higher-level statements.

The second language category for data-flow machines is single-assignment language. In such a language, a variable can only be assigned a value in a single expression, like a mathematical formula, and no variable can depend on itself. Expressions like $n = n + 1$, common in conventional languages,

are expressly forbidden in single-assignment languages because they implicitly refer to a central memory that keeps track of the value of n at any given time, while many data-flow machines lack such a central memory.

The third type of language suitable for these machines is functional language, also known as applicative language. A functional programming language consists exclusively of expressions to be evaluated and avoids the assignment of variables altogether [see "Function-level programming" by John Backus, the inventor of Fortran, p. 231].

In addition to the development of new languages, many other software issues have to be addressed. For one thing, how can problems best be posed to fit a data-flow computer? How should the data be structured? Some questions in turn may determine the type of data-flow machine that will be fastest for a given category of processors.

Dr. Amamiya, at NTT's Musashino Electrical Communication Laboratory, has begun to look at one of the issues that is of most interest to those seeking faster machines for artificial-intelligence applications. In artificial intelligence, list-processing languages—which manipulate categories of lists of items—have proven extremely useful.

Dr. Amamiya has developed various approaches to exploit data-flow parallelism in the processing of such lists. Much more of this type of software analysis will be necessary before practical data-flow designs are possible.

Data flow pro and con

While a growing amount of research is being devoted to data-flow machines, some computer scientists have raised serious questions as to whether such machines will eventually perform as well as expected, or if they will surpass more conventional designs. Critics say that data-flow designs have trouble in dealing with large arrays, have excessive computational overhead, and perform poorly on some classes of nonparallel problems.

Perhaps the most serious flaw is the difficulty in manipulating large arrays of data. Take, for example, a process that modifies only one element of a large array. If the entire array must be sent through the data flow because there is no one spot where it can be stored, there is a tremendous waste of transmission capacity. Dr. Arvind's machine provides for storage of arrays, distributed in pieces over the processing elements, but this too raises problems. If one processor has to access information physically stored elsewhere, enormous traffic problems can develop. As D.D. Gajski and his colleagues at the University of Illinois at Urbana–Champaign commented, "While data-flow people claim to be trying to eliminate the Von Neumann bottleneck between CPU and memory, they have created several new bottlenecks of their own."

However, Dr. Arvind and other data-flow researchers believe that there are ways around this obstacle. For one thing, data can be mapped onto the processors so that most communications to access stored arrays can be done locally at little cost and faster than with centrally stored data.

A second potential concern in data-flow designs is the amount of computation that has to be devoted to bookkeeping operations, such as creating the tags that accompany data in tokens. Some designs do without the tags but

[3] Experiments with small-scale prototypes of data-flow computers show that, as more processors are added, calculations go faster. However, above a certain point, the rate of gain of actual MIPs tapers off (lower curve), while potential MIPs increase with the number of processing units. Ian Watson, John Gurd, and their colleagues at the University of Manchester in England, who performed these tests, believe that this leveling off occurs when too few instructors are passed from the matching units to the processing units. The cure, they think, is to provide a reservoir to expand the number of matched tokens, so that the fluctuating number of successful matches passed to the processors over time will be smoothed out. When the matching unit is by-passed in programs where only one argument is needed to calculate a result, there is no leveling off (upper curve).

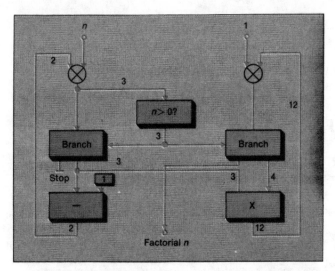

[4] Data-flow machines are programmed using data-flow languages that are quite different from conventional programming languages. The machine-level language is a graph showing where data go and what is done with them when they get there. Here is a graphical program for calculating factorials. On the left, the value enters the loop. If n is more than zero, the loop produces the series n, n-1, n-2. On the right, the results of the left-hand loop are multiplied together. When the left-hand loop gets down to zero, both loops terminate, yielding the answer, n! (Values illustrate 4! when n = 3.)

sacrifice some flexibility. Those designing the tagged token machines point out that if the machines are eventually as fast as seems theoretically possible, then the sacrifice of speed involved in tag creations will be amply compensated for by the inherent gains through parallelism.

Finally, many experts have noted that data-flow machines tend to be slower than conventional machines if there is insufficient parallelism in the computation itself. This point generally is acknowledged by data-flow designers: data-flow machines are intended for problems that are inherently parallel.

Hybrids tried

Some researchers are attempting to overcome the problems that crop up in data-flow designs by introducing ideas from other approaches, thereby creating hybrid machines. One common strategy is to integrate into a data-flow design a key feature of reduction machines: the requirement that processors only calculate results when they are needed. Such machines are then called demand-driven.

An example of this strategy is the loosely coupled parallel processor proposed at the University of Utah by Robert Keller and his associates. This machine, like reduction machines, is demand-driven; however, several features of its operation are similar to pure data-flow machines, so it is something of a hybrid.

The basic structure of the machine is treelike, with each process having several subordinate processes and cells, down to a base of thousands of leaf cells. Computing work is distributed through the tree in the form of tasks—operation and their associated data. The tasks are divided into two lists: a result list that contains the result of an evaluation of an operator and a demand list that contains an operator to be evaluated. A processor with a demand task will try to obtain the data needed to evaluate the operator by calling for the data from another processor. If the data is not yet available, the processor will do something else on its list. Once another processor makes the needed data available, it will notify the demanding processor and send the data along.

The demand list in effect constitutes a list of priority items to be evaluated before others. The idea is that instead of working on whatever comes to hand, as does a pure data-flow machine, each processor will work first on what is demanded of it, assuming that it has the data available. If the data are not available, each processor will demand the results of another processor, while working on lower-priority items. The net result is to avoid the mindless passing along of the data that can be calculated quickly, which then sits in storage waiting for the data that are calculated more slowly.

In the office or factory work-flow analogy, the system that relies on each worker working on whatever comes to hand has the danger of most workers doing quick and easy tasks, while a few are stuck with the hard jobs that hold up everything else. Large inventories are then needed to avoid bottlenecks. A demand-driven system simply means that one worker tells another, "Hey, I need such-and-such now—work on that first."

Another feature of Dr. Keller's design is that it allows parent cells to redistribute task lists among child cells in order to balance the load. Each parent cell is informed of the number of tasks on the list of each child cell and can transfer tasks from those with long lists to those with short ones. Again, the aim is to avoid accumulating too many tasks in one place and to cut down on the buffering required to keep all units busy.

Where is data flow going?

The key tests for the data-flow concept still lie ahead, as prototypes that have sufficient numbers of processing elements to give a realistic idea of the capabilities of the machines are constructed and tested over the next few years. Can they in fact handle large arrays of data reasonably efficiently? How large will buffers need to be to ensure that processors keep busy? Most critically, how do data-flow machines compare in speed and cost with demand-driven hybrids, reduction machines, and parallel control-flow machines?

Once such testing is well under way, the direction in which computer architectures of the late 1980s and 1990s are likely to go may become evident. One possible outcome that several computer scientists think likely is that there will be no single winner: computers of different designs will be used for different applications. One design may be preferred for large-scale business applications, another for simulations, and still another for massive numerical problems with low parallelism. Another possible outcome is that elements of all present designs will be incorporated into future machines. While it is still too early to tell what the role of data-flow machines will be, most in the field agree that at least some viable computer architecture will be based on the concepts used in today's experimental data-flow computers.

To probe further

A more detailed examination of the technical issues in data-flow computers is provided by Phillip C. Trelevan *et al.*, in "Data-Driven and Demand-Driven Computer Architecture," *Computing Surveys*, Vol. 14, no. 1, March 1982, pp. 93–143. The special issue of *IEEE Computer* on data-flow systems (Vol. 15, no. 2, February 1982) is also very useful, especially for the critique of data flow provided by D.D. Gajski *et al.*, pp. 58–68, which is used in this report.

For more information on the systems mentioned in this article and not covered in *Computer*, the following articles are helpful: "A Data Flow Processor Array" by Makoto Amamiya, *Proceedings of the International Symposium on Applied Mathematics and Information Science*, Kyoto University, March 29–31, 1983, pp. 7.1–7.8; "Procedure Level Data Flow Processing on Dynamic Structure Multimicroprocessors" by Tatsuo Suzuki *et al.*, *Journal of Information Processing*, Vol. 5, no. 1, March 1982, pp. 11–16; and "Data Flow Concepts for Hardware Design" by Robert M. Keller *et al.*, *Digest of Papers*, IEEE Compcon '80, February 1980, pp. 105–111.

A.L. Davis presents a general discussion of the problem of parallel computer architecture in "Computer architecture," *IEEE Spectrum*, November 1983, pp. 94–99 [see p. 66].   ◆

VLSI

MORE HARDWARE MEANS LESS SOFTWARE

The trend is toward using ever-cheaper VLSI circuits in place of costly software—but some would reverse the trend

Recent trends in the semiconductor industry indicate that very large-scale integration (VLSI) will offer microprocessor designers two conflicting approaches to designing future systems: (1) They can continue the mainstream trend, where VLSI is used to build increasingly complex microprocessors—and where greater complexity is exhibited as more hardware to do functions previously done by software alone; or (2) They can, as proposed by a small number of designers, take the opposite tack and build simpler processors, where more functions are done by software.

Greater complexity lets designers use ever-cheaper VLSI circuits in place of increasingly expensive software. What's more, the takeover of many software functions by hardware is said to help programmers develop high-level language (HLL) programs that are shorter, more efficient, and easier to write, compile, and debug. More complex systems would, in theory, reduce the high cost of developing software and thus reduce the total life-cycle cost of a system.

But David A. Patterson, professor of computer science at the University of California, Berkeley, and David Ditzel, a computer scientist at Bell Laboratories in Murray Hill, N.J., disagree with this approach. The more complex machines, they say, do not offer worthwhile gains in performance or reductions in system cost. They propose a return to simpler—and therefore cheaper—processors, where they think compilers can be used more efficiently to optimize debugging and run-time performance.

A more cost-effective solution to the problem of soaring software costs, as they see it, would be the development of improved compilers that further simplify the programmer's job. Simpler systems are potentially faster, they add, since simpler chips have more area available for such speed-enhancing circuits as additional cache for pipelining instructions or data.

The fact is, however, that no generally accepted models exist for weighing the benefits of various architectures against the life-cycle costs of the final products.

Complex systems in the spotlight

The recent trend toward more complex microprocessors was highlighted by reports earlier this year that the Intel Corp. of Aloha, Ore., and Hewlett-Packard Inc. of Fort Collins, Colo., had developed micromainframes—32-bit processor chips with far more transistors and complex architecture than previous microprocessors, as well as processing rates that were competitive with some modern mainframes [Figs. 1 and 2].

Growing complexity had already been shown in the unusually powerful microprocessors—as powerful as minicomputers— introduced in 1980 by other companies: the 16-bit Z8000 from Zilog Corp. of Cupertino, Calif.; the MC68000 from Motorola

Inc. of Phoenix, Ariz.; and the 32-bit NSC16000 from National Semiconductor Corp. of Santa Clara, Calif.

These machines have instruction sets with varying amounts of complex instructions. A complex instruction is one that replaces a number of simpler ones and usually corresponds to a statement in such HLLs as Fortran, Pascal, and Ada. For example, a single such instruction may control the transfer of an entire data file between main storage and the central processing unit. In simpler machines, by contrast, software routines implement that transfer. The main point is that executing a complex instruction requires more hardware or microcode—code stored in read-only memory that controls the steps the machine must take to perform functions specified in the instruction set.

Recent examples of the simpler approach to design are the IBM 801 minicomputer, developed at the company's Watson Research Center in Yorktown Heights, N.Y., and an experi-

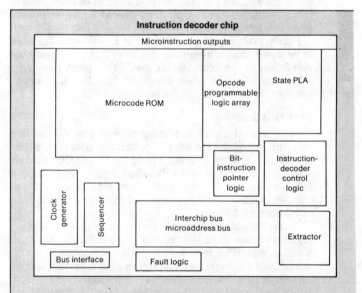

[1] Increasingly complex microprocessors—such as the Intel iAPX432 micromainframe shown above in a multiprocessor configuration—are the mainstream approach of the semiconductor industry to the cost-effective application of VLSI. Increasing complexity is defined as a trend toward using additional hardware to do functions previously done by software. The 432, for example, has a larger number of complex instructions that are done automatically by hardware (microcode). A complex instruction is one that replaces a number of simpler ones and usually corresponds to a statement in a high-level language.

Robert Bernhard   Associate Editor

mental 32-bit microprocessor under development by Professor Patterson and a Berkeley colleague, Professor Carlo Sequin.

The IBM 801 is reported to be comparable in performance to the IBM 370/168 mainframe yet architecturally simpler, cheaper to build, and three times faster.

Simplified machines that are commercially available are represented by the TMS99000 family of microprocessors, introduced recently by Texas Instruments Inc. in Houston. The simpler memory-to-memory architecture of these systems is more cost-effective than the standard register-to-register architecture of other microprocessors, says Harvey Cragon, senior fellow at TI and adjunct professor of computer science at Southern Methodist University in Dallas. The TI systems are, indeed, in a class by themselves; they do not have general registers, accumulators, or stack pointers, and only by looking deeply into their architecture is it understood how they do any computing at all.

Throwbacks to earlier mainframes

The architectures of today's complex processors, at any rate, are similar in some ways to the revolutionary architectures of several past mainframes: the B5000, introduced in 1962 by the Burroughs Corp.; the Symbol computer, conceived in 1964 at Fairchild Camera and Instruments Corp. in Palo Alto, Calif., and introduced in 1971—but reclining now as a museum piece at Iowa State University in Ames; the IBM 360 and 370 series, introduced in the late 1960s and 1970s, respectively; and the recently introduced IBM System/38.

The Symbol computer was remarkable in that its designers believed future VLSI would require computers to be controlled solely by hardware. The resulting machine was the ultimate complex–instruction-set computer (CISC), since hardware alone implemented such traditional software functions as compiling, text editing, memory management and timesharing, arithmetic, and variably sized data structures. The project was a commercial failure, its designers point out, because hardware and compiler technology were not advanced enough at that time to meet the system specifications.

The present-day microprocessor that comes closest to the ultimate CISC is the Intel iAPX432 micromainframe. The objections that some computer scientists have raised to CISCs may be better understood after a brief description of the controversial features of the 432 and other complex processor chips.

Intel innovates for programmers

Conventional proceedings have ample descriptions of how the iAPX432 achieves its mainframelike processing rates [see "For further reading," p. 275]. However, some industry observers believe that the key innovation in the system is its unequaled emphasis on hardware or microcode implementation of an HLL—in this case Ada, the language adopted as a standard by the U.S. Department of Defense. Though other microprocessors have some similar features designed to speed the development of HLL programs, Intel is perhaps the first to unite all of these and more in a single architecture. The key architectural characteristics include the following:

• The instruction set is designed for efficient translation of Ada into machine-language programs. In many cases, therefore, an HLL instruction is translated into a single machine instruction, whereas conventional processors would need six or more instructions. There are send and receive instructions, for example, that

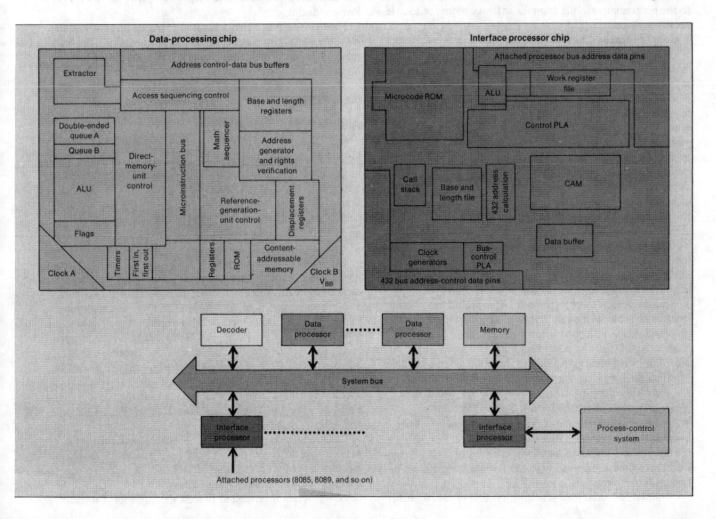

perform through hardware all the buffering and synchronizing operations needed to transmit such data structures as vectors, arrays, and files between programs.

• Microcode automatically performs various traditional operating system functions—for example, it distributes processing loads between different processors configured as a multiprocessing system. (In multiprocessing a single task is divided into subtasks that are processed concurrently by a system of coupled processors; this often yields far higher throughput at less cost than dividing the process load among many independent, single processors.) The distribution of loads is reported to reduce the time for programmers to develop custom operating systems for different applications. The programmer specifies only the parameters needed by a task scheduler, which is controlled by microcode. The parameters include task identification, user identification, and tasks to be performed.

• The most radical architectural characteristic is similar to the descriptor tables of the B5000 and the "object-oriented" architecture of the IBM System/38. Among nonspecialists the concepts of objects and descriptors may be widely misunderstood, though they have been publicized in the technical press.

Reliability and efficiency increased

The significance of object-oriented architecture is that it allows the hardware, the operating system, and the system programming language (Ada) to share in controlling automatically certain operations that help programmers develop reliable, efficient programs. These operations include such traditional compiler activities as type checking, range checking, and consistency checking. In previous microprocessors such functions were left to the programmer, to the compiler software alone, or to safeguards built into the HLL.

Object-oriented architecture has the following characteristics:

• The specification of data in programs (that is, what the data mean) is kept separate from how the data are referenced by program instructions or represented in memory. Programmers therefore can use data objects (or instructions as objects) without any knowledge of how the objects are implemented. The programmer uses them as if they were black boxes; the objects are abstractions in the sense that programmers have no direct access to the raw data but can access them indirectly through built-in hardware or software algorithms. Starting with simpler objects (integers, arrays, programs, lists, and so on), the programmer can build more complex objects, such as records, queues, lists of lists, lists of programs, and symbol tables.

• Hardware or software controls access to different types of data with passwords called descriptors. Through these a given object representation in memory (the actual physical data in a group of memory cells) may be accessed only by authorized programs. In theory programmers can thus use modular programming and structured design more efficiently. The programmer would design each program module (bubble in a typical bubble chart) to process a single task with a single data object. Access to the module would then be controlled automatically by hardware algorithms to ensure the required isolation of the module. Modular programs may be written for any microcomputer, but the 432 architecture is the only microcomputer system that enforces modular techniques through built-in algorithms.

• Hardware algorithms check whether each type of object is associated with operators that make sense for it. For example, the instruction "branch to data" would represent an illegal combination of data and operation (branch), since programs can only branch to instructions.

Examples of increased complexity are found in other

microprocessors in the form of additional hardware or microcode. The HP chip, for example, has special machine instructions for debugging HLLs; they let programmers step through each instruction of a program to trace errors in either the source code or machine language. Special instructions help programmers develop operating systems.

Other complex processors

Designers of the Z8000 and MC68000 may have gone the furthest in appealing to programmers through additional complex instructions and addressing modes (different paths for information, such as between different types of working or index registers, or between registers and main memory). Operands may reside in general registers or main memory; this and the freedom of movement offered by various addressing modes reportedly lets compilers optimize programs more easily.

The MC68000 also has several unique instructions (LINK and UNLK) that are said to simplify implementation of HLLs because they maintain a linked list of data areas and parameters on the stack. (LINK is used at the start of a subprogram to keep track of program execution status, where frequent interrupts occur in nested subprograms; UNLK, used at the end of a subprogram, clears the stack prior to transferring program control to a higher-level subprogram.)

The NSC16000 supports HLLs with instructions and addressing modes that directly implement the manipulation of arrays, records, strings, and so on. The 16000 family is also the first to implement a true, demand-paged virtual memory system (through a separate memory-management unit), according to Subash Bal, product marketing director at National Semiconductor.

The iAPX432 has a unique method of paging that is also complex, but not as costly as a separate management unit. The Intel memory is segmented; each segment has a descriptor that indicates when a physical segment is present in memory and which of the current segments should be swapped (moved to fast, working memory) or overwritten by the new segment.

Alternative to complexity

The original reason for adding HLL instructions to microprocessors was that in years past memory was far slower and more costly than logic circuits in the central processor. HLL instructions executed much faster and needed less memory space than simpler instructions implemented with software subroutines. This imbalance between memory and the central processor no longer holds, in the view of Prof. Patterson, Dr. Ditzel, and TI's Mr. Cragon.

The memory-to-memory architecture of TI's 16-bit microprocessors is, in fact, based on the proposition that memory circuits are more compact and cheaper than processor logic circuits, and the speed gap is no longer significant. Whereas all other microprocessors locate their working registers (work spaces or stacks) on the processor chip, the TI processors have their work spaces in the system random-access memory. Because it is a less complex architecture to implement—fewer steps are needed to manipulate operands—memory-to-memory design allows speedier switching to and from work spaces in the face of interrupts, according to TI designers John Hughes, Peter Chappel, and John V. Schabowski.

To service interrupts (or switch contexts) in register-to-register architecture, the contents of 16 stack registers must be moved to memory at the start of the interrupt; this is done to keep track of the information needed to restore the previous context, since the stack registers will be used to process the interrupt. On return,

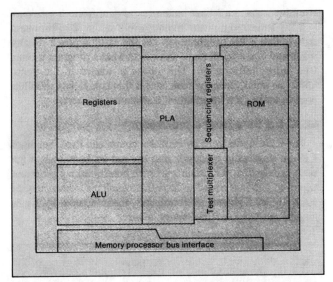

[2] A single-chip micromainframe built by Hewlett-Packard has 430 000 transistors on a chip area of 40 mm²; it has a stack-oriented instruction set that includes complex instructions to help programmers develop operating systems as well as do special stack manipulations that past processors did with software. The programmable logic array (PLA)—which holds the instruction decoder and controller—is a standard approach today in VLSI design. It provides the regular array of components that allows designers to use computer-aided design tools more cost-effectively. The interactions of PLA, test multiplexer, and sequencing registers implement conditional microcode skips, jumps, and subroutine calls.

the offloaded words must be reloaded in the stack. Besides the circuits and instructions needed to carry out these operations, the entire process entails one memory cycle to store and another to fetch each of many words.

The memory-to-memory architecture, its designers point out, requires just three programmable registers—a program counter, a work-space pointer, and a status register—along with a virtually unlimited supply of work space in virtual memory. Context switching is thus performed in two memory-read cycles and three memory-store cycles. The contents of the program counter are exchanged with those of the work-space pointer, the contents of the status register are saved, and data words stay in place. The overhead does increase as the number of different possible interrupts increases, but the TI designers contend that the overhead increases far more in register-based machines, since register capacity must be added in addition to control and housekeeping circuits.

Tagged, or descriptor, memories are not worth the cost, TI's Mr. Cragon believes, noting that the additional hardware complexity does not necessarily lead to more reliable, complex programs. Complexity itself, he says, is a significant source of errors. The run-time protection afforded by descriptor memories—although a benefit—tends, in his opinion, to suppress the innovativeness of programmers.

Benefit to compilers doubted

Complex instruction sets, Prof. Patterson and Dr. Ditzel say, appeal to designers who are unfamiliar with modern compiler technology.

Whereas HLL-oriented architecture serves largely that portion of the compiler that generates code from the HLL program, the size of the code-generating software is often dwarfed by the remaining portion of the compiler, which programmers generally find more important. The more important code includes the automatic lexical and syntax analyzers, parser generators, optimization routine, loaders, error detectors, and routines for error recovery and diagnostics.

The most complex architecture therefore would not significantly change the makeup or function of the compiler, Prof. Patterson and Dr. Ditzel maintain. Their long experience with compilers indicates that complex instructions are often impossible to generate from compilers; complex instructions are so specialized, moreover, that they are prone to implementing the wrong functions for languages other than those for which the machine was specifically designed.

The main point of their argument is that most of the presumed power that designers have put into CISC architecture is wasted; the machines would serve programmers better if the compilers were more intelligent and the architecture were simpler (and thus placed less burden on the compilers).

Another point about CISCs that critics challenge is the contention that they allow compilers to generate more compact code. The more compact code requires less memory and executes faster and so is cheaper, the argument goes. The critics raise these three points about code compaction:

1. Because the cost of memory is falling rapidly, more compact code offers insignificant savings in total system cost. The speed gap between memory and central processing unit has narrowed as well, and the recent use of pipelining (prefetching of instructions) has virtually closed the gap in fetching instructions from memory in microprocessors.

2. Experience indicates that more compact programs do not necessarily lead to significantly shorter execution times unless they result in at least a 20-to-30-percent savings. The limiting factor in execution speed is the rate at which data instructions are transferred from memory; but pipelining has greatly reduced the effect of this limitation.

3. Few systems are bought where the purchaser intends to run one particular fixed-size algorithm with one HLL; thus memory savings will differ for various HLLs. It is doubtful that under such conditions one instruction set could lead to significantly large savings.

Symbol of simplicity: the IBM 801

The designers of the IBM 801 conceived the machine about six years ago as a radically simpler alternative to the complex IBM 360 and 370 mainframes, according to Joel Birnbaum, formerly director of the computer science department at the Watson Research Center, but now at Hewlett-Packard. No performance details of this new minicomputer are available; however, the machine is currently used to monitor the hardware and software of the Model 3 370/168, where the 801 executes three or four instructions in a single memory cycle of the 168. Observers have extrapolated this to mean that the 801 can execute 10 MIPS (million instructions per second), compared with 2.4 MIPS for the 370/168 and 5 MIPS for the IBM 3033, one of the largest mainframes available.

The design of the 801 was based on the analysis of trace tapes carried out by IBM Fellow John Cocker and his colleagues at the Watson Research Center. Such analyses compare the patterns of instructions that are actually executed by the software of a given machine in daily use to the patterns that are possible in theory based on the machine architecture.

The analysis indicated, Dr. Birnbaum reports, that such relatively simple instructions as load, store, and branch are used far more often than the hundreds of other more complex instructions that CISCs may have in their instruction sets. The designers of the 801 therefore used hardwired logic to implement all such "primitives" (load, store, and so on) in one instruction cycle. As many higher-level instructions as possible were then implemented by software subroutines that use the primitives. The designers also made maximum use of the compiler to speed program execution through two techniques:

1. The compiler develops the best mix of hardware and software to minimize the number of machine cycles during run-time.
2. When the program is first compiled, the compiler and operating system execute those instructions that need to be performed only once, instead of on every execution of the program.

The execution of instructions in a single cycle is possible because the designers separated the caches for data from those for instructions. In a single cycle, therefore, the machine can simultaneously execute an instruction, fetch the next instruction from the cache, and either load or store data from the cache.

What is most significant about the 801 design, Dr. Birnbaum says, is that it lets programmers use the existing power of compilers and operating systems to analyze what a program is doing with stored information. This power is wasted in the typical CISC, he notes, since the basic idea is that complexity should be used to make such information transparent to users.

RISC-I: a bare-bones processor

The RISC-I, designed by Prof. Patterson and Prof. Sequin, is a 32-bit single-chip processor that has not yet been built; it has been simulated at the circuit level with benchmarking programs, however, and is reported to have the overall performance of the VAX 11/780 high-end minicomputer, manufactured by Digital Equipment Corp. of Tewksbury, Mass.

More power to computer-aided design

What some microprocessor makers have achieved in recent years seems amazing, considering the highly publicized reports that the industry is short of both engineers and computer-aided design (CAD) tools for designing very large-scale integrated systems. Either the existing manpower or CAD tools are more productive than the publicity indicates, or else the problems of VLSI design have been overstated.

The point is illustrated by the two micromainframes that are the current showpieces of VLSI: the three-chip iAPX432 from Intel Corp., with 200 000 transistors (110 000 on the data-processing chip alone), and a single-chip system from Hewlett-Packard Inc., with 430 000 transistors on a chip area 40 millimeters squared.

These are record IC densities for logic chips (64-kilobit random-access memories have about 100 000 transistors on a chip 25 mm^2 to 36 mm^2). Yet Intel and HP designers achieved those densities through state-of-the-art circuits and optical lithography with line widths of from 1.5 to 5 micrometers [see figure]. In addition, gates were placed and interconnected on the chip, and the logic and circuit designs were checked by less powerful CAD systems than many experts predicted would be needed for such complex systems.

The HP designers used an in-house CAD system to place and interconnect an average of more than 180 devices per engineer-day. That was more than the minimum productivity that experts had said was needed for systems of the late 1980s with a life cycle of three years. (The design cycle must be less than the life cycle, of course, so manufacturers can make timely introductions of new products.) The Intel team, also using its own CAD systems, placed and interconnected about 25 devices per engineer-day. Yet the layout was completed in less than two years. This achievement defied some expert predictions that systems of this size could not be built in less than three years unless productivity was more than 250 devices per engineer-day.

"Considering the unprecedented complexity of the two systems, their circuits were designed and debugged with relatively little trouble," says Carver Mead, professor of computer science at the California Institute of Technology in Pasadena, who was a consultant on the Intel project. He attributed this to the so-called structured hierarchical design method that he pioneered several years ago with a colleague, Lynn Conway.

Designing 'regular' structures

The structured method emphasizes the design of "regular computer structures"—that is, the logic circuits are built up from more or less repeated patterns of identical devices and interconnections. For example, the control portion of microprocessor chips had traditionally been made with logic devices placed at random in the available space between other circuits; in the structured approach, however, programmable logic arrays implement the control units, resulting in more regular layouts that are easier to design, debug, and modify. A similar example, at a lower functional level, is a shift register cell (made with an inverter) that can be concatenated for as many bits as desired. The power, ground, and output lines of one cell align with the corresponding lines of the next. Each cell has a gating transistor that is driven by clock signals.

In designing a register, therefore, the designer can specify the entire register by drawing just one cell on the chip and then specifying such parameters as bit length and timing. Regular arrays increase design productivity, as measured by the "regularization factor," which was introduced some years ago by Intel's William W. Lattin, general manager of OEM microcomputer operations. The factor yields the effective number of devices that designers get for each one they draw. It is defined as the total number of devices on the chip (excluding memory arrays) divided by the number of devices that the designers had actually drawn.

In the hierarchical aspect of the Mead-Conway approach, the functional design is partitioned into successively smaller pieces to yield circuits of manageable complexity with as little as 20 to 50 transistors. For example, a frequency divider may be split into one counter plus one register, and the counter can be split further into individual bit positions. Most of the circuit design is then performed in bits and pieces that are later integrated.

Because of the reduced complexity and data in each piece, designers can use interactive graphics systems to generate the layouts for a given partition.

Separating the design into simpler pieces is not new. What is new in VLSI design is the need for computerized methods to integrate and speed the vast number of separate design activities.

No more 'paper dolls'

Prior to the development of modern CAD systems, designers used the "paper doll" approach, where they drew individual polygons by hand on Mylar sheets to represent IC mask patterns. With that method, it would have taken, by some estimates, at least 100 years to lay out either the HP or Intel chips.

Modern CAD systems, whether made by IC manufacturers themselves or commercial suppliers, have one or more stand-alone interactive graphics terminals linked to a computer system. Each terminal, or work station, allows a designer to build circuits from different combinations of progressively larger standard cells stored in a data base in the computer. The designer uses the interactive graphics as a sketch pad, where he can edit, add, or delete polygons or interconnections, as well as define standard cells and experiment with different layouts or IC densities.

In the structured design approach at HP, for example, the designer used a library of regular block structures. The blocks had a matching cell pitch and bus structure in the length dimension, but they varied in width. Similar cells with well-defined interfaces could be placed in regular patterns forming larger blocks. These structured cells differ from standard cells used in other CAD systems only in that they were designed to satisfy a given computer architecture and general interconnection pattern.

CAD systems therefore are basically data-base management systems that assist designers by placing and routing IC devices and verifying the correctness of a logic or circuit design through simulation. The systems are available from such suppliers as Applicon Inc. in Burlington, Mass.; Calma Inc. in Sunnyvale, Calif.; Avers Inc. in Scott's Valley, Calif.; AMI in Santa Clara, Calif.; Compeda Inc. in Palo Alto, Calif, and Computervision in Bedford, Mass.

The designers ascribe the excellent performance to their unique implementation of the call/return instruction, which their studies of programs showed was the most time-consuming instruction in most HLL programs run on the VAX, the PDP-11 (also manufactured by DEC), and the MC68000. The call/return instruction is used when the program jumps from one procedure (subroutine) to another, perhaps through a number of procedures nested one inside the other. It involves such time-consuming operations as saving or restoring register contents on each call or return and passing parameters and data to and from the procedures. (Procedures are programs in a program library that make code written by one person available to others; they are written so that subsequent users need not know their inner workings, but only the external details of what parameters and data they require.)

As envisioned by the Berkeley computer scientists, the RISC-I architecture would be based on four rules:
1. Instructions shall be executed in one cycle in as little time as are the microinstructions on such machines at the PDP-11 or VAX-11; yet instructions shall be so simple that no microcode is needed for their execution. A cycle is defined as the time to read a register, perform an arithmetic-and-logic-unit operation, and store the result back in a register.
2. Higher-level instructions, such as those found in CISCs, shall be implemented as software subroutines.
3. To simplify implementation, all instructions shall have the same word length.
4. The architecture shall support HLLs through implementation of the fastest method of executing such instructions as call/return, or of supporting the allocation of local (confined to

---

CAD tools for production IC artwork are of two general types:
1. Systems for custom layout performed with computer graphics, where the designer closely controls the IC density and may achieve maximum coverage of the chip area at the cost of relatively long development time.
2. Automated layout systems, where the designer submits logic diagrams and the system either automatically places and interconnects standard logic cells or routes the cells in a gate-array chip. This approach is far speedier than the first, but it results in relatively inefficient use of chip area.

The symbolic layout system

A recent development is the symbolic layout system, which represents an attempt to bridge the gap between the two general types. Symbolic systems have been developed by Applicon, AMI,

Calma, HP, National Semiconductor, and Intel, among other companies. They are divided roughly into static and dynamic types, depending on whether the symbols refer to cells that are in fixed positions or to cells that can be moved to optimize the layout or meet design rules.

In both types, for example, the designer can symbolize an enhancement-mode transistor on the interactive sketch pad as follows: he uses software commands to draw a horizontal line that crosses a vertical line on one mask level and a rectangle on a second, higher level. These lines define a polysilicon rectangle, which serves as a gate contact, and a vertical rectangle that serves as a diffusion line. The X and Y coordinates of the vertices of any geometric shape on the mask are declared through such software descriptions as LL, for lower left, or UR for upper right.

Static symbolic systems, however, use the symbols to represent

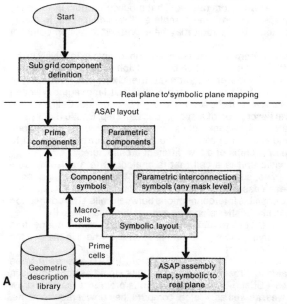

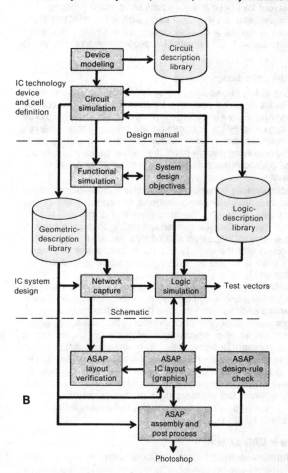

Advanced symbolic artwork preparation (ASAP) was used by Hewlett-Packard in Colorado Springs, Colo., to manage the design of its single-chip micromainframe, which has 430 000 transistors on a 40mm² chip. The IC designer writes a symbolic description of the desired circuits in the system language. The ASAP system generates a description of the IC mask by extending the software concept of mapping a program into a one-dimensional array of memory to that of mapping a symbolic hardware description into the two-dimensional physical planes of IC masks (A, above). Macrocells are groups of components with a given logic or circuit function. In the remainder of the design cycle (B), the ASAP assembly map, now stored in the geometric description library, involves device modeling, circuit simulation, and so on.

one procedure) as opposed to global variables (used in many different procedures). Studies of HLL programs had also shown that local scalar variables were the most frequent operands.

The so-called register windows in the RISC-I, the designers report, is a unique technique for maximizing the speed of execution of procedure calls [see Fig. 3]. The high speed, they say, stems from the reduction in off-chip memory accesses, compared with the way other processors perform the same operation.

In other processors the call instruction is implemented through a dedicated register (stack pointer) that saves a return address in the stack before the instruction causes the program to jump to the called procedure. Parameters are usually passed along to the stack through the help of another register (frame pointer) that points to the beginning of the parameters and the end of the local variables. The parameters are referenced by their memory addresses, so that each time the procedure refers to the parameter, it refers to the address.

The RISC-I, by contrast, has multiple register banks (32 registers per bank), so that each call causes a new bank to be allocated to the called procedure. Thus the contents of registers are neither saved on jumping nor restored on return; on return a frame pointer simply indicates the bank that contains the current procedure.

The unique register windows are implemented as follows:
• Each bank of registers is divided into three parts: high, containing parameters passed from that portion of the program above the current (calling) procedure; local, where local scalars are stored; and low, for parameters passed to the procedure "below" the current procedure.
• On each procedure call, a register bank is allocated. The low

---

combinations of mask layers at a fixed position on the mask. Examples of such systems are AMI's SLIC (symbolic layout for integrated circuits), Applicon's CASL (computer-aided symbolic layout), and Calma's GDS II. Since the design rules may not be the same for all mask layers, the systems use variable grid spacings. For example, one grid spacing is used for metal lines and a different spacing for polysilicon, whereas different grids apply to horizontal and vertical lines.

National Semiconductor has extended the variable-grid concept with a program that varies the grid spacing continuously, subject to design rules, to maximize the amount of chip area covered by circuits.

A major drawback of the static type is reported to be that the designer must draw symbols exactly and place them carefully, to avoid violating design rules. Design rules must therefore be checked after the layout has been done—a time-consuming process.

Dynamic systems, on the other hand, adjust the final positions of the cells on the mask to obey design rules. Designers cannot violate the rules, and so no checking is required when the layout is finished.

Sticks: a dynamic design system

The most widely known dynamic system is Sticks. Developed at Hewlett-Packard several years ago by John Williams, now consultant in Palo Alto, Sticks is undergoing further commercial exploitation at Calma and HP. It is based on the principle that whereas human designers are inferior to computers in analyzing local details and observing design rules, they are superior in analyzing the overall characteristics of drawings and spotting areas of low circuit density.

The Sticks system, for example, allows designers to control the spacing of circuits by drawing windows in various parts of the mask and then specifying a direction; the result is that only the circuits inside the window are spaced according to design rules in the given direction. Repeated use of this procedure allows the designer to control the density of circuits over the entire mask. Designers may also use a "fencing" procedure to prevent excessive dispersion of circuits over given mask areas.

The symbolic drawings, referred to as sticks, can be rendered imperfectly by designers, since the system software can recognize valid drawings and indicate when the designer has made an error. The system can connect any stick structures that lie within certain distances of one another, since the drawings are not required to be fixed in any position. Designers can insert new structures between any number of existing stick structures by zooming in through interactive graphics, drawing in the structures, and connecting them. However useful these CAD tools may be, they do not help designers achieve the ultimate goal of design automation: to generate an entire mask set from a high-level description of chip architecture or function.

The ultimate CAD system

The ultimate automated system would implement the transition from a high-level description of architecture through the four remaining levels of the design process: (1) high-level internal design, or the general floor plan of the microprocessor; (2) logic design; (3) circuit design; and (4) masks.

The ideal software package to accomplish that goal is generally called a silicon compiler, by analogy with traditional software compilers (which transform programs written in high-level languages into machine instructions). The silicon compiler is still in its infancy, largely at universities. Briefly the concept is this: the geometry of cells on the chip is described by various procedures in a programming language. Parameters are then passed to the procedures to generate cell structures representing either such logic blocks as adder/subtractors or shift registers, or such circuit elements as inverters.

For example, in the design of an inverter, the parameter would specify the circuit loading for the inverter amplifier. A procedure in the silicon compiler would use that parameter to compute the sizes of the transistors needed. That procedure would be linked to other procedures until the complete IC was described. In theory any architecture or circuit may be expressed in silicon compiler language.

The silicon compiler has been developed most extensively in the Bristle Blocks system written by David Johannsen, associate professor of computer science at the California Institute of Technology, based on the integrated-circuit language developed by Ronald Ayres of the Xerox Corp., in El Segundo, Calif. Given a high-level description of a microprocessor chip, Bristle Blocks produces a layout, a sticks diagram, and diagrams for transistors, logic, and functional blocks. The system is currently tailored to produce only chips of a few different architectures.

The basic unit is a cell that is analogous to a software subroutine. The subroutine manipulates lines, boxes, and polygons—each associated with a given mask layer—and it has a list of all the possible interconnections between cells. (The connection points are like bristles along the edge of the cells; hence the name.) For example, cells requiring inputs from pads have a connection point specifying the type of pad needed and where in the cell the pad should connect.

Whereas the cells in conventional CAD are data-base cells—akin to "frozen" frames of circuits stored as coordinates in data files—Bristle Blocks cells are little programs that can draw themselves, as well as stretch, compute their power requirements, and even simulate themselves.

The input to the silicon compiler has three parts:
1. The number of bits in each microcode word that is assigned to, for example, the register-select field, the arithmetic-and-logic-unit field, and so on.
2. The data-word width and the list of buses.
3. A list of the core elements, exclusive of pads, instruction decoders, the upper and lower buses, and the microcode.

The compiler is a three-pass type in which a core pass lays out the core elements, a control pass adds the instruction decoders, and a pad pass places the pads on the perimeter of the chip and routes wires to points in the core and decoders.

—R.B.

registers of the calling procedure then become the high **registers** of the called procedure; yet no information is moved, since the low registers of the calling frame overlap the high registers of the called frame.

• Associated circuitry intervenes when no free bank is available. Studies indicate that with four to eight banks, overflow occurs in only 1 percent of cases.

RISC's superiority questioned

The main criticisms of the RISC approach are stated most succinctly by Douglas W. Clark and William D. Strecker, architects of the VAX series of complex minicomputers, and Justin Rattner, architect of the iAPX432. The criticisms include the following:

1. RISC is still just a paper design. Before it can be realistically compared with modern processors, it must be completely designed and built, compilers and operating systems must be written, and performance measurements must be made in various applications.
2. A pillar of the RISC approach is that few operating codes account for most of a typical program's execution. However, the dominant codes differ for different HLLs, so that a RISC will always be less flexible than a machine with multiple instructions. (In the VAX 11/780, for example, the top 10 Fortran instructions account for 60 percent of all instruction executions, whereas the top 20 in Cobol account for a mere 8 percent of executions.) The execution time for an instruction is, in any case, more important than its frequency of execution. The RISC, in optimizing only the most frequently executed instruction, may degrade performance because rarely executed instructions can have very long execution times.
3. In the absence of any metric or model, there is no proof that a RISC—though implemented in less silicon than a complex machine—is more cost-effective.
4. A complex machine offers more opportunities to use specialized hardware to improve performance for specific applications. For example, a complex machine with a multiply instruction offers the potential of speeding the multiplication process through additional data paths and control; but a RISC that uses software for multiplication could speed the arithmetic only if the whole processor were speeded up.
5. Though the cost of memory is indeed decreasing over time, it will remain true that a small amount of cheap memory costs less than a large amount. What's more, the microcode cost for a machine is a one-time cost, whereas the memory for a given computer is added on for each system.

For further reading

Microcomputer Architecture and Programming, by John F. Wakely (John Wiley & Sons Inc., New York, 1981), is one of the rare textbooks with a detailed discussion of the trade-offs between microcomputer architecture, performance, and ease of programming.

In a debate over operating systems, published in *Interface,* Vol. 2, pp. 78–82, Harold Stone of the University of Massachusetts and Peter Denning of Purdue University discuss how computer architecture can close the "semantic gap"—the distance between the concepts in the computer instruction sets and the more powerful concepts in modern programming languages.

D.A. Patterson and C. Sequin generalize on the RISC concept in "Design considerations for single-chip computers of the future," *IEEE Journal of Solid-State Circuits,* SC-15 (1980), pp. 44–52.

The trade-offs in designing single-chip microcomputers—

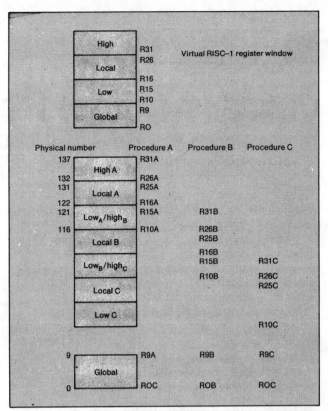

[3] *The register windows in the RISC-I (Reduced Instruction Set Computer-I, proposed by Prof. David Patterson of Cal Tech) maximize the execution speed of procedure calls by reducing the number of accesses to off-chip memory. Multiple-register banks (32 per bank) are allocated by each call instruction to the called procedure, so that the contents of registers are neither saved on jumping nor restored on return. The "high" portion of each bank of registers contains parameters passed to the part of the program above the current calling procedure; the "local" portion contains local scalars; and the "low" portion contains parameters passed to the procedure from below the current procedure. On each call instruction the low registers become the high registers of the called procedure, yet no information is moved, since the low registers of the calling frame overlap the high registers of the called frame.*

which differ from those well-proven in the design of computers, minicomputers, and microprocessor systems—are described by Harvey Cragon in "The elements of single-chip microcomputer architecture," *Computer,* October 1980, pp. 27–41. Unlike many articles of this type, the discussion is quite thorough and includes architecture trade-offs, memory-design factors, instruction and data word length, data-memory addressing, instruction-memory addressing, and so on. What's more, it weighs the classic alternatives in computer architecture: the von Neumann machine versus the Aiken machine. In the von Neumann machine, data words are not separate from instruction words; in Aiken machines, data and instructions are separate.

Richard J. Markowitz of Intel offers a well-balanced discussion of the relation between software and microcomputer architecture in "Software impact on microcomputer architecture," *Compcon 81* digest of papers pp. 40–48. Mr. Markowitz concludes that no quantitative method exists that "goes beyond these emotional arguments and can be applied dispassionately" to estimating the benefits of a new computer architecture. "Without metrics," he closes, "architecture remains a matter of taste." ◆

VLSI

VLSI WITH A VENGEANCE

The Pentagon's Very-High-Speed Integrated Circuits project requires revolutionary advances in systems and IC technology

The VHSIC program was initiated by the U.S. Department of Defense to develop VLSI signal processors with several hundred times higher speed and computing power than today's LSI devices. The planned processors must also consume less power and be smaller and more reliable than current integrated circuits would allow. They will be used in military applications with no counterparts in commerce or industry—mainly real-time signal processors for weapons systems of the next decade.

The weapons systems herald a new breed of military equipment that will radically change the way military force is applied in the decades ahead. The systems—containing processors capable of performing up to billions of operations/s—will allow unprecedented ability to rapidly collect, analyze, and disseminate battlefield information, and to attack targets effectively. The enormous boost in computational power resulting from VHSIC will produce a "force multiplier" effect tending to offset any numerical disadvantages that U.S. forces might face in the future.

The goal of the program is pilot production in 1986 of processors containing 250 000 gates, operating at clock speeds of at least 25 MHz, and performing several million to several billion operations per second. The gates would be fabricated by MOS or bipolar technology and have minimum dimensions of 0.5 to 0.8 μm. The required speed and circuit density would be obtained both by scaling down current LSI circuits—proportionately reducing such basic parameters as channel length, oxide thickness, and supply voltage—and by developing new types of system architecture and software.

The processors—termed subsystems in the program—will include spectrum analyzers and associative memories for identifying the sonar images of targets; processors for using sensor data to guide missiles and bombs; image processors for enhancing target images and implementing bandwidth compression techniques; devices for encoding and encrypting communication signals; and signal analyzers for synthetic aperture radar.

The subsystems will fit into such weapons systems as sonar devices for the Trident strategic attack submarine, radars for the E2C and E3A airborne early-warning systems, guidance and target recognition processors for the Phoenix air-to-air missile and the Pershing II tactical ballistic missile, and modulators and demodulators for the SeekTalk battlefield communication system (Table I).

Contracts awarded for the initial nine-month period of the program, termed Phase Zero (Table II), will address systems analyses of various weapons systems designated for VHSIC, as well as definitions of the architecture and design of processors for those systems. Plans will also be drawn for developing the integrated circuits, testing procedures, software, and packaging.

Why embark on VHSIC development? Because future weapon systems cannot be implemented simply by combining more LSI

Larry W. Sumney   U.S. Department of Defense

chips (Table III). They require VLSI chips with several hundred times higher power, as measured by their functional throughput rate (FTR)—gates per chip multiplied by clock speed per gate. LSI chips now have FTRs up to 10^{11} gate-hertz, whereas future military systems require FTRs of about 10^{13} gate-hertz.

The point is illustrated by the processors required for next-generation military aircraft. The processor load is estimated to be about 3×10^9 operations per second. If built with LSI circuits, these processors would weigh 10^4 kg and consume 100 kW.

VLSI circuits are also needed to reduce the power consumption, weight, and size of military electronics. These reductions will, in turn, lead to lower life-cycle costs—costs for primary power, deck space, air-conditioning, and the like. Such costs far exceed the cost of procuring integrated circuits for applications in satellites, submarines, missiles, and high-performance aircraft.

The costs of primary power and weight in a satellite, for example, are at least \$2000/W and \$5000/kg, respectively. About \$20 million would be saved on power costs alone by a reduction of 1 mW in the average operating power. The cost for integrated circuits, by contrast, is several hundred thousand dollars.

VLSI means higher reliability

VLSI systems will be more reliable than equivalent assemblies of LSI or MSI circuits, since they will contain fewer major sources of failure, such as power chips and external connections. The primary limitation on system reliability today is the fact that systems contain from five to 20 MSI chips—discrete components, power supply, and input/output—for each LSI chip. The increased reliability of VLSI circuits will reduce the cost of unscheduled maintenance, which is the major reason for lost operational time in many weapons systems.

Military electronic subsystems have grown so complex that, despite the steadily improving reliability of integrated circuits, the failure rate of aircraft avionics systems has become a serious problem. The point has been reached where the military can no longer devote increased computing power to improving performance alone. The higher complexity of VLSI circuits must also be used to increase reliability. This can be done by assigning circuits and software for fault-tolerant computing and on-chip functional and diagnostic testing.

Scaling down raises FTR

Advances in silicon fabrication techniques alone can contribute to increased FTR on a chip in three ways: by increasing chip area, by introducing innovative circuits, and by scaling down the dimensions of gates and interconnections.

Experience indicates that the greatest contributions will come from scaling down the minimum dimensions of gates and interconnections. Scaling down accounts for a tenfold increase in the complexity of the 64-kb dynamic RAM over the 1-kb RAM—whereas increased chip area and circuit innovations each account for about a twofold increase in complexity.

The scaling principles of MOS and bipolar devices allow the performance of VLSI chips to be extrapolated from the characteristics of present LSI chips.

A scale-down factor of $1/K$ applied to MOS gate parameters would scale down gate-delay and power-delay product by factors of $1/K$ and $1/K^3$, respectively. But the power per unit area would be unchanged, since both the power per logic gate and the area per logic gate scale as $1/K^2$. The FTR would scale up by a factor of K^3.

As a reference point for LSI, let us assume an MOS logic chip with 3.75-μm gates and a FTR of about 10^{11} gate-hertz. A scale-down factor of one-third would result in 1.25-μm gates and 27 times higher FTR. This gain is insufficient for VHSIC. However, a scale-down to 0.5-μm gates ($K = 7.5$) would raise the FTR of a chip to about 10^{13} gate-hertz—the basic capability required for future military systems.

No single set of scaling principles applies to all bipolar gates, since the devices are more varied and complex than MOS gates. However, I^2L may be used for illustrative purposes.

The scaling of voltages is generally inapplicable to I^2L, as well as to other bipolar technologies—supply voltages are already at the physical minimums—and so constant-voltage scaling must be used. This type of scaling removes one degree of freedom, and so the power-delay product scales as $1/K^2$ instead of $1/K^3$. The scaling factor for FTR is probably K^3—the same as for MOS at LSI dimensions. Scaling at constant power density leaves the propagation delay unchanged and scales up FTR by a factor of K^2.

The interconnections hang-up

Interconnection lines and contacts do not scale as advantageously as other IC elements. Both the resistance and response time of lines increase as the lines are made shorter and narrower. Interconnection current density also increases, along with the resistance and voltage drop at contacts.

A scale-down factor of $1/K$ applied to line width and average length would result in K-times higher resistance, current density, and normalized response time—or response time divided by gate delay. Contact resistance would be K^2 times higher, and the voltage drop at contacts would be K-times higher.

Scaling down also reduces the median-time-to-failure due to electromigration. This contribution to the failure rate is believed to be proportional to the cross-sectional area of interconnections. The failure rate due to electromigration scales by a factor between K and K^4—or worse.

Simulations bear out predictions

Detailed scaling simulations and available data have confirmed the major predictions derived from scaling principles (see figure). The system requirements for the next decade, therefore, can be met by VLSI chips using submicron patterning technology.

Unforseen problems may yet remain, however. Certain parasitic effects that may not be recognized now could significantly interfere with plans for scaling down current gates. Failures of the simple theory are known in the 1-μm-to-5-μm range, but these can be compensated for in the design and fabrication stages. We are not certain, however, that all scaling factors that scale improperly have been identified.

Fabrication poses problems

The scaling down needed for VLSI requires methods for fabricating submicron devices in production quantities. These methods are not yet available. Substantial development work is required to solve three principal problems (Table IV): alignment and exposure of circuit patterns with the required accuracy; the dissolution of exposed resist material; and metallization, or making reliable interconnections of submicron widths.

Submicron patterning will probably be feasible with direct-writing electron beams. Promising future techniques include X-ray lithography, deep ultraviolet light for contact or projection printing, direct-writing ion beams, and electron beams for projecting printing. Alignment and exposure must have resolutions of at least 0.1μm to achieve gate dimensions of 0.5μm. For economical chip yields, the defects may not exceed 1/cm².

Today's technology is inadequate for fabricating VLSI compatible interconnections. Serious difficulties are expected in attempts to extend LSI technology—doped aluminum/doped polysilicon stripes—to submicron line widths. No better alternatives are at hand, although various refractory metal silicides are promising.

VLSI-compatible interconnections pose problems in satisfying three basic requirements:
1. They must be capable of multilevel organization involving three to four levels on the same chip.
2. They must exhibit both low contact resistance and no tendency to form metal spikes or spears in contacts measuring 0.5 μm² in area or 0.5 μm in depth.
3. Electromigration must be insignificant for metal stripes 0.5 μm wide and 0.1 to 0.2 μm thick.

The multilevel challenge

Multilevel interconnection is the most severe requirement, since it embraces the other requirements and also certain problems of overall fabrication technology.

Metal interconnections, for example, must adhere to underlying dielectrics, and interlevel dielectrics must adhere to underlying interconnections. Gold has the desired electromigration characteristics, but it is a much poorer candidate than aluminum for underlying dielectric materials.

Metals at lower levels must be compatible with processes for removing material to form interlevel vias. Interlevel dielectrics must have minimal tendencies to become polarized or to support the migration of charged species or to undergo charge-spreading

---

I. Military equipment that will use VHSIC

Sonar—Acoustic signature analyzers used in the BQQ-5 and BQQ-6 processing subsystems in strategic (Trident) and attack submarines; the MK-48 processor in homing torpedoes; and in the Proteus processor used in antisubmarine warfare aircraft.

Radar—Signal processors for radar systems in the E2C and E3A airborne early warning systems; in advanced fighters (F-14, F-15, F-18) and interdiction aircraft (A-6) for all weather bombing; and in stand-off target acquisition systems (SOTAS).

Missile Guidance Satellites—Processors of radar and infrared sensor data for inertial navigation (Global Position Satellite), and processors for target recognition, proximity fusing, and clutter rejection in air-to-air missiles (Phoenix, Sparrow, Sidewinder), surface-to-air missiles (Patriot, Hawk), and submarine-launched cruise missiles.

Communications—Spread spectrum and time dispersion modulators and demodulators, error correction coders and decoders for digital voice transmission (ANDVT) and battlefield communications (REMBASS, SeekTalk, SINGGARS).

Signal Intercept Analysis—Signal modulation analyzers and signal classifiers for scan receivers (ALR-66, ALR-67)

Electro-Optical Processors—Processors of electro-optical data for more detail and for estimation of target trajectories, in such infrared surveillance systems as the Halo satellite

at interfaces between dielectrics. All dielectrics must be relatively insensitive to ionizing radiation.

Resistance and stability are the most serious problems associated with VLSI-compatible contacts. Contact resistance is important because the voltage drop across this resistance actually increases as interconnections are scaled down. When both the width and average length of a line are scaled down by a factor K, the voltage drop at a minimum-area contact becomes K-times higher. No problem should arise as long as the "typical best" values of resistance for Al or PtSi are obtained through good ohmic contacts and clear contact windows. These best values of specific contact resistance are about 10^{-6} ohm-cm^2 and result in a contact resistance of a few hundred ohms for a 1-μm^2 contact. This resistance can be a hundred times higher where contacts are unstable.

A major cause of contact instability is the formation of metal spikes or spears during such high-temperature processes as contact sintering. Spikes of aluminum penetrate vertically into the silicon surrounding the contact window. Spears penetrate laterally. Spikes or spears in Al-based systems may be prevented by interposing a barrier metal between the Al and the silicon substrate.

Detailed simulations and available data confirm the major predictions of scaling theory applied to MOS and bipolar (I²L) gates. The curves indicate the scaling relationships for power-delay product for gates with a fanout of 1. The dotted line indicates the approximate scaling of power-delay with the minimum dimension, d.

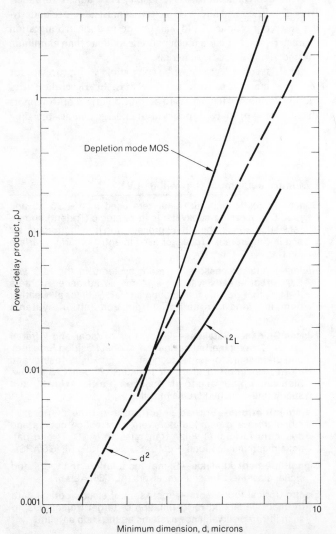

Power-delay product, pJ

Minimum dimension, d, microns

But this solution may not be applicable to VLSI because the material layers may be too thin.

The effect of electromigration in VLSI interconnections is controversial. Migration in thin aluminum films has been studied extensively for stripes several microns wide. However, little is known about migration in stripes no wider than 0.5 μm, or not wider than the median size of metal grains.

Some studies indicate that these small dimensions would not make VLSI lines less reliable than LSI lines—that is, when grain boundaries extend across the width of the line, the electromigration characteristics are believed to approach those of a single crystal. However, some investigators contend that grain boundaries spanning the full width would impede the diffusion of metal atoms and result in a lower median-time-to-failure. Failure would occur sooner, they say, because of the relatively early depletion of metal atoms on the more negative side of a grain boundary.

Standard chips vs. custom

New architectural concepts must be developed to maximize the number of standard chips that may be used in all applications. This will minimize the need for more costly custom chips. Standardization will reduce the cycle time for design and manufacture, as well as decrease costs and establish a data base for future developmental work.

Trade-offs will be made between three options:
1. Designs using cell/macrocell libraries and computer-aided design for placing cells and routing interconnections.
2. Designs using configurable gate arrays and CAD for emulating logic and routing interconnections.
3. Custom design, with computers for designing circuits and verifying logic.

Custom design for VLSI may be desirable for optimizing both critical processing functions and the elements of cells or macrocells. The cell/macrocell option is best for many high-speed VLSI chips, since it maximizes the FTR per chip. However, it does have a longer turnaround time and less flexibility than other options. Configurable gate arrays have the shortest turnaround time, since they are made from stockpiled prediffused wafers. They are inherently limited in performance, circuit density, and gate loading, but will be useful where short turnaround time is required and moderate FTR per chip is tolerable.

Architecture and design will be integrated by a CAD system that operates at all levels, from IC fabrication up to the system layer. The CAD system will include models of devices and gates, as well as software for placing cells/macrocells and for generating optimal test vectors and simulating chip performance in the intended environments.

Test procedure defined

Two types of testing are required for chips:
1. During chip development diagnostic tests must be performed to detect flaws, and prognostic tests are needed for making reliability projections.
2. Finished chips must be tested to assure their functions.

There is no experience yet with prognostic testing of submicron gates, and so it is not clear now how this will be done. Functional testing of VLSI chips presents an even greater challenge, since it will be comparable to testing complete subsystems or systems built with LSI chips.

Cell/macrocell architecture could partly alleviate testing problems, if built-in test modules are associated with macrocells.

On the other hand, the generation of test vectors by built-in testing is relatively easy and would be done during the chip-design

II. Milestones for the VHSIC project

	1980	1981	1982	1983	1984	1985	1986
Definition of concepts	▬▬						
Detailed program specified	▬▬▬	▬					
Subsystem brassboard development		▬▬▬▬▬▬	▬▬▬▬▬	▬▬▬▬▬	▬▬▬▬▬		
Submicrometer technique development		▬▬▬▬▬	▬▬▬▬▬	▬▬▬▬▬	▬▬▬▬▬	▬	
System brassboard fabrication						▬▬▬▬	▬
System demonstration						▬▬▬▬▬	
Subsystem capability demonstration						▬▬▬▬	▬
Pilot production of submicrometer chips							▬▬▬

III. Current and projected system processing requirements

Application	Platform	Equivalent signal processing required, million instructions per second	
		Current	Future
Army tactical signal intelligence	Land based mobile	0.4	40
Cruise missile terminal guidance	Small missile	0.1	50
Data correlation for over-the-horizon fire control	Ship/land based	1	50–100
Airborne synthetic aperture radar	Aircraft/spacecraft	3	100–500
Electronic warfare radar pulse processor	Aircraft/spacecraft	2	200–300
AJ/LPI spread spectrum communications	Small missile/RPV aircraft/spacecraft	5	500
Wideband data links 1 Gb/s	Spacecraft	10	500
U/SEA global search (SOSUS)	Ship/land based	0.5	2 000
ELINT/ESM processor (10 Hz digital spectrum analyzer)	Aircraft/spacecraft	10	10 000

IV. VLSI Fabrication and Circuit Technology Barriers

Technology	Relative Importance (1 = Most Important)	Solution
Patterning		
Align and expose	1	E-beam slice write/ X ray
Resist	1	Resist development
Material removal	2	Dry processing
Metalization	1	Unknown
Doping	3	Ion implant/annealing
Oxide & oxide quality	3	Evolution
Epitaxy	3	Low temp (solid phase?)
Circuit technology	2	Unknown (several contenders)
Process integration/ automation	2	Evolution

stage. Far harder is the implementation of testing at word rates of 100 to 200 MHz, since no testers of this speed are now available.

No plans for gallium arsenide

Gallium-arsenide gates are at least five times faster than silicon gates, and GaAs microwave monolithic ICs could be used now in all military communication, early-warning, and radar systems, but GaAs digital IC technology is far less mature than silicon digital technology. The gap is closing rapidly and GaAs VLSI will be achieved by 1985. Still, the VHSIC program includes no plans to develop GaAs chips. The Department of Defense is funding the development of GaAs technology for other applications, but the decision was made several years ago to concentrate VHSIC funds in the more mature silicon technology.

GaAs MESFETs do not yet have a reliable oxide-insulated gate, but they have been fabricated by existing silicon techniques. Impressive gains have been made in the last three years. Researchers are optimistic about the future of GaAs technology in microwave and digital applications at frequencies up to 10 GHz.

GaAs monolithic preamplifier and mixer chips operating at 10 GHz have been demonstrated. GaAs MESFETs have much lower power-delay products than silicon FETs, and GaAs logic gates operating at 10 fJ per gate have been fabricated at the MSI level. Shift registers and ring oscillators containing 100 to 500 gates per chip have been demonstrated. GaAs FET technology has used 1-μm gates for several years.

Industry observers predict the following developments:
• GaAs digital LSI will be achieved in the next two years. VSLI will be achieved by 1985.
• GaAs digital LSI will not compete directly with silicon chips for the same applications. Silicon will continue to dominate for the next 10 to 20 years. But GaAs ICs will complement silicon ICs for gigabit/gigahertz applications beyond the capability of silicon.

During the next several years, GaAs technology will be reviewed for possible application in VHSIC II.

About the author

Larry W. Sumney is research director of the Naval Electronics Systems Command, but was recently assigned to the Office of the Under Secretary of Defense for Research and Engineering as manager of the VHSIC program. From 1962 to 1972, he engaged in basic and applied research in microelectronics at the Naval Research Laboratory. He joined the NESC in 1972 and became research director in 1977. Mr. Sumney received his B.S. in physics from Washington and Jefferson College in 1962 and the M.S. from George Washington University in 1969, and completed his course work toward the D.Sc. in systems engineering at the latter in 1973. ◆

VLSI

VHSIC: A STATUS REPORT

The first two years of the program's lifespan is viewed by some as gestation and others as incubation. When will the baby walk?

With more than $400 million pledged for research and development over six years, the Very High-Speed Integrated Circuits (VHSIC) program of the U.S. Department of Defense is certainly the most ambitious and probably the most important Federal program since the United States embarked upon space exploration a quarter of a century ago. Up to now, the DOD has relied mainly on methods developed during World War II to organize and operate its aircraft, tanks, ships, and weapons-delivery systems. The radically altered future toward which VHSIC is rapidly leading is one in which there will be a pervasive dependence on electronics, and thus on very large-scale integration (VLSI), in all defense operations. Modifications will be needed in operating systems, work-force commitments, training, logistics, and, above all, management of the military establishment.

Not surprisingly, the program has generated a wide swing of reactions. To some observers, the program is an inadequate U.S. response to Japanese semiconductor competition. To others, VHSIC is a Machiavellian attempt to impose strictures on VLSI technology for defense applications. And to a few, it appears to be an expensive purchase of unnecessarily complex silicon chips that will never be used. But to the military and legislative leaders who created it, VHSIC is aimed at developing silicon chips that will be fast enough and reliable enough to ensure continuing U.S. superiority in defense electronics.

What exactly the program will yield is still far from clear, because it is only two years old and has at least two years to go before it produces its first applicable chip. But in that span, VHSIC has evolved from amorphous objectives to specific chip designs, and it has identified problems that must be overcome in creating subsystem brassboards. In response to changing DOD system requirements, the program is fostering high-speed signal-processing VLSI and efficient chip design, fabrication, and insertion techniques. Many specific VLSI chips are being made, demonstrated, and applied in present military defense machinery. In addition, a distinct organizational break with the past is being initiated: DOD managerial innovations are being tested that will permit more productivity for generic research and investments in technology.

Having directed VHSIC from its inception to last May, I propose to update *Spectrum* readers on the current state of the program. I will discuss some of the problems that have arisen, their resolutions, and what changes they have brought about. Finally, I hazard some hypotheses concerning both the future of the VHSIC project and what impact it may have on the future of the VLSI industry. Understandably, some aspects of the program, and many of the details, cannot be discussed in the public forum that *Spectrum* presents. But the progress and influence of the VHSIC program can be rightfully discussed without treading on classified ground.

The challenge: complexity with speed

Early on, industry and academic technologists concluded that high-throughput signal-processing VLSI would meet defense reliability and environmental requirements. The ultimate goal was pilot production in 1986 of processors containing 250 000 gates, operating at clock speeds of at least 25 megahertz, and performing several million to several billion operations per second. The processor chips were to perform their respective functions with a functional throughput rate of 10^{13} gate-Hz/cm^2 while having minimum dimensions of 0.5 micrometer. It was also deemed necessary to insert this technology into existing military hardware while providing radiation hardness for doses up to 10^{11}/cm^2. Built-in testing at the chip level was also desired. The required speed and circuit density were to be obtained by scaling down integrated circuits, reducing channel length and oxide thickness, decreasing supply voltage, and developing new types of system architecture and software.

The program has been divided into several phases over a six-year period [see table on facing page]. The effort involves major contracts to a small number of the country's most prolific electronic systems companies—six in Phase I—to cover the competitive technologies and to provide sufficient resources in each contract to obtain major progress. The supporting research effort, on the other hand, consists of a larger number of smaller contracts that are enlisting the innovative efforts of the much broader community of semiconductor researchers in industry, universities, and research institutions.

Each of the six major contractors in VHSIC is applying one of the competitive integrated-circuit technologies—NMOS, bulk CMOS, CMOS on SOS, and bipolar—to the design and fabrication of chips for applications in a specific system brassboard for each division of the military. Progress reported so far is on schedule and providing early harbingers of both technical and structural changes in the semiconductor industry [see "VHSIC contractors tell their story," p. 36]. Signal processors for electrooptical guidance, secure antijam communications, acoustic signals, multimode fire-and-forget missiles, electronic warfare, and advanced tactical radars comprise the existing brassboards. Others will be added.

In Phase I the contractors are required to obtain a 5×10^{11} gate-Hz/cm^2 functional throughput rate in these chips of 1¼-μm resolution. The complexity is typically 20 000 transistors on a chip, but it ranges from about 3000 to well over 100 000. The larger numbers apply to chips with integrated memory or those that are all memory. Twenty-eight chips are being designed and fabricated. Submicrometer chips some 20 times faster will be designed and built during Phase II, at which time the developed brassboard using these chips will also be demonstrated in actual military systems.

More than $30 million has been committed at this time to sup-

Larry W. Sumney
Semiconductor Research Cooperative

porting research. Over a quarter of the effort is on high-resolution lithography to meet the $1\frac{1}{4}$-μm and submicrometer goals, beyond the limits of contemporary commercial processing capabilities. Work has focused primarily on electron-beam, direct-write lithography, because of its flexibility and compatibility with small production runs. Optical and X-ray techniques, more suited to large-volume production, were initially not funded; it was felt that these were adequately exploited by existing industrial development. Other elements of the processing technology—plasma techniques, metallization, materials, reliability, ion milling, implantation, laser annealing, device design, packaging, and interconnections—are receiving selective attention as required for the fabrication of VHSIC chips.

Although the device and processing technologies are being pushed to their limits, it has been found that chip design and testing are even more demanding and will require larger shares of the program's resources. The changing nature of integrated-circuit technology is most visible at the design level. The development of operations systems—other than memories and other highly repetitive architectures—with 20 000 to 50 000 transistors is one of the most challenging tasks faced. Developing chips with 100 000 to a million transistors will require design-automation systems, automated production processes, and a user-support structure with capabilities well beyond those now available. For both defense and commercial VLSI, the definition of what to design and the development of affordable design methods are recognized as the most important needs.

Which technology? A mix is indicated

Commercial VLSI is largely based on NMOS technology, which is neither the fastest semiconductor technology nor that with the lowest power. Neither is it the most radiation-resistant. It is, however, inexpensive, and may be useful for expendable systems, among other applications. Speed, power, and radiation resistance are all important military requirements, however. Thus VHSIC includes several bipolar, CMOS, CMOS on SOS, and NMOS approaches. It is not clear, even now, which technology, if any, will dominate future defense VLSI. Indeed, the application might dictate NMOS for expendable systems (for cost benefit), bipolar for systems where the highest speed or highest radiation tolerance is required, or CMOS where very low-power requirements predominate.

Where digital electronics are applied, though, VHSIC is a "silicon only" program, because the mainstream of VLSI is totally silicon-based, and VHSIC is aimed at returning DOD electronics to that mainstream. Gallium arsenide gates are faster than silicon ones, and GaAs microwave monolithic integrated circuits could be used now in all military communication, early warning, and radar systems. But GaAs digital integrated-circuit technology is far less mature than silicon digital technology. Although the gap is closing rapidly, the VHSIC program includes no plans to develop GaAs chips at this time.

While bipolar devices are generally easier to harden against radiation damage, ways to harden MOS technologies are improving. The Defense Nuclear Agency has initiated a $5 million-a-year program to further harden selected VHSIC device technologies to present military satellite levels.

Closing the 'technology insertion' gap

A major concern of the military has been the unconscionable delay between the creation of a new technology and its application in operational systems. This "technology insertion" gap has extended to 10 years or even longer. While measures to provide state-of-the-art VLSI for new systems were originally outlined for selected portions of the program and the military hardware they would apply to, it rapidly became apparent that a more expeditious approach was needed, one that would reach all technological and institutional levels associated with the program. Technology-insertion targets were thereupon redirected to include any operational military equipment or production system in which VHSIC would provide cost, size, weight, or reliability improvements, as well as significant improvements in performance. Included in the planning were products still in the conceptual phase, including those that would not be possible without the equipment being generated by the VHSIC program.

This broader target for VHSIC insertion is stimulating intense efforts to apply the new chips. In 1984 added funding will become available to accelerate this process. In parallel with the technology-insertion effort is a broad educational activity to acquaint the defense establishment, contractors, the uniformed services, defense agencies, and DOD management with VHSIC. Without this top-to-bottom support, technology insertion cannot succeed. Education is being accomplished through presentations, publications, and involvement, rather than through any formal process—but it has proven amazingly effective.

The VHSIC program has recently been reviewed by a Defense Science Board Task Force, which determined that the program was progressing well and accomplishing its intended mission. Among its several recommendations for strengthening the program, the task force focused most strongly on inserting VHSIC technology into operational military systems. It recommended that this transition be abetted by including all DOD people con-

VHSIC program structure

	Goals	Budget
Phase 0 March–November 1980	Develop detailed concepts and plans Nine contractors	$10.5 million
Phase I May 1981–April 1984	Design, develop, and pilot-produce $1\frac{1}{4}$-micrometer chips with a 5×10^{11} gate-Hz/cm^2 functional throughput rate Develop subsystem brassboards Develop submicrometer chip technology Six contractors	$167.8 million
Phase II 1984–86	Demonstrate Phase I brassboards in actual military applications Develop and pilot-produce submicrometer chips with 10^{13} gate-Hz/cm^2 functional throughput rate	$75 million
Phase III 1980–86	Provide innovative R&D in support of program goals with some 60 contractors	$60 million

cerned with technology in the management of the program and by increasing funding for this part of the program. The added funding would be applied to an increased number of system brassboards, system demonstrations of the technology, and to the now unfunded testing, qualification, and development steps that will apply the technology to operational systems.

Unifying DOD research—a breakthrough

In the bureaucratic category, the major challenge encountered in the first two years of the VHSIC program was in melding the legal, acquisition, and technical procedures of the Department of Defense and the Army, Navy, and Air Force so that a single military proposal would be possible for each of the phases of the program and simultaneous contracts by the three services could be awarded. Although each service has procedures based on the same policy guidelines, these had become so different that a major effort to resolve the differences was required before a unified approach could be adopted.

A second challenge stemmed from the fact that VHSIC—a DOD program—was funded as an Air Force budgetary line item. Obtaining effective control of these funds, and avoiding diversions, consumed more than its rightful share of management attention. In solving these problems, the program directors have cleared the way for similar joint-service technology projects.

This success has also changed attitudes in many segments of the armed services toward joint technology efforts. Almost

VHSIC contractors tell their story

Technical work in the Department of Defense's Very High-Speed Integrated Circuits (VHSIC) program is divided between six major contractors during Phase I. Each contractor is making a different brassboard for insertion into existing military hardware, and each has developed a unique approach to develop the VLSI circuit for its brassboard. Honeywell Inc., Plymouth, Wis., and IBM Corp., Manassas, Va., are depending on macrocell libraries and TRW Inc., Redondo Beach, Calif., and Westinghouse Defense Electronics Center, Baltimore, Md., on standard chip sets, while Hughes Aircraft Co., Malibu, Calif., and Texas Instruments Inc., Dallas, have come up with more programmable chip sets. The following status report is based on information provided for *Spectrum* by five of the VHSIC Phase I contractors. For a quick summary of the precise technology and design approach each of the contractors has taken, see the table on this page. Due to time limitations, TRW was unable to furnish a detailed account.

Honeywell Inc.

Honeywell is using an oxide-isolated bipolar process in making two highly programmable chips. They will consist of macrocells that will be automatically interconnected by an autorouter to gain fast turnaround time. The necessary software has been written and has so far automatically routed over 700 interconnections between macrocells. Honeywell's Phase I goal is to manufacture a prototype electrooptical signal processor for a number of military applications that will typically require billions of operations per second. The processor will be made using a 23 000-gate programmable parallel processor and a 30 000-gate controller.

Manufacturing high-density metal interconnections became an early concern. A corrosion-free dry plasma-etching process was sought because of its high resolution, and it has since been demonstrated in producing 1.5-micrometer metal lines in copper-doped aluminum. Chlorine, a by-product of the process, was initially corroding the metal, but Honeywell has found a way to eliminate this problem. The company has also processed 0.4-μm minimum-geometry bipolar transistors.

Honeywell has also completed processing and begun testing all 43 of its macrocells for its VHSIC macrocell library. Macrocells are the building blocks for the brassboard chips, and they vary in complexity from 50 to 2500 gates per macrocell.

In conjunction with the 3M Co., St. Paul, Minn., Honeywell has completed the 180-pin area array package for forthcoming 1.25-μm circuits and has fabricated a mock-up of the brassboard based on the package.

The company has yet to demonstrate three-layer metal on a working chip level. This will be its next goal, the focus of early 1983 work. In addition, Honeywell has contracted Motorola as its second source for processing 1.25-μm IC chips. Motorola Inc., Phoenix, Ariz., was chosen because its manufacturing process is similar to Honeywell's, making it easier for designers and manufacturers from the two companies to understand each other's requirements and methods. Honeywell has finished designing its test chips. The design and layout information has been encoded on Calma tapes from which Motorola will generate fabrication masks.

In reaching its Phase I objectives, Honeywell is using integrated Schottky and current-mode logic to achieve a unique combination of high-speed RAM, ROM, and random logic on the same VLSI chip. Maintaining reliability while decreasing the size of interconnections is limiting density, however. In the long term, initial low yield is expected, as it is at all the companies involved. Reducing defect density will also be necessary if production yields are to improve, but Honeywell has made this a major part of its program and is confident the necessary improvement will be made.

Hughes Aircraft Co.

Standard and custom reconfigurable CMOS-on-SOS chips are being designed by Hughes for the Army's battlefield information-

VHSIC Phase I contractors

Contractor (service)	Technology	Brassboard
Honeywell (Air Force)	Bipolar ISL*, CML†	Electrooptical signal processor
Hughes (Army)	CMOS on SOS	Antijam communications
IBM (Navy)	NMOS	Acoustic signal processor
Texas Instruments (Army)	Bipolar-STL‡, NMOS	Multimode fire-and-forget missile
TRW (Navy)	Bipolar-3d** TTL, CMOS	Electronic-warfare signal processor
Westinghouse (Air Force)	Bulk CMOS	Advanced tactical radar processor

unobtrusively, VHSIC has become recognized as the most important technological program in the Army, Navy, and Air Force. The long-range impact of this cooperative approach could be of major importance. All technologies are becoming increasingly generic to the three services, and, with escalating costs, there is no basis for continued inefficient duplication of research efforts. The VHSIC program has successfully established a model for DOD management that integrates the needs of each of the services into one coherent investment strategy.

In considering export control of VHSIC technology, the Defense Science Board Task Force concluded that there was no risk-free course of action. The free flow of information in U.S. research is one reason for U.S. leadership in VLSI, but the export of information is of great value to our military and economic adversaries. A system to classify the most sensitive technologies is presently being proposed.

New plants needed to fill DOD needs

Because VLSI defense electronics will require special attention, with its demands for high-speed, low-power, and radiation-hardened devices, few design and fabrication plants are expected to be able to fill the full gamut of DOD needs. Such facilities would entail major investments beyond the resources of most semiconductor companies. For example, design automation for the next generation of VLSI components will require an investment in excess of $100 million. Consolidating resources of many

---

distribution-system brassboard and their position-location reporting-system brassboard. To do this work, Hughes has upgraded its Hercules computer-aided design (CAD) system to VHSIC design and layout specifications. The first pilot-line test chip, a preamble acquisition correlator, has been successfully fabricated, validating the Hughes baseline SOS-III process, which will be used to fabricate all of the company's VHSIC chips. Hughes developed their design rules in cooperation with RCA, Camden, N.J., and Rockwell International, Newport Beach, Calif., to ensure compatibility between all three companies' CMOS-on-SOS processes. RCA has, in fact, processed a Hughes-designed VHSIC test chip.

Automatic layout tools are being integrated with the Hercules CAD data base, and this will allow Hughes to design a spread-spectrum subsystem chip in 1983. A third chip, an algebraic encoder/decoder, is currently in the layout and simulator stage. The next critical benchmark, Hughes says, will be functional operation of the correlator chip.

Realizing the time it might take to insert VHSIC technology successfully into existing military machinery, the Hughes radar systems group has simultaneously embarked on a multimillion dollar Navy-funded program to develop a radar processor for the F-18 fighter plane. The Hercules CAD system will be used to design a bipolar chip set for this purpose.

Hughes reports that its main difficulty to date has been meeting a stringent program schedule, forcing its researchers to do many tasks in parallel which they would have preferred to do sequential-

Design approach	Chip set	Gate density (gates/mm²)	Gate power (μmW/gate)	Special features
Custom-chip–based macrocell library	Parallel programmable pipe-line Controller	480	30	Radiation hardness Responsive generic architecture
Standard and custom reconfigurable chips	Digital correlator Algebraic encoder/decoder Spread-spectrum subsystem	400	2	Radiation hardness Electron-beam direct-write lithography Highly specialized chips
Master image with macrocell library	Complex multiplier/accumulator	570	100	Software strength Design approach

Programmable chip set	Data processor
	Array controller and sequencer
	Vector address generator
	Vector arithmetic logic unit
	Static RAM
	Multipath switch
	Device interface unit
	General buffer unit
		390	37	Operational
				  fabrication facility
				Design utility
				  system

Standard chip set	Content addressable memory Window addressable memory Registered arithmetic logic unit Address generator Matrix switch 15-bit multiplier/accumulator Microcontroller Four-port memory	TTL: 390 CMOS: 300	240 20	Innovative memory chips Versatile chip set
Standard chip set	Pipeline arithmetic unit Extended arithmetic unit Controller Gate array Static RAM Multiplier	1000	4	Highest speeds

*) Integrated Schottky logic   †) Current mode logic   ‡) Schottky transistor logic   **) Triple diffusion

companies into programs that allocate them against improving generic R&D will ease the burden [see "The future of VLSI corporations," p. 39]. The likely result, though, is the emergence of several DOD-owned, contractor-operated defense VLSI facilities for digital systems, software, and artificial intelligence operations of DOD. However, a big portion of defense VLSI requirements will still be met with standard components from commercial suppliers.

Educational activities in microelectronics also need to change. The creation of 100 000 transistor chips requires engineers who are knowledgeable in system architectures and device performance, plasma processing and computer-aided design, physical phenomena and software, and testing and hierarchical languages. No one professional can deal with this array of knowledge in the necessary detail. Universities today are faced with the major challenge of implementing new curricula when qualified instructors are being lured away by attractive industrial careers.

Cooperative semiconductor research begins

A significant sign that the integrated-circuit industry is maturing is the decision by producers and users of VLSI devices to conduct cooperative research. This is based on recognition that progress in industry will flow from improved understanding of semiconductor materials and phenomena, as well as from more powerful design and manufacturing techniques. And these ad-

---

ly. For example, VHSIC chips were designed with a CAD system that was still under development; therefore the first chips have not been as efficiently designed as later ones will be when the system is perfected. In addition it has been necessary to initiate some layout work before the circuits have been fully simulated and debugged.

From here on, Hughes says, the challenge will be to manufacture working chips to military specifications while retaining a satisfactory process yield. Producing quantities of VHSIC chips efficiently may require additional process refinements.

IBM Corp.

IBM's brassboard will be an acoustic signal processor for planes and ships that will process data being sent from sonar buoys. The company has decided to use a "macrochip architecture" that interconnects custom macrocells, like memories and processors, with gate arrays. This approach allows designers to choose from a library of macrocells that are then connected at the CAD level. The result will be chips that can be tailored to the requirements of the specific system in which it will be installed.

The macrocells have been designed to the VHSIC 1.25-μm rule, as have the packaging and brassboard into which they will be fitted. The final result is a 36 000-gate complex multiplier and accumulator chip that is at present in IBM's process line, being fabricated along with the macrocells. Hardware for the brassboards is also being made.

IBM says its biggest difficulty to date was in wiring the 36 000 gates efficiently. IBM agrees with Hughes that obtaining an acceptable yield during pilot production will be the greatest impediment to future progress.

Texas Instruments Inc.

TI's brassboards will improve the radio-frequency and infrared guiding systems for multimode fire-and-forget gun-fired missiles.

Of the brassboard's eight defined chips, seven are logic-programmable system components using Schottky transistor logic (STL), and one is an NMOS memory. STL was selected because of its reliability, radiation tolerance, and exceptional speed and power characteristics. Minimum pinouts for each component have been achieved by distributing read-only-memory–encoded microcode across the logic chips. The entire chip set is TTL input/output–compatible and will be packaged in Jedec standard leadless chip-carriers. To date, circuit design rules have been completed for STL and NMOS. The design of the memory is finished, as are the logic designs of the array controller/sequencer and multipath switch.

A 16-bit, fixed-point array processor will handle repetitive data-independent operations on fixed-size blocks of data. The performance at a 25-megahertz clock rate is 75 million operations per second, and typical calculated power density is less than 1 watt per square inch. VHSIC Phase I implementation of the array processor will follow a writable control-store configuration with user-defined microcode. This will give the needed flexibility for brassboard development and low-volume production applications. The support software has been successfully demonstrated to support microcode development and simulation.

A 16-bit fixed-point data processor will provide data-dependent arithmetic, logic, and control operations on unstructured data streams. It will process 2 to 6 million instructions per second at a typical power density of 0.7 watt per square inch.

The data-processor support software consists of a Pascal-based microprocessor and executive for use on the Air Force's standard 1750A processor. The software contains utilities necessary to implement and maintain 1750A application systems in Pascal and 1750A assembly languages on a host processor. The 1750A software tool set is operational and currently undergoing tests. Both the array and data processors will be packaged in a single Phase I brassboard prototype.

At this time, the programmable system-component logic and gate-level designs are being defined and verified with hardware description language and simulation software developed at TI.

Subsequent to its current program, the company plans to make available a 4000-gate array for special-purpose processing and interface supplements to the basic chip set. The chip-design tools will provide a method to define and simulate such additions.

TI's next goal is to obtain functionally correct parts from its initial fabrication release data. The company says the key to doing this is making it easier for designers to use its hardware description language in VHSIC applications and chip simulation.

Westinghouse Electric Corp.

The Westinghouse brassboard, being developed at the company's Baltimore facility, will be an advanced radar signal processor for the Air Force's next generation of tactical fighter planes. The bulk-CMOS VHSIC chip set includes four signal-processor chips, each with over 30 000 gates, a 10 000-gate array, and a 64-K static RAM. The original program goals called for the chip set to be designed by the end of 1982 and to have a CMOS process with yield sufficient to obtain performance data on the chips' logic macrocells on their first pass. The focus would then be on optimizing the process to yield fully functional chips by the last quarter of 1983.

The VHSIC chip-set logic design is 80-percent complete. Layout of the first designs ranges from 10 percent to 100 percent complete across the chip set, and the CMOS baseline process is in place. The 10 000-gate array with logic cells from Westinghouse's minicell library and larger logic macrocells is at present being processed along with the 64-K static RAM. Devices have been tested at the first level of metal interconnections, and test data indicate that the basic device structures are sound. Westinghouse says its next critical benchmarks are design verification and fabrication of the first pass of these test chips.

A concerted effort to refine a two-level aluminum interconnection process using bias-sputtered quartz by year-end is in progress. Perfection of the process through the second level is now receiving most of Westinghouse's research attention. Meanwhile, static 64-K RAMs and 10 000-gate arrays are being fabricated, so that the performance of second-level metal interconnections on them can be demonstrated. Future success, again, will hinge on Westinghouse's ability to improve yield, they say.

—Mark A. Fischetti

vances depend directly upon the availability of enough highly trained scientists and engineers.

The first of these cooperative efforts is the Semiconductor Research Cooperative (SRC) in Research Triangle Park, N.C. The cooperative provides support and guidance to nonprofit semiconductor research entities in the United States, primarily universities, without the direct participation of the Government. Because of overlapping interests and the fact that many of the research groups supported by the cooperative will also receive Government support, some coordination of the research agenda with Government activities will be sought.

Also, in the advanced planning stage is a microelectronic computer technology corporation, spearheaded by the Control Data Corp. in Minneapolis. It will complement SRC research with other industry-oriented projects.

The pooled resources of the participating semiconductor corporations will represent superior efforts in critical research areas where capital or personnel requirements are beyond the reach of individual cooperating corporations. In generic research areas, the programs are expected to lessen the many fragmented, duplicative efforts undertaken in the industry in the past. The new cooperative will broaden the scope and number of university-industry contracts, enhance the quality and quantity of technical people available to the industry, create a technical bargaining position with respect to similar efforts in other countries, and accelerate the interchange of knowledge on generic science and technology.

A form of vertical integration among the manufacturers, suppliers, and users in this cooperative effort is being implemented. It has been fully recognized that the semiconductor technology of the 1980s encompasses a much broader agenda than that of the 1970s. Systems-on-silicon is the game of the future.

To probe further

For a perspective on the VHSIC program when it first began, see "VLSI with a vengeance," by Larry W. Sumney, *Spectrum*, April 1980, pp. 24–27 [see p. 276].

The magazine *Defense Electronics* periodically charts various aspects of VHSIC progress. See "VHSIC processors take shape," by James E. Fawcett, August 1982, pp. 33–38, and "VHSIC and commercial VLSI: two sides of the same coin?" by Jeffrey Frey, September 1982, pp. 79–80. Contact E.W. Communications, 1170 East Meadow Drive, Palo Alto, Calif. 94303.

A wealth of information on the latest innovations in VLSI design automation is contained in the ACM IEEE Nineteenth Design Automation Conference proceedings, Las Vegas, Nev., June 14–16, 1982. Order by the IEEE no. 82CH1759-0, IEEE Computer Society order no. 416, or ACM order no. 477820.

Other conferences covering VLSI technology, which usually cover VHSIC-related material, are the International Electron Devices Meeting, sponsored by the IEEE, Dec. 13–15, 1982, San Francisco, Calif. Contact Melissa Widerkehr, Courtesy Associates, 1629 K St., N.W., Washington, D.C. 20006; and the Government Microcircuit Applications Conference (Gomac), Nov. 2–4, Orlando, Fla. 32800. Gomac includes several classified and nonclassified sessions on VHSIC, but all proceedings are being handled by the conference chairman Bob Weck, U.S. Army, Eradcom. Attention: DELET-MH-W, Fort Monmouth, N.J. 07703.

About the author

Larry W. Sumney (SM) became executive director of the Semiconductor Research Cooperative, Arlington, Va., in May 1982, after directing the planning and the first two years of the

---

The future of VLSI corporations

Although only two years old, the Very High-Speed Integrated Circuits (VHSIC) program already is pointing to changes that will be required of semiconductor manufacturers who wish to remain in the very large-scale-integration market. While the current budget of VHSIC is $70 million per year—only about 7 percent of what U.S. industry is spending for semiconductor research and development—VHSIC should be an important sign of the kind of substantial effort in research and funding that will ultimately be needed. Two examples will illustrate the point.

The new three-piece Intel micromainframe chip set, the 432, was developed at a cost of approximately $40 million. That translates to about 400 man-years. It is estimated, however, that an additional 300 man-years will be invested in system development, primarily software, before the set is fully usable. How many companies will be willing and able to make similar investments in the future?

The production of 64-kilobyte RAMs is expected to be in excess of 60 million a year in 1982. This device is complex, and only in the last several years has it become possible to make it. While the price of a 64-kilobyte RAM is currently around $8, any manufacturer with an important share of the market will necessarily have a design and production-line investment approaching $100 million and produce in excess of 10 million chips a year to make this profitable. The 64-kilobyte RAM is the easiest of the new generation of VLSI chips to design and produce, but the size of investment and the difficulty in achieving a competitive design already limits participation to a few powerful companies. In the United States these include the IBM Corp., Western Electric Co., Motorola Inc., Texas Instruments Inc., Intel Corp., National Semiconductor Corp., and a few others.

The micromainframe and 64-kilobyte RAM are examples of the coming generation of billion-dollar chips. Others will include communications signal-processing chips, microprocessors, voice-synthesis and -recognition chips, and display interfaces. Even with large gains in design and processing technologies, each of these chips will represent an investment on the order of $100 million. In light of this, producers in the future will probably be dominated by a few very large, vertically integrated corporations. They will all be organized differently, but will most likely operate a large design center and highly automated production lines at strategic sites around the world. Since they will be selling mostly systems and not digital circuits, their success will hinge on service, software, and interface (sensing, display, and actuator) technology. The total annual integrated-circuit market is projected as approaching $100 billion before the present decade is over. If there are no more than 10 of these large integrated-circuit producers, their annual sales volumes will exceed $5 billion apiece. Other companies that focus only on devices, components, or special microelectronic niches can also expect to do well, but they will operate on a secondary tier of the industry. Their total share of the market will account for the second $50 billion.

—*L.W.S.*

Very High-Speed Integrated Circuits program in the Department of Defense's office of the under secretary of defense for research and engineering. Mr. Sumney began his Government career at the Naval Research Laboratories in Washington, D.C., in 1962, where he subsequently became responsible for applications of digital electronics in a variety of Navy systems. He holds a B.S. in physics from Washington and Jefferson College and an M.S. in applied mathematics from George Washington University.   ◆

VLSI

AUTOMATING CHIP LAYOUT
New computer-based layout systems are fast and produce designs that almost match those created manually

Only a small portion of new large-scale and very large-scale integrated-circuit designs are laid out automatically today. But that picture is changing. IC fabrication costs are now so low that the design process offers the only major avenue for reducing IC costs further. IC producers are certain to adopt automated layout tools—sophisticated programs that translate functional specifications into physical descriptions of chips—increasingly over the next few years, and by 1990 layout will probably be predominantly automatic.

Automating layout not only eliminates the need for highly skilled layout people, but it also virtually eliminates mistakes and greatly reduces the turnaround time for new IC designs. These features all reduce costs, of course.

Automated layout tools have been criticized because they use silicon chip area less efficiently than a human layout designer would and produce ICs that operate more slowly and consume more power. To some extent, these charges are true; some automated layout tools do waste chip real estate and use excessively long internal connections, resulting in speed and dissipation that are not optimum. Some automated designs use half again as much area as a manual design for the same function. But such faults often fade in comparison with the benefits of guaranteed correctness and fast turnaround. Moreover, improvements are continually being made in automated tools.

Indeed, a new automated layout tool known as the standard floor-plan system comes close to human proficiency and occasionally exceeds it. Although the standard floor-plan approach is currently limited in the types of ICs it can accommodate, the repertory is being expanded.

Industry giants automate

Today two industry giants—IBM Corp. and the Bell System—use the automated layout for virtually all their LSI and VLSI designs. Their IC chips are designed for in-house use. To a lesser extent, large commercial IC suppliers, such as Texas Instruments Inc., Dallas, and National Semiconductor Corp., Sunnyvale, Calif., also use automated tools for laying out random-logic chips and others. The smaller custom design houses use automated layout hardly at all, except for memories, which require only simple software because of their repetitive structures. But under pressure to stay competitive in cost and delivery time, large and small manufacturers inevitably will turn to automation more and more.

How will automated layout tools affect the people who lay out ICs? Automated layout specification requires different talents from those necessary to hand layout. Automated layout is more like programming; designers who use it do more textual specification and less graphic specification than those who use

Stephen Trimberger
California Institute of Technology

hand layout. They are much less concerned with the precise geometrical form of patterns on silicon and more concerned with the function of the circuit. The effects of job displacement have not yet been felt in the IC industry because of the acute shortage of qualified designers and the relatively small number of designs being made automatically.

Four basic ways to automate

IC layout—the process of translating a description, or specification, of an integrated circuit into photolithographic masks for fabricating the circuit—is being totally automated with four basic methods [Fig. 1]:

1. **Standard cell.** A large library of predefined cells (small logic elements, such as three-input NAND gates or 4-bit counters) is stored in the layout system. The designer of a circuit tells the system which cells are needed and the kinds of connections that will be required between the cells. The standard-cell-system software then assigns the cells to positions on the silicon chip and determines metallization routes, or "wiring," for connecting the cells.

2. **Gate array.** A prefabricated chip contains hundreds of thousands of identical cells, such as NAND-gates, arranged in arrays. The designer tells the layout system the logic functions the chip is to perform and the system selects the cells needed and establishes wiring routes among them.

3. **Programmed logic array (PLA).** A chip contains two arrays—consisting of NAND-gates or NOR-gates—that in series perform any Boolean logic operation. The designer supplies the PLA layout system with the general logic equations. The system selects the signals to be included in the array gates to implement the equations.

4. **Standard floor plan.** The system contains a generic structure for the chip that is much like a housing developer's basic floor plan for a house, which gives the relative positions of rooms and hallways and the means for connecting utilities to the rooms, but leaves unspecified room sizes and contents. Similarly, the chip floor plan specifies the positions of functional units, bus orientation, and wiring strategy, without predetermining the kinds of elements that will be connected.

The floor plan generating the most interest is known as the microprocessor data path. Here a designer tells the layout system the number of bits in the data path, the kinds of processing elements, and the input conditions that cause each element to perform its function. For each element, the system calls a subprogram to lay out the subcircuit with requisite parameters derived from the floor plan.

Each of these layout tools accepts a functional description of the circuit and may also accept some clues to the placement of logic on the chip. The functional description varies widely among automated layout tools and is tailored to the particular tool and the designer's needs [see table]. Each tool embodies a characteristic layout strategy that gives the additional information needed to

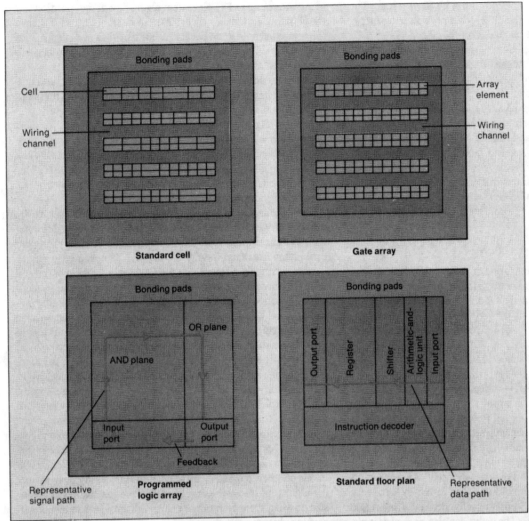

Cell

Wiring channel

Standard cell

Bonding pads

Array element

Wiring channel

Gate array

Bonding pads

OR plane

AND plane

Input port

Output port

Feedback

Representative signal path

Programmed logic array

Bonding pads

Output port

Register

Shifter

Arithmetic-and-logic unit

Input port

Instruction decoder

Standard floor plan

Representative data path

Bonding pads

[1] Among the four major automated layout concepts for IC chips are standard cell and gate-array layout, which are place-and-route schemes; circuit elements are assigned positions, and connections ("wiring") are routed among them as necessary. Unlike standard cells, the gate-array chip image is predefined, so wiring space is limited. The programmed logic array and standard floor plan emphasize wiring rather than placement; regular wiring paths are determined first, and elements are positioned to accommodate them. PLAs perform combinational logic, whereas the standard floor plan here is restricted to microprocessor data paths.

[2] A standard-cell chip made by ZyMOS Corp., Sunnyvale, Calif., contains wiring in channels of various widths between rows of cells. A relatively modest effort for a telephony application, this metal-gate CMOS chip contains 1110 transistors. The company has applied its automated layout system to design chips containing 10 000 random-logic devices in addition to memory on a single chip.

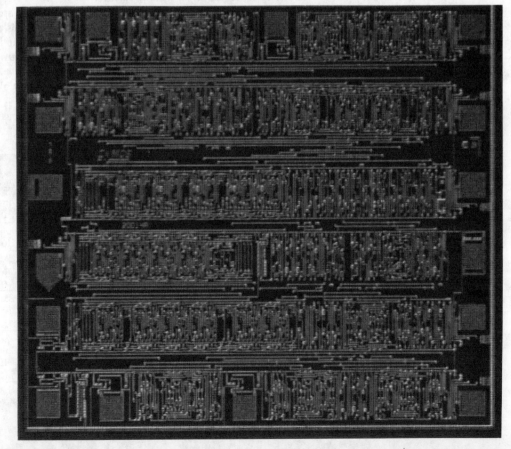

translate the functional description into a physical layout. The output of the layout tool is the mask geometry specification, or the geometrical patterns to be placed on the silicon.

An advantage of human over automated techniques is the ability to select different strategies in different situations. Most engineering organizations using automated layout have only one tool with one strategy. A good match between problem and strategy yields an efficient implementation. Standard cell layout, for example, does well on shift registers, PLA layout produces excellent control circuits, and standard floor-plan layout yields efficient processor circuits. A bad match, on the other hand, yields a messy implementation that may require extensive human intervention to complete, or one that cannot be completed at all. Some semiconductor manufacturers are now experimenting with hybrid layout systems that incorporate two or more layout strategies.

The straightforward approach

The standard cell approach is one of the most straightforward for automating the layout process. To the designer, it is similar to PC-board layout; the tools and methods to solve the layout problem are the same.

Standard cell technology was developed at Bell Laboratories and is now used there for virtually all LSI designs. A few of the more recent circuits from Bell include PLA or other large structures on the chips.

The logic cells selected by the designer from the standard cell library are positioned by the layout software in rows, between which are wiring channels [Fig. 2]. Power and ground wiring are laid out along the sides of the chip so that it does not interfere with the data signals. To ensure that all connections to a cell can be made, the cells are designed with a few simple rules, such as: "All inputs and outputs lie on the edge of a cell." Input to standard cell systems is in the form of a so-called netlist—a list of cells and connections between cells—usually derived from logic diagrams or logic equations. (The netlist can also be used as input to a simulator, to verify that the logic performs the required function before the chips are made.) The standard cell system examines the netlist, determines the positions of each of the cells on the chip, and creates the wiring pattern to connect the cells into a working system. Thus, both the input language and the design constraints are much the same for standard cell design as they are for PC-board layout.

The two steps to the standard-cell layout process are place-

ment and routing. The placement algorithms assign positions on the chip to logic-function cells. With some standard cell systems, the user can enter some placement information in a hierarchical specification that determines which cells will be placed close to one another. Ordinarily, however, an algorithm has much leeway in determining the precise placement of cells. Those that communicate directly are placed close together, and those that connect to bonding pads are placed near the edge of the chip.

Routing algorithms select wiring paths to make the connections given by a designer in a functional specification. Most routing algorithms route one wire at a time, remembering the used wiring channels and avoiding them with future wires. This causes problems when one wire blocks another, so some routers attempt to route all wires simultaneously.

The amount of logic that can fit on a chip is limited by the number of wiring channels used. Long wires require additional wiring channels that make the chip larger, thereby increasing the probability of a fatal flaw in fabrication. Signals take longer to travel across long wires, so a chip with short wires will not only be smaller, but will also run faster. Therefore, most standard cell-optimization routines attempt to minimize total wire length, wiring channel use, or both. Although this does not guarantee minimum chip area or optimum performance, the quantities are easy to measure and well correlated with area and speed.

Finding the absolute minimum wire length is not practical from a computational standpoint. Therefore, no systems try to find it but instead look for an acceptable local minimum, using an acceptable amount of computer time. A clustering algorithm is used in the placement step, and an iterative improvement algorithm is used in the routing step to achieve local minima.

Clustering algorithms attempt to group cells that have many connections among themselves, so those cells may be placed close to one another to make their connections short. A typical clustering algorithm stops when the clusters have reached a maximum size or when there are no more cells with enough connections to existing clusters.

If the designer provides a hierarchical specification—that is, describes the chip in terms of cells containing smaller cells—the user's specification is used as the initial clustering. Since cells defined hierarchically vary greatly in size, systems that allow hierarchical descriptions often relax the restriction that the cells must lie in rows, and the largest blocks of cells are positioned anywhere on the chip.

Iterative improvement algorithms come into play after the first

Layout tools at a glance

Tool	Applications	Percent of space for wiring	Input	Major users
Manual	All	Low	Cells and connections	Virtually universal
Standard cell	All	High (up to 80)	Cells and connectons	Bell Labs, others
Gate array	All	High	Logic specification	IBM, Motorola, others
Programmed logic array	Combinational logic, state machines	Low	Logic equations	IBM
Standard floor plan	Frequently designed large structures (such as processors)	Low	Functional parameters	Caltech, IBM, Bell Labs (experimental)

Note: Place-and-route systems—that is, standard cell and gate-array layout systems—are versatile but use cnip area extravagantly for wiring. Programmed logic arrays and standard floor plans, by contrast, conserve area almost as much as manual layout, but they have limited applications.

cell placement: they exchange the positions of pairs of cells if this reduces the total wire length or channel use. The iterative improvement proceeds until no further improvement can be found by any exchange, yielding a local minimum for the total wire length or channel use.

Some standard cell layout systems employ Karnaugh minimization to find similar gating configurations. The system can then implement the same logic with fewer cells.

In addition, many layout systems recognize that there usually are several possible physical forms of a cell for a given function. The forms differ in the orientation of their inputs and outputs and the driving power of their output. The system chooses the form that minimizes the wiring and can drive the fanout at a reasonable speed. Further, some systems perform critical path analysis and optimize critical paths so the chip will run faster. For example, an algorithm checks all logic stages from input to output to identify the signal paths having the most gates and hence the greatest delay. The system gives these critical paths special attention, selecting particularly fast gates from the library and positioning them for minimum wiring length.

Standard cell layout is fast because the positioning of the cells and routing of the wiring are done entirely by computer. A relatively modest LSI circuit—one, say, with about 10 000 gates—can be laid out and fabricated in perhaps two months, whereas the lead time for hand layout of a similar circuit is well over a year.

Designers need not know details of the IC technology that will be used to execute the design; the layout rules for CMOS, TTL, and other technologies are built into the algorithms. A design may be reimplemented when more advanced fabrication technologies become available.

On the other hand, standard cell layout undeniably wastes chip real estate, with as much as 80 percent of the area taken up by wiring. Moreover the automatic placement and routing system may not be able to produce a chip within the desired size, performance, and power-consumption limits. When this occurs, a human designer must modify the placement and wiring, and much of the advantage of automated layout is lost.

Exploiting mass production with gate arrays

Gate-array layout—also known as master-slice layout at IBM and uncommitted logic-array layout by Japanese and European manufacturers—is a variant of standard cell layout that takes advantage of the manufacturing economics of integrated circuitry. A gate-array chip consists of hundreds or thousands of identical structures placed at regular points on the surface of the chip [Fig. 3]. The structures can be sets of transistors and resistors, complete NAND-gates (the usual form), or other functional elements. The gates in an array are separated by wiring channels, which contain the user-specified interconnections and predefined power routing to ensure good power connections to all parts of the chip.

A manufacturer produces identical gate-array chips by the thousands—with all gates in position but without connections between the gates—and stores them. Then when a user orders a few or a few hundred chips to perform a given function, the manufacturer customizes the gate-array chips merely by adding the interconnections needed for the function.

IBM is the pioneer in gate-array technology. Layout techniques have matured there over the last 15 years or so and gate-array technology is now the mainstay of the company's IC design effort. Virtually every IC in IBM's computers is a gate-array circuit. Gate arrays are also catching on elsewhere; many custom IC fabricators are using the technology, including Silicon Systems

Inc., Tustin, Calif.; Interdesign Inc., Sunnyvale, Calif.; International Microcircuits Inc., Santa Clara, Calif.; Dionics Inc., Westbury, N.Y.; Motorola Inc., Phoenix, Ariz.; and Exar Integrated Systems Inc., Sunnyvale, Calif.

Gate-array layout algorithms map the logic specification onto the logic gates by first defining the correspondence between logic in the functional description and physical structures on the chip, then specifying the wiring between the gates to implement the circuit. These two tasks in a gate-array system are essentially the same as the placement and routing tasks in a standard cell system. However, gate-array layout is more constrained than standard cell layout because all cells are identical and the amount of wiring space available is defined when the structure of the gate array is defined. As with standard cell layout, the input specification may contain information about the placement of the gates on the chip, but the system will function without it.

A gate-array layout system requires the same input as a standard cell system: a list of components and the connections to be made between them. The components are either broken down into the array elements—for example, NAND-gates—or mapped into "macros," structures made up of several array elements with predefined wiring within those elements—for example, a two-bit adder. Macros speed up layout and use chip space more efficiently.

Advantages of gate arrays

Gate arrays offer all the advantages of standard cells: the designers need not know details of the fabrication technology, and the designs can be reimplemented in many different technologies with a minimum of human intervention. The same functional description used to generate the layout can be used for simulation; therefore, the simulation is likely to model the implementation accurately.

But gate arrays have a great advantage not found in standard cells: the identical gate pattern is used by the manufacturer for all gate-array chips, regardless of the end use. Most of the processing steps are identical for all gate-array chips; only the final wiring is unique. The cost of new masks and separate production runs is avoided. Gate-array chips can be processed in advance, shortening the delay from product specification to delivery to a few weeks instead of several months.

One challenge to manufacturers, of course, is estimating the best number of wiring channels for the number of gates and I/O pads on the chip. Although the amount of wiring needed is not known until the customer's needs are known, probability calculations are fairly reliable guides in setting aside chip area for wiring. Naturally, there are some chips for which the wiring capacity of the gate array is exceeded, leading to a condition akin to overbooking on airlines. At such times, lack of wiring channel space makes it difficult or impossible to wire a particular function on a gate array, so that a human must often complete the wire routing after the layout system's initial guess.

With some layout systems, the wiring can trespass over areas occupied by gates when more wiring space is needed. Then there may not be enough gates left on the chip to implement the function and the design may have to be partitioned into several chips. Partitioning creates its own problems, since there may not be enough pins on the chips to accommodate the input and output connections among chips. If a human finally must solve such problems, the fast turnaround and other automation advantages of the gate array may be lost.

Layout problems do not ordinarily crop up with gate arrays. But there is a fundamental assumption in place-and-route systems that, on an integrated circuit, as on a printed-circuit

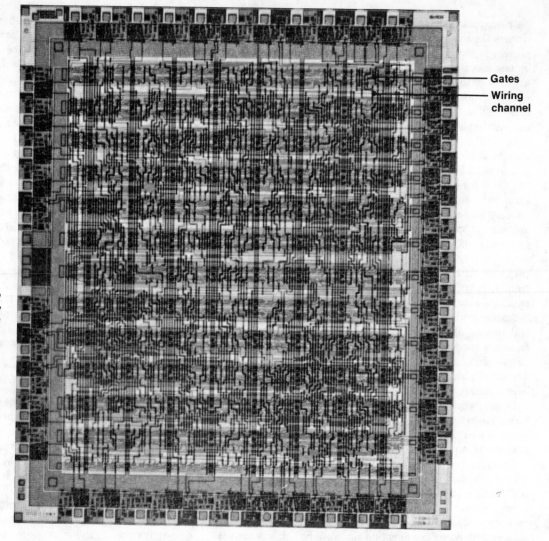

Gates

Wiring channel

[3] Gate-array chip manufactured by Digital Equipment Corp., Maynard, Mass., for its computers consists of a custom wiring pattern on prefabricated gates. The wiring runs predominantly in a horizontal direction between rows of cells. Unlike standard-cell rows, the gate-array rows are equally separated—an indication of their identical geometries.

board, wiring is cheap and logic expensive. This is a false assumption: since logic function and wiring are made by the same processes, there is no additional expense for additional functions. In fact, as ever larger chips are made, the space required for wiring grows faster than the space required for devices, and the priorities are reversed: wiring is more expensive than logic in terms of chip real estate. Programmed logic-array and standard floor-plan layout systems recognize the new priorities with layouts in which the wiring is predetermined and logic is placed where it is needed on the wiring.

A programmed logic array, sometimes called programmed array logic, brings all inputs along parallel connections into the AND plane, where they are used selectively as inputs to several gates. The outputs from the gates in the AND-plane, called minterms, run perpendicularly into the OR-plane, where the minterms become the inputs to the OR-plane gates. The outputs from the OR-plane are the outputs of the PLA and run parallel to the inputs. Outputs may be run back into the inputs, in which case they are feedback signals [Fig. 4].

The AND-plane and the OR-plane may both contain NAND gates, giving the AND-OR combination of inputs (hence the terms AND-plane and OR-plane); they may both be made of NOR-gates, giving a NOT-AND-OR-NOT function; or the AND-plane may be NAND-gates, the OR-plane may be NOR gates, and the minterms may be inverted with extra logic between the planes to give an AND-OR-NOT result. If necessary, inputs and outputs are inverted at the respective ports. The choice of

gate types in the arrays depends on the preferred structures in a particular fabrication technology—for example, NMOS makes better NOR gates, while a NAND-NOR combination is preferred in some CMOS schemes.

Gates in the AND-plane are spread horizontally across the entire array, so a minterm is the AND of any set of inputs. The PLA system simply lays a transistor on top of the wiring where the input line meets the minterm line. The same strategy is applied to build the OR-plane.

The regular grid pattern of wiring in PLAs allows them to perform complex logic functions without long wiring connections. PLA layout is similar to read-only memory programming: locations in the PLA are connected if the Boolean operation in that part of the PLA includes the input signal.

Some algorithms generate PLA layout directly from state machine equations, synchronous logic equations (equations with clocking information), or microcode specifications. Indeed, the PLA technique excels at circuits based on state machines—for example, microcode controllers. With the PLA scheme, inputs can be latched and held and outputs can be recycled from the output drivers to the inputs on the next clock cycle, where they provide the state needed by a state machine. But the PLA approach is less successful at implementing such chips as shift registers, which contain little or no logic. Forcing such functions into the PLA mold means very large chips.

PLAs were originally developed by IBM, although they were never widely used in that company. More recently there has been a resurgence of interest in them throughout the industry, because of their regular form and because they can be used to build new types of controllers quickly and economically.

PLA layout systems cannot optimize gate positions and wiring routes, but they can take one of three actions to reduce chip size: logic minimization, partitioning, and folding. Traditional logic minimization, which attempts to reduce the number of Boolean functions, does not necessarily reduce PLA area, because the size of the PLA chip depends on the number of inputs, outputs, and minterms.

Instead, since the inputs and outputs are fixed by the chip function, PLA minimization algorithms attempt to reduce the number of minterms. Current software eliminates redundant, unused, and constant minterms and recognizes simple recoding possibilities when a minterm can be eliminated by OR-ing together existing minterms. No efficient minimization algorithms have been developed, so the goal is to find PLAs that are small enough, but do not entail excessive computer time.

Often a space or performance advantage can be gained by separating disjoint or nearly disjoints sets of equations—those with few or no terms in common—into distinct PLAs. Partitioning algorithms collect outputs that require the same minterms and compare the total area of the smaller PLAs thus generated with the area of one large PLA.

Folding algorithms split rows or columns in the PLA so they can be used by more than one signal. A common form of folding allows inputs and outputs at both the top and the bottom of the PLA, with two signals sharing the same AND-plane and OR-plane column. Some layout systems insert logic in front of the inputs to give precalculated terms to the PLA, thereby eliminating some PLA inputs and minterms. An important advantage of PLAs is that their straightforward point-to-point wiring avoids excessively long connections.

PLAs can be made as electrically programmable units in which unwanted connections are burned out by the user after the chip has been fabricated, just as in electrically programmable ROMs. Electrically programmable PLAs can be mass-produced like ROMs and later customized, thereby gaining even greater replication advantages than gate arrays. They are offered by such manufacturers as Monolithic Memories Inc., Sunnyvale, Calif.; Texas Instruments Inc., Dallas; and Signetics Corp., Sunnyvale.

More commonly, though, PLAs are included as parts of larger designs, because of their rectangular shapes. PLAs are very good for functions with inputs numbering in the dozens that require complex operations on those inputs. PLAs are inefficient at handling very simple functions. The function $C = A$ or B, for example, would take two input columns, two minterm rows, and one output column. Also, PLAs implement functions of many inputs and outputs poorly; chip size becomes excessive, and speed is adversely affected by long wiring paths.

Knowing what to look for

Designers who have experience with several processors develop a generalized mental model of a processor. When called on to implement a processor, they use the mental model as the initial structure. Given the logic elements in the processor data path, the fields of the microcode that controls those elements, and the processor word size, the generation of the implementation is routine.

A program that embodies this knowledge is called a standard floor-plan system. Floor plan refers to the overall structure, which is predefined with open slots like empty rooms to be filled as the user sees fit. A standard floor-plan system may produce a layout as efficient as a human's from a very abstract description of a chip. For this reason, such systems are sometimes called silicon compilers.

Researchers at the California Institute of Technology, Pasadena, have developed a standard floor-plan program they call Bristle Blocks, after a toy consisting of modules that can be joined in complicated shapes by meshing bristles. Bristle Blocks is a system for constructing a microprocessor data path—the calculation portion of a processor, which includes registers, arithmetic-and-logic units (ALUs), and shifters on a shared bus. The control portion of the microprocessor, including the microcode and the microsequencer, must be laid out by other means (a PLA, for example).

The Bristle Blocks data path consists of data-processing elements strung along two buses. A processing element is defined as a 1-bit slice of a particular processor function—for example, a shifter, register, I/O port, or an ALU. The elements are stacked vertically to form the complete functional unit. Functional units are strung horizontally along the data buses [Fig. 5]. Externally supplied microcode enters at the bottom, and the fields required by each data-path element are decoded from the microcode and supplied to the core from the bottom.

The elements are parameterized cells; they are defined by a program capable of laying out elements having the required parameters, rather than by the geometrical representation of a functional element, as in standard cell systems. Because the core elements are parameterized, they can be used in various situations for diverse chips.

A designer gives Bristle Blocks the width of a data path in bits, the kinds of elements in the core, the microcode, and the microcode conditions for each element that cause that element

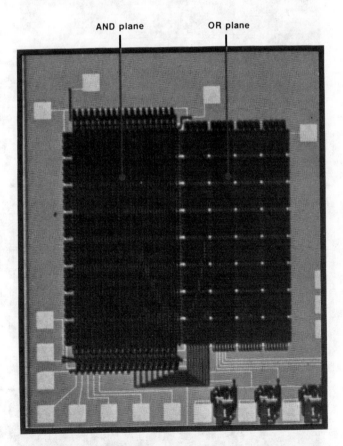

[4] Programmed logic array built at Caltech contains AND plane and OR plane. Both planes are made up of NOR gates, so the input port inverts inputs and the output port inverts outputs, resulting in AND-OR combinations of signals. Feedback loops linking the output and input ports of the chip appear at bottom.

to perform its operation. With that information, the Bristle Blocks system calls each of the core element programs, supplying the parameters to generate the chip layout.

Construction of a data path proceeds in two phases: query and layout. A query algorithm asks the core elements selected by the user for their minimum height and power consumption. The algorithm sums the power consumption to determine the width of power and ground lines. Then it positions the core elements horizontally in the order specified in the input. The algorithm gives core element programs instructions on where to connect the power, ground, and buses. These conventions are determined from the largest minimum size constraint acquired in the query phase. Small elements stretch to make the connection, lengthening vertical wires inside the element as necessary to reach the horizontal bus [Fig. 6].

Because of stretching, there is no need for routing between core elements, and so multiwire routing channels are unnecessary. The speed of the resulting data path is improved, since the connections between elements are shorter. Since each element is given its bit position in the data path, carry chain buffering or carry look-ahead for the ALU can readily be inserted by the program at the appropriate bit positions.

The control signals for each core element are supplied by the externally generated microcode. The proper microcode signal for

each input is routed from the pads along the bottom of the chip through a simple decoding array that resembles one plane of the PLA. The decoder is made as large as necessary to generate the signals required by the core elements. The decoded signals are routed to the data-path elements by means of a "river route," a simple route between parallel sets of connectors. The system places the decoder section below the routing area, places bonding pads on the chip, and connects them to the microcode decoder and to the data-path I/O ports.

Bristle Blocks implements processor data paths using no more than 10-percent more area—and sometimes even less area—than hand layout. The routing area, including routing to pads and the area lost by stretching core elements, is typically around 20 percent of the total area. Routing is virtually nonexistent inside the core.

No commercial data-path chips have been produced yet, but Bristle Blocks has been used to lay out 8-, 12-, and 16-bit data paths. Also, IBM and Bell laboratories are developing data-path systems of their own.

Most optimizations of standard floor-plan systems can be implemented as improvements in the core elements, rather than changes in the floor plan itself. With one floor-plan–optimization algorithm, data-path elements can trade off width for length, and the algorithm can find the combination of width and

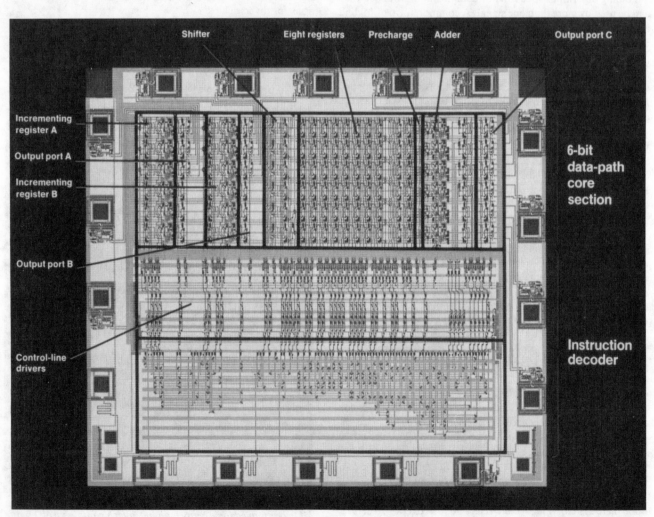

[5] A standard floor-plan program developed at the California Institute of Technology is known as Bristle Blocks, after the popular toy. This recently completed Bristle Blocks layout, a "stock market predictor," is being built as a demonstration. It analyzes a stream of 6-bit input numbers to detect trends in real time. The diagram combines NMOS mask layers: for example, one for metal wiring, another for polycrystalline silicon, and another for diffused areas.

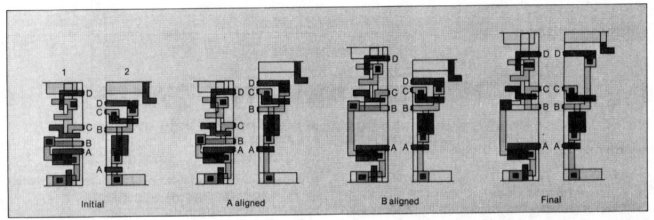

[6] *Cell stretching is used when two cells in a data path whose connectors are not at the same vertical positions must abut. To avoid generating wires for the interconnections, the Bristle Blocks software converts such cells into cells that can abut directly. For example, to align the A connectors in cells 1 and 2 at left, the system must increase the distance between the bottom of cell 2 and connector A. Accordingly, the layout system stretches cell 2 as shown in the center left diagram. It then stretches cell 1 as shown at center right to align the B connectors. The stretching process continues until all corresponding connectors have the same vertical position, at which stage the connections are made by merely abutting the cells.*

length that leads to the smallest chip.

Standard floor-plan layout makes a powerful ally of PLA layout; one produces processors, the other controllers. Together they produce an automatically laid out microcomputer, complete except for memory, either on multiple chips or, recently, on the same chip.

Because some of the data-path elements stretch when they are assembled, there is no good control of an element's electrical properties. Some designers consider this cause for alarm, but stretching has no more serious effect than the routing it replaces. Besides, the electrical properties of a cell can be estimated as a function of the stretching.

A more serious drawback of standard floor-plan systems is their limited applicability. Bristle Blocks can implement only processor data paths and not general logic functions. Many logic operations can be forced into the data-path form, but the conversion can be difficult. However, limitations in applicability can be cured by development of additional special floor plans.

The goals of research in automated layout are to produce tools that can implement any function very quickly, to implement the function as well as a human can, and to get to market as quickly as possible. Toward these ends, much work is going into better general placement and routing techniques, especially for gate arrays, which have the advantage of low fabrication cost. Better medium-scale macros are being developed for standard cell systems, and parameterized cells such as those used in Bristle Blocks, may make for more generally useful standard cells. New floor plan definitions will allow standard floor-plan systems to implement more chips efficiently.

Composite layout systems will also help by allowing designers to implement each function on a chip with the layout tool that makes the best design. Hybrid layout systems eventually may generate paths with a standard floor-plan system, state machines with PLAs, and general logic with a place-and-route system. The latter would allow the system to implement general functions; inefficiencies would be limited to a small part of the chip.

To probe further

Many engineering schools offer courses on LSI and VLSI circuit design, but they usually touch only lightly on automated design tools. A better source of up-to-date, detailed information is the yearly Design Automation Conference, sponsored by the IEEE and next scheduled for June 14–16 in Las Vegas, Nev. Contact Harry Hayman, P.O. Box 639, Silver Spring, Md. 20901. Phone 301-589-3386 for further information.

A new publication, the *IEEE Transactions on Computer-Aided Design*, features "original contributions and tutorial expositions relating to the design, development, integration, and application of computer aids for the design of integrated circuits and systems," according to the editors. Vol. CAD-1, no. 1, was published last January.

For a tutorial article on methods of integrated-circuit design, including automated and hand layout techniques, see J. Tobias' "LSI/VLSI building blocks" in *Computer*, August 1981.

Several proceedings of the Design Automation Conference merit special attention. In those for the 13th conference (1976), G. Persky, O.N. Deutsch, and D.G. Schweiker describe the basic Bell Laboratories standard cell system in "LTX—a system for the directed automatic design of LSI circuits." Other papers by the same authors cover placement and routing of standard cell circuits. In the proceedings for the 14th conference (1977), K.A. Chen and others give an introduction to wiring in gate arrays and describe optimizations in "The chip layout problem: an automatic wiring procedure." The original paper on the Bristle Blocks system, "Bristle blocks: a silicon compiler," by D. Johannsen, is in the proceedings for the 16th conference (1979).

The March 1975 edition of the *IBM Journal of Research and Development* contains three papers on programmed logic arrays, including an introduction to the concept and a description of PLAs for a small system.

About the author

Stephen Trimberger (M) does research on integrated-circuit design systems at the California Institute of Technology in Pasadena, where he is working on his Ph.D. in computer science. His recent work includes defining an interchange format for symbolic layout data and research into methods for combining graphic and algorithmic design techniques. He was previously deputy director of Caltech's Silicon Structures Project, an industry-supported program in which researchers from Caltech and industry work side by side in developing new IC systems. Mr. Trimberger received a B.S. in engineering and applied science from Caltech in 1977 and an M.S. in computer science from the University of California at Irvine. ◆

VLSI

FAST ELECTRON-BEAM LITHOGRAPHY

High blanking speeds may make this new system a serious challenger in producing submicrometer ICs

For the first time, electron-beam lithography may become competitive with optical methods, the leading production process today for making integrated circuits. The step that could make this possible is an electron-beam lithography system developed at Hewlett-Packard that is potentially many times faster than previous such machines for making ICs through direct writing on wafers or generating high-precision masks.

The new system is the first to operate at a blanking rate of 300 megahertz. This is the rate at which the beam can be turned on and off to make IC patterns on a substrate by scanning the exposure field and writing a 1 (exposure) or 0 (no exposure) in appropriate picture elements, or pixels. The patterns are written in an electron-sensitive resist, where the beam induces cross-links between polymer chains (negative resist) or breaks bonds between polymers (positive resist). Cross-linked polymers are less soluble in a developer solution.

The fastest electron-beam systems in commercial use today, by contrast, are the Bell System EBES, which operates at 40 MHz [see box on p. 297], and the IBM EL-3, at 45 MHz.

The Hewlett-Packard system has a beam spot—corresponding to the smallest pixel that can be written—with a diameter that can be varied from 0.5 to 0.25 micrometer. These sizes are comparable to those of previous systems. However, the high speed, beam current, and accuracy of the new machine required the solution of unique design problems in five subsystems:

1. The electron-optical column, where it was necessary to minimize the enlargement of the beam spot caused by secondary effects of the high beam current
2. Blanking circuits capable of operating at more than 300 MHz
3. Circuits for scanning a sufficiently large exposure field (a portion of the total substrate to be exposed), so that the target wafer or mask is restaged a minimum number of times for scanning the remaining fields
4. The high-speed data processors needed to transform the streams of bits representing IC patterns into signals for controlling beam position and exposure
5. Improved circuit design, in conjunction with calibration techniques and dynamic corrections, to position the beam within 0.125 μm of any address over the entire writing area

The new system has, among other unique circuits, a beam deflector that uses electrostatic deflection, which is faster than state-of-the-art magnetic deflection circuits. The source of electrons is a field-emission cathode that provides a higher beam current than that of previous systems and at the same time allows the beam to be deflected over relatively large exposure fields.

Electron-beam lithography offers higher resolutions than optical lithography because it uses electrons (15 to 25 kiloelectronvolts) that have shorter wavelengths than light. Because the electron-beam spot is relatively large, the resolution is not limited by diffraction. However, fundamental limits are set by electron scattering in the substrate—causing unintentional partial exposure of adjacent pixels—as well as by the molecular structure of the resist itself.

Electron-beam systems have long excelled the widely used optical methods for making masks of the highest precision. Their main advantage is 10 to 100 times higher speed for complex chips.

The throughput for direct writing on wafers, however, is far lower for electron systems than for optical or X-ray systems. The scanning electron beam writes IC patterns serially, through raster or vector scanning, whereas the other systems can expose the entire pattern at once. But in recent years direct writing has been used to make such special products as microwave transistors as well as some custom logic or memory chips.

Electron-beam lithography machines are similar to electron microscopes. Electrons emitted by a cathode are accelerated by a high voltage gun and the resulting beam is focused onto the

At the console of HP's electron-beam lithography system, the operator faces the equipment's exposure end. The dome-shaped structure is the electron-beam column, and below that is the X-Y stage that holds the target. On the right, cassettes holding substrates go into a system that transports targets to the X-Y stage.

John C. Eidson   Hewlett-Packard

substrate by a system of magnetic lenses (Fig. 1).

The beam scans the substrate by means of voltages applied to electrodes that produce an electric field perpendicular to the beam axis. Blanking is accomplished by a similar electrode system that deflects the beam off the beam axis, where it is collected by an aperature.

The total time required to generate an IC pattern by stepping through N exposure fields is equal to N multiplied by the sum of three main terms: (1) the time needed to expose each field; (2) the time needed to restage the wafer or mask; and (3) the overhead time—equal to the computer dead time plus the total settling time, per field, for the digital-to-analog converter (DAC) in the deflector system. The DAC converts digital addresses into analog signals for positioning the beam on the substrate.

High beam current for high speed

The Hewlett-Packard system was designed for a beam current of 600 nanoamperes (Fig. 2). When the beam spot is 0.5 μm, the resulting beam density is 306 amperes per square centimeter, or

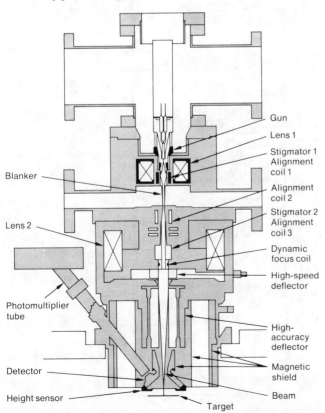

[1] The electron-beam column is a two-lens system using a field-emission cathode. The cathode, a very small, bright source of electrons, lets the required current be focused into a small spot while permitting large deflections of the electron beam. Both lenses are magnetic. The gun lens (1) produces a magnified crossover used for blanking the beam (turning it off by deflecting it to a blank target). The second lens (2) transfers the blank crossover to the target plane. Beam blanking is done with an electrostatic deflector. A wide-angle, high-accuracy deflector just below the final lens deflects the beam to the corner of the exposure field to initiate the scanning process. A high-speed deflector inside the final lens deflects the beam to the extremes of the raster-scan field. The column is aligned through three sets of magnetic deflection coils, in conjunction with the movable first lens. Backscattered electrons, which cause unwanted exposures, are detected by photomultipliers.

high enough to expose the fastest resist commercially available at the maximum data rate of 300 MHz. At that rate only 3.3 nanoseconds are needed to expose each pixel. With the 0.5-μm spot, the electron optics provide an exposure field five millimeters square that has 10^8 ($10^4 \times 10^4$) pixels.

Each five-millimeter-square exposure field is divided into an 80×80 array of blocks. Each block is 64 micrometers square and is subdivided into a 128-$\times$-128-pixel array. The octopole deflector positions the beam at the center of a block, and the block is then raster-scanned by a quadrupole deflector.

The data defining the IC pattern are sent from a special solid-state memory to the beam blanker in synchronism with the raster scan. After one raster is completed, the octopole deflector repositions the beam to the center of the next block. The process is repeated until the entire five-millimeter-square field is exposed. The substrate is then restaged, and the next field is exposed.

The heirarchy of pattern exposure is pixels within a block, blocks wtihin a "stripe" (up to 80 blocks), stripes within a "pass" (a row of up to 80 stripes), and passes within a chip.

In the octopole deflector, each plate is driven by a separate 16-bit DAC and amplifier with a settling time of 10 microseconds. The quadrupole deflector is driven by high-speed circuits, synchronized to the data stream, which generate a ramp in the X direction and stepping action in the Y direction.

Blanking is achieved by deflecting the beam onto a knife edge. The beam formed by electrons emitted from the cathode passes through a lens that focuses it near a knife edge in the beam-blanker region of the column. A potential applied to the blanker plates deflects the beam so that it strikes the edge. A very small deflection is needed to move the entire beam, since the beam that is focused near the edge is only a few micrometers in diameter. The blanking amplifier has rise and fall times of less than a nanosecond.

The hardest problem in designing the blanker was to guarantee that the exposure would fall in the proper place during the transition periods, when the beam switched. Moreover, a beam attenuation factor of at least 10^5 was needed so that exposure would not occur on the substrate during settling or off periods.

Tradeoffs in the optical column

It was not noticeably difficult to obtain the small beam spot, since commercial scanning electron microscopes have far smaller

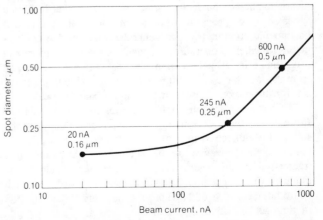

[2] A theoretical performance curve for the electron-beam column shows how the size of the beam spot increases with beam current. At the operating point of the system—600 nA and 0.5 μm—the current density is 306 A/cm², enough to expose the fastest commercially available resists at the system's full data rate of 300 MHz.

spot sizes. The problem was to achieve the small spot size along with the high beam intensity and the relatively large scan field. The solution required tradeoffs between the shortest possible column, the largest possible beam half-angle, optimal deflector performance, minimal spherical aberration, and dynamic focus and astigmatism.

The basis for making the tradeoffs was developed through a computer simulation of the effect of high beam currents on beam spot size. Earlier work with such columns had proved that high beam currents enlarged the spot considerably. However, that contradicted traditional theories indicating that the major influence on spot size—the effect of the space-charge cloud—was insignificant. Hewlett-Packard engineers calculated the beam enlargement more accurately through computer simulation and found that each electron acts on its neighbors, causing small angular deflections that build up along the length of the column. Larger beams are the result, although the electrons are sufficiently far apart so that no space charge cloud forms.

Two further major contributors to the size of the undeflected beam are spherical and chromatic aberrations. The enlargement effect caused by electron interactions decreases as the beam's half-angle increases, whereas spherical aberration increases as the third power of the beam's half-angle. The spot enlargement is also proportional to the length of the electron-optical column and the beam current. Tradeoff curves were derived from these relationships.

Aberration in lenses and deflectors

To produce a highly accurate system it was necessary to design electron optics with minimum distortion that would still be compatible with other system parameters. Two of the most critical components are the octopole deflector used to address blocks and the dynamic focus coil. The octopole can scan the five-millimeter field with only minimal dynamic corrections. Typical uncorrected field distortions are two micrometers. This distortion and astigmatism are corrected by applying the appropriate correction voltages to the octopole. The dynamic focus coil—a small, 20-turn winding centered on the upper part of the final lens—must also be free of uncorrectable aberrations. Along with the driving amplifier, it must have a fast settling time. The major settling problems are eddy currents in the surrounding conductors and, since the coil is outside the vacuum chamber, the time required for the field to penetrate the chamber wall.

System controlled by computer

Overall coordination of the system is controlled by a 16-bit HP 1000 computer. It is used as a process controller, in that it coordinates the activity of special-purpose hardware for beam and deflection control, data handling, and analog processing. Attached to the computer are various peripherals that include a system disk for program storage; a magnetic tape system for backup and program transfer from other machines; several terminals for entering operator commands; and four 124-megabyte disks for storing IC pattern data. The vast pattern storage stems from the fact that a direct bit map of a typical chip requires 10^8 bits for just a single five-millimeter-square exposure field.

The pattern is kept in a semiconductor memory capable of storing more than 150 million bits. This is more than enough storage for a direct bit map of $10^4 \times 10^4$ pixels. Specially formatted memory arrays store the pattern information until it is transferred to the beam. The array section is made of six modules, where each module has eight memory boards, and each board has eight rows of 24 chips. The chips are 16-kilobit MOS random-access memories.

At exposure time, data are transferred through error-correcting circuits into one of two units. Data in bit-map format are transferred directly into one of four block buffers. Block buffers hold 128×128 pixels of information, or what is needed to expose one block. Data in compressed format, adapted for mask generation, are first routed through a data decompresser and then into the block buffers.

Beam-blanker data synchronized

The block buffers provide temporary storage needed to synchronize the data that goes to the blanker. A synchronizing stage is necessary because the memory modules operate with fixed cycles and require refresh intervals, and data errors in transfer may require several retries before correct transmission occurs. The beam blanker, on the other hand, may operate at rates of several kilohertz to 300 MHz.

From the block buffers, the data are transferred through error-correcting circuits to the shifter system, which is a parallel-

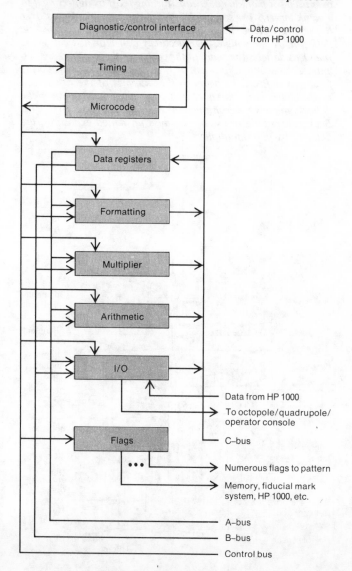

[3] "Hal," a high-speed processor implemented in emitter-coupled logic, controls the beam deflection. Calculations are done in real time by a microprogram that can execute a program of 512 steps. The microcode is generated by an assembler on the host computer—an HP 1000—and then downloaded into Hal. This allows flexibility in changing the beam-deflection protocol.

Diagnostic/control interface — Data/control from HP 1000

Timing

Microcode

Data registers

Formatting

Multiplier

Arithmetic

I/O

Flags

Data from HP 1000

To octopole/quadrupole/operator console

C–bus

Numerous flags to pattern

Memory, fiducial mark system, HP 1000, etc.

A–bus

B–bus

Control bus

to-series converter. To save space in memory, there is provision for skipping or filling empty or full blocks.

The shifter system can transmit data to the blanker at rates up to 300 MHz. Shifter control is not implemented with the normal system of combinatorial logic but rather through control signals generated by high-speed shift registers. Four signals are needed to control the data shifter and to synchronize data transfer: (1) a signal specifying the state of the main data shifter, commanding it either to load or shift data; (2) a ramp-reset signal, to indicate the start of a new scanning cycle in the raster generator; (3) a gating signal, to allow loading of data from the pattern memory into a temporary register before it is transferred to the main data shifter; and (4) a master signal, to control the state of all the control shifters. The two possible states for the master signal are to load data from a register associated with each shifter or to shift the data.

Hal does calculations

A special-purpose high-speed processor dubbed Hal, separate from the HP 1000, does the numerous calculations to set the voltages on the octopole plates block by block, in real time. Hal is implemented with emitter-coupled logic and is microprogrammed to execute a special program of 512 steps. In addition to microcode storage registers, the processor has 128 32-bit registers for arithmetic.

The microcode for Hal is generated in the HP 1000 and downloaded into Hal. This allows greater flexibility in changing the beam-deflection protocol.

Hal is built around several buses (Fig. 3). The first is the operation-code bus. When the microcode memory places an operation code on the bus, the code is transmitted to all the processor's printed-circuit boards. Each board is designed to execute different instructions. A board that receives an operation code and is free to execute the operation does so, and it then signals the control system that it is finished. This architecture allows adding of new instructions or modifying of previous ones simply by implementing the changes on a board that may be inserted into the system. Neither the control system nor the timing have to be modified, since the boards operate asynchronously.

The Hal instruction set now includes add, subtract, multiply,

VLSI lithography at the crossroads

As integrated-circuit makers push toward submicrometer devices, they may need to rethink the conventional wisdom concerning which lithographic technology will dominate production lines in the 1980s.

Until several months ago, the conventional wisdom was expressed in the following prediction:

Electron-beam systems that can pattern 0.25-micrometer to 1.5-micrometer lines will be used increasingly for making chips by direct writing on wafers. But those systems will not be widely used until the late 1980s, when they will probably become more economical than optical lithography—the dominant technology today—and optical methods have reached their limiting resolution of 0.7 μm to 0.8 μm. X-ray lithography will not be competitive in the foreseeable future, since the equipment is unreliable and too expensive, and X-ray masks are fragile and easily broken, even with moderate use.

The trouble with the prediction is that X-ray technology surged ahead unexpectedly when Bell Laboratories engineers reported a new X-ray system with a potentially higher production throughput than optical or electron-beam systems, as well as the ability to make the smallest MOS field-effect transistors ever reported—0.3 μm to 0.4 μm (see M. Lepselter, "X-ray lithography breaks the submicrometer barrier," *Spectrum*, May 1981, pp. 26–29). The Bell engineers also indicated that they had developed a more durable mask made of boron nitride, instead of the usual silicon compound or mylar.

The conventional wisdom may yet prove correct, however, if two future conditions are met: (1) the semiconductor industry finds significant markets for ICs with geometries smaller than 0.8 μm; and (2) electron-beam systems prove to be more economical than X-ray systems on production lines.

The military is at this point the only certain market. The VHSIC (Very High Speed Integrated Circuits) program of the Department of Defense envisions the need for 1.5-μm-to 0.8-μm geometries by the late 1980s, on chips with throughputs of billions of instructions per second. However, commercial IC makers may be satisfied at that future time with 1-μm to 1.5-μm production chips, within the range of optical methods.

IBM and TI challenges Hewlett-Packard

Electron-beam systems are made now by many firms, either for their own use or for the market. These include Texas Instruments, the Extrion Division of Varian, Perkin-Elmer (through its subsidiary, Etec), Bell Labs, IBM, Phillips, Cambridge Instruments, Thomson CSF, Electron Beam Microfabrication, Hughes, and, most recently, Hewlett-Packard.

The systems used most widely today are the EBES (developed by Bell Labs, but licensed for manufacture by Extrion and Etec) and the IBM EL-2. The new Hewlett-Packard system is faster than previous systems for direct writing on wafers, but it is rivaled by two other new systems, the IBM EL-3 and the Texas Instruments EBM-5. The three systems have roughly comparable throughputs of from 20 to 45 wafer levels per hour for a 2-μm geometry and 10 to 20 wafer levels per hour for a 1.5-μm geometry (7 to 10 wafer levels are exposed in making a typical chip). At submicrometer geometries, however, the HP system has a higher throughput—10 wafer levels per hour—according to Frank Ura, director of that company's electron-beam system project. The EMB-5 has been used to make a 16-microprocessor with a 1.5-μm geometry and I^{2}L circuits and a 4-kilobit static RAM.

Whereas the Hewlett-Packard system has an electron beam with a fixed spot size and uses a raster scanning technique, the IBM system has a variably shaped beam and uses both vector scanning (in subfields) and raster scanning. The EBM-5 has a fixed spot and vector scanning.

"The variably shaped beam does not require a high blanking rate because the system is capable of exposing many pixels at once," notes Richard D. Moore, manager of electron-beam lithography at IBM's General Technology Divison in East Fishkill, N.Y. "We also use a high-current-density beam, so we can use a resist that is 10 times less sensitive than that used in other systems."

Bell Labs engineers, meanwhile, recently finished the design of a 500-megahertz second-generation EBES. Ironically, the microwave-speed MOS in the new EBES will be manufactured through Bell's new X-ray lithography system. That system is reported to have a potential throughput of 75 wafer levels per hour, compared with 40 levels per hour for current optical methods and 10 to 20 levels per hour for previous electron-beam systems. Figures supplied by Bell indicate that the X-ray system is also far cheaper: $225 000 for the X-ray exposure system, compared with $1.5 million to $3 million for the electron-beam exposure system.

Various companies have been attempting to develop an electron projection system that, in theory, would be faster than any current scanning process. A large beam would perform parallel exposure of a large area, if not all, of the wafer. In the 1:1 projection system developed by Westinghouse, a quartz mask patterned with cesium iodide is placed pattern down on the wafer; ultraviolet radiation is then shone on the back of the quartz substrate to produce photoelectrons in the pattern (cathode).

—Robert Bernhard

and a variety of logical operations and format conversions, as well as special handshakes and flags. The flags are used, for example, to signal the pattern memory to dump a block of data, to command circuitry to generate pulses of specified width, or to signal Hal to execute specified subroutines or coordinate data transfers to the HP 1000.

Compressed format is more efficient

The average feature size for most IC patterns is much larger than the pixel, so it is more efficient to store patterns in a compressed form. In this form, termed EBIC (Electron Beam Internal Compressed), patterns are represented by sets of rectangles, which are converted in real time into bit streams that control beam exposure.

EBIC rectangles are described by integral numbers of pixels. The compression occurs within stripes, and EBIC rectangles are restricted so their sides are parallel to the X axis. Each rectangle is confined within a single stripe, and adjacent rectangles may not overlap.

As pattern geometries become finer, however, compressed format becomes less advantageous than a pure bit-map representation. The crossover point occurs at about 2.4 million compressed format rectangles in a 9984-$\times$-9984-pixel octopole field. This corresponds to a checkerboard where each square is 4.6 pixels on a side.

Patterns are stored initially on magnetic tape as a series of rectangles—or "flashes"—of varying location, width, length, and rotation. The flashes are then broken down, or "clipped," into rectangles or trapezoids contained within stripes. Each rectangle or trapezoid is placed in a bin according to its stripe and pass. Each bin has an internal memory buffer, and when the buffer for a stripe is full, its contents are transferred to a disk file. The file content is then converted into EBIC form.

Proximity effects corrected

The proximity effect is the unwanted exposure of resist caused by backscattering of electrons in the resist and from the substrate beneath the resist. This leads to pattern features differing from those designed and is a major limitation to the fabrication of high-resolution devices by electron-beam lithography. Two general methods have been used previously to limit the proximity effect; both involve preprocessing the input data and modifying the dose at exposure time. However, the HP system uses a method without preprocessing that achieves a substantial reduction in proximity effects.

The most widely used earlier method employs preprocessing in vector scan systems. In the second method using preprocessing, beam scans are added or subtracted to achieve a uniform dose.

The HP method of correcting is based on special resist modifications that minimize the effects of backscattered electrons as well as reduce their number. Proximity effects are further reduced by using a small beam spot and multilayer resists.

Adaptive filters to register patterns

Index (fiducial) marks on substrates must be quickly and accurately detected to attain high thoughputs in pattern registration and equipment calibration. This is done by detecting and processing the energy waveform of electrons that are backscattered by the index mark and its substrate as the electron beam is scanned across the substrate. (The mark is made of two strips in a '+' pattern.) The problem, therefore, is to detect a partially known signal in the presence of additive noise caused by a layer of resist covering the mark, or poor contrast between the mark and its surroundings.

The problem is solved by making the desired energy waveform an odd or even function. (An odd function, defined as $Y(-X) = -Y(X)$, is symmetric about the origin of coordinates, or the center of the '+'. An even function, $Y(-X) = Y(X)$, is symmetric about the Y axis.) Adaptive matched filters are then used to detect the even or odd signal embedded in the noise. When the electron beam is at the center of the '+', the detector output is maximum for the even function, but minimum for the odd function.

R&D experiments using the HP electron beam

Although the HP machine is still in the research and development laboratory, in the final stages of development, a number of interesting results have been obtained.

One of the first applications was to produce high-resolution Surface-Acoustic-Wave-Resonator devices (SAWR) in cooperation with HP's Applied Physics Lab. Two types of devices were made, one with critical dimensions of 500 nanometers and the other with 300 nm. The operating frequencies were 1.6 GHz and 2.6 GHz.

For further reading

R.K. Watts discusses extensively all forms of advanced lithography in *Very Large Scale Integration,* D.F. Barbe, *ed.,* Springer-Verlag, N.Y., 1980, pp. 42–88. Most significant for those interested in comparing optical, electron-beam, and X-ray lithography are the sections on accuracy and resolution, as these are affected by wafer throughput as well as complexity (number of wafer levels that must be exposed per chip). A good comparison appears on pp. 67–73 of the relative advantages of raster-scan and vector-scan systems. The X-ray lithography discussion is somewhat out of date since the development of a radically new X-ray system by Bell Labs.

A complete description of the Hewlett-Packard system is found in the *Hewlett-Packard Journal,* May 1981, Vol. 32, pp. 3–34, seven articles by 20 members of the project team.

Details of the IBM EL-3 may be obtained from Richard D. Moore, IBM General Technology Division, East Fishkill, N.Y. The differences between the EL-3 and HP systems are not readily translatable into comparisons of throughputs. Blanking speed alone is a significant indicator of the speed of a raster scanning system, whereas it is less significant for systems, such as the EL-3, which have a variably shaped beam and, in some measure, vector scanning. The larger the region of solidly exposed substrate, the more efficient the EL-3.

A twist on electron-beam systems—internal testing of microprocessor chips using electron-beam techniques—is described by E. Wolfgang *et al* in *IEEE International Conference on Circuits and Computers, 1980,* Vol. 1., pp. 548–51. The basic principle is that with a modified scanning electron microscope in the voltage-contrast operating mode, the internal execution of instructions in microprocessors can be visualized. Waveform measurements at various internal nodes are then used to determine the instruction execution speed.

About the authors

John C. Eidson (M) is project manager for electron-beam electronics at Hewlett-Packard, where he has been since 1972, contributing to the design of an optical spectrometer and the electron-beam system. He received B.S. and M.S. degrees in electrical engineering from Michigan State University in 1958 and 1960 and a Ph.D. degree from Stanford University in 1964. Before joining HP, he taught electronics and electromagnetic theory at Stanford University. He is the author of eight papers. ◆

VLSI

X-RAY LITHOGRAPHY BREAKS THE SUBMICROMETER BARRIER

A new X-ray lithography system allowed Bell Labs engineers to make the smallest, fastest MOSFETs yet reported

Device engineers at Bell Labs have used a new X-ray system to make circuits with MOSFETs that are among the smallest and fastest digital devices ever reported. The MOSFETs have channel lengths of 0.3 to 0.4 micrometers, switching speeds of 30 to 75 picoseconds, and speed-power products of 5 femtojoules (5×10^{-15} Ws) to 50 femtojoules.

The X-ray system is smaller, less expensive, and more reliable than previous X-ray systems, and it also has a higher throughput—potentially 75 wafers per hour (see table). It uses an exposure power of 4.5 kW, compared to the 20 to 40 kW in other systems. The key to a short exposure time with a low power source is the use of a novel resist that is more radiation-sensitive than conventional resists. Another advantage of the system is exceptional linewidth control—better than 0.1 micrometer across the wafer.

A further benefit of this new generation of processing technology is the apparent ability to break the cycle of ever-increasing capital costs burdening the manufacturers. The cost predictions make it an attractive contender in the burgeoning market for cheaper lithographic systems.

Most commercially available MOS ICs today have gate lengths down to 2 or 3 micrometers, and they are made primarily through optical lithography; however, optical patterning does not have high-enough resolution in commercial design to break through the micrometer barrier. When higher resolution is required and line widths in the IC are shrunk to dimensions comparable to the wavelength of the light used for exposure, the quality of the replicated pattern is degraded primarily by two effects: (1) diffraction at the pattern edges, and (2) reflection from various surfaces, causing interference fringes in the resist.

In contrast, X-ray printing using 4.36-angstrom wavelength radiation is far from any diffraction limit, and X-rays are not reflected from the surface because they strike it at a near-perpendicular angle.

X-ray system is more cost-effective

The cost-effectiveness of the Bell Labs X-ray system over other exposure systems is shown by comparing their respective figures of merit (see table). The figure is based on the wafer throughput (N), the first cost of the exposure system (C), and a factor relating to the clean-room space required (10 A). The figure of merit is inversely proportional to both C and A. The presumed resolution (R) is assumed to be an inverse-square term because linewidth depends on area. That is, the finer the design rule, the more devices may be placed on the chip.

The potential cost-effectiveness of the X-ray system, based on the assumed parameters, is two orders of magnitude higher than that for optical systems, and more than 10 times that for ad-

vanced electron-beam machines. Even allowing for large discrepancies in these assumptions, the X-ray system still appears to be an attractive approach to greatly reducing capital costs in the semiconductor industry.

The high resolution of the X-ray system stems primarily from the dependence of resolution on engineering design rather than on fundamental laws of optics. The fundamental limit for resolving an optical image, by contrast, is twice the wavelength of the radiation source. If one assumes an exposure wavelength of only 2500 angstroms (although 4360 angstroms is typical), the fundamental limit of the resolved image is 0.5 micrometer. However, the *useful* resolution would be reduced—about one micrometer in this example—after adjustments are made for scattering, reflection, and other factors.

Electron beams have equivalent wavelengths less than 1 angstrom, while the Bell Labs system uses X-rays with wavelengths of 4.36 angstroms. At these short wavelengths, diffraction is insignificant.

The useful resolution of the Bell Labs X-ray system is actually 0.25 micrometer. One reason for the limit is that the X-rays produce electrons in the resist that are emitted isotropically, with a lateral range of almost 1000 angstroms. Additional limits on the resolution are due to the dimensional instability of both the mask and wafer. However, previous workers have demonstrated that X-ray systems have a useful resolution of at least 0.1 micrometer. The choice of 0.25-micrometer resolution for the Bell Labs system—about 2.5 times the lower limit—seems to be a reasonable one at this time.

Conical, stationary target—source of X rays

When an accelerated electron beam strikes a metal anode, X rays are generated within the metal. In Bell Labs' new system, a 25-kV, 4.5-kW electron beam is generated by a ring electron gun, and this is focused into a palladium cone-anode (Fig. 1). This geometry allows a large increase in absorbed power, compared with the power absorbed by a flat surface.

While maintaining an equivalent spot size of 2 to 3 mm, the whole cone length is available to act as a cooling surface. The power density to be dissipated is 10 to 15 kW/cm^2, and it is carried away by boiling water. This high-velocity stream carries the bubbles formed by nucleate boiling, preventing formation of a vapor barrier at the back of the cone.

Use of a stationary cone target has led to a marked improvement in reliability and freedom of vibration when compared with other typical sources. These other sources are high-power, water-cooled, flat targets that are rotated at high speed to dissipate the large amounts of power needed when less sensitive resists than those reported here are used.

The resist materials are a blend of chemicals called guest-host mixtures (Fig. 2). They contain a monomer (guest) that is bonded

Martin P. Lepselter   Bell Laboratories

(locked) to a polymer (host) upon exposure to X rays under open regions of the mask. Fixing, by heating in a vacuum, removes the unlocked monomers and results in a negative relief image.

The host polymer serves as the main X-ray absorber, the initiator of polymerization or locking reactions, and also as a container, or binder, for the monomer. The final pattern is developed in an oxygen plasma that has been excited in a radio-frequency glow-discharge apparatus. In this step, the unexposed regions are removed faster than the exposed regions, thus enhancing or intensifying the original negative relief image.

Dry plasma development (etching) avoids the resist swelling that commonly occurs with other solution development methods. Resolution is much better with dry-developed resists.

The polymer host must, of course, contain atoms with high absorption coefficients for X rays and must be easily removed in an oxygen plasma. Upon exposure, it must yield species that initiate efficient locking of the monomer. The monomer, on the other hand, should be locked into the polymer readily, should have moderate volatility, and should be resistant to plasma removal in the locked state.

A previously reported sample of this resist class contains 81 percent polymer component (2, 3-dichloro-1-propyl acrylate) and 19 percent N-vinyl carbazole, the monomer component. With it, 0.3-micrometer features have been printed in 0.3-micrometer-thick resist. This would normally be too thin a layer to cover the stepped surfaces encountered in modern silicon devices. The steps lead to thickness variations and, as a result, patterns would be underdeveloped in valleys when properly developed on hills.

To circumvent the problem of thin layers not covering undulations, multilayer resist technology is under development for the various proposed fine-line lithographic technologies. Only the top layer is sensitive to the exposure source, and a large choice of materials can be used for the lower layers.

Bell's X-ray technology uses a tri-level resist technique: an X-ray resist top layer, a very thin SiO_2 middle layer, and any of a variety of organic polymers for the bottom layer. The bottom layer may be relatively thick and serve to fill in the hills and valleys. The X-ray resist is deposited onto a flattened surface, allowing the use of layers as thin as 0.3 micrometer. The pattern transfer through the bottom layer is accomplished by anisotropic etching in a reactive-plasma etch station.

Other problems encountered during plasma development stem from the need to develop the resist uniformly over the entire wafer surface and to control accurately the endpoint of the development process. Good control of submicrometer patterning requires the development nonuniformity to be less than ± 200 angstroms. New resist compositions and processes have been developed for which the development nonuniformity is ± 100 angstroms. The materials require only 18-second exposure to X rays and are fully compatible with batch processing.

Since X rays cannot be simply focused, it is necessary to use a shadow mask to print the required features in the resist pattern.

The mask structure consists of a composite-material membrane secured to a rugged glass ring. X rays are strongly attenuated in the desired feature area by a gold absorber formed on the membrane.

The membrane is fabricated by deposition of sequential layers of boron nitride and polyimide onto a sacrificial silicon substrate. The boron nitride is formed by the reaction of ammonia

[1] The Bell X-ray printer is smaller and cheaper than previous X-ray printers (A). It uses a 4-kW electron beam focused on a stationary, cone-shaped palladium target (B) that relieves the maintenance and reliability problems associated with conventional rotating targets. The cone angle shrinks the size of the apparent source at the wafer—thus improving resolution while allowing incident electrons to be absorbed over a wider area.

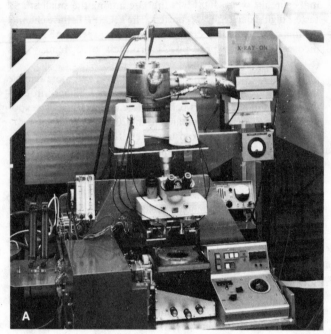

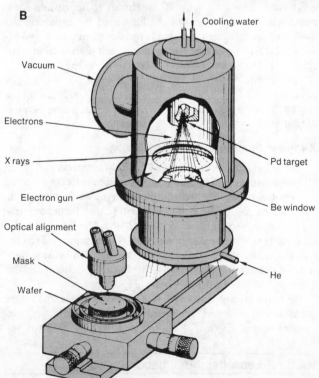

Comparison of lithographic technologies

	Optical S & R	Full Wafer X Ray	E-Beam
Useful resolution (R), micrometers	1.0	0.25	0.1
Throughput (N), wafer levels per hour	40	75	10
Exposure system cost (C), dollars	700 K	225 K	3 M
Clean room area (A), square feet per system	50	12	65
Figure of merit, $N/(C + 10 A)R^2$	33	3480	274

Silicon neck-and-neck with gallium arsenide

Two questions are raised by the newfound ability to build practical circuits with submicrometer MOSFETs that are among the smallest and fastest logic devices ever reported—faster even than the gallium arsenide MOSFETs that were previously the speediest state-of-the-art devices at room temperature.

Will the ability to mass produce the submicrometer MOSFETs in the near future discourage further development of gallium arsenide (GaAs) logic circuits?

Defense contractors have been developing GaAs for digital systems requiring higher data rates than most authorities believe silicon can handle—from one to five gigabits per second. Applications of GaAs logic have been slowed, however, by factors limiting the fabrication of GaAs LSI circuits. The new Bell devices, by contrast, are reported to be already suitable for LSI, as well as able to handle data rates of one to two gigabits per second.

Is there a flaw in the widely held belief that physical laws limit the miniaturization of MOSFETs to channel lengths approaching 0.25 to 0.2 micrometer?

The short-channel (submicrometer) MOSFETs made through Bell's new X-ray system have channel lengths of about 0.3 micrometer, with switching speeds of 30 to 50 ns, corresponding to speed-power products of 40 fj and 75 fj, respectively. Yet, they have the same threshold voltage characteristic as the long-channel (3- to 5-micrometer) devices that are the state-of-the-art for silicon ICs. They exhibit none of the breakdown effects that conventional theory predicts will occur as channels approach the limiting range—including punchthrough and tunneling of electrons from the channel to the gate. Indeed, Bell investigators report that their scaling-down model allows one to choose optimal device parameters to preserve long-channel behavior down to 0.1 micrometer channel length.

GaAs has room for improvement

The list of companies that have been developing GaAs logic technology includes Westinghouse Research and Development Center in Pittsburgh, Pa., Bell Labs in Murray Hill, N.J., and various California-based firms: Rockwell International Science Center in Thousand Oaks, Hughes Research Laboratories in Malibu, Lockheed Microelectronics in Sunnyvale, TRW Defense and Space Systems Group in Redondo Beach, and Hewlitt-Packard in Santa Rosa.

Most GaAs logic circuits are now being developed for such military applications as microwave-speed multipliers, A/D converters, memories, fast-Fourier-transform processors, frequency dividers, and statistical correlators in systems for data-acquisition or image processing. State-of-the art digital ICs made with depletion-mode MESFETs and Scotty diodes have channels of 1.1 micrometers and switching speeds of 75 to 100 ps. The ICs are currently at the 100 to 1000 gate level of complexity, whereas silicon is capable of at least 5000-gate bipolar ICs and 10 000-gate MOS ICs.

Various studies indicate, however, that GaAs MESFET circuits are inherently several times faster than their silicon counterparts. Groups developing GaAs explain that its higher speed stems primarily from a five to eight times higher electron mobility than silicon. A further advantage of the GaAs device is that it is fabricated on a semi-insulating Cr-doped GaAs substrate with a much smaller parasitic ground capacitance. The smaller capacitance results in higher transconductance, and thus a larger available current drive. The larger current drive and lower parasitic capacitance allow potentially higher switching speed, since circuit capacitances can be charged and discharged more quickly.

GaAs designers expect to improve the state of the art later this year by introducing 1 micrometer depletion devices with 60 ps switching speed and speed-power product of 35 fj. Researchers at Fujitsu Laboratories in Japan report 0.6 micrometer depletion devices with 30 ps speed. U.S. defense labs have similar devices, and they expect to achieve switching speeds of 10 to 20 ps within several years, by shrinking channels to 0.5 to 0.25 micrometer. A combination of submicrometer geometry and low temperature (but well above cryogenic) could result in speeds comparable to Josephson junction devices.

State of the art GaAs devices, in summary, are not yet comparable in size to Bell's MOSFETs. GaAs designers point out that, considering the current size discrepancy, GaAs now has a speed advantage of about two.

LSI poses problems

The major problems in achieving LSI with GaAs devices occur in the first processing step, where the active channel is formed by a thin n-type layer on the semi-insulating GaAs substrate. The layer—0.1 to 0.3 micrometer thick, with a doping density of $10^{17}/cm^3$—must be highly uniform over the wafer to ensure that both drain current and pinchoff voltage are uniform from one device to another. However, the various techniques now available for fabricating the layer are either too expensive, while yielding poor results, or still unproved.

Until recently, the most widely used method involved epitaxial formation of the layer in the vapor or liquid phase on the Cr-doped substrate. GaAs designers predict better results in the future with a new, ion-implantation method. However, two hurdles must be overcome: (1) the combined densities of the Cr doping and material impurities reduces the electron mobility in the channels formed by ion implantation; and (2) Cr accumulates near the surface during annealing, thus skewing the doping profile and also interfering with the ohmic contacts that are made later to the channel. The depletion of Cr from the region under the surface also results in nonuniformity of the pinchoff voltage across the wafer.

Many groups are investigating a promising new approach, where the semi-insulating substrate can be grown with much less Cr, and perhaps an order of magnitude fewer impurities. The new technique is a modification of the standard Czochralski method, where the crystal is grown while encapsulated in liquid.

Even if the fabrication problems are solved, however, GaAs may never achieve MOS levels of integration because of the further barrier of power dissipation. The barrier is already apparent in circuits made with Schottky diode FET logic (SDFL), which is the prime candidate for GaAs LSI. State of the art ICs, such as the 8-by-8 multiplier introduced recently by Rockwell International, have 1000 gates and dissipate 2.2 W. SDFL may, therefore, be infeasible for LSI beyond 5000 gates.

One alternative to SDFL—buffered depletion-mode FETs—is faster than SDFL, but is already limited by power dissipation to about 20 gates. The only remaining possibility now—enhancement-mode FET logic—is far slower per fanout than SDFL.

—*Robert Bernhard*

and diborane in a suitable chemical vapor deposition. The polyimide film is spun on top of the boron nitride from a liquid source, and it is used to cover small defects. This membrane is highly transparent to the 4.36-angstrom characteristic *Pd* radiation, with an attenuation of only 1.2 dB (75 percent transmission).

The absorption pattern is formed in a two-layer vacuum-deposited film of tantalum-gold. The desired silicon integrated-circuit features are formed in the gold film by plasma etching that uses a resist mask written by an electron beam.

Registration between successive lithographic-mask levels is required during the process sequence in device fabrication. This is accomplished by optical alignment, with matching patterns used between the silicon wafer and the X-ray mask. Measurements of mask dimensional stability indicate that the average pattern distortion is less than 0.1 micrometer.

In the early days of semiconductor technology, before better lithographic tools became available, designers merely used finer line widths for their devices and left the remaining processing steps the same. However, as 10-micrometer line widths were approached, it was recognized that this procedure would no longer work well. Most IC designers adopted a scaling law under which all device parameters were changed by some predetermined power of the line-width reduction factor. This procedure works well for line widths down to approximately 3 micrometers, the current production state of the art. For channel lengths possible with this dimension, short-channel effects occur when the source-to-drain current is no longer effectively controlled uniquely by the gate voltage. These effects were investigated by Bell Labs.

An advanced two-dimensional computer modeling scheme was developed to simulate both the processing steps and electrical behavior of the devices, and the calculations were performed on a Cray-1 computer. The results agree very well with the experimental devices and have been used to obtain a formula that relates structure and voltage levels with long-channel behavior in a manner more general than the strict scaling law. The formula may be applied in cases where oxide thicknesses are as thin as 0.01 micrometer, junction depths as shallow as 0.1 micrometer and channel lengths as short as 0.2 micrometer. This design tool now allows designers to optimize processing and device performance trade-offs with much more flexibility than before and with confidence that the results will be viable.

Among the ICs fabricated and tested with the new design techniques and X-ray lithography were ring oscillators. A ring oscillator, widely used for testing propagation delay and power dissipation and comparing different devices and technologies, is a convenient test circuit for high-speed technologies, since it provides its own signal source. It is a chain of an odd number of inverter gates, N, connected in a ring so that the frequency of oscillation, f, depends on the intrinsic propagation delay as $f = 1/2Nt$. The results on devices having channel lengths of 0.3 to 0.4 micrometer were switching speeds ranging from 75 ps at a power-delay product of 5 femtojoules to 30 ps at 40 femtojoules.

On the same chip a divide-by-16 counter, in which the high-speed input gates had a fanout of three, was run at a clock rate of 2.5 GHz. This result was consistent with the ring oscillator results.

A recently designed analog-to-digital converter was operated at clock rates up to 750 MHz. The 4-V, square-wave output had a rise time of less than 0.25 ns into a 25-ohm load.

For further reading

"X-ray lithography source using a stationary solid Pd target," by J.R. Maldonado *et al*, *Journal of Vacuum Science Technology*, Vol. 16, Nov./Dec. 1979, pp. 1942-1945. This short paper describes the basic X-ray source that was developed at Bell Labs to make the circuits reported by Mr. Lepselter. The description includes design considerations of the anode, the electron gun and the X-ray target source, and the cooling system.

"Plasma developed X-ray resists," by G.N. Taylor and T.M. Wolf, *Journal of the Electrochemical Society*, Vol. 127, Dec. 1980, pp. 2665-2674. The article describes in detail both the resist that optimized X-ray sensitivity and the plasma development method using an oxygen plasma.

"Boron nitride mask structure for X-ray lithography," by D. Maydan *et al*, *Journal of Vacuum Science Technology*, Vol. 16, Nov./Dec. 1979, pp. 1959-1961. The properties of the new boron nitride mask structure for X-ray lithography are discussed. The mask is especially noteworthy because is does not suffer excessive mask distortion as do the widely used Kapton masks.

About the author

M. P. Lepselter (F) has worked on semiconductor device development since joining Bell Telephone Laboratories in 1957. He holds over 50 patents on silicon device technology, including beam lead integrated circuits; structure, metallurgy, and process; platinum silicide Schottky diodes; ion-implanted semiconductor devices; and the shallow-junction contacts developed for the Telestar solar cells currently in use on many satellites. He is presently director of the Advanced LSI Development Laboratory at Murray Hill, N.J., following four years as director of the Bipolar Device Laboratory at Allentown, Pa., and four years as director of the MOS Integrated Circuit Laboratory at Murray Hill.

He has been awarded the Daniel C. Hughes Jr. Memorial Award by ISHM. He was awarded the IEEE Jack A. Morton Award in December 1979.   ◆

This work is the result of the efforts of many members of the Advanced LSI Development Laboratory and the Chemical Research Laboratory of Bell Laboratories. All have made significant contributions.

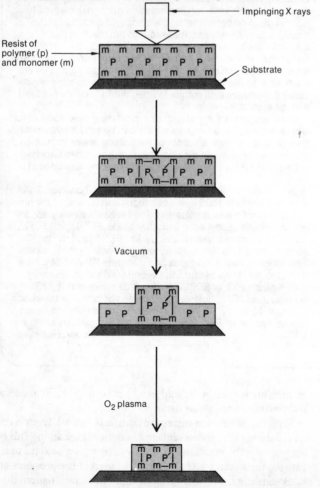

[2] The high efficiency of the X-ray system stems from the use of a novel resist that is more sensitive than other resists to the system's main spectral line at 4.36 angstroms. The resist material contains a monomer (guest) that is bonded to a polymer (host) upon exposure to X rays through windows in the mask. Heating in a vacuum removes the unbonded monomers and results in a negative relief image. The final pattern is developed in an oxygen plasma that removes unexposed regions faster than exposed ones, thus enhancing the original relief.

Impinging X rays

Resist of polymer (p) and monomer (m)

Substrate

Vacuum

O_2 plasma

Negative tone

RETHINKING THE 256-KB RAM

Creativity in the factory may be more important than innovation in product design

Now that the Japanese dominate the market for 64-K dynamic random-access memories, will they also crowd out United States competitors in the market for 256-kilobit RAMs? At least two Japanese companies—Hitachi Ltd. and Fujitsu Ltd., both in Tokyo—will start commercial production of 256-kb chips as soon as 1983, two years earlier than most industry observers had predicted and at least one year earlier than U.S. merchant companies. Hitachi is already the leading supplier of 64-K chips, with 40 percent of the international market, while Fujitsu ranks second with 20 percent of the market, according to Dataquest Inc., market researchers in Cupertino, Calif.

But do these first efforts guarantee Japanese leadership in the 256-kb field? Not necessarily.

The problems with the chips are such that production-line experience, once thought to be the forte of the U.S. semiconductor makers, may be more important than simply being first in the marketplace. And, though the Japanese appear to be in a position to gain the most experience, in time the learning curve on the production line tends to flatten for all competitors, leaving them on an even footing. Moreover, it is widely accepted in the industry that no single group of RAM makers will ever be able to meet the ever-expanding market for RAMs, so that even giant producers will not dominate for long as other companies gain increased production experience. As Andrew G. Varadi, vice president of National Semiconductor Corp. in Cupertino, Calif., puts it, the current scene is "just a healthy competitive challenge."

Some of the key manufacturing issues, at any rate, are the tightly related questions of chip yield, chip size, and the merits of redundancy for the 256-kb part. (Yield is the percentage of chips that pass inspection at a given stage of production, beginning with "probe" yield, when the chips are still on the wafer, and ending with the yield after final testing of packaged chips.) The most significant future problem for U.S. semiconductor makers may lie in achieving the economic yields that would allow them to enter the market on schedule [Fig. 1].

A rule of thumb is that a new-generation chip is not introduced until its yield is at least 10 percent; by that time, the yield of the previous generation—in this case the 64-K chip—should be about 50 percent, representing final product maturity. Industry consultants observe that typical yields for U.S. 64-K chips are now 25 to 30 percent. No Japanese figures are available.

Chip size and redundancy debated

Whereas RAM makers try to make the smallest chip possible for a given density—since larger chips have more defects that may render them unusable—256-kb RAM makers in the U.S. will use chips that are 30 to 60 percent larger than typical 64-K chips. The memory cells will be correspondingly larger and thus enhance stored charge and improve noise immunity. Present plans call for chips of 40 to 50 millimeters squared, with the memory cells 70 to 100 micrometers squared. Some critics think this approach will not be cost-effective.

For U.S. companies to compete with the Japanese, these critics contend, 256-kb RAM chips should be no larger than 25 to 30 mm^2 and memory cells 30 to 50 μm^2.

"If our RAM designers go after the smaller cells and chips," one such critic said last February, during a panel discussion at the International Solid State Circuits Conference, "we'll get the novel approaches that will give us a product that stands out above the Japanese products."

Nevertheless, U.S. 256-kb RAM makers believe that the lower yields anticipated for larger chips can be compensated for by on-chip redundancy—or extra rows or columns of memory cells that can be switched in to replace bad cells. In a typical redundancy system, a new chip is tested and a "bit profile" is generated of good and bad cells. The profile identifies defective word and bit lines; defective lines are disabled either by a laser that burns open the links at the outputs of drivers or by blowing fuses electrically.

This type of redundancy, which has been used by IBM and Bell Laboratories, as well as by Intel, Inmos, and Mostek in their second-generation 64-K RAMs, is reported to multiply chip yields by a factor of from 3 to 10.

However, debate still goes on over the merits of redundancy, whether in 64-K or 256-kb RAMs. Some of the debated penalties of redundancy include higher testing costs, slower speed (though access time may be increased by only 3 nanoseconds in some designs), higher power dissipation, and—most controversial of all—apparently reduced long-term reliability.

Finally, manufacturers will in any case have to resolve a key disagreement among RAM users: whether to shift from the traditional emphasis on bit-wide architecture—16 K by 1 bit, 64 K by 1 bit, and so on—to byte-wide 256-kb RAMs configured as 64 K by 4 bits or 32 K by 8 bits, instead of 256 kb by 1 bit. Hardware designers may prefer one architecture and programmers may want another.

U.S. to enter in 1984–85

Two U.S. firms—IBM Corp. in Essex Junction, Vt., and Bell Laboratories in Allentown, Pa.—report that their 256-kb chips could be mass-produced next year if need be, but that they are not commercial vendors. Merchant RAM makers, on the other hand, have scheduled volume production of 256-kb chips for 1984 at the earliest—as is the case with National Semiconductor—or for some time in 1985, as with Texas Instruments Inc., Dallas. TI now has 7 percent of the international 64-K RAM market, while Motorola Inc. in Austin, Texas, leads all U.S. RAM makers with 20 percent, according to the Dataquest survey.

However, some industry consultants believe the U.S. will enter the 256-kb RAM market too late, and thus lose out again to Japan, just as it lost the initiative several years ago in the 64-K

Robert Bernhard   Senior Associate Editor

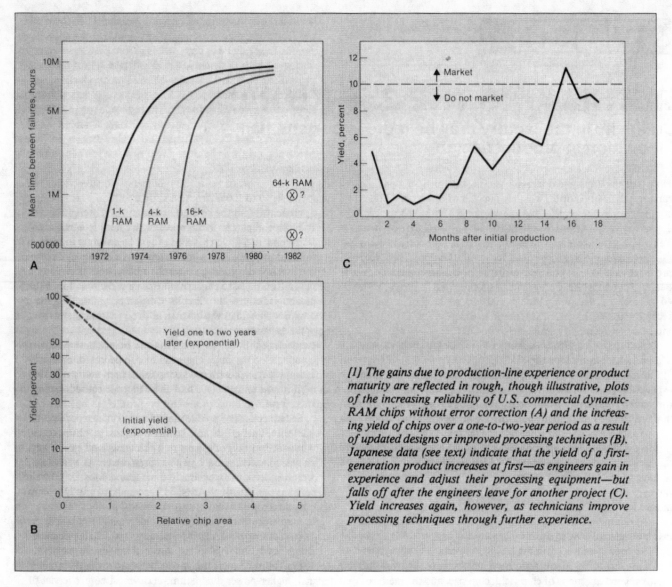

[1] The gains due to production-line experience or product maturity are reflected in rough, though illustrative, plots of the increasing reliability of U.S. commercial dynamic-RAM chips without error correction (A) and the increasing yield of chips over a one-to-two-year period as a result of updated designs or improved processing techniques (B). Japanese data (see text) indicate that the yield of a first-generation product increases at first—as engineers gain in experience and adjust their processing equipment—but falls off after the engineers leave for another project (C). Yield increases again, however, as technicians improve processing techniques through further experience.

market. They predict that those who enter in 1984 will be seriously behind the Japanese competition—with only a slim chance of catching up—whereas those who enter in 1985 will stand no chance unless they have a far superior product.

According to other market analysts, however, the RAM market can never be dominated by a few giant producers who may gain an advantage in price competition by getting an early foothold among users. They point out that a producer can, in theory, gain a high profit if it enters the market early and sets the price of its RAMs low and sacrifices initial profit in order to enlarge its market share; in doing so, its total production volume will increase as demand goes up, so that its production cost will drop sooner than that of other producers. But in reality, marginal suppliers who are behind at first could stay in the running, as long as the historical trend continues in which the RAM market has enlarged so rapidly on average (give or take some sluggish periods) that supply has never kept up with demand. If that is so, then both the 64-K and 256-kb RAM markets will tend toward an equilibrium where many producers can have more or less equitable shares.

U.S. firms still optimistic

Despite some gloomy forecasts, other U.S. firms that may enter the 256-kb RAM market in 1985 include Motorola; Intel

Corp. in Santa Clara, Calif.; Fairchild Camera and Instrument Inc. in Palo Alto, Calif.; Mostek Corp. in Carrollton, Texas; and Inmos Corp. in Colorado Springs, Colo. Semiconductor industry executives contend they will be timely in introducing their 256-kb chips, when the 64-K chip is past its peak in sales.

In theory, then, U.S. RAM makers face no surprises of the type that struck so unexpectedly to delay volume production of the 64-K RAM. The biggest of those surprises were the tenacious noise problems that arose initially when RAM designers, in shrinking the 16-K RAM to the first-generation 64-K RAM, strained circuit margins to the vanishing point or created unwanted couplings between circuit elements that also caused timing problems and degraded speed-power products.

Two of the biggest hangups that delayed the 64-K RAM and may yet delay the 256-kb chip were pattern sensitivity and capacitive coupling between the substrate and rapidly switching address signals. The problems arose because the charge stored in a memory cell was so small that the slightest noise disrupted memory operation. In pattern sensitivity, memory failures occurred only for certain patterns of bits that were being written, read, or merely retained; failures resulted from coupling between adjacent bits, subthreshold leakage in transistor gates, or a different form of coupling—either through the substrate or RC-noise—between stored bits and sense amplifiers, data lines, or

Comparison of 256-kb and 64-K random-access memories*

RAM	Cell size, μm^2	Chip size, mm^2
256-kb: Toshiba	71	low 40s
IBM Corp.	106	about 50
Bell Laboratories	117	54
Texas Instruments Inc.	60–70	low 40s
Motorola Inc.	84	46.2
Hitachi Ltd.	98	46.8
Mitsubishi Corp.	96	33–40
NEC-Toshiba and NTT-Musashino Laboratories (cooperative effort)	68	43
64-K	150–235	25–30

*Critics of U.S. 256-kb RAM makers' approach to the higher-density chip contend that the planned chips will be too large and, therefore, not cost-effective since larger chips have lower yields. The larger chips are needed to increase stored charge, which, in turn, will increase signal margins. U.S. firms are banking on redundancy to increase yields, whereas Japanese firms, though prepared to use redundancy, believe their products may mature fast enough to make it unnecessary.

on-chip clock generators. Millions of electrons, injected at clock and sense-amplifier nodes during address switching, diffuse freely in the substrate and occasionally cause a memory cell to discharge its capacitor.

Why Japanese firms were not delayed noticeably by such problems is as debatable as any other topic having to do with dynamic RAMs. But whatever the reason, Japanese firms have had a longer time to resolve these difficulties because they started developing their high-density RAMs earlier than U.S. merchant firms.

The Japanese have a head start

U.S. manufacturers admit, of course, that Japanese firms will take an early lead in the 256-kb market. They attribute the lead to the head start the Japanese had in initiating the development of such memories about five years before U.S. firms did. They believe Japanese firms also had the advantage of pooling their research and development in such cooperative ventures as the VLSI Cooperative Research Laboratories in Tokyo, which was dissolved in 1980. Before disbanding, in fact, some members of that laboratory introduced a 512-kb dynamic RAM at the 1980 International Solid State Circuit Conference; they also hinted that they knew how to make the almost legendary 1-megabit chip. Few, if any, RAM designers doubt that 256-kb or 1-Mb chips can be made; the question is whether a firm can make a cost-effective chip with cycle times of less than 360 ns and a mean time between failures of 1 million hours.

Be that as it may, any number of technical hangups could upset the timetables that 256-kb RAM makers have set for themselves. The techniques they use for increasing signal margins or for combatting noise are so varied as to create confusion, perhaps, in the minds of those who believe there are well-defined "right" ways to design products, as distinct from wrong ways. TI, for example, attacks the noise problem by building its circuits in an epitaxial layer of silicon deposited on a silicon substrate, whereas all other manufacturers build their circuits right in the silicon substrate. Then TI grounds the substrate—others give it a negative bias; the idea proved successful in the 64-K chip despite widespread initial doubts. The question now is whether it will also work in the 256-kb chips, should the company choose that approach.

Getting away from specific circuit problems for the moment, some industry consultants question whether U.S. firms can, in the first place, mass-produce 256-kb RAMs in the 1984–85 time frame. They point out that, judging from past experience, each leading supplier of dynamic RAMs will take at least three years to proceed from initial samples to volume production. As yet, however, no commercial U.S. manufacturer has shown such samples, whereas Japanese firms introduced sample 256-kb chips as long ago as 1980—including Hitachi, Toshiba Corp. in Kawasaki, and NTT-Musashino Laboratories in Tokyo. Motorola may be the first U.S. firm to introduce samples, perhaps early in 1983.

Chip yield—a major cost factor

High chip yield, like high reliability, is a well-publicized attribute of Japanese RAM makers, whereas it is reported that U.S. firms had to work hard last year to catch up in these areas. Whether or not a gap still exists, Japan's efficiency on the production lines is widely considered to have two roots: (1) its RAM designers are said to use less complex circuits, which are naturally easier to mass-produce and have higher reliability than the more complex U.S. RAM designs; and (2) Japanese workers are presumably more conscientious and take greater care during the production process. There is evidence, however, that if Japanese companies really have higher yields, these can be attributed to longer experience with producing the densest modern RAMs and with product maturity, since the Japanese started earlier than U.S. firms.

Because experience and product maturity are both correlated with the quality of the process engineers and production workers, it is fairly obvious that the quality of manpower, not circuit complexity, may be the major factor in achieving high yields. Indeed, the conventional wisdom among U.S. manufacturers is that the final test yield is not related strongly to circuit complexity but to testing experience and product maturity. This is consistent with Japanese thinking as stated in a report, "Characteristics of the IC Industry and IC Production," in *Long-Term Credit Bank of Japan Monthly Report No. 185*, 1981, Tokyo. According to the report, the difference in yields from one IC manufacturer to another is due largely to the disparity in the quality of suggestions coming from production engineers and technicians as to how to improve yield. Initially, the report notes, yield is relatively high because of suggestions from engineers; but after the engineers leave for another project, yield gradually drops—slowly rising again, however, as technicians gain experience.

Reliability and redundancy may not mix

Some computer makers are not convinced that chips with redundancy are as reliable in the long run as those without. Texas Instruments, in fact, originally rejected redundancy for its 64-K chip, in the belief that a defective chip is always a bad risk. The methods for invoking redundant cells—laser or electrically blown links—also have questionable long-term reliability. Though the technology for blowing fuses has been perfected in read-only memories (not for redundancy but for programming them), it has not yet been perfected in volume production of RAMs. One consultant notes, moreover, that ROM manufacturers took about 10 years to learn how to blow fuses reliably. Moreover, MOS RAMs have trouble generating the current to blow fuses, so they use additional area for high-current transistors. Laser systems, on the other hand, are expensive to develop—IBM, Bell, Intel, and Mostek had to make the equipment themselves—and the investment may go for naught if lasers are replaced soon by more efficient and cheaper electrically programmable ROMs to do the same job.

Japanese firms have always used larger chips than U.S. firms to increase signal margins and yet do not seem to have suffered undue yield penalties. NEC, Toshiba and NTT-Musashino Laboratories report no plans for using redundancy to increase their chip yields, whereas Hitachi—which rejected redundancy on its 64-K chip—has enough redundancy on its 256-kb chip to achieve, if it wished to use the spare cells, a reported 5-to-10-times higher yield. At this time, however, Hitachi and other

Japanese firms believe that redundancy may not be necessary if the 256-kb chip matures as quickly as the 64-K chip.

Users disagree on tradeoffs

Users would pay less for the bit-wide architecture than for the byte-wide; but three factors suggest that a 256-kb-by-1-bit chip is undesirable for many applications from mainframe and minicomputer memories to microprocessors and graphics terminals, according to Robert D. Chew, a design manager at Tektronix Inc. in Beaverton, Ore. These factors are: (1) micro-

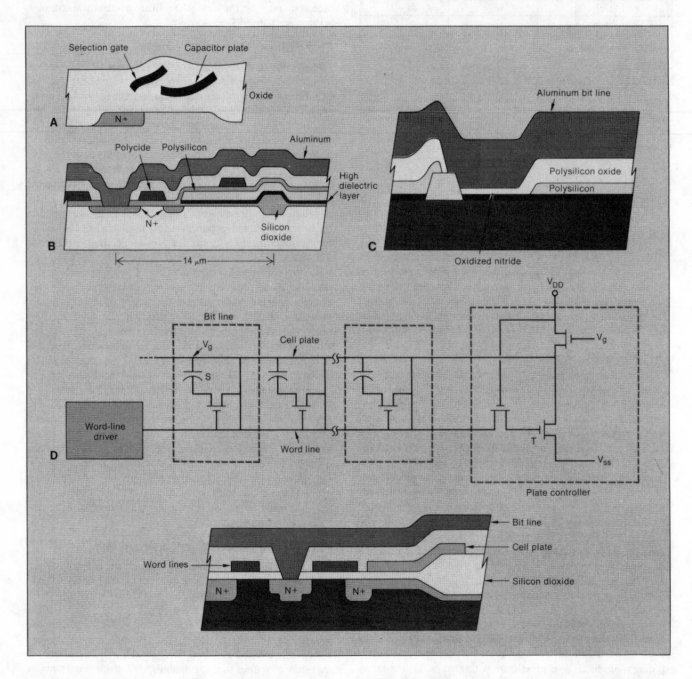

[2] Most U.S. manufacturers have turned to a double polysilicon process for making dynamic-RAM cells (A) and are expected to use a related process in their 256-kb RAMs, though metal or silicides will be used for gates or bit lines, as in the Hitachi cell, (B); however, IBM (C) and Mitsubishi (D) will use a single-level process. While IBM uses metal bit lines, Mitsubishi will continue to use the "old-fashioned" single polysilicon cell. But Mitsubishi has introduced a novel method for doubling the stored charge

(E). When a word line is accessed, a cell plate controller discharges the bias, V_g, on the memory cell through T at the end of the word line; the stored charge, S, is then pushed completely onto the bit line without any loss of threshold voltage in the gate. After reading into the bit line or refreshing the cell, the bit line is switched to V_{DD} for a stored 1 or V_{SS} for stored 0. Then V_{SS} is boosted to about 1.7 V_{DD} if the cell previously stored 1 or is clamped at V_{SS} if a 0 was stored.

and mini-computers expand their memories by increments of 8, 16, and 32 bits; (2) mainframe memories are generally interleaved by bytes, not bits; and (3) the best tradeoff for raster graphics terminals is to "broadside" load (a byte at a time) the cheapest byte-wide RAM, and then multiplex inputs and outputs to access bits at the required high rates of 60 hertz (40 ns/pixel).

However, wider architectures are a waste of money, contended William R. Sanders, a vice president of Apple Inc., Cupertino, Calif. "I have yet to find a programmer who thinks byte-wide RAMs are necessary," he said. "Furthermore, memory is a dollar market—not a bit market—meaning users try to buy as big a memory as they can afford instead of looking for just the right-size memory for their system. So, the cheaper the better. The 'by-1-bit' architecture has the lowest packaging cost, and you don't need costly multiplexing. The fanouts are also cleaner; when you have only one pin to drive, you can make it a great big drive with lots of fanout."

The disagreements at this level extend downward to problems with the memory cells themselves. Although each cell is simply an insulated-gate field-effect transistor connected in series with a capacitor—which stores a charge representing a 0 or 1—the high cell density causes enough problems with signal margins, noise, and short-channel effects to fill a textbook. Some of these problems are held over from the 64-K RAM but are more difficult to solve in the smaller geometries of the 256-kb chip, whereas others are new to 256-kb chips.

Circuit problems abound

Some circuit problems in 256-kb RAMs, especially those concerning substrate bias, are readily understood in terms of several of the many process and design parameters that control the threshold voltage of a memory-cell insulated-gate FET: substrate bias, gate-insulator thickness and materials, substrate doping, and drain voltage, as well as channel length and width. Threshold voltage can also increase during memory-cell operation as a result of the back-gate bias (or body) effect, where, as the capacitor is charged, the reverse bias increases between the source diffusion and the substrate. Switching speed, meanwhile, can be reduced by such parasitic capacitances as the p-n–junction capacitance, which is inversely proportional to the width of the depletion layer. The main point is that no matter how carefully a designer selects the threshold voltage, it will vary statistically over the chip because the above-mentioned parameters vary randomly over the chip (due to processing tolerances) while local fluctuations, such as the body effect, occur. The same problem affects all RAMs, regardless of size, but it became more difficult to manage as designers went from the 5-μm design rules of the 16-K RAM to 3-μm rules in the 64-K RAM—and now, to 1.4- to 2-μm rules in the 256-kb chip.

A negative substrate bias (about -3 to -5 volts) is desirable, because it controls injected charge carriers in the substrate—thus helping to keep the entire memory operation immune to the statistical scattering of threshold voltages, while reducing junction capacitance and body effect. (High-resistivity substrates are also used to reduce junction capacitance.) Another important detail is that substrate bias together with folded bit lines reduce substrate coupling and allow the RAM to tolerate negative dc-input pattern sensitivity; with the bias the RAM also can tolerate negative dc input levels (undershoots in input clock and address signals) of -2 to -3 V for up to 30 ns.

Taking a completely opposite tack, TI may build the 256-kb RAM with a highly resistive epitaxial layer on a low resistivity grounded substrate. The two layers combat noise and pattern sensitivity by segregating unwanted charge in the low-resistivity grounded substrate—where minority carrier (electron) lifetime is very short; the high-resistivity layer, on the other hand, stabilizes the stored charge in memory cells by *increasing* the minority carrier lifetime. Meanwhile, electrons injected into the substrate through various coupling mechanisms are swept away through recombinations.

Since the small amount of stored charge was such a decisive factor in 64-K RAMs, it is expected to be even more important in the 256-kb chip, with its smaller geometries.

Seek more efficient capacitors

Whereas the 64-K RAM had 2- to 3-μm design rules and a 400-angstroms-thick dielectric (capacitor), the 1.5- to 2- μm rules in the 256-kb RAM require a 200-Å-thick dielectric with a minimum storage charge of 45 to 50 femtofarads. Hitachi, Toshiba, and Musashino seem to have solved the process-technology problem—as shown by the 256-kb RAMs they introduced at the last ISSCC and IEDM (International Electron Devices Meeting); the problem is primarily that such thin oxides easily develop pinhole defects that cause a cell to short out. U.S. firms have been silent about their work in this area, though Motorola and TI have probably solved the problem too.

A novel approach to increasing stored charge may be taken by Toshiba, and perhaps other Japanese RAM designers, by using materials with higher dielectric constants than those used now. One such possibility is a layer of silicon nitride sandwiched with a layer of tantalum oxide, said to be capable of storing significantly more charge than a comparable area of the single silicon dioxide layer on the 64-K RAM.

To increase stored charge in the 64-K chip, most U.S. firms used larger capacitors or "boosted" word lines (when bits are read or written, the word line is boosted 2.5V above the 5-V supply to attain almost a 5-V charge in the cell), though National Semiconductor took the unique step of wrapping the capacitor plates in oxide dielectric to reduce leakage. These measures will also be applied in some U.S. 256-kb RAMs. The Japanese, on the other hand, increased storage charge in the 64-K chip merely by using larger cells (and chips)—thus rejecting boosted word lines as an unnecessary complexity. However, Hitachi will use boosted word lines on its 256-kb chips.

Mitsubishi recently introduced a controversial technique to double the currently stored charge, called storage-node boosting (SNB); the company will use it in its 256-kb chip and, when the time comes, a 1-Mb RAM [Fig. 2D]. Instead of boosting word lines, a circuit pulses the cell plate during the refresh or write cycle, so that the capacitor stores a charge equal to 1.7 times CV_{DD}, where C is the storage-cell capacitance and V_{DD} is the voltage to which the cell capacitor is connected in series. As a result, the Mitsubishi 256-kb RAM reportedly can read out twice the charge level of conventional RAMs.

SNB could spell trouble

Wary of the SNB approach are Richard Foss, president of Mosaid Inc. in Ottawa, Canada, and Jerry Moench, design manager for 256-kb RAMs at Motorola, whereas TI's Mohan Rao thinks the concept is worth trying.

SNB could be the answer to a persistent problem in RAMs in which the charge read out of the cell is about 50 percent of the stored charge, according to Dr. Rao. "The reason for this," he notes, "is that we already start to [strobe] the sense amplifier while the word line is still rising—so we really don't utilize the signal because the word-line level isn't high enough. The SNB approach may be one way to get around this—that is, by pulsing the cell plate and pushing charge out of the cell, somewhat like the way charge is read out of CCD memory cells."

Mr. Moench, by contrast, sees the SNB concept falling victim to substrate coupling because junction capacitance is directly coupled to the cell plate. "Another problem," he points out, "is the same problem as in the 16-K RAM, where the plate is essentially tied to a high supply, and as you slew the power up or down you can push charge onto data lines."

Dr. Foss, too, foresees trouble with SNB because the polysilicon cell plate is parallel to the word line—recalling a problem that was raised when this configuration was used in early dynamic RAMs. "When the cells were accessed," Dr. Foss says, "the middle of the cell plate went bouncing because the potential would vary along the strip of plate. So, I would be frightened of the Mitsubishi cell unless it was combined with disilicide (very low resistance) plates to guarantee equipotential along the plate."

The mention of disilicides, with their very low resistance, brings up another problem in designing the 256-kb chip: the increasing resistance of the ever-thinner lines that interconnect devices. This would seem to rule out the metal or polysilicon lines commonly used in 64-K chips because of their relatively high sheet resistance. Many experts have therefore advised designers to use metal silicides or polycide (polysilicon and silicide), which have one tenth as much sheet resistance as metal or polysilicon lines. Hitachi and Toshiba will indeed use the most advanced polycide and molybdenum silicide technology, respectively, in their 256-kb chips, while Bell will use similarly advanced tantalum disilicides. However, IBM will use the same aluminum and polysilicon lines and gates that they used in their 64-K RAM, whereas Mitsubishi will use conventional polysilicon and yet reports having one of the smallest, fastest 256-kb chips—33 mm^2 and with 100-ns access time.

In addition to the preceding problems of providing the required electrical performance at the time a chip is first tested, two further key problems concern the reliability of 256-kb RAMs long after the first tests: (1) gradual deterioration caused by hot electrons and (2) "soft," or random, errors caused when alpha particles strike the circuits. Solutions for the 64-K chip may be questionable for the smaller circuits in the 256-kb devices.

Smaller geometries—hotter electrons

Hot electrons may be viewed as especially energetic electrons that "evaporate" from the silicon and "condense" in the gate insulator and distort the device characteristics. They arise because of the high electric fields—at least 100 000 volts per centimeter—that occur near the drain in devices with channel lengths less than 2 to 3 μm; the high fields can accelerate channel electrons to such high energies that, when they collide with atoms of the silicon lattice, they cause the emission of secondary electrons that lead to the generation of a substrate current. Some of the electrons have enough energy to penetrate the interface between the silicon-gate and the insulator.

The solution might appear simple: restrict the electric field near the drain, where the secondary electrons collect, or increase channel length slightly. But that requires device models that simulate circuit performance and device degradation after a typical operating time of more than 50 000 hours. These models, though highly developed now, may not be all they are cracked up to be. Some device designers—those at Bell Laboratories in Murray Hill, N.J., for example—say they have models that allow them to design practical devices down to channel lengths near the theoretical limit of .25 μm; but others contend that all models may be accurate in theory but do not provide what is needed on practical RAM assembly lines: the models have too many independent variables that cannot be changed in practice—cannot be adjusted by turning knobs during the production process.

Regardless of the circuit design, however, the rate of soft errors of a dynamic RAM is generally thought to depend mainly on the stored charge; but designers differ over which areas of the chip are most sensitive to alpha radiation, or what to do about it. Moreover, whereas designers previously believed that naturally radioactive materials in the chip package were the only significant source of alpha radiation, an IBM researcher reported recently a new and harder-to-manage source of alpha particles: contaminated metal on the chip itself.

Most manufacturers have attacked the packaging aspect of the problem by placing some type of protective material, such as polyimide, on the chip surface, or using folded bit lines. The epitaxial layer used by Texas Instruments is also reputed to be a partial solution, on the theory that free electrons created when alpha particles strike the chip recombine in the low-resistivity substrate before they can do harm. These approaches are reported to have succeeded in reducing errors when alpha particles strike bit lines or memory cells—but manufacturers may still need to make improvements to reduce those errors caused by hits on the sense amplifers or the lines connecting the bit lines to the amplifiers. Therefore 256-kb RAM makers have redesigned their amplifiers or used higher impedance links from the bit line to the amplifiers. Another approach, which was used by Bell in its 64-K RAM, is to change the timing between successive clock pulses to reduce the "float time" most circuit nodes go through during a refresh, read, or write cycle, when the nodes are most susceptible to alpha rays.

Soft errors due to metal contamination require a combination of approaches, including new processes to increase the purity of the metals and improved error correction.

Production and circuit problems aside, Dr. Foss observes that U.S. 256-kb RAM makers must avoid two mistakes they made in producing the 16-K RAM in the late 1970s: (1) their production capacity fell so far short of demand that users turned to Japanese suppliers for, in some cases, all of their RAMs; and (2) when U.S. firms increased production of new generation 16-K RAMs—they stocked the shelves with new chips while users were gearing up to use them—until the chips were in oversupply. Prices then dropped so low that many industry observers have questioned whether the RAMs were at all profitable.

To probe further

The designs for 256-kb RAMs for IBM, Bell Labs, and Hitachi are described briefly in the *ISSCC-1982 Digest of Technical Papers*, pp. 68–69, 76–77, and 74–75, respectively. The storage-node–boosted RAM from Mitsubishi Laboratories is found on pp. 66–77 in the same volume.

The 256-kb RAMs designed by NTT-Musashino Laboratories and NEC-Toshiba are described briefly in the *ISSCC-1980 Digest of Technical Papers*, pp. 232–34. Details of the molybdenum-disilicide, buried-channel MOSFETs used in the Toshiba 256-kb chip may be found in the *International Electron Devices Meeting 1981* digest of papers.

"The 64-kb RAM teaches a VLSI lesson" [*IEEE Spectrum*, June 1981, pp. 38–42] discusses the problems in developing 64-K RAMs that will also affect the 256-kb chips, through an interview with Richard Foss, president of Mosaid Inc. in Ottawa.

A scholarly treatment of the problems with VLSI devices may be found in the second corrected and updated edition of "VLSI device fundamentals," by John L. Prince of Zymos Corp. in Sunnyvale, Calif., in *Very Large Scale Integration*, edited by D.F. Barbe, Springer-Verlag, New York, 1982.   ◆

NETWORKING

TELEPHONE NETS GO DIGITAL

Digital communication links promise flexible, economical telephone services for both home and office

While digital information plays an ever larger role in today's economy, anyone transmitting digital data from one place to another faces a number of obstacles. A residential user with, say, a home computer terminal is limited to transmitting or receiving at a rate at or below the 4-kilohertz bandwidth allowed by analog telephone lines. As a result, services requiring higher bandwidths, such as single-frame video, are out of reach for such users. Businesses can get special, high-capacity hookups for various purposes, but every time their requirements change, new circuits must be installed, often at considerable expense.

These problems exist because the only ubiquitous communications network, the international telephone system, is at present designed largely for analog voice, and not for digital data, transmission. But this situation is rapidly changing. Telephone companies and administrations in the developed countries are starting to convert their systems to digital. Their goal is the development of what has come to be known generically as integrated-services digital networks (ISDNs) to give telephone users all the digital communication links they require for both voice and data through a single set of standardized interfaces.

As ISDNs are implemented during the 1980s and 1990s, any telephone user will be able, for a fee, to access such digital services as facsimile transmission, teleconferencing, and eventually even video conferencing. The bandwidths available to residential users will begin to increase in the next few years from the present few kilobits per second to 80 to 144 kb/s. Businesses will have access to digital communications that are much more flexible and economical than those available today.

Already some limited steps toward ISDNs have been taken, and a number of digital services will be available in the next few years. Ultimately the new network will encompass most telecommunications, supplanting current analog networks.

Economics and flexibility dictate a new network

The primary reasons for establishing ISDNs are economy and flexibility. It is far more efficient to supply all the various digital communications services through a few standard hookups than by installing individual circuits for each application, whether it's facsimile, teleconferencing, computer-to-computer, voice, or other services. In addition, digital switches, loops, and transmission systems are becoming increasingly cost-effective in telecommunications networks. In fact, due to the nature of the technology, the more digital technology elements the network uses in switching, the more cost-effective it is to install other digital elements for transmission.

By analogy to the electric power system, one can imagine how costly it would be if every time the user bought a new piece of electrically powered equipment—a dishwasher, a television set, or an electric oven—a separate new power line had to be connected. Instead, power customers draw the power they require for all their equipment simply by plugging into a standardized interface—the wall outlet. Similarly, with ISDNs all communications services will be integrated into a single link to each user from the telephone net. This link could be called a digital pipe.

For large businesses, the primary attraction besides cost will be flexibility. If a business requires one sort of service in the morning—say, facsimile—and another in the afternoon—perhaps teleconferencing or computer links—it can shift back and forth easily without leaving its communicating capacity idle. At present, the hookup for a given service might take a substantial amount of time to complete. With the ISDN, new capacities can be added automatically just by asking for them through a terminal.

For a residential user, the ISDN will be essential if many of the services of the "wired home" are to be economical. Such services as shopping at home or home information networks will become much faster and of higher quality, as the higher transmission rates made possible by the digital network become available.

Varied applications for ISDN

The applications that will use the ISDN are extremely varied, ranging from data rates of less than 300 bits per second to over 100 megabits per second. The lowest data rates are applied to meter reading, energy management, and security. At somewhat higher rates, interactive data applications use terminals to access data bases, word processors, computers, and other terminals, usually at less than 4.8 kb/s. Since most of these applications involve polling, human entry of data into a terminal, or computer responses to inquiries, they generate traffic in bursts.

Image applications include facsimile, graphics, and slow-scan or single-frame TV. These are characterized by the transmission of data representing fixed images, such as a page of text or an individual TV frame, usually at 64 kb/s or less. These applications can use an array of processing techniques to reduce the transmitted bit rate and to improve quality. In addition to document transfer, such high-speed facsimile and graphics applications, when combined with a conferencing bridge, can be used for multilocation business meetings.

Audio applications include voice and music. Voice is by far the dominant component of telecommunications traffic today. Although forecasts show data and other traffic increasing significantly, voice needs will continue to dominate for many years to come.

Voice has usually been encoded at 64 kb/s for transmission within telecommunications networks. However, many techniques have been developed to transmit voice at less than 64 kb/s. Speeds of 32, 16, and 8 kb/s or less have been attained with acceptable quality for different applications. On the other hand, voice can be encoded at rates exceeding 64 kb/s for broadcasting, or advanced coding techniques can be used at 64 kb/s to improve voice fidelity.

Bulk data encompasses the transmission of large data files or

---

Irwin Dorros　Bell Central Services Organization

the use of distributed processing among computers. One application is the nightly transfer of data from remote locations to a central host site at up to 1.5 Mb/s or even higher.

Full-motion video can be provided in a number of ways with digital transmission. Straightforward encoding of a signal of broadcast quality requires about 100 Mb/s. With signal-compression techniques, high-quality full-motion signals can be sent at 6, 3, or 1.5 Mb/s or even lower. The applications for full-motion video include multilocation business meetings and entertainment.

Highly flexible design needed

Since it is not yet clear exactly what mix of services they will be required to handle, ISDNs must be designed with considerable flexibility. The key to this flexibility is a small family of standard interfaces for all users. Initially the access channels of this so-called digital pipe will have fixed bit rates, such as 64 or 16 kb/s. ISDN will give customers "integrated access" through use of one or several of these channels through a common interface. The channels can support simultaneous applications (voice, data, and video) from a given customer. Eventually, the capacity of the channels will be varied under customer control with the only constraint being the maximum bit rate, just as power companies today supply electricity measured by maximum amperage. The user will have access to a service center of the network and will be able to link up with packet- and circuit-switched services [Fig. 1].

Both the number of multiplexed information signals and the bit rates of the information presented by a customer may vary as long as the total signal rate at the interface does not exceed the maximum bit rate, or size, of the digital pipe. Thus many services can be supported simultaneously.

Control and signaling information is also multiplexed in the digital access pipe to instruct the serving center on what to do with the bit stream—that is, how to sort the stream out in time and space to reach various services or networks.

Within the access network, at either a remote terminal or a serving center, the signals of several customers are multiplexed. Inside the network, no fixed bandwidth is assigned to an application. A variable bandwidth assignment is made each time a customer accesses the network with a particular application. The network may convert the customer's information into a protocol to transport it efficiently and then convert it back to the original form before it reaches the network interface at the other end.

This local-access architecture can be viewed as a gateway to data bases, alarm bureaus, intercity network services, and a multitude of other potential services supported by an ISDN.

In circuit switching, a single circuit is dedicated to a particular connection between users for as long as the information interchange lasts. Such hookups are useful for continuous traffic, such as communications between computers. However, where there may be long gaps between data transmissions, as in a link between a computer and terminals, packet switching allows individual "packets" of information from different users to be interleaved on a single circuit, thus using the circuit capacity more efficiently.

As technology progresses, the customer may not need to choose in advance between packet and circuit switching; the techniques may merge. This merger might come through the development of "fast" packet switches. These could take advantage of the characteristic bursts of voice traffic and the development of

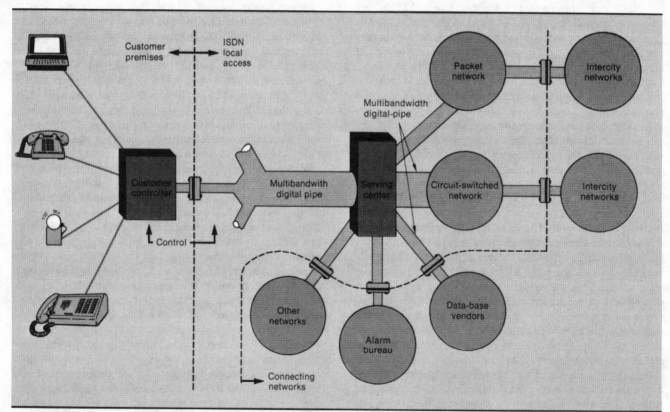

[1] The integrated-services digital network (ISDN) will give each user a single access, or digital pipe, that will handle all digital communication services. Included will be teleconferencing, facsimile, computer connections, data-base networks, and video conferencing. Through a service center, the customer will be able to use circuit-switching networks, in which each circuit is devoted to a single linkup, and packet-switched networks, in which packets of data will be interleaved on a single circuit.

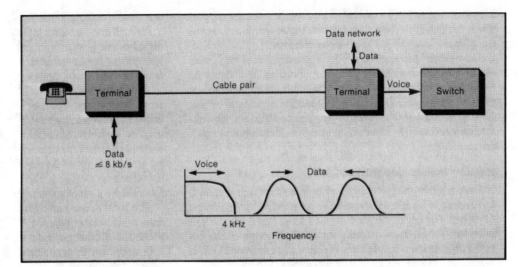

[2] ISDN users will be able to send data and voice information simultaneously over a single cable pair. Voice will occupy a frequency band below 4 kHz, while data in one direction will occupy a high band and data in the opposite direction a still higher band.

low bit-rate voice to packet-switch both voice and data at speeds of millions of packets per second. Then the separate packet and circuit networks shown in Figure 1 could be merged.

The local loop

To develop a digital-pipe type of access is a long-term ISDN goal. In the near term, however, ISDN will use a channel format over existing loops. Several simultaneous ISDN services can use these channels as long as they follow the channel format.

Work is under way on several methods to achieve full duplex (simultaneous, two-way) digital transmission over a two-wire, nonloaded loop. (A nonloaded loop is a loop with no inductors added. Loops under 18 000 feet are generally nonloaded.) One uses time-compression multiplexing to provide a digital transmission channel, giving full duplex transmission on one wire pair by transmitting in one direction at a time with a silent interval between. The line-transmission rate is slightly higher than twice the terminal–network interface rate. Terminal–network interface rates of 56 to 80 kb/s will be used initially. Eventually, this will likely rise to 144 kb/s or higher.

Another technique, data over voice [Fig. 2], uses channel equipment to put data on the order of 8 kb/s in the frequency spectrum above the voice band. A two-wire, nonloaded wire pair can be used to carry simultaneous analog voice and digital data.

For applications up to 1.5 Mb/s or more, either multiple lower-capacity channels, such as multiplexed 64-kb/s channels, or broadband channels can be employed. The broadband can use such media as paired cable, radio, satellite, or lightguide. (The table shows various ISDN capabilities over time.)

Switching and transmission

In addition to digital access to connect users to ISDN switching offices, the capability to switch digits within the offices as well as digital transmission lines to connect the offices and digital signaling to control the network will be needed. Components of this digital network have been developed and gradually introduced over the last 20 years. As telecommunications companies and administrations in North America, Europe, and Japan have modernized their facilities, they have deployed digital transmission and switching systems that now transport a growing volume of voice and data traffic. Such systems have cost, service, and operational advantages over analog systems.

The digital evolution began in 1962 with the installation in the Bell network of the first T-carrier system, a 1.544-Mb/s digital transmission system that carries 24 channels, each of 64 kb/s. This was followed by a rapidly growing family of digital

transmission systems around the world. The evolution continued through the 1960s, 1970s, and early 1980s, as stored program-controlled switching, digital subscriber loop carriers, and common-channel interoffice signaling were introduced.

In the United States there is a variety of specialized digital services, such as digital private line services (Dataphone Digital Service from American Telephone & Telegraph Co. in New York), packet-switched services (Tymnet from Tymnet Inc. of San Jose, Calif., and Telenet from GTE Telenet Inc. of Morristown, N.J.), and digital satellite services (Communications Network Service from Satellite Business Systems in McLean, Va., and Satellite Data Exchange Service from the American Satellite Co. in Rockville, Md.). In addition, the analog public-switched network offers some "digital" services through modems that convert digital input signals into the 4-kHz analog bandwidth of the network.

With this as a technological base, new elements are being developed for the existing communications networks in each country as part of their evolution to ISDNs.

Some switching already available

Existing software-controlled switches, called stored–program-controlled (SPC) switches, already supply most of the capability needed for ISDN circuit switching. SPC switches use both space-division switching, with input signals linked to outputs along different physical paths, and time-division switching, with signals assigned to different time slots. These switches have replaced the earlier electromechanical types on 60 percent of the lines in the Bell Operating Co. networks in the United States and will be used on 90 percent of the lines in the networks by 1990.

Independent telephone companies are also investing heavily in time-division SPC switches. For example, Continental Telephone, Atlanta, Ga., has 20 percent of its loops on time-division digital switches. This is expected to increase to 85 percent by 1987.

In addition to the SPC switching systems, telecommunications networks will use statistical multiplexers and packet switches increasingly for data transport. Statistical multiplexers package together input traffic from several users, giving each user a portion of the output line only when the user has actually transmitted data. The multiplexers will funnel individual, low-speed customer demands into a higher-speed output line for accessing packet switches. Bigger customers will be able to access packet switches directly over high-speed lines—for example, 56 kb/s.

Once an ISDN signal has been switched, it needs a digital transmission link to get to its destination. In metropolitan areas a significant number of digital transmission systems, such as T-carrier, already exist. The Bell System's 130 million circuit miles of digital systems represent more digital transmission circuit miles than all others combined worldwide.

By 1990, metropolitan area digital transmission systems, including lightwave systems, are expected to account for approximately 80 percent of the Bell Operating Cos.' metropolitan area circuit miles. In combination with digital loop systems and SPC switches, these digital transmission systems will give the Bell Operating Cos. a strong technological base for their ISDNs.

AT&T, planning for intercity transmission, is focusing on expanding long-haul digital connections whenever economic factors permit. In the early 1980s, digital terminals will be used for tranmission over existing radio and coaxial cable systems. Such terminals include 45-Mb/s units on microwave radio and 140-Mb/s systems on coaxial cable. Long-haul digital radio systems may also be constructed. In February 1982, a lightwave system between New York and Washington, D.C., became operational. Current estimates are that by 1990 digital transmission systems will account for at least 25 percent of AT&T's intercity circuit miles.

Independent telephone companies have also made a major commitment to using digital carrier on wire pairs and lightguide cable. General Telephone in Stamford, Conn., first began using lightwave systems in 1977 in a field trial connecting central offices in Long Beach and Artesia, Calif. General Telephone is now using lightwave systems at many sites, including an experimental long-wavelength, repeaterless system on a 20-mile route in Hawaii. United Telephone, United Telecommunications Inc. in Kansas, and Continental Telephone also have significant lightwave system installations.

Signaling: new interfaces and protocols

Many future ISDN services will require sophisticated network control. Signaling between the network and customer terminals will use new, standardized interfaces and protocols based on message-oriented signaling channels.

A major feature of ISDNs will be an out-of-band signaling channel for user–network signaling. This channel will handle such features as call setup, specification of special features for a call, and information on incoming calls. Using this channel and special messages, the customer will be able to request initiation of services directly from the network. In addition, because of their packet nature, telemetry, digital signaling messages, and packet traffic can all be carried on this out-of-band channel.

Near-term capabilities

Based on such technology, a number of new capabilities will become available in the United States over the next few years. All will provide switched, digital, full-duplex data connections using existing two-wire loops for network access.

One capability of interest will be circuit-switched digital capability (CSDC), for a full-duplex, circuit-switched, 56-kb/s digital channel using time-compression multiplexing for access. AT&T announced the interface specifications for CSDC in 1981.

The CSDC will let users alternate between a digital channel and an analog channel on the same call if they so choose. A key feature of this capability is that it uses existing transmission systems and switches. Some software and channel circuitry modifications will be required within the telephone network before the customer can switch from analog to digital and before operations functions can be added. The capability can be used for bulk data transfer, secure voice, facsimile transport, backup for private lines, and possibly access to packet-switched networks.

Another capability in the offing is local-area data transport, based on packet switching [Fig. 3]. The packet-switching portion of this transport will be accessed via statistical multiplexers in the central office to concentrate many users onto a single 56 kb/s line.

Customers will have access to the statistical multiplexer in two ways, each via a two-wire metallic loop. The occasional user, through a terminal with a modem, will be able to dial up a compatible port in the multiplexer on a regular telephone line. Using this line for data will preclude using it simultaneously for telephone conversations. A typical application for this transport capability will be home information systems.

The residential or business customer requiring more continuous service or multiple simultaneous data applications can have direct access to the multiplexer through the data-over-voice method. The advantages here are simultaneous voice and data, as well as continuously available data channels for simultaneous use of such services as home or business information, energy management, and security.

A third potential capability will be the packet transport network. This is planned as a network of packet switches with access via a standard packet protocol. Enhanced services, such as packet assembly, disassembly, and storage, would be provided outside the packet transport network. AT&T's basic packet-switched service, for private packet-switched service on shared switches, is expected to be available soon.

Networks outside the U.S.

Meanwhile, the other industrialized countries are also moving toward digital telecommunications networks, though each has shaped its ISDN program somewhat differently from the U.S. approach. The Nippon Telegraph & Telephone Corp. in Tokyo, is placing heavy emphasis on fiber-optic transmission in its 20-year plan to convert into digital. Field trials of two 400-Mb/s lightwave systems have already begun, and optical fibers are planned for use in sophisticated services to residential users.

The Japanese government is sponsoring an ambitious project for a two-way interactive video system based on lightguide cables in the new model city of Higashi-Ikoma, near Osaka. The project, called HI-OVIS (high interactive optical visual interactive system), will offer videotex and cable TV, as well as an interactive TV service. A videotex service called Captain (character and pattern telephone access information network system) has been in field trial since 1979.

A second major emphasis is on facsimile, since the written Japanese language is best transmitted this way. Considerable research and development have been done in facsimile services. In 1981, the Japanese tested a packet-switched digital facsimile service connecting Japan, France, and the United States. The packet switches and the terminals were connected by 9.6-kb/s lines.

Britain is also moving rapidly to establish lightwave transmission lines in its effort toward nationwide ISDN service by the end of the 1980s. Since the distance between exchanges in the United Kingdom rarely exceeds 30 kilometers, the British have concentrated on developing repeaterless single-mode lightwave systems within this range. The first commercial system is expected to be installed in 1984.

British Telecom in London has been a leader in establishing videotex services. A videotex system called Prestel has been in public use since September 1979. Over 200 000 pages of information are available on this system, which has some 27 000 subscribers. Two new features, "mailbox" and "gateway," were introduced in 1982. These are expected to increase greatly the demand for the service among residential users.

With mailbox, messages are stored and retrieved remotely. Gateway allows advertisers, businesses, and information suppliers to link their own data bases to the Prestel system. This permits interactive services, such as telebanking, remote booking of airline reservations, and teleshopping.

On the European continent, France has established a lead in the installation of digital switches. By the end of 1981 the Postal Telephone & Telegraph (PT&T) in Paris had close to 1.9 million lines served by its E-10A and E-10B time-division local switching systems. In the future, the French expect to install only digital exchanges.

The French also have widespread penetration of digital transmission in their microwave radio networks at 8, 34, and 140 Mb/s. Nearly 50 percent of the local network and 25 percent of the long-haul network in France is digital. A switched 64-kb/s service is planned for 1984, when the French PT&T will also start a time-division, multiple-access satellite service called Telecom 1. It will offer digital services to large-business customers via small earth stations close to the customer's premises. The system, designed for up to 256 earth stations, will provide service at 2.4 kb/s to 2 Mb/s.

The French packet network, called Transpac, was first introduced in 1978. It was connected worldwide via a French gateway switch located in Paris the following year. The first connections were to Tymnet and Telenet in the United States. Connections have since been established or are planned with other countries in Europe, Asia, and Africa.

Italy and West Germany are not yet as far along as France. However, SIP, the major Italian telephone company, has scheduled a 1983 field trial of two digital subscriber local-access methods. Each will provide 80-kb/s full-duplex subscriber access on a single two-wire loop with the following channel format: a 64-kb/s channel for circuit-switched voice or data and a 16-kb/s channel for signaling information and packet-switched data. One access method will employ time-compression multiplexing, while the other will use a hybrid approach that includes echo cancellation. At the exchange, the subscriber access channel will be broken into its component circuit and packet-switching parts. Services supported in the trial will include digital telephony, single-frame video, digital facsimile, circuit-switched access to X.25 packet switching, videotex, and teletext.

In West Germany, the *Bundespost* is planning a 64-kb/s switched network as an expansion and enhancement of the existing public digital data network. Using 64-kb/s channels and constructed so that digital time-division switching can be used at the nodes, this network will have data and text-services as well as voice capabilities. The expanded services will not be generally available until digital switching systems are introduced starting in 1985. A 64-kb/s model network for 4000 residential and business subscribers is planned to be available by year-end.

The beginning of an international digital network, connecting the systems of different countries, is emerging in Europe. An international packet-switched network called Euronet has been established. It has more than 30 host computers with more than 200 data bases containing scientific, technical, and socio-economic data. Access to Euronet is available by direct connection or from various European national networks.

In Canada, the TransCanada Telephone System (TCTS), Ottawa, Ont., of which Bell Canada is a member, has offered the Dataroute digital transmission service since 1973. This service supports a wide range of asynchronous and synchronous speeds up to 56 kb/s. TCTS also has a circuit-switched digital service called Datalink, which handles synchronous full- and half-duplex connections at speeds up to 9.6 kb/s to more than 60 serving areas across Canada. Still another packet-switched data service from TCTS, called Datapac, was first introduced commercially in 1977. Datapac supports a wide range of synchronous and asynchronous terminals and includes X.25 as an access option. Also, Datapac offers international packet-switched connections to points in the United States, Europe, and Asia.

With a plethora of digital technology available to support an ISDN, the need for equipment, configuration, service, and inter-

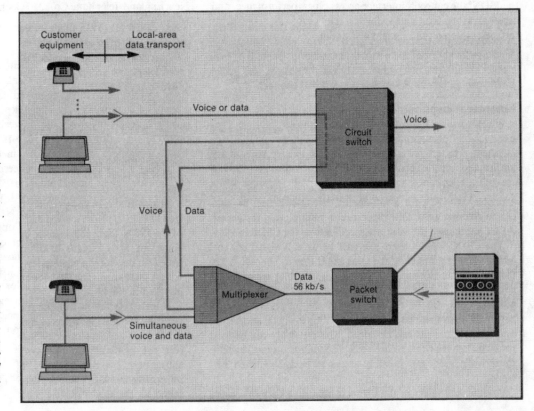

[3] *One of the first ISDN capabilities that will be available in the United States will be local-area data transport. With this, a customer will be able to access packet-switched networks through a statistical multiplexer, which will concentrate many users onto a single 56-kb/s line. The frequent or continuous user (bottom) will access the multiplexer directly, while the occasional user (top) will dial up on a public telephone line.*

Expected progress in ISDN capabilities

1983	Mid-1980s	1990s
Individual applications utilize individual circuits at incompatible interfaces: Videotex Single-frame video Low-speed facsimile Video conferencing Energy management Terminal–computer Electronic mail	Several applications on single ISDN access (16 kb/s to 1.5 Mb/s) at common interfaces: Integrated-circuit- and packet-switched access Integrated voice and data access High-speed facsimile Low-bit-rate voice	Wideband (20-to-100 Mb/s) ISDN access: Switched full-motion video Very high-speed data Customer control of bandwidth in digital pipe

face standards is obvious. Regional and domestic organizations involved in such standards include the American National Standards Institute (ANSI), the European Computer Manufacturers Association (ECMA), the Conference of European Administrations of Post and Telecommunications (CEPT), and the Electronic Industries Association (EIA). A key role in establishing international ISDN standards is being played by the International Telegraph and Telephone Consultative Committee (CCITT). Together these organizations represent a wide range of equipment manufacturers, telecommunications networks, and other interests. All these groups have important stakes in ISDNs, including deciding which ISDN functions will be done in equipment on the customer's premises and which will be done within the telecommunications networks.

Setting standards: an international effort

CCITT is a part of the International Telecommunications Union (ITU), a specialized treaty agency of the United Nations headquartered in Geneva. Participation by U.S. entities is administered by the Department of State's Office of International Communications Policy. CCITT studies technical, operations, and tariff questions and issues recommendations for endorsement by its worldwide membership.

Several CCITT study groups are working on various aspects of the ISDN: the concept, interface access types, performance, and access arrangements; data switching, data protocols, and data interfaces; switching and signaling, including digital subscriber line signaling; and common physical interfaces for a wide variety of data applications, including modems on analog networks and terminations. One study group is examining the establishment of fundamental service elements, including call control, testing and addressing features.

While it will be more than a decade before all ISDN services are available throughout North America, Europe, and Japan, sufficient progress has already been made to give preliminary confirmation of the feasibility of ISDN architecture. By 1990, a user of the telephone system will be able to plug a terminal into a standard ISDN interface at home or in the office and access any one of many ISDN services.

To probe further

More detailed information on the progress toward ISDNs can be obtained in "Aspects in the Evolution toward ISDN," a session at the International Conference on Communications, Philadelphia, June 1982. Copies are available from the IEEE Service Center, 445 Hoes Lane, Piscataway, N.J. 08854.

The approach of telephone carriers to the ISDN is outlined in "Challenge and opportunity of the 1980s: ISDN," by Irwin Dorros, *Telephony* (55 E. Jackson Blvd., Chicago, Ill. 60604), Jan. 26, 1981. The Bell System's specific innovations in ISDN are explained by C.R. Williamson in "Opening the digital pipe—Bell

System overview," National Telecommunications Conference, 1981.

For an in-depth description of ISDN services to be offered in the near future, see "Planning switched data transport capabilities in the Bell System," by G.J. Handler, International Conference on Communications, Denver, June 1981. Copies are available from the IEEE Service Center, 445 Hoes Lane, Piscataway, N.J. 08854.

Specific user applications of ISDN are detailed in the January 1982 special issue of *IEEE Transactions on Communications*, "Communications in the automated office." A second special issue, "Bit-rate reduction and speech interpolation," April 1982, describes advanced techniques for voice and data processing and their relevance to ISDN.

For a glimpse at some of the issues in ISDN standards setting, a useful article is "Progress toward user access arrangements in integrated services digital networks," *IEEE Transactions on Communications*, September 1982.

Field trials of advanced fiber-optic systems are discussed in "Single-mode fibers outperform multimode cables," March 1983, p. 30–37.

The next meeting of the International Conference on Communications will be June 19–22 in Boston. For more information on this upcoming conference, contact C. William Anderson, New England Telephone Co., 350 Cochituate Rd., Framingham, Mass. 01701.

About the author

Irwin Dorros (F) has been designated executive vice president, Technical Services, of the Bell Central Services Organization. Prior to this designation, he served as assistant vice president, Network Planning, at American Telephone & Telegraph Co. He has been deeply involved with the technical issues arising from the AT&T divestiture. From 1956 to 1978, Dr. Dorros worked at Bell Laboratories in many areas, including data communications. He led network systems engineering and planning activities for a wide spectrum of programs, including Picturephone, cellular radio, and the evolution of ISDN.

He has been a member of the National Research Council Board on Telecommunications—Computer Applications. He holds six patents and is the author of many technical papers published in the *Bell System Technical Journal* and other journals. He is a member of Tau Beta Pi, Eta Kappa Nu, and Sigma Xi. Dr. Dorros received the bachelor of science and master of science degrees in electrical engineering from the Massachusetts Institute of Technology and the doctor of engineering science degree in electrical engineering from Columbia University in 1962.   ◆

The expertise and careful research of Frank Gratzer and John McLaughlin are deeply appreciated.

NETWORKING

LOCAL AREA NETS: A PAIR OF STANDARDS

Confronted by marketplace needs, the IEEE 802 Committee is proposing standards for two kinds of networks: contention access and token passing

As factories and offices move toward automation, local networks for sharing information and computer-related resources are bound to proliferate. To avoid a veritable Babel as myriad devices built by different manufacturers attempt to communicate, there must be standards for the networks. But which?

The IEEE 802 Committee, which is considering such standards at the two lowest protocol levels, believes a single standard will not satisfy the demands of the marketplace. It is thus proposing that two incompatible systems be standarized: contention, a fairly simple method in which devices compete for access to a common communications link, but may not get access at all during periods of heavy traffic; and token passing, a more complex and expensive method in which access is parceled out in a predetermined order, limiting possible delays.

Neither standard is intended for heavy industrial applications or other areas where immediate communication between two devices may be necessary, but rather for office and light industrial information and resource sharing. Once the IEEE 802 standards are in place, a great step will have been taken toward compatible local networks made up of devices from different manufacturers. Much work must still be done on the IEEE 802 standard, and standards efforts for higher-level protocols are even further off, since major computer manufacturers each have their own proprietary standards. Work toward higher-level uniformity is just beginning through such organizations as the American National Standards Institute (ANSI) and the International Standards Organization (ISO).

Once full standardization is achieved, system designers will be able to put together a compatible local network composed of computers, terminals, printers, and other equipment down to connectors and cables from a variety of vendors. The design will not require much custom hardware or software, and the engineer should be able to complete it in a minimum of time. With standards, a big market, and competition among manufacturers, all of the equipment will become cheaper. And this, of course, will lead to more and more local networks.

Such networks will differ from present global networks only in size and distance covered. Consider the present typical reservation system, a global network, for an international airline. From each terminal a user can request information about the status of the reservation system, get data from it, and add information to it. The network connects computers, terminals, electronic file-storage devices, and ticket printers around the world.

An example of data sharing in a local area might be a purchasing system. An engineer wanting to buy an oscilloscope might fill out the purchase requisition on a terminal and route this to the manager via the network. The manager can "sign" this requisi-

tion and route it to the purchasing department. Purchasing can then generate a purchase order on a terminal and have it automatically typed and sent to the vendor. When the oscilloscope is received, the receiving dock can log its arrival into the terminal and send it on for incoming inspection. After examining the oscilloscope, incoming inspection can notify accounts payable via the network that the invoice can be paid. At any time the engineer can interrogate the system to find out if the manager has signed the requisition, if purchasing has placed the order, if the equipment has been received, and where it is located.

Local area networking can also be applied to design automation. Marketing, for example, might specify a product through a terminal. Using this information, engineering can design the product with a computer-aided–design system and test the product by simulation. With this data base, manufacturing can generate the programs to run the numerically controlled machines that make the product. Using the data base, a manuals group can write the operations and maintenance manuals with network-based word processing.

Managing the standards task

But developing the standards for such local networks is not easy. There are many aspects of data communications to consider: the cable, connections, and electrical signals of the interface; how the data are to be sent between different devices; the formats and meaning of the data; and more. To make the standards effort manageable, ISO has developed a general model for data communications called the Open Systems Interconnection Model.

If there are two things that must communicate, such as computers or programs executing on different computers (these are, in general, called applications), the model separates the applications from the communications task. It then subdivides the communications task into seven subtasks, or layers. These layers support one another in hierarchical fashion: layer 2 is served by layer 1 and in turn serves layer 3 and so forth. Layers also communicate with their peers—equivalent layers in other devices—by protocols, or prior agreements on how a particular task is to be carried out.

With a given device, a layer communicates with the layer above and the layer below through interfaces. The most commonly recognized interface is the one between the physical layers—that is, the connector seen on the back of various equipment. The other interfaces are logical, meaning they are only a description of how the layers pass data to one another.

For devices from different manufacturers to be compatible, standards must be established for each layer. Specific protocols and interfaces must be developed.

As the first order of business, the IEEE 802 Committee is setting the standards for layers 1 and 2, which are the physical and link layers. This work has been undertaken first because many

Maris Graube Tektronix Inc.

aspects of these two layers will before long be integrated into semiconductor chips. The immediate goal of the standard is to have the different manufacturers make chips that are functionally equivalent, so that devices using them will be compatible.

Before a standard can be set out in technical terms, it must be set out conceptually. The IEEE 802 Committee has laid down the following requirements for a standard local network:

• The 802 standard network should be usable for commercial and light industrial applications. Networks for the home and for heavy industrial applications, such as nuclear power stations, are not within its scope.

• The transmission line may be up to 2 kilometers long. The data rate on the cable should be between 1 and 20 megabits per second. As many as 200 devices should be able to use the same cable.

• The standard should, as much as possible, be independent of the type of transmission line and signaling technique—it should be media-independent.

• The network should have reasonable reliability. There should be only one undetected data-transmission error per year. A failure of any device on the network should not make the network inoperational.

• The network should provide peer-to-peer communication: any device should be able to talk to any other without use of intermediary devices.

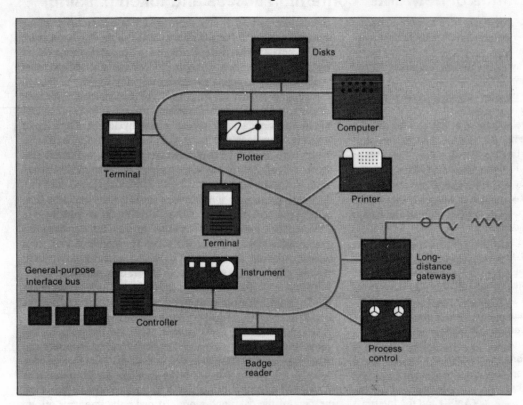

Local networks permit resource sharing, so that users or devices at any point on the net can have access to any information or device at any other point. If network traffic is fairly light, each user appears to have sole ownership of the full resources of the system, in addition to being able to communicate with all other users.

Applications and other high-level parts of the ISO model communicate by means of protocols, in which messages of specified format are sent down through the various layers, out to the media-access unit, along the bus, and back up again. The IEEE 802 standard deals only with the physical and logical link layers; the higher levels have yet to be standardized, and many manufacturers already have their own higher-level protocols in place.

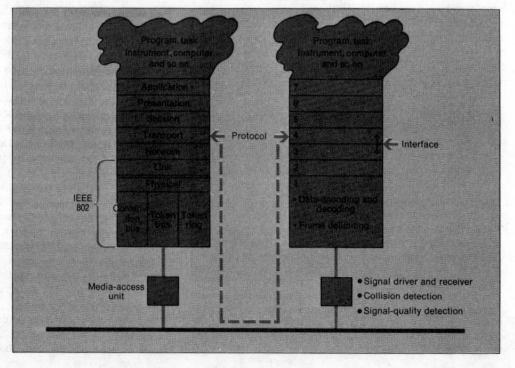

• The IEEE standard should be cognizant of other, related standards activities to prevent duplication of effect and to be compatible with the higher-layer protocol standards being developed.

Flexibility for transmission lines

To make a standard for the physical layer, a transmission line with its connectors must be selected and electrical signal levels defined. Because it is not clear what transmission lines (coaxial cables, fiber optics, and so on) will be most effective for future networks, the IEEE standard provides for a small box called a media-access unit (MAU). One side of the MAU will have a fixed standard interface that connects to particular equipment, such as a computer or terminals. The other side will have an interface for a particular transmission line. There will be a small number of standards for the transmission-line interface. The techniques currently being standardized include:

• A coaxial cable with baseband data signaling (no carrier for the data).
• A coaxial cable commonly used for cable television with data signaling done by radio-frequency carrier.

With either method, the data will be sent and received serially. The MAU will simply contain the needed line drivers and receivers tailored to the particular transmission line. The cable in the MAU interface can be up to 50 meters long. The standard data rates for the network will be 1, 5, 10, and 20 Mb per second. If a different and superior transmission technique is developed, only the MAU will become obsolete, rather than all the equipment on the network.

Most of the physical layer's functions will be carried out on the equipment side of the MAU interface. These functions include data coding and decoding, synchronization, and recognition of the start and stop of a data unit. It is envisaged that these functions, together with many of the link-layer functions, will be integrated onto a very large-scale-integrated semiconductor chip.

The link layer will be responsible for sending and receiving a unit of data. Each data unit consists of a destination address, a source address, a control code, the information to be sent, and a frame-check sequence. The two addresses will identify the source and recipient of the information, the control code will tell the

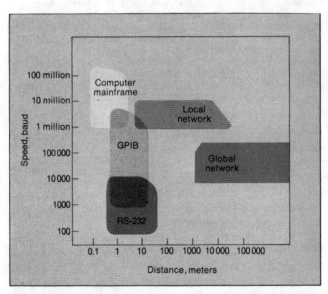

The local network is intermediate in data rate and distance between the mainframe bus and the global network. The general-purpose interface bus and the RS-232 are examples of early, highly specialized local interconnections, but are not generally considered true networks.

receiver what kind of data is being sent, and the frame-check sequence will allow detection of transmission errors.

Two access methods planned

When the link layer (layer 2) is requested by layer 3 to send a unit of data, the link must determine when to send the data. This is a problem since the serial-transmission link will be shared by all the devices on the network, much like telephones on a party line. The question here is which device can use the transmission line at any given time? There are numerous methods for determining access rights to the transmission line. The two currently being considered in the IEEE 802 Committee are:

1. **Contention.** In this method a link layer needing to transmit listens first to hear if any other device is transmitting. If the transmission line is busy, the device waits; if the line is not busy, the device transmits. Because of signal-propagation delays on the transmission line, two or more devices can start transmitting simultaneously or nearly simultaneously. If they do, the data on the transmission line will "collide." The protocol then is for each device to detect the collison and stop transmitting for a random amount of time, so the devices' messages do not collide again when they retry. If a collision does recur, each device refrains from transmitting for a random time twice as long as before. This method is called carrier sense multiple access with collision detection, or CSMA/CD.

2. **Token passing.** In a network of devices there can be a line-access protocol that lets only one device at a time hold a "token," or access rights. When that device is through using the transmission line, it passes the token to another device via a special data unit. The token can be passed around from device to device, giving each access rights to the transmission line.

CSMA/CD is very simple to implement. However, access to the line is statistical rather than deterministic, so it is possible (but highly unlikely) that a device's transmission could repeatedly collide with others and never be sent. Also, the transmission line must be limited to a maximum length for a given data rate and data unit size if collision detection is to work. The token-passing scheme, on the other hand, is deterministic (in the absence of noise or device failures) and is not as constrained by transmission-line length, frame size, or data rate.

It is, however, more complex. For example, protocols must be established for how a new device just added to the network will get the token, what happens if the device then holding the token loses power, what happens if two devices pick up a token, and so on. These are not insurmountable problems, but they do make the token line-access method more involved.

Besides the data-unit structure and the line-access method, another consideration for the link layer (layer 2) is the type of service it will give the network layer (layer 3). The simplest service is called a datagram. Here a source can send one data unit and no more to a destination. The transmitting link layer takes no further responsibility for ensuring that the data have been transmitted correctly or for retransmitting the data if there were errors. With datagram service, the higher-layer protocols, typically the transport layer (layer 4), must make sure the data are getting through correctly. In other situations, very complete services must be performed at the link level.

Connection service ensures that data are being correctly transmitted at the link level. This service involves numbering the frames to make sure they are received in proper sequence and that duplicate frames are not received. To do this, any particular source-destination pair must exchange information about their connections, such as the synchronizing of source and destination frame counters and the acknowledging of received data. The

The rocky road to setting a standard

Formulating standards for local area networks is particularly difficult because of the large amount of equipment already in the field and the *de facto* standards of each manufacturer. These factors alone explain why the local networks standard is not as easy to set as the IEEE-488 bus apparently was.

But developing any IEEE standard requires much writing and rewriting before it is set in final form, with the following hurdles to be cleared:
• The project must be proposed and approved by the IEEE Standards Board and other standards bodies.
• A technical committee must be appointed and it must prepare a draft standard and circulate it for comment.
• The draft must be revised until it receives approval from three quarters of those commenting on it.

To achieve wide acceptance, an organization in the IEEE must be found to sponsor the standards activity. For the local network standard, that organization is the Technical Committee for Computer Communications in the Computer Society.

The sponsoring organization prepares a project proposal detailing the standard's scope and objectives and submits it to the IEEE Standards Board. The Standards Board checks with other standard-setting organizations, such as ANSI, to ensure that similar standards activity is not already under way. If all goes well, the standards project is authorized, a number is assigned to it, and a chairman is appointed to produce the requisite technical document. The number assigned to the local-network-standard project is 802.

Technical committee organized

The chairman organizes a technical committee by inviting experts in the field and other interested parties to help formulate the standard. Committee meetings are open; anyone may participate. The committee refines the scope and objectives of the standard; experts and committee members submit proposals on how particular goals of the standard are to be met.

Often sections of a standard will resemble existing products, for the simple reason that some companies find it in their long-term interest to make substantial, detailed contributions to the committee. Without these contributions, the committee would find it difficult to complete the detailed engineering design of a standard in a reasonable time. On the other hand, some companies keep details proprietary, and their technology is not incorporated in the standard.

Of course, even the most complete participation in the standards-making process will not guarantee that a particular manufacturer's products will meet the standard. Political considerations alone mandate that the standard cannot be based directly on a single product, and close resemblance of a product to the final standard will be just that, not compatibility.

Because some possible standards are easier for manufacturers to adapt their machines to, lively discussion takes place in the technical committee, and eventually compromises are reached. A draft of the standard is written and then refined until the committee believes it is technically sound. Then the draft is submitted to the sponsoring organization to determine if it will be widely acceptable.

Reaching a consensus

To determine the acceptability of the standard, the sponsoring organization sends it with a ballot to representative vendors who would use the standard to build equipment and to users who eventually would buy such equipment. The ballot has three voting choices:
1. Abstain. A person may not have the time, the interest, or the expertise to evaluate the draft standard.
2. Approve.
3. Not approve. The not-approve vote must be accompanied by a statement of what it would take to change the "not approve" to "approve."

To gain the widest possible consensus, all the "not approve" comments are examined, and an attempt is made to incorporate the proposed changes into the draft. Care must be taken, however, to see that those who voted to approve the draft are not offended by the proposed changes. A consensus is attained when 75 percent of the sponsoring organization votes to approve the draft standard. It is then sent on for higher-level approvals.

Approval and production

The local network draft standard will first be approved by the Technical Committee for Computer Communications and will then be sent to the Computer Society's Standards Board. The board will review it to verify that all procedures were correctly followed, that a consensus has been reached, and that no one was arbitrarily ignored in the consensus process.

After this level of verification approval, the draft standard will be forwarded to the IEEE Standards Board for its approval. There, again, the development processes for the standard will be examined. When the standard has been approved, a draft will be put into final form, as specified by the IEEE Standards Manual. After the standard is printed, it will be ready for official distribution.

Standards efforts often encounter unexpected twists and turns. Those involved are all volunteers; they may have to give up IEEE work if they change jobs or interests. It takes financial support to attend week-long standards meetings six times a year all over the United States, and though support is often available from forward-looking companies, these resources may vary with time.

Finally, as with any other human activity, it simply takes time to make compromises and reach a consensus. —*M.G.*

---

control field is used for this purpose, and it also indicates if a datagram or connection service is used.

Former long-distance networks relied exclusively on connection link-level service, and much communications software uses that service. The newer networks rely on datagrams only. The IEEE 802 standard will embrace both.

Basic network configurations

Local networks can be configured in several ways, with the basic configurations being buses, rings, and stars. In a star network, the central hub is responsible for switching messages between the communicating points at the periphery, and though this has been a common topology in timeshared computer applications, it does not fulfill the requirement that failure of a single node not affect the rest of the system and has not been considered by the IEEE 802 Committee. (Some manufacturers currently produce systems that use a star topology to connect several devices to the same node on a bus, but that is a different matter.)

The bus configuration can be used for both token passing and collision sensing, so the committee has drafted standards for both CSMA/CD and token buses. The ring topology can be used for token-passing, though not for CSMA/CD, so there will be a single standard for token rings.

In attempting to cover most of the applications for local networks, the IEEE committee has been unable to define any one standard. Rather, a family of standards is emerging. There will be a CSMA/CD (bus) standard, a token bus standard, and a token ring standard. CSMA/CD devices will not be compatible with token bus or token ring devices, though the logical link protocol will be the same for all devices. Thus the IEEE 802 standards will uniformly support the higher-level protocols, and this will pave the way for standards for these other protocols.

Manufacturers will conform to standard

When the IEEE 802 local network standard becomes final, widespread compliance appears guaranteed because of two factors: good timing, and the standard's accommodation of most kinds of equipment already in the field.

The development and acceptance of any standard depends heavily on its timing. If proposed too soon, the best approach or technique may not yet have been found. The result could be an inefficent and costly method that is difficult to change. If proposed too late, the proliferation of approaches would make agreement on one unlikely. With local network standardization, the timing seems about right.

Starting in February 1980, before many of the more than 100 manufacturers of local network systems had even demonstrated their offerings, the IEEE 802 Committee met to formulate a local network standard. Although the work to date covers sufficiently different media-access techniques to give the appearance of multiple standards to many people, it has indeed limited the types of commercial local networks produced, while remaining fairly "friendly" to most major manufacturers.

One technology covered by the proposed standard is a contention network using "carrier sense multiple access with collision detection" (CSMA/CD). The interfaces and protocols defined for this network type are very close to the Ethernet approach put forward by Xerox Corp., Digital Equipment Corp., and Intel Corp., and 802 requirements could easily be met. No changes have been made in Ethernet to date because the 802 standard is not yet final. When the standard is announced, conformance will be widespread.

Twenty-eight companies have announced Ethernet products or have bought product rights. 3Com Inc., TCL Corp., Interlan, and others make Ethernet-compatible products; Zilog Inc., DEC, Intel, and others plan to offer them. In addition to offering an Ethernet-compatible network (the Net/One), Ungermann-Bass Inc. even supplies Xerox with Ethernet interface/controller boards. In addition, a number of manufacturers who have participated in the 802 effort intend to build equipment similar to Ethernet. The many CSMA/CD manufacturers who will be able to conform to the local network standard should ensure its longevity.

Another major network type defined by the IEEE 802 is the token ring, where the symbol of authority is passed between stations around the ring to indicate which is in control. Apollo Computer's Domain, Gould-Modicon's Modway, and Proteon's Associates' Pronet are commercial examples of this approach. And in what appears to be an unprecedented preliminary disclosure of product plans, IBM has given the 802 Committee a detailed presentation on the company's view of a token-ring scheme. IBM sources have indicated that the company's contributions are intended to ensure that it can meet any forthcoming standard, but the presentations have been taken as a clear indication of network product plans. It appears that the token-ring portion of the local network standard will have IBM's support, and if so, it will not be long before other manufacturers offer compatible versions or products. Many existing token-passing rings will be modified to conform to the standard. The result will be similar to that for CSMA/CD: manufacturers will build in conformance with the standard, thereby ensuring further widespread use.

A third technique endorsed so far by the 802 Committee is that of a token media-access method on a bus. This has not been widely implemented or endorsed, and it is not clear whether it will be part of the standard. Control Data Corp.'s Loosely Coupled Network is an example of a token bus; Datapoint Corp.'s Arcnet is another, but details are proprietary.

If balloting by the IEEE 802 Local Network Standard Committee shows acceptance and the final details of the standard are worked out at the next meeting in August, the standard will become a reality. A shakeout in the local network market will follow, and manufacturers that conform to one of the standardized approaches will survive.

A note of caution: some local networks are not covered by the 802 effort. These include computer-controlled voice/data PBX networks, military local networks, real-time local networks, and several others targeted for specific environments or equipment. How to standardize these network types has yet to be determined.

—Harvey Freeman
Architecture Technology Corp.
Minneapolis, Minn.

To ensure compatibility among devices made by different manufacturers, standards are needed at all protocol layers, not just layers 1 and 2. Work on standards for the upper-level protocols is just beginning in ANSI and other standards groups, and it will be many years before a consensus is reached. Thus, even with the IEEE 802 standard, the goal of total compatibility between different vendors' equipment will not be achieved.

The National Bureau of Standards is developing a set of Federal information-processing standards (FIPS) for use with local networks. These standards will incorporate the IEEE 802 for the lower two protocol layers. Standards for the higher-level protocols have been developed by industrial contractors and tested by the bureau. The hope is that the Federal standards will provide the impetus for equipment manufacturers to design their devices for industrywide and worldwide compatibility.

To probe further

Copies of the IEEE 802 draft standard are available from the IEEE Computer Society, 1109 Spring St., No. 201, Silver Spring, Md. 20910, or by calling the Society at 301-589-3386.

For more information about the Open Systems Interconnection Model, see "Network Protocols," by A.S. Tannenbaum, in the *Communications of the ACM*, Vol. 13, no. 4, December 1981, pp. 453–89, or "Overview and status of the ISO/ANSI reference model of open systems interconnections," by R. DesJardins, in the *Proceedings of the IEEE Computer Society*

Compcon '80, Washington, D.C., September 1980, pp. 553–57. A copy of the January 1982 International Standards Organization draft standard (ISO DIS 7498, Data Processing—Open Systems Interconnection—Basic Reference Model) is available from ANSI in New York; phone 212-354-3300.

Various organizations sponsor seminars and symposia on local area networks. One such seminar will be held in Washington, D.C., June 24–25 by McGraw-Hill Inc.'s *Data Communications*. Contact the Special Projects Center, 1221 Avenue of the Americas, 42nd Fl., New York, N.Y. 10020; 212-997-2015.

Another seminar will be held in Washington, D.C., on the same dates by Architecture Technology Corp. Registration is $550, and inquiries about the seminar or any other of the company's local area networks should be sent to Architecture Technology Corp., P.O. Box 24344, Minneapolis, Minn. 55424; 612-935-2035.

About the author

Maris Graube (M) is manager of corporate interface engineering at Tektronix Inc., Beaverton, Ore. His group is responsible for compatibility among the company's products and for compliance with relevant data-communications standards. Mr. Graube is the chairman of the IEEE 802 Committee for local network standards and has been active in other standards efforts, such as the IEEE-488 bus. He holds a B.S. in science engineering from the University of Michigan.   ◆

SUPERCOMPUTERS

'SUPERPOWER' COMPUTERS

The omnipresent microprocessor can hardly supplant the large high-speed computer in modeling complex systems and phenomena

The science of computing has advanced tremendously in 30 years, but computing for science is still—relatively—in the Eniac era. Yet, the need for powerful scientific computers is greater than ever. Three-dimensional computer modeling of the world's energy resources, its weather, and its inhabitants has become a major concern of scientists and engineers.

Energy and power modeling is now a key part of the search for oil, for workable nuclear fusion, and for ensuring nuclear reactor safety. Weather modeling is necessary for short-range forecasts and for longer-range hazard predictions about man-made atmospheric pollution. People modeling includes both computer-assisted tomography (CAT) and the modeling of future developments, like the artificial heart.

Such modeling requires state-of-the-art computing at speeds approaching 100 million floating-point operations, or flops, per second. As scientists refine their models in the 1980s, effective speeds well beyond 1000 megaflops will be needed, and computers with that speed would be purchased today if they were available.

To double the number of grid points of a two-dimensional model takes a fourfold increase in computing power. To do so in three dimensions and in time takes a sixteenfold increase. Thus, every twofold increase in the refinement of computer modeling takes an order of magnitude increase in computer speed.

The maximum number of grid points used in fluid dynamics—including, for example, aircraft and spacecraft design—has grown sevenfold every 10 years, with a 10^6 maximum in present use. The factor shows no sign of diminishing. Such growth rate is typical of all modeling requirements, since each model designed to correct the deficiencies of the last one also points to new possibilities with the next version.

Commitments in four fields

U.S. Government-sponsored commitments to increase computer power tenfold have been made in at least four fields. The Geophysical Fluid Dynamics Laboratory in Princeton, N.J., is pursuing such a commitment in weather modeling; the National Aeronautics and Space Administration Ames Research Center, in Mountain View, Calif., is pressing ahead with aircraft and spacecraft lift and turbulence studies; the Nuclear Regulatory Commission is seeking faster simulation of hypothetical accidents in light-water reactors; and the Mayo Clinic in Rochester, Minn., is developing, under National Institute of Health sponsorship, a research CAT scanner for stop-action motion pictures of internal human organs, such as the heart.

Although no supercomputer plans are in the budgets of nuclear fusion researchers, some reseachers say they would push to buy a computer 100 times more powerful than any existing one, if it were available, for modeling the plasma instabilities of proposed

fusion power generators. In the private sector, Chevron Oil says it also would buy such a computer to analyze seismic data in oil exploration; to help calculate how much it can expect in a new field and how best to exploit removal of that oil; and to help determine how best to pump in steam and/or chemicals for later secondary and tertiary recovery. Scientists at New York University's Courant Institute of Mathematical Sciences in New York City would like someday to build a computer thousands of times more powerful than any in commercial production, both to see if it can be done and for computational problems in artificial intelligence, hydrodynamics, fusion, transsonic flow, and quantum chemistry. The U.S. armed forces, particularly the Air Force, have requirements for tactical computers of prodigious speed to process and analyze incoming sensor data and to integrate it with mission tasks on a real-time basis.

If there is one common denominator in all these requirements, it is that there is no common agreement about how such a computer should be built nor any forecast that such agreement is possible in the next several years. Array processors, analog computers, microprocessors, clusters of microprocessors, large scientific mainframes, singly and in combinations, have all been suggested.

The Geophysical Fluid Dynamics Laboratory in Princeton is open to any kind of computer, provided it meets its software speed benchmarks. Ames would probably do the same. The Mayo Clinic is developing its own system, which is really a superfast array processor micro-program sequencer or state machine. The NRC is willing to consider either microprocessor clusters or a combination of analog and digital computers. [See Best Bits, March, 1980.] At least one oil company is close to buying a superarray processor. The Department of Defense is pushing for high-speed VLSI special- and general-purpose building blocks, and the Courant Institute wants to explore the creation of a computer from several thousand VLSI processor chips.

'Ideal' computer proves elusive

The reason for the lack of unanimity is not because of a failure in communication between the groups, but rather because of the complexity of the problems and the fact that every approach appears to have disadvantages.

If floating-point operations per second or their equivalent were the only criterion, analog computers would probably be the leading choice. They are constantly being upgraded to include, for example, microprocessor-controlled function lookups. They are the workhorses in missiles, antisubmarine warfare, and some spacecraft research. Still, it is hard for many researchers to conceive of them as the wave of the future. Researchers are inclined to suspect the accuracy of the analog computer, and the dwindling number of analog computer designers and programmers in the world has led some researchers to suggest that they be protected as an endangered species.

The next choice would be array processors (Fig. 1), which are

Robert Sugarman Associate Editor

essentially computers good at repetitive operations. They excel at a long vector calculation, which is defined as the same instruction—like "multiply" or "take the fast-Fourier transform of"—operating on a very large field of data. And, after that, come scientific mainframes, which excel at shorter vectors and at scalar operations, defined as one instruction operating on one word. (Fig. 2).

When one scientific program with a lot of long vectors—say, signal processing—has to be repeated often and at least cost, array processors would probably be preferred over big mainframes. When a whole mix of research problems has to be run around the clock with maximum speed, the big mainframe would get the nod. The table shows the relative performance of both in nonlinear filter analysis, as compared by R. Bucy of the University of Southern California and K. D. Senne of the M.I.T. Lincoln Laboratory. When the problem mix is well known in advance, a combination of array processors driven by a scientific mainframe might come out on top. The experts agree on only one thing: The choice is difficult and depends on the detailed parallelism of both the program and the computer. By parallelism is meant the number of vector instructions in the software and the amount of vectorizing hardware in the computer. Nobody has found a good way to accurately determine program parallelism without running a real problem on a real machine. Guesstimates of the run time without such a check can be off by a factor of two or three.

The predicted performance of microprocessors interconnected in parallel isn't known yet for general classes of problems, because the efficiency of such machines depends on the problem, the solution algorithms, and the hardware interconnection scheme, all of which are still under preliminary study. (See *Spectrum*, January, pp. 34–35).

It is easy to give relative performance figures for particular problems, on particular computers, but the more specific the problem, the less likely that many people will be interested in an optimum solution. Consider the very specific problem of real-time processing of satellite side-looking radar: Only one such radar system was orbited, and it is now inoperable, with no immediate plans for another. While it was working, though, the satellite was sending data to the Jet Propulsion Laboratory in Pasadena, Calif., at some 120 Mb/s. JPL did occasional data analyses to reconstruct photographs on a state-of-the-art array processor at the rate of 10 h of data reduction for every 15 s of data transmission. As an alternative, JPL converted the data to film strips and used a very much faster, but cumbersome optical analog computer.

Had the satellite transmission continued to transmit, JPL might have started on a very ingenious solution, using a single silicon wafer containing thousands of VLSI processors and capable of real-time reduction of the satellite data. None of these well-defined choices would, however, have been applicable to other more general imaging problems.

Scientific software needs fine touch

How best to write software for scientific processing is another problem. Scientists at Carnegie-Mellon's computer science department, for example, have always tried to write software that is independent of the number of parallel microprocessors operating in their experimental systems. That way, the problem can be simulated with only one processor, albeit a lot slower. If one processor is down, the computer continues to operate. By adding processors, one can easily determine the effect on solution speed.

That ideal is far from achievable with present production hardware. The Geophysical Fluid Dynamics Laboratory reports, for

example, that 15 man-years will have to be spent retuning its existing programs to the architecture of its planned computer, to best match the parallelism of the program with that of the computer.

Some compilers are better than others, depending on the effort made either in software or in hardware to exploit the parallelism of any problem:

One user of a Texas Instruments ASC computer that TI has discontinued benchmarked the Cray-I and found it no substantial improvement over the ASC. The user (not the Geophysical Laboratory) had expected the Cray-I to be faster; the fact that it wasn't may have been caused by initial lack of efficient compiler software.

Some uses of present compilers for array processors and large mainframes report a five to tenfold slowing of computer speed unless there is additional hand tuning of the program. Other users say there is only a two or threefold slowing. Answers depend on the user, the problem, the computer, and the sophistication of the compiler or other software aids.

To be fair to the manufacturers, though, they have tried to reduce hand tuning by direct execution of high-level languages, or by providing language extensions so that the parallism implicit in the users' algorithms can be more easily expressed, or by employing a software "vectorizer" to detect the parallism implicit in programs written in standard Fortran.

The technique depends on the machine. The vector instructions of the new Burroughs BSP, for example, are designed to execute directly Fortran assignment statements under the indexing control typical of DO loops. Assembly language is not needed in the BSP. How well the machine will handle a large variety of problems is now being studied by user groups.

That marginally useful software aids save money in scientific programming is not debatable. Since the typical programming

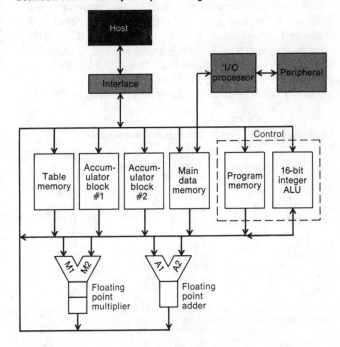

[1] Array processors like this Floating Point Corp. AP-120B achieve high speed by use of parallel processing elements and pipelines. The processor has three arithmetic-logic units —a floating point multiplier, anlogic adder, and a dedicated ALU for generating memory addresses. It has two independent blocks of accumulators and multiple data buses that provide connections between each memory and processing unit.

cost for a big scientific processor runs about $4 million a year, any aids that made only a 2 percent improvement in programming productivity over a three-year period would have a break-even value of a quarter million dollars. The time lost by scientists who have to do hand tuning is not measurable in dollars.

If that means that some scientist-programmers will continue to spend 90 percent of their time programming and 10 percent in research, as a few do at the Geophysical Fluid Dynamics Laboratory, then that appears to be a price they must pay for state-of-the-art modeling tools.

There are well-proven application programs for scientists who are exploring aircraft and spacecraft lift and turbulence characteristics, as well as for weather forecasting, real-time CAT scanning and other advanced medical research, and seismic oil exploration, and all of the scientists involved are looking forward to faster computers. What can they expect to gain? The answer differs in each case.

NASA seeks 3-dimensional modeling

NASA's Ames Research Center is seeking to supplement its Illiac-4 so it can do three-dimensional modeling of aircraft wing lift and turbulence at gigaflop speeds. The Illiac's speed of about 100 megaflops limit it to two-dimensional modeling of airfoil cross sections (Fig. 3). Two proposed 1000 megaflop systems have been suggested by the Burroughs Corp. and by the Control Data Corp. that are both substantially more complex than their present supercomputers, the BSP and the Star, respectively.

The Star has taken about 15 years to become a useful machine—about the same time that Burroughs has taken to come up with a much-modified Illiac-4 architecture, the BSP. The first Star, for example, was very fast at vector instructions, but took a very, very long time for scalar operations. This in no way implies that the two companies are incompetent, but only that it takes 10 or 20 years to come up with workable solutions to complex architectures.

Seymour Cray, the architectural genius who designed the Cray-I in a shorter time, cannot be considered an exception to the rule of long gestation, since he gained considerable experience as the designer of CDC's scientific machines.

Improving weather forecasts

As for weather and climate researchers, they presumably will never run out of their need for faster computers. Present 24-h computer forecasts are made on about a 240-mile grid, roughly the distance from New York to Washington, D.C. That leaves unanswered such questions as: How does New York's weather compare to Wilmington's? To halve the grid size, giving the Wilmington weather, requires 16 times more computing power. The reason is that weather prediction is a four-dimensional process. To produce a prediction (Fig. 4), it is necessary to solve the weather equations over a two-dimensional surface of the Earth at a number of altitude levels and at each of many time steps. Halving the grid means four times as many surface points, twice as many steps and twice as many altitude planes.

To do such a hemispheric 24-h forecast with a 270-mile grid requires about 10^{11} data operations. If the computer could run at a peak speed of 100 million operations per second, it could complete the forecast in, say, 10 min. Since even a Cray-I can't run at such an average peak speed, halving the grid spacing to increase the load 16 times might stretch the time to more than 24 h. Such a forecast would be useless, since it has value only if distributed in a fraction of the forecast time period.

To get more accurate 24-h forecasts, more computing power and more extensive initial data seem to be all that are needed. But to get more accurate weather information a few months ahead and to find the climate effect of CO_2 and particulates from fossil fuel burning, a lot more exploratory data and computer modeling are also going to be necessary. That, at least, is the opinion of Dr. Syukuro Manabe of the Geophysical Fluid Dynamics Laboratory, who specializes in problems of climate dynamics.

Scientist-programmers at the Geophysical Laboratory continually fine-tune their programs to exploit the parallelism of the present ASC computer. They could devise software probes to indicate when the machine is operating efficiently—that is, when the ASC is spending most of its time executing long vectors, at which it is most efficient, and not scalars, at which it is relatively inefficient compared with the performance of the Cray-I, but the structure of the TI machine permits a much simpler hardware probe, which also records a graph of the changes of parallelism in the program.

The idea for the probe came from Jim Welsh, the senior computer systems analyst at the laboratory. He just attaches a pen chart recorder to one or more of its four vector computing sections. The chart recorder is connected to a flip-flop that is in one state when the machine is doing scalar calculations and in the other when it is using its vector sections. Its output is a weighted time average of the two states. The maximum vector efficiency is

[2] Present computers can operate at about 100 floating-point operations per second, as shown in the figure. To reach 1000 Mflops for fluid-dynamic problem-solving, the Burroughs Corp. and Control Data Corp. have proposed highly parallel computers. The Burroughs proposal, for example, would use 512 separate processor-plus-memory sections, each capable of operating either in lockstep with the others for vector instruction or independently. One potential customer is NASA, which funded the proposals and would use such a computer for aerodynamic simulation.

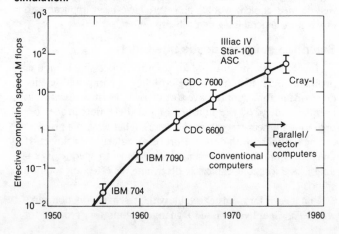

Cost/speed comparison for scientific computers

Computer	Maximum Megaflop Rate	Average Megaflop Rate	Software Development, Man-months	Hardware Cost, Millions of Dollars
AP 120/190	12	5.9*	6	0.18
AP 120/190	12	1.0†	1.2	0.18
Cray-I	160	23.5	.5	7.76
Star 100	40	16.8	2	8
CDC 7600	10	3.3	1.1	3
Illiac IV	80	9.1	3	10
PDP 11/70	0.2	0.09	1.2	0.15
370/168	3	0.75	1	2

* Hand coded assembly language
† Estimated for compiler performance

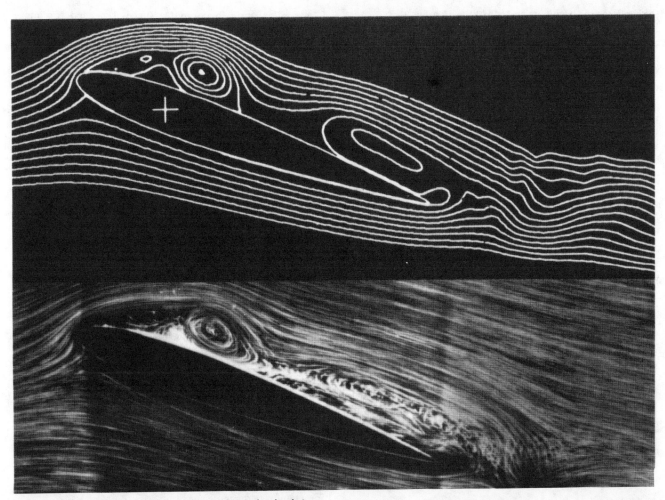

[3] One frame of a computer-generated movie depicts a helicopter blade cross section moving at low air velocity (top) and is compared with a wind-tunnel result (bottom). The agreement is good at the forward edge of the blade, but less so at the rear because of turbulence. To obtain such a movie at high velocity, in 3-D, and with accurate analysis of turbulence would have required a computer much more powerful than the CDC 6600 used by Dr. Unmeel Mehta of NASA's Ames Research Center.

[4] Monsoon winds over the Indian Ocean, are shown in one frame of a computer-generated movie. The white arrows show the direction and velocity of the winds at sea level, and the grey arrows at 40 000 feet. The length of the arrows is proportional to the wind speed. A computer model was used to generate a frame every 3 min over a total simulated time of three years to analyze the rapidly changing wind patterns.

given by $N/(N+K)$, where N is the vector length or number of data words in a single instruction and K the number of clock cycles to load the vector pipeline. For the four-pipe ASC at the Geophysical Laboratory, K is 25 clock cycles. Vectors that are much longer than K will have nearly 100 percent efficiency. For shorter vectors the efficiency drops, and the recorder tracks the drop. The idea is to code the application program so that the recorder reads high most of the time. No two programs show the same pen chart signature.

The degree of vectorization as an ASC runs through the weather forecast for the Northern Hemisphere is shown in Fig. 5. The horizontal grid has 161×161 data points, and there are nine atmospheric levels at each point. The equator is described in the random memory of the computer by an inscribed circle tangent to the square grid. The hemispheric weather is calculated only within the circle. At the beginning and end of the program, these vector lengths are short because much of the square is outside the circle—in the opposite hemisphere. Toward the middle of the run the parallelism is high, with the vector lengths approaching 159×9 elements. The trapezoidal shape of the recording accurately reflects this parallelism of the program, which on the average spends 70 percent of its time doing vector arithmetic.

However, other programs running on the same ASC have totally different patterns. Also, if the same programs were run on a different computer, it would produce different patterns. For example, the Cray-I can load its vector pipeline in two clock cycles, whereas the ASC takes 25 cycles. The Cray, on the other hand, can handle only vectors up to 64 words long, whereas some of the vectors in the ASC program are 20 times longer.

When vectors aren't being processed, the scientific machines revert to scalar operation. Here, the Cray is a lot faster than the ASC. TI planned to increase the scalar speed of the ASC, but the idea was abandoned when the company dropped out of the scientific mainframe business.

Pursuing the artificial heart

At the Courant Institute of Mathematical Sciences, Dr. Charles Peskin, associate professor, and Dr. David McQueen, research scientist, have been using a CDC 6600 for time-sequence, two-dimensional modeling of blood flow in the heart, with the goal of understanding how best to make an artifical heart valve (Fig. 6). Each time frame takes 40 minutes to compute. They see the need to work in three dimensions rather than two and, with 64-grid spacing, they would require 64 times more computing speed. This is out of the question with their present computer. The researchers feel that the solution may be to construct an array of 64^3 microprocessors, as envisioned by one of the institute's computer scientists, Dr. Jacob Schwartz.

[5] Variations in parallelism in a single computer program are evident in this pen-chart recording of a vector pipeline of a Texas Instruments ASC machine as the computer runs a Northern Hemisphere weather forecast. The recording shows low vector activity as the program starts at the equator (left), highest at about the North Pole (center), and low again as the program ends at the equator (right).

A similar jump in computer speed is needed for image reconstruction of human anatomy. The present typical CAT scanner, using conventional array processors, needs a few seconds to produce an image (Fig. 7), but the Mayo Clinic's super CAT scanner that is nearing completion will produce high-resolution three-dimensional images of the beating heart and other organs at 60 frames per second. (see *Spectrum*, January 1979, p. 77).

X-ray CAT scanners need only two algorithms. One of these reconstructs the image; the other removes the star-shaped aberrations unavoidably produced at each image point by the reconstruction. The detailed nature of both algorithms determines image quality, and is kept highly confidential by the scanner manufacturers.

Cross-sectional CAT images used to take 6 to 10 minutes to generate on a conventional computer, but streamlining the algorithms and switching to an array processor has cut this to 5 to 20 s. If this still seems like a long time, remember that each cross-sectional view has from 256^2 to 512^2 pixels or picture elements. Each pixel may be reconstructed from up to several hundred different viewing angles. To do a reconstruction with the maximum number of viewing angles per pixel then takes about 200 ns. This can be achieved with specially designed reconstruction processors even more efficient than general-purpose array processors.

However, such reconstructions are both two-dimensional and generated too slowly (5 s) to freeze the motion of organs such as the heart or the lungs. To reconstruct cross-sectional images of the lungs, for example, the patient must hold his breath. And to generate an accurate cross-sectional image of a beating heart is not possible with present X-ray CAT scanners. A physician may also need dozens of cross-sectional images—for example, of the liver—where some five to 20 cross-section slices may be needed for a complete diagnosis.

To solve such problems of three-dimensional, stop-action viewing, scientists at the Mayo Clinic are developing a research scanner, not meant for commercial production, that in 11 ms will take from 60 to 240 thin adjacent cross-sections that can be stacked one upon the other to form a truly three-dimensional image. The entire scan can be repeated at 60 sets per second for several

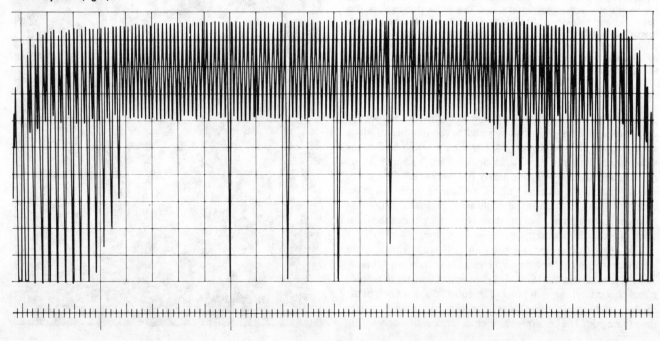

seconds, generating data for thousands of cross-sectional images. Because of the short processing and exposure time, three-dimensional, stop-motion pictures of a beating heart will be possible for the first time. And dye injection may be used to trace blood flow.

The computational speed to assure computer processing of a scan in a few minutes will require processing times of about 1 ns per pixel per view, or from 2 billion to 3 billion arithmetic operations per second.

To accomplish this, Barry Gilbert, a researcher in the Mayo Clinic's Dept. of Physiology and Biophysics, has designed and is now constructing the prototype of a specialized array processor with an architecture unique to image processing. Having examined the performance of 16-bit microprocessors, he concluded that they could do much better by using a few microprogram sequencers to drive two dozen or so computing elements, each performing only arithmetic functions.

The prototype uses two wide-word microprogram sequences, one for the prefiltering operation and one for the image construction algorithm. The final computer, Mr. Gilbert says, will probably use 29 computing modules and two microsequencers. It will probably be fabricated with subnanosecond emitter-coupled logic and execute 2 billion to 3 billion arithmetic operations per second. The controllers, the researcher adds, need very few instructions, typically no more than 100, divided into 10 subroutines.

While the control code is written for CAT processing, Mr. Gilbert sees no reason why similar computer architectures couldn't be used for other imaging applications that need high speed, but only simple programs.

Array processors help find oil

Many oil companies are investing in even more elaborate array processor systems to help in the discovery of oil and gas and the management of its recovery. Although seismic exploration accounts for only 10 to 15 percent of the money being spent to find oil, the industry processed some 10^{15} bits of seismic data in 1979. One company alone, Western Geophysical of Houston, Texas, is outranked only by the U.S. Government as the world's largest user of magnetic tapes. The company has about two million reels of geophysical data in inventory, according to its technical director, Carl Savit, and 300 000 reels are awaiting processing. The inventory is so large, he said, that he has been searching for a way to use video disks instead, but so far no manufacturers will undertake to supply the large number of disks needed.

Seismic exploration, Mr. Savit explained, usually involves setting off a sonic shock wave, either by explosives, by firing a huge air gun, or (on land) by jamming a 14-ton hydraulic ram into the ground and vibrating it in a computer-controlled pattern. A few thousand phones scattered about the shot are used to pick up echoes.

The data are used, in most cases, to draw two-dimensional cross-sections that display the geometrical arrangement of underground strata such as that shown on the cover of this issue. A new approach involves reconstructions that identify the types of rock that make up the strata and can tell which bear oil, according to Mr. Savit, a pioneer in this technique. Had such techniques been used recently off the Florida and Atlantic Coasts, he said, many dry holes might not have been drilled. A few surveys today are being conducted with three-dimensional data and rock-identification methods, but at heavy cost for computer power.

Analyzing the data doesn't take many complex algorithms, since most of today's analysis assumes that sound rays obey the simple laws of ray reflection, their wavelength being small compared with any reflective bodies. Reassembling the echoes does take many square roots of sums of the squares in Pythagorean arithmetic to calculate the time delay of different paths. More time-consuming is the need to remove redundant data. A typical field record for the response of the earth to one sonic input has 3000 different time values, each at say, 48 different locations. This produces about 150 000 floating-point numbers. One signal input is applied typically to every 30 to 60 m along a survey line, so the survey produces about 2 million to 5 million floating-point numbers per kilometer, with redundancy ranging from 12 to about 100.

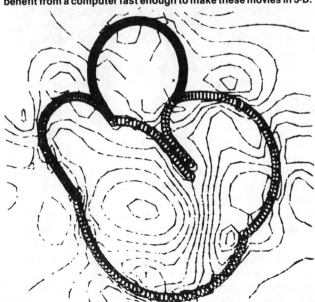

[6] Blood flow within the heart just after the mitral valve (the two contacting surfaces) has closed is shown on a single frame of a computer-generated movie. Artificial heart valve studies would benefit from a computer fast enough to make these movies in 3-D.

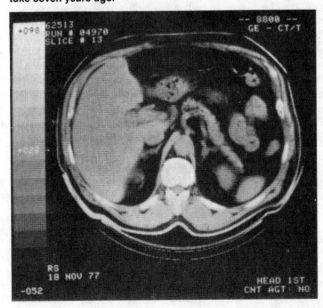

[7] Midsection scan of the human body with General Electric computer-assisted tomography equipment. Such body scans would have been badly blurred five years ago and impossible to take seven years ago.

If the sonic source is not even approximately an impulse, then the data must also be deconvolved with the source waveform to reconstruct what the echoes would have been with an impulse source.

Mr. Savit uses commercially available array processors for seismic analysis, but in a very complex interrelationship. Western Geophysical's associated company, Litton Resources Systems, has developed a high-speed bus system for interconnecting tape drives, array processors, host processors, and intelligent memories with self-contained microprocessors for memory address formatting.

One array processor might be used for the Pythagorean ray-tracing arithmetic, for example, while another processes the same data to compensate for the spectral response of the sonic driver. The bus has a communication rate of 40 megabytes per second and allocates bus time according to needed resources. If two units need to communicate with each other at 6-Mb rate, the bus assigns that bandwidth to them and uses the remainder of its bandpass for other allocations.

If array processors had not arrived on the oil scene in 1967, Mr. Savit calculates that, by 1985, the industry would have needed 3000 of the most powerful computers then available, a figure exceeding estimated production of such machines.

Mr. Savit believes that the oil industry's production of data power will go up by a factor of 10 every three or four years. As the seismic survey models become more elaborate, more data points will be needed, with the processing rate going up even faster than the square of the number of datapoints. Present calculations require about 50 to 100 flops per data point, but for three-dimensional calculations and modeling of oil reservoirs, the total may go up to 1000 flops.

Superarrays to the rescue?

If array processors are so effective, why not just enlarge their instruction repertoire and turn them into general-purpose scientific processors? No one is attempting such an architecture at present, but DataWest of Scottsdale, Ariz., and International Computers Ltd. of London are building very sophisticated array procesors for attachment to large scientific computers. The cost of such machines approximates that of the large general scientific computers.

The DataWest processor is designed to work with a Univac 1184 computer. Using one Univac and two DataWest attached processors at a cost of $8 million, the company says it can get a peak rate of 250 megaflops. This compares with 160 megaflops with a $10 million Cray-I. At least one major oil company that operates Univacs is negotiating with DataWest and may buy its machine for modeling oil field recovery operations. Besides a lot of very expensive parallel and pipelining hardware, the DataWest processor has two key features to overcome the data and instruction bottlenecks between the host and processing machines:
1. To speed data flow, a cache memory is added to the host computer, so the four ports of the DataWest processor can transfer data to it at 40 megawords per second.
2. To speed instruction flow, each subroutine in the DataWest processor is linked by a series of hierarchically arranged firmware indices, so the next subroutine can be quickly pulled either from its own internal memory or from the host.

The DataWest processor has four parallel internal processing sections to speed data flow. The data array processor being constructed by International Computers Ltd.—the company calls it a DAP—has a thousand processors, and the company plans to go up to 4000. But, while the DataWest processor handles 36 bits of arithmetic, each DAP processor handles only one bit. The DAP processors are connected in a matrix array of 32 × 32 or 64 × 64, with each processor able to communicate with its four neighbors. Each processor has a few thousand words of fast random-access storage.

Since the combined memory of all the DAP processors is bit-organized, it can also serve as part of the random memory of the host processor. This solves, in theory, the problem of communicating between the host machine and the attached DAP, since they are both mapped into the same space.

The DAP is capable of some unique on-the-fly reconfigurations: When one instruction has to handle much data, as in matrix multiplication, each processor stores all the bits of a word, with one processor for every matrix or submatrix element. This makes for very fast matrix operations. For vector operations on a string of data, each row of processors holds one bit of the data, with ripple carry between rows. The vector string is then formed of columns of processors. The Goodyear Aerospace Staran IV is organized architectually like the DAP. Four Staran IV machines and one DAP have been sold.

Scientific mainframes forever?

Must scientific computers always remain outside the mainstream of large computer development, whose primary thrust is for business use? Only about 100 CDC 7600 machines and about 20 of the present generation of supercomputers have been sold.

And even if the scientific computers remain a class apart, is there a better architecture than that used in the present scientific supercomputers, the Cray-I, the Burroughs BSP, the CDC Star, and Cyber 200 series? At Yorktown Heights, N.Y., George Paul, manager of vector architecture for International Business Machines, doesn't know the answer yet, but has been engaged for several years in research projects to find some answers.

Mr. Paul doesn't think that array processors with canned algorithms are a reasonable alternative to a general-purpose scientific machine, and certainly not to one that can also double as a business mainframe. The array processors made by IBM are primarily designed for seismic data reduction.

The key to evaluating an architectures' effectiveness, Mr. Paul believes, is not its peak processing rate, but the degree to which it can exploit the parallelism in its application programs. A program with a lot of vector or matrix instructions is highly parallel, in the sense that a single instruction simultaneously operates on all the elements in the row or matrix. Such parallelism is easy to obtain in problems like seismic data reduction for petroleum exploration, where the parallelism, Mr. Paul says, is as high as 85 percent. But, when considering an array processor for more general problems—even an array in which the algorithms can be loaded dynamically—one must take into account total system performance. This includes the time it takes to transfer data back and forth to the array box and the cost of translating programs to use the box.

All of the big scientific mainframes, Mr. Paul feels, have specialized architectures that use one or more features to exploit this parallelism, but he is searching for an optimum architecture that would exploit the best features of all such machines and also serve as a business mainframe.

Some business problems display algorithmic parallelism and some data parallelism. For example, computing breakout of parts needed to assemble a product is, in principle, a matrix operation. Computing a payroll is a vector operation, with some conditional vector operations thrown in for contingency modifications. Today's architectures, Mr. Paul feels, are not well-suited to either of these problems. ◆

SUPERCOMPUTERS

BEYOND THE SUPERCOMPUTER

NASA is developing ultrafast machines to process satellite data that would choke a mere supercomputer

Computers 1000 times faster than today's fastest supercomputers are needed to process the radar or television pictures satellites will be capable of broadcasting to earth stations in the late 1980s. Computations will be needed on 10^{13} bits of data every 24 hours—representing at least 500 maps or scenes that satellites will send as they monitor the earth's weather, mineral and water resources, food crops, and atmospheric pollution. The goal, which the National Aeronautics and Space Administration has been attempting to meet since 1971, is to develop a new family of computers: ultrafast image processors that can do up to 10^{11} operations per second, whereas current computers can do a maximum of 10^8 such operations. The 10^{11} operations per second are needed since each picture element (pixel) must be processed at the rate of 10^2 to 10^4 operations per second to identify a single map in the required time.

While research has proceeded throughout the world, a single-instruction multiple-data–stream computer known as the massively parallel processor (MPP) is being built for NASA by the Goodyear Aerospace Corp. in Akron, Ohio. The machine, scheduled for delivery in 1983, will have a 10-MHz clock rate and be able to do 6 billion 8-bit additions every second and almost 2 billion 8-bit multiplications. Similar but less powerful computers are operating in England.

These computers descended from the Solomon computer, reported in 1962 by Daniel L. Slotnick, W. Carl Borck, and Robert C. McReynolds of the Westinghouse Electric Corp. in Baltimore, Md., and concepts advanced at about the same time by Stephen H. Unger of Bell Laboratories in Whippany, N.J.

These early efforts were premature, because the circuitry necessary to achieve ultrafast processing was too expensive and bulky. What's more, almost nothing was known at that time about programming the thousands of simultaneous operations these machines must do to achieve such high speed. However, the development of large-scale integrated circuits and advances in software for multiprocessors has made the project economically feasible and the goal reachable.

As envisioned by the NASA planners in 1971, the ultrafast computers would have a spatially parallel architecture that would enable them to recognize automatically in just milliseconds the details in satellite pictures. To accomplish this, thousands of computing units would be organized to process simultaneously each pixel in an array of thousands; meanwhile, the separate processors would be interconnected to do the tasks required to identify details over the entire picture. These tasks would include the correction of distortions, image registration (matching input images against reference images), calculation of correlation functions, and classification of the multispectral characteristics of im-

ages (the identification of crops, land areas, water, and so on by their different colors).

Whereas conventional computers manipulate individual 0s and 1s as the basic computational objects, the new parallel machines would manipulate arrays of 0s and 1s—an entire black and white image—as the unit of computation. By the same token, instructions would also have the format of an array that would simultaneously control the operations of every processing unit. The processing of real, gray-level pictures would be achieved through analog-to-digital conversions that generated separate bit planes—planes corresponding to 2^0, 2^1, 2^2, and so on—so that each black and white plane could be processed [Fig. 1A]. Arithmetic operations involving adjacent processing units would, therefore, be implemented by sequences of shifts within a plane and Boolean operations on the contents of adjacent planes.

Spatially parallel machines may be pictured as conventional computers in which every data wire has been replaced by thousands of wires or fiber-optic tubes, while every logic gate has been replaced by thousands of logic gates and every memory element by thousands of memory elements. The result would be thousands of architecturally identical computers. In future image-processing computers built along these lines, image data will be sensed on a two-dimensional array. Analog-to-digital conversions will then be carried out and the results passed to one massively parallel computer [Fig. 1B]. All spatial data will be processed in parallel in semiconductor chips stacked one on top of another.

In 1978, NASA authorized Goodyear Aerospace to design and build a spatially parallel computer, the massively parallel processor, for use at earth stations. The MPP performs 16 384 simultaneous operations per second with a 10-MHz clock rate and an array of 128 by 128 processing units [Fig. 1C]. The addition of 32-bit floating point numbers can be done at 430 million operations per second and multiplications at 216 million operations per second, compared with 50 to 100 million for such computations on today's supercomputers. Ultimately, spatially parallel computers may be built with 1024 by 1024 processing units that can do at least one million simultaneous operations in approximately every 10 nanoseconds.

In London the massively parallel machines that have been in use for several years include the cellular-logic image processor (CLIP) at University College, which can do 9216 simultaneous operations, and the distributed array processor (DAP) at Queen Mary College, which can do 4096 operations.

Major design improvements must still be made, however, before spatially parallel computers can reach their full processing potential. The improvements include: (1) optimization of the interconnection pattern between processing units [Fig. 2]; (2) optimization of application software in both high-level and assembly language; and (3) development of methods for rapid, simultaneous analog-to-digital conversion at every pixel in a sensor array, compared with slower-current methods in which the

David H. Schaefer George Mason University
James R. Fischer
National Aeronautics and Space Administration

array is scanned serially and conversions are done 1 pixel at a time.

Interconnections simplify processing

Computing the two-dimensional fast-Fourier transform of an image, transposing a matrix, or matching two images involves communication between units: the shifting of the numbers associated with a group of pixels to the processing units at other

pixels [Fig. 3]. An operation called "sliding" is the simplest form of communication between units. The simplest form of slider is basically made from two data buses, one offset from the other. This device can shift an image one element north, south, east, or west. In this operation one row or column at the edge of the input array is lost, while an output array receives (at the opposite edge) a row or column of 0s. A "loop slider" does not lose data; instead the row or column that would be lost in a basic slider moves

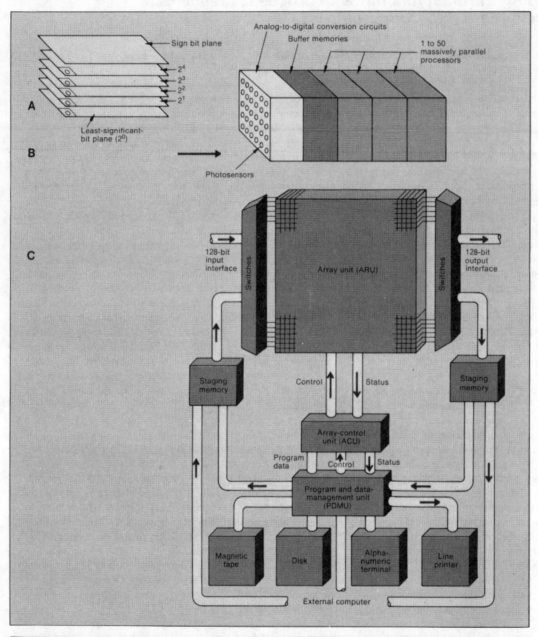

[1] Spatially parallel machines—which manipulate entire images, not just individual 0s and 1s, as the basic units of computation—process gray-level pictures by generating separate bit planes (A). Image data is passed to buffer memories (B) and parallel computing units (C) for further processing.

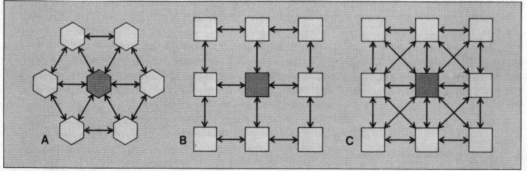

[2] Processing units are commonly interconnected in either a 6-connected hexagonal array (A) or 4- or 8-connected square arrays (B, C). Interconnections are minimized to avoid excessive communication delays or off-chip connections.

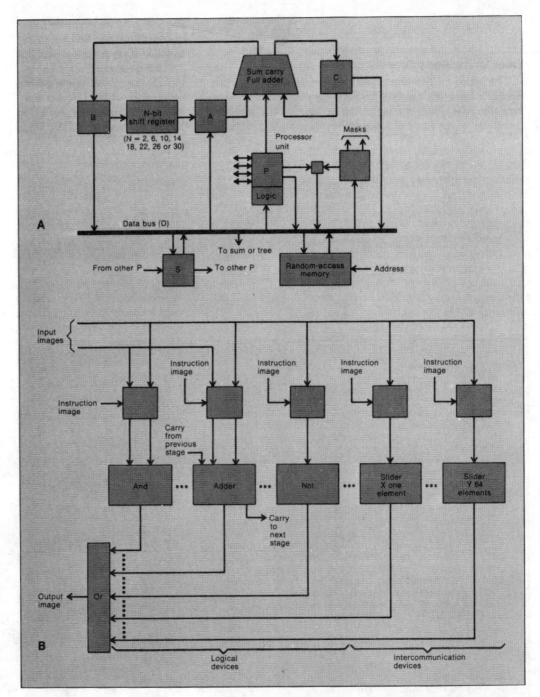

[3] A single processing unit in the massively parallel processor being built by Goodyear Aerospace (A) receives the same instruction as all other units when the instruction image (B) is all black or all white. A masking register alters the instructions in individual units.

to the opposite edge of the output array.

Additional connections on a slider can be used alternately for input or output of single rows or columns of data. A four-way programmable slider is capable of sliding north, south, east, or west and is made of arrays of switches and elementary sliding components.

Increasing the number of more distantly communicating neighbors may contribute to the speedier execution of some algorithms; however, the longer connections to distant neighbors lead to circuit delays that may slow execution speed. Such delays may pose no problems when the number of communicating units ranges to several thousand, but they are a serious problem when 16 384 units are interconnected.

A communication pattern called the shuffle/exchange network has long been studied for potential use in future machines. A so-called perfect shuffle is analogous to shuffling a deck of cards, or rearranging the elements of the vector so that the

elements of the first half of the vector alternate with those of the second half [see "The perfect shuffle," opposite]. Another view of the shuffle is that it can be implemented by a sequence of sliding operations.

Still poorly understood is the effect of shuffle or any other overall interconnection pattern on the computational speed of massively parallel machines. Some patterns are optimal for certain parallel algorithms, but the optimal patterns vary greatly from one algorithm to another.

In CLIP-3 and later models, at any rate, each unit communicates with eight neighbors that can slide diagonally. In the MPP, however, communication is only with nearest neighbors (up, down, left, right), except at the edges of the array.

Goodyear designers chose the simpler square array because their studies indicated that the nearest neighbor interaction would suffice for tasks specified by NASA. Special staging memories serve the input/output operations that require the disassembly of gray-level images into component bit planes, or the reassembly of gray-level images into gray-level format [Fig. 1C].

Programs can change the connections between processor units at the edges to allow data to enter or leave the array. They can also change the communication pattern so that units in the top edge are linked to units in the bottom edge, or links are set up between the left and right edges.

Images control processor units

The spatially parallel computer instructions, in the form of images, use the sliding operation and AND gates to coordinate the actions of the processing units. The simplest types of instruction are completely white or black fields. A white instruction is analogous to opening the shutter of a lens; it opens logic gates while a black one closes them. With the uniform-field instructions, a conventional computer can be used as a host to control the arithmetic units of the MPP; the host can generate the instructions as voltages that control the shutters. The uniform instruction field is equivalent to an instruction in an SIMD (single-instruction-stream, multiple-data) architecture. Instructions for individual devices can be changed by masking.

When an instruction is a uniform field, any operation done on one point of an image is also done on every other point. When half the instruction image is black and the other half is white, half the image will be extracted, or filtered out. Through such non-uniform instruction images, programs can be written, for example, that simultaneously locate cotton in land areas while searching for cod in water. A uniform instruction field, by contrast, can initiate only one process at a time.

A typical program in the MPP is illustrated by the following algorithm for detecting the eastern edge of a pattern stored in memory [Fig. 4]:

• Machine cycle 1: load image A into processor through logic programmed for negation. (At the end of this cycle, the negative image of A is in the processor.)
• Machine cycle 2: slide the processor west. (Image C is now in the processor.)
• Machine cycle 3: (image C) AND (image A). (Image D is now in the processor.)
• Machine cycle 4: load image D into memory.

Though this example represents a natural application of parallel processing to images, it is less obvious that parallel pro-

---

The perfect shuffle

When massive parallel machines were first conceived, the square mesh was thought to be the best compromise for handling the largest variety of algorithms; however, computer scientists later developed mathematical proofs that the mesh was far from optimal for such computations as fast-Fourier transforms, matrix transportation, and sorting. Although computer designers still debate whether a single optimal interconnection pattern can ever be found, the pioneering concept of the perfect shuffle was introduced in 1968 by M.C. Pease and in 1971 by Harold S. Stone, now professor of computer science at the University of Massachusetts in Amherst.

The pioneering investigators demonstrated mathematically that the perfect shuffle, though not necessarily optimal for all algorithms, fit those commonly used in image processing better than the simple square or hexagonal mesh. During the last decade many investigators have expanded this early concept into an abstract mathematical specialty that is applied to designing "universal" networks for parallel processing. A universal network can implement any permutation of the input and output lines if multiple passes through the network are allowed. A number of shuffle-type networks have since been proved capable of generating any permutation of inputs and outputs in three passes, according to D. Stott Parker Jr., professor of computer science at the University of California at Los Angeles.

A key concept behind such networks is the perfect shuffle. As defined by Prof. Stone, it is a shuffle of the elements of a vector that is analogous to viewing the vector as a deck of cards shuffled so that the elements of both halves of the vector alternate. The importance of the shuffle is shown in the accompanying figure, where a parallel processor has been implemented with the perfect shuffle to perform the fast-Fourier transform algorithm at peak efficiency.

The perfect shuffle of the vector, $e(0)$, $e(1)$, $e(2) \ldots$, $e(n/2) \ldots$ $(n-1)$, yields $e(0)$, $e(n/2)$, $e(1)$, $e(n^2 + 1) \ldots$, $e(n-1)$. The shuffle may also be viewed as an operation that cyclically rotates the bits in the binary representation of each element of the vector one bit position to the left. The network shown in the figure, which was advanced by Prof. Stone, computes the fast-Fourier transform through a perfect shuffle by combining pairs of numbers with indexes that differ by 4 in their binary expansions. After one shuffle, the pairs combined will differ by 2, and finally by 1.

Each of the modules labeled MA is a multiply-add unit that computes two weighted sums of its inputs simultaneously. For n samples of a time-varying function, the processor com-

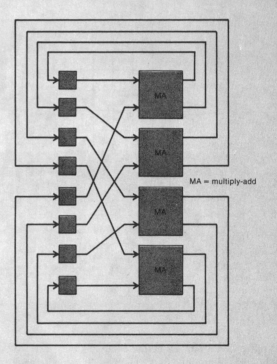

MA = multiply-add

putes the fast-Fourier transform by repeating the following sequence $\log_2 n$ times: (1) shuffle; (2) multiply-add; and (3) transfer results back to the input of the shuffle network.

The perfect shuffle may also be applied to such two-dimensional matrix processing as matrix multiplication, where it is necessary to align the rows of one matrix with the columns of another. Prof. Stone has shown that such processing can be done most efficiently by generating the matrix transposition with a shuffle interconnection pattern. If the elements of a 2m-by-2m matrix are stored in special order in the memory, the matrix transposition can be generated by doing m perfect shuffles of the elements. After m such shuffles, the indexes of the matrix will have undergone m cyclic shifts of their binary representations; this corresponds to moving every element (i, j) of the matrix to the position occupied by (j, i)—which is the definition of transposition.

—Robert Bernhard

cessors can excel at arithmetic, except in such specific cases as the fast-Fourier transform, matrix transposition, and polynomial evaluation.

Conventional circuits are used

Today's spatially parallel computers use conventional techniques of computer fabrication. Both the CLIP and MPP use custom microcircuit chips that have a two-column-by-four-row version of the computer. The MPP chip has no random-access memory, but the system has commercially available RAMs.

The DAP uses standard, medium-scale–integrated TTL. Whereas the CLIP is controlled by a commercially available computer, the MPP and DAP have their own specialized control units. For high-speed operation, the control computer or unit must do such bookkeeping operations as address calculation, loop control, and subroutine calling, while simultaneously sending control signals and memory addresses to the array.

The present computers have similar I/O problems. For example, although the two 8-bit images can be added in 24 machine cycles in the MPP, input and output of data takes 3096 cycles. The most cost-effective use of these computers, therefore, is for applications that are computationally intensive and require relatively little input/output. One example of a cost-effective application is the production of images from data sent by synthetic aperture radars.

Because today's spatially parallel machines have such small amounts of memory, a staging memory is needed for buffering input and output. The MPP has a staging memory that not only provides buffering but also can be used in reformatting data. Such reformatting operations include the "corner turning" function, where conventional byte-oriented data are converted into the bit-plane form normally processed by such computers.

A further problem with today's spatially parallel machines is that the software for such systems is still in a primitive state of development. The CLIP, for example, has only recently begun to utilize a high-level programming language (the C language developed at Bell Laboratories in Murray Hill, N. J.), whereas the DAP uses a new, parallel version of Fortran called DAP-Fortran.

The MPP, on the other hand, is still being programmed in assembly language (an intermediate language between machine and high-level languages); however, compilers are now being developed for both Parallel Pascal and Parallel Fortran. The major shortcoming in previous languages was that the machine architecture remains relatively visible to the programmer. However, with Parallel Pascal—an extension of standard Pascal—programmers use the MPP array architecture implicitly.

The MPP will be used both as an element in an operational

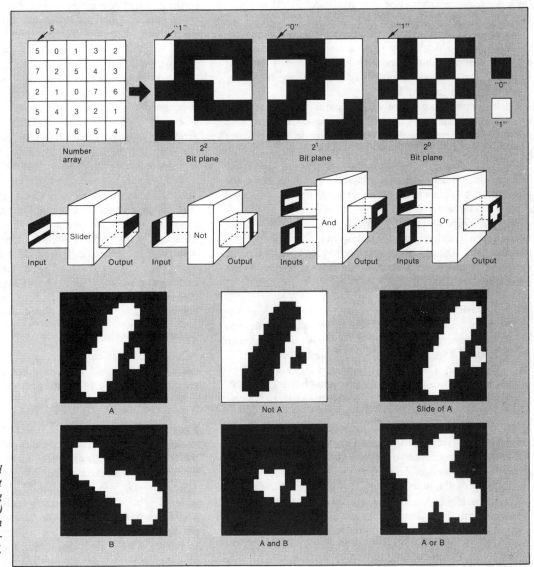

In a spatially parallel machine, the bit planes representing gray-level images (top) are processed through four logical operations: sliding, NOT, AND, and OR.

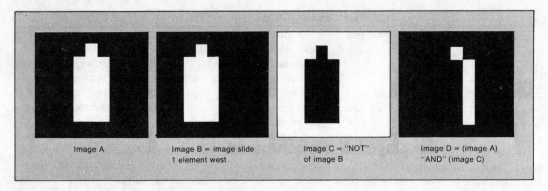

Image A

Image B = image slide
1 element west

Image C = "NOT"
of image B

Image D = (image A)
"AND" (image C)

[4] The algorithm for detecting the eastern edge of a pattern, when applied to pattern A, produces the contour D.

data-processing system and as a research tool. An example of operational use is for the Landsat (satellite) Thematic Mapper data. The MPP that is now being built will be able to process over 500 scenes daily. Another example is a system to process data from an array with 18 000 sensing units—a task requiring three MPPs. Proposals have also been made to use the MPP for running programs that will test various climate models.

Electronics in the future

Future spatially parallel image-processing machines may well be multiple-data, multiple-instruction (MIMD) machines where every element can receive a unique instruction. The front ends of these image processors may be large array-sized SIMD machines that will feed into smaller, very sophisticated MIMD arrays.

Although the only interconnection network shown in this article is the slider, which gives a direct connection only to nearest neighbor elements, shuffle and exchange components for direct connections to distant elements will be among a large class of interconnection options available.

Optical implementations of spatially parallel computers seem most attractive, since light is a method of transmitting thousands of image points simultaneously. Work on an optical embodiment of digital spatially parallel systems has recently been carried out by Sing H. Lee and R. Athale at the University of California. These systems utilize lasers, liquid-crystal logic components, and phenomena of polarized light; the present, slow liquid-crystal devices will be replaced with high-speed silicon-lithium-niobate devices. Tomorrow's spatially parallel processors may well use both electronic and optical components in a single machine. By the mid-1990s, therefore, we may see a 1024-by-1024-element computer capable of performing 1 million simultaneous operations every 10 nanoseconds.

To probe further

The general philosophy and specific circuits of massively parallel machines are described in "Tse computers," by David H. Schaefer and James P. Strong III, in *Proceedings of the IEEE*, 1977, Vol. 65, pp. 129–38. These computers are called tse (pronounced "see") because they use pictograms (images) instead of single bits, and tse is the English transliteration of the Chinese word for "pictogram character." This article preceded the design and building of the prototype massively parallel processor (MPP) by Goodyear Aerospace, and so it emphasizes the potential role of fiber-optic and optoelectronic state-of-the-art large-scale–integrated semiconductor circuits.

The MPP itself is described fully in two articles: "Design of a massively parallel processor," by Kenneth Batcher of Goodyear Aerospace, in *IEEE Transactions on Computers*, 1980, Vol. C-29, pp. 837–39; and "The massively parallel processor," by D.H. Schaefer *et al.*, in *AIAA Third Conference on Computers in Aerospace*, 1980, pp. 187–90. The first article has block diagrams of the overall machine and the identical processing units. Each unit is a bit-serial arithmetic unit with auxiliary shift registers, control logic, random-access memory, and masks that control all functions of the unit. Like the control units of other parallel processors, an array-control unit performs scalar arithmetic of the application program, for overlapping of scalar arithmetic, input/output, and array arithmetic. Staging memories, located between the I/O ports of the control unit and the program-management unit, reorder the arrays of data in memory (satellite images) so that they can be processed more efficiently.

The origins of the massively parallel image processor go back to the articles "A computer oriented toward spatial problems," by Stephen H. Unger, in *Proceedings of the IRE*, 1958, Vol. 46, pp. 1744–50; and "The Solomon computer," by Daniel Slotnick *et al.*, in *AFIPS Proceedings of the Fall Joint Computer Conference*, 1962, Vol. 22, pp. 97–107.

Pattern Recognition, edited by B.G. Batchelor (Plenum Press, New York, 1978) has a chapter about the cellular-logic image processors (the CLIP series) by its chief architect, E.J. Duff of University College, London. The CLIP series and the distributed array processor at Queen Mary College in London, along with the Illiac IV at the University of Illinois, offer the only operating experience so far with massively parallel machines.

Though parallel-processor hardware is widely described, few articles discuss software or the related subject of interconnection patterns between processor units. The perfect shuffle, as applied to sorting, matrix transposition, and computing the fast-Fourier transform is analyzed by Harold S. Stone in "Parallel processing with the perfect shuffle," *IEEE Transactions on Computers*, 1971, Vol. C-20, pp. 153–61. The universality of various shuffle/exchange networks is the focus of "Notes on shuffle/exchange-type switching networks," by D. Stott Parker Jr., in *IEEE Transactions on Computers*, 1980, Vol. C-29, pp. 213–22.

About the authors

David M. Schaefer is adjunct associate professor of engineering at George Mason University in Fairfax, Virginia, where he is setting up a facility to do research on spatially parallel computers. Prior to joining the university, Mr. Schaefer was head of the Computer Development Section at NASA's Goddard Space Flight Center in Greenbelt, Md. There he brought about the program to build the massively parallel processor. Mr. Schaefer is the author of over 20 papers in the computer field and holds patents for 12 computer-related inventions. He graduated from Tulane University in 1949 with a B.S. in physics.

Jim Fischer (M), an aerospace engineer at Goddard Space Flight Center has worked in the field of spatially parallel computing since receiving his B.S.E.E. from North Carolina State University in 1974. He is now project engineer at Goddard, planning the use of the massively parallel processor. ◆

SUPERCOMPUTERS

THE LIMITS TO SIMULATION

Despite the promise of superfast computers, turbulence and nonlinearity cause problems no foreseeable machine can handle

Computer simulations are used to model the behavior of many systems, from tomorrow's weather or next year's economy to new generations of integrated circuits or aircraft or the next century's fusion power plant. The basic concepts for simulation are well understood: develop a mathematical model—a series of differential equations—of a system's behavior over time, reduce it to a form that can be numerically integrated by a computer, set up the initial conditions, and let the model run. With the expected development of computers a thousand times faster than the current generation of supercomputers, will engineers be able to run simulations currently considered unfeasible?

In many cases, the answer is yes. But in other cases, increases in computer power alone will not improve current results significantly. And in some areas of simulation, no conceivable increase in computing power can improve simulations beyond a certain limited extent. Instead, improvements will have to come from better understanding of the problems being modeled and from better ways of turning differential-equation models into algorithms. Particularly important is the understanding of which interactions can be ignored to simplify computation and which must be retained to stay fairly close to the real world.

The reason some simulation problems may be amenable to increased computing power while others are not is that the intractable problems involve mathematically ill-conditioned behavior, in which input and output are not proportional and systems cannot easily be scaled up or down. Turbulence in the air flowing over an aircraft wing or a continent or turbulence in the flow of electrons in a plasma are examples of such phenomena, and the mathematical study of them, begun 50 years ago, is still in its infancy. Theoretical studies of ill-conditioned turbulent phenomena suffer from a lack of sufficient computing power just as the practical studies do, even though some impressive analytical results have been achieved with no more than a hand calculator.

Some phenomena could be modeled by applying basic physical principles—airflow simulations, for example, could be attacked by models so detailed that no averaging of flows or other approximations would be necessary. But such a simulation would require trillions of grid points for an airplane wing, and even the next generation of supercomputers, expected to be capable of hundreds of billions of operations per second, would take weeks or months to run such a model.

Many of the most intractable problems in simulation are known as continuous simulations; their equations model pressure, temperature, velocity, or other quantities that vary smoothly through space and time. Values at grid points are only an approximation of the actual situation. There is, however, another class of simulations, known as discrete simulations, that models individual interacting elements. Digital circuit simula-

tions are one example of this class; every circuit element can be represented and modeled individually.

Discrete simulations often suffer from "combinatorial explosion," in which more than a few interacting objects cause possibilities to increase geometrically. Heuristic methods are being used to limit the possibilities examined in such cases. The level of understanding of such heuristics may be compared to the level of understanding of techniques for accurately and completely representing turbulent behavior.

Turbulence: the elusive variable

Some scaling may be possible to test general parameters of turbulent phenomena. This is why wind tunnels are used to test models of aircraft. But detailed behavior depends on the interaction of size-dependent factors, which is why aircraft manufacturers test full-scale models in wind tunnels and flight-test finished aircraft extensively. Consider transsonic flow over a wing: if both wing and airspeed were scaled down to a reasonable size, the model would then be dealing with a gentle breeze.

In simulations of flow, the nonlinear forces involved are the frictional shear forces of a viscous fluid. Every traveling parcel of air, water, or plasma exerts a force on every other traveling parcel dependent on the direction and magnitude of their relative velocities. This is true of descriptions on the continental or molecular scale. When a fluid is forced to flow fast enough, or heated quickly enough, the interactions lead to turbulence, in which large-scale descriptions of the flow depend significantly on small-scale disturbances. Unstable behavior results. In the turbulent regime, flow never settles down to a consistent pattern, but rather changes continually and unpredictably. Furthermore, past behavior cannot always be used to predict the future.

Turbulence is particularly intractable in plasma physics simulations for fusion reactors because of the interactions between the plasma and its containing magnetic field. The field is generated in part by outside coils and in part by the very flow of electrons it is supposed to contain. Thus, plasma simulations must take into account not only normal physical interactions between parcels, but electromagnetic ones as well, where electrical resistivity is the analog to frictional shear.

In economic models, the changing velocity of money through the economy and the time lags between causes in one sector and effects in another lead to nonlinear, ill-conditioned behavior. Policy changes lead only slowly to changes in deficits or employment levels, but their effect on interest rates can be almost instantaneous. The inherent nonlinearity of the models is complicated by the human factors involved: models assume purely rational behavior, but actual decisions are made by people.

Still, some success has been achieved in the mathematical study of weak turbulence and other nonlinear behavior. The concept of "strange attractors"—areas around which the solutions to certain equations tend to converge, although they do not stay there—has been helpful [see "Strange attractors: turbulent

Robert Sugarman   Contributing Editor
Paul Wallich   Associate Editor

Strange attractors: turbulent mathematics

Certain differential equations, including those used to model weak turbulence, have associated with them points known as strange attractors. These attractors are points in whose neighborhood the solutions of the equations are to be found, much like the asymptotes familiar in more conventional equations. A typical example of asymptotic behavior is the voltage in a resonant RLC circuit, which oscillates at a continually decaying amplitude. However, unlike conventional systems with asymptotic solutions, systems of equations with strange attractors never actually settle down to any single value.

Instead, an equation with a strange attractor will jump unpredictably between the neighborhoods of several different points, staying for a while near each and then moving on. Real-world examples of such jumpy solutions are systems with frictional forces and also turbulent systems, where the behavior of an airflow or plasma constantly fluctuates in a near-random fashion. Sometimes such a system will remain in one "metastable" state for a long time, then suddenly change to another; even detailed knowledge of past behavior does not necessarily point to future events.

In strict mathematical terms, the concept of strange attractors applies only to a few weakly turbulent systems: it refers to equations whose behavior over time is so unpredictable that, no matter how similar a set of initial conditions may be, final behavior will diverge widely. However, many systems behave in a manner similar to that of those possessing strange attractors, even though they are not strictly strange, and mathematical studies of turbulence include them. Studies of turbulence also include strongly turbulent systems, which are not well understood at all. The concepts of strange attractors have not yet been extended to cover strongly turbulent systems, and so models must be developed on a case-by-case basis from the physical description of the system, be it plasma, airflow, weather, or other.

While turbulence itself is not yet understood, mathematicians are beginning to make some headway in understanding the transition some systems make between regular and irregular behavior. For example, many systems begin with periodic fluctuations and go through a process known as period doubling, in which the time scale of fluctuations increases, and subperiodic disturbances appear. After a sufficient number of doublings the original periodicity vanishes, and the system becomes turbulent, with no discernible regular behavior. Many different systems undergo period-doubling phenomena as part of their transition to turbulent behavior; one encouraging sign for mathematicians is that the properties of the period-doubling phase are remarkably similar, even for systems with widely varying physical properties. For example, the length of time between successive doublings is identical for a large number of weakly turbulent systems. This common behavior holds out some hope that similar unifying principles may be found for turbulent phenomena that have not yet yielded to mathematical analysis.

Although the behavior of turbulent systems is extraordinarily complex, their mathematical basis may be quite simple. The figure below shows a fairly simple equation with two strange attractors; the solution of the equation spirals between them in an unpredictable manner. If any of the initial conditions or coefficients of the equation were changed even slightly, a completely different pattern would result. If the system below were merely irregular, instead of possessing strange attractors, small changes in initial parameters would yield quite similar curves.

—P.W.

The system of differential equations shown below has two strange attractors, causing it to behave irregularly. The value of z changes in a semiperiodic fashion, as shown by the peaks in the power spectrum (A), but there is a great deal of "noise" in the function, as indicated by the broad-band contributions to the spectrum. The curve (B) shows a plot of 50 loops of the solution to these equations when R = 28.

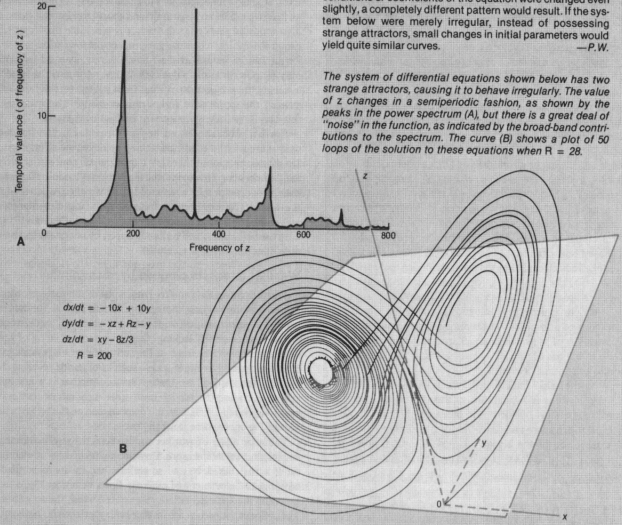

$$dx/dt = -10x + 10y$$
$$dy/dt = -xz + Rz - y$$
$$dz/dt = xy - 8z/3$$
$$R = 200$$

mathematics," p. 334]. Often a turbulent system may be described by a number of attractors and jump from one to another in an unpredictable manner. Mathematical research on such systems is continuing, but its applicability is uncertain.

The impossible job of modeling the economy

Economic modeling, which usually involves the forecast of conditions from present and past information, is one of the most difficult applications for simulation. It combines all of the uncertainties that can beset a model: unmanageable complexity, an uncertainty of how different parts of the system being modeled interact, and a lack of adequate real-world data against which to measure the model.

Stephen K. McNees, an economist at the Federal Reserve Bank of Boston, in analyzing the performance of 13 leading forecasting organizations, noted that "forecasts not based on formal [computer] econometric methods appear to be generally as accurate as or more accurate than econometrically based forecasts." This observation is borne out by the research of Ray Fair, an economist at Yale University, who has analyzed a series of econometric models, not for their accuracy in predicting the real world, but simply for their repeatability.

Dr. Fair's models operate by means of a matrix that describes the way in which different economic variables interact. One

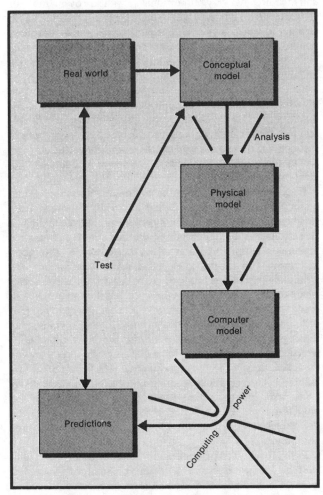

Assumptions are made and realism is sacrificed at each step of refining a model, from concept to mathematical expression to algorithm. The more simplified a model is, the more easily it can be computed, but tests of its predictions against the real-world behavior it was derived from may be disappointing.

model that gives results whose quality is comparable to that of the others has all off-diagonal elements of the matrix set to zero, implying that there is no interaction whatsoever and that the future behavior of any economic indicator depends only on a time-weighted function of its past behavior. Clearly this does not coincide with economists' understanding of the way real economies work. Rather it reinforces the notion that current economic models have basic conceptual problems.

Jared Enzler, an econometrician at the Federal Reserve Board in Washington, D.C., noted that economists are well aware that their models do not correspond to the economies being modeled. He blames part of the shortcoming on inadequate computing resources. Running current models on more powerful computers would simply produce erroneous results faster, he said, but more powerful machines might make possible the running of qualitatively different models that better emulate the real world.

At the most primitive level, one could build models "out of atoms," simulating the behavior of individuals trying to optimize their assets over time; this approach would require machines several orders of magnitude more powerful than current ones, although something of the "atomistic" approach is being taken by Jay W. Forrester of the Massachusetts Institute of Technology, Cambridge, in a model that has been in development for more than a decade.

A more realistic possibility, Dr. Enzler said, is the iterative running of models—feeding in assumptions about final conditions and repeating until consistent results appear. This practice is too expensive for economists to attempt today. One example of an iterative model involves long- and short-term interest rates. If a government plans huge deficits, it is inevitable that rates will rise in the future, when the government borrows more money. Predictions of long- and short-term interest rates can be made only by putting initial values for future rates into the model, watching the progression of rates from present into future, and running the model until future rates converge. Unfortunately, this cannot be done given current computing budgets.

Another problem with economic forecasting is that the data used as input and the indicators being predicted are all imprecise. Dr. Enzler noted that there is "a tremendous conceptual problem" in deciding how to weight the National Income Accounts data, produced by the Commerce Department, on which models are based. The data are extrapolated from statistical samples, and without far larger, more expensive data-gathering efforts, even the best models will be handicapped by uncertainties in the quantities they attempt to model.

Weather forecasts plagued by uncertainties

Weather forecasting suffers from some of the same problems as economic forecasting, though for the most part the fundamental laws governing atmospheric phenomena are well understood. A few factors are still lacking. One is an understanding of how events at small scales, such as the formation of ice crystals in a cloud, propagate to larger scales, such as blizzards covering the Eastern Seaboard of the United States. Another is a machine powerful enough to model small-scale atmospheric behavior over long periods. And a third is detailed data on the actual behavior of the atmosphere at small scales.

The basic driver of weather conditions is the seasonal change of pressure and temperature. Pressure highs and lows sometimes move across the globe and sometimes halt in the same place, blocking the movement of cyclonic flows with a high-pressure ridge and precipitating hot, dry summers or cold, snowy winters. The cyclones themselves are smaller-scale phenomena, lasting for a week or so before dissipating and causing local disturbances

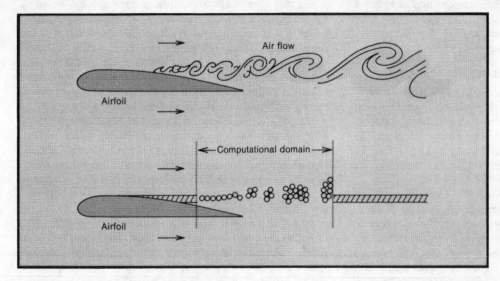

When two airflows moving at different speeds mix, they exchange irregular eddies at their boundary. Such turbulence may be more easily modeled by assuming that the irregular eddies can be represented by combinations of mathematically idealized vortices.

along their paths—thunderstorms that last for a few hours or clouds that sometimes form and dissolve in minutes.

The limit of predictability for any of these scales is usually no greater than the life cycle of a single ridge, cyclone, storm, or cloud, assuming no outside influence. And prediction at one scale gives little information about smaller scales, so forecasts of cyclonic paths give almost no information about local storms and none whatsoever about the shape of an individual cloud. The theoretical limits of general weather forecasting are about two or three weeks. Typical forecasts are good for four or five days, and highly sophisticated models may reach an eight-day level.

An ever finer grid of weather-recording stations might give data for better forecasts by reducing small-scale errors. But even with a 40-meter grid, small-scale errors would double in magnitude every two or three days; such a fine grid would only add 72 hours to the time scale of forecasts. And it would involve 50 billion grid points over the continental United States alone.

Climate forecasting is in much the same position as weather forecasting. According to Jerome Namias of the Scripps Institution of Oceanography in La Jolla, Calif., climate forecasts as to whether winters will be colder or summers hotter than average, are right about 65 percent of the time. Even random chance would give 50-percent accuracy. Such performance results because although many external influences are expected to have long-range impacts on climatic variations, the quantitative effects of such factors as changes in world snow and ice cover, volcanic deposits of ash into the atmosphere, and changes in atmospheric carbon dioxide are unknown.

Since 1965, for example, many scientific papers have established the concept of ocean-atmosphere coupling, but not whether atmospheric temperatures drive ocean surface temperatures or vice versa. The general problem is that the 30 years of weather observations available for study, although long on a cyclonic scale, are far too short on a climatic scale.

Chasing airfoil eddies

Aerodynamic models at the National Aeronautics and Space Administration and elsewhere attempt to calculate lift, drag, buffeting, and average pressure over aircraft surfaces. One goal, thought to be attainable in 10 minutes or so with a 1000-megaflop computer, would be to calculate such values for entire aircraft traveling at transonic speeds. Such a turnaround time would allow many different aircraft designs to be explored more quickly than a few can be explored today.

The most accurate equations governing airflow are the so-called Navier-Stokes equations. However, computational aerodynamicists have no intention of solving them directly for turbulent flows, either now or in the foreseeable future.

Eddies of varying sizes are the major feature of turbulent flow, and their lifetimes vary proportionally with size over a range of 10 000 to 1 for a typical wing. To model flow directly over such a large range would require a three-dimensional grid of 10 trillion points, and even a 1000-megaflop computer would require the better part of a year to run such a model, even if the necessary billions of words of main memory were available.

Two approximation methods are being used by modelers. One involves averaging the effects of eddies over short time scales, so that they cancel out without distorting actual flows, and the second involves separating the effects of large eddies from those of small ones and making separate calculations for each class. The first method, which is known as Reynolds-averaged modeling, is most common.

Eddy-averagers separate turbulent flow into average and fluctuating velocity components. To handle the latter, the models assume either that the shear stress between parcels of fluid has a single value, or that it depends on the directions the parcels are moving—a tensor force. Reynolds-averaged models give good agreement with experimental pressures and temperatures for steady-state conditions as well as for shock-wave conditions where the flow separates from the wing. But they do not do well predicting steady-state pressure profiles over a wing, or in predicting the frequency of buffeting caused by shock waves.

Eddy-chasers, unlike eddy-averagers, calculate the actual interactions between the larger eddies. The most important area of the flow is the so-called boundary layer, in which most of the turbulence occurs, and it is theoretically possible to calculate by brute force all the eddies larger than a few percent of the boundary-layer width. This size limit is about 10 times the "Kolmogoroff limit," below which eddies generate only heat, not motion.

In the first successful application of this method, reported in 1981 by Parviz Moin and John Kim of Stanford University, working at the National Aeronautics and Space Administrations' Ames Research Laboratory in Moffett Field, Calif., the boundary layer modeled was simply for airflow between two flat plates. A half-million-point grid took 92 hours to compute. Since most cases of practical interest would require far more points, it is not clear how the Moin-Kim techniques can be extended.

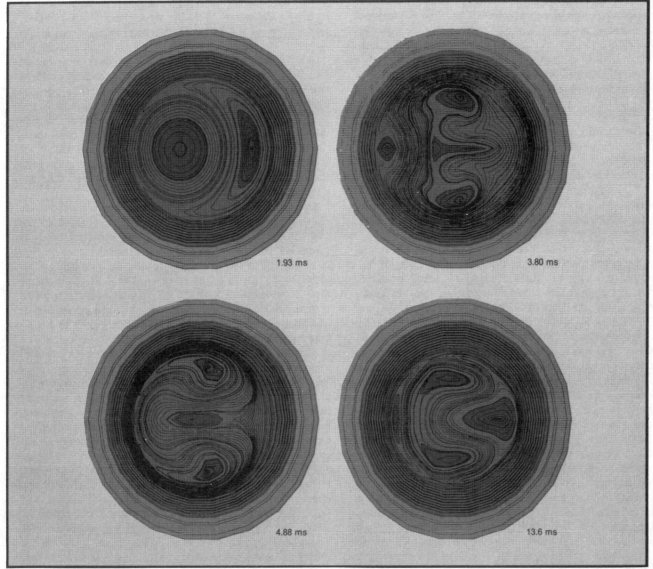

1.93 ms

3.80 ms

4.88 ms

13.6 ms

This simulated slice from a toroidal plasma demonstrates the growth of magnetic islands. The contour lines, which initially form near-concentric cylinders, represent surfaces of constant magnetic energy. As time passes, the contours become more and more distorted; eventually, the plasma will no longer be contained, or the field will reshape itself into a symmetrical configuration.

Another eddy-chasing technique starts with the assumption that eddies look like vortices, or whirlpools, and makes the vortex the basic mathematical element of turbulent flow. At the interface between two layers of air moving at different velocities, for example, the layers interact by interchanging irregular chunks of eddies; it is possible to replace these chunks in a computer by idealized mathematical vortices.

According to Paul Rubbert of Boeing Military Airplane Co. in Seattle, Wash., not only are practical applications of computational aerodynamics being limited by lack of computer power, but that same lack also hampers theoretical work that could lead to better models. The way to do useful research in turbulence, he said, is to construct models and design experiments to test them. Then one revises the models and redesigns the experiments to provide whatever new information may be needed, iterating the process until models work and can be refined into viable applications programs. But without the computational resources to construct more detailed models than those of today, theoretical work cannot proceed rapidly.

Dr. Rubbert noted that computer architecture is particularly important, since even today it affects algorithm design. "There are algorithms that will be viable on a CRAY that wouldn't be viable on a Cyber, for example," he said, because the two machines are organized differently. But one area that limits all current machines is memory, he said: once a model must transfer large amounts of information to and from disks, the central processing unit is being wasted.

The amount of memory required for a model depends on the size and spacing of the grid used for modeling. Current techniques are not always successful at producing good three-dimensional grids, said Dr. Rubbert. Not only are there difficulties in matching the complex contours of modern aircraft shapes, but it is also not initially clear where grids should be finer and where coarser. Techniques being explored today include a grid whose spacing changes in different areas, and a completely regular grid, which ignores aircraft surfaces and uses pseudoflow techniques to arrive at consistent results.

The ideal solution, he noted, would be a so-called solution-adaptive grid, whose spacing would depend on the airflow conditions at any given point. Such a grid would have to be generated iteratively, since only by solving the airflow equation could one find out what grid spacing was required. And convergence is not guaranteed; in most cases, one might assume that the most "interesting" airflows occur near aircraft surfaces, but in some situations, such as rapidly maneuvering fighter aircraft, flow separates from surfaces and the most important regions—the boundary layers—are at large distances from any surface.

Charting islands of plasma

Modeling fusion reactors requires a search for pockets of stability in the generally unstable evolution of a rapidly heated plasma. Both the plasma and the magnetic field that confines it are in excited states, and it is energetically favorable for them to move out of their intended positions. When plasma instabilities develop, they quickly lead to a disruption of the symmetric configuration needed for confinement and fusion.

If the plasma hits any part of its containing vessel often enough and with enough energy, the vessel will be weakened, and replacement or repairs will be necessary. The frequencey of such disruptions in a hypothesized commercial fusion reactor has not been successfully modeled. Some experimental data is becoming available from the operation of the tokamak fusion test reactor (TFTR) at the Princeton Plasma Physics Laboratory, and more will follow as the TFTR approaches break-even power.

Most physicists assume that the disruption of plasmas is caused by the deformation of magnetic field lines along which electrons in the plasma move into islands—self-contained loops of magnetic field that have lower magnetic energy than the surrounding magnetic "ocean." The islands can either collapse or grow so large that they thermally short-circuit the plasma.

Alternatively, if two islands approach each other, they will become distorted, and the magnetic field lines in the area between them will become so complexly twisted as to be virtually random. Such randomly oriented flux lines do not contain a plasma well, according to Roscoe White, principal research physicist at the Plasma Physics Laboratory. Plasma disruptions are thought to be due to the growth of a single large island to the point where it interacts with other islands and destabilizes them.

It may be possible to prevent disruptions by altering tokamak magnetic fields as islands form. Island formation leads to oscillations of plasma current and is thus detectable, and island growth is dependent on the density gradient of the plasma current. The resistivity of the plasma allows the normally self-stabilizing magnetic field lines to shift into lower-energy configurations.

Exploration of island behavior would be aided by either faster-running models or faster computers. Current models are only beginning to explore the behavior of plasmas in three dimensions, and models with more physics in them will be required to understand the phenomenon more fully.

Current plasma simulations take about a half hour per time series on a CRAY, but accurate three-dimensional models would take far longer. Modeling even a small section of a plasma torus would require calculating the values of 10 or 20 functions at a million different points—estimated running time on a CRAY: 30 hours, at a cost of a few dollars per second.

As in computational aerodynamics, the theory of fusion plasmas is not yet fully worked out. The interactions of high-energy beams—thought to be useful for injecting energy into the plasma—with certain modes of plasma oscillation is not understood, for example. "It's clear from experiments that it's important," said Dr. White, but the theory is still in the process of being developed. Computer limitations slow the development of theory, but not always as much as one might expect, he noted. Soviet plasma physicists, with much more limited computing power, have applied analytical techniques to a number of problems with fair success, but, Dr. White pointed out, computationally derived understanding of general behavior may greatly accelerate the search for analytic solutions.

When the next generation of supercomputers comes along, said Dr. White, plasma physicists will no doubt find problems that those supercomputers cannot handle, but for today, even an order or two of magnitude in computing power would make a significant difference. The ability to run simulations of new theoretical models is one example, and the calculation of three-dimensional simulations is another. But algorithms will also be important. Dr. Rubbert spoke of the "folklore" involved in "learning how to squeeze the last megaflop out of a CRAY," and the same holds for plasma physics.

One example is in the calculation of magnetic-island growth. Currently, models calculate the behavior of the entire plasma and examine island growth within that context. However, the actual formation of islands depends on a "tearing layer" where magnetic field lines are detached from the uniform field and attached to the field of a growing island. The width of the tearing layer depends on the resistivity of the plasma, and for ignited plasmas whose resistivity is very low, the tearing layer can be quite narrow, just as the turbulent boundary layer in airflow over a wing becomes narrower at high speed.

It may be possible to compute island growth rates by examining the magnetic field changes across the tearing layer, rather than throughout the entire plasma. The problem presents complex topological difficulties, because the shape of an island and its tearing layer may not be simple, but could still lead to shorter calculations. Such a model has been developed by Raymond Grimm, deputy head of the theoretical plasma physics branch at Princeton, and by his associates.

Of course, verification may be difficult, since conventional models do not run quickly enough to model ignited plasmas, and direct experimental measurements are impossible. Better diagnostics for plasma are constantly being developed, noted Dr. White, but still almost everything must be measured indirectly. The modeling of fusion plasmas is thus beset, like economic modeling, by the inaccessibility of the quantities it attempts to model, even though it proceeds from the first principles of electromagnetism.

To probe further

An analysis of economic forecasting problems can be found in the article, "Recent records of 13 forecasters," by Stephen K. McNees in the *New England Economic Review*, or in "An analysis of four macroeconomic models," by Ray Fair (Cowles Foundation Papers 489, Yale University, New Haven, Conn.). Jay W. Forrester of the Massachusetts Institute of Technology has constructed a large-scale "realistic" economic model and has found that it shows some of the same long-term behavior as real economies. His article, "Growth Cycles," in *De Economist* (Vol. 124, no. 4, 1977, pp. 525-43), is useful.

For weather forecasting, the major specialized medium is *Journal of the Atmospheric Sciences*.

The American Institute of Aeronautics and Astronautics in New York is a major source of information on computational aerodynamics, as are NASA's research laboratories. *The Journal of Computational Physics* contains information on both aerodynamic modeling and on plasma modeling for fusion research.

The *Joint U.S.-Soviet Handbook of Plasma Physics*, from North-Holland Publishing Co., furnishes a review of many areas of fusion research, including a chapter on the various models of island growth and their associated instabilities.   ◆

Author Index

Subject Index

About the Editor

Edward A. Torrero, *IEEE Spectrum's* Technical Editor, launched his career in electronics intent on becoming an R&D engineer in the field of high-frequency electronics. After working on advanced radar systems in the early 1960s, he returned to school to specialize in fusion research—an area he regarded as critical 10 years before the energy crisis brought it to the forefront.

Mr. Torrero got his start in technical journalism in 1971 as solid-state editor of *Electronic Design,* covering the emerging world of microprocessors. Articles and stories he developed on this burgeoning field became highly regarded and were reprinted in book form. It was this same trenchant editorial style that brought him recognition in one of his first major assignments at *Spectrum*—the widely acclaimed special issue on Japanese electrotechnology. In 1981, he was issue editor for the special issue on reliability, and in 1983 he was the principal editor for the "Tomorrow's computers" issue—the basis for this book.

More recently, he was issue editor for "Education: the challenges are classic," which entailed a survey of IEEE members' perceptions regarding lifelong education. The survey was cosponsored by IEEE Educational Activities Board and was funded in part by the National Science Foundation.

Mr. Torrero has organized a number of panel discussions. The two most recent concerned the intensely controversial topic of possible health effects of electromagnetic fields. Reports of these discussions were published in "The drive to regulate electromagnetic fields," and "Biological effects of electromagnetic fields," in the March and May 1984 issues, respectively. He also organized panel sessions on microprocessors and computer graphics for the annual Electro meeting, and was session chairman for the former.

He was the U.S. Department of Commerce's industry trade representative at a weeklong trade fair in Yugoslavia. He is also an involved member of the IEEE.

Mr. Torrero acquired his design experience at Wheeler Laboratories and Sedco Systems. He was a Research Fellow at the Polytechnic Institute of Brooklyn and a first lieutenant in the U.S. Army Corps of Engineers in France for two years. He received his bachelor's degree in electrical engineering from the City College of New York and his MS in electrophysics from the Polytechnic Institute of Brooklyn.